MW00799217

The Whole Book of Psalms

Medieval & Renaissance
Texts and Studies

Volume 557

Renaissance English Text Society
Seventh Series

Volume XXXVII (for 2011)

The Whole Book of Psalms

*Collected into English Metre by
Thomas Sternhold, John Hopkins,
and Others*

A Critical Edition
of the Texts and Tunes

VOLUME TWO

Beth Quitslund
Nicholas Temperley

Arizona Center for Medieval & Renaissance Studies
Tempe, Arizona
2018

Arizona Center
for Medieval &
Renaissance Studies

Published by ACMRS (Arizona Center for Medieval and Renaissance Studies)
Tempe, Arizona
© 2018 Arizona Board of Regents for Arizona State University.
All Rights Reserved.

Library of Congress Cataloging-in-Publication Data

Names: Sternhold, Thomas, -1549, author. | Quitslund, Beth, editor, author. |
    Temperley, Nicholas, editor, author.
Title: The whole book of Psalms collected into English metre by Thomas
    Sternhold, John Hopkins, and others : a critical edition of the texts and tunes
    / Beth Quitslund and Nicholas Temperley.
Other titles: Whole book of Psalms
Description: Tempe, Arizona : ACMRS, 2018. | Series: Medieval and
    renaissance texts and studies ; Volume 387 | Series: Renaissance English
    Text Society seventh series ; Volume XXXVI | Includes bibliographical
    references and index. Contents: The whole book of Psalms -- Historical essay
    -- Development and publication -- The Elizabethan Psalm book -- Later
    history of the Psalm book.
Identifiers: LCCN 2018047359| ISBN 9780866984355 (hardcover : alk. paper)
    | ISBN 9780866986151 (hardcover : alk. paper)
Subjects: LCSH: Bible. Psalms--Paraphrases, English. | Bible. Psalms--
    Paraphrases, English--Criticism, interpretation, etc. | Psalms (Music)
Classification: LCC BS1440 .S8 2018 | DDC 223/.205209--dc23
LC record available at https://lccn.loc.gov/2018047359

∞
This book is made to last. It is set in Adobe Caslon Pro,
smyth-sewn and printed on acid-free paper to library specifications.
Printed in the United States of America

Contents

List of Figures, Tables, and Music Examples

HISTORICAL ESSAY

The Whole Book of Psalms, Collected into English Metre by Thomas Sternhold, John Hopkins, and Others (*WBP*) was almost certainly the single best-selling book in early modern England.[1] For much of the seventeenth century, its production significantly outran that of the Bible and the Book of Common Prayer as well as every other devotional manual, music book, and collection of verse. From the first edition in 1562 to the middle of the nineteenth century, English printers produced over a thousand editions, with at least fragments of 150 surviving from before the Stationers' Company took over the patent in late 1603.[2] As the first widely-used hymnal for congregational singing in English, it carried that practice into nearly all parish churches and remained essentially unchallenged as a fixture of public worship in the Church of England for well over a century. As a hymnal, it did not die out entirely until well into the Victorian era. The texts that made up the *WBP* must thus have been among the most familiar in the English language for close to three centuries, and the tunes to which they were sung a musical vernacular common to everyone in the kingdom and many English settlements abroad.

Such ubiquity is all the more striking in that the *WBP* was never an official part of the English liturgy. One of the results of its unofficial status is that it was far more flexible than any other text used over a long period in public worship, requiring no authority other than the printer's to alter its contents. In the

---

[1] The most likely exception is what Day's royal patent refers to as "the ABC with little catechism"; as surviving seventeenth-century examples generally fit onto a single sheet (sixteen pages in octavo), these are more appropriately classed with broadside ballads and chapbooks than with bindable books. See pp. xxv–xxvi n.9.

[2] A complete list of known editions through 1603 appears in App. 1. Ian Green counts approximately 819 surviving editions between 1562 and 1729: *Print and Protestantism in Early Modern England* (Oxford: Oxford University Press, 2000), 509. Not only did publication continue after that for more than a century, but any census should account for the loss of a great many smaller-format editions (see below, pp. 567–8); see for the sixteenth century Christopher L. Oastler, *John Day, Elizabethan Printer* (Oxford: Oxford Bibliographic Society, 1975), 24, and for the seventeenth century Green, 520–1. For comparative numbers of editions of Bibles, *BCP*s, and psalm books, see Green, 52–3, 247–8, 513. Nicholas Temperley, in the *Hymn Tune Index* (1777), 1.7, counts 452 surviving editions with tunes, the last dating from 1688.

first twenty-five years of its publication, it was in fact deliberately revised several times: the texts of the psalm versifications themselves were tweaked, additional psalm versions added, the hymns reordered, tunes added and revised and reassigned, the prose arguments to the psalms abridged, the prefatory materials replaced, and the private prayer book at the end of the volume expanded. Some of these changes must reflect market conditions and the practice of actual congregations, while others register the aesthetic and religious inclinations of the publishers, John Day and his son Richard (and perhaps Richard's early assignee, John Wolfe); a handful may represent careful negotiation with members of Elizabeth's Privy Council over the patent for this increasingly influential title. The net result is a book that was unstable in ways that have not been recognized in discussions of either the music or the texts. This edition is intended to provide a clear version of both the tunes and the words while indicating the nature of the book's changes over the Elizabethan period and the range of variation in the music, ditties, and prose apparatus.

Development and Publication

Henrician Prehistory

Devotional, liturgical, and literary trends in early sixteenth-century culture, including but not limited to the Reformation, together made it extremely probable that something like *The Whole Book of Psalms* should have come into being. It took the form it did, however, as a result of the idiosyncratic ways that these trends combined with each other and with political contingencies of the English Reformation in particular. This is not by any means to discount the specific talents, tastes, and limitations that the various authors, composers, and editors brought to the collection. Still, the *WBP* at every stage of its development responded to its contexts in Christian psalmody, vernacular biblicism, courtly poetics, liturgical change, and interactions between Reformation ideas and popular culture as well as to the specific circumstances of the writers and (mostly anonymous) composers themselves.

From the beginning of Christianity, the Book of Psalms has had a privileged status within the Old Testament. There are more citations from the Psalms in the New Testament than from any other book of the Hebrew Bible, reflecting not only the usefulness of the Psalms as a prophetic source but also their significance in first-century Jewish devotional practice. [3] Church Fathers beginning at

---

[3] Steven Moyise and Maarten J. J. Menken, eds., *The Psalms in the New Testament* (London and New York: T. & T. Clark International, 2004), 1–2. Alexander F. Kirkpatrick listed well over 100 Psalm quotations in the New Testament, even disregarding

the latest with Origen also turned to the psalms as a source of doctrine and devotion. Though not all are as thoroughly saturated with the psalter as Augustine of Hippo (who cites the psalms some 10,000 times in his collected writings), it was conventional by the fourth century to point to the psalms as either an epitome of the Bible as a whole, a treasury of wholesome prayer and spiritual comfort, or both.[4] In the fourth century, the monastic round of psalm chanting—the whole psalter every week, spread over a varying number of liturgical hours—began to influence not only cathedral liturgies but lay devotion.[5] Lay books of devotional prayers followed the monastic hours for centuries, and even the French and English tradition of Books of Hours that supplanted psalters *per se* retained a significant number of psalms. Although these were mainly in Latin until after the Reformation and thus required more than rudimentary literacy, the *Horae* were extremely widely produced and disseminated.[6] Both psalters and Books of Hours (or "primers") formed the textbooks for early reading practice throughout the Middle Ages. The psalms themselves, then, were dependent on neither early modern culture nor Reformation theology for their general prominence in sixteenth-century Christian life and thought. Their traditional importance explains why they became a focus of Reformation exposition and vernacular translation: if the Bible was to be the foundation of the Church, the psalms would naturally form the threshold.

The explosion of psalm paraphrases in vernacular verse during the sixteenth century, however, was triggered by the Reformation. Inheriting the centrality of the psalms and returning to the pre-scholastic Fathers to defend differences with Rome, the Reformers redeployed psalmody for their own radically purified purposes. One of the most important was lay singing, both within the liturgy and outside it. Although it was Erasmus (echoing Jerome) who wished that the farmer and weaver would sing the psalms in their work, they seem to have been able to do so largely as a result of Lutheran and especially Reformed efforts. The first Lutheran hymnal contained nine psalm paraphrases among its thirty-two selections. Other versions of reform not only mined the Book of Psalms but drew sharp distinctions between it and humanly-authored hymns. Thus congregational singers in Calvin's Geneva gave voice only to songs that had explicit divine

---

duplicative passages from the Gospels; see Kirkpatrick, ed., *The Cambridge Bible: The Book of Psalms* (Cambridge: Cambridge University Press, 1903), 839–40.

[4] Michael Fiedrowicz, "Introduction," *Expositions of the Psalms 1–32*, Works of Saint Augustine 3.15 (Brooklyn, N. Y.: New City Press, 2000), 13.

[5] The liturgical spread of psalmody is summarized by James McKinnon, "The Book of Psalms, Monasticism, and the Western Liturgy," *The Place of the Psalms in the Intellectual Culture of the Middle Ages*, ed. Nancy Van Deusen (Albany, NY: SUNY Press, 1999), 43–58.

[6] See Roger S. Wieck, *Painted Prayers: The Book of Hours in Medieval and Renaissance Art* (New York: George Braziller, 1997), 9.

approval—that is, the psalms and a small handful of other scriptural canticles. As he put it in the preface to the 49-psalm volume of 1543 (a preface reprinted in the expanding metrical psalter for decades), "what St. Augustine said is true, that no one is able to sing things worthy of God unless he has received them from Him. Wherefore, when we have looked thoroughly everywhere and searched high and low, we shall find no better songs nor more appropriate to the purpose than the Psalms of David which the Holy Spirit made and spoke through him."[7] The rationale is not so different from monastic chanting of the psalter, but the form, with people of all ages and both sexes singing inventive stanzas of rhyming French verse to tunes newly-composed by the best musical talent in France, made for a quite different experience of psalmody.

Reformers did not, though, forget about laborers and extra-liturgical singing. Luther also inaugurated the wide-spread Protestant crusade to replace immoral recreational songs with improving ones. In the preface to the Wittenberg Hymnal of 1524, he notes that "these songs were arranged in four parts to give the young—who should at any rate be trained in music and other fine arts—something to wean them away from love ballads and carnal songs and to teach them something of value in their place, thus combining the good with the pleasing, as is proper for youth."[8] This earnest hope for musical rehabilitation recalls a recurrent patristic comparison between the lascivious pagan songs of feast or theater and the sweetly decorous music of psalmody.[9] Luther, in turn, is echoed in the title pages or prefaces of many early psalm and hymn collections of the Reformation, including not only Calvin's for Geneva but Miles Coverdale's *Goostly Psalmes* (London, [1535–6?])[10], the anonymous *Souterliedekens* [Psalter Songs] (Antwerp, 1540), and John Wedderburn's *Ane Compendious Buik of Godly and*

---

[7] Clément Marot, *Cinquante Pseaumes de David mis en françoys selon la vérité hébraïque* (Geneva: Jean Gérard, 1543); translation by Charles Garside, Jr., *The Origins of Calvin's Theology of Music: 1536–43* (Philadelphia: American Philosophical Society, 1979), 33.

[8] Johann Walter, *Geystliche Gesangbüchlin* (Wittenberg, 1524). The preface, in a translation by Paul Zeller Strodach revised by Ulrich S. Leupold, is in *Luther's Works*, vol. 53: *Liturgy and Hymns* (Philadelphia: Fortress Press, 1965), 316.

[9] James McKinnon notes in the introduction to his collection of patristic writings on music that "[t]here is hardly a major church father from the fourth century who does not inveigh against pagan musical practice in the strongest language," and many of the examples he gathers go on to praise the psalms by contrast or to recommend their use instead. McKinnon, ed., *Music in Early Christian Literature* (Cambridge: Cambridge University Press, 1987), 2; for examples, see McKinnon, pp. 70, 80–1, 86–7, 126–7, 133–4.

[10] Coverdale's title page justified the work thus: "And to make theyr songes of the Lorde / That they may thrust under the borde / All other balettes of fylthynes," reproduced in Robin A. Leaver, *'Goostly Psalmes and Spirituall Songes': English and Dutch Metrical Psalms from Coverdale to Utenhove, 1535–1566* (Oxford: Clarendon Press, 1991), 63. For additional English examples, see Beth Quitslund, "Singing the Psalms for Fun and Profit," *Private and Domestic Devotion in Early Modern Britain*, ed. Alec Ryrie and Jessica

Spiritual Songis [Edinburgh?, c.1546?].[11] The core of the French metrical psalter, in fact, began as pious aristocratic entertainment. The first thirty of Clement Marot's psalm paraphrases enjoyed enormous favor at the French court, where they were sung with great enthusiasm up to the point at which the poet himself fled to Geneva, in 1542.[12]

Such activity also flourished at the English court in the last years of Henry VIII, as we know from the memoirs of Thomas Whythorne, which date from the 1570s. After studying music at Oxford he was apprenticed for "three years and more" [c.1545–8?] to the court musician and dramatist John Heywood, for whom he "did write out . . . diverse songs and sonnets that were made by the Earl of Surrey, Sir Thomas Wyatt the elder, and Mr. More the excellent harper, besides certain psalms that were made by the said Mr. Wyatt, and also Mr. Sternhold."[13] This leaves no doubt that the context of Sternhold's psalms was an existing tradition of solo song at the Tudor court, with accompaniment of lute, keyboard, or harp.

The formal variety and literary refinement of Marot's lyrics also points us to non-musical impulses in sixteenth-century metrical psalmody.[14] Though Coverdale's *Goostly Psalmes*, a songbook greatly indebted to Lutheran hymnals, was probably the first early modern experiment in putting psalms into English poetry, the second was almost certainly Wyatt's paraphrase of Psalm 37.[15] This precursor to his better-known versification of Aretino's Penitential Psalms is, like those in the later sequence, a long block of *terza rima* and formally quite different from Wyatt's poems that present themselves as songs, all of which are in stanzas suitable for singing to a repeating tune. Instead, it is a lyric meditation, similar in voice if not in form to Wyatt's other poems on the vanity and danger of the court,

---

Martin (Aldershot: Ashgate, 2012), 237–58. Early modern quotations are regularized to modern conventions for i/j and u/v.

[11] ". . . with diveris utheris ballattis changeit out of prophane sangis in godlie sangis, for avoyding of sin and harlatrie" (1578 title page). The earliest surviving edition (1567) lacks title page; there is reason to believe that the book was first published by 1546. See A. F. Mitchell, ed., *A Compendious Book of Godly and Spiritual Songs*, Scottish Text Society, 1/39 (Edinburgh: W. Blackwood and Sons, 1897, repr. New York: Johnson, 1966), cxvii, cxxix.

[12] On the reception of Marot's psalm paraphrases at court, see Claude A. Mayer, *Clément Marot* (Paris: Editions A.-G. Nizet, 1972), 460–7.

[13] James M. Osborn, ed., *The Autobiography of Thomas Whythorne* (Oxford: Clarendon Press, 1961), 13–14; spelling modernized.

[14] Michel Jeanneret describes Marot's innovations at length in *Poésie et tradition biblique* (Paris: J. Cortis, 1969), 71–8.

[15] Jason Powell deduces from the scribal hand of Ps. 37 in Egerton MS 2711 that the poem was entered into the volume during 1537. See Powell, "Thomas Wyatt's Poetry in Embassy: Egerton 2711 and the Production of Literary Manuscripts Abroad," *Huntington Library Quarterly* 67/2 (2004): 261–82.

adapted from Seneca.[16] That the psalms could be models for vernacular poetry depended at least as much on their recognized status as poetry as on the Reformers' desire to see the scriptures in the vernacular. Humanist-influenced writers could find praise for the art of the psalms in some of the same Fathers who described the importance of their content, as well as in modern admirers like Petrarch.[17] On the other hand, as Whythorne's evidence establishes, the musical associations of the psalms were such that even Wyatt's *terza rima* was eventually pressed into service for singing.[18]

Edwardian Origins

Around 1548, the evangelical[19] printer Edward Whitchurch put out a small octavo volume entitled *Certayne Psalmes Chosen out of the Psalter of Dauid, & Drawen into Englishe Metre by Thomas Sternhold Grome of ye Kinges Maiesties Roobes*, and containing paraphrases of nineteen psalms, each prefaced by a quatrain summarizing its purport.[20] A second edition appeared in the first half of 1549. Following Sternhold's death in August, Whitchurch prepared an expanded collection of his versifications, *Al Such Psalmes of Dauid as Thomas Sterneholde Late Grome of y[e] Kinges Maiesties Robes, Didde in his Life Time Draw into English Metre*, dated 24 December 1549. With eighteen more psalms by Sternhold and a separate set of seven by John Hopkins, this anthology formed the nucleus around which the texts of the *WBP* would accrete over the course of the next thirteen years.

---

[16] Zim noted the similarity of Wyatt's self-positioning in Ps. 37 and "Who lyst his welthe and eas Retayne"; see Rivkah Zim, *English Metrical Psalms: Poetry as Praise and Prayer, 1535–1601* (Cambridge: Cambridge University Press, 1987), 72.

[17] See Hannibal Hamlin, *Psalm Culture and Early Modern English Literature* (Cambridge: Cambridge University Press, 2004), 2, 87. For English writers who praised the poetry of the Psalms, see Zim, *English Metrical Psalms*, 32–4.

[18] Also looking back from the (probably) mid-1570s, the poet Thomas Sackville recalls singing Wyatt's psalms in what must have been the Edwardian court: "and wyates psalmes while that i synge and saie / in court amyd the heavenly ladyes bright" ("Sacvyles olde age," ll. 92–3). See Rivkah Zim and M.B. Parkes, "'Sacvyles Olde Age': A Newly Discovered Poem by Thomas Sackville, Lord Buckhurst, Earl of Dorset &c. (1536–1608)," *Review of English Studies*, 40 (1989): 1–25. The ambivalence of "synge or saie" echoes the directions for using the *BCP* psalter, but may also reflect the difficulties of setting *terza rima*.

[19] We use "evangelical" or "reformist" to describe mid-Tudor people and attitudes resembling those championed by Luther, Calvin, or other anti-Romanist Continental reformers; the term "Protestant" was not yet in general use and is potentially misleading.

[20] The first edition (*STC* 2419.5) is undated; we refer to it as *1548*. It could not have been printed before August 1547, and the first imitations do not appear until the beginning of 1549; see *RR*, 27–8.

Although it seems likely that Sternhold paraphrased at least a few psalms before the death of Henry VIII in January 1547, both *Certayne Psalmes* and *Al Such Psalmes* are distinctively Edwardian books. In dedicating his efforts to the young king, Sternhold praises Edward's personal piety by means of the contrast between wicked ballads and godly songs: "youre tender and godlye zeale doeth more delyght in the holy songes of veritie, than in any fayned rymes of vanitie." More pointedly, Sternhold also refers in glowing terms to Edward's precociously wise reliance on scripture as the "very meane to attayne to the perfect government of this your realme" and efforts to disseminate vernacular scripture among the laity. These amount to a policy very different from Henry's—particularly in light of the old king's objections to hearing God's word "disputed, rymed, song and jangeled in every Alehouse and Tauerne."[21] The selection of psalms that Sternhold included in his first publication (1–5, 20, 25, 28, 29, 32, 34, 41, 49, 63, 78, 103, 120, 123, and 128) and the choices he made in paraphrasing them strongly suggest that he intended the little book as a contribution to the evangelical political advice with which Edward's ears were filled in the late 1540s. Sternhold both includes a high proportion of wisdom-type psalms in his selection and emphasizes moralizing didacticism in his versifications of other psalms, like Psalms 28 or 41, that might seem to lend themselves better to expressions of subjective experience. Many of the subjects on which Sternhold moralizes were popular evangelical *topoi* during Edward's reign: the importance of the Bible as the highest political authority; the Deuteronomic justice that rewards godly nations and punishes those that go astray; the danger of hypocritical flatterers; and the importance of distributive justice for the godly commonwealth. Reading Sternhold's metrical psalms next to, for example, the printed court sermons of Hugh Latimer makes it hard to avoid the conclusion that both were printed at least in part to portray Edward as the recipient of godly counsel and his regime as founded on scriptural imperatives.[22]

The contributions of the collection's second Edwardian writer, John Hopkins, participate in similar evangelical sentiments without the element of courtly counsel. For example, he chooses to paraphrase Psalm 82, a stern admonition to oppressive rulers, but departs from the majority of his sources in criticizing not princes but the more ambiguous "men of might" and, uniquely in the period, "judges."[23] He also displays a greater interest than Sternhold in the psalms as the expressions of a godly community. The quatrain arguments to two of his seven

---

[21] *1548*, A2r–3v; Edward Hall and Richard Grafton, *Hall's Chronicle*, ed. Henry Ellis (London: J. Johnson, 1809; repr. New York: AMS Press, 1965), 866. It is not clear what scripture was being sung in alehouses by 1546, although Coverdale's psalms and manuscript versions of some of Sternhold's are both possible. Sternhold's original preface was reprinted in all editions of *Al Such Psalmes*.

[22] These matters are treated at length in *RR*, 19–57

[23] See Notes on the Individual Texts and Tunes, below, pp. 623–781.

psalms refer to the psalm's speaker as "the Church," and his versifications depart from the originals and his vernacular sources by adding assertions of collective identity: "As we always with one accord" (Ps. 33.79); "So we thy folk, thy pasture sheep" (Ps. 69.4).[24] It is not clear how or whether early readers distinguished between the two authors; Sternhold's name, position, and reputation seem to have controlled the psalms' reception. The preface to Hopkins's psalms is signed merely "I.H.," and given that his full name never appeared in any pre-Elizabethan collection containing his paraphrases, it is unsurprising that no contemporary in the 1550s mentions him. Nevertheless, Hopkins's interpretive strategy and sense of his audience would end up being a better fit than Sternhold's for the eventual audience of the *WBP*.

Sternhold also established the dominant metrical pattern for the English singing psalm tradition. The meter that he employed for the majority of his psalms (all but two of his total thirty-seven) is a version of fourteeners, rhymed couplets with fourteen syllables in each line of the pair. Until Day's single-column folio editions of the *WBP* in the 1560s, however, his paraphrases were never printed as long couplets, but rather as *abcb* quatrains of eight and six. Full fourteener lines in a respectably-sized font would not have fit the octavo pages of the early editions, but they are always broken into the same metrical units. (The occasional failure to do this in *1548*, as at Psalm 49.45–6, suggests that the lines were divided at the time of printing, rather than before.) In addition, some of the unrhymed first and third lines end with extra unstressed syllables like the feminine endings that one not infrequently finds in iambic lines. These extra syllables never occur in the middle of printed lines, which suggests that Sternhold heard a strong caesura after the first eight syllables that at least resembled a line ending — a pause that may be related to the musical idiom he expected his words to fit, as we shall see shortly. In only four instances does Sternhold break a word across the eighth and ninth syllables (shown by the printer with a hyphen), again indicating a normative division between the two parts of the fourteener line.[25] Hopkins followed Sternhold's usual meter but definitively turned it into quatrains of eight and six by rhyming them *abab*. Most Edwardian editions of the psalms did recognize a distinction between Sternhold's meter and Hopkins's in capitalization and indentation of lines (see App. 2); the difference in indentation was lost during the Marian expansion of the metrical psalter beginning in *1558*, while the capitalization started to slip in the first Elizabethan edition (*1560a*) and became uniform for all CM psalms in the next enlargement of the collection (*1561c* and *1561d*).

Although the meter of these psalms would become the standard ballad stanza and a regular medium for nursery rhymes, its relationship to earlier popular

---

[24] On this tendency, see *RR*, 96–7.

[25] One of these occurs in Ps. 49, but the other three are all in Ps. 78 — far and away the longest psalm that Sternhold undertook and quite possibly early in his Edwardian efforts. For the significance of the psalm to Sternhold's project see *RR*, 38–40, 44–5.

form is more tenuous. Certainly there are examples of similar meters among medieval collections. A handful of late medieval narrative songs in (roughly) fourteeners survives, although these are not generically much like metrical psalms.[26] The carols and shorter devotional lyrics that are generically close to psalms generally rely on fairly short lines (certainly nothing as long as fourteeners). Some, however, resemble Sternhold's lines in the form of quatrains. While continuous four-stress lines seem to have been more common, there are some survivals of alternating lines of eight and six or variations such as 4.4.6.4.4.6.[27] Because our knowledge of popular song before widespread literacy or printing requires deduction from a relatively small number of samples, it is entirely possible that Sternhold patterned his paraphrases after a body of popular devotional songs in the same or a closely related meter. On the other hand, Sternhold's was a meter that had seen use at court previously: Wyatt had used versions of the form, and it is fairly close to Surrey's beloved poulter's meter, which Sternhold employed for his version of Psalm 25.[28] Finally, whatever the meter's origins, it was an extremely practical choice. The relatively long distance between rhymes, in Sternhold's version, allowed him considerable freedom for shaping meaning; the paired, parallel structure of the fourteener couplets could easily reflect the logical organization of the Hebrew psalms; and short units are easiest to assemble into poems of highly variable length. In any event, Edwardian versifiers who wrote either fourteeners or Hopkins's quatrains regularly referred to the form as "Sternhold's meter," implying that it was the signature of a particular author rather than a recognized appropriation from popular culture.

Twelve editions of *Al Such Psalmes* survive, nine of them printed between December 1549 and mid-1553. (Whitchurch's press was silenced by Mary's accession, and first the partnership of John Kingston and Henry Sutton and then Richard Tottel helped themselves to the copy for three Marian editions before such projects became plainly dangerous in late 1554.) Most of these editions are represented by only one surviving example, so it is not unlikely that other editions of this small and fragile book have been lost as owners replaced them with

---

[26] Examples include "Robin Hood and the Monk" and "The Battle of Otterburn." See Charles Read Baskervill, *The Elizabethan Jig and Related Song Drama* (Chicago: University of Chicago Press, 1929), 30.

[27] Out of 502 carols listed in Richard L. Greene, *The Early English Carols,* 2nd edn (Oxford: Clarendon Press, 1977), ten are in what would become Sternhold's meter (nos. 71, 149, 154, 162, 219, 251, 252, 255, 270, 441). None of them are later than c.1500. For examples with music see *The New Oxford Book of Carols,* ed. Hugh Keyte and Andrew Parrott (Oxford: Oxford University Press,1992), nos. 23, 26, 39, 40.

[28] Baskervill (*Elizabethan Jig*, 30) has suggested a connection between the Earl of Surrey's poulter's meter and popular ballads, but his argument essentially rests on the fact that both Surrey and some authors of Robin Hood and chivalric narratives used long lines — a fairly tenuous demonstration of influence.

the Elizabethan *WBP*. The known editions alone, though, represent a rate of production extraordinary for a private prayer book in a relatively novel format with no ecclesiastical imprimatur—the official primer in English survives in only thirteen editions from the same period—and unprecedented for a book of songs or vernacular poesy.

We can also measure the popularity of Sternhold's psalms in terms of the imitations they inspired. In an appendix to *The Reformation in Rhyme*, Quitslund lists eleven Edwardian sets of scriptural versifications written after the appearance of *Certaine Psalmes* that mention Sternhold in the title or apparatus, use Sternhold's meter, borrow some of Sternhold's phrasing, have titles conspicuously modeled on Sternhold's inaugural collection, or show his influence in a combination of those ways.[29] The majority are psalm paraphrases, with printed works by Robert Crowley (the first complete English metrical psalter), John Hall, Elizabeth Fane, William Hunnis, and Francis Seager and manuscripts by Thomas Smith and William Forrest.[30] Other parts of scripture also saw treatments inspired by Sternhold, however. The bulk of Hall's collection came from Proverbs and Ecclesiastes, while William Baldwin added a version of the Song of Songs, Christopher Tye did fourteen chapters of Acts, and William Samuel compacted the Pentateuch into verse at the rate of one octave for each biblical chapter. To these newly-written works showing Sternhold's influence should be added the publications of two Henrician authors. The only early modern print edition of Wyatt's Penitential Psalms was brought out in December of 1549 under the Sternholdian title *Certayne Psalmes Chosen out of the Psalter of Dauid, . . . Drawen into Englyshe Meter by Sir Thomas Wyat Knyght*. Three of Surrey's psalms were printed with his versifications from Ecclesiastes and some of Hall's paraphrases: the whole collection was erroneously attributed to Sternhold. Though none of these books sold as briskly as *Al Such Psalmes*, some did extremely well by Edwardian standards: Hall's *Certayne Chapters Take[n] out of the Prouerbes of Salomon* survives in four editions after the one misattributed to Sternhold, and Tye's *Actes of the Apostles*, first printed in 1553, was twice reprinted before Edward's death called a halt to most evangelical publishing. The Sternhold–Hopkins metrical psalms were thus the leaders in a major literary and publishing phenomenon.

The evident popularity of this body of song gives rise to an obvious question: how were these songs sung? Most earlier studies have had little to say on the subject, or have resorted to speculation. In dedicating the psalms to Edward, Sternhold commented that "your grace taketh pleasure to heare them song somtimes of me," and hopes that others will sing them to the king in the future. We know that this practice was already familiar at court. The most direct way of replacing naughty words with pious ones was to fit the sacred words to existing secular songs, and this was certainly done by German, French, Dutch, and Scottish

---

[29] *RR*, 277–8.
[30] For detailed description of these works see *RR*, 72–93.

compilers. It undoubtedly occurred in England also. Yet the only surviving religious parodies of ballads in English sources of this period are two anonymous psalm paraphrases set for four voices in the Lumley partbooks,[31] where the music of decidedly salacious songs by William Cornyshe was adapted to anonymous paraphrases of Psalms 8 and 13. If any of Sternhold's psalms were treated in this way, there are no extant sources of the music from this period. More generally, the *idiom* of secular song or dance could be applied to sacred texts, and that was what Sternhold evidently expected for his psalms. Some evidence that this did happen comes from William Forrest's preface to his own metrical psalms of 1551. Nowadays, he writes,

> In steade of balads / dissonaunte / and light.
> godlye Psalmes / received are in place:
> conveyed in meatre of number and feete right:
> as unto Ryme / apperteynethe the grace.
> songe to the Vyall / lute / treble: or base.
> or other Instrument/ pleasinge to the eare:[32]

In the next stanza, he names Sternhold as the first to versify psalms for this purpose.

The form of the tunes was harder to describe than the instruments, but there is evidence that they may have been dances. Many years later Edmund Howes reported that "In the first and second yeare of [Edward VI's] Raygne, the mass was wholly suppressed, and part of king Davids Psalmes were turned into English verses, by Hopkins & Sterneholde, Gromes of the kings chamber and set them to severall tunes consisting of gallyards and measures."[33] John Milsom has pointed out that King Edward and his half-sisters Mary and Elizabeth were all accomplished lute players. He has drawn attention to a setting of Sternhold's

---

[31] British Library MSS Royal Appendix 74–76. For a modern edition see Judith Blezzard, ed., *The Tudor Church Music of the Lumley Books*, Recent Researches in the Music of the Renaissance, 65 (Madison, Wis.: A-R Editions, 1985), nos. 17 and 18. As Blezzard points out (viii), the four metrical pieces "intended to be sung to pre-existent popular tunes . . . show regular rhythmic patterns and homophonic textures with balanced phrases, stable harmonies, and easily memorable phrases." The same partbooks contain dances for two to seven instruments in similar style (not reproduced in Blezzard's edition).

[32] William Forrest, "Certaigne Psalmes of davyd in meeatre," British Library Royal MS 17.A.xxi: fol. 1v.

[33] Edmond Howes, "Historical Preface" added to John Stow, *The Annales, or, a Generall Chronicle of England* (London: Thomas Adams, 1615), fol. 6v. Galliards and measures were types of dance. It was not until the seventeenth century that efforts were made by English authorities to resist such secular associations, and even to suppress the fact that they had ever occurred: in the 1631 edition of this passage Howes deleted the words "consisting of gallyards and measures" (*MEPC*, 1:36). See also Quitslund, "Fun and Profit," 239–41.

Psalm 4 for voice and lute in the Osborn Commonplace Book,[34] and shown how it could have been sung as a solo or partsong with lute accompaniment (see Ex.1 and μ1).[35] The piece is similar in style to a pavan, a moderately slow dance in common time, and is in the company of a number of songs and dances transcribed for lute, cittern, or guitar. Milsom further advances the idea that the ubiquitous iambic meters of Sternhold's verses "may actually grow out of the rhythms of the courtly dances to which they were sung." He continues:

> Certainly it is relevant that Sternhold's metrical psalms, unlike those of Wyatt or Surrey, seem to have been conceived from the start as words-for-music, and perhaps for music drawn from the world of pavans, galliards and passamezzo basses. If so, then their 'jogtrot' rhythms merely mirror the manner of courtly dance, and they are bound to sound mechanical when read as words alone. Only when viewed holistically as words-and-music do they properly make sense.[36]

Ex. 1. The "Osborn Psalm": Psalm 4, verse 1

Thomas Sternhold, *ca.* 1548   Anonymous, *ca.* 1550

---

[34] Yale University Library, James Marshall and Marie-Louise Osborn Collection, Music MS 13. The music has no verbal text, but is headed "O god that art my ryghtu-usnes," the first line of Sternhold's paraphrase of Ps. 4, and could fit a common-meter verse. The lute part is transcribed in John Ward, ed., *Music for Elizabethan Lutes*, 2 vols. (Oxford: Clarendon Press, 1992), 2:86. In Ex.1 and μ1 (see n. 35) an editorial voice part is added, set to Ps.4, verse 1.

[35] Citations of live music examples (μ1 to μ29) refer to the Audio Supplement, which is available to the public without charge and may be found at https://www.retsonline.org/psalms.audiosupplement.html.

[36] John Milsom, private communication.

hear — me when I — call: Thou

hast set me at li - ber - ty when

I was bond — and — thrall.

Source: Yale University Library, James Marshall and Marie-Louise Osborn Collection, Music MS. 13, f. 9. The voice part is editorial.

The piece could indeed be a pavan, as can be seen by comparing some actual pavans from the contemporary Lumley partbooks.[37] It shares with them the clear organization in four- or eight-measure phrases and the occasional use of

---

[37] See Paul Doe, ed., *Elizabethan Consort Music I*, MB 44 (London: Royal Musical Association, 1979), nos. 76–111, especially nos. 83, 84, 94, and 95.

dotted-minim-and-crotchet pairs, but a feature added to the dance itself is the initial upbeat to accommodate the first syllable of the iambic verse.

As we have noted, one of many publications modeled on Sternhold's psalms was *The Actes of the Apostles* (1553), a metrical paraphrase of Acts 1–14 set to music for four voices by Christopher Tye (c. 1505–c. 1572), with one tune for all the verses of each chapter.[38] Like Sternhold, Tye was a minor courtier, and he too dedicated his volume to the king. He may have been one of Edward's music masters: unlike Sternhold, he was a composer, and could set his own verses to music. Each tune sets two (short-line) quatrains of "Sternhold's meter" (known to hymnologists as double common meter, or DCM). The title page says the paraphrases are "to synge and also to play upon the Lute, very necessarye for studentes after theyr studye, to fyle theyr wyttes, and also for all Christians that cannot synge, to read the good and Godlye storyes of the lyves of Christ hys Apostles." The settings are mildly contrapuntal, but have a clear melody in the top voice (see Ex. 2 and μ2). They are an almost perfect fit to the iambic meter of the text: every stressed syllable coincides either with a beat, or (as in mm. 9 and 13) with a syncopation. Again the organization is in four-measure phrases (with interludes for the lower voices), and the frequency of dotted notes suggests dancing. Indeed, the prevailing pavan rhythm of Exx. 1 and 2 is almost a cliché of English secular songs in common time, from those of Cornyshe (who died in 1523)[39] to early Elizabethan examples like Richard Edwards's well-known partsong "In going to my naked bed."[40]

Relics of a more sustained Edwardian effort to provide polyphonic settings of Sternhold and Hopkins's psalms are to be found in an early Elizabethan manuscript, British Library Additional MS. 15166, which has only recently attracted much attention.[41] It is a single surviving treble partbook from a set of four that contained strophic settings by John Sheppard (c. 1515–58) of each Sternhold psalm in *Al Such Psalmes* [c. 1549], followed by four of Hopkins's, with the music repeated for several verses in each case.[42] Some of them are distinctly "tunes" in

---

[38] An advance, undated issue (*STC* 2983.8) has only three tunes; the complete editions are *STC* 2984 and 2985, both dated 1553. The tunes are set out in score in Frost, nos. 295–308, and are encoded as *HTI* 43–45 and 49–59.

[39] See examples in John Stevens, ed., *Music at the Court of Henry VIII*, MB 18 (London: Royal Musical Association, 1962).

[40] See Edmund Fellowes, ed., *The English Madrigal School*, 36 (London: Stainer & Bell, 1924), 4th group.

[41] It was first discussed in *MEPC*, 1:45, and in John Milsom, "Songs, Carols and Contrafacta in the Early History of the Tudor Anthem," *Proceedings of the Royal Musical Association* 107 (1980–81), 34–45.

[42] It is for the uppermost voice (usually called "mean" or "superius"), but it has clues to the existence of other voice parts, including brief passages of silence. A table of contents, bound in with the MS but not conjugate with it, does not correspond exactly with the foliation of the existing book, and presumably comes from one of the other partbooks. The MS is Elizabethan, copied after Sheppard's death. Although most of the pieces have

Ex. 2. *The Actes of the Apostles,* chap. 2, verse 1

Christopher Tye, 1553

Barlines are editorial.

the Osborn/Tye domestic style already discussed. In almost every case, the last two lines of the four-line tune are repeated (*ABB* forms)—an increasingly common practice in secular songs.[43] These are followed by six more elaborate settings of some of the earlier Sternhold psalms (2, 3, 4, 5, 28, 32), all of which had

---

the unrevised texts of *Al Such Psalmes,* Ps. 1 is mixed: all after the first stanza, presumably left untexted by Sheppard, was underlaid by the copyist with the post-1556 version of the text as revised by Whittingham in 1556. Later in the manuscript are some undoubtedly Elizabethan versions. According to Katherine Butler, the decorative music paper dates from 1568 or later ("Printed Borders for Sixteenth-Century Music Paper and the Early Career of Music Printer Thomas East," *The Library* 19 (2018): 201).

[43] See Milsom, "Songs, Carols and *Contrafacta,*" 39–41. The earliest examples found by Milsom are in "Henry VIII's Manuscript" (British Library Add. MS 31922), dated c. 1515 by John Stevens, *Music and Poetry in the Early Tudor Court* (Cambridge: Cambridge University Press, 1979), 4.

appeared in *Certayne Psalmes*: on this basis Milsom concludes that they are earlier settings than the others, and calls them the "First Set."[44] The copyist firmly attributes all the settings so far to "mr Shepardes doinge." Most of the settings use from sixteen to twenty-eight lines of the psalm text, selected to make sense as a whole; only one (Psalm 11) breaks off in mid-sentence. The longest is forty lines, consisting of the whole of Psalm 6. The manuscript also includes prose anthems by Sheppard, Thomas Tallis, and others. Sheppard was a leading composer of church music for both the Latin and English rites, and a member of the Chapel Royal under both Edward and Mary. Fortunately, the music of Psalm 1 is also found in the contemporaneous Mulliner Book[45] in the form of an organ reduction that likely corresponds to the full four-voice setting (see Ex. 4 below, and μ4), displaying the same mildly contrapuntal support for the melody that we have already found to be typical of the period. Since this is scored for organ, it is always possible that it is an example of domestically conceived settings of metrical psalms being adopted in church. Milsom, however, considers that Sheppard designed the settings to be extended to cover the whole psalm in each case, and that they are more likely to be for devotional recreation than for church use, like Tye's *Actes* and some of the other sources we have considered.

These examples indicate that in Edward VI's time metrical paraphrases of scripture were regarded primarily as a private intellectual pastime tending to moral improvement, not differing stylistically from other kinds of secular verse or music. Singing them in church was another matter. It hardly seems likely that settings modeled on secular ballads, courtly songs, or dances were introduced in worship, even by reformers. Their idiom was radically different from the chant-based and learned polyphonic styles that had been customary, and they would have required instruments of an unchurchly kind. There is no trace of such a practice in England. Moreover, Sternhold's introduction, along with Whitchurch's title page highlighting the poet's place in the royal household, positions the collection as a courtly rather than an ecclesiastical volume. If his and Hopkins's paraphrases were used in churches, then, it was through an improvisatory appropriation of texts designed for another purpose.

---

[44] Four of these (Pss. 2, 3, 5, and 29) are found in another treble partbook, BL Harley MS. 7578, fols. 89r–91v.

[45] British Library Add. MS. 30513, fol. 80v. The Mulliner Book, consisting mostly of keyboard music, is thought to have been compiled over a considerable period, between 1545 and 1570. Neither Denis Stevens's edition of 1951 (MB 1) nor John Caldwell's revised edition of 2011 mentions the concordance between this piece and MS. 15166. Caldwell (122) offers an arrangement for four voices.

Soon after Henry VIII's death on January 28, 1547, a wide variety of experiments began towards the introduction of English services.[46] The Book of Common Prayer, which appeared in March 1549, "was formed, not by a composition of new materials, but with a careful observance of the order of the several elements or parts of the earlier [Latin] Services."[47] It was predominantly a translation and revision of parts of the Sarum version of the Roman Catholic liturgy, and much of it was undoubtedly sung by choirs to music adapted from that tradition, as exemplified in the Litany in English (published in 1544) and Marbeck's *Booke of Common Praier Noted* (1550).[48] In the words of a hostile witness, "the mass priests, although they are compelled to discontinue the use of the Latin language, yet most carefully observe the same time and manner of chanting to which they were heretofore accustomed in the papacy."[49]

As far as the psalms were concerned, the issue was not about metrical versions, but about how to adapt the prose translations of Coverdale's Great Bible to the chanting traditions already known to choirs, who would need guidance. At Matins the rubric says "Then shalbe saied or songe without any Invitatori this psalme *Venite exultemus* &c. in Englishe, as foloweth." Psalm 95 is then set out in the Great Bible translation, in a form adapted for chanting, with each verse beginning on a new line, and with a colon dividing every verse into two parts to indicate where the half-cadence should occur. This was followed by a second rubric: "Then shal folow certaine Psalmes in order as they [have] been appointed in a table made for the purpose, except there be propre Psalmes appointed for that day."[50] All churches had been required to display the Great Bible since 1536; now, those with choirs would need copies of *The Psalter or Boke of the Psalmes where unto is Added the Letany and Other Devout Prayers*. This had appeared as a separate publication in July 1548[51] in the form adapted for chanting, just as the *Venite* was set out in the Prayer Book. This important feature is recognized in the title of a later edition, dated 27 November 1548: *The Psalter or Psalmes of David after the Translacion of the Great Bible, Poincted as it Shalbe Song in Churches.* Many

---

[46] See Susan Brigden, *London and the Reformation* (Oxford: Clarendon Press, 1989), 423–46; Peter le Huray, *Music and the Reformation in England 1549–1660* (London: Herbert Jenkins, 1967), 9–18.

[47] Francis Proctor, *A History of the Book of Common Prayer* (London: Macmillan, 1864), 26.

[48] Le Huray, *Music and the Reformation*, 18–23.

[49] Bishop John Hooper to Heinrich Bullinger, December 27, 1549: Hastings Robinson, ed., *Original Letters Relative to the English Reformation*, 1 (Cambridge: Cambridge University Press, 1846), 71.

[50] The Prayer Book included an unprecedented calendar allocating all 150 psalms to morning and evening prayer in a monthly cycle.

[51] STC 2373.

churches acquired copies of this work, and indeed parts of it seem to have been available as early as 1547.[52]

The wording of the rubrics did not specifically exclude metrical versions, however. Indeed one source backed by royal authority, a special order of prayer for relief of the sweating sickness that had spread quickly over the country in 1551, replaced prose psalms with Sternhold versions taken from *Al Such Psalmes*, to be sing by "the Quere," with added metrical doxologies of unknown origin.[53] One of them is headed "After the lesson sing this Psalm." In the absence of published or widely known metrical tunes it seems most likely that these too were chanted to the familiar Gregorian psalm tones.[54] Robert Crowley, an activist evangelical clergyman who would later join the Marian exiles, had shown how this might be done (see Ex. 3). In a published version of all the psalms and canticles in Sternhold's meter, he had provided by way of example the first verse of his paraphrase of Psalm 1, set to the seventh psalm tone in the tenor, harmonized for four voices in faburden style.[55] The two eight-syllable lines are set to the reciting note, which would have carried a varying number of syllables in a prose psalm; the short lines are set to the half-cadence and full cadence of the chant.

Hymn tunes were readily available for adaptation to metrical psalms. Latin metrical hymns, most of them in long meter (iambic tetrameters), had been used in worship for centuries, sung strophically by choirs to monophonic tunes.[56]

---

[52] We examined fourteen published sets of churchwardens' accounts (those of Ashburton, Devon; Bishop's Stortford, Herts.; Boxford, Suffolk; Cambridge: St. Mary the Great; Lambeth, Surrey; London: St. Andrew Hubbard, St. Martin-in-the-Fields, St. Mary Woolnoth, St. Michael Cornhill; Ludlow, Shropshire; Marston, Oxfordshire; Mildenhall, Suffolk; Preston, Lancs.; and York: St. Michael Spurriergate). All but three of them recorded the purchase of one or more psalters between 1547 and 1552. At Cambridge they were described as "iii saulter bookes in ynglyse to sing or say the salmes of the servys," echoing the rubric in the Book of Common Prayer. St. Mary Woolnoth bought "vi Salters in English for the quyere" in 1547.

[53] *A Thankes Geuing to God vsed in Christes Churche on the Monday, Wednisday and Friday* [London, 1551], *STC* 16504; modern edition in Natalie Meares et al., eds., *Special Prayers, Fasts and Thanksgivings in the British Isles 1533–1688* (National Prayers, I; Woodbridge: Boydell Press, 2013), 34–41. This service was enjoined in an order to the bishops dated 18 June 1551.

[54] Later in the same source the prose Nunc dimittis, taken from the 1549 BCP, is followed (curiously) by the same metrical doxology as the one appended to two of the psalms, suggesting that chanting was equally suited to both.

[55] Robert Crowley, *The Psalter of David Newely Translated into Englysh Metre in Such Sort that it Maye the More Decently, and wyth More Delyte of the Mynde, be Reade and Songe of All Men.* [London:] Robert Crowley, 1549 (*STC* 2725). See Ex. 3 and μ3.

[56] For an edition of those used in England see Walter H. Frere, ed., *Hymn-Melodies for the Whole Year from the Sarum Service-Books and Other Ancient English Sources* (London: Plainsong & Medieval Music Society, 1903).

Ex. 3. Chant for Psalm 1, verse 1

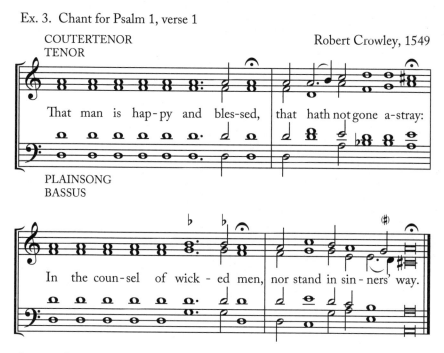

Source: Crowley, *The Psalter of David* (STC 2725)

One of them was now translated and explicitly authorized for use in the re-
formed church. The hymn "Come, Holy Ghost, eternal God," a common-meter
translation of the long-meter *Veni, Creator*, was prescribed in March 1550 for or-
dination services, and may well have been sung by choirs to its ancient melody
(see p. 633 for details). We have found no example in print or manuscript from
the sixteenth century of an English hymn or metrical paraphrase deliberately set
to a traditional Latin hymn tune. Probably the religious and political gulf of ref-
ormation was too wide for such a development. In 1561 the metrical *Veni, Creator*
would appear in the psalm book with its own Geneva-style tune.[57]

A more acceptable model for use in the reformed church was to treat metri-
cal psalms like prose texts in vocal polyphony, in the manner of a Latin motet or
English anthem. There are a few surviving anthem-like settings of single stanzas,
allowing for strophic repetition, that probably found their way into choral ser-
vices between 1549 and 1553, when the reformed liturgy in English was in regular
use. Robin Leaver plausibly speculates that such pieces were sung before or after

---

[57] In an ironic development, however, the fiercely anticatholic "Preserve us, Lord"
would eventually be joined to the tune of an ancient Catholic hymn, St. Ambrose's *Veni,
redemptor gentium*. See p. 780.

services on certain major festivals.[58] Seager provided one for some of his own psalm paraphrases.[59] Two settings of Sternhold psalms are found in the Wanley partbooks, the most important surviving source of Edwardian choir music. One is strophic, with a text consisting of Psalm 49:1 and Psalm 4:1, 3–9.[60] The other is a through-composed setting of Psalm 128, headed "Wedding."[61]

Psalm 128 was indeed in demand as the customary choice for wedding ceremonies. A more ambitious five-voice setting of Sternhold's Psalm 128 was composed by his fellow-courtier Philip van Wilder, who died on 24 February 1554. This, Van Wilder's only known anthem, seems to imitate the pealing of church bells. Milsom proposes that it originated as an occasional piece for a royal wedding, either in church or at a banquet following the ceremony.[62] It is extant in as many as nine Elizabethan and later manuscript sources associated with church choirs, and was still in use after 1660.[63]

What about congregational singing? Some writers have advanced the notion that it was widely practiced in Edward's reign, perhaps following the example of the Continental religious refugees at the Strangers' Church of Austin Friars, London, and that some of the later tunes originated in England at that time.[64] While it is always possible that communal singing was tried out here and there, and a solitary piece of evidence seems to support this hypothesis,[65] there was

---

[58] Leaver, 'Goostly Psalmes,' 136.

[59] See Frost 293.

[60] The tenor partbook is missing. Modern reconstructions of this piece can be found in James Wrightson, ed., The Wanley Manuscripts, Recent Researches in the Music of the Renaissance, 99–101 (Madison, Wis.: A-R Editions, 1995), 2, no. 42, and in MEPC, 2, no. 40. It seems likely that the peculiar text selection for this piece, with a semantic disconnect between the two psalms, was the result of an error or misunderstanding.

[61] For a modern reconstruction see Wrightson, Wanley Manuscripts, 2, no. 25.

[62] For a modern edition see Philip van Wilder, Collected Works, ed. Jane A. Bernstein, Masters and Monuments of the Renaissance, 4 (New York: Broude Bros., 1991), 1–9, 124–6. We have recorded the anthem as µ4.

[63] The evidence for this is in James Clifford's The Divine Services and Anthems Usually Sung in His Majesties Chappell, and in all Cathedrals and Collegiate Choirs in England and Ireland, 2nd ed. (London: Nathaniel Brooke and Henry Brome, 1664). Van Wilder's anthem is on p. 82, headed "Epithalamium," with the same attribution to "Mr. Phillips" that is found in some of the manuscript sources.

[64] Leaver goes so far as to list a selection of 12 tunes from the WBP that he believes originated in England between 1547 and 1553: 'Goostly Psalmes', 317. Alec Ryrie strongly supports this possibility, while admitting it to be unproven: "The Psalms and Confrontation in English and Scottish Protestantism," Archiv für Reformationsgeschichte, 101 (2010), 114–37: 122.

[65] François van der Delft, Emperor Charles V's ambassador to England, wrote in a letter to the Imperial Council on 7 December 1547 (cited and discussed in RR, 106): "Mass is still celebrated here, but the common people are beginning to sing psalms in

Ex. 4. Psalm 1 (Sternhold)

John Sheppard

The man is blest that hath not gone by wick–ed rede a - - - stray,____ Ne sate in chair of pes - ti-lence, nor walked in___

Sources: Text and voice part, British Library Add. MS. 15166, fol. 1r–2r; organ part, British Library Add. MS. 30513, fol. 80v.

certainly no widespread movement in that direction such as would occur later on. No purchase of metrical psalms by any church before 1558 has come to light, nor are there any English sources of the Elizabethan psalm tunes dating from before *1556*. When Henry Machyn (1496/8–1563) recorded the introduction of congregational singing in London after Elizabeth's accession, at morning prayer in St. Antholin's church on 21 September 1559, he described with evident astonishment how a psalm was sung: "in Geneva fashion: . . . men and women all do sing, and boys."[66] Six months later, at the installation of a new incumbent at St. Martin,

---

their own language in the churches." This could not have been more than a few months after the publication of Sternhold's *Certayne Psalmes* (see *RR*, 27–8). Van der Delft may have seen a copy of Coverdale's *Goostly Psalmes* [1535–6]. But that book was explicitly designed for private use; there is nothing to suggest that it was ever used in church, and it had been ceremonially burnt in 1546 (Leaver, '*Goostly Psalmes*', 68–83). See Ryrie, "Psalms and Confrontation," 121–2.

[66] *The Diary of Henry Machyn*, ed. John Gough Nicholls (London: Camden Society, 1848), 212, quoted *MEPC*, 1:43; Leaver, '*Goostly Psalmes*,' 240; and *RR*, 196–7. The boys

Ludgate, "all the people did sing the tune of Genevay, and with the base of the organs."[67] There is no hint here of an indigenous tradition being restored. Since 1549 at the latest, Machyn had been parish clerk of another London church, Holy Trinity the Less, where he would have had charge of the music and the choir. He had kept his "chronicle," largely a record of public events, since 1550, and his report shows clearly that this kind of singing was new to London in 1559. It also tells us where it came from. As we shall see, surviving churchwardens' accounts from several London parishes of the early Elizabethan period specifically refer to the purchase of "Geneva psalms."[68]

Marian Expansion

The real beginning of English congregational singing, and of the tunes that went with it, was among the Marian exiles. It represented an almost total break with the English past, and the version of the Sternhold–Hopkins collection that would become the *WBP* was effectively rewritten as a part of the anglophone liturgy at Geneva. To the people of England, Geneva was the immediate source of the new kind of singing, and this accounts for the common name "Geneva psalms" (satirized by some slightly later as "Geneva jigs").[69] In fact, though, congregational song was a feature of worship in most of the scattered exile churches. The practice may well have started at Strassburg,[70] where the first English exiles arrived in April 1554, and it certainly flourished at Frankfurt and Wesel.

The exiles' first collection, *One and Fiftie Psalms of David in Englishe Metre, whereof, 37. were made by Thomas Sterneholde: and the Rest by Others*, was printed in February 1556 as part of *The Forme of Prayers and Ministration of the Sacramentes, &c., Used in the Englishe Congregation at Geneva*, the new service book for the Anglo-Scottish community in Geneva.[71] The fifty-one psalms consist of the forty-four from *Al Such Psalmes*—most of them extensively revised—to which were

---

may have included choristers; some parish churches still had boys to assist the paid men singers: see Jonathan Willis, *Church Music and Protestantism in Post-Reformation England: Discourses, Sites and Identities* (Farnham: Ashgate, 2009), 119–20.

[67] *Diary of Henry Machyn*, 228.

[68] Willis, *Church Music and Protestantism*, 126. For details see Appendix 7.

[69] The term "Geneva tunes" was still in use after 1603: see British Library Royal MS. 18.B.xix, fol. 8r, quoted Nicholas Temperley, "John Playford and the Metrical Psalms," *Journal of the American Musicological Society* 25 (1972): 334.

[70] Leaver (*'Goostly Psalmes,'* 194) plausibly suggests that the hymns and psalms by Becon, Coxe, Grindal, and Wisdom that found their way into the *WBP* originated in Strassburg. Coxe's Lord's Prayer, Grindal's "Da pacem, Domine" and Wisdom's "Preserve us, Lord" are associated with German-derived melodies to which they may well have been first sung there.

[71] Geneva: J. Crespin, 1556 (*STC* 16561: hereinafter *Form of Prayers or 1556*). The *Hymn Tune Index* dated this edition 1557 (new style), on the basis of the preface dated 10

added seven new psalm versifications and a metrical version of the Ten Commandments that would all be attributed in the next edition to William Whittingham. The compilation's explicit purpose in the volume was to provide the singing psalms that the *Form of Prayers* required during public services, though the marginal glosses clarifying and applying psalm verses suggest that the editor (almost certainly Whittingham) also imagined household use and even reflective private reading. In addition to glosses, he replaced the summary quatrains that had headed the psalms in their Edwardian printings with prose arguments, lest anyone should be tempted to sing them: this reflected Calvin's view that only the words of God were fit for singing in worship. A tune was attached to the first stanza of each paraphrase. The result is that the English metrical psalter now looked very much like the Huguenot psalter as it had developed in Geneva and much less like the recreational verses initially published in London.

That does not mean that it was a purely Genevan effort. Published less than five months after Whittingham, Knox, and other leaders of the Anglo-Scottish church had left Frankfurt as a result of ecclesiological and personal conflict, the *1556* edition of the metrical psalms is probably as much a product of the exiles' needs there as in Geneva. Arriving on 27 June 1554, the pioneering English group in Frankfurt (which included Whittingham) was soon given permission by the Frankfurt Senate to form a congregation and to share the building in use by the Francophone church, on the condition that they "shulde not discent from the frenchmen in doctrine / or ceremonies."[72] The English liturgy instituted there at the end of July seems, in fact, to have followed an essentially Calvinist form of worship, including congregational psalm singing. Such singing can only have been possible by employing a set of psalm versifications already in the congregants' possession. While Whittingham must have worked on revising and expanding the collection as time allowed over the next eighteen months, they would have started with *Al Such Psalmes*. Virtually every other aspect of the English church's public worship seems to have quickly become a matter of contention within the larger exile community, resulting in four separate liturgies within nine months, but psalm singing evidently continued through it all as a rare instantiation of harmony amid the rest of the conflict.

Although the theological leaders of the Anglo-Scottish party at Geneva were John Knox and Christopher Goodman, it was Whittingham who seems to

---

February 1556 (presumed old style). I now accept that new-style dating must have been in use in the Republic of Geneva (N. T.).

[72] *A Brieff Discours off the Troubles Begonne at Franckford in Germany anno Domini 1554 abowte the Booke off off* [sic] *Common Prayer and Ceremonies* ([Heidelberg: M. Schirat], 1575), 6. This account of the Frankfurt period is largely derived from *RR*, 115–20, which in turn relies heavily on *A Brieff Discours*. The Frenchmen in question were in fact the Walloon Protestants led by Valérand Poullain, previously settled at Glastonbury, England. See also *MEPC*, 1:28 and p. 539, below.

have most zealously worked to create the materials that would underlie the devotional practices of a fully reformed English Church, bringing to it the liturgical innovations and vernacular resources associated with Calvin's own church. These include not only the metrical psalter but also the Geneva Bible and, in all likelihood, the parts of the *Form of Prayers* translated or adapted from French originals.[73] In all of these efforts, he took his cue from Calvin or from the innovations and scholarship that Calvin fostered at Geneva. He was, moreover, at Frankfurt when the congregational singing of metrical psalms began, and moved to Geneva with Knox in September 1555. With regard to the singing psalms, Whittingham seems to have set himself three tasks: adding to the number of available metrical versions, with a particular focus on psalms appropriate to the exiles' circumstances; revising the Edwardian versifications to make them more suitable for Calvinist-style hymnody; and providing tunes suitable for public worship. In all of these efforts he took his cue from Calvin and looked to the French metrical psalter for guidance. The most obvious textual change is his addition of seven psalms and the Ten Commandments. Though he put four psalms into Sternhold's meter and one into poulter's meter (later termed double short meter, or DSM)—forms already used in *Al Such Psalmes*—his Psalm 51 and Commandments are in eight-syllable quatrains (DLM) and Psalm 130 uses quatrains alternating seven and six syllables (7.6.7.6.D). Unlike most of those in the French psalter, all of the meters are too close to fourteeners to give any real sense of metrical variety, but the Ten Commandments and the (for English) quite odd stanza of Ps. 130 match their counterparts in the Genevan psalm book and employ the same tunes.[74] Even where the stanza form is different, most of the new psalms also show the influence of Marot or Beza in the distribution of the psalm texts between lines, diction that favors cognates with the French versions, and some interpretive similarities. In the revisions to Sternhold and Hopkins's earlier psalms, we can find a Genevan emphasis on scriptural purity in congregational song. The *Pseaumes octantetrois* describes Beza's new contributions as "mise en rime françoise au plus près de l'hebreu," echoed on the internal title page of 1556 in the claim that the paraphrases had been "co[n]ferred with the Hebrewe, and in certeine places corrected, as the text and sens of the Prophete required."[75]

---

[73] See *RR*, 159–60, 176–92. Jane E.A. Dawson has argued for Goodman's (and Anthony Gilby's) authorship of the *Form of Prayers* preface, and it is difficult to imagine that the two ministers were not involved in its formulation, but the extensive use of Calvin's own preface to the French metrical psalter virtually assures that Whittingham wrote large pieces of it. Jane E.A. Dawson, "The Early Career of Christopher Goodman and his Place in the Development of English Protestant Thought," Ph.D. diss. (Durham University, 1968), 183.

[74] In fact, the 7.6.7.6 pattern of Ps. 130 is enough like Sternhold's meter that I mischaracterized it in *RR*, 144. (B. Q.)

[75] *Pseaumes octantetrois*, 1.

Despite having some Hebrew himself, Whittingham's method for turning the recreational Edwardian verses into accurate enough reflections of David's psalms for liturgical use was to work through French and Latin: Beza's metrical psalms, the annotated French psalter prepared by Louis Budé, and Calvin's own manuscript psalm commentaries. With these aids, he supplied verses shortchanged or missing in Sternhold's paraphrases, altered emphasis, clarified imagery, and imposed his own aesthetic preferences on the diction (not always with results that gratify a modern reader).[76] The prose arguments are in a number of cases translated from the French psalter.

The most pressing matter to settle in making the Sternhold and Hopkins psalms available for the new liturgies in either Frankfurt or Geneva, however, would have been tunes. Unlike all musical settings discussed so far, the tunes printed in *1556* were explicitly designed for congregational participation in worship, after Calvin's principles, as the preface makes clear. Discussing the validity of "prayers . . . with songe joyned ther unto," the writer (again, most likely Whittingham) declares that "as well for lack of the true use therof, as due consideration of the same, [it] is called by many into dout, whether it may be used in a reformed church." He goes on to assert biblical authority for singing of psalms, and explains how Satan had corrupted this natural gift, "chieflye by the papistes his ministers in disfiguring it, partly by strange language, that can not edifie: and partly by a curious wanton sort, hyringe men to tickle the eares, and flatter the phantasies."[77] This rules out any imitation of traditional Latin chants, motets, or hymns. As for using tunes in the style of secular song, let alone dance, as Tye, Sheppard, and others had done, such a practice had been banished by Calvin himself, that "learned and godly man" whose approval was claimed on the title page and in the preface of the service book:

> One should always see to it that the singing is not light or frivolous: but has weight and majesty, as St. Augustine said. And so there should be a great difference between music made to entertain men at the table and in their home, and the Psalms, which are sung in Church, in the presence of God and his Angels.[78]

---

[76] For a more detailed overview of these revisions, see *RR*, 158–65.

[77] *Form of Prayers*, 1:16–18.

[78] Il y a tousiours à regarder, que le chant ne soit pas leger & volage: mais ait pois & maiesté, comme dit sainct Augustin. & ainsi, qu'il y ait grande difference entre la musique qu'on fait pour resiouir les hommes à table & en leur maison: & entre les Pseaumes, qui se chantent en l'Eglise, en la presence de Dieu & de ses Anges. "Jean Calvin à tous Chrestiens et amateurs de la Parole de Dieu," in *Pseaumes octantetrois de David, mis en rime françoise par Clément Marot et Théodore de Bèze* (Genève: Jean Crespin, 1551), A5v. Translation ours.

Even if the Frankfurt magistrates had not stipulated that the English church should follow the "doctrine" and "ceremonies" of the Calvinist French church there, Whittingham clearly wished to pattern the English metrical psalter after the one in use at Geneva.

So, when after prayers "the people" were directed to "singe a Psalme all together, in a playne tune,"[79] there could be little choice as to its musical character. It was to follow the French model, that new and pure mode of singing uniquely suited to the people's zeal for a truly reformed religion. Several characteristic melodic features of the French tunes were imitated in the English ones, which are indeed radically different in character from any English music so far discussed. They are solemn and plain, with no dotted rhythms: indeed they use only semibreves and minims, except for the concluding longs. They are monophonic, with no hint of either vocal or instrumental accompaniment. They are syllabic, with no melismas or textual repetitions or *ABB* forms. Almost every line begins with a long note on the beat.

The developing French corpus had reached eighty-three psalms, each with its own tune, by 1551 (plus the Nunc dimittis and the Decalogue). The vast majority had phrases beginning and ending with semibreves, but with a varying number and arrangement of minims and semibreves between them. In accordance with the principles of French verse they had a strict syllable-count pattern, but the only regular stresses occurred at the end of each line (masculine or feminine), and in some cases before a caesura in the middle of the line.

The English exiles could not simply adopt the French tunes wholesale, as the Dutch and German Reformed Churches would do in 1566 and 1573 respectively, after preparing their own translations to match the tunes.[80] They had the extremely popular Sternhold and Hopkins collection, and even if Whittingham was willing to revise the texts, commitment to this version seems to have been very strong. Given the opportunity to add psalms, after all, Whittingham began not by adapting French stanzas for French tunes but by replicating the Edwardian fourteeners and carefully choosing meters that did not look too much like a departure from the established English form. This meant, however, that he was stuck with a set of verses entirely in DCM and related iambic meters. He searched the French Genevan psalter for tunes that were near enough to those meters for possible adaptation, but found few candidates.[81] One Sternhold

---

[79] *Form of Prayers*, 1:56.

[80] See Walter Blankenburg, "Church Music in Reformed Europe," in Friedrich Blume and others, *Protestant Church Music: A History* (New York and London, 1975), 566, 549 respectively; Waldo Selden Pratt, *The Music of the French Psalter of 1562* (New York: Columbia University Press, 1939), 21. Leaver discusses Utenhove's Dutch translations in detail (*'Goostly Psalmes,'* 141–74).

[81] All tunes adapted from French sources by the English compilers appear to have been taken from the 1551 edition of the French psalter, *Pseaumes octantetrois de David,*

paraphrase in DCM (Psalm 128) was accommodated to the French tune for the same psalm, which was close to its syllable count (7.6.7.6.D), by simply repeating one note in each of the seven-note phrases.[82] By a more hazardous process, involving the omission of some notes, a French tune in 9.8.9.8.D was adapted for Whittingham's Psalm 114.[83] The translations of Psalm 130 (7.6.7.6.D) and the Commandments (LM) were written to fit the French tunes syllabically for those texts, and both of these would survive into the *WBP*.

The remaining forty-eight tunes were all new, and all but seven are in DCM.[84] They represent an awkward compromise between Sternhold's meter and the idiom of the French tunes. There was indeed a profound difference in prosody between French and English verse, which amply accounts for the difficulties faced by the exiles in creating effective tunes on the French model for the English psalms.[85] To take the most obvious example: of 414 fourteener phrases in these tunes designed for iambic verses, 313 begin with a semibreve. This is in marked contrast to Tye's *Actes of the Apostles*, also in DCM, where only one of the fifty-six fourteener phrases in the tune-carrying upper voice begins with a semibreve.[86] As already pointed out, Tye's system reflects the iambic meter of the verses, where every line, at least in prosodic theory, begins with an unstressed syllable. It also provides a regular and easily perceptible rhythmic framework for his tunes. Both of these virtues had to be sacrificed in deference to Calvin's views.

The new English tunes fell far short of their French models, as is generally agreed,[87] and they offered little to replace the lost rhythmic vitality of Edward-

---

or its successors of 1554 or 1556. An exemplar of the previously lost 1551 edition was acquired by Rutgers Library in 1966 and published in facsimile in 1973. Some of the tunes had originated in earlier sources, which are cited here in the notes on individual tunes.

[82] See Frost 147 (*HTI* 106a.)

[83] Frost 126, *HTI* 102: lines 1 and 4–8 are based on the French tune for Ps. 118 (Frost 131).

[84] Ps. 23 is CM; Pss. 30 and 79 are triple CM; Pss. 25 and 115 are DSM; Whittingham's new Ps. 51 is DLM; and Ps. 120 is 6.6.6.6.6.6.

[85] This is discussed in more detail below, pp. 557–8.

[86] The long notes at the beginning of phrases in tunes designed for iambic verse are a striking feature of many Elizabethan psalm tunes. They have in recent times been called "gathering notes," as if the need to wait for stragglers to catch up had to be reflected in the notation of most (but not all) phrases of most (but not all) tunes. Percy A. Scholes stated this as a fact under "Gathering Note" in *The Oxford Companion to Music* (London: Oxford University Press, 1938), and it is still assumed without discussion by Timothy Duguid, who calls the long notes "gathering tones": *Metrical Psalmody in Print and Practice: English 'Singing Psalms' and Scottish 'Psalm Buiks', c. 1547–1640* (Farnham: Ashgate, 2014), 158. In reality they are a survival of Calvin's model as realized in the French tunes.

[87] "Geneva had introduced new metres and a set of tunes, which, even when altered to suit English metres, retained a good deal of magnificence. The English tradition hardly

ian settings. Most of them are notably lacking in interest or direction, failing to take advantage of elementary, universal melodic principles such as symmetry, repetition, sequence, or climax that could have made them striking or memorable. Only eight of the forty-eight new tunes would find their way into the Elizabethan canon. Their indifferent quality is not surprising. In addition to their lack of natural affinity with the verses, the circumstances of their creation were unpropitious. The English and Scottish exiles had no master musician of the stature or experience of Walter, Franc, Goudimel, or Bourgeois among their number, who might have been equal to the daunting task of creating a new musical idiom from scratch.

The composer of the new tunes may never be positively identified, but we now advance the hypothesis that it was Whittingham himself, with assistance from one or more French or Genevan musicians.[88] As with the texts, he was anxious to adopt a French model. According to his biographer, he was "skillfull in musick," and later, as Dean of Durham, would be "very carefull to provide the best songs and anthems that could be got out of the Queen's Chapell to furnish the quire with all."[89] His personal property on his death included a virginals.[90] On the other hand, Whittingham was not a professional musician and left no

---

ever got away from the jog-trot D.C.M.; after the modal tunes [i.e. those in modes that later fell out of use] of that metre had been eliminated, those that remained were for the most part uniformly dull, and those that took their places were certainly no less so." Walter H. Frere, ed., *Hymns Ancient and Modern: Historical Edition* (London: William Clowes, 1909), xlix; repeated word for word by Maurice Frost, *Historical Companion to Hymns Ancient & Modern* (London, 1962), 43. See also Robert Bridges, "A Practical Discourse on Some Theories of Hymn-Singing," *Journal of Theological Studies* 1 (1899–1900): 55–56; Kenneth Long, *The Music of the English Church* (London: Hodder & Stoughton, 1972), 208–9; Erik Routley, *The Music of Christian Hymns* (Chicago: G. I. A. Publications, 1981), 38; Christopher Marsh, *Music and Society in Early Modern England* (Cambridge: Cambridge University Press, 2010), 412.

[88] Assistance with the music, including the notation, could have come, for instance, from French musicians in Calvin's circle at Geneva, such as Pierre Dagues (d. 1571?), cantor at St. Peter's church from 1556, whom Blankenburg identifies as the "Maître Pierre" said to have composed the later melodies published in the French Genevan psalter of 1562 ("Church Music in Reformed Europe," in Friedrich Blume and others, *Protestant Church Music: A History* (New York and London: Victor Gollancz, Ltd., 1975), 520–1). The French influence is not limited to rhythmic matters: the tunes of *1556* reflect a more traditional use of the modes than was common in English music of the time, where modern tonality was more developed (see Jessie Ann Owens, "Concepts of Pitch in English Music Theory, c. 1560–1640," in Cristal Collins Judd., ed., *Tonal Structures in Early Music* [New York and London: Garland, 1998], 191), which helps to explain why so few of them survived into the Elizabethan psalm books.

[89] A. M. E. Green, ed., "Life of Mr William Whittingham, Dean of Durham," *Camden Miscellany* 6 (London: Camden Society, 1870), 23

[90] David Marcombe, Whittingham, William," *ODNB*.

attributed compositions, which helps to account for the relatively poor quality of the tunes of *1556*.

The near-uniformity of verse meter, deplored by later critics, could have been a boon to these early reformers: the bulk of the psalms might have been sung to one or a few tunes, a quick and easy way to realize both biblical injunctions and Calvin's prescriptions. Whittingham did not at once seize on this possibility, however. Instead, he dutifully followed French precedent by providing a unique tune for each psalm. Quite apart from the strain this placed on the limited creative skills available, it must have posed difficulties for the congregation, which was asked to learn a large number of unfamiliar and rather nondescript tunes in short order. What people did, no doubt, was to learn the most accessible ones, then apply those to several different psalms. This is attested by the fact that twenty-seven of the forty-eight new tunes were abandoned in the second edition (*1558*) and replaced by cross-references, such as "Sing this, as the 3. psalme" for Psalms 4 and 5. (Here began an English practice that would lead eventually to common tunes — those with unspecified texts — and the tune-name system. The references were generally to tunes on nearby pages, with no discernible effort to find a tune that matched the psalm in mood.[91]) Evidently the dropped tunes were no longer needed; probably they had not been very successful in congregational practice. It is a striking fact that seven of them were in the obsolescent Phrygian mode.[92]

The second edition (*1558*) continued to expand the psalm and hymn corpus while showing some modifications of Whittingham's original conception of the metrical psalter's format. Whittingham himself contributed a version of the Nunc dimittis and his last nine new psalm paraphrases, including the 704-line

---

[91] Timothy Duguid considers, on the contrary, that both tunes and cross-references (which he aptly terms "tune suggestions") were deliberately selected to suit the character of the psalms to which they were assigned (*Metrical Psalmody*, 66–7, 74–6). But he provides no convincing evidence to support this belief, and there is much reason to doubt it, as will be pointed out below. In later editions many cross-references are to tunes in the wrong meter, or to psalms without any tune at all. These erroneous suggestions were often reprinted unchanged over many years. Had any tune suggestions been widely adopted one might expect the resulting tune/text combinations to appear later on in other publications, as did many of the tunes printed with their texts in the *WBP*. This did occur for nine psalms in the first edition of East's Companion (*East 1592*), but they were all replaced in the second edition (1594), showing that they were not generally accepted. The *HTI* records no other instance of a *WBP* "tune suggestion" being adopted in any other musical publication.

[92] A good example is the *1556* tune for Ps. 7 (μ7). Only one Phrygian tune survived into the canon: DA PACEM (see p. 776), incorporated in *1561a* and *1561d* from German sources. But even in that case the final was changed to G; presumably English singers would not accept E as a final because of its unfamiliar or archaic effect. (Small capitals are used in this study for tune names.)

Psalm 119. His name was printed this time to distinguish his versifications from the two by another exiled Englishman, John Pullain. Both writers were willing, by this point, to move away from the dominant DCM form. Six of Whittingham's new versifications were fitted to the French tunes for the same texts, without changing the syllable count.[93] Some of these (most notably Psalms 50 and 127) essentially translate their French counterparts. He worked without a French model for Psalm 119 (DCM), and the tune shows German influence.[94] Pullain's two psalms, 148 and 149, abandon fourteeners and, in the case of 149, iambs, even without borrowing French tunes; the latter (5.5.5.5.5, anapestic) has a tune largely made up of fragments from Martin Luther's famous tune "Ein' feste Burg ist unser Gott."[95] Despite the increase in the number of texts, the total number of tunes fell from fifty-two to forty-two. Perhaps because Whittingham had published an annotated prose psalter in 1557, which would presumably take care of reading and study needs, the marginal glosses also disappeared from the psalms in meter. This edition sets the pattern for the layout of the rest of the metrical psalm editions that would be printed in Geneva. The Genevan editions, however, would soon have competition from the renewed Protestant publishing industry in Elizabeth's London.

Elizabethan Compilation

After Elizabeth's accession the Anglo-Genevan school of psalmody split into two distinct lineages of texts and tunes. The first, which would ultimately lead to the Scottish psalm book, came from the Anglo-Scottish Protestant community still based in Geneva. The second began to cater to English use, and culminated in *The Whole Book of Psalms*.[96]

The fourth edition of the Genevan service book to contain the metrical psalter (*1560b*)[97] included twenty-five new psalms by the polemicist William Kethe, and raised the number of tunes to sixty-one, dropping only one.[98] Its twenty-one

---

[93] Pss. 50(1), 121, 124, 127, 129 and the Nunc dimittis (*HTI* 116, 122–125, 112 respectively). Those for Pss. 50(1), 121, and 124 would survive into the canon.

[94] See the note on PSALM 119, p. 742.

[95] Of the other new tunes in *1558*, five were for old psalms whose *1556* tunes had been dropped: Sternhold's Pss. 14, 25, 68, and 120, and Hopkins's Ps. 79. Two were for new paraphrases by Whittingham for Pss. 37 (DCM) and 71 (DSM). One triple-CM tune (for Ps. 84) was reduced to DCM; the other was among the rejects.

[96] For a thorough comparison of the two streams, see Duguid, *Metrical Psalmody*.

[97] The third edition, referred to in the preface of the fourth, has not survived, but, given textual variants shared by the 1560 London and Genevan editions, was probably subsequent to *1558* but nearly identical in its contents. *1560b* is misdated 1561 in the *Hymn Tune Index*: see pp. 528–9, n. 71 (N. T.).

[98] PSALM 114 (*HTI* 102), to be restored in *1561b* and *1561c*.

new tunes include nineteen based on French ones, all accompanying Kethe's texts. His method and goals in these French-influenced paraphrases were distinct from Whittingham's, however. Kethe would choose a French tune that had not hitherto been used by the English, and write for it a paraphrase of a psalm that was not yet in the English repertoire. In fifteen of the nineteen cases, though, it was a different psalm from the French one. These were in no sense translations from the French—Kethe shows no textual debt to the Marot-Beza psalms at all, and in many cases his versifications precede the French versions of the same psalms—but new verses inspired in part by the tunes, or at least designed to fit them. Kethe must have realized, however, that wholesale departure from the beloved Sternhold's meter would be risky. He composed four paraphrases in DCM and one in DSM, and whenever possible he made slight changes towards iambic meter in the French tunes, usually by omitting or repeating one or two notes in a phrase. But the seemingly immovable semibreve at the beginning of every line was again an obstacle (see, for instance, PSALM 111, discussed on p. 735 and recorded with both French and English texts in μ8). Eight of these French-derived tunes would be adopted in the Elizabethan canon, most notably PSALMS 100 (μ9), 113, and 124. A unique addition to this book was a new tune for Whittingham's Psalm 67,[99] which differs in character from both French and English norms and sounds much like a popular ballad. But it did not survive into the *WBP*.

This edition contains some purely textual innovations as well. There are two more hymns outside of the psalms, both of them versions of The Lord's Prayer in eight-syllable quatrains attributed to Whittingham. In addition, the prose arguments to all of Kethe's metrical psalms match those of the Geneva Bible Book of Psalms, which had been published ahead of the whole Bible in 1559. The textual relationship between the Geneva Bible prose psalter and the Anglo-Genevan metrical psalms is highly complex, but inserting the arguments from the one into the other served to bind the singing psalms even closer to the community's new standard version of pure scripture. Finally, for the first and only time the compiler added a preface to the metrical psalter, explaining why a community of now (mostly) voluntary expatriates, many of whom were planning their imminent departure from Geneva, would reprint the liturgy and devotional materials specific to their sojourn there. It was intended, according to the preface, to meet voluble demand for these materials in England and Scotland, where private use of the form of prayers, catechism, and singing psalms during the reign of Mary Tudor and under the Catholic regency of Marie de Guise had allowed there to be in "everie familie, to the comfort of all those that feared God, . . . a Church or Congregation erected."[100] That such comfort was still needed in England after the reconversion of the public Church and the establishment of the 1559 Book of

---

[99] Frost 82.
[100] *1560b*, 101.

Common Prayer is a difficult case to make clearly while maintaining enthusiasm for "a moste verteous Quene, suche one as is moste desirous her selfe to set forthe Gods glorie in all her dominions." The editor thus made it in a nearly-incoherent set of defensive paragraphs instead. Nevertheless, the implication is that the Prayer Book had not sufficiently set forth God's glory and that the Anglo-Genevan documents should serve as a model for speedy further reformation. They actually did so in Scotland, which adopted the service, catechism, and psalms with very little change, but the effects on English worship were largely limited to the metrical psalter.

A curious pair of 1561 editions reprinted the *1560b* version of the metrical psalter and its tunes. One (*1561c*) is without imprint but looks as if it was published in London. It includes a solitary prose prayer, "A Prayer to be said before a man begin his work," and Richard Cox's paraphrase of the Lord's Prayer with its German tune (referred to below), both apparently to fill leftover leaves, but otherwise reproduces only the psalms and hymns from *1560b*. The other (*1561b*) is a haphazardly printed volume from the Genevan press of Zacharie Durand, who seems to have taken the bulk of the Genevan service book from *1558* or a lost reprint but copied the metrical psalter (with the prose prayer, extra hymn, and many new errors) from *1561c*.[101] Their contents suggest that both books were designed for English exiles who had remained in Geneva, but the half-concealed suggestion in *1560b* that ardent reformers might still find a use for the *Form of Prayers* in Britain makes the publishers' intentions harder to judge.

Meanwhile, English editions were appearing that brought in texts and tunes from other branches of the exile, which had been less immediately dominated by Calvin. The *WBP* and thus the corpus for English congregational singing takes most of its DNA from this London lineage, and despite language on early title pages referring to private singing, it seems to have flourished from the beginning as a source for church music. Within months of Elizabeth's accession on 18 November 1558, some London churches began purchasing psalm books, often calling them "Geneva psalms." Some acquired what appear to have been printed sheets of additional psalms and hymns that would eventually form part of the *WBP*, a cheap and practical way of teaching the texts and tunes to choirs and then to congregations.[102] Unfortunately, none of these unbound psalm publications survive.

The bibliography of even the extant early London editions is extremely complex. In addition to the difficulties imposed by several centuries' distance, we are hindered by some intentional obscurity that the printers seem to have employed

---

[101] In *RR* (206–7), I accepted the *ESTC*'s attribution of *1561c* to John Day's shop and called it a copy of *1561b*. Closer examination of both volumes has convinced me, however, that *1561c* represents an infringement of Day's patent and that *1561b* was set from it, rather than the other way around. (B. Q.)

[102] For details see Appendix 7.

to avoid the unpleasant consequences of piracy, violating bans on foreign religious texts, or both. The first known edition of the psalms in meter, John Day's 1559 edition, is lost; we know it existed only because William Seres owned the copyright and Day was fined for infringement that October.[103] The following month, Day received a royal patent that included the rights to any unpatented works that he "compiled" at his own expense, and this patent could have been the one subsequently invoked to include the metrical psalms.[104] Why it should have taken precedence over Seres's previous entry of the same material into the Stationers' Register is a puzzle, however; Day's relationship with William Cecil allowed him to more or less legally poach the copyright, but there may also have been a now-lost patent for the psalms in meter in late 1560 or early 1561.[105] It is also hard to tell who controlled the English production of the psalms from late 1559 to the start of 1561.

The first surviving Elizabethan edition (*1560a*) took its title and the majority of its contents from *1558* (or a reprint of it). It contains all of *1558*'s psalm paraphrases with their arguments, as well as Whittingham's Ten Commandments ("Attend, my people"), and bases their tunes and the tune cross-references on the same edition. It is not a simple reprint, however: the editor both added texts with tunes from other sources and heavily revised the tunes from Geneva. As a result, this compilation essentially represents a melding of Genevan metrical psalmody with the congregational singing from other exile communities. At the same time, the title page cautiously contextualizes the metrical psalms as Edwardian-style private recreation rather than as a part of public worship: "Very mete to be vsed of all sorts of people priuatly for their godly solace and confort, laiyng aparte all vngodly songes & ballades, which tende only to the norishing of vice, and corrupting of youth."

The largest group of additions in *1560a* comes from another publication of the Marian diaspora, *The Psalmes of Dauid in Metre* (*1556w*). This book, another expansion of *Al Such Psalmes*, may have been printed by Hugh Singleton during the latter part of his time at Wesel, but the imperfect surviving copy bears

---

[103] See Edward Arber, *A Transcript of the Registers of the Company of Stationers of London: 1554–1640 A. D.*, 5 vols. (Birmingham, 1875–94), 1:124.

[104] Christopher L. Oastler, *John Day, Elizabethan Printer* (Oxford: Oxford Bibliographic Society, 1975), 70; Brian P. Davis, "John Day," in *The English Literary Book Trade: 1475–1700*, James K. Bracken and Joel Silver (eds.), *Dictionary of Literary Biography*, vol. 170 (Detroit: Gale, 1996), 858.

[105] Evenden and Freeman assume that there was a specific patent for the metrical psalms, and the date of the next patent, in 1567, would support the existence of a seven-year privilege beginning later than October 1559. See Elizabeth Evenden and Thomas S. Freeman, *Religion and the Book in Early Modern England: The Making of Foxe's 'Book of Martyrs'* (Cambridge: Cambridge University Press, 2011), 112.

no colophon.[106] Wherever it was printed, it contains—in addition to the (unrevised) Edwardian psalms—Whittingham's psalms and Ten Commandments from *1556*, a new version of Psalm 95, nine other hymns (with space for another in missing leaves), a dialogue with God in two poems, and a variety of prose prayers. No tunes are printed. In this assortment, congregational songs from at least three of the exiled congregations are represented, depending on how one counts: the congregation that began at Wesel and moved to Aarau; the Knoxian faction of the Frankfurt congregation that ended up in Geneva; and the more conservative branch at Frankfurt led by Richard Cox, which drew from and overlapped with the group at Strassburg. The prose works, nearly all anonymous, may have been gathered from a wider field still, but the sole attributed prayer is by Miles Coverdale, who ministered mainly to the Wesel/Aarau community but also spent some weeks in Frankfurt during the height of the intracongregational conflicts there. The only hymn from the Wesel book included in *1560a* that can be definitely attributed is Cox's own Lord's Prayer. The other five—Psalm 95 (the Venite), Benedictus, Creed, Magnificat, and a different Nunc dimittis, all from the daily services in the *BCP*—are anonymous, but may be the work of William Samuel, whose initials do appear on several of the other hymns in Sternhold's meter and who was a leader in the Wesel congregation.[107] Added to these in *1560a* are paraphrases of Psalms 67 and 125 by Robert Wisdom, neither known from any earlier source. It is likely, however, that he wrote them either in Frankfurt (where he arrived in 1555) or in Strassburg, where he moved in early 1558. Finally, "Attend, my people" receives "An Addition" in the form of a prayer that continues the hymn. The unique exemplar of *1560a* lacks the final leaves, which may well have contained the other hymns brought home from exile that appear in *1561d* after the ones already listed.

Incorporating these texts meant adding seven new tunes.[108] All the additions from the Wesel book except Psalm 95 are printed with tunes probably representing the way that they were sung at Frankfurt after Whittingham and Knox departed. The Benedictus tune bears some resemblance to the French tune for Psalm 118 (not used in *1556*), while the Nunc Dimittis is the one for Psalm 19 from *1556*. The Lord's Prayer (2) tune is the Lutheran "Vater unser." *1560a* also offers tunes for Wisdom's versions of Psalms 67 and 125, both adapted from German hymns; more surprisingly, it reprints Whittingham's ballad-like Psalm 67 as well.

---

[106] For discussion of dating and attribution, see Nicholas Temperley, "The Anglican Communion Hymn," *The Hymn* 30 (1979), 178–86, repr. *SECM*, 122–30; Leaver, *'Goostly Psalmes,'* 195–215; *RR*, 126.

[107] See Temperley, "The Anglican Communion Hymn," 180; *RR*, 130; and Leaver, *'Goostly Psalmes,'* 196–7.

[108] For details see Appendix 5.

Ex. 5. Psalm 44 in *1560a*

Thomas Sternhold, *ca.* 1549
rev. ?William Whittingham, 1556

Anonymous, 1560

As noted, the *1558* tunes were also modified for *1560a*, mostly in the matter of rhythm. They reflect a consistent policy of inserting a longer note, usually a dotted semibreve, in the middle of a line, especially for the fourth syllable in an eight-syllable line.[109] The long notes do not always coincide with final syllables, important words, or other obvious features of the underlaid verses. The same characteristic is found in three of the new DCM tunes in *1560a* (BENEDICTUS, MAGNIFICAT, CREED).[110] This could have been to permit breathing in the middle of a line. But it also in many cases allows an underlying meter to be sensed: in Ex. 5 this would be 3/1 with an upbeat, though it is not followed consistently through the whole tune.[111]

The surviving copy of *1560a* lacks its colophon, where the printer's name would have appeared (as it does on the similarly formatted *1561d*). The problem with simply attributing the production to Day[112] is threefold. First, the music font does not appear in other Day versions of the metrical psalms; Donald W. Krummel next finds it in Thomas Marsh's printing of John Hall's *Court of Vertue* (1565), and it subsequently turns up in ballad sheets.[113] Second, twenty of the tunes printed in *1560a* (listed in Appendix 5), as well as the rhythmic idiosyncrasies just described, were ignored by Day in all later editions. Third, the first edition surviving with Day's colophon makes some slightly different editorial choices about the presentation of the psalms (see below). It is possible that Seres in fact brought this edition out after Day was disciplined in 1559.[114] On the other hand, Day's *1561d* did use the liturgical hymns from *1560a* with the tunes printed for them there, after bringing their rhythms closer to the Anglo-Genevan norm.

Another early edition (*1561c*) must now be regarded as Elizabethan, though it has not hitherto been so classified: *Psalmes of David in Englishe Metre*, surviving only at the Bibliothèque Nationale, Paris (shelfmark A 6234), where it is bound with *1561a*, the 1561 edition of the *Form of Prayers* (*STC* 16562).[115] It lacks

---

[109] Compare Ex. 5 (and μ5) with Ps. 44 in vol. 1, which shows the Genevan version of the same tune.

[110] These tunes as printed in *1560a* are set out in Frost, nos. 3, 4, 181. In the present edition the *1560a* rhythms are shown as variants to these three tunes.

[111] There is clear evidence of an attempt to impose 3/1 time on at least 13 pre-existing tunes in this edition, and 3/2 or 4/1 time on several others. This may well reflect Wesel practice..

[112] As the *ESTC* does and Quitslund does in *RR*, 201–2.

[113] Donald W. Krummel, *English Music Printing 1553–1700* (London: The Bibliographical Society, 1975), 42–6.

[114] The Seres hypothesis originated with Donald W. Krummel, by word of mouth.

[115] The revised *STC* treats it as part of 16562, but it is clearly an independent publication. Although "Psalmes of David in metre" is listed in the table of contents of 16562, there is no space for any such item in the structure or pagination of the book. The table appears to be copied directly from *1560b*, which does include the psalms. Our tentative date for the separate psalm book is [London? 1561?].

date, imprint, and colophon, although it includes a version of Zacherie Durand's candlestick device with its text from Matthew 5:15 translated into English.[116] The title page is copied from *1560a* except that it omits the language about private use; set in a matching (roman) font and format, this edition was probably intended to accompany *STC* 16562 and thus had no reason to pretend that it was primarily for recreational singing. It does, however, include from *1560a* the citation of the 1559 Royal Injunction on religious printing: "Newly set fourth and allowed, accordyng to the order appointed in the Queenes Majesties Injunctions."[117] While the title page image and the font look ostentatiously Genevan, then, the book also advertises its compliance with the regulation of English printers. This may well point to an English rather than a Genevan origin, and the tune and text selection reinforce that hypothesis. Wherever printed, it and the matching Genevan *Form of Prayers* squarely target an audience in England.

The relationship between *1561c* and *1561d*, to which we will turn next, shows that John Day must have shared some materials with the printer of *1561c*. Its texts and tunes are nearly all the same as those in *1561d*, but neither book is set primarily from the other. A number of bizarre misprints in the tunes in *1561c* strongly suggest that at least its music was copied from a manuscript by an underequipped printer, and thus that it precedes *1561d*.[118] Another piece of evidence pointing in the same direction is the woodcut illustrating a new prose work at the front, "A Short Introduction into the Science of Music" (see p. 873). Both books seem to have used the same block, but in *1561d* and *1562a* it has sustained damage, with a chunk of the bottom border missing. In *1561c* the border is intact. Most of the discrepancies in content are items present in *1561d* and not here, but one hymn, The Complaint of a Sinner, appears for the first time in *1561c* and is not in *1561d*. Its tune (see p. 472) has a sense of form and direction not generally found among

---

[116] Although the design is essentially the same, the block used is neither the one recorded for Durand's in 1557 by both Paul Heitz and Bettye Thomas Chambers nor the slightly different version Chambers reproduces from two 1561 volumes. Heitz, *Genfer Buchdrucker und Verlegerzeichen im XV., XVI. und XVII. Jahrhundert* (Strassburg: J.H. Heitz, 1908), 28–9; Chambers, *Bibliography of French Bibles: Fifteenth- and Sixteenth-Century French Language Editions of the Scriptures* (Geneva: Librairie Droz, 1983), 244, 282, 359. The verse is a new English translation from the French or Latin of a Durand edition rather than taken from an English Bible.

[117] Injunction 51; see Paul L. Hughes and James Francis Larkin, eds., *Tudor Royal Proclamations*, 3 vols. (New Haven: Yale University Press, 1964–9), 2:128–9. On the confusion this reference has caused, see *RR*, 201.

[118] There are no dots in the music of the kind that lengthens the preceding note by a half. In 12 instances a dotted note (the correct reading, found in *1561d*) is replaced by two notes, the second on the space where the dot should have been, making nonsense of the word-setting. In another instance a sharp is interpreted as an extra note. Many of the textual variants also suggest misreading of handwriting by an incompetent typesetter. These errors do not recur in *1561d*.

the original English ones, and displays an accomplished composer at work. It is the only tune that calls for repetition of the last line of text in the first stanza, a common feature of secular music of the time; the writer probably modeled it on an existing song. The tune's conclusion on a sharpened third also points to an origin in a solo or consort song with instrumental bass (μ12).[119]

The other member of this pair, *1561d*, is the first edition with Day's imprint on an extant copy. It has the same title (except for restoring the language about private singing) and nearly the same contents as *1561c*. Musically, there are no major differences except the absence of The Complaint of a Sinner, but the music looks like a more professional copy of the manuscript source. Considered as a pair, the two editions contain the first Elizabethan London expansions of the *1558* metrical psalter, without any of the material introduced in the fourth Geneva edition (*1560b*) except William Kethe's Psalm 100 with its famous French tune. It seems likely that the primary editor, probably Day, did not have access to that collection in late 1560 or early 1561 when compiling this version, but received the Old Hundredth as a separately-circulating composition. The metrical psalter proper also adds eighteen other paraphrases. Thirteen are attributed to John Hopkins, who here begins his very large set of Elizabethan contributions, and the anonymous Psalm 75 would be attributed the next year to Thomas Norton. The surprise is the four new versifications attributed to Sternhold, as if there had been a lost cache by the Edwardian master. In fact, three (18, 22, and 23) are probably by Norton and the last (66) by Hopkins.[120] Surrounding the psalms at the heart of the collection are two sections of hymns, including all those from *1560a*, but significantly augmented and arranged into two sections (before and after the psalms).[121] To accompany these additions are fifteen new tunes. Twelve of them are in DCM, either replacing old ones (PSALMS 1, 21 and 78) or accommodating new psalms by Hopkins. In addition to the liturgical hymns from *1560a*, there is a notable incursion of non-scriptural texts with tunes (*1560a* had only one, the Creed): the Veni, Creator from the prayer book, probably by Cranmer; Thomas Norton's Athanasian Creed ("Quicunque vult") and a Te Deum which is probably also his; and, most significantly, three original hymns, two of which ("Da pacem, Domine" and "Preserve us, Lord") are translations from German to match German-derived tunes. There are also alternate paraphrases of the Lord's Prayer and the Ten Commandments by Norton. These texts and

---

[119] See p. 777. Normally an unaccompanied tune will end on the tonic (final) of the scale in use. A harmonized tune can end on the third scale degree if the bass supplies the necessary tonic.

[120] For discussion of the basis for emending these author attributions, see the Notes for these psalms and *RR*, Appendix D.

[121] On the motives for splitting the hymns, see pp. 552–3 below.

tunes are apparently a combination of those originating among the non-Genevan exiles and in England after Elizabeth's accession.[122]

The divergences between *1561d* and *1561c* mainly occur in the prose materials before and after the music. After "A Short Introduction into the Science of Music," *1561d* adds a pair of lists suggesting circumstances in which particular psalms might be sung. The first of these translates a portion of Athanasius' *Epistula ad Marcellinum de interpretatione psalmorum*, while the second supplies uses for "the rest of the Psalms not comprehended in the former table."[123] Day makes one subtle change in the metrical psalter itself, going back to the very first Genevan edition (*1556*) to add most of the marginal glosses for those fifty-one psalms. The largest difference, however, is that *1561d* ends with "A form of prayer to be used in private houses, every morning and evening" (pp. 483–95). This reprints all but one prayer from the section of the same name in *STC* 16562 (*1561a*) — the edition of the Genevan *Form of Prayers* with which the unique copy of *1561c* is bound. Adding these domestic prayers to the metrical psalms reproduces the form of the Wesel psalm book, but it also adds a substantial piece of the Anglo-Genevan devotional program to a book meant for worshipers in England. Moreover, Day chose his copy text from this particular edition of the *Form of Prayers* deliberately: it was edited after Elizabeth's accession to reflect the crucial change in England's confessional status and for the use of English people at home as well as abroad.[124]

At last, in 1562, Day offered his complete edition, with its proud title *The Whole Book of Psalmes*.[125] In terms of the texts, the main addition was seventy-seven new psalm paraphrases. The lion's share, thirty-eight, were supplied by Hopkins, who apparently undertook to fill in gaps up to Psalm 100. Norton provided twenty-six, while John Marckant (responsible for The Lamentation of a Sinner in *1561c/d*) contributed four. The remaining nine psalms are versifications by Kethe taken from *1560b*. The Complaint of a Sinner, left out of *1561d*, was added into this edition. A number of other psalm texts and a few tunes were, however, removed. With the exception of Psalm 51, which appeared in versions by both Whittingham and Norton, Day decided to print only one paraphrase of each psalm. Of the newly-written paraphrases, six replace earlier Genevan versions in *1561d*. Three psalm paraphrases printed among the hymns also disappeared in the first edition of the *WBP*.

The number of new tunes was much smaller than the number of new texts: eighteen tunes appeared in *1562a* for the first time, nearly completing the

---

[122] The origins of the texts are surveyed in *RR*, 121–3, 202–6.

[123] See pp. 7–16.

[124] Details of the changes can be found in *RR*, 232–5.

[125] *1562a*. In the same year he printed an ephemeral publication, *The Residue of All David's Psalmes in Metre* (*1562b*), for people who already possessed *1561d*. Minor differences in the tunes and a new Ps. 129 show that it was printed after *1562a*. See p. 564.

Elizabethan canon. Fourteen of these are in DCM. Since they were all presumably composed in England after 1558, one might expect an overall improvement in musical quality. What could prevent Day, armed with a royal patent, from drawing on the talents of experienced English composers of the time, as he would for his Companion[126] in the following year? But he did so in only one recorded case: Thomas Tallis's tune for The Lamentation (μ13), which shows its superiority by a consistent rhythmic pattern precisely fitting the iambic text, by melodic repetition and sequence, and by a clear overall direction, rising to a climax in its seventh phrase. These features enable the tune to convey emotional intensity.

The tune for The Complaint of a Sinner from *1561a*, also well adapted to iambic verse, now appears in corrected form. But most of the remaining tunes are in the same dull idiom as the Anglo-Genevan ones on which they are evidently modeled. A slight innovation is the tentative re-emergence of dotted rhythms, found in PSALMS 77, 141, 145, and 147, faintly recalling the Edwardian style. Tunes were now provided for two texts with repeated refrains, Psalm 136 and the Benedicite; but it cannot be said that their composers took much creative advantage of this novel opportunity. It seems that the Calvin-inspired censure of lightness and frivolity still restrained the English reformers, or at least those who controlled the selection of music for congregational singing.

Two pairs of tunes in *1562a* are varying versions of one (new) melody: PSALM 35 and HUMBLE SUIT, and PSALMS 77 and 81. The latter pair is a solitary instance of tunes with identical pitches but fundamentally different rhythms. PSALM 77 is in a regular duple time, while PSALM 81 has a consistent triple-time pattern, slightly disguised by its musical notation. With COMPLAINT OF A SINNER they are the only tunes in the canon whose style suggests a possible origin in secular song or dance. In the 1586 revision[127] PSALM 81 would be duplicated as the tune for Psalm 77, showing that the triple-time version had proved the more congenial of the two. In further evidence of its popularity, it spawned several shorter tunes that also enjoyed a long life, including the new (1569) PSALM 120.[128]

The Whole Book of Psalms of 1562, termed "the final London edition" by Illing,[129] was in reality the beginning of an almost interminable series. It was "complete" in the sense of containing all the biblical psalms, but by no means contains all the texts or tunes that would regularly appear in the *WBP*, or even

---

[126] *The Whole Psalmes in Foure Partes* (4 partbooks; London: John Day, 1563), *STC* 2431. The term "Companion" is used here to refer to any of the published sets of harmonized psalm tunes for domestic use. They are listed and described in detail in Appendix 6. Individual Companions are referred to by the compiler or publisher and year of publication, e.g. *Day 1563*.

[127] See Appendix 4.

[128] See pp. 711–12 for details.

[129] Robert Illing, *English Metrical Psalter 1562*, 3 vols. (Adelaide: Robert Illing, 1983), 1.30.

in Elizabethan editions. The subsequent printing history presents a study in the variety of contents that the same title could cover. (Or, at any rate, the same short title — the title page itself took another five years to stabilize.) As far as tunes are concerned, there would be no less than 452 distinct editions, the last appearing in 1688. Among them would be found a newly invented music type incorporating solfa letters in 1569 (see Figure 1), a wholesale revision of the rhythmic scheme of the tunes in 1586, a gradual introduction of new tunes, especially after Ravenscroft's Companion had appeared in 1621, a complete overhaul by John Playford in 1661, and a radical revision of 1688 in which every verse was supplied with musical notes in the Dutch manner. Like the tunes, the texts could appear in varying combinations in different editions, but the book also underwent distinct phases of revision to the selection of texts and to the readings of the texts themselves. The *WBP*, that is, continued in material ways to be a living text during its varied use over the next three centuries.

The Elizabethan Psalm Book

Whatever changes were in store, there was never any doubt, from 1562 onwards, that *The Whole Book of Psalms* was a single, continuing entity. Most of the texts and the basic structure that Day had chosen proved to be popular and long-lived: editions looking very similar continued to be printed after the Restoration. His own fortunes, indeed, depended heavily on his two best-selling titles, the metrical psalms and the A.B.C. with shorter catechism. In 1566, when Day was preparing to print the second edition of *The Acts and Monuments*, John Foxe told William Cecil that that expensive project would require a renewal of the patent for the psalms in meter because "from this one thing his whole household is sustained."[130] A patent for ten years duly arrived in 1567, and in 1577 was renewed again through the end of his son Richard's life. So until 1604, when James I granted the right to print psalms in both prose and meter to the Stationers' Company, the contents of the *WBP* were legally in the hands of its original editor and then his son's. In addition, psalm singing in public worship grew extremely rapidly and was entirely based on Day's book, creating a need for a very large number of copies with the same texts. It is thus not surprising that the volume was referred to in the book trade as simply "the psalms" or "the psalm book."

There were, nevertheless, significant changes in the book over the Elizabethan period as well as an expanding variety among editions. In the mid-1560s, a Londoner wishing to buy a copy of the *WBP* might have some choices to make — between a quarto edition in a large, clear blackletter font, an even more impressive folio that could be bound with a grand, pulpit-sized Book of Common

---

[130] British Library, Lansdowne MS 10, fol. 211r; quoted in translation from Evenden and Freeman, *Religion and the Book*, 164–5.

Prayer (*BCP*),[131] a more intimate octavo that may have recalled the popular Edwardian editions of Sternhold and Hopkins, and—possibly—other lost, smaller formats (see pp. 567–8). The same shopper would not really have been choosing between different contents, however. Although the number of tunes and psalm texts did change from edition to edition early on, these were changes that John Day initiated to get the collection right, not to court different audiences. By 1603, our original Londoner's daughter could choose from volumes resembling the ones her father examined, but also two-column octavos bound with New Testaments, two-column quartos or folios printed to match any bible on the market, an assortment of other octavo, duodecimo, 16° editions in different fonts, and certainly 24° and 32° pocket copies. Furthermore, if she purchased an edition meant to stand on its own, she would often be choosing between more and less deluxe versions, some with larger apparatus than was available in the 1560s and others stripped down to the bare words of the psalms and hymns, lacking even printed tunes. Those tunes themselves would be rhythmically different from the ones published in the early editions, and the most complete editions would feature new texts and new versions of old ones, while even the cheapest editions would register revisions to the psalm texts themselves. The phases by which these alterations occurred included a rapid period of adjustment and edition-by-edition changes in the early years of publication, followed by some systematic editing in 1569, a more comprehensive set of changes in 1577–8, a final round of tweaks to individual lines of the psalms in the 1580s, and the revision of the tunes in 1586. In the process, a standard selection of psalms and hymns was settled for most printing formats, while the prose contents and the number of tunes became far less predictable from edition to edition. This section describes in detail the many changes that occurred over the course of Elizabeth's reign.

Reading the Psalm Book

The *WBP* as a whole is very much an Elizabethan creation, a work carefully arranged by John Day to take advantage of and to promote the popularity of Continental-style congregational singing in the newly re-Protestantized English Church. At the same time, it bundles together in that arrangement texts that reflect quite different original uses and intentions, in addition to the different skills and styles of the writers and composers. Roughly half of the psalms, hymns, prose material, and tunes came from exiles during the Marian diaspora or their editions of Edwardian originals, and the other half from writers in Elizabethan England. Day's compilation of these materials is conservative in the sense that he very frequently accepts the decisions of previous editors as to what to include (particularly if the first extant London edition, *1560a*, is not in fact his). He also,

---

[131] As William Allen, Lord Mayor of London in 1571–2, had done with his copy of *1567* (British Library shelfmark C.108.aaa.3). See also App. 7.

however, commissioned new texts and added others from Marian sources that situate the metrical psalms both firmly within the Elizabethan Church and as a continuation of the pugnacious, sectarian piety that characterized the exile congregations. The verse itself in Day's collection continues the journey it began in exile, moving away from the cultural space of poetry and into that of liturgy.

The heart of the *WBP* is, of course, the metrical psalms, and it is certainly the portion of the book that saw the most actual use by owners. With the exception of one psalm not added until 1577, the number and order of psalm versions was settled by 1565. Comments on the *WBP* by contemporaries also suggest that at least some readers did not rigorously distinguish between the biblical psalms and the other hymns, a reasonable enough position given that a substantial number of the hymns outside the metrical psalter itself were in fact alternate psalm versions or were based on other biblical texts. In addition, about half of the hymns either emerged from the same Marian exile communities that were singing the psalms congregationally or were actually printed with the psalms in the exiles' publications. If we are thinking of the *WBP* as a collection of lyric poetry, then, it makes sense to consider the psalms and hymns together.

Superficially, the song texts are highly uniform. All the Elizabethan contributors returned to (or, in Hopkins's case, stuck with) the fourteener couplets or 8.6.8.6 quatrain that dominated the Edwardian editions, and, as noted above, any visual difference between Sternhold's *abcb* rhymes and Hopkins's *abab* variation disappeared. More than eighty percent of the songs in the *WBP*—132 of the 156 versifications that would end up in the psalter section and fourteen of the twenty-three hymns[132]—are in this form and, except for Norton's Ten Commandments, set to DCM tunes that treat two quatrains as a complete song verse. An additional six of the psalms are in the quite similar poulter's meter (6.6.8.6, or SM), with, again, no distinction in the printing between different rhyme schemes. The remainder, however, present considerable metrical variety. The somewhat curious result is an anthology neither consistently in one or two similar meters, as seems to have been Sternhold's mature intention, nor consciously creating a range of metrical (and thus also musical) effects, as the French psalms did.

Since roughly the middle of the seventeenth century, the critical consensus on the poetry of the *WBP* has alternated between sneering and giggling. There are a number of reasons for this disdain, including powerful ideological ones that we will treat below. Still, it would be an unusual modern reader who could make her way through the metrical psalms and hymns with unalloyed pleasure and reverence. Part of the problem is the dominant metrical form. Dickinson and Housman aside, Sternhold's meter has for several centuries now been more associated with folk songs and nursery rhymes than sophisticated verse. Worse

---

[132] The psalm count includes all the alternate versions from 1577 on except for those always placed among the hymns and often not identified as psalm paraphrases (Pss. 95, 117, and 134).

is Hopkins's version of CM, with its *abab* quatrains. In choosing to rhyme all of the short lines in long poems, he created a situation that would have challenged even a poet of great verbal ingenuity—which he was not. The result is a great deal of formulaic phrasing. In Hopkins's psalms, for example, the word "God" rhymes a total of forty times, thirty-six of those with "abroad." Sternhold's meter is also a form that at times calls for either compression (if fitting a whole psalm verse into one fourteen-syllable unit) or padding (to stretch a verse to the length of a quatrain). This was less of a problem for Sternhold than for some of his successors, because in songs meant for the court rather than the church he was willing to choose economy over completeness.[133] For example, for Psalm 68:7–8, the Great Bible gives "O God, when thou wentest forth before the people: when thou wentest through the wilderness. The earth shook, and the heavens at the presence of God: even as Sinai also was moved at the presence of God, which is the God of Israel." Sternhold's original paraphrase distills this to the bare essence, while Whittingham's revision, which tries to capture the full literal meaning of what Sternhold has left out, also expands on the verses to take up metrical slack:

> *1549b*
>   When thou wentest out in wilderness,
> thy majesty did make
> The earth to quake, the heavens drop,
> the mount Sinai to shake.

> *1556*
> When thou didst march before thy folk
>   the Egyptians from among,
> And brought them through the wilderness
>   which was both wide and long,
> The earth did quake, the rain poured down,
>   heard were great claps of thunder;
> The mount Sinai shook in such sort
>   as it would cleave asunder.

A different line length might have made it easier to avoid syllabic place holders like "which was both wide and long" or "in such sort."

It is reasonable to ask whether the majority of the post-Edwardian versifications were, in fact, ever meant to be more than aesthetically *acceptable* renderings of the biblical and ecclesiastical texts into a form that could be sung. Sternhold wrote psalm paraphrases in the context of a court culture that saw biblical art as a way of purifying recreation and demonstrating wit in the service

---

[133] On Sternhold's method of paraphrasing, see *RR*, 21–2.

of godliness, and his Edwardian contemporaries applauded his work in aesthetic terms as "fyne englysh meter" and "moost exquisite dooinges."[134] By the time Whittingham revised these paraphrases in Geneva, however, he consciously subordinated the fineness of the text to the requirements of literal meaning. "[W]e thoght it better to frame the ryme to the Hebrewe sense," he explains regarding the changes to Sternhold's work in the Preface to the *Form of Prayers*, "the[n] to bynde that sense to the Englishe meter."[135] The same preface does defend versifying the Psalms by remarking that the originals are in Hebrew poetry. Moreover, despite lines like those above the contributors in Geneva were not indifferent in practice to the aesthetic effect of their versifications. Some of the paraphrases written in exile, like Whittingham's Psalm 23, are quite lovely. Nevertheless, their efforts were probably encountered by most people in England not as poems to be read but as a sequence of words and syllables to sing. Furthermore, Norton and Hopkins in 1561 seem to have been charged with completing specific ranges of psalms on a tight deadline (one which, judging from where Marckant's new psalms and the ones extracted from *1560b* fall, Norton missed). All the previous paraphrasts had the luxury of choosing which particular psalms they wished to render into verse; even Sternhold, beginning to fill in paraphrases toward a complete metrical psalter in 1549, skipped Psalm 18. It is thus not surprising that the versifications added in the final stages in London are on average less appealing than those done earlier. Contemporaries, however, may not really have noticed. We have found no recorded comments on the poetic quality of the songs in the *WBP* from the 1560s to the late 1590s.[136] For most of Elizabeth's reign, then, the devotional and liturgical ends of the singing psalms displaced the question of whether they worked as art.

The book also contained much more than the psalms, or even psalms and hymns. The texts that Day assembled for his complete metrical psalter in 1562 go well beyond what might be considered necessary in a volume for either public or private psalm singing, and its arrangement is clearly rhetorical rather than strictly practical. In fact, it takes a moment to find the psalms themselves when picking up the book for the first time, as they are sandwiched between groups of hymns, and the whole songbook is in turn embedded in a frame made up of substantial prose sections. Taken together, the texts around the metrical psalter create a set of highly orthodox contexts for psalm singing while providing

---

[134] William Baldwyn, *The Canticles or Balades of Salomon, Phraselyke Declared in Englysh Metres* ([London: William Baldwyn], 1549), sig. A3v; John Hopkins's epistle "To the Reader," in *1549b*, sig. G2v.

[135] *1556*, p. 21. Whittingham did, in fact, make some changes to Edwardian versions that can only reflect his literary taste, and it is unfortunate that his taste is often farther from our own than Sternhold's was; see *RR*, 164–5.

[136] See pp. 611–15 below.

devotional materials designed to replicate the zeal of oppositional Marian Protestantism within the Elizabethan Church.

The prose texts preceding the psalms are guides to using them.[137] "A Short Introduction into the Science of Music" confronts the practical problem of sight-singing, while the two lists of uses of the psalms (one adapted from Athanasius and one newly written) instruct the reader how to choose which psalm to sing. Day seems to have been concerned that some churches did not have—or would not use—choirs to teach the tunes to the congregations, explaining that he has included the guide to reading music so that "the rude and ignorant in song may with more delight, desire, and good will be moved and drawn to the godly exercise of singing of Psalms, as well in common place of prayer . . . as privately by themselves or at home in their houses." This is the earliest surviving English treatise on music theory, and it is of unknown authorship or model. The author makes it very clear, especially in the closing sentence, that its purpose is strictly limited to teaching "such knowledge as shall be requisite to the singing of psalms contained in this book, for which cause only they are set out." It may be doubted, however, whether it achieved even this goal. The primary problem in reading the pitches of the notes was to distinguish between whole and half steps. The traditional method of overlapping hexachords, each containing six notes, is pedantically explained, allowing the reader to learn how to "solmize" (provide the correct name for) each note; and the note-values represented by the shapes of notes are fully interpreted. But the treatise does not help the reader to determine where the half steps occur, or how to move from one hexachord to another (the necessary process of "mutation"). Not surprisingly, the "Short Introduction" appeared in few editions of the *WBP* after 1565 and none after 1583.[138]

It may be that "A Treatise of Athanasius" and "The Use of the Rest" were intended as much to provide parish clerks with help in selecting psalms as for private devotion, but both lists are interesting hodge-podges of personal and communal or liturgical situations. For instance, the Athanasian recommendations include singing Psalm 137 "If thou be captivated with strange cogitations and hast perceived thyself to be led out of the way," which, barring episodes of mass delusion, is irrelevant to a congregation. We also, however, find that Psalm 16 declares Christ's "kingdom and power to judge and his presence in the flesh," which is a perfectly suitable topic for collective celebration. Likewise, the second list suggests Psalm 124 for "When thou art delivered out of prison, captivity, or any distress," but also a large number that could be sung congregationally. One of these is the first psalm listed, Psalm 21, for anyone or everyone who "would praise God because he hath given us a good prince"; another comes a few items down, in the recommendation of Psalm 29: "If thou seest the nobility, the Council, the

---

[137] See App. 3 for the full texts.

[138] See Samantha Arten, "The Origin of Fixed-Scale Solmization in *The Whole Booke of Psalmes*," *Early Music* 46:1 (Feb. 2018), 149–65.]

magistrates, and princes not given to religion nor to the praising of God." All
these texts, that is, position the metrical psalms for use in a range of settings and
for a range of purposes. Most of those purposes are uncontroversial forms of de-
votion, but a handful suggest that the people can also sing psalms to push for re-
ligious reform or to chastise both authorities and community members for their
insufficient commitment to Protestantism. The patristic commentary here seems
to be providing cover for the more daring contemporary list. Athanasius not un-
commonly gave multiple psalms for some circumstances, and in some places the
translator removed those, *creating* the need for a supplement to cover "the rest."

A similar goal—to use unexceptionable materials to balance and draw at-
tention away from slightly riskier ones—seems to have governed Day's strategy
in arranging the hymns into two sections, one before and one after the psalms.
In the first section, Day placed versions of all the ecclesiastical hymns and scrip-
tural songs other than psalms in the Morning and Evening Prayers of the *BCP*,
along with three other important Prayer Book texts, the Lord's Prayer, the Ten
Commandments, and the Athanasian Creed ("Quicunque vult"). Only two of
the eleven hymns preceding the psalms in 1562, The Lamentation of a Sinner
and The Humble Suit of a Sinner, are not drawn from the *BCP*. Both are uncon-
troversial penitential songs. While Day may have envisioned that the metrical
versions of liturgical texts would sometimes be used in place of the prose ones
during common prayer, the real importance of the first group of hymns is that it
allies the *WBP* with the ecclesiology of the *BCP*. It also distances Day's volume
from Calvin's restriction of congregational singing to psalms.[139] The translation
of the very first hymn, Veni, Creator, came from the 1550 Ordinal and was the
only text in meter that had been officially endorsed by the Church of England
for regular use. In addition, these prefatory hymns are nearly as metrically uni-
form as they are ecclesiologically conformist. Only the Benedicite was not writ-
ten in Sternhold's meter, a deviation resulting from the paraphrast throwing up
his hands in the face of the song's refrain in every biblical verse. (Norton did the
same thing with the similarly-structured Psalm 136.)

After the psalms, however, Day inserted both hymns not in fourteeners
and a handful of others, both newly-written and older, that are in Sternhold's
meter but may have seemed too daring for the prefatory group. Included here
from Marian exile publications also represented elsewhere in the volume are sec-
ond versions of the Ten Commandments (Whittingham) and the Lord's Prayer
(Cox). There are also hymns specifically for public worship but that were not

---

[139] The French metrical psalter from 1543 on included a handful of Marot's other
scriptural and non-scriptural songs, including versions of the Nunc dimittis, the Lord's
Prayer, the Ten Commandments (translated in the *WBP* by Whittingham), and the
Apostle's Creed, along with two meal-time prayers to sing. Calvin's recommendation for
congregational singing, however, speaks only about the Psalms of David, and the pran-
dial songs make it clear that the metrical psalter was not exclusively for liturgical use.

authorized by the *BCP* for singing by a choir, like "Come, Holy Spirit" to precede the sermon or "The Lord be thanked" to follow communion. Thomas Becon's paraphrases of Psalms 117 and 134, to be sung before and after common prayer, respectively, are not metrically similar to anything else in the *WBP*, as they almost entirely eschew accentual meter in favor of French-style syllable-counting. (Unfortunately, the direction to sing them to the French PSALM 100 still results in a poor fit with the tune.) The Complaint of a Sinner is perhaps most obviously unlike the other hymns, given its far more secular tune style and the repetition of the last line of each stanza. Ending the songs with a sectarian flourish is Wisdom's long-meter "Preserve us, Lord," with its plea for protection from Pope and Turk. This section is thus, both in form and content, a good deal more heterogeneous and unruly than the first set.

Closing the volume is "A form of prayer to be used in private houses every morning and evening," a set of twelve prayers taken from one of the two editions of the Anglo-Genevan Form of Prayers published in 1561 (*1561a*). This edition altered the private prayers as they existed in *1558* and *1560b* by adding two from the public Anglo-Genevan liturgy, removing four, and selectively editing three. While the two public prayers are unchanged in the service book itself, both they and the Morning Prayer in the section for household devotions drop their references to England's bondage and to Catholic persecution in England. The "Prayer for the Whole State of Christ's Church" replaces prayers on behalf of the Genevan authorities with prayers for the Queen, Council, and English magistrates. Two of the prayers that were omitted had also been specifically devoted to the situation of the congregation in Geneva and to the trials of the faithful in Britain. What Day adopted, then, was the set of devotions originally composed for the exiles in Geneva but now stripped of any obvious (and inappropriate) contextual specificity. Remaining is the sense of general penitence, opposition to the enemies of true faith, and national covenant that characterized the Anglo-Genevan religious attitudes.[140] It is not impossible to imagine Day including a miniature private prayer book in his metrical psalter both as a way of appealing to the brisk demand for such devotional materials and, at the same time, promoting the singing of psalms in household prayers. By including *this* set, though, he more firmly tied the metrical psalms not only to their history in the Marian diaspora but also to the basic devotional worldview of the exiles — and the exiles in Calvin's Geneva, at that.

The psalm book as Day brought it out and, in large measure, as it continued over the rest of Elizabeth's reign, conspicuously and consciously provided texts for both public and private devotion. This double purpose is one of the principles that underlies the selection of materials to accompany the central metrical psalter. In addition, these other texts guide the way that users should think about the

---

[140] For a more detailed discussion of the Anglo-Genevan *Form of Prayers* and its private prayers, see *RR*, 176–92.

psalm versifications. Though the lists of the uses of the psalms and the arguments that preceded each one suggest that the paraphrases should be read for understanding, they also frame the psalms as prayers and divine comfort rather than as delightful poetry. The hymns before the psalms (and the presence of non-scriptural hymns in both sections) make a strong case that psalm singing should be part of ecclesiologically moderate worship fully conformable to the practices authorized in the Act of Uniformity. At the same time, the private prayers and the content of some of the original hymns position the singer and reader as members of a Church that is largely defined through a fierce sectarian zeal. And regardless of whether English people used the *WBP* at home or read the additional materials designed to guide their use, orthodox congregations shared the experience of singing its psalms together.

The Canon of Elizabethan Tunes

By 1562 the music of the psalm book had nearly settled down to its permanent canon.[141] Of a total of 125 early Anglo-Genevan and English tunes,[142] sixty-six (slightly more than half) survived the winnowing process that had taken place between *1556* and *1565*.[143] The proper tunes[144] printed in *1565* would become indissolubly linked with their texts:[145] names like "The 100(th) Psalm Tune" or PSALM 100 (later OLD HUNDREDTH), MAGNIFICAT, and COMMANDMENTS became definitive modes of identification. For the rest of Elizabeth's reign and

---

[141] A few adjustments were made between 1562 and 1565. The tune content of *1567* is identical to that of *1565; 1567* was chosen as copy-text for this edition for reasons arising from the texts rather than the tunes.

[142] *HTI* 60–184. The exact total depends on whether certain similar but not identical tunes are counted once or twice; 125 is the most conservative figure, and excludes tunes 185–194, which were printed only in Day's Companion, *The Whole Psalmes in Foure Partes, whiche may be Songe to Al Musicall Instrumentes, Set Forth for the Encrease of Vertue: and Aboleshyng of Other Vayne and Triflyng Ballades*, 4 partbooks (Medius, Contra Tenor, Tenor, Bassus) (London: John Day, 1563). Fourteen more Genevan tunes (195–208) were used only in the Scottish psalm books, of which the earliest is *The Forme of Prayers and Ministration of the Sacraments &c Used in the English Church at Geneva, Approved and Received by the Churche of Scotland . . . with the Whole Psalmes of David in Englishe Meter* (Edinburgh: Robert Lekprevik, 1564).

[143] The *Hymn Tune Index* (under sources ✳P E8 a, b) shows 65, not 66, tunes for *1565* and *1567*. This is because the rhythmically distinct PSALMS 77 and 81, having an identical sequence of pitches, were counted as one (*HTI* 175) for indexing purposes.

[144] A "proper tune," in both early modern and recent scholarly usage, refers to a tune intended for the specific text to which it is allocated. The contrasting term, "common tune," means one that can be used with any text of the same meter.

[145] With one exception: the tune for Ps. 120 would soon be replaced by another, which became permanent.

long after, these tunes held their place in England as the normal settings of their texts.

The sixty-six proper tunes, even if their quality and popularity were uneven, represent a remarkable achievement: nothing less than the coming-of-age of a new and revolutionary musical tradition, worked out abroad under pressure, then successfully imposed in short order on the bulk of the population. Day was almost exclusively responsible for their dissemination in print.[146] The extraordinary number and variety of editions attests to their widespread use, and contemporary witnesses testify to the speed at which the singing psalms spread, as we shall see when we consider the character of congregational singing.

All the tunes, unlike most of the paraphrases themselves, were printed without attribution. At that time, and for many years to come, few musicians were proud of inventing a melody. Tunes were in the public domain. Louis Bourgeois, still credited in many hymnals for tunes taken from his famous four-part tunebook of 1547,[147] spoke in its preface only of polyphonic setting and made no mention of original melodic creations. A hundred and fifty years later, one of the most successful English inventors of hymn tunes, William Croft (1678–1727), was still content to have ST. ANNE's and HANOVER and many others printed without attribution when they first appeared in 1708. Even Bach, who harmonized and arranged hymn tunes in every conceivable fashion, never claimed to have authored one.[148] The musician's skill was held to lie rather in the arrangement of tunes: this is reflected in the very word "composer." So we find that the tunes of the *WBP* carry musicians' names only when they appear in harmonized form. This is true of LAMENTATION, which made its first printed appearance fully harmonized in four parts under Tallis's name, but lost its attribution when reduced to a melody alone in the *WBP*. All the other English tunes were first printed anonymously as melodies, and had arrangers' names attached to them when they appeared with harmonies in the Companions. One result was that

---

[146] It has been suggested that Thomas Caustun was Day's musical editor or proof reader, on the grounds that only this can explain the inclusion of so many of his compositions in *Certaine Notes Set Forth in Foure and Three Parts* (London: John Day, 1560 [1565]). See Elizabeth Evenden, *Patents, Pictures and Patronage: John Day and the Tudor Book Trade* (Farnham: Ashgate, 2008), 75–8. A similar argument has been proposed to identify William Parsons as the editor of Day's Companion (1563): see Maurice Frost (following Walter Frere), *Historical Companion to Hymns Ancient & Modern* (London: Hymns Ancient & Modern, 1962), 45. There is no direct evidence connecting either man with the *WBP* itself.

[147] *Pseaulmes cinquante . . . mis en musique par Loys Bourgeois à quatre parties à voix de contrepoinct égal consonante au verbe* [Fifty psalms set to music by Louis Bourgeois for four vocal parts in syllabic homophony fitted to the text] (Lyons: Godefroy et Marcelin Beringer, 1547). See Blankenburg, "Church Music in Reformed Europe," 518, 532–3.

[148] His contemporary, Handel, composed three, for hymns by Charles Wesley, but they were not published or even attributed until long after his death.

many of them in later generations were mistakenly credited to men who were not in fact their authors. PSALM 100 was probably composed by one of the three French musicians responsible for the tunes of the 1551 Huguenot psalter: Bourgeois, Guillaume Franc, or "Maître Pierre" (most probably Pierre Dagues, who was cantor at St. Peter's church, Geneva, from 1556); but we cannot know which. Later, it was often attributed to John Dowland, whose name had appeared over his harmonization in *East 1592*; to John Playford, who had printed his own version in *A Brief Introduction to the Skill of Music* (1658); or to Claude Le Jeune, who had harmonized it as Psalm 134 in *Les 150 Pseaumes* (Paris, 1601). Other books ascribed it, without even a semblance of a reason, to Martin Luther.

Apart from Tallis, the only musicians whom we can identify as the likely originators of *WBP* tunes are French or German. Franc (c. 1505–1570) is believed to have composed the new tunes for a lost edition of Calvin's *La forme des prières et chants ecclésiastiques* [(Geneva, 1542)], one of which was for Marot's paraphrase of the Ten Commandments, adapted as COMMANDMENTS (2) in *1556*.[149] The tune adopted for the French Psalm 113, and then for Kethe's translation of it, had been composed by Matthias Greiter (c. 1494–1550) for the Lutheran version of Psalm 119, verses 1–16, in *Psalmen, Gebett und Kirchenubung* (Strassburg, 1526). LORD'S PRAYER (2), for which the earliest extant source was published in 1539, has been generally credited to Luther himself.[150]

Regardless of their specific origins, the twelve French-based[151] and five German-based[152] tunes in the canon have an air of confidence and purpose that is lacking in most of the English ones. We may attempt to identify the precise musical features that might be the basis of such an impression. Most of them have a consistent but individual rhythmic pattern reflecting their often distinctive verse structures. Many seem to grow out of their opening phrase: subsequent phrases are audibly related to it, whether by direct repetition (PSALMS 111, 113, DA PACEM), melodic sequence (partial repetition at a different pitch level, as in PSALMS 100, 122 and 124), or complementarity (PSALMS 50 (1), 122, 126, 130, where the second phrase seems to answer the first, reversing its direction). Later in the tune there may be repeated lines (as in 50 (1), 111, COMMANDMENTS (2)) or references to earlier cadences (104, 122), contributing to a tune's audible form and predictability. Several of the French tunes have a distinct overall shape, with a climax at

---

[149] See Blankenburg, "Church Music in Reformed Europe," 518.

[150] However, this too has been questioned for want of evidence.

[151] PSALMS 50 (1), 100, 104, 111, 121, 122, 124, 125, 126, 130, 134, COMMANDMENTS (2). Of these, however, PSALM 134 only used part of its model, and the resulting torso proved to be problematic (see pp. 757–8). PSALM 113, though taken from French sources, was of German origin. PSALM 120 (first tune) is not counted because it dropped out of the *WBP* in 1569.

[152] The Lutheran tunes for PSALMS 119 (in part), LORD'S PRAYER (2), and PRESERVE US, and the Reformed tunes PSALM 113 and DA PACEM.

or soon after the middle, often characterized by an upward leap of an octave. As Pratt pointed out, "the most salient feature among the line-openings [of French psalm tunes] is a triple repetition of the same tone."[153] This is found at the point of climax in two of the French tunes of the *WBP* (104, 111) as well as two German ones (113, Da pacem). Perhaps the grandest of the foreign tunes are Psalms 100, 113, 124, and Lord's Prayer (2). Their majestic tones have continued to uplift English-speaking congregations until the present time.

While some of these characteristics can also be found here and there in the English tunes, most suffer from their absence, which tends to produce a feeling of aimlessness. The overwhelming predominance of iambic meter had produced a strong rhythmic structure in the Edwardian tunes, ultimately based on dance, but this had been given up in deference to Calvin's views. The new DCM tunes created by the exiles were guided by certain characteristics of the tunes in the French psalter. Only semibreves and minims were used, except for the long or breve on the final note.[154] Ideally each line should begin with a semibreve.[155] In French prosody, lacking lexical stress, composers were free to create any combination of minims and semibreves for each line.[156] But for English iambic verse there was a profound clash with the strong underlying rhythm. We have seen how this led to false stresses in French tunes adapted to English paraphrases by Kethe and others.

Fifty-four of the new English tunes were in iambic meter. Ex. 6 shows three possible rhythmic templates for setting the opening lines of Psalm 1. Pattern A is in triple time, and would no doubt have been disapproved by Calvin because

---

[153] Pratt, *French Psalter*, 54.

[154] The minim-and-dotted-crotchet group, which as we have seen was characteristic of Edwardian tunes, was evidently banned for the exiles. It is not found at all in either the French or the Anglo-Genevan psalter. It crept back in a few of the latest tunes of the *WBP*, beginning in *1562a*: Psalms 35, 59, 141, 145, 147, and Complaint.

[155] Pratt's analysis, based on the completed *Pseaumes de David mis en rime francaise* (Paris: Adriane le Roy & Robert Ballard, 1562), shows that of 860 lines all but 7 begin with a semibreve. See Pratt, *French Psalter*, 40–3.

[156] French verse meters are defined not by stress patterns but by syllable count, along with rhyme and the mid-line caesura. See Frédéric Deloffre, *Le Vers français*, 3rd edition (Paris: Société d'édition d'enseignement supérieur, 1973), 15; Jacqueline Flescher, "French," in *Versification: Major Language Types*, ed. W. K. Wimsatt (New York: Modern Language Association, 1972), 177–90; Nicholas and David Temperley, "Stress-Meter Alignment in French Vocal Music," *Journal of the Acoustical Society of America* 134 (2013); 520–7. That this was already true in the 16th century is confirmed in Deloffre's chapter on "L'Œuvre poétique de la Renaissance": "Le vers français, reposant sur le syllabisme, la césure et la rime, était evidemment adapté au caractère phonétique du français, avec ses syllabes nettes et la richesse de ses timbres vocalicaux finaux": *Le Vers français*, 102. Frost (*Historical Companion*, 36) and Pratt (*French Psalter*, 26) misguidedly classified most of the French psalms as "iambic," but the term has no application here.

Ex. 6. Three possible settings of iambic lines

of its secular aura: in the French psalter, minims tended to come only in pairs. It was used for only three tunes in the *WBP* (PSALM 81, PSALM 135, LAMENTA-TION), all introduced in *1562a*. Four others (PSALM 77, MAGNIFICAT, CREED, PRESERVE US) are in or close to pattern B: they too were only introduced after the return to England. The remaining forty-six iambic tunes are based on pattern C. Though it fits clearly into duple time, it is an imperfect match for iambic meter, because each six- or eight-note phrase begins with a long note carrying musical stress, which will most often fall on an unstressed syllable, such as *The* or *to* in the example.

The musical editors, from Whittingham onwards, tried to mitigate this problem by tinkering with the rhythms. Not a single DCM tune in the *WBP* follows pattern C note for note; indeed, Robert Illing was able to find only one that did in the entire corpus of 125 early British psalm tunes, the one for Psalm 66 in the Scottish psalm book of 1564 (Frost 81).[157] The great majority of the modifications were motivated by a desire to make the tune a better fit for the first stanza of a text — the one printed with the tune. No regard was paid to the later stanzas, let alone those of other psalms or hymns referred to the tune. Many of the changes deprived the tune of any consistent underlying beat, such as pattern C itself provides.

---

[157] Illing, *English Metrical Psalter*, 1:148. However, PSALMS 113, 122 and 125 (1) and LORD'S PRAYER (2), in various other meters combining 8- and 6-syllable lines, follow the pattern fully. The revisions of 1586 added four more examples: VENI CREATOR and PSALMS 44, 100, and 119 (see Appendix 4).

The only paraphrase clearly in anapestic meter is Psalm 104.[158] But the expected triple-time rhythm is not present in the French tune adapted to it, so it has false accents on the first and fourth syllables of several phrases. Psalm 136 (1) has alternating iambic and anapestic lines; the tune meets the situation well by setting each line to its own rhythm. The Benedicite has an irregular metrical scheme where, again, the note-lengths are fitted to the stress patterns of each of the three lines of text.[159]

In sum, the sixty-six proper tunes of the Elizabethan canon show a prevailing French pattern of semibreve beginnings of phrases, which is sometimes modified in various ways to accommodate the nearly ubiquitous iambic meter. In this process, only the opening stanzas were considered by the musical editors. Singers were left to their own devices to make similar modifications to suit the verbal rhythms of the subsequent stanzas — or to accept any false stresses that were found there. As printed, the musical phrases themselves are of differing arithmetical duration and show some variety in their internal rhythms. These distinctions may have been observed by singers in the early years, when the tunes were sung at a brisk pace.[160] As the tempo slowed in the course of several generations of unaccompanied singing, the tunes would have tended to sound more and more like a succession of undifferentiated long notes. Thus any sense of an underlying regular beat tended to be weakened. In 1586 John Wolfe attempted to recover the Calvinist spirit of the original "Geneva tunes" by means of a systematic revision of their rhythms, restoring a unified "pattern C." This process is described and analyzed in Appendix 4.

Rhythm apart, the sense of purpose present in most French tunes is found in only a few of the English ones. A few benefit from a perceptible structure, such as *AABC* (Nunc Dimittis, Psalm 44) or *ABB'B"* (Psalm 77/81); in several others the last six-note phrase recalls an earlier one (Veni Creator, Magnificat, Psalms 30, 35). Rather more have repeated cadences that confer some shapeliness and order (Creed, Te Deum, Quicunque vult, Humble Suit, Psalms 3, 25, 50 (2), 51, 59, 69, 78); a few also take advantage of melodic sequence (Psalms 77/81, 132, 137, Lamentation). Psalms 1, 41, and 68 are well shaped, with their highest note near the middle of the tune. Benedicite and Psalm 136 gain some structural interest from their refrains. But too many of the DCM tunes contain no perceptible features of these kinds, and wander from phrase to phrase with little sense of direction or meaning.

A separate question concerns the matching of tunes to their texts. The general mood or theological slant of a psalm could have influenced the choice of tune. For instance, Psalm 51, "O Lord, consider my distress," one of the traditional

---

[158] Pullain's version of Ps. 149 was also anapestic, with a tune to match it in *1558*, but it did not survive in English psalm books after *1560a*.

[159] Further discussion of individual tunes will be found in the Tune Notes.

[160] Questions of performance will be discussed below: see pp. 585–93.

sequence known as the seven penitential psalms, is a tortured expression of misery and rejection by God—a feeling that may well have been particularly intense among the exiles in Geneva, where the tune was first printed in *1556*. A minor mode[161] was chosen; all eight phrases are in clear common time, beginning with a solemn semibreve, and most move downward to their cadence; a plaintive three-note motive that ends the first phrase is repeated in five others, the last ending on the lowest note of the tune. In total contrast PSALM 81, "Be light and glad, in God rejoice," first printed in London in 1562, is one of only three *WBP* tunes in triple time, giving it a jaunty, even dance-like flavor; it is in a major mode, its cadences move upward, and it makes unusual use of a cheerful melodic sequence.[162] It is easy to believe that Whittingham and Day, or their musical advisors, chose or created these tunes to fit the mood of their texts.

It is another matter, however, to look for deliberate tone-painting of individual lines of the psalms, as Timothy Duguid has done in a recent study. He concludes: "Psalm tunes were intentionally paired with or composed for each psalm text in the 1556 *Forme of prayers* [here termed *1556*], in order to ensure that the psalms could be more easily sung and more clearly understood."[163] He bases this theory chiefly on finding phrases in the tunes that could have been designed to match particular words.[164] But such minute attention to word-setting could not apply to the other stanzas of a psalm set to a single tune, let alone to other psalms referred to the same tune. It seems equally unlikely that a composer would want to shape a repeated tune so precisely to fit just one stanza of the text—and not even the underlaid first stanza, which, as we have seen, was generally the only one whose fit to the tune received any editorial attention. The situation is different when a psalm paraphrase was written to go with an existing tune, as was the case with Whittingham's and Kethe's adaptations of French tunes. In those cases it is at least conceivable that wording was deliberately chosen in more than one, or even in every, stanza to fit the tune in rhythm and meaning. But Duguid does not raise this possibility.

---

[161] That is, a mode with a minor third degree (actually the Dorian mode in this case). See the Glossary of Musical Terms, p. 1038.

[162] Richard Allison's arrangement can be heard in µ28.

[163] Duguid, *Metrical Psalmody*, 33.

[164] For example, in discussing the *1556* tune for Psalm 7, he prints the second half of the tune underlaid with the texts of the first, second, and seventh stanzas. On the setting of the lines "Lest lyke a lyon he me teare, and rent in pieces small," from the second stanza, he remarks: "The minim rhythms paired with the verse . . . de-emphasize 'he' by quickly passing over it to arrive at the word 'teare'. The melody then follows the action in the text, as it uses the largest leap—a fifth—between the words 'and' and 'rent' to express violent tearing. This is followed by two pairs of notes that are a third apart, suggesting the small pieces rent by a lion." Duguid, *Metrical Psalmody*, 30–1, and Ex. 1.3. Considered in isolation, this is a plausible example of musical word-painting, or "tone-painting."

The negative view of many of the tunes that has long prevailed among scholars and critics, as much as the widespread contempt for the texts, may be a product of connoisseurship that has little to do with sixteenth-century ideas or needs. Certainly many Elizabethans adopted the tunes quickly and soon made them a part of their culture and of their lives. On the other hand, while the custom of singing psalms to these tunes was firmly enforced in some quarters, it is difficult to find any specific or discriminating praise of the tunes as music. They had come to England as "Geneva Psalms," part of a Reformed package that had been fully worked out abroad and was seized on by some as the embodiment of the new godliness. Additional tunes created in England after 1558 followed the new style, with little attempt to improve on it. Tallis's more sophisticated approach was represented in the *WBP* only by his Lamentation (μ13); his tunes for Parker's metrical psalter were never given a chance to compete, and went nowhere.[165]

Soon the proper tunes of the canon were so entrenched that they were hard to challenge. They were loved—because they were familiar. Yet, as will be seen, they would rapidly lose ground to the shorter and more accessible common tunes in the 1590s. Only a few of the proper tunes remained popular enough to survive in regular use into the 18th century. By contrast, the Huguenot, Dutch, and German Reformed churches continued to use the tunes of the French Genevan psalter until recent times. It seems likely that their greater durability was at least partly due to better quality, which can be traced to the strong group of professional musicians who had produced them.

The Psalm Book to 1567

From the 1562 *editio princeps* through 1603 the contents of the *WBP* altered in several ways. One psalm version in the central metrical psalter dropped out, and six others were restored from previous partial editions or newly added, along with four tunes. Psalm versions previously printed among the hymns returned to their positions there, while the order of the other hymns shifted slightly. The essay on reading music for singing disappeared—replaced, in editions using the new solfa music type, with a short note on how to use it, but otherwise simply discontinued. The extract from Athanasius on "The Use of the Psalms" gave way to a different translation of the same passage at the same time that the companion "Use of the Rest of the Psalms" dropped out. The prose arguments to most of the psalms were largely rewritten. Some new prayers were added to the collection for household use at the back of the volume, two of which recurred frequently over two or more decades, and several of the original Genevan prayers began to appear only sporadically. A text from a different section of the Anglo-Genevan

---

[165] Until Ravenscroft adopted one in 1621: see pp. 771–2. For a conjecture that they were originally intended for the *WBP* see Milsom, "Tallis, the Parker Psalter, and Some Unknowns," 10–11.

service books, the Confession of Faith, was added to the *WBP* and appeared there regularly well into the seventeenth century. The psalm texts were repeatedly (and inconsistently) tweaked up through 1567, then underwent further deliberate editing three times before John Day died in 1584. Throughout this period, varying selections of tunes dropped out of different editions. Shortly after Day's death, the tunes as a body underwent revision. The reasons for the changes were various and certainly at times interrelated, but encompass at least the following: repeated adaptation in response to market demand; a broadening of available versions to take advantage of market differentiation; the aesthetic, religious, and political tastes of the editors and publishers; recognition of changes that had taken place in the process of oral transmission of the tunes and quite possibly texts; and, probably, accommodation to the sometimes different preferences of ecclesiastical authorities. Complicating the effects of these intentional editorial interventions are both the printing house practices that allowed the book to be rapidly and efficiently reproduced, and inevitable errors, which were reproduced with equal facility.

Perhaps the most immediately striking early change was to the title page. The first edition proclaimed that it was "faithfully perused and alowed according to thordre appointed in the Quenes maiesties iniunctions. Very mete t [sic] be vsed of all sortes of people priuately for their solace & comfort: laying apart all vngodly songes and ballades, which tende only to the norishing of vyce, and corrupting of youth."[166] Two points here are notable. First, Day ostentatiously foregrounded the book's compliance with the royal injunction stipulating that religious works must be examined by licensors before publication.[167] Second, he describes the psalms as wholesome recreation, as if this version of Sternhold

---

[166] The formulation reorders the one originally found on *1560a*: "Very mete to be vsed of all sorts of people priuatly for their godly solace and confort, laiying aparte all vngodly songes & ballades, which tende only to the norishing of vice, and corrupting of youth. Newly set fourth and allowed, according to the order appointed in the Quenes Maiesties Iniunctions."

[167] The Injunctions of July, 1559 declared that "no manner of person shall print any manner of book or paper of what sort, nature, or in what language soever it be, except the same be first licensed by her majesty by express words in writing, or by six of her Privy Council, or be perused and licensed by the Archbishops of Canterbury and York, the Bishop of London, the chancellors of both universities, the bishop being ordinary, and the archdeacon also of the place where any such shall be printed, or by two of them whereof the ordinary of the place to be always one. . . . And touching all other books of matters of religion, or policy, or governance, that hath been printed either on this side of the seas or on the other side, because the diversity of them is great and that there needeth good consideration to be had of the particularities thereof, her majesty referreth the prohibition or permission thereof to the order which her said commissioners within the city of London shall take and notify." (Hughes and Larkin, *Tudor Royal Proclamations*, 2:128–9).

and Hopkins would be used the same way that the Edwardian ones were. Adding the wholly unnecessary word "privately" looks like a reassurance that no one is attempting to interfere with the official uniformity of public prayer. This text remained unchanged until 1566 (*STC* 2437), when a new title page startlingly appeared to alter the relationship between allowance and singing: "Newly set foorth and allowed to bee soong of the people together, in Churches, before and after Morning and Euening prayer: as also before and after the Sermon, and moreouer in priuate houses, for their godlye solace and comfort. . .." This phrasing does not actually claim that Elizabeth or her injunctions "allowed" the metrical psalms to be sung in churches—wisely, given that singing before and after sermons is never mentioned in the injunction that does permit congregational singing.[168] Nevertheless, a reader would naturally draw the conclusion that some relevant authority had given a more or less official nod to the practices that the title page describes.[169] The final form of the title, which would continue for more than a century to be printed on all title pages large enough to hold it, first appeared in *1567* and put the churches even before the people: "Newly set forth and allowed to be song in all Churches, of all the people together, before & after morning & euenyng prayer: as also before and after the Sermo[n], and moreouer in priuate houses. . .."

Internal changes up to 1567 are of essentially two kinds: corrections to *1562a* and the gradual resumption of some psalms, hymns, and tunes dropped in that edition. They repaired, that is, different kinds of shortcomings in the first complete metrical psalter; if misprints resulted from a lack of attention impressive even by the standards of the mid-sixteenth century, the restoration of texts shows Day backing away from a conscious editorial decision.

The textual problems in *1562a* indicate that the printing was rushed, the manuscript materials not uniformly finished, and the proof-reading somewhat cursory. Among other general problems, there are a high number of similar-letter substitutions, so either compositors had imperfect English—Day employed a high number of foreign typesetters—or the cases were fouled. Less-familiar Hebrew names were a problem, and it's easy enough to imagine how a stray speck on the copy text might have looked enough like a macron to transform the desert of Maon into *1562a*'s "desert of Mammon" in the argument to Psalm 116. Nor did

---

[168] After first insisting on the maintenance of singing-men and allowing for the liturgy to be sung in such a way "that the same may be plainly understood as if it were read without singing," the Injunction goes on to add, "And yet nevertheless, for the comforting of such as delight in music, it may be permitted that in the beginning or in the end of common prayers, either at morning or evening, there may be sung an hymn or such like song to the praise of Almighty God, in the best sort of melody and music that may be conveniently devised, having respect that the sentence of the hymn may be understood and perceived." (Hughes and Larkin, *Tudor Royal Proclamations*, 2.129–30.)

[169] For evidence of episcopal support, see pp. 588–9 below and *RR*, 240–1.

the compositors work from impeccable sources. Hopkins's new paraphrases contain several formal errors. At least two lines (Psalms 36.36 and 59.49) were written with too many syllables, and the author rather than the compositor may be responsible for another line that is too short (88.55). Hopkins also seems to have given up on his rhyme scheme in places: a total of twelve quatrains rhyme *abcb* in five psalms that otherwise hew to his usual *abab* cross-rhyming. The combination strongly suggests that he had no time for proper revision. Norton's psalms do not display these kinds of problem, but he did not finish his work as quickly as Hopkins did—or, indeed, in time for the edition. The new psalms from *1560b* all occur in Norton's section (Psalms 101–150), and, as noted above, John Marckant's four psalms seem to have been commissioned to fill in what neither Norton in London nor Kethe in Geneva had paraphrased. Either because he submitted it after *1562a* was printed or due to a compositor's error, Norton's Psalm 129 was belatedly added to *1562b*, replacing in all subsequent editions the *1558* version by Whittingham that appeared in *1562a*. More damagingly, neither Norton nor anyone else provided verse numbers for his new paraphrases before the edition was set. Not only are they thus inconsistent with the other metrical psalms, but the absence of numbering together with the unvarying verse form and frequently similar sentiments of the psalms made it difficult to tell if manuscript pages had gotten shuffled. They had: Psalm 109 lacks verses 3–22, and the missing eighteen quatrains of versification turn up between verses 12 and 13 of Psalm 115. (The errant passage recounts the speaker's unjust persecution by relentless enemies—in the context of the psalms, in other words, it could go nearly anywhere.) Day must have known that there was a very large profit potential in the metrical psalter. Given that, the best explanation for his sloppiness with the first complete edition is that he needed the revenue quickly, because during 1562 he had an enormous amount of capital and three of his four presses tied up in the first English edition of John Foxe's *Actes and Monuments*.[170] Foxe's great work probably engrossed his best workmen, as well. This view is supported by the fact that the tunes in *1562a* are relatively free of new errors; Day's best music setters were not involved with Foxe.

The next several editions gradually cleaned up the mess. In the "Residue" (*1562b*), most of the serious metrical defects in *1562a* were straightened out, although Psalm 109 is still in its incomplete state there; the missing verses were transferred back from Psalm 115 (not present in *1562b*) in *1563*. While the most obvious problems with the most obvious solutions were permanently fixed early on, the correction process as a whole was not undertaken systematically, nor was a corrected copy used as a guide for subsequent editions in different formats. So some of the psalms initially without verse numbers received them in *1563*, and nearly all have them—in some places corrected—in *1564* and the two 1565

---

[170] Andrew Pettegree, "Day, John," *ODNB*.

editions, but the quarto of 1566 introduced brand-new errors in the numbering for some psalms and left the numbers off others altogether. Errors without a single obvious solution tended to end up with several over the first few years of publication. For example, *1562a* gives Psalm 56.23 as "They spie my pathes & snares haue tred." This is obviously wrong, and *1562b* corrected the last word to "tryd." The second edition of the whole book, *1563*, left "tred." In *1564* (octavo), we find "layd": this makes better sense than "tryd," but is not a plausible restoration of whatever "tred" mistook. In 1565, Day brought out a folio (*1565*) that picked up a number of readings from *1562b*, including "tryde," and *1567* agrees. The quarto edition of 1565 (*STC* 2435), however, set from *1563* and once again grappling with the original misprint, launched "spred." This emendation was reproduced in two further one-column quartos from 1566 and 1569 (*1569a*). The line did not stabilize until the more thorough revision of *1569b* supplied "tied."

Beginning in 1564, the text was further adjusted through a determined assault on awkwardly contracted verb endings. Virtually throughout the volume, third-person singular conjugations were changed from "-eth" to "-s" wherever it was desirable not to voice the ending as a separate syllable. So, for example, at Psalm 7.57, where *1562a* gives "He digth a ditche, and delueth it depe," *1564* has "digs" and "delues." These changes, unlike the other corrections, are consistent in nearly all the subsequent editions, which suggests a policy decision in the print shop that was applied reasonably uniformly: normal lines of textual transmission show a good deal more variation.

In the same set of early editions, Day was also in the process of working out exactly which texts and tunes from his earlier publications needed to be in the *WBP*. With the exception of the two paraphrases of Psalm 51, *1562a* had eliminated all redundant psalm versions, including those that had appeared among the hymns before and after the complete set of psalms. In each case within the metrical psalter, Day preferred a new paraphrase by Hopkins or Norton to those he had inherited from the exile communities.[171] In fact, it seems entirely possible that the *WBP* included both Whittingham's and Norton's Psalm 51 because Day found Norton's insufficiently penitential but felt obligated to print it anyway. The contents of the next several editions, however, suggest that purchasers missed some—but not all—of the versions that Day had jettisoned.

Unlike the inconsistent corrections to the psalm texts themselves, the reincorporation of alternate psalm paraphrases looks like a continuous experiment in trying to accommodate popular demand. The catalogued copies of *1563* are, unfortunately, incomplete, but almost certainly contained the same selection as *1564* and the 1565 quarto. In both these editions, Day restored the *1556w* Venite (Psalm 95) to the first group of hymns. The quartos of 1563 and 1565 add a new section between the main metrical psalter and the second group of

---

[171] The newer version of Ps. 23 is attributed to Sternhold from its first appearance in *1561d* on, but is probably by Norton; see p. 659.

hymns comprising "Sertayne other Psalmes that be vsually song"; in *1564*, the additional psalms are appended without notice to the end of the hymns. These "usual" psalms include Whittingham's Psalm 50, Kethe's Psalm 100, and Wisdom's Psalm 125, and they brought with them the tunes PSALM 50 (1) and PSALM 100. Finally, Becon's versions of Psalms 117 and 134, not identified as psalms but marked as hymns for morning and evening prayer, respectively, returned to their position at the start of the second group of hymns. For the folio *1565*, however, Day did away with the separate section for the "usual" psalm versions and put them back into the main sequence, where a singer might more reasonably be expected to look for them. In the same edition, he added one further alternate psalm version, Whittingham's Psalm 23. Subsequently until the final addition in 1577, nearly all editions of the *WBP* contained two back-to-back paraphrases of five psalms (23, 50, 51, 100, and 125). It is likely that, at least in London in the 1560s, the Anglo-Genevan versions really were more commonly sung than the Elizabethan ones, because Day placed them before the Elizabethan paraphrases that he had previously favored. Wisdom's Psalm 125 may have been less of a runaway winner, inasmuch as it consistently appeared after the other version by Kethe. In the 1566 edition, Day reversed the order of the two versions of Psalms 50 and 125, but apparently quickly thought better of it: all later editions order the psalms as in *1565*. The same folio, moreover, saw changes in tunes for existing texts. A competing tune for Psalm 1, first printed in *1561c* and *1561d*, finally prevailed over the one from *1556*, and two others dropped out—PSALM 115 for good, and PSALM 22 to resurface occasionally in later editions.[172]

Day also tweaked the prose accompaniments to the psalms and hymns. A 1564 octavo, *The First Parte of the Psalmes Collected into Englishe Meter*—clearly intended to complete and thus help sell leftover copies of *1562b*—added the shorter catechism to the front of the volume and the Litany with associated prayers to the household prayer book at the back. Day had the copyright to the "little catechism," but did not print it with the *WBP* or its parts again. Presumably he realized that there was better margin in selling the two works separately. All editions through the quarto edition (*STC* 2435) of 1565 (but not *1565*, which was probably printed second that year) contained "A Short Introduction into the Science of Music." Subsequently, however, it only appeared in black-letter octavo editions, quite possibly as an oversight perpetuating itself through reprinting from similar copies. The folio of 1567 also printed in full Day's new, ten-year royal patent, the first surviving one to give him specific rights to the *WBP* and for a longer term than the previous grant "per septennium" (see pp. 5–6).

---

[172] App. 5 gives a complete account of tunes not in *1567* that are found in other Elizabethan editions of the *WBP*.

1569 Revisions

Editions up to *1567* determined which parts of Day's early Elizabethan metrical psalters would become standard, essentially finalizing the "complete" volume of 1562. Rather than settling on a series of stable and uniform editions, however, Day almost immediately began to revise that project. Editions of 1569 inaugurate new printing formats, offer a novel music type and a new tune, rearrange some hymns, add new prose texts, and give the first systematic set of revisions and corrections to the texts. Although there were some experiments that would not be much repeated, most were long-lasting changes to the *WBP* that persisted in many or most of the subsequent editions.

Surviving editions of the *WBP* up through 1567 are quartos (like *1562b*), folios, or (like the earlier, incomplete editions) octavos, and all are a single column of black letter. This means that the quartos as well as the folios use a large font and a great deal of paper. (The folios do avoid the choice between gigantic type and huge amounts of white space by using fewer line breaks: they not only print common meter as long fourteener lines but combine lines in some other short-line forms as well). By 1569, Day introduced what would become extremely popular formats of the *WBP* for the next sixty years: a two-column quarto (*1569b*) and a 32° (*1569c*). Both were in black letter, though most extant later 32°s are in roman type, which miniaturizes far more cleanly. Most surviving two-column quarto copies of the *WBP* are bound with bibles in a matching print format, and seem to have been produced for that purpose. While the 32° edition used a fraction of the paper required by earlier editions, its other obvious virtue was portability. By 1569, that is, Day anticipated a demand for tiny personal copies to carry in a pocket to church and sermons. The first surviving 16° is from the following year, evidence of the widened range of *WBP*s available for use in different settings (home, school, church, outdoor sermon) and by purchasers with differently-sized purses.

It is nearly certain, in fact, that these little volumes were a great deal more popular than the *STC* suggests. Though library holdings would seem to show that the Elizabethan market favored quartos and octavos, often bound with bibles or New Testaments, a significant number of small format editions—probably the vast majority of those produced in the sixteenth century—have not survived to be catalogued. John Barnard has calculated astronomical loss rates of small books (including prose psalters) not bound with other works from the late seventeenth century.[173] There is no reason to think that Elizabethan psalm books fared any better. Moreover, other Elizabethan evidence shows that editions are missing.

---

[173] John Barnard, "The Survival and Loss Rates of Psalms, ABCs, Psalters and Primers from the Stationers' Stock, 1660–1700," *The Library* ser. 6th, vol. 21 (1999), 148–50. Barnard's figures depend on records not available for earlier periods; see pp. 604–6 below.

The list of books that the bookseller Thomas Chard sent to Cambridge between the fall of 1583 and spring of 1584 includes fifty-two copies of the *WBP*, alone or bound with other works. Of these, thirty-six are 16°s, twenty-one are 32°s, one is a duodecimo, two are quartos, one is in folio, and one is unspecified but (based on price) either a 32° or 16°.[174] The first three 32° editions of the *WBP* recorded in the *STC* are from 1569, 1577, and 1590. Even if the Cambridge market was atypical, those proportions would not be possible without further editions during that period. Furthermore, when the Stationers' Company in December 1587 reiterated its prohibition of standing type, it included the *WBP* in 32° among the tiny number of books permitted to be printed in double impressions of 2,500 copies. Such permission only makes sense in the face of high enough demand that these technically-challenging little volumes were being produced on a regular, probably at least annual, basis.[175] The number of innovations in 1569 makes it seem likely that this was the first 32° *WBP*, but it must have had a huge, now impossible to calculate, number of successors.

The same year also saw two new ways of printing the tunes. In *1569c* they were printed in a new fashion, possibly from wood blocks. These could have been reused, saving the cost of music type-setting, but there is no other surviving example, possibly because of objections by Day's compositors or the Company of Stationers.[176] For the quarto *1569b* he introduced a new type with solfa letters accompanying each note, so that the reader might "know how to call every Note by his right name" and thus "by the vewing of these letters come to the knowledge of perfect *Solf[a]yng.*" The device was a French invention dating from 1550: Day's immediate model seems to have been *Pseaumes de David* ([Geneva]: Pierre Davantes, 1560).[177] Unhelpfully for buyers of the *WBP*, the prefatory explanation of the system refers back to "the Introduction Printed heretofore in the Psalmes" for the full description of solfa-ing. This reference would only have become more obscure as the decades rolled on and the brief solfa preface continued to be reproduced verbatim without any guidance for its use. The type was largely restricted to two-column quartos, though Day also employed it in 16°s and one series of two-column folios. It or a very close successor passed down, after John Day's death, to Richard's assigns—first John Wolfe, and then John Windet, for use in two-column quartos through the end of the Day patent and beyond. It is found as late as 1634 (*STC* 2649) in a musically unrevised edition printed by William

---

[174] Robert Jahn, "Letters and Booklists of Thomas Chard (or Chare) of London, 1583–4," *The Library*, ser. 4, vol. 3 (1923); 219–37.

[175] Arber, *Transcript of the Registers*, 2: 883. The list of works eligible for double impressions comprises two basic grammar school textbooks, 8° Bibles in nonpareil (a very small type), proclamations, statutes, almanacs, and "anie booke in ye nonpareil letter."

[176] See Krummel, *English Music Printing*, 59.

[177] See Krummel, *English Music Printing*, 71–3. For an explanation of the system as used in the *WBP* see pp. 583–5.

Stansby, of which the prototype (*STC* 2594) had appeared in 1625, but even in these editions it was not used for new or revised tunes, suggesting that it had not in practice helped singers to learn unfamiliar music.

On the other hand, Day must have been responding to evolving patterns of use in making his first change to the order of the hymns. In both *1569b* and *1569c*, "The Complaint of a Sinner" shifted from its position in the middle of the original hymns in the section after the metrical psalter to become the last item in the first section of hymns, immediately before Psalm 1. At the same time, "The Humble Suit of a Sinner" moved from near the end of the first hymn section to be slotted in immediately after *Veni, Creator* as the second song in the collection. Both songs are, as a result, significantly easier to find. These changes also, however, make a difference in the shape of the first section of hymns, both interrupting the opening sequence of traditional ecclesiastical texts and adding a third newly-written one to the section as a whole. As we have noted, the original arrangement of the hymns seemed designed to (literally) foreground the *WBP*'s Elizabethan orthodoxy by prefacing the psalms with hymns associated with the rites of the *BCP* and tucking the Anglo-Genevan songs and the majority of the original hymns (including the most potentially controversial ones) at the back.[178] While the altered order does not much change those basic categories, it does compromise the first section's mirroring of the Prayer Book. These changes came after the 1567 patent gave Day a form of official endorsement for the volume; by that point the preferences of singers were in some respects becoming as important as negotiating with ecclesiastical authority.

The publisher also tinkered with the prose texts around and after the metrical psalms. Beginning with *1561d*, Day had reproduced many of the marginal glosses to the psalms from *1556*—an untidy decision, since *1556* only contained 51 psalms and there was no attempt to add comparable glosses for the remainder of the psalter. Some of these notes continued to appear in most editions through *1569a*, although the 1566 edition and *1569a* abruptly stop after Psalms 14 and 13, respectively. (The exceptions are the folios *1565* and *1567*, with the result that the glosses are not printed with the text in the present edition but in the notes to individual psalms.) With the revised editions of 1569 Day appears to have actively decided to abandon the glosses: they subsequently appeared only in the handful of editions directly descending from *1569a*. He, did, however, try a new experiment in adding a group of additional prayers at the end of the volume, following the ones from the Anglo-Genevan collection. For *1569c*, Day gathered nine of these out of popular books of private prayer, including Catherine Parr's *The Queen's Prayers*. While the only surviving edition to reprint any of these is *1577*, it seems likely that some of the lost 32° editions in the intervening years were similarly expanded, as well as some after 1577.

---

[178] See p. 552 above.

Much more surprisingly, Day went back to the Anglo-Genevan *Form of Prayers* for a final borrowing, the exiles' confession of faith. In *1556*, this is headed "The Confession of our faithe, Which are assembled in the Englishe Co[n]gregation at Geneua." For the Elizabethan context, Day chose a version of the title given in the *1556* table of contents, calling it in *1569c* "The Confession of Christen Faith" (see pp. 903–8). Having had a difficult enough time with the Thirty-Nine Articles, the English Church had not ventured an official confession of faith, so the Anglo-Genevan one could be seen as filling a gap for English Protestants. Any authorized confession would, however, have looked rather different from this, with its Knoxian assertions that a legitimate Church could be recognized by three "tokens & markes": obedience to the written Word of God as the only guide to salvation; proper administration of the two legitimate sacraments of communion and baptism; and ecclesiastical discipline, including excommunication of offenders by consent of the Church. Whether the Elizabethan Church adequately reflected scriptural imperatives in its outward rites was a subject of contention throughout the reign, but no one could pretend that it had a discipline in the sense implied by the Anglo-Genevan confession. In effect, then, Day included a text that at the least called for tangible ecclesiastical reform.

That he meant to do so is suggested by the events of the next parliament, which convened on 2 April 1571. On 6 April, the puritan MP William Strickland noted that "the Professors of the Gospel in other Nations, had writ and published to the World the Confession of their Faith," and declared that England ought to do the same. He concluded by asking fellow MP Thomas Norton to produce a relevant book in his possession. This turned out not to be a confession of faith at all, but rather an Edwardian draft of a Reformed-style church discipline. This work by Archbishop Cranmer had just been edited by John Foxe and printed by John Day as *Reformatio legum ecclesiasticarum* (1571). Thomas Freeman and Elizabeth Evenden argue that Strickland may have impoliticly spoiled a parliamentary maneuver for a wider set of reforms that would have included both new canon law and changes to the *BCP*, but his association of these goals with a confession of faith implicates Day's addition to the *WBP* in the plan. Day did, at any rate, collaborate in making the *Reformatio* available to take advantage of the next legislative opportunity: he sent Foxe a note asking for the preface because "the parliamente draweth neare."[179] Day's inclusion of the confession of faith in his revised version of the *WBP* between parliaments looks very much, in light of the events of 1571, like a preview of or even preparation for this ambitious project.[180]

---

[179] Evenden and Freeman, *Religion and the Book*, 237–8.

[180] Because I had not been able to examine a complete copy of *1569c*, in *RR* I erroneously contended that the confession was first printed in 1572 (*STC* 2442). I argued as a result that Day intervened in the battle for a discipline as it was unfolding. Instead, it seems to be the case that he fired the first shot. Further discussion of the relationship between the confession of faith and *Reformatio* can be found in *RR*, 235–8. (B. Q.)

As it turned out, the reformers made little progress, and the frequent presence of the confession in editions of the *WBP* well into the seventeenth century was their chief legacy.

Finally, the psalm texts themselves were given careful copyediting prior to printing *1569b* and *1569c*. These did not receive identical editing, but they do share a substantial number of revisions. Intentional changes to lines of poetry and the prose arguments prior to this had been limited to places where the sense or the meter was clearly faulty, and the emendations appear to have been largely a matter of common sense and deduction—which explains the large range of proposed solutions. In 1569, an editor went back to earlier editions and restored readings that had been mistaken in or before *1562a*. For example: at Psalm 45:8, *1562a* and the next seven editions give "With mirth and sauours swete, / thy clothes ar all be spreade." In the revised 1569 editions, however, we discover that the clothes are in fact scented with myrrh, and are not literally glad rags. *1562a*'s Bunyanesque "desert of Mammon" in the argument to Psalm 116 also finally turns back into the merely Mediterranean "desert of Maon." There may also have been an attempt nudge the text further in the direction of the Geneva Bible. For example, the same editions emend Psalm 1:3, "He shall be like the tree that groweth, / Fast by the riuer side" to "riuers side." This could be a possessive, though "riverside" is colloquial in the sixteenth century. The greater likelihood is that it's a plural, derived from the Geneva Bible "rivers of waters." Although complete consistency was never a feature of the *WBP* texts, many of the changes from *1569b*, *1569c*, or both were carried through a large number of later editions.

Finally, Day began unobtrusively reducing the number of printed tunes. Psalms 6, 35, and 95 were dropped from *1569b* and replaced by cross-references to other psalms or hymns with tunes, saving about one column in all; some of these were also omitted from the other editions of that year. Already a certain nonchalance was creeping in: Day did not correct the cross-reference "Sing this as Psalm xxxv" that headed Psalms 39, 40, 42, and 43, though it now led to a psalm without a tune. In *1569b* he also replaced the old tune for Psalm 120 with a new one closely related to the popular Psalm 81.

Later Elizabethan Changes

Although the 1569 alterations to the *WBP* were mostly permanent, editors continued to tinker with the book, introducing both more changes intended to affect all editions and greater variety in the contents. Some of the prose apparatus was revised, some dropped out, and by the 1580s the amount of prose included was highly inconsistent between editions in different formats. A final psalm text was added in 1577, but the publishers elected in some subsequent editions to forgo duplicate versions of some psalms or to reduce the number of hymns. The number of tunes in any given edition also became much more variable as the century went on. In 1586 the tunes themselves underwent their only systematic, permanent Elizabethan revision, which evidently reflected a desire of the puritan party to reenforce the original Calvinist principles on which psalm singing had been based.

A curious set of changes, one a precedent for others and the second more fleeting, appear in the folio printing series that Day initiated in 1576, beginning with *STC* 2446. This is the first two-column folio of the *WBP* as well as the first folio in roman type; it was no doubt set to be bound with the first London editions of the full Geneva Bible, which Christopher Barker published in the same year. Although it was printed handsomely enough, Day also appears to have wanted to cut costs on what was, after all, essentially a supplement to Barker's bibles. This is most evident in the music: he eliminated ten more tunes than he had left out of any previous edition, leaving only fifty-three in the volume. Apparently this did not cause widespread indignation from customers, because from this point the number of tunes varied widely (see Appendix 1). The most drastically pruned series began with an octavo edition in 1581 (*STC* 2459.3), designed for binding with a New Testament. It crowded the entire book into 108 octavo pages mainly by reducing the tune content from sixty-six to forty-seven. Its tune selection was adopted in eleven later Elizabethan editions, presumably sold at cut prices.

What, in such cases, was the basis for deciding which tunes should stay and which should be cast out? The hymns and canticles were exempt from tune cutting, for reasons unknown.[181] Of the psalms the obvious victims were those in common, short, or long meter, since a discarded tune could then be replaced by a cross-reference to another. In the 1581 edition mentioned above, eleven of the nineteen discarded tunes are in DCM, two in DSM, and one in SM, and most of these psalms are referred to others in the same meter. But the other five (PSALMS 111, 120, 125 (1), 126, and 136 (1)) are in meters not shared by any other texts in the book. Naturally they have no cross-references—or, in the case of Psalm 120, are referred to a tune with a different meter, leaving the hapless singer to attempt the necessary musical modifications. As a practical matter, then, Day in 1581 was content to assume that the tunes were generally known by heart, or if not, to let certain unpopular psalms go unsung. A similar assumption lay behind the uncorrected misprints that gradually multiplied in editions from about 1580 onwards, to the point where some tunes were barely recognizable; it also accounts for the eventual introduction of editions without any tunes at all.

We must assume, as for *1558*, that the tunes chosen for exclusion were ones that had failed to catch the public fancy and were rarely used in church. Those in unusual meters, mostly of French origin, were certainly dropping out by the 1590s, as both East and Allison recognized (see Appendix 6). In 1603 Henry Dod would publish *Certaine Psalmes of David, Heretofore Much out of Use: Because*

---

[181] Until 1603, when a new 24° series, beginning with *STC* 2510.5, omitted "Preserve us, Lord" with its tune, along with two tuneless hymns.

of Their Difficult Tunes. . . . Reduced into English Meter Better Fitting the Common Tunes.[182] Later efforts to rescue these tunes, most notably in *A Supplement to the New Version of Psalms* (1700), would prove unsuccessful until the antiquarian movement of the 19th century.

An odd decision in the folio edition of 1576 was to drop "Come, Holy Spirit," a hymn in the back section "to be sung before the sermon" which gives a version of a prayer for the whole state of the church (similar to that in the Communion service of the *BCP* and one found in the household prayer section of the *WBP*). While different readers might quibble with different parts of this hymn, it is a challenge to find anything in it that might offend purchasers of the Geneva Bible. If its absence is not an oversight, however, it seems most likely that Day wondered whether especially forward, Genevan-inclined bible readers might object to the supplication to "keep us from sects and errors all." The hymn did not, however, disappear from the general run of *WBP* editions, though other folios in the same printing series and several printing series of two-column quartos descended from it also lack "Come, Holy Spirit."

A round of changes to the *WBP* at least as substantial as those of 1569 occurred in 1577 and 1578. As in 1569, not all the lasting changes emerged in any one edition, and some experiments were quickly abandoned. Possibly because some shifts were experiments, they appear first in two small-format editions (a 16°, *STC* 2449.3, and a 32°, *1577*), and only afterward move into the quartos and folios. What stuck most consistently were new arguments to the individual psalms; an additional version of Psalm 136; and the replacement of the two older lists for how to use the psalms with one, a different translation of Athanasius. From this point, too, the potential purchaser begins to find a much larger variety of textual contents in different editions. In 1578, Day produced a 16° with no prose arguments for the psalms, a choice repeated in some smaller format editions thereafter, often corresponding with other space-saving measures. The section called "A Form of Prayers to Be Used in Private Houses" is first abridged in 1577, and after that it is as common to find some selection from it as to find the whole. Often in the place of some of these Anglo-Genevan prayers are two with quite different English histories.

Two events probably influenced the timing of this set of revisions. First, in 1575 John Day's son Richard came down from Cambridge and began working for his father; he gave up his fellowship late the next year without completing his intended M.A.[183] Second, the 1567 patent on the *WBP*, as well as on the little catechism and ABC, was expiring in 1577 and would take the mainstays of Day's for-

---

[182] He provided a DSM version of Ps. 104, headed "Sing this to the tune of the 25. Psalme," and DCM versions of Pss. 111, 120, 121, 122, 124, 125, 126, and 130. All but one of these had, in the *WBP*, been adapted from French tunes. No musical settings or reprintings of Dod's revised texts have come to light

[183] Evenden, *Patents*, 151–2.

tune with it. Richard was given responsibility for securing a new patent, which he handled by asking the diplomat Henry Killigrew (brother-in-law to William Cecil) to advance their cause with his patron, the Earl of Leicester.[184] The patent that resulted in late August was, generously, a lifetime one—but, probably unexpectedly to John Day, it was to *both* father and son for the longer of their two lifetimes.[185] Richard was thus financially interested in the *WBP*, and it is not unlikely that he had time to devote to textual changes during 1577.

In the little books of 1577, two alterations affect the metrical psalter directly. First, the Days added John Craig's versification of Psalm 136, taken from the Scottish Psalm Book—a rare instance of textual borrowing between the British metrical psalters running from north to south. It was, however, attributed in the *WBP*, initially and apparently forever after, to "T.C." Because written for PSALM 148, it did not require the admission of a new tune. In both of the 1577 editions, as with the majority of printing series afterward, the Craig version preceded the old Norton one. Second, a ruthless red pencil was taken to the prose arguments preceding the psalms. Many arguments had come from *1558*, which, in turn, had combined some original pieces with translations of French psalm arguments or those included in Whittingham's 1557 prose psalter. These had their literary limits, but were often models of clarity compared to the arguments taken directly from the Geneva Bible. In the Geneva Book of Psalms, the arguments break the Psalm into groups of lines and give a summary for each piece, signaling a new section with the number of the first verse in each. The headers were adapted for the metrical psalter by simply taking out the verse numbers. This left phrases not originally intended to be syntactically related jostling against each other, with or without benefit of punctuation. The 1577 editor shortened and tightened most of the arguments. The only systematic agenda seems to have been to impose clarity, and perhaps to reduce slightly the amount of paper being dedicated to sloppy writing. A probably unintended but not insignificant effect was to shift the *WBP* away from some of its closest resemblance to the Geneva Bible.

A change in both of the same 1577 editions that probably does demonstrate someone's ideology at work is the replacement of the two lists of uses for the Psalms—the one excerpted from Athanasius and the sixteenth-century supplement—with a different translation of the Athanasian list alone. The new version of "A Treatise made by Athanasius the Great" (see pp. 882–94) was taken from Matthew Parker's 1567 metrical psalter, also published by Day; in *1577*, it is surrounded by three more passages of ancient writing celebrating the Psalms from Parker's volume (these are also found in *1593*, suggesting that they may have been included in other lost 32° editions as well). As we have already noted, "The Use of the Rest of the Psalms," first printed in *1561d*, included some rather pointedly political occasions and uses. Given that Richard Day was in the process of or had

---

184 Evenden, *Patents*, 156.
185 Oastler, pp. 65–7.

just concluded the negotiations over the *WBP*'s patent renewal, it is easy to imagine that purging an edgy bit of non-patristic devotional material and including the recently deceased archbishop's translation of the patristic treatise might have played some role in those arrangements. Though speculative, such a conclusion is supported by the fact that this is virtually the only textual change that was implemented in *every* later printing series; indeed, no edition after 1577 came out with either of the original lists of uses. To accomplish that required a level of sustained carefulness unique in the production of the *WBP*, suggesting that it was unusually important to the publishers.

The archbishop's translation certainly has features that are more conservative than the *1561d* version. Where *1561d* gets a bit garbled trying not to assign individual psalms to days of the week (in Athanasius a kind of repeated Passion liturgy), Parker enthusiastically assigns three psalms (compared to Athanasius's one) to "Good Friday." He also prescribes Psalm 51 for "penance" rather than *1561d*'s "repentance." At the same time, Parker takes liberties with the text far beyond what the original *WBP* translator did. The version in *1561d* and subsequent editions makes some substitutions in the psalms allotted to particular uses (beyond the errors in typesetting), but is otherwise reasonably faithful to versions of the Athanasian letter in sixteenth-century circulation. Parker adopts some of the psalm substitutions from the *WBP*, adds more of his own, reorders the list of uses to match the (new) list of psalms, and even adds a handful of situations in need of prayer that never appear in Athanasius. The most interesting is taken nearly straight out of "The Use of the Rest": "If thou wilt exhort and provoke kings and princes to submit their powers to God and to regard his honour, sing the 29th, 82nd Psalms." In other words, Parker camouflaged the prescriptions of a *WBP* editor as the work of a fourth-century Father for his own purposes, and the Days later reincorporated the result, with its authoritative and orthodox pedigree, back into the book—a superb example of laundering a questionable text.

Finally, editions of 1577 introduced alterations to the prose prayers that would affect the book's whole printing future. One change is a set of additions, the only ones that would regularly join the material from the Anglo-Genevan *Form of Prayers*. The 1577 16° added a "Prayer Against the Devil," taken from a collection of pseudo-Augustinian devotions that Day first printed in 1574 (and reprinted with some regularity thereafter).[186] The text vividly evokes Satan's flashier forms, but focuses on the theologically uncontroversial idea that God defends the soul from temptation (see pp. 900–02 below). The little 32°, however, added a very different prayer, one taken from John Foxe's 1570 Good Friday sermon at St. Paul's Cross, published the same year by John Day (and subsequently reprinted several times). Evenden and Freeman describe *A Sermon of Christ Crucified* as "anti-Catholic" but "not political"; the prayer that follows and that the Days

---

[186] *Certaine Select Prayers Gathered out of S. Augustines Meditations* (London: John Day, 1574).

inserted into the *WBP*, however, is at great pains to point out the immediate threat that Catholic treason poses to English stability, and it prays that disobedient subjects will not compel the Queen to unwillingly draw her sword "out of the scabbard of long sufferance" (see pp. 895–9 below). That it was Richard Day who added this prayer is suggested by its appearance the next year in his extensively reworked edition of *A Booke of Christian Prayers*.[187] Although the "Prayer Against the Devil" and the longer one by Foxe came out in different editions in 1577, they are present together in the roman type 16° printing series (16/53) that began in 1578. A substantial number of editions printed one or both of these prayers through the sixteenth century and well into the early Stuart period, with the "Prayer Against the Devil" occasionally included after the Restoration.

Just as importantly, the revisions of 1577 also included the first *abbreviation* of the private prayers. *1577* contained an expanded set of household prayers and the Confession, making it one of the most capacious surviving editions. The 16°, however, not only omitted the Confession but dropped the six prandial prayers. After 1577, more printing series lack them than include them. As the century wore on, moreover, the private prayer section became highly variable. While two prayers stand out as most frequently included ("A godly prayer to be said at all times" and "A confession of all estates and times"), there are at least thirteen different selections of prose contents after the psalms in editions printed between 1577 and 1603. The most radical (and the most arbitrary) truncations occurred after John Day's death in 1584. Richard — or his assigns — clearly did not feel the same attachment to the prayer book of the Marian exiles, and it seems probable enough that their mid- and late-Elizabethan audience didn't either.

In 1579, the Days took further steps to shorten some editions of the *WBP* by removing the prose arguments to the metrical psalms in a new 16° edition (*STC* 2451). The same volume cut the number of tunes to fifty (the same selection as in a 1578 quarto, *STC* 2450.5), and is the first surviving evidence of a set of small-format budget editions for the lower end of the market. By 1590, Richard Day's assigns were bringing out 32°s with no printed tunes, no psalm arguments, a shortened roster of hymns, and just two private prayers to fill out the gathering. There are no surviving sixteenth-century copies of any larger format stripped quite as bare as that, but 16°s for individual sale and octavos for binding with

---

[187] Often known as "Queen Elizabeth's Prayer Book." *A Booke of Christian Prayers* (London: John Daye, 1578). Jesse Lander makes a good case that Richard Day's index and its foreword in the 1576 edition of *Acts and Monuments* are meant to lead readers to support Bishop Whitgift's view on church ceremony against his Presbyterian opponents in the Admonition Controversy: Lander, *Inventing Polemic: Religion, Print, and Literary Culture in Early Modern England* (Cambridge: Cambridge University Press, 2006), 66–9. Richard was clearly not an ecclesiological radical, and was probably more conservative in that way than his father. His attachment to Foxe's polemical prayer, however, along with the Parker "translation" of Athanasius, do suggest that his anti-popery was relatively militant.

Geneva New Testaments would also continue to appear without psalm arguments and with both the tunes and prose apparatus considerably reduced.

What Richard Day did not tamper with much in 1577–78, beyond Psalm 136 (2), was the psalm texts themselves. While subsequent Elizabethan editions of the *WBP* do not include any further new texts or permanent deletions of old ones, there was at least one more round of revisions to lines of the metrical psalms. This is a group of textual changes that tended to carry through later editions together, if not consistently, aside from the gradual accretion of sporadic single-line "corrections" and errors. It seems to have occurred after 1577 and before John Day's death in 1584. Unlike the 1569 revisions, this one favored the Great Bible over the Geneva in cases where the line is close enough to any of the prose translations for there to be influence. At Psalm 1:3, for instance, which 1569 had shifted toward Geneva's "rivers of waters," the tree in most editions of the 1580s and 1590s echoes Coverdale by growing "fast by the water side." Additionally, the -eth endings of third-person singular verbs without any metrical rationale made an unexpected reappearance in the early 1580s, though this reversion was even less consistent in later editions. It is hard to tell how much of this process constituted an articulated editorial policy and how much relied on the whims of press correctors, but the eventual result was a large number of lines that sounded rather different from the texts that John Day settled on in the 1560s.

There was also some experimentation with the presentation of editions meant to be sold and bound only with matching books of scripture. One surviving octavo edition, *STC* 2459.3, was issued as a supplement to Christopher Barker's 1581 Geneva Bible. Instead of the usual title page, the first signature of the *WBP* has "The Whole Booke of Psalmes with the Note" in place of a running-head. The strategy does not seem to have been long-lived, but it reflects the evolving role of the *WBP* as part of a suite of personal devotional texts.

Although the patent for the psalm book reverted to Richard Day after his father's death, he was unable to exercise it himself. A series of nasty family quarrels over what share of John's business Richard might be able to take on led to Richard pirating the senior Day's monopolies. As a Warden of the Stationers' Company, John Day confiscated his son's presses and financially crippled him.[188] Subsequently, Richard's privileges were assigned to a coalition of five printers, who appear to have operated largely independently from Day aside from paying him rents, but in coordination with the Stationers' Company.[189] John Wolfe printed nearly all legal editions of the *WBP* until 1591, when John Windet took over.

---

[188] Evenden and Freeman, *Religion and the Book*, 292–3.

[189] Evenden, *Patents*, 175–6. For instances of the assigns working in Richard's place in publishing disputes, see e.g. Walter W. Greg and Eleanore Boswell, eds., *The Records of the Court of the Stationers' Company, 1576–1602* (London: The Bibliographical Society, 1930), 16, 39, 76.

A major revision of the tunes was undertaken by Wolfe in all five editions of
1586, apparently based on John Cosyn's Companion, published by Wolfe the pre-
vious year. Cosyn's versions of the tunes differed in more than 200 details from
the standard versions, and probably reflect in part some of the changes that had
occurred in the process of oral transmission. They also, no doubt for ideological
reasons, return to a stricter compliance with Calvin's ideals for congregational
song.[190] Henry Denham, beginning in 1588, took the first step in printing a few
of the four-line tunes (CM and SM) that were already in widespread use, and
was gradually followed in some editions by Wolfe and Windet. Here the motiva-
tion was more probably financial.[191]

A radical departure came near the end of Elizabeth's reign, known in the
printing trade as the "Middleburg Psalms," beginning with Peter Short's edition
of 1601.[192] In 1599, the Scottish bookbinder John Gibsoun commissioned Rich-
ard Schilders of Middelburg in the Netherlands to print a 16° edition of the Scot-
tish Psalm Book with the Geneva Bible version in the margins.[193] On his own
initiative, most likely, Schilders modified the standing type for this edition to
produce a matching version of the English metrical psalter.[194] As a result of this
opportunism in publication, the result differed from London editions through
more than the presence of marginal prose. Although the basic psalm versions
matched editions of *WBP* circulating in the late-Elizabethan period, the ones
that overlapped with those in the Scottish psalm book often retained their Scot-
tish textual variants, with sometimes whole quatrains that would be unfamil-
iar to English audiences. Moreover, Schilders printed only one version of each
psalm, and the hymns were lumped together in jumbled order after the psalms.
Like the most inexpensive English editions, this one lacked prose arguments to
the psalms. Most importantly, for the pagination to correspond efficiently to the
Scottish book Schilders had to include more psalm tunes than were usual in the
English publication — a total of eighty-one. Thirty-two of the psalm tunes print-
ed had never appeared with that text in an English *WBP*, the majority of them

---

[190] For Cosyn's links to the puritan movement see pp. 910–11 and 1015 below.

[191] For details of the 1586 revisions and the new four-line tunes see Apps. 4 and 5
respectively.

[192] See Nicholas Temperley, "Middleburg Psalms," *Studies in Bibliography* 30 (1977):
162–71, repr. *SECM*, 10–19. The spelling of Middelburg was anglicized in English usage.

[193] *STC* 16587. See William Cowan, *A Bibliography of the Book of Common Order and
Psalm Book of the Church of Scotland: 1556–1644* (Edinburgh: Edinburgh Bibliographical
Society, 1913), 83, 24.

[194] *STC* 2499.9. See Temperley, "Middleburg Psalms," 165–6. Schilders had earlier
attempted to ply his trade in London, and in 1578 came to the attention of the Stationers
for being in violation of the section of their Charter forbidding independent printing by
aliens: see Cyprian Blagden, *The Stationers' Company: A History, 1403–1959* (Cambridge,
Mass.: Harvard University Press, 1960), 36. He would have been well aware that the mar-
ket for *WBP*s was considerably larger than that for Scottish Psalm Books.

following the Scottish tradition. The title page says that it was "for the vse of the English Church in Middelburgh," but the inclusion of the non-scriptural hymns rules out the Separatists there as Schilders's only intended audience. A dozen copies brought home by an English merchant in fact came to the attention of the Stationers' Company in the fall of 1600,[195] and in response Peter Short as joint assignee of Richard Day and William Seres (who held the patent for prose psalters) published a legally saleable reprint of Schilders's volume the next year. He copied Schilders's text closely, including the Scottish textual variants, but replaced all but one of the Scottish tunes, largely with those from East's Companion of 1592. These were presumably tunes in current English use, but the selection remained far larger than those in other editions of the *WBP*. He also added back the second versions of Psalms 23 and 51. With the number of tunes reduced to seventy-eight, this 16° printing series continued to at least 1631 and makes up the majority of surviving editions of Middleburg psalms.

A rather different version of the Middleburg psalms descends from Schilders's second attempt at a metrical psalter for the English market, this time an octavo. In 1602 he printed fresh versions of both the English and Scottish psalm books with the prose in the margins, but this time he set the English one first. Doing so made room for the arguments to the psalms, removed the textual debts to the Scottish tradition, and allowed for English tunes. The ninety-three tunes he printed in his *WBP* were paired with the same texts as in East's volumes. He did not, however, bother with the hymns in this edition. Adapting this new piracy under the auspices of the Stationers' Company in 1605, John Windet retained most of Schilders's tunes and added other traditional English ones back in, for a total of 115 when the hymns are included. (The number increased to 116 in 1613.) These octavo editions continued to be printed until at least 1629.

Middleburg psalms made up a small minority of *WBP*s published during these years, and their intended audience seems to have been puritan. Small format *WBP*s were at times bound with the Great Bible prose psalters used throughout the month in the liturgy of the *BCP*. That the Middleburg psalms include the Geneva version means that they were used domestically in psalm-singing households, an increasingly puritan activity during the seventeenth century. Additionally, placing the prose verses as references next to the corresponding metrical ones emphasizes the need to "sing with understanding"—an imperative not only voiced by Calvin but particularly emphasized in the seventeenth century by puritan writers. Because the format quickly became standard in Scottish psalm books, it might be tempting to associate the similar English metrical psalters with presbyterian ecclesiology as well. The publishing history of the Middleburg psalms does not support a wholly sectarian interpretation, however. In reprinting Schilders's edition, Windet's 1605 octavo gave the table immediately after the

---

[195] Greg and Boswell, *Records of the Stationers' Company*, 79.

psalms, and then, in a separate set of gatherings, added the hymns and a handful of prayers. As a consequence, buyers who did not want the non-scriptural material could choose a copy that did not contain it (and some surviving copies of this edition do lack those quires). The 16° editions from 1608 onwards end the psalms with quire Aa and use quires Bb-Ee for the rest of the contents, including the index, and copies of both varieties can be found. So it appears that the Stationers' Company wanted to cater to both schools of thought with minimal inconvenience and expense.[196]

The Middleburg psalms were adapted to actually promote Prayer Book practice in the 1630s and 1640s. In 1635, *WBP* editions with the Great Bible psalms in the margins were issued in both octavo and 16° formats, suggesting that the Stationers' Company either anticipated great demand for them or had been encouraged by authority to make a large supply available. The title page of the octavo edition (*STC* 2661) notes that the prose psalms are "according as they are appointed to bee read in the Church of England," and both editions divide the margins into the portions prescribed for morning and evening prayer each day. The prose text also retains the colons ("pointing") in the middle of each verse from the Prayer Book psalter. A reprint of the octavo appeared in 1641. A 1649 experiment (Wing B2436) replaced the Great Bible psalter with the KJV ("the new Translation of the English Bible"). In parceling the psalms out according to the *BCP* calendar, presumably for households that maintained a version of the Prayer Book services at home after its abolition for public worship in 1644, this last known edition of the Middleburg psalms is a nearly perfect mirror image of the first ones. Rather than supporting puritan sensibilities against the conformity of public prayers, it catered to conservatives whose established public worship had been abruptly changed. In this scenario, the *WBP* was not a mark of radical private zeal but a link to the long-established practices of the English Church.

The Character of Congregational Song

Once the psalms were introduced in 1559, they spread very quickly over the city and nation, as we know from several contemporary sources. According to the often-quoted 1560 account of Bishop John Jewel, this had been almost immediate:

> As soon as they had once commenced singing in public, in only one little church in London, immediately not only the churches in the neighbourhood, but even the towns far distant, began to vie with each other in the same practice. You may now sometimes see at Paul's Cross, after the

---

[196] E.g., the copy from the Huntington Library reproduced on EEBO lacks these quires. See Temperley, "Middleburg Psalms," 168.

service, six thousand persons, old and young, of both sexes, all singing to-
gether and praising God."[197]

Many returning exiles were soon given parish benefices or higher church posi-
tions, or made heads of colleges.[198] Edmund Grindal, a member of the "Prayer
Book" party among the exiles and the translator of "Da pacem, Domine" in the
WBP, was appointed bishop of London on 22 June 1559, and was "the most zeal-
ous in presenting his companions in exile for ordination." As many as a tenth of
the 294 clergy he ordained and placed in parishes in the large diocese of London,
which included Essex, Middlesex, and parts of Hertfordshire, were returned ex-
iles.[199] Others presided at the mass meetings at St. Paul's Cross.[200] The practice
of psalm singing had reached the universities and beyond by the time the first
English edition of the *WBP* was issued.[201]

It is not obvious how people learned the tunes so quickly—or the words, in
the case of those who could not read. The exiles abroad had sung without choir
or organ, and Archbishop Parker later recorded that this was a normal English
practice, though he also allowed for a four-part choir.[202] Ryrie assumes that the
crowds "had learned their tunes under Edward [VI]," without explaining how
this was done.[203] We conclude, on the contrary, that the tunes were new to most
English churchgoers. In some churches the parson and parish clerk,[204] perhaps
backed by a few returned exiles, or some well-educated churchgoers who could
read music notation, would have led the people. As we have seen, Jonathan Wil-
lis has found abundant new evidence of the purchase of psalm books for the use

---

[197] Hastings Robinson, ed., *The Zurich Letters*, 2 vols. (London: Parker Society, 1846),
1:71.

[198] Garrett, *Marian Exiles*, passim.

[199] John Strype, *The History of the Life and Acts of . . . Edmund Grindal* (London: John
Hartley, 1710), 49–50; Patrick Collinson, "Grindal, Edmund," *ODNB*.

[200] For instance John Mackbray on 3 September 1559 and Robert Crowley on 15 Oc-
tober 1559 (Garrett, *Marian Exiles*, 224, 138).

[201] See *MEPC*, 1:63; *RR*, 240–1.

[202] "The Tenor of these partes be for the people when they will syng alone, the
other parts, put for greater queers, or to suche as will syng or play them privatelye."
[Matthew Parker], *The Whole Psalter Translated into English Metre* (London: John Daye,
[1567]), sig. W4r.

[203] Ryrie, "Psalms and Confrontation," 125.

[204] The official duties of parish clerks did not include singing: see Gerald Bray, ed.,
Tudor Church Reform: The Henrician Canons of 1535 and the Reformatio Legum Ecclesias-
ticarum (Bury St. Edmunds: The Boydell Press, 2000), 347. But Jonathan Willis found
examples, one as late as 1577, of references showing that parish clerks were still able to
provide musical leadership in some parishes: see Willis, *Church Music and Protestant-
ism*, 115–16. Their musical duties continued in places for centuries. see *MEPC*, 1.111, 154,
234–5, and 275.

of choirs. "Geneva books" and "psalm books in meter" were rapidly acquired by many parishes beginning in 1559, especially in London.[205] Purchases were usually of one to eight copies, suggesting that they were intended for those who could read music notation and lead the singing. Since the main evangelical impetus was for congregational singing, we must assume that their purpose was to enable choirs to lead the people. Of course, many individuals would have bought their own copies as the practice became established. In many London churches and some provincial ones an organ and organist were available to provide guidance, as Willis has shown.[206] Schoolchildren were taught the tunes by rote in some parishes and led the singing in church until frequent repetition made them familiar to all.[207]

For want of evidence we question Willis's conclusion that "the earliest purchases of metrical Psalms seem to have been designed to furnish choirs with confessionally appropriate material to sing during the service in place of traditional Latin liturgical works and motets."[208] Such a practice would have required the copying of manuscript partbooks with the psalms arranged in harmony, but Willis has not identified any such activity in his study of churchwardens' accounts, nor has any survived to our knowledge.[209] The practice of faburden, used in chanting without the need for music notation, was not well suited to tunes of this type and there is no evidence that it was ever used with them. Nor does Willis report a single purchase of Day's 1563 Companion, which could have supplied four-part harmony for choirs.

As we have seen, Day did attempt to build sight-singing aids into the *WBP* itself, but these were probably of limited utility. "A Short Introduction into the Science of Music," which he first printed in 1561, tried to teach basic music theory

---

[205] The quotations are from the accounts from St. Margaret Pattens (London: Guildhall Library 4570/2) and St. Mary Woolnoth (London: Guildhall Library 1002/1A–B), respectively. Dr. Willis has graciously made his transcriptions of these accounts available to us; see also his *Church Music and Protestantism*, 121–8. Appendix 7 is based on his findings, but distinguishes (as he does not) between "psalters" (prose) and "psalm books" or "psalms" (metrical). These terms were consistently used in those senses at the time, following the title pages of the respective books.

[206] Willis found evidence of the use of an organ in 47 (55%) of 85 parishes whose accounts he was able to examine, but reported that "records of disbursements relating to organs drop off rapidly during the first half of Elizabeth's reign" (Willis, *Church Music and Protestantism*, 90–103). Of course the more affluent parishes tend to be the ones whose accounts were well kept and have survived, so it would be wrong to assume that such a high proportion of churches in the country at large possessed functioning organs, even at the beginning of the reign.

[207] For some slightly later examples see *MEPC*, 1:81–2, 89.

[208] Willis, *Church Music and Protestantism*, 126, 128.

[209] British Library Add. MS. 15166, which may have been used by choirs (see p. 518 above), is not primarily based on the *WBP* tunes.

Ex. 7. The solfa letters.

for this purpose. The solfa letters placed beside the notes in some editions, start-
ing in 1569, offered another approach. This idea was borrowed from a Genevan
publication,[210] but the explanation offered in a one-page preface "To the Reader"
(see App. 3) did not represent the way the letters were actually applied.[211] Nor did
it explain the effect of a key-signature on the scale. Example 7, in modern clefs,
shows how the letters were actually used in the psalm book, but no such accurate
representation is to be found in any edition. The upper line represents their use
on the white notes only, the lower line when there is a key-signature of one flat.
The letters of the lower octave do not repeat in the upper octave, so that v and r
are only used for the two lowest notes.

Figure 5 shows a page from *STC* 2442 (1572), one of the early solfa editions;
it is the same edition whose preface is reproduced on page 881–82. One of the
few tunes that presents any problems for the notation is PSALM 148,[212] which has
an open key signature, and hence B naturals, but contains two B flats, marked

---

[210] [Pierre Davantes], *Pseaumes de David, mis en rhythme francoise par Clement Ma-
rot, & Théodore de Besze.* [Geneva:] Pierre Dauantes, 1560. See Krummel, *English Music
Printing,* 71–2.

[211] "This preface's implication of a hexachordal understanding of solmization is seri-
ously misleading" (Arten, "Protestant Advocacy", 11: see note 15). Moreover, the music
examples supposed to provide a key to the solfa syllables were erroneously printed in the
early editions (see App. 3), making them nearly useless for pedagogic purposes.

[212] For a transcription of this tune see pp. 453–4.

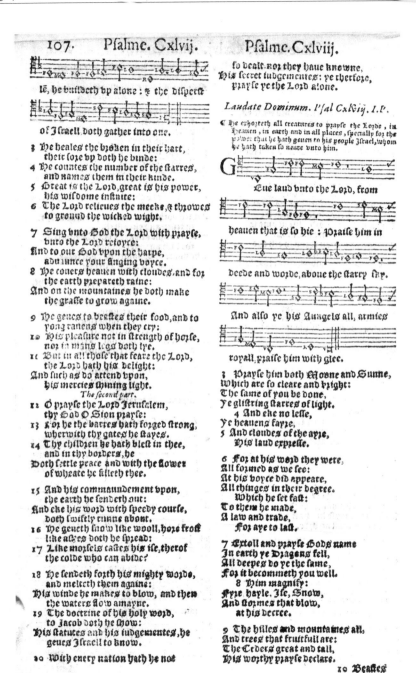

107.   Pſalme. Cxlvij.

iſ, he buildeth vp alone : & the diſperſt

of Iſraell, doth gather into one.

3 He heales the broken in their hart,
    their ſore vp doth he binde:
4 He countes the number of the ſtarres,
    and names them in their kinde.
5 Great is the Lord, great is his power,
    his wiſdome infinite:
6 The Lord relieues the meeke, & throwes
    to ground the wicked wight,

7 Sing vnto God the Lord with prayſe,
    vnto the Lord reioyce:
And to our God vpon the harpe,
    aduaunce your ſinging voyce.
8 He couers heauen with cloudes, and for
    the earth prepareth raine:
And on the mountaines he doth make
    the graſſe to grow againe.

9 He geues to beaſtes their food, and to
    yong ravens when they cry:
10 His pleaſure not in ſtrength of horſe,
    nor in mans legs doth lye.
11 But in all thoſe that feare the Lord,
    the Lord hath his delight:
And ſuch as do attend vpon,
    his mercies ſhining light.
         The ſecond part.
12 O prayſe the Lord Ieruſalem,
    thy God O Sion prayſe:
13 For he the barres hath forged ſtrong,
    wherwith thy gates he ſtayes.
14 Thy children he hath bleſt in thee,
    and in thy borders, he
Doth ſettle peace and with the flower
    of wheate he filleth thee.

15 And his commaundement vpon,
    the earth he ſendeth out:
And eke his word with ſpeedy courſe,
    doth ſwiftly runne about.
16 He geueth ſnow like the wooll, hore froſt
    like aſhes doth he ſpread:
17 Like morſels caſtes his iſe, therof
    the colde who can abide?

18 He ſendeth forth his mighty words,
    and melteth them againe:
His winde he makes to blow, and then
    the waters flow amayne.
19 The doctrine of his holy word,
    to Iacob doth he ſhow:
His ſtatutes and his iudgementes, he
    geues Iſraell to know.

20 With euery nation hath he not

Pſalme. Cxlviij.

ſo dealt: nor they haue knowne,
His ſecret iudgementes: ye therfore,
prayſe ye the Lord alone.

Laudate Dominum. Pſal. CxlViij. I. P.

¶ He exhorteth all creatures to prayſe the Lorde, in
Heauen, in earth and in all places, ſpecially for the
power that he hath geuen to his people Iſrael, whom
he hath taken ſo neare vnto him.

Gue laud vnto the Lord, from

heauen that is ſo hie : Prayſe him in

deede and worde, aboue the ſtarry ſky.

And alſo ye his Angels all, armies

royall, prayſe him with glee.

3 Prayſe him both Moone and Sunne,
Which are ſo cleare and bright,
The ſame of you be done,
Ye gliſtring ſtarres of light.
    4 And eke no leſſe,
Ye heauens fayre,
5 And cloudes of the ayre,
    His laud expreſſe.

6 For at his word they were,
All formed as we ſee:
At his voyce did appeare,
All thinges in their degree.
    Which he ſet faſt:
To them he made,
A law and trade,
    For aye to laſt.

7 Extoll and prayſe Gods name
In earth ye Dragons fell,
All deepes do ye the ſame,
For it becommeth you well.
    8 Him magnify:
Fyre hayle, Iſe, Snow,
And ſtormes that blow,
    at his decree.

9 The hilles and mountaines all,
And trees that fruitfull are:
The Cedars great and tall,
His worthy prayſe declare.
          10 Beaſtes

Fig. 5: *WBP* 1572 (*STC* 2442), sig. 3v. University of Illinois at Urbana-Champaign.

by accidentals. The notation uses M (mi) for the B naturals in the first and later phrases, but for the two B flats uses F (fa). This implies a change of hexachord.[213]

If the letters have any purpose it is to show where a note is in the diatonic scale: thus M (mi) should indicate that the next note upwards is only a half-step higher, and the rest indicate other positions in the scale. But, as Ex. 7 shows, this principle was not consistently followed. Some notes in the tunes have no letter, including those with an accidental, where it might be supposed that the singer needed special guidance. Altogether it is difficult to see how the notation could have provided any practical help in learning the tunes.[214]

As for the words, before psalm books were widespread there was always the possibility of "lining out," where someone such as the parish clerk read out each line or pair of lines before the people sang it. In 1644 lining out was ordered by the Presbyterian establishment, and would last in some churches for two centuries after that.[215] Only two earlier references to the practice have come to light. One was at Wesel in 1556, where, according to a deleted passage in a draft document now at Lambeth Palace, it was allowed "that some psalm or invocation may at sometyme be sung either in one tune, or in severall parts, at the discretion of all the elders provided alwayes that the verse wich shalbe so sung be befoer playnly & distinctly read of the minister."[216] This suggests that the purpose of reading the lines was to make sure that they were heard or understood before they were sung by a select group, not to allow the people at large to sing them in imitation of the reader. In 1636 Bishop Wren of Norwich asked the churchwardens of his diocese whether the psalms were sung "according to that grave manner (which first was in use) that such doe sing as can read the psalmes, or have learned them by heart: and not after that uncouth and undecent custom of

---

[213] From C fa ut to F fa ut. See App. 3, Fig. 3, for further explanation. The preface, however, makes no attempt to explain the system. In the last phrase of PSALM 147, shown also in the figure, a B natural is required on the fifth note from the end, available only in the G sol re ut hexachord. The editor did not attempt to attain this and contented himself with a B flat, copying the earliest solfa edition (*1569b*), though every earlier source had specified a B natural (by means of a sharp accidental).

[214] The final note of Ps. 147 is F sharp in most sources. Here (see Fig. 1) it does not carry either a sharp or a solfa letter.

[215] "For the present, where many in the Congregation cannot read, it is convenient that the Minister, or some other fit person appointed by him and the other ruling officers, do reade the psalme, line by line, before the singing thereof." *A Directory for the Publique Worship of God* (London: Company of Stationers, 1644), 83–4; *MEPC* 1:81–2, 89.

[216] Lambeth Palace Library, MS 2523, fol. 3v; quoted Leaver, *'Goostly Psalmes,'* 214. It is possible, of course, that the entire psalm was read out before the singing began; this depends on the meaning of "verse."

late taken up, to have every line first read, and then sung by the people."[217] This suggests that lining out had not been a normal practice in Elizabethan or Jacobean times, and no mention of it from those two reigns has come to light. Nevertheless it would have been an obvious way to introduce congregational singing in a church where it had not been known. In any case, lining out was reading, not singing, as all three sources confirm. It was not for teaching tunes. Whether or not a psalm was lined out, the parish clerk or another leader would begin the singing, identifying the tune and setting the pitch for the congregation.[218]

Not everyone would necessarily join in the singing, but in many churches a substantial portion of the congregation would sing—men in the tenor range, women and children an octave higher.[219] The opening pitch would normally be set by the parish clerk. As choirs and organs gradually disappeared from most churches by the middle of Elizabeth's reign, the singers in the congregation were essentially on their own. In such circumstances the more timid participants, including those unfamiliar with words or tune, would tend to hang behind the confident ones, and so delay the performance. Over time the expected or normal pace slowed down. Whether as additional cause or as effect of this tempo change, it was conventional from the late Elizabethan period onwards to distinguish sharply in rhythmic notation between the kinds of tunes appropriate for ballads and those intended for psalms.[220] By the early eighteenth century people seem to have found a slow and stately pace particularly appropriate for psalm singing as a part of public devotional exercises: in 1710 the high-church Bishop Beveridge testified that parishioners "love and admire" the psalms all the more for their

---

[217] Kenneth Fincham, ed., *Visitation Articles and Injunctions of the Early Stuart Church*, 2 vols. (Woodbridge, Suffolk: Boydell & Brewer, 1994–8), 2:148–9, quoted Marsh, *Music and Society*, 427.

[218] This is what was meant by the entry in the churchwardens' accounts of St. Michael Cornhill, London, charging the churchwardens to "provid a skylfull man to begyne the syngynge salmes," interpreted by Willis (*Church Music and Protestantism*, 124) as evidence that "the practice of lining out was in common use in some parishes." Similar assumptions have been made by others, e.g. Watkins Shaw in "Church Music in England from the Reformation to the Present Day" (Friedrich Blume et al., *Protestant Church Music: A History*, London: Victor Gollancz Ltd., 1975), 700. In fact no clear evidence of lining out has been found anywhere from Elizabeth's reign. For later instances and further discussion, and see Nicholas Temperley, "The Old Way of Singing: Its Origins and Development," *Journal of the American Musicological Society* 34 (1981): 532–5.

[219] The overall range of the tunes as printed in the *WBP* was c to a', with the exception of two that probably originated as upper voices in accompanied settings (COMPLAINT and LAMENTATION), both of which rise to c". Of course in unaccompanied singing the leader was always free to choose whatever pitch was convenient.

[220] See *MEPC*, 1:63–4; *RR*, 271–2; Marsh, *Music and Society*, 420–1.

"plain," "low," and "heavy" qualities.[221] Somewhat ironically, then, English practice had come to exemplify the "weight and majesty" that Calvin desired for the psalms much more dramatically than Huguenot practice did. There is no reason to doubt that the Geneva psalms, when first introduced, were sung at the brisk pace that their notation then defined: much the same as that of secular songs.[222] This fits with the pejorative nickname coined by Catholic critics, "Geneva jigs." There may have been some slowing down already during the Marian exile, and there surely was by 1586 (see Appendix 4). As the process continued, a consequence was the spontaneous introduction of intermediate pitches to fill in the gaps in a tune. All this led in some places, by the middle of the seventeenth century, to an unregulated heterophony, later known as the "old way of singing."[223]

The 1559 Injunctions allowed a "hymn or suchlike song" only "in the beginning, or in the end of common prayers"; and, as discussed above, this was extended, without the same explicit authority but presumably with tacit approval, to "before and after sermons" on the title pages of most editions from 1566. The Anglo-Genevan liturgy situated the congregational singing around the sermon, and Jewel's remark about singing at St. Paul's Cross suggests that the practice continued without interruption in England. It is thus unsurprising that sermons emerged as the most usual occasion for metrical psalms, at outdoor meetings as well as in parish churches and many cathedrals. Richard Harrison's description of Sunday worship in a parish church in 1577 mentions psalms *only* before and after the sermon.[224] Putting the seal of approval on this practice for the national church, forms of prayer for particular occasions issued in 1576 and 1580 specified which metrical psalms should accompany the sermon or homily.[225] Normally, the choice of psalm belonged legally to the priest conducting the service, but in practice was often left to whoever led the singing—in many cases, the parish

---

[221] William Beveridge, *A Defence of the Book of Psalms, Collected into English Metre, by Thomas Sternhold, John Hopkins, and Others* (London: R. Smith, 1710), 42. Marsh (*Music and Society*, 430–2) argues for aesthetic preference as a reason for the slow tempo of psalms, though without accounting for the retardation already evident in mid-Elizabethan psalm singing.

[222] The tactus, normally represented by the semibreve, was supposed to be at the normal heart rate, which we may call 72 to the minute: see George Houle, *Meter in Music, 1600–1800* (Bloomington, Ind.: Indiana University Press, 1987), 3–4. It may have slowed down at Wesel, however.

[223] Described in detail in *MEPC*, 1:91 8, and in Temperley, "Old Way of Singing." The hostile witness John Phillips transcribes a sample in *The Religion of the Hypocritical Presbyterians in Meeter* (London, 1661), 6.

[224] Holinshed, *Chronicles*, 1:232, quoted in full in *MEPC*, 1:44.

[225] *A Fourme of Praier with Thankes Giving, to be Used Every Yeare, the 17. of November, being the Day of the Queenes Majesties Entrie to her Raigne* (London: Richard Jugge, 1576); *The Order of Prayer, and other Exercises, upon Wednesdayes and Frydayes . . .* (London: Christopher Barker, 1580). See p. 592 below.

clerk. Robert Horne, bishop of Winchester, as early as 1562 ordered the Chanter [precentor] of his cathedral to "have in readiness books of psalms set forth in English metre to be provided at the costs of the church, and to sing in the body of the church both afore the sermon and after the sermon one of the said psalms to be appointed at the discretion of the Chanter."[226] It became customary in cathedrals, after choral service in the chancel, for people from the nearby churches to come to hear the sermon in the nave, and thus take part in the congregational singing that went with it. The custom was reinstated in many cathedrals after the Restoration, at least before the sermon.[227] The choir generally sang an anthem after the sermon, but in 1665 John Hackett, bishop of Lichfield, stipulated a metrical psalm instead, to the indignation of at least one of the canons: "it is not difficult to foresee how nauseous church music and common prayer will again become if Hopkins and Sternhold's rhythms may jostle out our anthems."[228]

So long as congregational singing from the *WBP* did not interrupt or displace elements of the *BCP*, there is no evidence that English episcopal authorities ever objected to the practice and considerable evidence over the early modern period that they encouraged it. When the metrical psalms or congregational singing intruded into the liturgy, the bishops and church courts could react with alarm. One trouble spot was early Elizabethan substitutions of the metrical psalms for the prose psalms ordered to be read or chanted in morning and evening prayer. It was reported to Archbishop Parker in 1565 that "while some keep precisely the order of the book, others intermeddle psalms in metre."[229] Bishop Bickley of Chichester inquired disapprovingly in his 1586 diocesan Visitation Articles whether any ministers "endeavour to have the parishioners say service and sing psalms in prose and metre with them in the Church?" At the same time, Bickley's are the *only* surviving Elizabethan episcopal Visitation Articles to include copies of the metrical psalms among the required furniture for parish churches. He could not have objected to the *WBP* as such, though he did wish to discourage its disorderly use during the parts of the service that should be read to the

---

[226] Walter H. Frere, *Visitation Articles and Injunctions of the Period of the Reformation*, 3 vols. (London: Longmans Green & Co., 1910), 3:138. The practice was similar at Norwich cathedral; see note 231 below.

[227] *MEPC*, 1:42–3. For examples after 1660 see Ian Spink, *Restoration Cathedral Music, 1660–1714* (Oxford: Clarendon Press, 1995), 18–19.

[228] James Clifford, *The Divine Services and Anthems Usually Sung in the Cathedrals and Collegiate Choires in the Church of England* (London: Henry Brome, 1663), A2v; Oxford, Bodleian Library, MS. Tanner 131, fol. 14, quoted in Ann J. Kettle and D. A. Johnson, "House of Secular Canons – Lichfield Cathedral: from the Reformation to the 20th Century," in The Victoria History of the County of Stafford (20 vols.), vol. 3, *Ecclesiastical History*, ed. Michael W. Greenslade (London: Oxford University Press, 1970), 181.

[229] Frere, *English Church*, 115.

congregation rather than voiced by it.[230] Similarly, Bishop Parkhurst of Norwich, his eye on some recent puritan disturbances, included in his 1571 Visitation Articles for the cathedral the order that "no ditties nor notes of psalms nor of other godly songs be used in the choir but such as be allowed by public authority or by the Ordinary." Evidently, the intention was to confine psalm singing to the nave, where the people would congregate after the choral service to hear the sermon.[231] It is entirely possible that in other places the full congregation sang the metrical canticles instead of the prose versions which were set out in full in the prayer book. Some of them — those derived from Scripture — had first been printed for the Wesel community, which, though generally loyal to the 1552 prayer book, did make some changes in the prescribed services.[232] The fact that they were included in the *WBP* suggests that this practice continued in England in some quarters. Many years later, Peter Heylyn wrote that "in very little time they [the Puritan party] prevailed so far in most parish churches, as to thrust the Te Deum, the Benedictus, the Magnificat, and the Nunc dimittis quite out of the Church."[233] No evidence has come to light of the use of the metrical commandments, creeds, or Lord's Prayer in place of the *BCP* prose versions.

Some other hymns in the psalm book had specific functions, with varying relationships to authorized liturgical practice. The metrical Veni, Creator was

---

[230] William Paul McClure Kennedy, *Elizabethan Episcopal Administration: An Essay in Sociology and Politics*, 3 vols. (London: A. R. Mowbray & Co., 1924), 3:214–15. The metrical psalms are awkwardly inserted into a conventional list of church furniture, requiring "two Psalters in prose and metre" rather than the usual "two Psalters" (210). (This unusual formulation is repeated in Thomas King's 1599 Articles for the Archdeaconry of Nottingham, which are largely taken from Bickley's 1586 list; Kennedy, 3:317–18.) Craig and Marsh give Bickley's inquiry about singing as evidence of episcopal disapproval of congregational singing without noting the equally unusual explicit insistence on parish churches buying the *WBP*, when parishes frequently purchased them without being told to. Two copies is not adequate provision for a choir, and rather suggests that they are, like the copies of the prose psalms, meant for the priest and a clerical assistant (the mandated "clerk, sexton, or deacon," 210). The natural conclusion is that Bickley was endorsing singing by the congregation, led by the clerk in the usual way. (Solo performances of metrical psalms by the minister or clerk have no place in the contemporary understanding of the *BCP* and no rationale outside of it.)

[231] The same articles also insist that "every Sunday after the service be ended all persons of the college do resort to the sermon and help to sing the psalms and not to depart thence until the last psalm be ended," reinforcing appropriate congregational singing. Kennedy, *Elizabethan Episcopal Administration*, 3:317.

[232] Leaver, *'Goostly Psalmes,'* 198–9.

[233] Heylyn, *Examen historicum*, 1:119–20. After 1604 in the diocese of York "there were frequent cases where the lessons at mattins and evensong were omitted and metrical psalms sung in place of the canticles": John Addy, "The Archdeacon and Ecclesiastical Discipline in Yorkshire, 1598–1714" (York: St. Anthony's Press, 1963), 13.

an authorized part of the ordination service, and was now (in 1561) provided with a tune. In explicit accordance with the 1559 Injunction, "Praise the Lord" and "Behold, now give heed" were directed to be sung before morning and evening prayer respectively, to the tune of PSALM 100. "Come, Holy Spirit" was "to be sung before sermons," and was under normal circumstances treated like a psalm sung in the same context. In 1564, Melchior Smyth, a Yorkshire vicar who repeatedly clashed with authorities over Prayer Book ceremony, answered the charge that he did "omytt and neclect to pray for the Quenes majestie" as required before sermons in the ante-communion service by ingenuously explaining that "for brevitie onlie and to avoyd tediousnes he appoynted the hympne to be sung called Come Holie Spiritt, at the begynnyng of everie sermon, Wherein the Queene hir Counsell the Nobilitie [and] the States bothe of the spiritualitie and temporalitie were praied for."[234] A mock church service staged at Wrington, Somerset, in 1605, suggests that another *WBP* text may have been creatively added in some congregations. The players "began a psalm, beginning the spiritt of grace etc, & song it to the end." This is no psalm but The Prayer that follows the Ten Commandments (see p. 462), presumably sung to COMMANDMENTS (2). The incident suggests that the Prayer was sometimes sung by itself in real services after the prose Commandments had been recited in the ante-communion service—the position that the song occupied in this parodic context.[235]

Most significantly, William Samuel's 124-line communion hymn ("The Lord be thanked") was sung in many churches. The custom of singing during and after the administration of the sacrament had its origin in the *communio* and *post-communio*, Latin prose psalm excerpts or antiphons chanted at that point in the Sarum Mass. Despite the fact that the meaning of the sacrament was hotly disputed among the reformers, the custom of singing as a part of the service was maintained even in the Genevan *Form of Prayers* of 1556, where Sternhold's Psalm 103 was prescribed to be sung by the people after communion. Samuel's hymn was first printed at Wesel. In Daman's Companion (1579) the title was changed from "A Thanksgiving after the Receiving of the Lord's Supper" to "A Thanksgiving to be Sung at the Ministering of the Lord's Supper." This practice seems to have generated some controversy in the Elizabethan period. The sporadically-conformist preacher William Burton, in a 1589 sermon defending a number of (puritan) practices attacked by his opponents, lists among the charges

---

[234] See John S. Purvis, ed., *Tudor Parish Documents of the Diocese of York* (Cambridge: Cambridge University Press, 1948), 212, 217. The description positively identifies the hymn of that name in *WBP*.

[235] James Stokes and Robert I. Alexander, eds., *Record of Early English Drama: Somerset*, 2 vols. (Toronto: University of Toronto Press, 1996), 1:398–9. As Marsh notes (*Music and Society*, p. 446), the performance does not suggest any theological agenda. He does not, however, identify the text. The Prayer had some independent existence and was set as an anthem in the 17th century (see p. 773).

against his party that "we sing psalmes in time of the communion, which were foysted in by the Geneua puritans."[236] An early Jacobean writer maintained that the puritans favored "the singing of psalmes in the Churche at Sermons by the whole multitude, and at other exercises (namely at the Comunion) . . . in a plaine *Geneva* tune."[237] Perhaps because of the custom's ancient pedigree, the consensus seems to have come down on the side of those puritans. In 1623, George Wither published under royal patent a new and even longer communion hymn; as he said in a prefatory comment, "Wee have a custome among us, that, during the administring the blessed *Sacrament* of the *Lord's Supper,* there is a long *Psalme* or *Hymne* sung, the better to keepe the thoughts of the *Communicants* from wandering after vaine objects."[238]

To the extent that they were used congregationally, most of the remaining original hymns would probably have been treated as interchangeable with the metrical psalms. There is direct evidence that Robert Wisdom's "Preserve us, Lord" was thus employed. The Jesuit Robert Persons said of it in 1580 that English Protestants "singe it, and make other simple men to singe it, in the beginning of sermons, and otherwise: as though it were scripture it selfe, and one of Dauids psalmes."[239] Three decades later, Christopher Sibthorp answered similar Irish Catholic criticism of the *WBP*: "yee alledge, that in a Psalme or Hymne which wee sometimes sing in our Churches, wee pray unto God, to keepe and defend us from the Pope and Turke: and why should we not doe so?"[240] The robust sectarianism of the text and, among later intra-Protestant debates, the fact that Wisdom's evocative name appeared as the only heading for the hymn drew attention that was not focused on the volume's other hymns. It seems likely that some at least would have been sung in the same way, with less attendant controversy.

Even after congregational singing was well established, the *WBP* could be a source for choral music. Several hymns, especially The Lamentation of a Sinner, were popular texts for polyphonic settings, both ecclesiastical and domestic. Towards the end of Elizabeth's reign several composers began using verses of the metrical psalms as anthem texts. St. George's Chapel, Windsor Castle, seems

---

[236] William Burton, *A Sermon Preached in the Cathedrall Church in Norwich, the xxi. day of December, 1589* [London: Robert Waldegrave, 1590], sig. D1r. For use in communion, see *RR*, p. 246–7 and *MEPC*, 1:49.

[237] British Library Royal MS 18.B.xix, fol. 8r. For full quotation and discussion see Temperley, "John Playford and the Metrical Psalms," 333–4, repr. *SECM*, 23–4.

[238] George Wither, *The Hymns and Songs of the Church* (London, for G. W., 1623), 63. For further information about the survival of this and other hymns in Anglican worship, see Temperley, "The Anglican Communion Hymn."

[239] Robert Parsons, *A Brief Discours Contayning Certayne Reasons why Catholiques Refuse to Goe to Church* (Doway: John Lyon, 1580), fol. 42v.

[240] Christopher Sibthorp, *A Friendly Advertisement to the Pretended Catholickes of Ireland* (Dublin: Societie of Stationers, 1622), 412.

to have pioneered this. A verse anthem based on Whittingham's Psalm 137 by Richard Farrant, who was master of the choristers at Windsor from 1563 to 1580, is "one of the very earliest of its kind," as Peter le Huray pointed out. His joint successors, Nathaniel Giles and John Mundy (see μ26), both published vocal partsongs that may have originated as anthems.[241] Mundy even composed an anthem based on both text and tune of the *WBP* Psalm 148 (see p. 768). It is perhaps no coincidence that the dean of St. George's from 1572 to 1596, William Day, has been characterized as "an extreme Puritan."[242] Anthems were not exactly puritan favorites, but if they were required in the chapel by the Queen's command, Dean Day may well have preferred them to have texts and tunes drawn from the popular metrical psalms. After 1600 Thomas Weelkes and others quite often selected metrical psalms as anthem texts (see μ29).[243]

Many of the psalms and several of the liturgical hymns were clearly too long to be sung in church, whether by choir or congregation. The psalm books had all the psalms in complete form, whereas most of the Companions had just the first stanzas with the tunes. Some of the longer psalms are divided into "parts" in the psalm book, but all the evidence suggests that these divisions were arbitrary and went largely unheeded.[244] The singing of a psalm almost invariably began with the first stanza; no more than the first four to eight stanzas were sung (four-line stanzas in the case of common, short, and long meters). That is how the texts are presented in the mid-16th-century choirbook already referred to.[245] Again, the directions for the first Accession Service, issued in 1576, appointed "The xxi. psalm in metre before the sermon, until the end of the vii. verse. And the c. psalm after the sermon."[246] These are clear indications of general practice. The first printed collection of texts intended to be sung in complete form appears

---

[241] Peter le Huray, "Farrant, Richard," Grove Music Online.

[242] Sidney L. Ollard, *Fasti Wyndesorienses: The Deans and Canons of Windsor* (Windsor: Otley and Son, 1950), 44. See also Brett Usher, "Day, William," in *ODNB*.

[243] Twenty-one anthem texts derived from *WBP* hymns and psalms are printed in Clifford, *Divine Services and Anthems*, 2nd ed. (1664).

[244] Many of the second and later "parts" begin with "And" or "But," or with other unlikely openings such as "Tush, God forgetteth this, saith he" (Ps. 10, part 2). The *Hymn Tune Index* shows that, of the 108 opening lines of subsidiary "parts" of psalms, only 13 were found with printed tunes up to the year 1820, in a total of 94 printings, compared with many thousand printings of the opening lines of all 156 psalms. The "parts" of Ps. 119, being specified in scripture by letters of the Hebrew alphabet, were treated as separate texts by a few 18th-century tunebook compilers: see p. 743.

[245] British Library Add. MS 15166: see pp. 518–20 above.

[246] *A Forme of Praier . . . to be Used Every Yeare, the 17 of November*, sig. B1v. Ps. 21 has 13 four-line stanzas, which was evidently too long for the purpose; Ps. 100 has only four. If an odd number of four-line stanzas was to be sung to an eight-line tune, such as PSALM 21, we must suppose that the second half of the tune was used to accommodate the last stanza sung.

to be George Wither's *The Hymns and Songs of the Church* (1623), with tunes by Gibbons, meant to be bound up with the *WBP*. The second part (Songs 45–89) provides hymns for church feasts and other particular occasions. With few exceptions these are between twenty-four and forty lines long, showing again that this was the length normally expected.[247] Some situations might, however, demand a lengthier performance. In his diary for 1725, Thomas Hearne records what one can only hope was an apocryphal anecdote of a preacher named Eustace Edward, who,

> being once to preach a funeral Sermon at Beckley, happened to forget his Sermon, and thereupon went home, at some distance, to fetch it, just as the Psalm was begun to be sung, upon w[ch] he desired the Clarke to keep on the singing 'till his Return, so that the whole 119th Psalm was sung out, a Thing never, I believe, heard of before.[248]

Although the argument for Psalm 119 insisted that "it is meet that all the faithful have it alway both in heart and mouth," the most zealous expositor could not have wished for congregations to sing all 704 lines in one sitting.

The Psalm Book Outside of the Church

Although the public, congregational life of the *WBP* was the most important to early modern culture, it came into the world advertising itself as a volume for "private solace and comfort" and an alternative to "ungodly songs and ballads." These uses, distinct from liturgy or even open-air sermons, contributed to the ubiquity of the metrical psalms among English Protestants and doubtless drove a proportion of the book's sales. The psalm book's several places outside of common prayer were, however, far more likely to be associated with particular cultural identities, including class, profession, and religious community.

Like earlier versions of the metrical psalms, the psalms and hymns of the *WBP* provided sophisticated singers and musicians with a form of improving recreation. The majority of the musical Companions to the *WBP* during the Elizabethan period are designed more as chamber music than accompaniments to public worship. They frequently echo Edwardian rhetoric about the psalms as a morally appropriate recreation. The earliest, published by Day in 1563, was "set forth for the encrease of vertue: and aboleshyng of other vayne and triflyng ballades."[249]

---

[247] Its longest hymn (Song 83, for Communion) has 200 lines, but this was for a special reason: see p. 590.

[248] Thomas Hearne, *Remarks and Collections*, 11 vols. (Oxford: Oxford Historical Society, 1885–1921), 8:326.

[249] *Day 1563*, title page. Presumably the recopying of John Sheppard's Edwardian settings of Sternhold's unrevised psalms and other sacred pieces, sometime after 1568 in British Library Add. MS. 15166, had a similar motive (see above, pp. 518–20).

John Cosyn, in the dedication of his 1585 volume, professes that he was urged to print his settings "for the priuate vse and comfort of the godlie, in place of many other Songs neither tending to the praise of God, nor conteining any thing fit for Christian eares."[250] Psalm settings participated in the triumphant climax of English vocal and instrumental music-making that took place in the late Elizabethan and Jacobean periods. Many composers drew on the *WBP* for the texts of madrigals, consort songs, and ayres; details will be found in the notes on individual psalms. Even the openly Catholic William Byrd in his *Psalmes, Sonnets, & Songs of Sadness and Pietie* (1588) offered sophisticated settings of *WBP* verses for those who were "disposed to praye." East had leading secular musicians provide music for the whole metrical psalter, which at least professedly was for the domestic entertainment of the godly: "'Some have pleased themselves with Pastoralls, others with Madrigalls, but such as are endued with Davids hart, desire with David to sing unto God Psalmes & Hymnes, and spirituall songs." The 1591 edition of William Daman's settings was "Published for the recreation of such as delight in Musicke."[251] Richard Alison's 1599 dedication emphasizes the scriptural centrality of the psalms, but the collection is said to be suitable for "the Lute, Orpharyon, Citterne or Base Violl, seuerally or together"—a distinctly domestic and recreational collection of instruments.[252] While Ravenscroft's Companion of 1621 and Playford's harmonized edition of 1677 did explicitly aim at amending church psalmody, they were also extensively used in private. In his advice manual for his grandson, the mid-seventeenth-century gentleman William Higford capped his general praise of the power of music with the recommendation to sing four-part psalms as "a singular ease and refreshment" from "weighty cares and business."[253] Samuel Pepys, too, sang from Ravenscroft for after-dinner entertainment on Sundays.[254]

Advanced musical literacy aside, the metrical psalms were available as well-known songs for any of the other situations in which early modern people sang to lighten tedious tasks or to pass the time. Along with the iconic plowboy whom so many early reformers wished to hear singing scripture were any number of other laborers who also sang or whistled. The godly idea that psalms should be chosen for such a use persisted into the seventeenth century: George Herbert's ideal Caroline country parson would ask his parishioners about whether household

---

[250] *Cosyn 1585*, sig. A2r.

[251] *East 1592*, A2r, v; *Daman 1591 (1)*, title page.

[252] *Allison 1599*, title page. For full discussion of the Elizabethan Companions see App. 6.

[253] William Higford, *Institutions, or Advice to a Grandson* (London: Edward Thorn, 1658), 78–80. Page 46 advises to read the Psalms appointed for the day in the *BCP* and recommends Hooker's *Ecclesiastical Polity*.

[254] G. Gregory Smith (ed.), *The Diary of Samuel Pepys* (London: Macmillan, 1905), 290.

members were engaged in "singing of Psalms at their work."[255] There is scattered evidence that some ordinary people did in fact employ the psalms this way. Marsh cites a mid-seventeenth-century Suffolk widow who sang psalms while milking cows. A Restoration argument for religious toleration pointed out that the English cloth industry depended on religious radicals, a group overrepresented among weavers, spinners, or cloth dressers because these professions allowed them to "think or speak of Religious things, or sing Psalms, and yet pursue their Trades."[256] The fact that it was puritans who were said to seek out the opportunity to sing psalms at work, however, suggests that few conformists were routinely doing so in 1661. In fact, psalm singing as a replacement for ballads outside of contexts or company that might specifically call for godliness does not seem to have ever been as common in England as it was in places like Calvin's Geneva, where that substitution was legally mandated. Specifically, the Ordinances there forbade the singing of any "immoral, dissolute or outrageous songs," which essentially meant secular ballads, on pain of fine and three days' imprisonment.[257] A Catholic pamphlet of 1616 lingered over the malign influence of psalms among the common people in Continental Calvinist communities: "There is nothing that hath drawn multitudes to be of therir [sic] Sects so much, as the singing of their psalmes, in such variable and delightfull tunes: There the souldier singeth in warre, the artizans at their worke, wenches spinning and sewing, apprentices in their shoppes, and wayfaring men in their trauaile."[258] That some ordinary Elizabethans did sing one in the place of the other is at least implied by the godly minister Nicholas Bownd's 1595 lament that ballads were making a comeback relative to psalms, but more than that is difficult to say.[259]

---

[255] Louis Martz, ed., *George Herbert and Henry Vaughan* (Oxford: Oxford University Press, 1986), 210.

[256] Marsh, *Music and Society,* 270; Peter Pett, *A Discourse Concerning Liberty of Conscience* (London: Nathaniel Brook, 1661), 64–5.

[257] *Selections from Ordinances for the Regulation of the Churches Dependent upon the Seigniory of Geneva* (1547), in George L. Burns, ed., *Translations and Reprints from the Original Sources of European History,* 6 vols. (Philadelphia: University of Pennsylvania History Department, 1898–1912), 1, no.3: 10.

[258] Thomas Harrab, *Tessaradelphus: or The Foure Brothers* ([Lancashire? Birchley Hall Press?], 1616), sig. D2v–3r, E3v. Because of an incautious reference by Helen Constance White, *English Devotional Literature (Prose)* (New York: Haskell House, 1966), 61, this passage has been misapplied to *English* psalm singing in several subsequent studies. The author, however, specifically ties this phenomenon to mockery of the versifications by Beza and Marot, along with the "wanton" and "light" tunes that go with them. In his subsequent critique of "Anglicanisme," Harrab mentions the singing of a "Geneua psalm" only as an accompaniment to sermons.

[259] Nicholas Bownd, *The Doctrine of the Subbath Plainely Layde Forth* (London: John Porter and Thomas Man, 1595), 241–2.

If the *WBP* in some circumstances expanded private musical choices by pro-viding familiar, godly songs for recreation, it also expanded the possible forms of prayer and thanksgiving for ordinary people into the realm of music. As the preacher Thomas Jackson noted in 1603, "[W]ho findeth not great vse of singing, both in prosperitie, and aduersitie? In prosperitie by singing of Psalmes, our zeale is quickned; fervencie in prayer, increased; and our earnestnesse to perfourme all laudable seruice vnto God, notably stirred vp . . .. Also in aduersitie by singing of some holy and godly Psalme, our heauie and pensiue hearts are refreshed."[260] Diaries and other first-person accounts in the late sixteenth and seventeenth cen-turies give examples of psalms having been sung as meditation, comfort, peti-tion, or celebration.[261] In the grip of spiritual crisis, John Bunyan wrote that he prayed "whether at home or a broad [sic], in house or field, and should also of-ten with lifting up of heart, sing that of the fifty first Psalm, O Lord, consider my distress."[262] Likewise, in his relief of unmasking a maleficent cat as a witch, Richard Galis in 1579 reported "singing Psalmes to the honor and glory of God which had vouchsafed of his meere mercie and goodnes to strenghthen [sic] me in this my afflictions."[263] Singing was, however, more often a communal activ-ity than an individual one, and it is easier to find references to using the metri-cal psalms as collective expressions even outside of regular worship. Woodfield provides several instances of late sixteenth- and early seventeenth-century sailors turning to the *WBP* in moments of danger or after narrow escapes.[264] Deathbed watches inspired psalm singing among the godly, whether or not the bed's occu-pant was physically capable of taking part.[265] More cheerfully, Londoners greet-ed both the detection of the Babington plot in 1586 and the defeat of the Armada two years later with bonfires, bell-ringing, and the singing of psalms.[266]

In the Geneva translation of Acts 16:25, Paul and Silas passed the time under confinement at Philippi by singing "a psalm," and psalm singing in early mod-ern England was particularly associated with private consolation during imprison-ment and the public rituals of execution. Reading, reciting, or paraphrasing

---

[260] Thomas Jackson, *Dauids Pastorall Poeme: or Sheepeheards Song* (London: Edmund Weaver, 1603), fol. 3r.

[261] One demonstrating both is *The Diary of Roger Lowe of Ashton-in-Makerfield, Lancashire*, ed. William L. Sachse (New Haven: Yale University Press, 1938), 15, 28–9, 36, 44; quoted in Marsh, *Music and Society*, 436.

[262] John Bunyan, *Grace Abounding to the Chief of Sinners* (London: George Larkin, 1666), 16.

[263] Richard Galis, *A Brief Treatise Containing the Most Strange and Horrible Cruelty of Elizabeth Stile* (London: J. Allde, 1579), sig. A4r-v.

[264] Ian Woodfield, *English Musicians in the Age of Exploration* (Stuyvesant, N.Y.: Pendragon Press, 1995), 46.

[265] See Quitslund, "Fun and Profit," 244.

[266] John Strype, *Annals of the Reformation and Establishment of Religion*, 4 vols., 7 pts. (Oxford: Clarendon Press, 1822), 1/1:607; 3/2:27–8.

psalms in either situation was commonplace both before and during the early Reformation, but the spread of the singing psalms created a new opportunity for audible display from prisoners and for audience participation in the condemned criminal's last act. Foxe records both kinds of performance among Marian Protestants in England, demonstrations of undaunted spiritual mirth in the face of persecution.[267] By the middle of Elizabeth's reign, English prisoners conventionally sang psalms for comfort during their sufferings. Thus Edmund Gayton, in his 1655 parody of a prisoner's memoir, staged a mock contest between the psalms and sack, "the two great cordialls and consolatories of human necessities."[268] Psalm singing was also a standard sign of repentance in criminals, distinguishing numerous accounts of new-found piety (as well as the ostentatious hypocrisy of the larcenous Londoners in *Eastward Hoe*).[269] Singing on the scaffold could show either confidence or repentance, as well. It functioned differently from prison singing, however, by including the witnesses to the execution. A psalm specified by the condemned man served both as an individual, occasional prayer and an assertion of community in the face of imminent death. The practice was routine enough to be used by ordinary felons, pirates, and royalist martyrs, and lasted well into the eighteenth century.[270]

The most common use for the singing psalms outside of congregational worship, however, was as an element of domestic worship. Devotional manuals from the late sixteenth century on frequently prescribe the singing of psalms as part of the routine for well-ordered households. The puritan minister Richard Rogers listed the daily "exercises of Religion" as "prayer, reading, chatechising [sic] and conference, with singing of Psalmes, &c." and urged "that these or such of them as are common to the whole family, be vsed at the most conuenient times when the family may come together." While Rogers preferred that the family perform all of these devotions "together twise in the day at least," psalm singing

---

[267] John Foxe, *The First Volume of the Ecclesiastical History Contaynyng the Actes and Monuments of Thynges Passed in Euery Kynges Tyme in this Realme* (London: John Daye, 1570), 2131 [corr. from 2301], 1867, 2113 [corr. from 2301], 2123, 2263.

[268] Edmund Gayton, *Wil: Bagnal's Ghost. Or the Merry Devill of Gadmunton* (London: W. Wilson for Thomas Johnson, 1655), 46–8. Gayton notes parenthetically that Paul and Silas's choice was "rare" in that they "knew not Hopkins and Sternhold."

[269] E.g., *Of the Endes and Deathes of Two Prisoners, Lately Pressed to Death in Newgate* (London: John Awdely, 1569); *The Most Cruell and Bloody Murther Committed by an Inkeepers Wife* (London: William Finebrand, John Wright, 1606), sig. C2r–v. See also George Chapman, *Eastward Hoe: As it was Playd in the Black-friers* (London: William Aspley, 1605).

[270] See, for example, John Burroughs, *A Narrative of the Conversion of Thomas Mackernesse* (London: John Dunton, 1694), 21; *The Lives, Apprehensions, Arraignments, and Executions, of the 19. Late Pyrates* (London: [E. Alldes] for John Busby the Elder, [1609]), sig. B8v–C1r, H1v; and *Anglia Ruina: or, England's Ruine* ([London, n.p.], 1647 [i.e.,1648]), 198, 200.

in particular belonged most often to the end of the day.[271] Lewis Bayly's astonishingly durable and popular *Practise of Pietie* gave its most extensive treatment of psalm singing in the section on evening prayers, including directions on how to sing reverently and which psalms to choose.[272] Injunctions to sing psalms domestically are supported by some accounts of actual singing, but even more frequently by references to the ungodliness of those households, whether Catholic or merely worldly, which failed to do so.[273] These contrasts took their meaning from the assumption that the readers' domestic prayers did in fact include the full complement of godly exercises.

Finally, other communities that functioned as surrogate households incorporated diurnal devotional practices that included the singing of psalms. For example, from the late sixteenth century psalm singing along with prayers accompanied the changing of the watch on English ships—the equivalent of morning and evening devotions for the sailors coming onto and leaving the deck, respectively.[274] Daily (or nightly) psalms were augmented, for households that sang them, by additional singing on the Sabbath. By complementing the public occasions of common prayers and sermons with catechizing, reviewing the sermon, and singing the psalms, the family recreated in itself a model of the larger Church and a godly social order.[275]

---

[271] Richard Rogers, *Seven Treatises Containing Such Direction as is Gathered out of the Holie Scriptures . . . : and may be Called the Practise of Christianitie* (London: Felix Kyngston, 1603), 335. See also Phillip Stubbes, *A Perfect Pathway to Felicitie* (London: Humfrey Lownes, 1610), sig. D7r–D8r, and Quitslund, "Fun and Profit," 246–7.

[272] Lewis Bayly, *The Practise of Pietie* (London: John Hodgets, 1613), 465–8. The first edition is lost, but the second was published in 1612, followed by 122 more in English recorded before the end of the eighteenth century. Bayly did not recommend any of the hymns in the *WBP*.

[273] For women leading psalm singing in their own houses, see Donne's description of Lady Magdalene Herbert Danvers, p. 614, below, and the posthumous account of Lettice Cary, Viscountess Falkland including evening psalm singing in the household's evening devotions in John Duncon, *The Returns of Spiritual Comfort and Grief in a Devout Soul* (London: for R. Royston, 1649), 167. For praise of psalm-singing households and castigation of those that engage in other forms of Sabbath recreations, see, for example, Robert Openshaw, *Short Questions and Answeares, Conteyning the Summe of Christian Religion* (London: Thomas Dawson, 1579), sigs A2r–v, A4r; Stephen Egerton, *The Boring of the Eare Contayning a Plaine and Profitable Discourse by Way of Dialogue* (London: William Stansby, 1623), 64–5; and Robert Bolton, *Two Sermons Preached at Northampton at Two Severall Assises There* (London: George Miller, 1635), 66. While all three of the preachers promoting household psalm singing were in the puritan wing of the Church, Lady Danvers was fully conformist and Lady Falkland a Laudian.

[274] See Woodfield, *English Musicians*, 41–5.

[275] See Quitslund, "Fun and Profit," 242–52.

While the demand for the musical Companions must have come in part from a desire for appropriate Sabbath musical recreation, few households are likely to have used instrumental settings or even vocal harmony in regular evening devotions. Precisely because these were imagined as a mirror and extension of public congregational worship, they called for similar musical decorum as well as the same kind of attitude in the singer. Sixteenth-century discussions of psalm singing as prayer do not generally differentiate between singing inside and outside of church,[276] but how to approach it as part of domestic exercises becomes explicit in Jacobean devotional manuals. Bayly, in the *Practise of Pietie*, delivers typical instruction:

> [B]e sure that the matter makes more melodie in your hearts, then the Musicke in your eares: for the singing with a grace in our hearts, is that which the Lord is delighted withall, according to that olde verse:
> *Non vox, sed votum, non musica chordula, sed cor:*
> *Non clamans, sed amans, psallit in aure Dei.*
> T'is not the voyce, but vow:
> Sound hart, not sounding string:
> True zeale, not outward show,
> That in Gods eare doth ring.[277]

As private psalm singing became increasingly associated with puritanism in the seventeenth century, it drew even further away from its recreational origins.[278]

Later History of the Psalm Book

Post-Elizabethan Development and Publication

On 29 October 1603, James I granted to the Stationers' Company the right "To imprynte or cause to be imprinted all manner of booke and bookes of Prymers Psalters and Psalmes in meter or prose with musycall notes or withoute notes both in greate volumes and small in the Englishe tonge which nowe be or anye tyme hereafter shalbe sett forthe and permitted."[279] This patent created the Company's lucrative English Stock and makes it impossible, from this distance, to

---

[276] See, for example, Jean Calvin, *The Institution of Christian Religion*, trans. Thomas Norton (London: Reynold Wolfe and Richard Harrison, 1561), fol. 229r; George Gascoigne, *The Droomme of Doomes Day* (London: [T. East for] Gabriel Cawood, 1576), sig. R8v–S2r.

[277] Lewis Bayly, *The Practice of Pietie*, 455–6.

[278] Quitslund, "Fun and Profit," 252–8.

[279] Arber, *Registers*, 3:42.

identify editorial control over the *WBP*. Thenceforth its production was parceled out among various printers needing work, the profits went to the Company's hierarchy of stockholders, and all subsequent legal London editions declared themselves to be printed "for the Company of Stationers."[280] Editions were regularly issued by the printers to the University of Cambridge from 1628 on, at first in competition with the Stationers but beginning in 1631 as essentially contract labor for the London Company.[281] Until after the Restoration the press at the University of Oxford was paid off, according to various arrangements, not to encroach on the English Stock; it began printing *WBP*s only in 1675.[282]

The physical volumes that embodied the *WBP* changed over the course of the seventeenth century, shifts that involved not only the bibliographic formats but also what works the book found itself bound with. Reflecting a widespread change in English printing practices, the most popular formats of the *WBP* got slightly larger, with duodecimos and 24°s completely replacing 16°s and 32°s before 1650.[283] In the later seventeenth and eighteenth centuries, the smallest books were often fatter as well as taller, because many were printed for the purpose

---

[280] It is not clear what Richard Day had to say about this. In March 1616, James I *reissued* the patent for metrical psalms to the Stationers, this time acknowledging that Elizabeth had, in 1591, granted the reversion of the Day patent to Verney Alley and his heirs for thirty years after Richard's death, "Which said letters patentes the Administrators and Assignes of the said VERNEY have assigned and sett over unto certaine persons in trust to the use of the master and keepers or wardens and Comynaltie of the Arte of misterie of Stacioners of the Cittie of London and theire Successors." (Arber, *Registers,* 3:679.) This formalized an agreement with Alley's executors in 1614, by which they received £600 for Alley's claims (Blagden, *Stationers' Company,* 101).

[281] The first surviving Cambridge edition is *1590,* a 32°; the University printer, John Legate, must have made a concerted push into the psalm book market that year, as Richard Day and his assignees lodged a complaint in 1591 about another edition that was part of a Legate-printed quarto bible (see Arber, *Registers,* 2:819). The *ESTC* next catalogues two 1623 Cambridge editions, which, after the Privy Council intervened, the Stationers' Company permitted to be sold. Further legal and personal wrangling ensued, with the eventual upshot that the University, for a price, agreed to print the metrical psalms only in quantities ordered and with paper supplied by the Stationers. See Blagden, *Stationers' Company,* 102–4; David McKitterick, *A History of Cambridge University Press,* vol. 1, *Printing and the Book Trade in Cambridge, 1534–1698* (Cambridge: Cambridge University Press, 1992), 53–4, 171–2.

[282] McKitterick, 216, 323, 326; Peter Sutcliffe, *The Oxford University Press: An Informal History* (Oxford: Clarendon Press, 1978), xx–xxii.

[283] The exceptions are a handful of 16° editions in shorthand from the last decades of the seventeenth century. Green notes the difference in *WBP* formats (Green, *Print and Protestantism,* 512–15). Only four 32° books of any kind printed in England survive from the last four decades of the seventeenth century, according to the *ESTC.*

of being bound with bibles or *BCP*s.[284] Duodecimo combined editions in particular seem to have taken the enormous market share that had, in the Elizabethan and early Stuart periods, gone to two-column quartos. While surviving sixteenth-century quartos tend to package together a bible (either the Bishops' or the Geneva) and/or prose psalter with the *WBP* and *BCP*, the number of titles in these volumes expanded in the 1590s. Robert Herrey's concordance swelled most Geneva quartos from 1595 on; a concordance to the KJV by George Downame is included in some copies from 1630. Beginning in 1611, John Speed (and later his son) held a patent allowing them to insert a copy of Speed's *Genealogies of the Scriptures* into every copy of the new bible translation, and it was added to Jacobean editions of the Geneva Bible as well. The Stationers seem to have borne this imposition philosophically, as a relatively small addition to the whole Bible. They loudly protested, however, the much more onerous requirement to bind George Wither's 1623 *Hymns and Songs of the Church* with every copy of the *WBP* as specified in Wither's royal patent for the work. Despite several attempts at enforcement by the Privy Council, the Stationers' united refusal to comply with the terms of the patent effectively prevented Wither's hymns from joining those of the *WBP* in England's congregational music.[285]

The contents of the *WBP* itself changed relatively little in the early Stuart period. Indeed, a half-dozen printing series begun during Richard Day's patent, representing folios, one- and two-column quartos, 24°s, and 32°s continued well into the reign of James I or even that of Charles I, with the text and tune selections remaining the same as in their predecessors. Among these continuing series are both some of the longest versions of the *WBP* (with the Athanasian preface, psalms arguments, and a generous selection of prayers) and some that eliminated tunes, arguments, prayers, and a third of the hymns. Nor did the printing series initiated from 1604 to 1640 introduce much textual novelty. The list of uses from Athanasius became much less common, and an increasing proportion of small-format editions omitted the arguments to the psalms. Though not all the combinations of prose prayers that appeared were anticipated by Elizabethan editions, the selections favored the same ones that had been included most frequently in late sixteenth-century copies. There was, however, a significant change in presentation: many of the quartos and folios during these years moved all of the hymns

---

[284] John Barnard calculates that 66% of the bibles printed in the mid-1660s for which *WBP*s were required were in the two smallest formats (Barnard, "The Stationers' Stock 1663/4 to 1705/6: Psalms, Psalters, Primers and ABCs," *The Library*, ser. 6, 21.4 (1999): 371–2). It is, however, likely that some of the consignments to the King's Printers were for binding with the *BCP* instead.

[285] See Allan Pritchard, "George Wither's Quarrel with the Stationers: an Anonymous Reply to *The Schollers Purgatory*," *Studies in Bibliography* 16 (1963): 28–43. The *ESTC* catalogs nine editions of Wither's *Hymns and Songes of the Church* from 1623 and none thereafter.

after the metrical psalter and began to shift their normal post-1569 order. There was also a belated recognition of the decline in popularity of some of the Elizabethan tunes: after the publication of Ravenscroft's Companion in 1621, many editions substituted short tunes he had introduced for some of the psalms.[286]

While some editions with contents very close to standard Elizabethan variations continued to appear from presses in London and Cambridge for the rest of the century, these became less common with each passing decade. The emergent Restoration and early eighteenth-century model of the *WBP* began with the metrical psalter, containing the 156 psalm versions usually included since 1577, but dispensing with both arguments and tunes. In most editions, the majority of the other hymns then immediately followed the psalms. By the middle of the eighteenth century, the two hymns for morning and evening prayer (paraphrased from Psalms 127 and 134) and the Venite (a second paraphrase of Psalm 95) were no longer commonly printed in the book at all. Duplication was further eliminated by removing Whittingham's Ten Commandments and Cox's Lord's Prayer; the other paraphrases of these texts were also gone by the turn of the nineteenth century. Also dropping out by 1800 were the Benedicite, "Quicunque Vult," "Da pacem, Domine," and "Preserve us, Lord." At the same time, the order of the hymns was rationalized by putting all the scriptural and ecclesiastical canticles before the original hymns. In a handful of editions, however, *new* alternative versifications found their way into the mix.[287] Most editions also capped off the hymns with the Gloria Patri in an assortment of meters to match many or most of the psalms and canticles. Both psalms and hymns underwent textual revision between 1690 and 1720, in some instances only to remove the most troubling archaisms but in other cases creating substantially different texts.[288] Finally, the average number of prayers included after the hymns decreased by the early eighteenth century to between three and five in most editions that included any. By 1750, one finds no private prayers in about half of the editions published.

Meanwhile, the custom of printing tunes in the smaller psalm books for the use of regular churchgoers had ended in 1648.[289] After the Restoration, only folio editions contained the tunes, presumably for the use of parish clerks. Two such editions were printed in 1661. One (Wing B2475) was a consciously conservative

---

[286] For instance, an octavo edition with solfa type printed in 1625 (*STC* 2590) has new short tunes for Pss. 72, 88, 134, and 147, all to the same texts to which they were set by Ravenscroft, and also Ravenscroft's new tune to Ps. 104. None of these tunes, however, have solfa notation, as many of the old ones do.

[287] For instance, *ESTC* T180242, a 1751 folio, which has a second DCM Apostle's Creed and versions of The Complaint of a Sinner and The Lamentation adapted into different meters.

[288] See Notes on individual texts.

[289] Editions of 1649 and 1653 are erroneously included in the *Hymn Tune Index*. (N. T.)

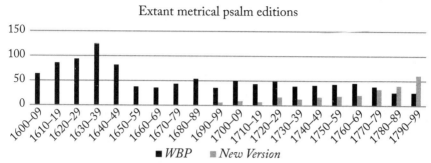

Fig. 6: Catalogued editions of the *WBP* and Tate & Brady

effort, based on the last pre-war black-letter folio (*STC 2693*). In the other, "The tunes of the psalmes . . . is [sic] carefully revised and corrected by J. P.," i.e. John Playford, the leading music printer of the day, who was promoted to the livery of the Stationers Company in that very year. It represents the second and last attempt at a thorough musical revision, newly setting psalms to tunes often deliberately chosen to suit their mood.[290] At least five reprints of this edition followed, the last in 1687. The following year saw an experimental edition edited by one Thomas Mathew (Wing B2565), an attempt to use the Dutch style of printing psalms, where every verse has musical notes provided.[291] After that, no edition of the *WBP* had tunes.

There are two important consequences of these changes. First, the diversity that characterized the *WBP* as a commercial product in the Elizabethan period had been radically diminished by the eighteenth century. Two centuries after John Day first assembled the *WBP*, it had become in essence what the title page promised: the whole of the Book of Psalms in meter, and very little more. Certainly the musical notes were no longer "joined withal." While most editions did provide many of the other hymns that Day had arranged around the metrical psalter, eighteenth-century printers signaled that these were supplementary by tucking them in at the end. Rather than comprising a brief but complete handbook of daily private devotion, what prayers lingered at the back of the book looked like a slightly miscellaneous afterthought. They did, however (along with the still unchanged title page contrasting the psalms with "ungodly songs and ballads") provide a vestigial sense of the *WBP* as a book for private use as well as congregational hymnody. Second, the *WBP* had shed the complex rhetorical

---

[290] For details of this edition (Wing B2475A) see Temperley, "John Playford and the Metrical Psalms," 346–53, repr. *SECM*, 36–43.

[291] This was no doubt influenced by the accession of William of Orange to the British throne. The Stationers Hall entry for the book states that it was "patronized by the Hon. Robert Boyle, Esq.," the famous scientist and enlightened defender of Christianity, and "approved by the Company of Parish Clerks, London."

organization and apparatus that tied it both to the practices of the *BCP* and to
the Calvinist commitments of the Anglo-Genevan community that contributed
so many of its early texts. Without the carefully divided hymns, the arguments
modeled on those of the Geneva Bible, or the private prayer book and Confes-
sion of the Genevan exiles, all that was left of the Elizabethan tensions that the
WBP originally attempted to balance were (most of) the words of the metrical
psalms themselves.

Tracking the size of the market for the *WBP* in the seventeenth and eigh-
teenth centuries is extraordinarily difficult. Thanks to the *ESTC*, the easiest part
is enumerating the surviving editions.[292] That census suggests that the produc-
tion of *WBP*s steadily increased for the first four decades of the seventeenth cen-
tury, from sixty-four editions from 1600–1609 to 125 from 1630–1639.[293] This was
probably the high point. The number of catalogued editions drops noticeably for
the period from 1640–49 (82), and then plunges in the next decade to 38, which
is still surprisingly high in view of the discontinuation of public Anglican wor-
ship. For the next century, the number of editions surviving from each decade is
close to flat, at a level slightly above the low of the 1650s. From the Restoration to
1700, the average number of editions per decade surviving is only 42.25, includ-
ing the not insubstantial number printed with bibles and sometimes *BCP*s.[294] The
numbers are slightly higher for the early eighteenth century, with between 48
and 50 editions each decade until 1730, after which it gradually declined to about
half as many in the last two decades of the century—the period in which Tate
and Brady's *New Version of the Psalms of David* (1696) finally began to displace

---

[292] "Easiest" is still relative. Due to differences in the ways that Wing and the *STC*
record variant imprints, as well as the frequency of mixed copies in the seventeenth cen-
tury and the possibility that the book was more or less continuously printed at times, all
figures are probably more precise than accurate. On this problem, see Green, *Print and
Protestantism*, 508–9, 673–77; Krummel, *English Music Printing*, 36–42. Numbers after
1640 are even sketchier than those up to that point due to inconsistencies in Wing's and
thus *ESTC* cataloging, although we have made every effort to flush out less completely
described editions and to eliminate duplicates.

[293] These numbers, taken from the *ESTC* in 2013, include Middleburg psalms but
not East's Companions with four-part harmonization. The figures are slightly larger than
Ian Green's (*Print and Protestantism*, 509); he appears to be excluding the Middleburg-
style editions. They are roughly confirmed by the number of editions held by the British
Library (see *MEPC*, 1:122).

[294] This number would be even lower were it not for the puzzling profusion of edi-
tions in 1682 (at least 17 of them, the largest mass of surviving editions for *any* single year).
Our count for every decade after 1640 is higher than Green's (*Print and Protestantism*,
520), probably because Wing does not give editions of the *WBP* printed with bibles or
*BCP*s their own number or cross-list them with the other books containing psalms only.

what had long been known as the Old Version.[295] John Barnard attributes the rise in production in the 1690s and 1700s to the Stationers' success in undercutting the market for pirated Dutch editions and to greater sales in Ireland and the colonies;[296] subsequently, as we shall see below, increased competition from yet other metrical psalms and hymns eroded demand. The last known edition was printed at Oxford in 1861.[297]

All of these numbers, however, require qualification, and unfortunately those qualifications change over time. Different kinds of information are available from which to draw conclusions about printing the *WBP* before and after the Restoration. Before, the main metric is the number and kind of surviving editions. After, there are notes on how many copies the Treasurer of the Stationers' Company ordered for each year. One thing those records tell us is that surviving numbers of editions are not an accurate indication of the number of copies in circulation. First, the surviving editions do not adequately represent the ones actually printed, but they are probably a worse guide earlier on. We have already seen evidence of small format editions disappearing disproportionately in the mid-Elizabethan period, and the same is true to some extent later as well. In the later seventeenth century, however, duodecimo *WBP*s were frequently bound with bibles or New Testaments, which increased their value and thus likelihood of being handed down to posterity.[298] As a result, a higher proportion of the editions produced during that period are probably exemplified in the *ESTC*. Second, impression sizes changed dramatically over time, and for much of the period in question it is impossible to know how many copies an edition represents. In 1587, the Stationers Company forbade impressions over 1,500 copies or standing type (in order to maintain employment for compositors).[299] Prior to that, John Day's edition sizes may well have been larger, and pirated editions certainly were.[300] Enforcement of impression size after 1604 with regard to the English Stock also

---

[295] Nahum Tate and Nicholas Brady, *A New Version of the Psalms of David, Fitted to the Tunes Used in Churches* (London: M. Clark for the Company of Stationers, 1696). William III in council officially "allowed" the *New Version* for public use in churches, giving it the same (perceived) legal status as the *WBP*. In fact, neither one had any valid legal priority for liturgical use. See *MEPC*, 1:121.

[296] Barnard, "Stationers' Stock," 374–5.

[297] Five editions published by Oxford University Press between 1829 and 1857 are held in the British Library. Birmingham University Library holds one "printed at the Clarendon Press, by Dawson, Bensley, and Cooke, printers to the University and sold at the Oxford Bible Warehouse, Paternoster Row, London, 1861."

[298] Although late seventeenth-century *WBP*s in small formats were more likely to disappear than folios and quartos, John Barnard shows that they still fared better than small ABCs, psalters, and primers. He, too, attributes their persistence to being bound with other works. Barnard, "Stationers' Stock," 148–9.

[299] Arber, *Registers*, II:43.

[300] Arber, *Registers*, II:791.

seems dubious, given the inherent conflict of interest that the limits presented for stockholders.[301] In 1635, the Company reiterated the ceiling on number of copies per impression for most books, but the occasion for doing so was a petition from journeymen about, among other things, printing houses producing too many outsized impressions.[302] By the close of the seventeenth century, impressions of the *WBP* in some formats were permitted to balloon to 18,000 copies. Sampling from the records of the Treasurer of the English Stock suggests a rough estimate of about 400,000 copies printed by the London Stationers in the last quarter of the seventeenth century, and in 1684 alone the Stationers collected fees from Oxford and the King's Printer allowing an additional 101,000 copies.[303] If Jacobean printers *did* observe the legal impression size, that half million books is more than would be represented by the surviving editions from the first quarter of the seventeenth century. The likelihood, however, is that they did not, and in any case the comparison does not take lost editions into account.

The sum of the problem is this: there is no precise way to figure out production trends in the *WBP* before 1660. Any figures calculated from surviving editions based on a constant, "official" impression size will be too low, with the worst undercounting in the mid-Elizabethan period and the early decades of the seventeenth century (due to the loss of small-format editions and either unregulated or illegal impression sizes). That would still imply that the highest production was shortly before the beginning of the Civil Wars—which is, happily, what a reading of the cultural place of the *WBP* would suggest, as well.

Psalm Singing in Church after 1603

The seventeenth century was a period in which it was taken for granted that the people would sing at least one metrical psalm from the *WBP* during any public service or sermon meeting. Even civil war, interregnum, and restoration did little to disturb that tradition. The closing down of cathedrals, disbanding of choirs, and destruction of organs made little difference, because few parish churches

---

[301] McKitterick collects a number of records from the 1610s to 1630s of books printed, apparently uncontroversially, in impressions of 3,000 copies or more (McKitterick, 272, 452, notes 40–1).

[302] John Bruce, ed., *Calendar of State Papers, Domestic Series, of the Reign of Charles I*, 23 vols. (London: Longman *et al.*, 1858–67), 8. 483–4; cf. Jackson, *Records of the Stationers' Company*, 266, 274.

[303] The figure for London is given by Ian Green (*Print and Protestantism*, 521) and represents an extrapolation from John Barnard's three-year samples in each decade from the 1660s to the 1700s. For those and for the payments to the Treasurer, see Barnard, "Stationers' Stock," 370. Permission paid for in 1684 might have covered multiple years.

possessed either organs or choirs in the Stuart times, and Laud's attempts to re-institute them in the 1630s were largely unsuccessful.[304]

The *WBP*, as we have seen, reached the height of its popularity in the reign of Charles I. Even during the Commonwealth it continued in wide use, since it was well loved by the people, and the kind of singing it represented did not offend either Presbyterian or Independent principles. On the other hand, the various separatist movements, once they had left the established Church, saw no reason to go on using it. After the Restoration, a handful of High Church controversialists made a point of linking the singing of metrical psalms with the political disruption of rebellion.[305] Literary culture had permanently adopted the names "Sternhold" and "Hopkins" as bywords for poetic ineptitude.[306] By and large, however, the *WBP* had begun to assume the character of a national trea-sure linked with church and state.

In 1671 Playford broke new ground with *Psalmes & Hymns in Solemn Mu-sick*, a book that contained enough verses of the approved psalms for singing in church (extending Wither's policy to the psalms as well as the hymns), but add-ing some alternate versions and hymns from other sources—the latter printed in roman type to distinguish them from the traditional versions in black letter. Playford added: "it were to be wished, that one of these Translations, (if Author-ity thought fit,) might be allowed and used in our Churches."[307] From the longer texts he made his own selection of up to eight four-line stanzas, always begin-ning with the first stanza and often adding a doxology at the end. Each text was set to a well-known tune in the tenor register, harmonized for four male voices. Though the book itself had little success, its editorial principle would make it a forerunner of thousands of hymnbooks in the sense we understand the term to-day. Playford used his full influence with both the Stationers and the Company of Parish Clerks to encourage the improvement of psalmody.

He had a more ambitious agenda with respect to the *WBP*, however. In 1677 he published *The Whole Book of Psalms with the Usual Hymns and Spritual Songs; with All the Ancient and Proper Tunes Sung in Churches, with Some of Later Use:*

---

[304] For details see *MEPC*, 1:51–2.

[305] See Peter Heylin, *Aerius redivivus* (London: for John Crosley, 1670), 248–9; Richard Watson, *The Right Reverend Doctor John Cosin, late Lord Bishop of Durham his Opinion* (London: F. Leach for Nicholas Woolfe, 1684), 48.

[306] For examples, see Abraham Cowley, "A Satire Against Separatists," *The Foure Ages of England* (London: n.p., 1648), 63; Thomas Duffet, "Prologue to *Psyche Debauch'd*," *New Poems, Songs, Prologues and Epilogues* (London: for Nicholas Woolfe, 1676), 94; Thomas Brown, *Amusements Serious and Comical* (London: for John Nutt, 1700), 52.

[307] John Playford, *Psalmes & Hymns in Solemn Musick of Four Parts on the Common Tunes to the Psalms in Metre Used in Parish-Churches* (London: W. Godbid, 1671), preface. For more details see Temperley, "John Playford and the Metrical Psalms," 355–60, repr. *SECM*, 45–50.

Composed in Three Parts, Cantus, Medius, and Bassus. It was essentially a revised edition of the *WBP*, printed for the Company of Stationers, with a tune for each psalm and hymn arranged for three voice parts. In a long preface he praised the "holy and godly men" who brought "the present use and manner of singing Psalms into the Publick Service of our Church." Nevertheless, "time and long use hath much abated the wonted reverence and estimation it had had for about an hundred years," he claimed, the chief reasons being faults in the translation, dislike of some of the tunes, and the custom of lining out. He therefore had undertaken to revise the translation, and in four cases (Psalms 111, 121, 124, and 130) substituted common-meter paraphrases for the difficult originals. He admitted that continental Reformed churches sang better, which he put down to the fact that they taught their children the psalms, and "had their psalm books printed most exactly with the Musical Tunes to each psalm, so that their Congregations are generally perfect in the Tunes." By this time the normal tempo for singing the psalms had reached the unimaginably slow level of twenty notes to the minute.[308] A byproduct of this process was the gradual loss of any distinction between the longer and shorter notes of a tune; this had long before caused the rhythmic standardization of the printed tunes, and was even more apparent now.[309] Playford also attacked "the late intruding Scotch manner" of lining out, and he went on to suggest that the clergy could well take more interest in the music of the church, a criticism that would be echoed by many later writers.[310] His book went into no less than twenty editions, the last in 1757.

Playford's book was an influential part of a growing movement to reform the psalmody of the established church, carried out at first through the high-church religious societies that were being formed in many parishes. This has been

---

[308] Among other evidence is that of Thomas Mathew, who defined the minim for psalm tunes as "two pulses at the wrist of a person in good health and temper," which works out at about 18 notes to the minute, four times slower than the original tempo (see Mathew, *Whole Booke*, preface, quoted *MEPC*, 1:93). Christopher Marsh (*Music and Society*, 430–1) believes that psalm singing is likely to have been slow from the beginning. But the evidence of music notation shows beyond doubt that by the early 1600s psalm tunes had slowed down to about half their original tempo, and continued to slow in later generations. See Temperley, "Old Way of Singing," 518–22.

[309] "The clerks are seldom so exact as to keep these distinct times [i.e. note-lengths] in the churches: they do generally observe but one time, . . . and that is (usually) about a minim and a half, or three pulses." Mathew, *Whole Booke*, preface. This was still usual in the 18th century, when "the common Psalm Tunes in the parochial Service . . . are every where sung without the least Regard to *Time* or *Measure*, by drawling out every Note to an unlimited Length": Charles Avison, *An Essay on Musical Expression*, 2nd edn. (London, 1753), 89–91.

[310] For further discussion see Temperley, "John Playford," 363–72, repr. *SECM*, 53–62.

described in detail elsewhere.[311] The results were of two kinds, which can broadly be termed urban and rural.

In the more affluent urban parishes, where an organ could be acquired and an organist employed, the singing was generally dominated by the children of the local charity school, who clustered round the organ, often in the west[312] gallery. They would be taught the standard tunes and lead the congregation, with harmonies provided by the organ, assisted in some cases by the young men who formed the local Religious Society.[313] An early example is the first published tunebook designed for a particular parish (or two parishes, in this case).[314] Of its twenty-nine texts, the first twenty-two are a selection of psalms from the *WBP*, in numerical order, headed "Lords Day the first. Morn[ing]", and so on, allotting two psalms to each Sunday morning and evening for a six-week cycle. The texts are heavily revised but still recognizable, and in all cases but one the passage selected is the first few stanzas, varying from eight to thirty-two lines: in the case of the shortest ones a four-line doxology is added. The Nunc dimittis (in a version by John Patrick) and The Lamentation of a Sinner function as the last two metrical texts for the sixth Sunday. The remaining texts are Patrick's paraphrase of the Te Deum (1679), the two authorized translations of the Veni, Creator (the one in the *WBP* and Bishop John Cosin's from the 1662 *BCP*), and two "Morning Hymns," one by John Austin (1668) which had been used by Playford in his 1677 psalm book, the other unidentified. Tables at the back prescribe special selections for the main feasts of the church, national days, and "occasional thanksgiving-days." [315]

At these two churches, then, there was a preponderance of *WBP* texts, but no monopoly, nor one for psalms as opposed to hymns. A relatively small number of texts and tunes sufficed for morning and evening prayer, each one being sung, on average, at least eight times a year; and moderate length was clearly an essential factor. The tunes were arranged for two trebles and bass, with the top voice carrying the tune. They are mostly the best-known of the common tunes, some used several times; only six of the old proper tunes remain: PSALMS 1, 51, 100 (used for three texts), 113, 119, and 148. The first stanza of each text

---

[311] *MEPC*, 1:97–108, 141–51.

[312] Because, by ancient custom, churches normally faced east (towards Jerusalem), the west gallery was at the back of the building, and in the 18th century it often contained the organ, the choir, and the less important part of the congregation.

[313] See *MEPC*, 1:108–38.

[314] *The Psalms and Hymns, Usually Sung in the Churches and Tabernacles of St. Martins in the Fields and St. James's Westminster* (London: R. Everingham for Ric. Chiswell, 1688), *HTI* #PHMF. "Tabernacles" in this case were Anglican chapels-of-ease subordinate to a parish church.

[315] Similar courses of psalms and tunes are found in many later books. For one used in Gosport, Hampshire, in about 1745, see *MEPC*, 1:125.

is underlaid for all three voices; the rest of the selected text follows. The score could be used by schoolchildren and male adult singers, and by an organist. In fact both churches mentioned on the title page had charity schools in 1688, in which the boys were taught to sing psalms, and a gallery was provided for them in the church. St. Martin's had an organ built in 1667; St. James's acquired one in 1691.[316] These were among the richest, most fashionable parishes in London, with newly built churches, and they were establishing a new model for urban psalmody, one in which the congregation, instead of praising God directly, would pay to have his praise sung by poor children and played on an organ.[317] So one cardinal principle of the Reformation had bitten the dust.

This would be the normal urban practice for much of the eighteenth century. Few churches could afford to commission their own private hymnal,[318] but it was a relatively easy matter for the organist to teach a limited number of standard psalms and tunes to the children. Lining out was no longer necessary, though it continued in some churches from sheer conservatism. The people, if they wished, could gently sing or silently follow the psalms in their books, which were more and more often bound up with prayer books. Gradually, in the course of the century, the Old Version gave way in some churches to the New.[319]

The situation was different in most village churches, where any reforms had to be achieved without an organ or charity school and without the services of a professional choir director. In the course of the eighteenth century a system of voluntary parish choirs developed in rural areas, taught by unaccredited singing teachers who competed in selling their own tunebooks. They sang increasingly elaborate tunes (some "fuging") as well as anthems, and generally discouraged the congregations from joining in.[320]

Both urban and rural reforms eventually succeeded in getting rid of the "old way of singing." As for the musical repertoire, the urban school of psalmody, which relied chiefly on rote singing led by children, offered little motivation to introduce new material, but it was in the interests of country singing teachers to innovate and hence keep up the demand for their printed collections. For this reason both the texts and the tunes of the Old Version survived longest in town churches. In 1801 it was still in use at the Chapel Royal, the Temple Church,

---

[316] A revised edition, for St. James's only (*Select Psalms and Hymns*) appeared in 1697, with the contents further reduced to 15 psalms and the Te Deum, and the vocal settings to two parts, treble and bass. This went into at least 13 editions, the last published about 1750.

[317] For further details see *MEPC*, 1:115–16.

[318] For a list of those with music (up to 1820) see *HTI*, 1:9–11, 13.

[319] It was not until the 1780s that the number of editions of the *New Version* in print decisively surpassed that of the *WBP*. See Fig. 6 above (p. 603).

[320] For a general account of these developments see *MEPC*, 1, chap. 6.

and at least seven parishes in the City of London.[321] One factor deterring change was the widely held belief that only the Old and New Versions were legal in the Church of England. Under the pressure of the Evangelical movement, this theory was laid to rest by a decision of the York Consistory Court in 1820,[322] which removed any remaining obstacle to the vast outpouring of hymnody from all quarters that would follow during the Victorian period. It was soon out of the question for a church to use a single collection of psalms, and anthologies became the order of the day, culminating in the most influential of all English hymnals, *Hymns Ancient and Modern* (1861). The old Calvinist insistence on singing scriptural texts was no longer a factor in the Church of England or in most nonconformist churches, and any survival of the old *WBP* texts—reduced to one (Psalm 100) in many hymnals—was accountable to habit rather than principle. Rather more of the early tunes were still in use, and others had been revived when old music acquired a romantic appeal; but they were, as often as not, assigned to new hymn texts. Details of such survivals may be found in the notes on individual texts and tunes.

For nearly three centuries the *WBP* was a focus of the spiritual life of the English, finding its way into many parts of everyday life as well as public worship. Even when most of its texts and tunes were forgotten, the popularity of congregational singing, which it had inaugurated, remained as strong as ever, and is still with us today.

Consensus, Criticism, and Competition

Such an overview of the place of the *WBP* in English life does not, of course, take account of the widely varying view of the singing psalms in general and the *WBP* in particular among different subcultures. The history of its reception—and rejection—is complex, and frequently requires us to conjecture from silence. Nevertheless, it is only a partial oversimplification to say that in controversial literature at least, the *WBP* started out portrayed as a characteristically Protestant work and ended its period of practical dominance by being painted as characteristically puritan, popular, or both—usually in a derogatory sense. By the late seventeenth century, in addition, both radical and Anglican commentators differed among themselves on its utility for private or public singing. These changes were accompanied by an enormous number of attempts to replace the *WBP* in

---

[321] *Gentleman's Magazine* 71 (1801): 811; cited *MEPC*, 1:123, where more details are given. The Old Version was still used as a physical source of texts for singing in some churches in 1831: see John Antes Latrobe, *The Music of the Church Considered in its Various Branches, Congregational and Choral* (London: Thames Ditton, 1831), 191–2. Ironically, Oxford may have been the last refuge of the *WBP*: the seven latest known editions were printed by the university at the height of the Oxford Movement, between 1829 and 1861.

[322] See *SECM*, 105–7, 305.

churches, chambers, kitchens, or all three. Important shifts in attitude toward the book become obvious around the beginning of the seventeenth century, and crystallize around the cultural upheaval of the Civil Wars.

For most of the Elizabethan period, there was virtually no adverse commentary on the *WBP*, its texts, its tunes, or the practice of singing congregationally *per se* from anyone who was not also opposed to the Elizabethan Settlement itself.[323] Early scuffles over congregational psalm singing happened in strongholds of religious conservatism, as at Exeter in 1559, or at the instigation of individuals who resisted other parts of the new religion, and they brought swift action from ecclesiastical authorities on behalf of the singers.[324] The first printed critiques both of the *WBP* and of the practice of congregational psalm singing in England came from Catholic polemicists. We have already encountered Robert Persons's 1580 castigation of "a Certayne Geneua Psalme" (i.e., "Preserve us, Lord") sung "in the beginnings of sermons and otherwise."[325] William Rainolds sneered three years later at "their Geneua, or rather Gehenna psalmes sung in their co[n]gregations."[326] As late as 1619, when George Wither noted that "some sectaries and fauourers of the Church of *Rome*, haue of late yeares disapprooued the translation of these *Psalmes* into the vulgar tongues, & scoffed at the singing of them in the reformed Churches," he was accurately reflecting the largest sources of animosity toward congregational singing.[327] (We will return shortly to the radicals who disliked psalm singing.) Given how little official warrant the metrical psalms had and how unrelentingly the bishops had to enforce the Act of Uniformity and the details of the *BCP* during Elizabeth's reign, it is actually surprising that the *WBP* was as well accepted as it seems to have been.[328]

Nevertheless, by the early seventeenth century, there are unambiguous signs that conspicuous enthusiasm for metrical psalms in public worship was seen as a puritan trait. John Boys, an indefatigable defender of the Prayer Book, asserted in 1610 that "the Geneua translation of the Psalmes in English meeter" was "vsed most, and preferred best of all Scriptures in their priuate and publike deuotions" by sectarians ("Nouelists"). He nevertheless refers to the *WBP* as a "godly labour," and implies that rejecting it because of its imperfections would be as intemperate

---

[323] For the scope of this silence, see *RR*, 259–65.

[324] Frere, *English Church*, 43–4, 66; see also *RR*, 240–1.

[325] Persons, *Brief Discours*, fols. 41v–r.

[326] William Rainolds, *A Refutation of Sundry Reprehensions, Cauils, and False Sleightes* (Paris, 1583), 331. Rainolds also took particular exception to "Preserve us, Lord."

[327] George Wither, *Preparation*, 8. He seems, in fact, to have been reading Harrab's 1616 *Tessaradelphus*, as he alludes to the attack there on the Huguenot psalm book.

[328] For further discussion of and some possible reasons for this acceptance, see *RR*, 259–65.

as rejecting the *BCP*.[329] In the 1620s, some of the Laudian Durham House divines raised hackles by abridging metrical psalmody. Richard Montaguc found himself in February 1625 defending his chaplain's omission of a congregational psalm before the sermon. In 1628, the marginalized Durham prebendary Peter Smart drew up an indictment against his colleagues that included the charge that they had "banished the singing of psalmes, in the vulgar tunes, and by authority allowed, and in all Cathedrall churches, before and after sermons."[330] When the situation at Durham Cathedral exploded in 1630 under the new bishop, John Howson, one of the main points of contention was the replacement of congregational psalms with anthems. Howson's insistence on psalms "sung by the whole multitude of the people in the common tunes of parish churches" is especially notable given that, until this dispute, he had been a champion of high ceremonialism and a close colleague of Laud.[331] In the early 1630s, opposition to the singing psalms in public worship was still very much a minority position even among the emerging High Church party.

Private singing from the *WBP* has a more complicated history of cultural meanings. There is no real evidence of friction over these psalms among English Protestants before the mid to late 1590s, which at least suggests that psalm singing was not, during most of the Elizabethan period, particularly contentious. After that, however, defenders of the *BCP* and the good order they associated with the royal supremacy began to adopt what had been a Catholic derogatory vocabulary for the metrical psalms and those who voluntarily sang them. A number of different kinds of sources indicate that singing metrical or "Geneva" psalms outside of public worship or sermon venues was beginning to be associated with puritanism and religious hypocrisy, a pair of ideas that were frequently entangled for the next century.[332] The most famous—and earliest—published instance of the association between hypocrisy and psalmody is Falstaff's assumption of victimized piety in the 1598 quarto edition of *Henry IV, part 1*: "a bad world, I say.

---

[329] John Boys, *An Exposition of the Dominical Epistles and Gospels Used in our English Liturgie . . .; the Winter Part from the First Aduentuall Sunday to Lent* (London: William Aspley, 1610), 8.

[330] John Cosin, *The Correspondence of John Cosin, D. D., Lord Bishop of Durham*, ed. George Ormsby (Durham: Andrews & Co., 1869–72), 52:5–6, 166.

[331] The words are those of the reprimanded prebendaries John Cosin and Augustine Lindsell. Laud and Charles I ultimately forced Howson to let Cosin and Lindsell alone. See Cosin, *Correspondence,* 52:200–2, 207, xxxviii–xxxix; Nicholas W. S. Cranfield, "Howson, John (1556/7–1632)," *ODNB*.

[332] Patrick Collinson, "Ecclesiastical Vitriol: Religious Satire in the 1590s and the Invention of Puritanism," in *The Reign of Elizabeth I: Court and Culture in the Last Decade*, ed. John Guy (Cambridge: Cambridge University Press, 1995), 150–70; Kristin Poole, *Radical Religion from Shakespeare to Milton: Figures of Nonconformity in Early Modern England* (Cambridge: Cambridge University Press, 2000), *passim*, but see esp. 16–44.

I would I were a weaver, I could sing psalms, or any thing."[333] In a 1602 sermon, William Burton imagined an interlocutor objecting to the performance of a godly life including "singing of Psalmes for our spirituall recreation" as "plaine Puritanisme (as they call it)."[334] Hostile neighbors of the puritan Sir Thomas Hoby and his wife Margaret in 1600 seized on psalm singing as an objectionable practice: invading the Hobys' home, they set up a din in order to drown out the household's psalms.[335] By the 1610s, singing psalms in various circumstances outside of church had become common in depictions of puritanism, signaling the increasing distance of private psalm singing from mainstream English Protestant culture.[336]

It is important to note, however, that up to the beginning of the Civil Wars this process was gradual, inconsistent, and rather idiosyncratic. As late as 1627, John Donne could eulogize Lady Magdalene Herbert Danvers by noting that she "did, euery Sabbath, shut vp the day, at night, with a generall, with a cheerfull singing of Psalmes," and in the same year the conformist and ultimately royalist minister John Reading preached that "the sweet singer of Israel endited Psalmes to bee sung, not onely in the publick seruice of God, but in priuate also, with singular profit."[337] Even the Laudian Peter Heylyn, who would write bitterly against the *WBP* after the Restoration, encouraged his future wife in the 1640s to refresh herself after study by singing the metrical psalms.[338] That Pepys happily sang the *WBP* psalms for fun is a warning against flattening out our sense of cultural contexts even in the second half of the seventeenth century. By the middle of the seventeenth century, though, it is largely self-consciously godly writers and preachers who endorse singing psalms outside of church, while Cavaliers and High Church ministers mock or condemn them. From the Restora-

---

[333] *1 Henry IV*, II.iv.130–4 in G. Blakemore Evans, ed., *The Riverside Shakespeare*, 2nd edn. (Boston: Houghton Mifflin, 1997). For an extensive discussion of this passage, see *RR*, 268–71.

[334] William Burton, *Ten Sermons vpon the First, Second, Third and Fourth Verses of the Sixt of Matthew* (London: Thomas Man, 1602), 62.

[335] See Ryrie, "Psalms and Confrontation," 120.

[336] In addition to Boys's 1610 comment on "priuate and publike deuotions," above, an early example is an anecdote on a hypocritical preacher singing "Geneva Psalms" printed in both Henry Parrot, *Laquei Ridiculosi: or Springes for Woodcocks* (London: Thomas Snodham for John Busby, 1618), sig. I5r, and John Harington, *The Most Elegant and Witty Epigrams of Sir John Harrington, Knight* (London: G[eorge] P[urslowe] for John Budge, 1618), sig. B5r. See also Quitslund, "Fun and Profit," 248.

[337] John Donne, *The Sermons of John Donne*, ed. Evelyn Simpson and George Potter (Berkeley and Los Angeles: University of California Press, 1953–62), 8:86; John Reading, *Dauids Soliloquie* (London: Robert Allot, 1627), 11.

[338] John Barnard, *Theologo-Historicus, or, The True Life of the Most Reverend Divine and Excellent Historian, Peter Heylyn* (London: Daniel Brown, 1683), 118. See Quitslund, "Fun and Profit," 245.

tion through the mid-nineteenth century, "psalm-singer" and its variants served as handy terms of derision for men given to mealy-mouthed piety or outlandishly enthusiastic religion.[339]

Further complicating reactions to the practice of singing psalms in the Stuart period was a set of emerging discontents with the versifications in the *WBP* itself. While Sternhold's skill as a poet had received lavish praise from Edwardian contemporaries, Elizabethans by and large seem not to have thought of the *WBP* as a set of poems, subject to literary judgment, until the last years of the century.[340] At that point, evaluations ranged from lukewarm to dismissive: John Marston in 1598 called the work of Sternhold and Hopkins "sencefull tollerable lines," while the next year Thomas Moffett referred to their psalms as "wronging verse."[341] Critics also began to point out the shortcomings of the psalms as translations. These strands were frequently wound together, as when James VI complained in 1601 about the Scottish psalm book (overlapping with the *WBP* by 106 psalms), "shewing both the faults of the metre and the discrepance from the text."[342] Both kinds of criticism became increasingly common over the next decades, and spurred first a trickle and eventually a torrent of new metrical psalms designed to replace the *WBP*.

Because the uses of the *WBP* were so various, it inspired at least two distinct kinds of rival. The first attempted to displace it altogether by providing a new set of psalms (and sometimes also hymns) for singing congregationally. From 1600 through 1640, at least eight writers or sets of collaborators published collections of psalms intended for public use.[343] These paraphrasts represent nearly the entire range of ecclesiological positions, from an exiled separatist (Henry Ainsworth) to James I. Most implicitly or explicitly aimed to provide a better translation than the *WBP* did, though the means differed; Ainsworth, for example, gave scrupulous attention to the Hebrew originals, while Henry Dod's 1620 psalms mined the KJV. These would-be public psalm books also evinced a variety of attitudes toward aesthetic refinement. At one extreme, Ainsworth expressed the hope that, in following custom by rhyming his verse, he does not "violate . . . the

---

[339] See *OED*, "psalm, *n*", C2. In "Nautical Rambles: The Leeward Station During the War," *The Nautical Chronicle and Naval Magazine*, 11 (1842): 829, the anonymous naval author understands "psalm-singer" to denote "a state of fanaticism."

[340] See Ramie Targoff, *Common Prayer: The Language of Public Devotion in Early Modern England* (Chicago: University of Chicago Press, 2001), 72–3, and *RR*, 265–8.

[341] John Marston, *The Metamorphosis of Pigmalions Image. And Certaine Satyres* (London: Edmond Matts, 1598), 62; T[homas] M[offett], *The Silkewormes, and Their Flies* (London: Nicholas Ling, 1599), 41.

[342] Millar Patrick, *Four Centuries of Scottish Psalmody* (London: Oxford University Press, 1949), 81.

[343] Including both collections intended as first installments and complete metrical psalters.

text"; "Yet," he notes, "rather than I would stray from the text, I streyn now and
then, with the rules of our English poësie."[344] By contrast, the former poet and
future bishop Joseph Hall justified launching his attempt to "better" the *WBP*
by observing that "it is well knowne howe rude & homely our English Poësy
was in those times, compared with the present."[345] All of the psalms in this cat-
egory, however, had to balance poetical ingenuity with the practical constraints
of congregational singing. This meant first of all a strong preference for com-
mon meter and other stanzaic forms taken from the *WBP*. Nearly all were meant
to fit tunes already in use (Ainsworth's was the only set of new congregational
psalms during this period printed with music).[346] In addition, these forms were,
by the early seventeenth century, very strongly associated with the popular idea
of metrical psalmody, and familiarity rather than novelty was better for public
use. Moreover, psalms for use by all the people together needed to be more or
less comprehensible to more or less all the people. "I have had more care," George
Wither wrote in the preface to his 1632 psalm paraphrases, "to suite the Capaci-
tie of the *Vulger* then to observe those *Criticismes* which arride the *Learned*."[347]
These constraints on both stanzaic form and diction, not to mention innovative
tunes, significantly limited the new metrical psalters' ability to make the singing
psalms beautiful. The extreme case was the "Bay Psalm Book," the New England
puritans' first attempt to revise the *WBP* in ways more faithful to the Hebrew
originals, though still fitting the common tunes.[348] To take an example, its anon-
ymous paraphrase of Psalm 137 begins thus:

---

[344] H[enry] A[insworth], *The Booke of Psalmes: Englished both in Prose and Metre* (Am-
sterdam: Giles Thorp, 1612), sig. **2r. For details of Ainsworth's tunes see Frost 318–31.

[345] Joseph Hall, *Holy Observations. Lib. I. Also Some Fewe of Davids Psalmes Meta-
phrased, for a Taste of the Rest* (London: Samuel Macham, 1607), sig. G4r–v.

[346] Of Ainsworth's 40 different tunes, 27 were shared with the *WBP* or were English
common tunes, 10 were newly adapted from French tunes, and only 3 were new. George
Wither's *The Psalmes of David Translated into Lyrick-Verse* ([Amsterdam]: Cornelis Ger-
ritis van Breughel, 1632) is the conspicuous exception. While most of its versifications
are in forms that would be suitable for tunes from the *WBP*, several are not. Due to the
hostility of the Stationers' Company, Wither had considerable difficulty getting the work
printed at all; adding tunes may have been simply too much to accomplish.

[347] Wither, *Psalmes of David*, sig. A6r. The psalms nominally by James I and VI
in fact drew harsh criticism from the Scots minister David Calderwood for their "hea-
thenish libertie and poeticall conceats" as well as their "French, Latine, and hard Eng-
lish tearmes, and harsh phrases" that would "have need of a dictionarie in the end of
the metaphrase." See John W. McMeeken, *The History of the Scottish Metrical Psalms*
(Glasgow: M'Culloch & Co., 1872), 180.

[348] *The Whole Booke of Psalmes Faithfully Translated into English Metre* ([Cambridge,
Mass.: Stephen Day], 1640). The few psalms not in common meter were referred to spe-
cific tunes "in our English psalm books." See Zolan Haraszti, *The Enigma of the Bay Psalm
Book* ([Chicago]: University of Chicago Press, [1956]); Norman S. Grabo, "How Bad is

The rivers on of Babylon
　　there when we did sit down,
Yea even then we mournèd, when
　　we remembered Sion.

The second type of competitor to the *WBP* was the metrical psalm collection meant for private singing. Unlike those for congregations, psalms to be used in domestic or recreational settings could cater to elite abilities with more challenging music, vocabulary, or—in the case of William Slatyer's parallel versifications into Latin, Greek, and Hebrew—a knowledge of scholarly languages.[349] The most prominent such version was that of George Sandys, published in 1636 with tunes by Henry Lawes. These were printed complete at least four times (again in 1638 and twice in 1648 as part of *A Paraphrase upon the Divine Poems*), and a selection also appeared in the 1648 *Choice Psalmes Put into Musick*.[350] By their nature, however, such private psalm books were likely to be niche publications that could not actually affect the market position of the *WBP* itself.

The kinds of criticism and sectarian polarization that had swirled around the use of the *WBP* during the first part of the seventeenth century took far more dramatic and dogmatic form in the 1640s and 1650s as each side demonized the other. If it was largely puritans who were understood to sing psalms outside of church, then satires of hypocritical puritans would prominently feature psalmody. A Cavalier description of a puritan private "liturgy"—a riotous dinner party—thus featured the howling of Psalm 119 as the final and most appalling act.[351] Discussions of the inaccuracies and aesthetic shortcomings in the *WBP* had been mostly moderate prior to the Civil Wars, but its association with puritan culture also now meant that its inadequacies and even violence to the scriptural text were figures for their errors and savagery. Sternhold and Hopkins "murdered the Psalmes over and over," the result "Barbarity, and Botching."[352] A

---

the *Bay Psalm Book?*," *Papers of the Michigan Academy of Science, Arts and Letters* 56 (1961): 605–15; Nicholas Temperley, "Bay Psalm Book," *CDH*.

[349] W[illiam] S[latyer], *The Psalmes of David in 4 Languages and in 4 Parts Set to ye Tunes of our Church* (London: George Thomason and Octavian Pullen, 1543). These are almost certainly the only extant samples of Greek and Hebrew in rhymed Common Meter.

[350] G[eorge] S[andys], *A Paraphrase vpon the Psalmes of David* (London, [1636]); Henry and William Lawes, *Choice Psalmes Put into Musick* (London: Humphrey Moseley, 1648). For Lawes's tunes see Frost 366–89.

[351] Agamemnon Shaglock van Dammee, *The Speech of a Cavaleere to his Comrades, in Answer to the Wardens Speech* (London, 1642), sig. A3r.

[352] John Sergeant, *Schism Dis-arm'd of the Defensive Weapons, Lent it by Doctor Hammond, and the Bishop of Derry by S. W.* (Paris: M. Blageart, 1655), 221–2; Peter Heylyn, *Ecclesia restaurata: or, the History of the Reformation of the Church of England* (London. II. Twyford et al, 1660–1), 50.

larger change was the polemical treatment of congregational psalm singing. The sound of the psalms at public worship, and particularly the "old way of singing," became, quite suddenly, a metaphor for popular disorder. John Phillips, a royalist nephew of John Milton, described it as following:

> Then out the people yaule an hundred parts,
> Some roar, some whine, some creak like wheels of Carts,
> Such Notes that Gamut never yet did know,
>
> . . . .
>
> Like untam'd horses tearing with their throats
> One wretched stave into an hundred notes.[353]

At the beginning of Elizabeth's reign, both sexes and all ages and social classes lifting up their voices had provided a metonymic representation of unanimity in the new national church. A hundred years later, it had become, for a time at least, a form of discord and resistance to proper hierarchical deference. It should be noted, however, that in practice royalists during the wars continued to sing psalms as a form of communal devotional expression, just as they had before the outbreak of hostilities.[354]

Somewhat ironically, many of the "hypocritical presbyterians" that Phillips satirized were themselves dissatisfied enough with the *WBP* that Parliament and the Westminster Assembly attempted to replace it along with the *BCP*. In 1643, the Commons ordered printed an edition of a metrical psalter by Francis Rous, in effect his second version of a thorough-going revision to the *WBP*.[355] This was also forwarded to the Westminster Assembly to be authorized for public use. Delays in its approval allowed the Lords to put forward a different alternate psalm book in 1645, a set of William Barton's paraphrases supplemented by some revised psalms from the *WBP*.[356] Although the Assembly ultimately endorsed

---

[353] Phillips, *Religion of the Hypocritical Presbyterians*, 5. The work was originally published in 1655 as *A Satyr Against Hypocrites*. This passage was quoted in the preface to a collection of psalms with music more than half a century later: Elias Hall, *The Psalm-Singer's Compleat Companion* (London, 1708); cited *MEPC*, 1:91.

[354] Thomas Mace records the royalist congregation of 1,000 singing psalms (with an organ) in the York Minster during the siege in 1644: Thomas Mace, *Musick's Monument* (London: T. Ratcliffe, and N. Thompson for Thomas Mace, 1676), 18–19. Additionally, Lady Falkland's household psalm singing took place as part of her secret use of the *BPC* during the 1640s (see 598 n. 273 above).

[355] Francis Rous, *Psalmes of David in English Meter* (London: Philip Nevill, 1643). The first version was *The Booke of Psalmes, in English Meetre* (Rotterdam, 1638; London, 1641).

[356] William Barton, *The Book of Psalms in Metre, Lately Translated, with Many Whole Ones, and Choice Collections of the Old Psalms Added to the First Impression* (London: G[eorge] M[iller], 1645).

Rous's book, it was not widely adopted in practice: there are no surviving English editions after 1643.[357] Barton's metrical psalms, in various revisions and configurations, continued to be printed sporadically into the early eighteenth century. Neither of these contending psalters, however, was produced in anything like the quantities that would have been required to make more than token inroads against the *WBP*. As we have seen, production of the *WBP* dropped during the 1640s and 1650s, but probably not as a result of competition from Rous or Barton. The spread of lining out may have caused a decrease in demand, but the commercial practice of printing editions of the *WBP* to match issues of the *BCP* was just as much to blame—when the use of the Prayer Book was outlawed, one source of metrical psalter sales vanished at the same time.

The last factor that may have caused some eclipse of the *WBP* during the middle of the seventeenth century was the growth of radical sects that rejected congregational singing altogether. Some fringe movements from the Elizabethan years on had eschewed metrical psalmody along with most other formal liturgical practice. The separatist Henry Barrow, for example, argued that paraphrasing of any kind falsified the scriptures.[358] As the seventeenth century progressed, both the number and size of such groups mushroomed. Among those that would go on to become major denominations, both Quakers and General Baptists regarded corporate psalm singing as unacceptable for essentially the same reason that they rejected set prayers: anything sung by the whole congregation together could not reflect the motion of the spirit within the heart of each individual at that moment. If the serious defenses of congregational singing during the late sixteenth century were largely undertaken to respond to Catholic critics, those of the later seventeenth century faced off against the arguments of anti-presbyterian radicals.[359]

The sneers of Interregnum and Restoration wits at the vulgarity and barbarism of the *WBP* far outlived the political circumstances that initially motivated them, and figures as diverse as the Dissenter Isaac Watts, the Methodist founder John Wesley, and the high-church literary critic Thomas Warton could all agree that the *WBP* was aesthetically unacceptable.[360] Notably, each of these men for

---

[357] Rous's versions did, however, form part of the basis for the 1650 revision of the Scots psalm book. See McMeeken, *History of the Scottish Metrical Psalms*. (Glascow: M'Culloch & Co., 1872), 38–50.

[358] Henry Barrow, "A Few Observations to the Reader of Mr. Giffard His Last *Replie* [1591/2]," in *The Writings of John Greenwood and Henry Barrow, 1591–1593*, ed. Leland H. Carlson, Elizabethan Nonconformist Texts: vol. 6 (1970; rpt. London: Routledge, 2003), 63.

[359] See N. Temperley, "The Music of Dissent," in Isabel Rivers and David Wykes, eds., *Dissenting Praise* (Oxford: Oxford University Press, 2011), 200–1.

[360] See Kate Horgan, *The Politics of Songs in Eighteenth Century Britain* (London: Pickering and Chatto, 2014), 61–92.

different reasons also rejected the idea that congregational singing should be limited to literal psalm paraphrase. A writer in the *Gentleman's Magazine* for 1781, calling himself "No Psalm Singer," quoted Warton as associating the Old Version with "manufacturers and mechanics": "It is certainly better calculated for the spiritual consolation of tallow-chandlers and taylors, than for the pious uses of the liberal and intelligent. Psalm-singing and Republicanism naturally go together. They seem both founded on the same levelling principle. . . . There is much philosophical truth in a ludicrous saying of King Charles the Second, that *the Presbyterian Worship was not fit for a Gentleman.*" "A Dissenter" retorted with some justice in a later issue that dissenters for forty years had sung Watts's or Merrick's much more poetical versions and had "abandoned the *ekes* and *ayes* of Sternhold to that church for the use of which they were translated."[361] This exchange highlights the fact that whereas neither side could find much to praise in the verses themselves, a low churchman's loyalty to the *WBP* could be traced primarily to the Calvinistic dictum that only the psalms should be sung in worship, while the more recent high-church devotion was more likely to be based on support of royal authority and tradition. This became clear, for example, when John Crosse (1739–1816), a high-church (Arminian) Evangelical, became vicar of Bradford, Yorkshire, in 1784, and on Sundays would allow only Old Version psalms to be sung—with the old tunes.[362] For some people these ancient relics were acquiring a romantic appeal, which reached its height when they were performed by opera singers, chorus, and orchestra at the Ancient Concerts in London (starting in 1806) and at the York Choral Festival (first in 1823).[363]

Rearguard action on behalf of the *WBP* as congregational music continued into nineteenth-century polemics. In 1822, responding to the recent decision that hymns outside the Old and New Versions were legal in public worship, the minister and literary scholar Henry John Todd published a little book of *Observations upon the Metrical Versions of the Psalms, Made by Sternhold, Hopkins and Others* which offers a comprehensive defense of the *WBP* on legal, practical, philological, and even aesthetic grounds.[364] His aim, as advertised on the title page, was to encourage the Church of England to "maintain . . . the usage of such metrical psalmody only as is duly authorized" and thus conducive to truly common forms

---

[361] *Gentleman's Magazine* 51 (1781): 266, 406.

[362] *MEPC,* 1:216–17.

[363] *MEPC,* 1:245; 2, no. 58. A movement to revive the Elizabethan tunes in church was already under way, led by William Crotch, professor of music at Oxford: see Crotch, *Tallis's Litany . . . A Collection of Old Psalm Tunes . . . for the Use of the University Church, Oxford* (Oxford: for the Editor, 1803).

[364] Henry John Todd, *Observations upon the Metrical Versions of the Psalms, Made by Sternhold, Hopkins and Others* (London: for F.C. & J. Rivington, 1822). See also Rev. E. Berens, *Observations on Parochial Psalmody, with a Selection of Psalms from the Old Version* (Oxford: W. Baxter, for C. and J. Rivington, 1825).

of prayer throughout the nation. Although Todd takes royal printing patents as evidence of "authorization" for not only the *WBP* but a number of seventeenth-century metrical psalm collections, and concedes that both the metrical psalms ascribed to James I and the *New Version* had explicit royal permission for congregational use, he stands by the *WBP* as the best version both "duly authorized" and suited for public use. Aside from the portions establishing the history of the *WBP* and comparing specific versifications to those in its rivals, the bulk of the treatise is devoted to extended quotations of other commentators, ranging from Fuller and Strype in the mid-seventeenth century to a short essay by the young church historian Henry Cotton only the year before. The result is both a history of responses to the *WBP* and a learned chorus of appreciation linking the metrical psalms to the whole lifespan of the English Church. An editor of Milton and Spenser, Todd also takes care to rest his case not on the revised editions that had been printed over the last century but on the Elizabethan texts in their full antique glory, "the old unsophisticated publication."[365] Having examined a copy of *Al Such Psalmes*, he knew perfectly well that Sternhold had been lauded by contemporaries for his "exquisite dooings." For the Regency churchman, though, the *WBP*'s old-fashioned plainness was a form of authenticity, and its lack of modern sophistication a reassurance of historical as well as geographical uniformity. Nostalgia, particularly for texts that had not been sung in their unrevised state for over a hundred years, would not suffice to revive the popularity of the *WBP* or forestall the explosion of original hymnody about to burst into English religious life. It does, however, mark a final evolution in the cultural place of the *WBP*, even as the metrical psalms themselves were slipping from use.

---

[365] Todd, *Observations*, 101.

NOTES ON INDIVIDUAL TEXTS AND TUNES

NOTES ON PREFATORY MATTER

An Extract of the Queen's privilege

This text is printed only in *1567*, the inaugural edition that Day published under the new patent. He had once previously reproduced a royal patent, the October 1559 license for seven years to print William Cunningham's *The Cosmographical Glasse* as well as "all suche Bookes, and workes, as he hath Imprinted, or herafter shall Imprint, being diuised, compiled, or set out by any learned man, at the procurement, costes, & charge, only of the said Iohn Day"[1] (the same language used in the 1567 patent, lines 11–14). This extension of the privilege to books commissioned by Day does not occur in the other important 1559 royal printing patents to William Seres for private prayer books, primers, and psalters, to Richard Jugge and Thomas Cawood for statute books, or to Richard Tottel for common law books.[2] Though inserted at the end of *The Cosmographical Glasse* rather than at the front as in *1567*, the 1559 patent was important enough to Day to expend an extra half sheet of paper in printing it with Cunningham's volume. The language of the 1567 patent is virtually identical to that of 1559, except that the specific works listed differ and the caveat that it only covers books that are not "repugnant to the holy scripture or the laws and order of our realm" (lines 14–15) is new. While it seems likely that this patent extends a seven-year privilege granted in late 1560 for at least the metrical psalms with notes, no copy of such a patent survives. (For discussion, see p. 538.)

---

[1] William Cuningham, *The Cosmographical Glasse* (London: John Day, 1559), sig. T3r.

[2] See "Seres' patent for Primers and Psalters," Westminster (1559), "Jugge and Cawood's printing patent for statute books," Westminster (1559), and "Totell's patent for Common Law Books," Westminster (1559), all in *Primary Sources on Copyright (1450–1900)*, eds. L. Bently & M. Kretschmer, www.copyrighthistory.org.

A Treatise Made by Athanasius the Great

This anonymous version of Athanasius' *Letter to Marcellinus* was first printed in *1562a*. The English text uses about a third of the *Letter* as it is known in modern scholarship, primarily ¶¶15–26 of Migne's *Patrologia graeca* edition.[3] It certainly derives from a Latin intermediary, probably one that looked similar to the version printed at the end of the 1534 edition of Jan van Campen's Latin psalm paraphrase, *Psalmoru[m] omnium*.[4] Campen's edition includes the first third of the treatise, nearly all missing from the *WBP* text, but omits everything after the list of psalm uses that is translated in the *WBP*. Also in common with the *WBP*, the directions for various uses of the psalms in Campen is arranged as a list, with the psalm numbers sometimes disentangled from the prose of the letter. The Campen text itself was not the one used by the *WBP* editor—it contains errors and omissions in the psalms listed that do not agree with the *WBP*. We have, however, noted instances where it coincides with the *WBP* against modern editions, because those may represent points in common with the *WBP*'s 16th-century Latin source.

The *WBP* text has other peculiarities, as well. In addition to some awkward translation, the editor frequently failed to correctly change the Septuagint psalm numbers used by Athanasius to the numbering found in Protestant Bibles and the *WBP* (Campen did not attempt to do so, despite the Hebrew numbering of his own paraphrase). The notes below indicate significant differences from Athanasius' text regarding what directions are included and which psalms indicated. Quotations of the original Athanasian text are from the English translation by Robert C. Gregg.[5] Unless otherwise indicated, psalm numbers are those used in the *WBP* and KJV.

The text appeared in essentially all complete editions of the *WBP* from 1562 through 1576, with the exception of two-column quartos, which uniformly omitted it. It was always accompanied by "The use of the rest." It is possible, as Ian Green has suggested, that the original idea to add it to the *WBP* was Matthew Parker's (Green, 538).[6] If so, however, the translator who undertook the task lacked both Parker's literary finesse and skill as a translator. That Parker himself considered it badly done is demonstrated by the fact that he prepared his own version, based at least in part on the *WBP* text but with a fresh translation from

---

[3] Athanasius of Alexandria, *Epistola ad Marcellinum*, in *Patrologia graeca*, ed. Jacques-Paul Migne, 162 vols (Paris: J-P Migne, 1857–86), 27: cols. 11–46.

[4] Jan van Campen, *Psalmoru[m] omnium* (Paris: F. Regnault for Thomas Berthelet, 1534), sig. X8r–BB8r.

[5] Athanasius of Alexandria, *The Life of Anthony* and *The Letter to Marcellinus*, trans. Robert C. Gregg (New York, Ramsey, Toronto: Paulist Press, 1980), 101–29. For clarity, this translation will be cited as "Gregg."

[6] Green, *Print and Protestantism*, 538.

the Latin, for inclusion in his 1567 *Whole Psalter Translated into English Metre* (sig. A5r–B3v).[7] Parker's text, in turn, was slightly adapted for the *WBP* in 1577 (for the 1577 text, see pp. 882–94; for discussion, see pp. 551–2 and 574–5).

1–8 The first sentences paraphrase the start of ¶14 of *A Letter to Marcellinus*.
8 The text skips to the start of ¶15.
24 115th: Should be 116th (114th in Septuagint). Omits Ps. 75 (also omitted in Campen).
28 37th: Should be 38th (37th in Septuagint).
35 81st: Replaces Ps. 84 (as Campen).
40 10th: Should be 11th (10th in Septuagint).
43 11th: Should be 12th (11th in Septuagint).
46 26th: Replaces Ps. 13.
50–51 what sort . . . heaven: Slightly garbled. Gregg gives "what sort of a person the citizen of the kingdom of heaven is" (Gregg, 115); Parker translates as "who is a citizen of heaven" (p. 885).
53 89th: Replaces 88th.
58 Omits Ps. 24 but adds Pss. 26 and 27.
71 46th: Athanasius has Ps. 27 (in his Septuagint numbering 26), which the editor here assigned above.
73 47th: Replaces 28th. Ps. 28 is reassigned to "The use of the rest."
75 48th: Replaces 29th. Ps. 29 is reassigned to "The use of the rest."
78 49th: Replaces 30th, although Campen gives Septuagint Ps. 49.
81 31st: Should be 32nd (31st in Septuagint).
89–90 In the 4th century, this was a warning against particular Gnostic doctrines. In the context of 16th-century debates about the implications of predestinarian soteriology, it would probably have struck readers as a comment on the culpability of the rebrobate.
90 36th: Should be 37th (36th in Septuagint), although Campen gives Ps. 36.
96 Omits an Athanasian item: "And if, when the enemies set upon you, you persevere in the face of the trials, and you want to learn the advantage of endurance, sing Psalm 39 [KJV 40]" (Gregg, 117). Also omitted from Campen.
97 try them . . . already: Either misconstrued or badly expressed by the translator. Gregg gives "approve those who already act with compassion" (Gregg, 117); Parker has "thyself receive them to mercy" (p. 886).
106 79th, 80th, 102nd: Replacing, intentionally or in error, what from Gregg would be Pss. 78, 89, and 105. Campen also replaces Ps. 105 with 102.
115 Pharisees did Christ: Not in Migne, though present in Campen.
120 142nd: Replaces Ps. 116; Campen has the same replacement.
126 4th: Replaces Ps. 55; possibly an error for the Septuagint 54th.

---

[7] [Matthew Parker], *The Whole Psalter Translated Into English Metre* (London: John Daye, [1567]), sig. A5r–B3v.

138 68th: Replaces Ps. 65; Campen makes the same replacement, as does Parker (see. p. 887).

142: 80th: Replaces Ps. 66 (or, according to Campen, Ps. 70).

148 71st: Replaces Ps. 10. Campen makes the same replacement, as does Parker (see p. 887).

150–52 Omits Athanasius' comment that "the knowledge of God does not reside in a single one among them, but in the Catholic Church alone" (Gregg, 119). Also replaces—possibly through typographical error—Ps. 76 with Ps. 86.

165 author: A compositor's error for "anchor," which must have seemed just plausible enough that it was never corrected in this translation of the text.

170 116th: Replaces (in error?) Ps. 126.

177 13th: Replaces (in error?) Ps. 24 (23 in the Septuagint).

178 second Sabbath: The Septuagint heading for Ps. 47 (48 in the KJV), which is given here in *A Letter*, is "deutera sabbatou." Parker translates the text here as "the second day of the Sabbath" (p. 889), Gregg as "the second day of the week" (Gregg, 146n46, 120). The replacement of Ps. 48 with Ps. 95 is consistent with Campen's text.

179 day of preparation: Good Friday. The editor considerably shortened this discussion; Parker gives a fuller translation (see p. 889).

186 fourth Sabbath: I.e., the fourth day of the week.

203 Omits Ps. 104.

205 113th, 127th, 133rd: These replace Pss. 105, 107, and 135 (or, according to Campen, 118, 119, and 135).

207 96th: Almost certainly an error for 116th (as in Athanasius).

208 Omits the Athanasian direction for reciting the Gradual Psalms (Pss. 120–134) as one is "progressing by deeds" (Gregg, 122).

216–17 5th . . . 144th: Should be 6th (5th in Septuagint) and 143; Pss. 141, 142, and 144 are added. Campen adds Pss. 141, 142, and 146.

221 85th: Replaces Ps. 145 (or, according to Campen, Ps. 105).

222 Replaces Ps. 93 with 96.

226 152nd or the 151st: Athanasias specifies Ps. 151, present in the Septuagint but not the Masoretic Hebrew text behind Protestant Bibles. The non-existent 152 is *1567*'s error for *1562a*'s 52, although given the tone of Ps. 52, that seems likely to be an error as well.

227–9 The Psalm numbers are only partly (or incorrectly) converted from the Septuagint. Of the list given in *1567*, Pss. 111 and 117 are superfluous, and 134 and 145 should be converted to 135 and 146, respectively. Missing from the list is Ps. 136. Campen does include Ps. 117.

230–33 In *A Letter*, Athanasius notes that Christ can be found in nearly every psalm, but that his generation and incarnation are shown in Pss. 45 and 110. Psalm 11 is not mentioned.

235–6 Pss. 2 and 119 replace Pss. 22 and 69 from Athanasius (Pss. 62 and 69 in Campen).

238 21st . . . 72nd: Replacing Pss. 3 and 109.
240 16th: Replaces Pss. 21, 50, and 72.
241–2 Replaces Ps. 15, which Athanasius lists here, with two that he discusses earlier (¶8) in reference to the resurrection.

The use of the rest of the Psalms

This anonymous text was first printed in *1562a*. It always accompanied "A Treatise made by Athanasius the Great," appearing with it in all extant printing series except two-column quartos from 1562 until 1576. No edition from 1577 or later containing this text survives; both it and "A Treatise" were supplanted by Matthew Parker's version of the Athanasian text (see pp. 882–94).

25–7 A trans-historical assortment of bogeys. **Syrians, Idumeans, Ammonites:** Hostile to Israel and/or Judah at various points in the Old Testament. **Antichristians:** possibly an error for or variant of "Antichrists," an epithet commonly applied to Catholics or to Catholic leaders in Protestant sectarian polemic. **Nullifidians:** unbelievers or atheists. **Neutrals:** reference to Rev. 4:16, in which the Lord spits out the lukewarm church at Laodicea; a common term of opprobrium among early modern Protestants for the insufficiently zealous. **Pelagians:** followers of a late-4th-century heresy maintaining that original sin does not prevent the human will from good works without the intervention of grace. Protestant polemic caricatured Catholic free will doctrine as virtually Pelagian.

Notes on Psalms and Hymns

Textual Sources for Psalm Versifications and Prose Arguments

The eight men who paraphrased the metrical psalms that were eventually included in *The Whole Book of Psalms* based their versions on a variety of previous translations, paraphrases, and commentaries in several languages. Most of these sources are used by more than one of the psalm versifiers, and, conversely, most of the versifiers used multiple sources for at least some of their paraphrases. The Text Notes to each psalm suggest the most likely sources for individual psalms and the prose arguments preceding them, but a few words are still necessary about these sources to avoid repetition in the Notes themselves.

In the late 1540s, both Thomas Sternhold and John Hopkins worked primarily from Protestant English versions. The Great Bible (1539) was the single most important source, but both consulted at least one *other* translation by Miles Coverdale. Both occasionally prefer the wording of the Coverdale Bible (1535), or perhaps one of its direct descendants such as the Matthew Bible (1537).[8] Sternhold also frequently echoes the English of Coverdale's parallel English-Latin psalter (1540), which, as a direct translation of the Vulgate, differs from his versions drawing on Protestant scholarship. Both writers also seem to have known and consulted George Joye's *Psalter of Dauid in Englishe* (1530), a set of prose paraphrases based on those by Martin Bucer. In addition to these, the Vulgate version used publically well into their adulthood continued to exercise some pull, for Sternhold especially.[9]

The writers in Geneva up through *1558* continued to rely heavily on the Great Bible, but they supplemented it with the texts and scholarship to be found in the community around Calvin. William Whittingham used French sources extensively, and many of his psalm paraphrases and their prose arguments translate or draw from the metrical psalms of Clément Marot and Theodore Beza as they had been printed in 1551 (while still borrowing diction from the Great

---

[8] *Biblia: The Bible, that is, the Holy Scripture* [Coverdale Bible] ([Cologne?: E. Cervicornus and J. Soter?,] 1535); *The Byble, whych is All the Holy Scripture* [Matthew Bible] ([Antwerp: Matthew Crom for Richard Grafton and Edward Whitchurch,] 1537). Great Bible quotations are taken from *The Byble in Englishe* (London: Edward Whitchurch, 1540).

[9] Miles Coverdale, ed., *The Psalter or Booke of Psalmes both in Latyne and Englyshe* (London: Ricardus Grafton, 1540); George Joye, ed., *The Psalter of Dauid in Englishe Purely a[n]d Faithfully Tra[n]slated aftir the Texte of Feline* (Argentine [i.e., Antwerp]: Francis Foxe [i.e., Martin de Keyser], 1530); Aretinus Felinus [i.e., Martin Bucer], ed., *Psalmorum libri quinque ad Ebraicam veritatem versi* (Strassburg: George Ulricher, 1529).

Bible).[10] He also drew on some of Beza's sources, including the annotations to the psalms by Louis Budé. These were published independently in 1551 and also appeared as marginal notes in some editions of the French Protestant Bible printed in Geneva.[11] It is likely, however, that Whittingham had to hand an edition of the Olivétan Bible—the translation most commonly used in Geneva—that did not contain Budé's notes, as the marginal notes that he added to the metrical psalms in *1556* often echo a different set of French annotations. The same French notes influenced some of the annotation for Whittingham's 1557 prose version of the Book of Psalms, referred to in the Text Notes as the 1557 Genevan Psalter.[12] Whittingham also seems to have consulted at least at times Martin Bucer's paraphrase and commentary, *Psalmorum libri quinque*, which had helped to shape the arguments that Beza affixed to the French metrical psalms and would contribute heavily to Jean Calvin's extensive *Commentary on the Psalms*. Most interestingly, Whittingham frequently echoes details from Calvin's *Commentary*, which was not printed (in Latin) until 1557.[13] He evidently had access to a manuscript copy of most of that work in late 1555 and early 1556. Calvin's explication also provided models for most of the *1556* and *1558* prose arguments that were not taken from the French metrical psalter.

William Kethe was among the company that prepared the Geneva Bible, and his paraphrases are usually very close to that version. (The Book of Psalms to the 1560 Geneva Bible was also published separately in 1559 with a dedication to Queen Elizabeth.)[14] In addition, all arguments added in *1560b* are taken from the ones in the 1559 Book of Psalms and Geneva Bible; these usually had their sources in the 1557 Genevan Psalter, Calvin's *Commentaries*, or the arguments to psalms in an Olivétan Bible. The poets working in London also made early use of

---

[10] *Pseaumes octantetrois de David, mis en rime françoise par Clément Marot et Théodore de Bèze. La forme des prières ecclésiastiques et Catéchisme par Jean Calvin* (Geneva: Jean Crespin, 1551; repr. New Brunswick, NJ: Friends of the Rutgers University Libraries, 1973).

[11] See the Introduction to Théodore de Bèze, *Psaumes mis en vers français (1551–1562), accompagnés de la version en prose de Loïs Budé*, ed. Pierre Pidoux (Geneva: Librairie Droz, 1984), 3–4. In addition to influencing Beza, Budé's translation from the Hebrew provided much of the scholarly underpinning for Whittingham's work on the 1557 Genevan Psalter. See *Pseaumes octantetrois*, 4–5; *RR*, 158–9. For Budé and revisions to the Olivétan Bible, see Rodolphe Peter, "Calvin and Louis Budé's Translation of the Psalms," in G[ervase] E. Duffield (ed.), *John Calvin* (Appleford: Sutton Courtenay Press, 1966), 191–200.

[12] [William Whittingham], *The Psalmes of Dauid Translated accordyng to the Veritie and Truth of th'Ebrue* ([Geneva: M. Blanchier,] 1557).

[13] Jean Calvin, *In Librum Psalmorum Commentarius* (Geneva: Robert Estienne, 1557).

[14] *The Boke of Psalmes* (Geneva: Rowland Hall, 1559). *The Holy Bible and Scriptures Conteyned in the Olde and Newe Testament* [Geneva Bible] (Geneva: Rowland Hall, 1560).

the Geneva prose psalms, though less consistently so in the psalms first published in *1561c* and *1561d*. The new arguments in those editions, too, are drawn from Whittingham's 1557 Genevan Psalter, rather than the newer 1559/1560 translation. By contrast, the arguments new in *1562a* and *1562b* are all taken from the Geneva Bible (or the identical 1559 Book of Psalms). Nevertheless, especially for Hopkins and John Marckant, the Great Bible continued to be an important source; Norton employs it more selectively. Finally, Robert Wisdom's psalms are unlike all the others in that they have relatively little connection to any English sources and instead simply translate German Lutheran hymns.

Quotations from the Great Bible and the Geneva Bible have been modernized in spelling and punctuation both for ease of comparison and because there is little rationale for reproducing the accidentals of such frequently reprinted works. As there are a number of editions of Calvin's *Commentary* available both in print and online, the Notes generally refer to the psalm and verse numbers rather than to page numbers. When quoting from the work, however, we have used Arthur Golding's 1571 translation.[15] It has not been possible to determine exactly which edition of the Bible in French either Whittingham or Kethe used, and the annotations could vary considerably in the early 1550s. The Geneva Book of Psalms, however, follows a model of apparatus that began in an Olivétan edition of 1555 and remained relatively standard for about a decade. We have consulted a 1564 edition that retains these paratextual features and which overlaps frequently enough with both Whittingham's and the Geneva Bible editors' notes that it is almost certainly very close to the earlier edition from which they actually worked.[16]

The Latin psalm incipits given for translation in the notes have been expanded to their conventional full length in order to provide intelligible phrases. The translations are based on those in Coverdale's parallel edition of the Vulgate, but modernized and edited to eliminate occasional interpolations of extra words or interpretations of the Latin incompatible with the *WBP* paraphrase.

The marginal notes to the psalms from *1556* were partially reprinted (in steadily decreasing numbers) in *1561d, 1562a, 1563,* the quarto edition of 1566 (*STC* 2437), and *1569a*. Those from editions collated for the main text (*1556, 1561d,* and *1562a*) are given in modernized form in the Notes following the procedures for the rest of the *WBP* text. Many of them echo either notes present in 1560s editions of the Olivétan Bible or observations from Calvin's psalm

---

[15] Arthur Golding, trans., *The Psalmes of Dauid and Others. With M. Iohn Caluins Commentaries* (London: [Thomas East and Henry Littleton], 1571), hereinafter Calvin, *Commentaries*.

[16] *La sainte Bible* (Lyon: Jean de Tournes, 1564). For a description of the evolution of the Olivétan Bible, see Bettye Thomas Chambers, *Bibliography of French Bibles: Fifteenth- and Sixteenth-Century French-Language Editions of the Scriptures* (Geneva: Librairie Droz, 1983), xii–xv.

commentaries. Those that take the form of cross-references to other parts of the Bible are keyed to the Great Bible, which, preceding the innovation of numbered verses, placed letters in the margins to create divisions within chapters. The Notes supply modern verse numbers in brackets for convenience in locating the passage.

In the last five years of the 17th century and again a few years later, the texts of the *WBP* underwent systematic revision. The first round of modernization uniformly eliminated much-maligned archaisms such as "eke" and "ay," and occasionally went considerably further in changes to style or meaning. The early-18th-century revisions, where present, targeted out-of-date or inelegant syntax as well as additional diction that the editor found too old-fashioned. Both sets of revisions sometimes also bring the psalm texts closer to the KJV translation. Because hymns have, since the early publications of the *WBP* itself, been indexed by their first one or two lines, notes on the later uses of the texts include the new first and/or second lines where 18th- and 19th-century editions have a standard version that differs from *1567* and its Elizabethan successors. These are usually taken from a Cambridge edition of 1751,[17] but were generally stable from at least 1710 through the middle of the 19th century. When the modernization extended beyond scattered words and phrases, the notes also reflect its scope, though without attempting detailed collation.

Origins of Tunes

There is no tune based on an Edwardian or earlier English source. Ten of the sixty-seven tunes were adapted from tunes in the French Genevan psalter of 1551,[18] and five came from German printed sources. In each of these cases the source has been collated with the Anglo-Genevan and English editions, and significant variants listed. Less direct relationships, such as that between PSALM 119 and the tune of the Lutheran Creed, have been discussed in the Notes but not treated in the lists of variants. The remaining tunes are believed to have been composed expressly for the Marian exiles or, after 1558, for the *WBP* or its incomplete predecessors. For the origins of tunes added to *WBP* editions after *1567* see Apps. 5 and 6. Sternhold's unrevised texts, and some of Hopkins's, were set for four voices by John Sheppard in the late 1540s: in most cases only the treble part has survived, and none of the music was used in the *WBP*. For a general discussion of these see pp. 518–20. The more popular texts were often used for anthems, or were set to various tunes, some of them new, in tunebooks of the 18th century and later. The most striking examples of these further uses have been mentioned.

---

[17] *The Whole Book of Psalms* (Cambridge: Joseph Bentham, 1751), hereinafter *WBP* 1751.

[18] *Pseaumes octantetrois de David.*

Hymns Before the Psalms

Veni, Creator

Text: Alone of all the psalms and hymns in the *WBP*, this text was part of the authorized liturgy. It is the only metrical hymn printed in the *BCP* and also almost certainly the earliest of those in the *WBP*. It was first printed in March 1550 in the Edwardian Protestant *Ordinal,* which was incorporated into the *BCP* in 1552. Archbishop Thomas Cranmer was the primary author of these liturgies, which makes him the most likely versifier of this 9th-century Latin hymn. It was, like much of the 1549 Prayer Book, translated from the equivalent service in the medieval Sarum rite. It does not appear printed with the metrical psalms until *1561c* and *1561d*, but was included in all Elizabethan editions thereafter. From 1575 (*STC* 16579.5) until 1650, it also appeared in some editions of the Scottish service and psalm book after the metrical psalms.

Later use of the text: In the 1662 *BCP*, this version became an alternative to a new versification by John Cosin, Bishop of Durham ("Come, Holy Ghost our souls inspire"). The 1550 text was revised at the same time, thoroughly if for the most part without replacing lines wholesale. Only Cosin's version survived in the 1928 *BCP* text (the American Episcopal Prayer Book replaced the older hymn with a third translation). The text in the *WBP* continued to closely follow its Elizabethan form until the early 18th century, when it first passed through a compromise revision adopting some of the 1662 alterations and then, by the middle of the century, conformed to the wording found in the *BCP*. In this form, or a very similar one, it continued to appear in other collections of psalms and/ or hymns in the 19th century. As a hymn for Whitsuntide, the 1889 supplement to *Hymns Ancient and Modern* (which became a standard part of that hymnal through 1924) included a 9-stanza abridgement (as no. 735).

Tune: DCM, D minor (*HTI* 168a, Frost 1). First included in *1561c*, though it may have been printed on a separate sheet and tried out at St. Margaret Pattens parish church, London, as early as 1559 (see p. 1024). The first three phrases bear a strong resemblance to the *1561b* PSALM 70 (*HTI* 140, Frost 87), which came from the French tune for Pss. 77 and 86 (Pidoux 77a, 86c). It also shares its first phrase with PSALM 15 from *1556* (*HTI* 74, Frost 33). But the structural reprise of the opening in phrase 7 does not occur in the others. *Cosyn 1585* used the tune for a five-voice setting of Ps. 34 and a six-voice setting of Ps. 40. The 1586 revision (see p. 915) recast it in strictly regular rhythm. In some Middleburg editions, starting with *1601b*, it was used also with Ps. 16; Playford in 1677 used it for Ps. 132. An anonymous setting of the tune for five voices is found, unusually, in a late

Ex. 8. Veni, Creator treated as plainsong hymn

Source of music: *Hymnorum cum notis opusculu[m], secundu[m] usum insignis ecclesie Sarisburiensis* [Antwerp: C. Ruremond], 1525 (*STC* 16131), fol. 67v, "In die penthecosten ad matutinas." Solid slurs represent ligatures in the source; the broken slurs are editorial, as is the underlaid text.

16th-century manuscript (Oxford, Christ Church, Mus. 984–88). It remained popular in England up to about 1740.

Other musical settings: The *BCP* rubric required the hymn to be "sayed or song" after the Gospel reading at services for the ordination of priests and the consecration of bishops. It is not clear what music was intended. Cranmer, if it was he, had chosen the popular "Sternhold's meter" rather than the iambic tetrameters (LM) of the Latin original, but it could still have been easily adapted to the 11th-century plainsong melody *Veni Creator Spiritus* (see Ex. 8), and may have been until 1554, and perhaps after 1558 in conservative circles.[19] Since ordination was

---

[19] Ex. 8 shows how it can be fitted to the tune, though we cannot be sure how the notes would have been redistributed to accommodate the CM text. A similar process was used by Robert Crowley in his *Psalter of David* (see p. 523, Ex. 3). The little available evidence suggests that plainsong hymns were sung in even notes, as the notation implies. See More, "The Performance of Plainsong," 126–9. For a dissenting view see Haar,

a cathedral service, choirs would generally have been available to sing the hymn in faburden (defined on p. 1038). It could also have been used at Whitsuntide.

However, the Catholic associations of the old tune probably hastened its banishment. In Edward Lowe's *Short Direction for the Performance of Cathedral Service* (1661) the hymn appears with its *WBP* tune, "To be sung at the Ordination of Priests," harmonized for four voices. In 1755 William Tans'ur matched the older translation to a tune of his own (St. Asaph's) as "Whitsunday Hymn." It was again becoming customary for a special hymn to be sung on that festival in parish churches. The Oxford Movement made the practice more widespread. Hymn-anthems based on the *WBP* text were composed by several 19th- and 20th-century composers, including Gilbert Heathcote (1820?), Hugh Blair (1907), and Bernard Naylor (1973).

Venite

Text: This versification of Ps. 95 first appeared in *1556w*, the only psalm paraphrase original to that collection. Although it was included in its numerical place (numbered as in the Vulgate as Ps. 94) among the psalms inherited from the Edwardian editions and *1556*, its addition can be explained by the fact that the psalm is part of the 1552 order for Morning Prayer. The paraphrast worked from the Great Bible, but expanded liberally on his source in places (e.g., ll. 7–8, 17–18). This text remained anonymous through its printing history; the most probable candidate for author is William Samuel, whose initials appear on five other *1556w* texts in "Sternhold's meter" following the metrical psalms (including the *WBP*'s "The Lord be thanked"). *1560a* also printed it with the psalms, replacing the metrical argument with a prose one apparently newly-written for the purpose. In *1561c* and *1561d*, the text was moved (with its argument) to the section of hymns before the psalms. For the first complete edition (*1562a*), Day eliminated nearly all duplicate psalm versifications, including this one. *1563*, however, saw it replaced among the *BCP* texts in the first section of hymns, now without its argument. The argument appeared for the last time in the editions of 1564, though one of them, *STC* 2433, gave the psalm its correct number for the first time. *Venite* was dropped from the small-format Elizabethan and Jacobean editions that included a reduced number of hymns, all following the psalms.

Musical settings and later use of the text: This version of Psalm 95 never earned its own tune in the *WBP*, but was marked to be sung to Benedictus when added in *1563*. It was set to that tune in the Companions from *Day 1563* onwards. By the early 18th century, the text had disappeared from the *WBP*. It appeared in only three 18th-century tunebooks, each time with a different tune.

"Monophony and the Unwritten Tradition," 240–7. We are grateful to David Hiley for guidance on this question.

Te Deum

Text: In the *BCP*, Te Deum is the first text printed after *Venite* as one of two alternative hymns following the lesson at Morning Prayer. This translation of the ancient Latin hymn was first printed in *1561c*. The *WBP* never included attribution, but the most likely author is Thomas Norton. Some of his other contributions to the 1561 editions were also unattributed there, and the compact, enjambed use of Sternhold's meter is typical of his work.

Later use of the text: In the mid-1690s, the text underwent at least two stages of very light revision, including the first line: by 1700, the first line was uniformly printed as "We praise thee, God, and thee confess" (*WBP* 1751, sig. G1v). This version was part of the standard contents of the *WBP* through its 19th-century editions, but elsewhere lost out to the versification in the 1700 *Supplement* to Tate & Brady's *New Version* ("O God, we praise thee, and confess").

Tune: DCM, D minor (*HTI* 166a, Frost 2). First included in *1561c*, though it may have been printed on a separate sheet and tried out at St. James Garlickhythe, London, in 1560 (see p. 1025). It is in all subsequent musical editions of the *WBP* and the Companions. *Cosyn 1585* set it to a scriptural text, Ps. 55. He changed the tonality by harmonizing the final on a chord of G major, and was followed in this by East and Allison. Playford in 1677 used the tune also for Ps. 41. One tune was written for the revised text in 1713 (*HTI* 754) but it found no favor.

Other musical settings: None are known.

Benedicite

Text: The Benedicite, a song of thanksgiving from one of the apocryphal sections of Daniel 3, is the alternative to the Te Deum in the *BCP* order for Morning Prayer. This versification was first printed in *1561c*. Although never attributed in the *WBP*, it is probably the work of Thomas Norton, who similarly paraphrased Ps. 136 as pairs of one iambic line and one refrain line without accentual meter. The Benedicite was dropped from the small-format Elizabethan and Jacobean editions that placed a reduced roster of hymns after the psalms.

Later use of the text: This versification continued to appear in most editions of the *WBP* until the 1640s, and some editions after the Restoration. *A Supplement to the New Version of the Psalms* included this text from the 6th (1708) edition through the 9th (1725?). In the middle of the 18th-century, this versification was replaced in the *WBP* with a new, anonymous DCM paraphrase ("O all ye works of God the Lord, bless him eternally"; *WBP* 1751, sig. G1v). The original version lived on after that primarily in various Scottish Episcopalian books, which continued to reprint it through the early 19th century.

Tune: 8.4.10, F major (*HTI* 169a, Frost 6). First printed in *1562a*. It appeared in all musical editions of the *WBP* and the Companions, but its unique structure of three unequal phrases did not lend itself to other texts, and it fell out of use after about 1750.

Other musical settings. Two later tunes for this text gained some popularity: John Playford's of 1677 (*HTI* 549, Frost 7), and an anonymous one in *A Supplement to the New Version of Psalms* (*HTI* 650a).

Benedictus

Text: From 1552 on, the *BCP* specified that either this canticle (Luke 1:68–79) or Ps. 100 should follow the second lesson in the order for Morning Prayer. The *WBP*'s versification was first printed in *1556w*. It was not attributed, but may be by William Samuel (see Text note to Venite, above). Whoever the writer was, he stayed close to the Great Bible translation. The text was reprinted after the psalms in *1560a*, and then moved to the section before the psalms in *1561c* and *1561d*.

Later use of the text: It remained a usual part of the *WBP* through the early 19th century, but was little reprinted outside of it.

Tune: DCM, C major (*HTI* 128a, Frost 3). Probably used by the exiles at Wesel, it was first printed in *1560a*. It may have been influenced in its general character by the French Ps. 118 (Pidoux 118b), which became the Scottish tune for that psalm (*HTI* 204a, Frost 131). If so, it had lost the structural repetitions that gave the French tune much of its character. It appeared in all musical editions of the *WBP* and the Companions. Some compilers also used it for the Venite. It retained some popularity in the early 18th century.

Other musical settings: None are known.

Magnificat

Text: The Magnificat, Luke 1:46–55, is the first canticle appointed to be read in the *BCP* order for Evening Prayer (with Ps. 98 provided as an alternative). This versification was first printed in *1556w*, and may be by William Samuel (see Text note to Venite, above). The text appears to be primarily paraphrased from the Great Bible, with some metrical padding. It was included after the psalms in *1560a*, and then moved to its place before the psalms in *1561c* and *1561d*. From

1575 (*STC* 16579.5) until 1650, it also appeared in some editions of the Scottish service and psalm book after the metrical psalms.

Later use of the text: This versification continued to be printed with the *WBP* into the 19th century. In the mid-1690s, a light revision of the text altered the second line to "my spirit evermore" (*WBP* 1751, sig. G2r), although this change was not consistently applied for several years. The text did not enjoy any real popularity outside of the *WBP* and its tune books.

Tune: DCM, Dorian transposed/G minor (*HTI* 131a, Frost 4). Probably used by the exiles at Wesel, it was first printed in *1560a*. It is a clear example of bitonality. In modern terms, the first half seems securely fixed in F major, but the second half moves to G minor and stays there, ending surprisingly on G. The use of dotted rhythms provides some individuality. It did not share the fate of some modally ambiguous tunes, but remained in all musical editions of the *WBP* and survived well into the 18th century, both with its original text and with Ps. 59 (first set to it by Ravenscroft). Joseph Fox, parish clerk of St. Margaret, Westminster, emended it to end on F in 1757 (*HTI* 131b); William Croft, organist of Christ Church, Oxford, went the other way and made it a wholly G-minor tune in 1818 (131c); but neither revision caught on. Ainsworth (1612) set the tune to his own version of Ps. 89.

Other musical settings: The text remained largely wedded to its tune. Richard Brimley, in *Day 1563*, set it instead to a tune of his own (*HTI* 185), in a four-voice arrangement (reprinted as Frost 5), but this is found in only one other publication, dating from 1700.

Nunc dimittis

Text: In the *BCP* order for Evening Prayer, the Nunc dimittis (Luke 2:29–32) follows the first lesson (with Ps. 67 offered as an alternative). This much expanded adaptation and versification was probably first printed in *1556w*, where it would have fallen between the Magnificat and The Lord's Prayer (2) in the leaves missing from the unique exemplar (sig. K1–3). Never attributed in the *WBP*, it may have been written by William Samuel (see Text note to Venite, above). The text first survives in *1560a*, where it appears after the psalms. It was moved to the section before the psalms in *1561c* and *1561d*. From 1575 (*STC* 16579.5) until 1650, it also appeared in nearly all editions of the Scottish service and psalm book after the metrical psalms.

Later use of the text: The versification was a regular part of the *WBP* through its 19th-century editions, albeit in a significantly revised form. In the first years of the 18th century, the first lines changed to "O Lord my God, because my heart /

hath longed earnestly," and other whole lines were replaced (*WBP* 1751, sig. G2r). These attempts at modernization apparently did not succeed in making the text popular enough to gain a place in other collections of hymns.

Tune: DCM, Mixolydian (*HTI* 77a, Frost 37). It was first set to Sternhold's Ps. 19 in *1556*; it survived in that role in the Scottish psalm books, but was linked instead to the Wesel version of the Nunc dimittis in *1560a* and afterwards in all musical editions of the *WBP*. One of the better-constructed tunes in the English repertory, it benefits from the repetition of its first two phrases and their subsequent development. The strong suggestion of triple time is not maintained consistently. All the Companions end their settings with a cadence on G major, undermining its originally modal character. (For Allison's setting see μ27.) John Playford in 1677 altered the cadence to anchor it more firmly in G major (*HTI* 77c), setting it also to Ps. 46, whereas Ely Stansfield in 1714 changed the final phrases to end in C major (77d).

Other musical settings: The text was almost entirely wedded to its tune; its last known appearance in a musical publication dates from 1757.

"Quicunque vult"

Text: The Athanasian Creed, referred to by its Latin incipit "Quicunque vult," was appointed in place of the Apostles' Creed on fifteen feast days in the 1559 *BCP* order for Evening Prayer (Morning after 1662). This versification by Thomas Norton was first printed in *1561c*. In paraphrasing, Norton stayed extraordinarily close to the phrasing of the translation in the *BCP*, and seems to have prioritized concision over clarity. This text was dropped from most small-format Elizabethan and Jacobean editions that reduced the number of hymns.

Later use of the text: The text continued to be printed in the majority of *WBP* editions through the late 17th century, but thereafter appeared only sporadically through the second half of the 18th. By this time, the second line had been altered to "salvation hopes to gain" (*WBP* 1751, sig. G2r-v). Other revisions were limited to untangling some of the most difficult syntax in the original and eliminating obvious archaisms.

Tune: DCM, F major (*HTI* 165, Frost 9). First printed in *1561c*. A very plain tune, it remained in all musical editions of the *WBP* and had its quota of harmonizations in the Companions, but it was not adopted by Playford, and it dropped out of common use, along with its text and prose counterpart, soon after 1700.

Other musical settings: None are known.

The Lamentation of a Sinner

Text: First printed in *1561c*. This is John Marckant's first contribution to the *WBP*; it is not based on a known source. That means that, unlike the previous hymns, there is no *BCP* precedent for the text, although it is possible that it is placed here in imitation of the penitential verses that open Morning Prayer and the confession that follows them. From 1575 (*STC* 16579.5) until 1650, it also appeared in some editions of the Scottish service and psalm book after the metrical psalms.

Later use of the text: The text was a regular part of the *WBP* through its 19th-century editions. In the 1690s, it received a modernizing revision; shortly after 1700 the first line in the *WBP* changed to "O Lord, turn not thy face away" (*WBP* 1751, sig. G3r), though tune books retained the old first line until the 1750s. With a yet different first line, "O Lord, turn not thy face from me," the hymn appeared in the 6th (1708) edition of *A Supplement to the New Version*, continued to appear in subsequent editions and associated hymn collections, and by the 19th century was printed as a part of the *New Version* itself. Various forms of the hymn are also easy to find in other hymn and psalm collections of the 19th and 20th centuries, including *Hymns Ancient and Modern* in virtually all editions.

Tune: DCM, D minor (*HTI* 155, Frost 10). First printed in *1561c*. It is in all musical editions of the *WBP* and the Companions, though *Cosyn 1585*, shunning hymns, matched it instead to Ps. 59. Some CM psalms (51(2), 56, 131) often carried the direction "Sing this to the Lamentation", presumably referring to this tune, since they do not fit Lamentation. There is a unique organ setting in the Mulliner Book, oddly titled "Psalmus, O Lorde turne not awaye." It is transposed to G minor, with the tune in the alto register over a rapidly running bass.[20] An anonymous five-voice setting is found in a late-16th-century manuscript (Oxford, Christ Church, Mus. MSS. 984–88). William Lawes used text and tune for one of his *12 Psalms* (c. 1640). Playford used the tune additionally for Pss. 77 and 141, and it was later coupled with Tate & Brady's version of Ps. 77, "To God I cried, who to my help / Did graciously appear."

Other musical settings: It is rarely found with any other tune in early sources. But the first stanza was set as a three-voice anthem by John Mundy in his *Songs and Psalmes* (1594), and there are also anthem settings by Edmund Hooper, Nathaniel Giles, and John Bull. Hooper's was still in use in 1664, when its text was listed in Clifford (1663). When the hymn was revised as "O Lord, turn not thy

---

[20] British Library Add. MS. 30513. For a modern edition see MB 1 (2011), no. 109. The rhythms correspond to those found in *1562a* and later editions.

face from me" for *Hymns Ancient and Modern* (1861) the editors chose the Welsh tune ST. MARY's (1621: *HTI* 542a, Frost 333a), which has since become standard.

The Humble Suit of a Sinner

Text: First printed in *1562a*. Like John Marckant's earlier penitential hymn "The Lamentation of a Sinner," it is not based on a known source. Initially the two hymns may have been printed next to each other because they share a genre. It seems to quickly have become popular, and it was moved up to a position immediately after Veni, Creator in *1569b* and *1569c*, where it would remain in all subsequent editions that had a section of hymns before the psalms. From 1575 (*STC* 16579.5) until 1650, it also appeared in some editions of the Scottish service and psalm book after the metrical psalms.

Later use of the text: The first line evolved into "O Lord, on whom I do depend" by the 1640s. In this form, the hymn continued to appear in a handful of other collections of psalms and hymns without printed tunes through the middle of the 19th century.

Tune: DCM, D minor (*HTI* 170a, Frost 8). First printed in *1562a*. Its first five phrases are essentially the same as those of PSALM 35 (*HTI* 170b, Frost 57: see pp. 132–3), also first printed in *1562a*. Parsons set both tunes for four voices in *Day 1563*, but most of the later Companions chose this version, which lasted through all the musical editions of the *WBP*. It was often referred to as the tune for certain psalms without proper tunes, especially Pss. 36–43 and 55. An anonymous five-voice setting is found in a late-16th-century manuscript (Oxford, Christ Church, Mus. MSS. 984–88). *Cosyn 1585* and Playford in his *Whole Book of Psalms* (1677) matched it to Psalm 38. William Lawes used text and tune as one of his *12 Psalms* (c. 1640), and it is in several 18th-century tunebooks.

Other musical settings: The first stanza was set as a four-voice anthem by John Mundy in his *Songs and Psalmes* (1594), and by John Amner (1579–1641) in his *Sacred Hymns* (1615). Anthem settings of the whole hymn by Nathaniel Giles (c. 1588–1633) and John Holmes (d. 1629) are listed in Clifford (1663, 1664). In 1794 John Randall of Cambridge, in his *Collection of Psalm & Hymn Tunes*, set it to the Welsh tune ST. MARY's (*HTI* 542a, Frost 333a), which he renamed PLAYFORD; but this pairing was not generally adopted, and the hymn is not found in modern hymnals.

The Lord's Prayer (1)

Text: First printed in *1561c*, and attributed in *1561d* to Thomas Norton. With this versification, the *WBP* returned to texts appointed in the *BCP* for common prayer. Before the final collects at Morning and Evening Prayer, "the Minister, Clarkes, and people shall saye the Lordes praier in Englyshe, with a loud voice." It is difficult to imagine a metrical paraphrase that follows the *BCP* wording more precisely. In most Elizabethan and Jacobean editions that reduced the number of hymns, however, this version was dropped in favor of The Lord's Prayer (2).

Later use of the text: By 1700, preferences between the two versifications of the Lord's Prayer had reversed, and Norton's version was more frequently printed in the *WBP* (though, given the lack of settings in contemporary tunebooks, was probably not sung). The second line became "hallowed be thy name" (omitting "Lord") in the middle of the 18th century, but the hymn disappeared from the *WBP* within a few decades afterward.

Tune: TCM, Dorian/D minor (*HTI* 156, Frost 11). First printed in *1561c*. This long tune, to be sung only once, has six pairs of 8.6 iambic lines, all of which are treated as fourteeners. There is a special effort to cater for the rare enjambment between lines 4 and 5, resulting in an unbroken succession of 26 minims. Phrase 9 treats "temptation" as four syllables by means of an additional note, adding a minim to the phrase length and hence subverting the otherwise regular duple-time pattern. In the Wolfe revision of 1586 (see pp. 923–4), and still more in *East 1592*, phrases were regrouped to match the various petitions in the prayer; this was feasible in the absence of subsequent stanzas sung to the same music. The tune survived in all the musical editions of the *WBP*, but was ignored by Playford and attracted few later compilers, probably because the paraphrase itself had outlived its usefulness.

Other musical settings: None are known.

The Ten Commandments (1)

Text: First printed in *1561c*. It was presumably added to echo the reading of the Commandments at the start of the *BCP* Communion service. The first 6 lines (Exod. 20:1–2) are not included in the *BCP*, so Norton must have been imitating Marot's French paraphrase or, more likely, Whittingham's translation of it (The Ten Commandments (2)). Aside from those first verses, which he took from the Great Bible, Norton worked from the *BCP* text of the Commandments. In most Elizabethan and Jacobean small-format editions that reduced the number of hymns, this version lost out to The Lord's Prayer (2).

Later use of the text: Either because it was more literal or because it had a greater number of tunes available, by the late 17th century this version was more frequently included in the *WBP* than Whittingham's. In the 18th century, the first line changed to "Hear Israel, and what I say" (possibly accidentally, given that most late 17th-century editions printed "Hark" as "Heark": see *WBP* 1751, G2v). It, too, however, dropped from the *WBP* by 1800, and there is no sign of it in other collections.

Tune: DCM, A minor (*HTI* 167a, Frost 12). First printed in *1561c*. This tune has a clear structure and tonality, but suffers from over-repetition of the five notes ending the first phrase. It appears in all musical editions of the *WBP* and the Companions, but was passed over by Playford and disappeared from musical collections soon after 1700, though it was briefly matched with Tate & Brady's version of the Ten Commandments, "God spake these words: 'O Israel, hear.'" Possibly by mistake, Benjamin Smith printed it in his *Harmonious Companion* (1732) with the wrong text, that of The Humble Suit of a Sinner. That was its last known appearance.

Other musical settings: None are known.

PSALMS OF DAVID

Psalm 1
The man is blest that hath not bent

Text: The **psalm** was one of Sternhold's original nineteen first printed in *1548* (see p. 799) and was revised for *1556*. As for most of his paraphrases, Sternhold drew primarily on the Vulgate and on the three English translations by Miles Coverdale: the Coverdale Bible, the Great Bible, and his parallel text of the Vulgate with English translation. Whittingham's revisions here most commonly replace obvious debts to the Vulgate in favor of readings from the Great Bible. Sternhold's "chair of pestilence" (*cathedra pestilentiae*), for example, became "scorner's chair" ("the seat of the scornful"). The **argument** was first printed in *1556*; it was reprinted in the 1557 Genevan Psalter and subsequently in the Geneva Bible. It is a translation of Calvin's summary of the psalm in his *Commentary on the Psalms*. The marginal notes first appearing in *1556* and reprinted in some early Elizabethan editions also come primarily from Calvin's commentary.

Incipit Beatus vir [qui non abiit in consilio impiorum]: Blessed is the man that hath not gone in the counsel of the ungodly

i Esdras: Latin (and Greek) form of Ezra, a scribe associated with the compilation of the Torah and psalms during the Babylonian captivity. His return to Jerusalem and role in enforcing Jewish law is narrated in Ezra 7–10.

1 *Marginal note to v. 1*: When a man hath given once place to his concupiscence, he beginneth to forget himself in his sin, and so at length falleth into a contempt of God, which the prophet here calleth the chair or seat of scorners. *1556*

9 *Marginal note to v. 3*: Jer. 17.b. [17:8] *1556*

17 *Marginal note to v. 4*: Although the wicked seem to bear the swinge in this world, yet the Lorde scattereth them like chaff with a blast of his mouth. *1556, 1561d, 1562a* [**swinge**: rule, authority].

Later use of the text: The opening lines changed in the late 17th century ("The man is blest that hath not lent / to wicked men his ear," *WBP* 1751), and the psalm underwent a more thorough revision early in the 18th, with the result that very few of the Elizabethan lines remained unchanged. It was, however, one of the more popular texts from the *WBP* while psalmody formed an important part of congregational singing. Collections of psalm and hymn texts continued to incorporate it until at least the middle of the 19th century.

Tune: DCM, D minor (*HTI* 158a, Frost 15). First printed in *1561c*. In the early English editions it competed with *HTI* 60 (see below) but from 1565 it was in every musical edition and all the Companions. Pss. 2 and 4 are referred to this tune. *East 1592* followed by using it for Ps. 2 as well as Ps. 1. The change of the 7th note from A to Bb, which prevailed from 1586, was doubtless influenced by LAMENTATION OF A SINNER. In this revised form (*HTI* 158b: see p. 926) it was one of the eight long tunes chosen by Playford for his *Introduction to the Skill of Musick* in 1658. An anonymous 17th-century setting for voice and instrumental bass survives in British Library Add. MS. 29481, fol. 3v. The tune, which benefits from its consistent underlying duple-time beat, remained popular in the 18th century, when it was sometimes misattributed to Thomas Morley, whose arrangement had appeared in Ravenscroft (1621). From 1702 it was often matched with Tate & Brady's Ps. 1, "How blest is he who ne'er consents." Sir John Hawkins included it as one of five ancient psalm tunes in his *General History of Music* (1776), 3: 515, and from there it entered antiquarian collections by William Crotch (1803) and William Cross (1818).

Other musical settings: Of 49 four-voice settings by John Sheppard of the texts in *Al Such Psalmes* (1549), this is the only one that survives in complete form, in the Mulliner Book: see Ex. 4 (p. 525) and µ5. Of the two Geneva tunes *HTI* 60 (see App. 5, p. 985) was the earlier, dating from *1556*, and would become the Scottish choice, but it is not found in English editions after *1564*. The text was introduced to the Magdalen House chapel in 1760 coupled with Philip Hart's PRESCOT (*HTI* 837a), which became the favored tune in England and the United States.

Psalm 2
Why did the Gentiles tumults raise

Text: The **psalm** was one of Sternhold's original nineteen first printed in *1548* (see p. 800) and was revised for *1556*. Along with the Coverdale sources that he regularly drew on and the Vulgate, Sternhold chose several phrases from George Joye's English paraphrase. These include "Gentiles" (l. 1) and "trouble them" (l. 19). In *1556*, the most important revision is to v. 6, which in Sternhold's original is spoken by the king who has been appointed and in Whittingham's version by God, who announces that he has annointed the speaker king. (These interpretations derive from the Vulgate and the Great Bible—as well as French Protestant scholarship—respectively.) The **argument** was first printed in *1556* and was reprinted with minor changes in the 1557 Genevan Psalter as well as the Geneva Bible. It slightly abridges Calvin's summary in the *Commentary on the Psalms*. The marginal notes first appearing in *1556* and reprinted in some early Elizabethan editions (see below) also come primarily from Calvin's commentary.

Incipit Quare fremuerunt gentes: Why have the heathen raged
10 *Marginal note to* **bonds:** In Hebrew, great ropes or cables. *1556, 1561d, 1562a*
28 *Marginal gloss to* **today:** That is to say, as touching man's knowledge, because it was the first time that David appeared to be elected of God. So it is applied to Christ, because he was then first manifested to the world. *1556*
42, 44 Fear and the second syllable of **manner** were, in the 1540s, closer in pronunciation than currently, though probably still not a perfect rhyme. *1548* spelled them "fere" and "manere."
45 *Marginal gloss to* **kiss:** In sign of homage. *1556*
49 *Marginal gloss to v. 12b:* For when they shall say "peace" and "safety," then shall the destruction suddenly come. 1. Thes. 5.a. [5:3] *1556*

Musical settings and later use of the text: John Sheppard composed two four-voice settings of Sternhold's unrevised text in Edward VI's time, but in each case only the uppermost voice part survives (see p. 518). In *1556*, and in Scottish psalm books starting in 1575, the revised psalm was set to *HTI* 61 (Frost 16), but in the English books this setting did not get beyond *1560a*; in the *WBP* it was usually referred to PSALM 1. *East 1592* followed suit, but from 1594 East used the common tune OXFORD, for which Ravenscroft (1621) substituted CAMBRIDGE. With the latter tune the psalm remained popular throughout the 18th century and beyond, and several new tunes were composed for it by country psalmodists. A number of lines of the text were thoroughly reworked in the late-17th-century revision, including removal of reference to Jews in the first verse.

Psalm 3
O Lord, how are my foes increased

Text: The **psalm** was one of Sternhold's original nineteen first printed in *1548* (see p. 801) and was revised for *1556*. Sternhold's original version shows a mixture of choices from Coverdale's three translations. The revision by Whittingham supplies the first half of v. 7, missing in Sternhold's version. Whittingham also restores the declarative mood of the prose sources in the last verse, which Sternhold had treated as an imperative. The **argument** was first printed in *1556* and was reprinted without change in the 1557 Genevan Psalter and with slight revision in the Geneva Bible. In addition to Calvin's summary in the *Commentary on the Psalms*, it is related to the argument from the French metrical psalter. The marginal notes first appearing in *1556* and reprinted in some early Elizabethan editions (see below) also come primarily from Calvin's commentary.

Incipit Domine, quid multiplicati [sunt qui tribulant me?]: Lord, why are they multiplied in number which trouble me?
i For the story of Absalom's coup d'état, see 2 Sam. 15.
4 *Marginal note to end of v. 2*: "Selah" signifieth a lifting up of the voice in singing, which declareth some notable matter and worthy to be well weighed. *1556*
12 *Marginal note to end of v. 4*: Selah *1556, 1561d*
17 *Marginal note to v. 6*: God's strength must not be measured by man's weakness, and therefore we ought to fear no dangers. *1556, 1561d, 1562a*
21 *Marginal note to v. 7*: He returneth to his prayer. *1556, 1561d, 1562a*
25 *Marginal note to v. 8*: God will deliver his Church from all dangers, because he favoureth it. *1556, 1561d, 1562a*
28 *Marginal note to end of v. 8*: Selah *1556*

Later use of the text: While it remained in some collections of psalms and hymns into the 19th century, there is little evidence of this paraphrase's popularity divorced from its tune. In the early 18th century, the second line became "who vex me more and more" (*WBP* 1751).

Tune: DCM, F major (*HTI* 62a, Frost 17). First printed in *1556*. The opening phrase recalls PSALM 100, but there is no further resemblance. It is not clear why a long note was chosen for the word "heart" in phrase 3. The last two phrases are unstable; the original ending was maintained in the Scottish psalm book, but the present version, first printed in *1561c*, prevailed in the *WBP*, where the tune was a permanent fixture, though the ending was revised in 1586 (see p. 927). Pss. 5 and 7–13 were generally referred to it, and often 15 and 17 as well. One series, beginning with *STC* 2472.5 (*1586c*), printed the first half of this tune with Ps. 10. *East 1592* used it for Pss. 3, 5 and 7, and some Middleburg editions starting with

1601b printed it with Ps. 7, but Ps. 3 remained its principal text until its popularity waned after 1750.

Other musical settings: John Sheppard composed two four-voice settings of Sternhold's unrevised text of this psalm in Edward VI's time, but in each case only the uppermost voice part survives (see p. 518). For the *WBP* text at least five other tunes were printed between 1730 and 1782, but none caught on.

Psalm 4
O God that art my righteousness

Text: The **psalm** was one of Sternhold's original nineteen first printed in *1548* (see p. 802) and was revised for *1556*. Among his sources, Sternhold drew most heavily from the Great Bible in paraphrasing this psalm. Whittingham thus revised this psalm unusually lightly, with the exception of providing a new quatrain for the second half of v. 1, which Sternhold had omitted. The **argument** was first printed in *1556*, reprinted unchanged in the 1557 Genevan Psalter, and included in the Geneva Bible without the final hortatory sentence. While the structure of the argument comes from Calvin's summary in the *Commentary on the Psalms*, Whittingham delves into the commentary itself for references to Saul's persecution. The marginal notes first appearing in *1556* and reprinted in some early Elizabethan editions (see below) also come primarily from Calvin's commentary.

Incipit Cum invocarem, exaudivi[t me Deus iustitiae me]: The God of my righteousness heard me when I called upon him
i Saul persecuted David: David's danger and flights from Saul take up most of 1 Sam. 19–27, but the argument may refer to their confrontation in 1 Sam. 24:8–14.
17 *Marginal note to v. 4:* David exhorteth his enemies to repentance for fear of God's judgements. *1556*
25 *Marginal note to v. 6:* He setteth his perfect felicity in God's favour. *1556*
35 *Marginal note to v. 8b:* That being solitary he shall live as if he were amongst many because God doth defend him. *1556*

Musical settings and later use of the text: John Sheppard composed two four-voice settings of Sternhold's unrevised text in Edward VI's time, but in each case only the uppermost voice part survives (see p. 518). Two other Edwardian settings survive: a domestic arrangement for lute, called the Osborn Psalm (see pp. 516–18, Ex.1, and μ1), and an incomplete four-part choral piece which, after the first stanza, switches to Ps. 49 (see p. 524). In *1556* the revised psalm was set to *HTI* 63 (Frost 18), a tune found in only one later source, a Scottish edition of 1575, with a different text. In the *WBP* it was most often referred to PSALM 1 or 3. *East 1592* set it along with 32 other psalms to the common tune LOW DUTCH (the setting is reprinted as Frost 19); Ravenscroft and Playford substituted OXFORD.

The text remained remarkably popular in Anglican circles throughout the 18th century and was set to at least twenty different tunes. By the early 18th century, the first line had changed to "O God, thou art my righteousness" (*WBP* 1751), but the rest remained very close to the Elizabethan original.

Psalm 5
Incline thine ears unto my words

Text: The **psalm** was one of Sternhold's original nineteen first printed in *1548* (see p. 804) and was revised for *1556*. Sternhold mixed readings from his accustomed Coverdale translations, but relied especially heavily on the 1540 version printed in parallel with the Vulgate text. While some of Whittingham's revisions bring the language closer to the Great Bible, his version also reflects some influence from Clément Marot's French paraphrase. See most notably the opening lines of the psalm: "Aux paroles que je veulx dire, / plaise toy l'aureille prester" (*Pseaumes octantetrois*, p. 18) as compared to the Great Bible's "Ponder my words, O Lord, consider my meditation." The **argument** was first printed in *1556*. It is a condensed version of Calvin's summary in his *Commentary on the Psalms*, although the association with Doeg and Achitophel comes (in slightly confused form) from the commentary itself. It was reprinted in the 1557 Genevan Psalter and modified for the Geneva Bible. The marginal notes first appearing in *1556* and reprinted in some early Elizabethan editions (see below) also come primarily from Calvin's commentary.

Incipit Verba mea auribus percipe: Hark my words with thine ears
i Doeg: an Edomite and the chief herdsman to Saul. He informed Saul that the fleeing David had received food and Goliath's sword from Ahimelech, the high priest at Nob, thus provoking Saul to order the execution of eighty-five priests. When none of the Israelites would lay hands on the priests, Doeg killed them all himself. See 1 Sam. 22:6–19. **Achitophel:** actually David's unfaithful counselor, rather than Saul's. He threw in his lot with David's son Absalom, during the latter's revolt against his father; see 2 Sam. 15:12, 15:31, and 16:15–17:23.
13 *Marginal note to v. 6:* The wicked cannot escape God's punishment, who will judge all the world. *1556, 1561d, 1562a*
21 *Marginal note to v. 8:* In the deepest of his temptations he putteth his full confidence in God. *1556, 1561d, 1562a*
43 *Marginal note:* Hebrew thou wilt crown him. *1556;* that wilt *1561d;* that will *1562a*

Musical settings and later use of the text: John Sheppard composed two four-voice settings of Sternhold's unrevised text in Edward VI's time, but in each case only the uppermost voice part survives (see p. 518). The revised psalm was set in *1556* to *IITI* 64 (Frost 20), a tune that was adopted for Ps. 109 in the Scottish series but did not appear in the *WBP*, where the usual cross-reference was to PSALM 3. *East 1592* followed suit, but East's later editions used CAMBRIDGE. Playford's choice in 1677 of *HTI* 536a, which he named LONDON, was decisive for the early 18th century, by which time the text had undergone extensive revisions (including the first lines, which became "Incline thine ears, O Lord, and let / my words have free access": *WBP* 1751). It nevertheless faded from view before the turn of the 19th century.

Psalm 6
Lord, in thy wrath reprove me not

Text: The **psalm** was first printed in *1549b* (see p. 805) and revised in *1556*. Sternhold consulted all three of Coverdale's prose translations as well as the Vulgate. Whittingham changed only two of Sternhold's lines (22 and 25), the first one without real difference in meaning. The second is a departure from the Great Bible's understanding of the Hebrew, which Sternhold followed ("My beauty is gone for very trouble") in favor of the reading that would later be given in the Geneva Bible ("Mine eye is dimmed for despite"). The **argument** was first printed in *1556*, and was reprinted in the 1557 Geneva Psalter and the Geneva Bible. It translates the argument from the 1551 French metrical psalter, with some reference to Calvin's summary from the *Commentary on the Psalms*. The marginal notes, first printed in *1556* and picked up in some early Elizabethan editions, engage with Calvin's commentary but in this psalm do not fully agree with him.

Incipit 1. Domine, ne in furore tuo [arguas me]: Lord, rebuke me not in thy heavy indignation [The numeral "1" is residual from the system of identifying psalms by incipit rather than number; it distinguishes this from Psalm 37, which opens with the same phrase.]

i his sins: This is the first of the seven Penitential Psalms, traditionally associated with David's repentance for adulterously appropriating Bathsheba and causing her husband, Uriah the Hittite, to be killed (see 2 Sam. 11–12). Calvin, however, frames the psalm as a recollection of and reflection on some unspecified affliction, possibly a grave illness.

17 *Marginal note to v. 5:* He feared not so much the death of the body but trembled as it were for fear of God's judgement, and so waxeth dumb and could not praise God. *1556*; waxeth dim *1561d*; waxed dim *1562a* [This interpretation departs from Calvin's, who wrote at length about David's fear of physical death.]

25 *Marginal note to* **sight:** Hebrew: mine eye is eaten, as with worms. *1556, 1561d, 1562a*

29 *Marginal note to v. 8:* God sendeth comfort and boldness in affliction. *1556, 1561d, 1562a*

Later use of the text: The text, in nearly its Elizabethan form, substantially outlasted the proper tune and was frequently incorporated into collections of psalms and hymns through the mid-19th century.

Tune: DCM, D minor (*HTI* 65, Frost 21). First printed in *1556*. The opening phrase recalls Luther's *Vater unser*, later used for LORD'S PRAYER (2). The gradually increased use of semibreves tends to undermine the tune's integrity. Beginning with *1561d*, some editions of the *WBP* omitted the tune, substituting a cross-reference to PSALM 1. But it continued to appear with its text in the Companions, and (although Playford ignored it) in some conservative tunebooks until 1732.

Other musical settings: John Sheppard composed a four-voice setting of Sternhold's text in Edward VI's time, but only the uppermost voice part survives (see p. 518). For the *WBP* text a few editions, starting with Henry Denham's (*1588b*), followed *Cosyn 1585* in assigning the common tune LOW DUTCH to this text, doubled so as to look like a DCM tune (see LOW DUTCH Version B, p. 1004). The opening stanzas were set as anthems by a number of Elizabethan and Jacobean composers including John Amner, William Byrd (*Collected Works*, 12:37), Richard Gibbs, Nathaniel Giles, and John Holmes; those by Amner, Gibbs, and Holmes are listed in Clifford (1663 or 1664). William Lawes used text and tune as one of his *12 Psalms* (c. 1640). In the 18th century the favorite tune among many was the one selected by Playford in 1677, BRISTOL (*HTI* 547a, Frost 22).

Psalm 7
O Lord my God, I put my trust

Text: The **psalm** was first printed in *1549b* (see p. 806) and revised in *1556*. Most of Sternhold's choices in paraphrasing can be accounted for among Coverdale's prose versions. The *1556* revisions are extensive, affecting thirty-one of the psalm's sixty-six lines. Where Whittingham made changes, he did so not to move the sense closer to the Great Bible but toward language that he would also use in the prose Psalter of 1557. The **argument** was first printed in *1556* and reprinted without emendation in the 1557 Genevan Psalter and the Geneva Bible. Its primary source is the summary from Calvin's *Commentary on the Psalms*. The marginal notes first appearing in *1556* and reprinted in some early Elizabethan editions (see below) also come primarily from Calvin's commentary.

Incipit Domine Deus meus, in te speravi: My Lord God, in thee have I put my trust
i Chus: The name comes from the Hebrew heading to the psalm, given thus in the Geneva Bible: "Shiggaion of David, which he sang unto the Lord, concerning the words of Cush [Chush] the son of Jemini." Calvin's commentary

associated the "words of Chus" with the slander the speaker complains of in v. 3 (Calvin, *Commentaries*, fol. 18v).

5 *Marginal note to* **lion**: Saul *1556*

9 *Marginal note to v. 3a*: Wherewith Chus chargeth me. *1556, 1561d, 1562a*

11 *Marginal note to v. 3b*: He rejoiceth that God only doth approve his cause. *1556, 1561d, 1562a*

17 *Marginal note to v. 6*: A sign of a pure conscience. *1556, 1561d, 1562a*

20 *Marginal note to end of v. 6*: Selah. *1556, 1561d, 1562a*

31 *Marginal note to* **righteousness**: As touching my behaviour towards Saul and mine enemies. *1556, 1561d, 1562a*

44 *Marginal note to v.12*: He derideth Saul's enterprises, being surely persuaded to be preserved by God's favour. *1556, 1561d*; enterprise *1562a*

53 *Marginal note to v. 14*: The wicked seem to labour of child till they have compassed their mischiefs; Isa. 26.c. [26: 17–18] *1556, 1561d, 1562a*

57 *Marginal note to v. 15*: The wicked man is beaten with his own rod. *1556*; beate *1561d, 1562a*

Musical settings and later use of the text: John Sheppard composed a four-voice setting of Sternhold's text in Edward VI's time, but only the uppermost voice part survives (see p. 518). The tune in *1556* (*HTI* 66a, Frost 23) is a pure specimen of the already archaic Phrygian mode, with its second degree a half step above the final and its prominent sixth degree (μ7). This became the Scottish tune for Ps. 7, but was not adopted in England after *1560a* and dropped out of use along with its mode. *East 1592* followed the usual *WBP* cross-reference by using the tune of PSALM 3 for this text, but in later editions East set it to OXFORD, imitated in Middleburg editions from *1601b*. Playford, followed by some 18th-century compilers, chose WORCESTER (382a) instead. The text was only lightly modernized except for the complete replacement of lines 21–4 (v. 6) with a more literal paraphase in the early 18th century. In 18th-century psalm collections other than the *WBP*, though, it was frequently supplanted by later versions of the psalm.

Psalm 8
O God our Lord, how wonderful

Text: The **psalm** was first printed in *1549b* (see p. 808) and revised in *1556*. Sternhold mixed readings from Coverdale's three prose versions. The revisions in *1556* do not, for the most part, represent substantial changes in meaning so much as shadings of interpretation. The **argument** was first printed in *1556*, and was adopted for the 1557 Genevan Psalter and (without the last phrase) for the Geneva Bible. It expands on Calvin's summary in his *Commentary on the Psalms*. The marginal note first appearing in *1556* and reprinted in some early Elizabethan editions (see below) also come primarily from Calvin's commentary.

Incipit Domine, Deus [*sc.* Dominus] noster [quam admirabile est nomen tuum]: Lord our God, how wonderful is thy name
5 *Marginal note to v. 5*: Herein appeareth the great love of God towards man: Heb. 2. *1556, 1561d, 1562a*

Musical settings and later use of the text: John Sheppard composed a four-voice setting of Sternhold's text in Edward VI's time, but only the uppermost voice part survives (see p. 518). As the first celebratory psalm after a series of penitential ones, this was allotted a joyful C-major tune in *1556* (*HTI* 67, Frost 24). But the tune did not reach the *WBP*, though a variant was adopted for Ps. 14. In the *WBP* it was usually referred to PSALM 3. *East 1592* set it to LOW DUTCH. Playford in 1671 chose a new tune he named LITCHFIELD (*HTI* 536a, Frost 25), but in his *Whole Book of Psalms in Three Parts* (1677) he settled on ST. MARY's (*HTI* 542a, Frost 333a). Revised aggressively in the late 17th century and further in the first years of the 18th, the updated text remained popular in Anglican use and accumulated many tunes in the 18th century. When Michael Beesly coupled a lively fuging tune (1942a) to Tate & Brady's Ps. 8 ("O thou to whom all creatures bow"), his tune assumed the name PSALM 8 and was then set to the present text in *A Choice Collection of Church Musick* (1749) by Joseph Watts, a Warwickshire singing teacher.[21] This caught on in country churches; the tune was sometimes named OTFORD. The psalm was sung at the Magdalen Chapel with the tune CROWLE (1084a) and at the Foundling Hospital with Croft's ST. ANNE's (664a). It persisted in common use, with several different tunes, well into the 19th century.

Psalm 9
With heart and mouth unto the Lord

Text: The **psalm** was first printed in *1549b* (see p. 809) and revised in *1556*. As usual, Sternhold appears to have selected readings from all three of Coverdale's prose versions and also employs cognates to phrases in the Vulgate. In *1556*, the revisions are numerous (affecting twenty-nine lines) but often very minor, such as substituting "may" and "might" for "should" in v. 14 or reversing the order of the ideas in v. 16. The most substantial change is an entirely new quatrain for v. 6 (see below). The **argument** was first printed in *1556* and reprinted without modification in the 1557 Genevan Psalter and the Geneva Bible. It is a paraphrase of Calvin's summary in his *Commentary on the Psalms*. The marginal notes first appearing in *1556* and reprinted in some early Elizabethan editions (see below) also come primarily from Calvin's commentary.

---

[21] For a modern edition of this setting see MB 85, no. 11.

Incipit Confitebor tibi, Domine: I will give thanks unto thee, O Lord

13 *Marginal note to v. 4*: God only defendeth the just cause. *1556, 1561d, 1562a*

21 As the variants show, this quatrain proved very puzzling to later readers. The Great Bible seems to suggest that the speaker's enemy has effectively erased all trace of the cities: "O thou enemy: destructions are come to a perpetual end, even as the cities which thou hast destroyed: their memorial is perished with them." Sternhold, however, reversed this meaning, with God taking away the enemies' force (and emendations in the 1580s would return to a similar interpretation). The Geneva Bible's far more ambiguous version is closer to Whittingham's: "O enemy, destructions are come to a perpetual end, and thou hast destroyed the cities: their memorial is perished with them." The marginal note in the Geneva Bible calls the verse "A derision of the enemy, that mindeth nothing but destruction: but the Lord will deliver his, and bring him into judgement." The mock-congratulations of "thou hast made good dispatch" is apparently Whittingham's rendition of this derision.

39 *Marginal note to* **suit**: We seek God either by prayer or by upright and godly life. *1556, 1561d*; god there by *1562a*

61 *Marginal note to v. 16*: The Hebrew willeth men to meditate diligently on this thing. *1556, 1561d, 1562a*

Musical settings and later use of the text: John Sheppard composed a four-voice setting of Sternhold's text in Edward VI's time, but only the uppermost voice part survives (see p. 518). An unreformed Dorian melody (*HTI* 68, Frost 26) was assigned in *1556* but was retained only in the Scottish psalm book. In the *WBP* the psalm was usually referred to PSALM 3. It was later set to several common tunes, first in *East 1592* to CAMBRIDGE (μ24), and it appeared with this tune in Middleburg editions from *1601b*. Ravenscroft chose LITCHFIELD (371a), Playford preferred GLOUCESTER (368e), and with these and other tunes it continued to appear in tunebooks until after 1800. The first line in these later publications appears as "With heart and mouth to thee, O Lord" (*WBP* 1751). Along with other modernizations, the late-17th-century revision also replaced the problematic quatrain beginning at line 21 and lines 61–4 (v. 16).

Psalm 10
What is the cause that thou, O Lord

Text: The **psalm** was first printed in *1549b* (see p. 811) and revised in *1556*. Sternhold alternates between phrasing from the Great Bible and the 1540 English/Latin parallel, but also allows himself some freedom with his descriptions of both the vicious oppressors and their victims. Whittingham's *1556* revisions largely bring the paraphrase into better accord with the literal meaning of the psalm, with some word choices taken from the Great Bible. He also, however, shows some influence from Clément Marot's French metrical version, taking, e.g., the "heaps of poor men" in line 39 from Marot's "Grand quantité de povres gens." The **argument** was first printed in 1556 and reprinted in both the 1557 Genevan Psalter and the Geneva Bible. It is a very close translation of the first half of Calvin's summary from his *Commentary on the Psalms*. The marginal notes first appearing in *1556* and reprinted in some early Elizabethan editions (see below) also come primarily from Calvin's commentary.

Incipit Ut quid, Domine[, recessisti longe?]: Why art thou gone so far off, O Lord?
25 *Marginal note to v. 7*: He meaneth that wickedness is so far overgrown that God must needs now help, or never. *1556, 1561d, 1562a*
28 travail: The primary meaning is "work," but the image of a tongue running on (traveling) is latent.
63 *Marginal note to v. 16b*: By the heathen he meaneth the hypocrites which gloried as if they had been of the Church. *1556, 1561d, 1562a*
69 *Marginal note to v. 18*: God helpeth when man's aid ceaseth. *1556*

Musical settings and later use of the text: John Sheppard composed a four-voice setting of Sternhold's text in Edward VI's time, but only the uppermost voice part survives (see p. 518). Ps. 10 was set to a transposed Phrygian-mode tune (*HTI* 69, Frost 27) in *1556*, but from *1558* and on into the Scottish editions it shared the tune of Psalm 2 (*HTI* 61, Frost 16). In the *WBP* it was usually referred to PSALM 3, until suddenly in *1585a* it acquired a strange four-line tune of its own (*HTI* 268: see p. 986), which was never seen again after a reprint of 1592. Next, in *1586d*, it was assigned the first half of PSALM 3, which made a plausible short tune; this also died after the last reprint of that series. *East 1592* set it to OXFORD. Some Middleburg editions, starting with *1601b*, used NUNC DIMITTIS for this psalm. By the early 18th century, the second line had been amended to "so far off now dost stand?" (*WBP* 1751), with altered rhyme scheme; only one other quatrain (lines 53–6) was as affected by the revision. Several other tunes were tried before it fell out of common use after about 1750.

Psalm 11
I trust in God, how dare ye then

Text: The **psalm** was first printed in *1549b* (see p. 813) and revised in *1556*. Sternhold based his paraphrase on Coverdale's various prose translations as well as the Vulgate. There were relatively few changes in *1556*, the most substantial a new version of v. 3. The argument was first printed in *1556* and reprinted in both the 1557 Genevan Psalter and the Geneva Bible. It translates Calvin's summary from his *Commentary on the Psalms*, with the addition of "governing the good and wicked men."

Incipit In Domino confido: In the Lord I put my trust

17 *Marginal note to v. 4b*: All things are governed by God's providence. *1556, 1561d, 1562a*

9–10 These lines, new in Whittingham's revision, draw on Calvin's commentary to interpret a fairly opaque half-verse given in the Great Bible and 1557 Genevan Psalter as "For the foundations will be cast down."

25 *Marginal note to v. 6*: As in the destruction of Sodom and Gomorrah. *1556, 1561d, 1562a*

Musical settings and later use of the text: John Sheppard composed a four-voice setting of Sternhold's text in Edward VI's time, but only the uppermost voice part survives (see p. 518). Its *1556* tune (*HTI* 70, Frost 28) was not adopted in the *WBP*, where it was usually referred to PSALM 3. It was later set to several common tunes, first in *East 1592* to LOW DUTCH. Some *WBP* editions starting in 1622 allocated it to GLASSENBURIE, renamed BATH, and later revised with its name spelled GLASTENBURY by Playford. Among lighter textual revisions, the first quatrain was entirely replaced in the late 17th century, changing the first lines to "In God the Lord I put my trust; / why say ye to my soul" (*WBP* 1751). In this form it continued to appear in many tunebooks; the immensely popular tune BANGOR (*HTI* 1390a) was composed for it by William Tans'ur in 1735.

Psalm 12
Help, Lord, for good and godly men

Text: The **psalm** was first printed in *1549b* (see p. 814) and revised in *1556*. In this paraphrase, Sternhold drew most heavily on the Great Bible and Coverdale Bible translations. Whittingham revised only six lines in *1556*, all of them retaining part of Sternhold's phrasing. The **argument** was first printed in *1556*, reprinted verbatim in the 1557 Genevan Psalter, and adopted for the Geneva Bible without the final half-sentence. It translates Calvin's summary from his *Commentary on the Psalms*.

Incipit Salvum me fac, Deus: Save me, O God

i the prophet: David.

19 *Marginal note to v. 6b*: The Lord doth deliver his from all dangers. *1556, 1561d, 1562a*

25 *Marginal note to v. 7*: God cannot deceive them that put their trust in him. *1556, 1561d, 1562a*

Musical settings and later use of the text: John Sheppard composed a four-voice setting of Sternhold's text in Edward VI's time, but only the uppermost voice part survives (see p. 518). In *1556* it was assigned an unreconstructed Phrygian-mode tune (*HTI* 71a, Frost 29), beginning on the 4th scale degree, which never reached the *WBP*, where it was usually referred to Psalm 3. It was later set to several common tunes, first in *East 1592* to Cambridge, with which it appeared in Playford's *Introduction to the Skill of Musick* (1658). But in *The Whole Book of Psalms in Three Parts* (1677) Playford chose Canterbury instead (related to Low Dutch: *HTI* 250h) and that was its usual setting in 18th-century collections. In 1763 Aaron Williams, a Dorset singing teacher, provided an ornate new tune, Buckingham (2924a), and in that form the psalm entered the American repertory in 1767. The text survived well into the 19th century in English collections, but was more popular in the United States.

Psalm 13
How long wilt thou forget me, Lord,

Text: The **psalm** was first printed in *1549b* (see p. 815) and revised in *1556*. Sternhold drew most of his readings from the Great Bible with some admixture from the Coverdale Bible, but also expanded the text slightly in several places. When Whittingham revised for *1556*, he generally removed these expansions in favor of more literal paraphrase, with the exception of the last two lines (see below). The **argument** was first printed in 1556 and reprinted in both the 1557 Genevan Psalter and the Geneva Bible. Whittingham slightly adapted Calvin's summary from his *Commentary on the Psalms*.

Incipit Usquequo, Domine[, oblivisceris me]: How long, O Lord, wilt thou forget me?
17 *Marginal note to v. 5a*: The mercy of God is the cause of our salvation. *1556, 1561d, 1562a*
21 The KJV (and all contemporary English translations) begin v. 6 here.
23–24 These lines, new with Whittingham's *1556* revision, are actually farther from the literal meaning of the text than Sternhold's original paraphrase. The Great Bible and Whittingham's 1557 prose translation both give "because he hath dealt so lovingly with me."

Musical settings and later use of the text: John Sheppard composed a four-voice setting of Sternhold's text in Edward VI's time, but only the uppermost voice part survives (see p. 518). Its *1556* tune (*HTI* 72, Frost 30) was never reprinted. In the *WBP* it was usually referred to Psalm 3. *East 1592* set it to the common tune Oxford. No single tune became widely associated with it, but it continued in occasional use through the 18th century with relatively light revision except at the beginning of the psalm, where more substantial textual changes include the emendation of the second line to "shall it for ever be?" (*WBP* 1751).

Psalm 14
"There is no God," as foolish men

Text: The **psalm** was first printed in *1549b* (see p. 816) and revised in *1556*. Sternhold shows influence from all of Coverdale's prose translations as well as the Vulgate. He carefully omitted, however, several sentences present in all of his sources but shown in the Great Bible in a smaller font, one reserved for passages from the Septuagint that are missing in the Hebrew. In his revision for *1556*, Whittingham frequently inserted language from the Great Bible. He was, however, also looking at Clément Marot's metrical paraphrase, which influenced his new quatrain for v. 5. The **argument** was first printed in *1556* and reprinted in both the 1557 Genevan Psalter and the Geneva Bible. Whittingham based it on Calvin's summary in his *Commentary on the Psalms*, though it is not, in this case, a precise translation.

Incipit Dixit insipiens [in corde suo]: The unwise man hath said in his heart **29** *Marginal note to v. 7b*: Where wicked men reign, all felicity is but very slavery, like to Egypt or Babylon. *1556, 1561d, 1562a* [Calvin comments that the captivity in question is "an oppression at home, whe[n] y[e] wicked beare sway like Tyrants in the Churche" (Calvin, *Commentaries*, fol. 24v)].

Later use of the text: This paraphrase was not frequently selected for eclectic collections of psalms, ceding its place to later versions. Editions of the *WBP* from the late 17th century altered the first line to "There is no God, do foolish men" (*WBP* 1751). It dropped out of musical publications after 1740.

Tune: DCM, C major (*HTI* 113b, Frost 32). First printed in *1558*. The first three and last two phrases are almost the same as the *1556* tune for Ps. 8 (*HTI* 67, Frost 24). Perhaps for this reason, the original second phrase (shown here as a variant) was changed to its present form in the London editions from *1562a*. The tune appeared in most editions of the *WBP*, but starting with *STC* 2450.5 (1578) some dropped it, leaving the psalm tuneless, with a reference to PSALM 3. Pss. 16, 19, 20, and 26, and sometimes later ones, were generally referred to this tune. *East 1592* used it for Pss. 20 and 26 as well as Ps. 14; Playford transferred it to Ps. 86. It was chosen by Sir John Hawkins to illustrate ancient psalmody in his *General History of Music* (1776), 3:515. It remained in use into the 19th century, sometimes under the name THORNTON.

Other musical settings: John Sheppard composed a four-voice setting of Sternhold's text in Edward VI's time, but only the uppermost voice part survives (see p. 518). *HTI* 73 (Frost 31), the transposed-Phrygian tune in *1556*, was never reprinted. Later, as a psalm with a proper tune, Ps. 14 was not generally sung to common tunes, but Playford matched it to YORK (*HTI* 331a) in his *Whole Book of Psalms in Three Parts* (1677), and was followed in this by a few later compilers.

Psalm 15
O Lord, within thy tabernacle

Text: The **psalm** was first printed in *1549b* (see p. 817) and revised in *1556*. Sternhold in this psalm relies on his most common sources, Coverdale's three English prose translations and the Vulgate. For *1556*, Whittingham revised very little: a total of four lines are affected, of which only two are completely replaced (11–12). The **argument** was first printed in *1556* and reprinted in both the 1557 Genevan Psalter and the Geneva Bible. It translates the summary from Calvin's *Commentary on the Psalms*. The marginal note first appearing in *1556* and reprinted in some early Elizabethan editions (see below) also come primarily from Calvin's commentary.

Incipit Domine, quis habitabit [in tabernaculo tuo]: Lord, who shall dwell in thy tabernacle
25 *Marginal note to v. 6*: Them the which do not this shall be cast out of the Church with Ishmael and the hypocrites. *1556, 1561d, 1562a*

Musical settings and later use of the text: John Sheppard composed a four-voice setting of Sternhold's text in Edward VI's time, but only the uppermost voice part survives (see p. 518). The *1556* tune (*HTI* 74, Frost 33) became the standard Scottish tune but was not adopted in England. In the *WBP* it was usually referred to PSALM 3. William Byrd wrote a consort song on this text, with four viols (*Collected Works*, 15:1). *East 1592* assigned LOW DUTCH, followed in Middleburg editions starting with *1601b*. Playford chose MARTYRS (330a). Although the permanent textual revisions in the late 17th century were not unusually extensive, the first line did entirely change to "Within thy tabernacle, Lord" (*WBP* 1751). SION (*HTI* 672a), the tune composed for Tate & Brady's version of the psalm ("Lord, who's the happy man, that may to thy blest courts repair?"), was adopted for the revised *WBP* text in many collections, beginning with Thomas Orme's *A Collecion* [sic] *of the Choicest and Best Psalm-Tunes*, 2nd edn. (Nottingham, 1717) and continuing until the 1760s.

Psalm 16
Lord, keep me, for I trust in thee

Text: The **psalm** was first printed in *1549b* (see p. 818) and revised in *1556*. In paraphrasing, Sternhold selected from among his most common sources, including three English prose translations by Coverdale and the Vulgate. He omitted the first half of v. 4, which Whittingham supplied as a new quatrain in *1556*. These lines and the other twelve that Whittingham revised are heavily indebted to Theodore Beza's French metrical version of the psalm. The **argument** was first printed in *1556* and reprinted in both the 1557 Genevan Psalter and the Geneva

Bible. It is similar to Calvin's summary in his *Commentary on the Psalms* but appears to come more directly from the argument in the French metrical psalter. This argument was not abridged in 1577. The marginal notes first appearing in *1556* and reprinted in some early Elizabethan editions (see below) also come primarily from Calvin's commentary.

Incipit Conserva me, Domine: Preserve me, Lord
9 Cf. the revised metrical version by Beza: "Mais mal sur mal s'entassera sur ceux / Qui vont courans après ces dieux estranges" (De Bèze, *Psaumes mis en vers français*, p. 21)
13 *Marginal note to v. 4b*: He would neither by outward profession nor in heart consent with idolatries. *1556, 1561d, 1562a*
29 *Marginal note to v. 8*: The faithful are sure to persevere to the end. *1556; at v. 7 in 1561d, 1562a*
37 *Marginal note to* **soul**: That is to say his life. *1556, 1561d, 1562a*
41 *Marginal note to v. 11*: Where God favoureth there is perfect felicity. *1556, 1561d, 1562a*

Musical settings and later use of the text: The *1556* tune (*HTI* 75, Frost 34) was adopted in Scotland but did not reach the *WBP*, where the psalm was usually referred to PSALM 3 or 14. Some Middleburg editions, from *1601b*, set it to VENI CREATOR. East fitted it to CAMBRIDGE, Playford to the second tune named LONDON (536a), while Francis Timbrell in about 1720 matched it to ST. JAMES'S (582a). The text was extensively revised in the 1690s; it remained in occasional use in the 18th century.

Psalm 17
O Lord, give ear to my just cause

Text: The **psalm** was first printed in *1549b* (see p. 820) and revised in *1556*. Sternhold combined readings from various prose translations by Coverdale and some direct cognates from the Vulgate. Revising for *1556*, Whittingham removed those cognates. Other emendations bring the paraphrase closer to the Great Bible and, in the last verse, to the French translation by Louis Budé. The **argument** was first printed in *1556*, reprinted in the 1557 Genevan Psalter, and adopted without the final sentence for the Geneva Bible. It is mainly a paraphrase of Calvin's summary from his *Commentary on the Psalms*, although the last sentence comes from the argument in the French metrical psalter. The marginal notes first appearing in *1556* and reprinted in some early Elizabethan editions (see below) also come primarily from Calvin's commentary.

Incipit Exaudi, Domine, iustitiam meam: Hear my righteousness, O Lord
i **Saul**: See note to Ps. 4.i.

25 *Marginal note to v. 7*: This is an effectual kind of prayer, for it containeth God's promise. *1556*

41 *Marginal note to* we: Meaning himself and his companions. *1556, 1561d, 1562a*

65 *Marginal note to v. 15*: When he awaketh out of his heaviness he shall be fulfilled with God's image, which shineth in his gospel and in his benefits. *1556*

Musical settings and later use of the text: John Sheppard composed a four-voice setting of Sternhold's text in Edward VI's time, but only the uppermost voice part survives (see p. 518). The *1556* tune (*HTI* 76a, Frost 35) is an unreconstructed Phrygian melody, which became the Scottish tune for this psalm but was not adopted in the English books. In the *WBP* it was usually referred to PSALM 3 or 14. East set it to OXFORD, Playford to WINDSOR, which was its most usual setting in the early 18th century, but it never became widely popular. The second line from the early 18th century on reads "attend unto my cry" (*WBP* 1751). The accompanying revisions were light, except for the replacement of the final quatrain.

Psalm 18
O God, my strength and foritude

Text: The **psalm** was first printed in *1561c*. Although all early editions attribute it to Sternhold, the author is almost certainly Thomas Norton, whose Ps. 75, also present in *1561c* and *1561d*, was not attributed until *1562a*. Because the metrical form and rhyme scheme are identical to Sternhold's, the compositor appears to have simply inserted Sternhold's initials for all three new psalms that filled gaps in an otherwise continuous run of paraphrases by Sternhold (18, 22, and 23). A number of word choices from the Geneva Bible conclusively date the paraphrase after early 1559, when the Geneva Book of Psalms was printed.[22] Norton used Sternhold's stanzaic form for all his versifications except the two with a refrain in every verse (Benedicite and Ps. 136). In addition to the Geneva Bible, he relied here on the Great Bible. The **argument** was first printed, in a slightly different form, in the 1559 Geneva Book of Psalms and subsequently the complete Geneva Bible; that version is an extract from the very long argument in the 1557 Genevan Psalter. The version there is a close paraphrase of Calvin's summary in his *Commentary on the Psalms*.

Incipit Diligam te, Domine [fortitudo mea]: I will love thee, O Lord my strength

i salutation: In the Geneva Bible, the word is "gratulation" (i.e., rejoicing). Initially corrupted to "salvation" in *1561d*, it was emended apparently at a guess

---

[22] Because this metrical psalm was not known to the Genevan metrical psalter compilers, it cannot have been written by Whittingham or Kethe (who participated in the preparation of the Geneva Bible). For further discussion, see *RR*, 293–5.

in *1563* to correct a misprint that had resulted in a theologically questionable assertion.

27–28 Basan: The quaking mountains or hills are not named in the psalm text. Norton appears to be associating them with the description of Sinai at Psalm 68:15: "The mountain of God is like the mountain of Bashan: it is an high mountain, as mount Bashan" (Geneva). There are also earthquakes at Sinai in Psalm 68:8.

37 cherubs and cherubins: In Hebrew, "cherubim" is the plural of "cherub," although in sixteenth-century English usage "cherubin" could be singular or plural. Norton, who may have thought that these were different creatures, combined the plural "cherubins" from the Great Bible with the Geneva Bible's "cherub" (here made plural as well).

163 sweep them out: The alternate image in *1601b*, "tread them down," comes from the Scottish psalm book via Schilders's 1599 edition (see p. 578); it reproduces the Geneva Bible phrasing verbatim.

Later use of the text: Aside from Ps. 100 (1), stanzas of this versification are the longest-lived psalm paraphrases from the *WBP*. An anonymous anthem, based on stanzas 1–6 plus a doxology, had its text printed in Clifford (1664). This was the only Elizabethan metrical psalm other than Ps. 100 listed as appearing in several hymnals in a survey dated 1869.[23] The text remained, to a surprising degree, Elizabethan as well; while a few scattered lines were rewritten (along with the last quatrain, handicapped by both "I say" and "ay"), the vast majority survived intact, at least in the *WBP* itself. Various selections beginning with the first stanza appeared in both English and American hymnbooks throughout the 19th and 20th centuries; the *Harvard University Hymn Book* added one version in 1926 and retained it until the 4th edition of 2007.[24] A colorful excerpt, stanzas 9 and 10 (beginning "The Lord descended from above"), gained an independent following in the 18th century and is still in print (see below).

Tune: DCM, Dorian transposed/G minor (*HTI* 159a, Frost 36). First printed in *1561c*. Once it was part of the *WBP*, this well-constructed tune appeared in almost every musical edition and in all the Companions. It distinguishes between fourteener lines 1–2 and 3–4, and clearer breaks between phrases in the second half; but of course this does not necessarily suit subsequent stanzas. Pss. 26 and 27 were generally referred to this tune. There are manuscript settings by John Mundy and William Lawes. Ainsworth in 1612 coupled it to his own versions of Pss. 27 and 106. In 1702 it was matched to Tate & Brady's Ps. 18, "No change of time shall ever shock." Still a proper tune with its original text, it traveled in 1698 to Ireland (as LINCOLN). The tune and its text maintained some popularity

---

[23] See Miller, *Singers and Songs of the Church* (1869).
[24] *Harvard University Hymn Book*, 2nd and 3rd edns. (1926, 1965).

through the 18th century. It was chosen by Sir John Hawkins to illustrate ancient psalmody in his *General History of Music* (1776), 3: 516, and in 1786 it was revived in Scotland as EDINBURGH.

Other musical settings: Apart from the Middleburg editions, which assigned this psalm to Low DUTCH beginning in *1601b*, the text-tune bond remained strong. But in 1760 the psalm was set to the four-line Scottish tune LONDON NEW (497b) in the Magdalen Chapel collection, and from there was taken up in American sources under the name MAGDALENE. Several English publications used other tunes, and the text remained popular into the 19th century; Thomas Clark of Canterbury wrote a new tune for it (*HTI* 15627) as late as 1818. On 5 February 1806, at the Concert of Ancient Music, Thomas Greatorex staged a setting of the psalm with soloists, chorus and orchestra to William Croft's tune ST. MATTHEW, and in 1822 John Clarke-Whitfeld published a sacred song based on this text, allied to the same tune.

Of the various tunes allied to "The Lord descended from above" (see above), FROOM (*HTI* 1931) by William Tans'ur (1748) had some currency, but its greatest popularity was in America, where William Billings's flamboyant tune MAJESTY (*HTI* 4014) was an inspired match to the text. First printed in 1778,[25] it had appeared in more than 100 American tunebooks by 1820, and is still in the last revision of *The Sacred Harp*.[26]

Psalm 19
The heavens and the firmament

Text: The **psalm** was first printed in *1549b* (see p. 821) and revised in *1556*. Sternhold relied on Coverdale's English prose translations, mixing readings from all three. His paraphrase is fairly literal excepting compression in v. 5, which Whittingham corrected in *1556* by rewriting a quatrain and also adding a new one. In general, Sternhold's version is closer to Coverdale's readings than Whittingham's; Whittingham instead anticipated changes that would be made in the Geneva Bible. The **argument** was first printed in *1556*, reprinted in 1557 Geneva Psalter, and given in the Geneva Bible without the final clause. It translates Calvin's summary in his *Commentary on the Psalms*. The marginal notes first appearing in *1556* and reprinted in some early Elizabethan editions (see below) also come primarily from Calvin's commentary.

Incipit Coeli enarrant gloriam Dei: The heavens declare the glory of God

---

[25] For a modern edition see Billings, *Complete Works*, 2: 203–5.
[26] *Sacred Harp: 1991 Revision*.

9 *Marginal note to v. 3*: Rom. 10.d. [10:18]/ Acts 14.c. [14:16–17] *1556, 1561d, 1562a* [Calvin references these passages in commenting on the next verse; they were apparently misplaced in the margin in *1556*.]

15 *Marginal note to v. 5*: He noteth three excellent qualities in the sun: his beauty, swiftness and heat. *1556, 1561d, 1562a*

29 *Marginal note to v. 8*: Mans inventions are crooked, without comfort, filthy and blinde *1556, 1561d, 1562a*

35 *Marginal note to v. 9*: Whatsoever man's fantasy doth invent is but lies, and vanity. *1556, 1561d, 1562a*

43 *Marginal note to v. 11b*: The effect of this reward is contained in the covenant of our adoption, for here he maketh all men sinners. *1556, 1561d, 1562a*

Musical settings and later use of the text: John Sheppard composed a four-voice setting of Sternhold's text in Edward VI's time, but only the uppermost voice part survives (see p. 518). The *1556* tune (*HTI* 77a, Frost 37) was used with this psalm in the Scottish psalm books, but in the *WBP* it was transferred to the Nunc dimittis (see p. 32). The usual cross-reference was to PSALM 14 or 3. *East 1592* set the psalm to LOW DUTCH (250b), and Playford chose YORK (331a). Cumulative revisions in the late 17th and early 18th century left the first lines as "The heav'ns and firmament on high / do wondrously declare" (*WBP* 1751), with a number of other lines also rewritten. The text continued to appear in some tunebooks until the early 19th century

Psalm 20
In trouble and adversity

Text: The **psalm** was one of Sternhold's original nineteen first printed in *1548* (see p. 823) and was revised for *1556*. Sternhold worked from both Coverdale's various English prose translations and the Vulgate. Whittingham's revision for *1556*, which was fairly modest, mainly brought some of Sternhold's lines into closer agreement with existing English prose versions, though he also consulted Budé's French translation. The **argument** was first printed in *1556* and reprinted in the 1557 Genevan Psalter, while the Geneva Bible reprinted only the first half. It expands the argument given in the French metrical psalter by specifying the enemy as the Ammonites (a suggestion from Calvin's commentary) and further summarizing the end of the psalm.

Incipit Exaudiat te Dominus [in die tribulationis]: The Lord hear thee in the day of trouble
ii–iii Ammonites: Inhabitants of present-day Jordan. For David's resubjugation of the Ammonites, see 2 Sam. 10.
4 *Marginal note to* **defend** (?): Hebrew exalt. *1556*

18–19 banners . . . Lord: The image is not found in the English psalm text until the Geneva Bible; it derives from Budé's French version: "nous . . . dresserons la banière au nom de nostre Dieu" (*Pseaumes octantetrois*, p. 36).

Musical settings and later use of the text: John Sheppard composed a four-voice setting of Sternhold's text in Edward VI's time, but only the uppermost voice part survives (see p. 518). The *1556* tune (*HTI* 78, Frost 38), strictly in the Dorian mode, was adopted in the Scottish psalm books but never reached the *WBP*. Day's *Certaine Notes* (1560) contains an adaptation by Thomas Caustun of an instrumental *In nomine* by John Taverner (c.1490–1545) set to the first stanza of the psalm.[27] The usual cross-reference was to PSALM 14. *East 1592* followed this suggestion, as did some later Middleburg editions. But in 1594 East substituted the common tune OXFORD. Ravenscroft instead chose ELY (366); Playford preferred HEREFORD (276g, Frost 152b); each of these was adopted by some 18th-century compilers. An elaborate new tune (*STC* 18072) was composed for this text in 1788 by a later John Mundy, a country psalmodist of Brixworth, Northamptonshire. This was the psalm's last known appearance in a printed tunebook, and it did not enjoy greater popularity in collections of psalm texts.

Psalm 21
O Lord, how joyful is the king

Text: The **psalm** was first printed in *1549b* (see p. 824) and revised in *1556*. As he usually did, Sternhold mixed readings from Coverdale's three printed English prose translations. For *1556*, Whittingham accepted nearly all of Sternhold's original paraphrase, modifying only four lines (and only ll. 45–46 substantially). To the extent that he emended Sternhold, Whittingham was influenced by Budé's French psalter. The **argument** was first printed in *1556* and reproduced in the 1557 Genevan Psalter. The Geneva Bible adopted it in a condensed form without identifying the victory. It adapts the argument in the French metrical psalter, though with much more detail about the specific battles involved. The marginal notes first appearing in *1556* and reprinted in some early Elizabethan editions (see below) come primarily from Calvin's *Commentary on the Psalms*.

Incipit Domine, in virtute [tua laetabitur rex]: Lord, in thy power shall the king rejoice
ii Syrians and Ammonites: Whittingham seems to have extrapolated from Calvin's summary in his *Commentary on the Psalms* (fol. 74v) that "the meening of this and the last [psalm] before is muche alike." 1 Sam. 10–11 recount Saul's anointing as king by Samuel and his first victory over the Ammonites; David receives

---

[27] See *Tudor Church Music*, 3: 199–200.

the king of Ammon's crown in 2 Sam. 12:30 after a victory in which he did not
directly participate.
13 *Marginal note to v. 4*: David did not only obtain life, but also assurance that
his posterity should reign for ever. *1556, 1561d, 1562a*
29 *Marginal note to v. 8*: Here he describeth the strength of Christ's kingdom
against the enemies thereof. *1556*; Hereof *1561d, 1562a*
49 *Marginal note to v. 13*: The wicked fall into despair and feel no comfort in
conscience to praise God for. *1556*

Later use of the text: The 1570s form of the Elizabethan prayer service for Ac-
cession Day (November 17) specifies singing "The xxi. Psalme in Metre before
the Sermon, vnto the ende of the .vii. verse."[28] This paraphrase was usually sup-
planted by later versions in collections of psalm texts, and survived longer in the
WBP itself than in secondary anthologies.

Tune: DCM, Dorian/D minor (*HTI* 160a, Frost 40). This well-constructed mel-
ody (μ11), with all eight lines suited to iambic verse, replaced the *1556* tune in
1561c and *1561d*, and thereafter was present in most editions of the *WBP*. Pss. 22,
23 (both versions), 24, 28, and 29 were generally referred to it. But when space-
saving affected a 1578 quarto edition (*STC* 2450.5) the tune was replaced by a
cross-reference to PSALM 18, and this example was followed in many later edi-
tions. Nevertheless it figured in all the Companions and maintained its status as
a proper tune through the first half of the 18th century, sometimes with Tate &
Brady's version of the psalm, "The king, O Lord, with shouts of praise."

Other musical settings: John Sheppard composed a four-voice setting of Stern-
hold's text in Edward VI's time, but only the uppermost voice part survives (see
p. 518). The *1556* tune (*HTI* 79, Frost 39) was dropped after *1560a*. At some time
after 1605 the whole psalm was used for a five-voice verse anthem "for the Fifth
of November" by Thomas Weelkes (1576–1623).[29] Several short tunes were tried
after 1700, but none became widely known.

Psalm 22
O God, my God, wherefore dost thou

Text: The **psalm** was first printed in *1561c*. Its author is almost certainly Thomas
Norton rather than Sternhold; see the Text note for Ps. 18, above. This psalm
has phrasing taken directly from the Geneva Bible, including the colorful de-
scription of the scornful in l. 27. It also reflects the large stretches of translation
shared by both the Geneva and Great Bibles and occasional understanding taken

---

[28] *A Fourme of Prayer to be Vsed the 17. of Nouember*, sig. B1v.
[29] See MB 23: 99–108.

from the Vulgate or even from Coverdale's 1540 Latin/English parallel text. The **argument**, first printed in this form in *1561c*, is a shortened version of the one in the 1557 Genevan Psalter (which was also slightly but differently edited for the Geneva Bible). It translates Calvin's summary in his *Commentary on the Psalms*.

Incipit Deus, Deus meus respice [in me]: God, my God, attend to me
9–10 sanctuary and holy place: Translating "the praises of Israel" via the gloss to the Geneva Bible: "He meaneth the places of praising, even the Tabernacle."
33–4 But . . . request: The alternate version of these lines in *1601b* comes from the Scottish psalm book, via Schilders's 1599 edition of the *WBP* (see p. 578).
67, 69 heathen: This is how Coverdale translates the Latin *gens* in the 1540 parallel Vulgate version (both the Great and Geneva Bibles give "nations").
90, 92 These lines, with two extra syllables each, escaped correction in the *WBP* until 1569. The wording in *1601b* is the Scottish version reproduced by Schilders.

Musical settings and later use of the text: The *1556* tune for Ps. 16 (*HTI* 75, Frost 34) was set for four voices to this text by Hake in *Day 1563*, and was then occasionally printed with the psalm in the *WBP* (eight Elizabethan editions in all, the first being *1564*) and in *East 1592* and *Allison 1599*. Other editions of the *WBP* generally referred it to Psalm 21. In an unusual plan William Lawes provided three tunes, one for each of the three parts of the psalm, in his *12 Psalms* (c. 1640). The link with *HTI* 75 continued in some quarters into the early 18th century, despite Playford's choice of Salisbury (279c). The text, lightly modernized except for a wholly new last quatrain in the 1690s, seems to have dropped out of collections other than the *WBP* by the mid-18th century. The tune was revived as Old 22nd in *The English Hymnal* (1906).

Psalm 23 (1)
The Lord is only my support

Text: This **psalm** was first printed in *1556*. It appeared in all subsequent editions until *1562a*, when Day dropped it in favor of Ps. 23 (2). Day first restored it to the *WBP* in *1565*; it is absent from the 1565 quarto edition (*STC* 2435), but appears in all editions of the *WBP* from the 1566 quarto (*STC* 2437) on. As he did several times, William Whittingham adopted the familiar Sternhold's meter from the Edwardian metrical psalms. Several phrases are recognizable from the Great Bible, but the paraphrase tends to explicate or interpret the psalm's images as much as restate them. Whittingham seems to have Clément Marot's metrical version in mind, but much more Calvin's discussion in his *Commentary on the Psalms*. The **argument** also first appeared in *1556* and was reprinted in the 1557 Genevan Psalter and the Geneva Bible. It is paraphrased from the argument in the French metrical psalter.

Incipit Dominus regit me: The Lord governs me

5 cotes: Calvin's commentary dwells on the advantages of translating the Hebrew to mean a shelter rather than merely an open pasture.

13 death's door: Cf. Calvin's commentary: "And Dauid alludeth to the dark swales or the dens of wyld beastes: wherinto if a man come, by and by at the first enterance he meeteth with the fear of death" (Calvin, *Commentaries*, fol. 86v: "swales" = shady places).

18 despite: The emphasis is here on the first syllable.

Musical settings and later use of the text: The *1556* tune (*HTI* 80, Frost 41) is a rare early example of a four-line CM tune, and in an unusual key (B flat). But after *1560a* it was adopted only in the Scottish psalm books, and the paraphrase was referred to PSALM 21 (to which it is sung in µ11). *East 1592* matched it to CAMBRIDGE, as did the Middleburg editions starting with *1601b*. It was also set as a consort song with four viols (µ17) by William Byrd (1543–1623).[30] Ravenscroft selected WINCHESTER, followed in some late editions of the *WBP*, and this competed with Playford's choice of CANTERBURY (250h) as the text maintained its popularity through the 18th century. It is printed in 229 tune books up to 1820, as compared to 120 for the second version, and continued in use through the middle of the 19th century. An anonymous anthem, using the complete psalm, had its text printed in Clifford (1664).

Psalm 23 (2)
My shepherd is the living Lord

Text: The **psalm** was first printed in *1561c*. Its author is almost certainly Thomas Norton rather than Sternhold; see the Text note for Ps. 18, above. Unlike Pss. 18 and 22, this does not owe any obvious debts to the Geneva Bible; Norton instead remained very close to the Great Bible version.

Musical settings and later use of the text: This version never acquired its own tune in the *WBP*, which generally did not even provide a cross-reference, perhaps because it would fit the tune suggested for Ps. 23 (1). It was set to CAMBRIDGE in *Daman 1579* (the setting is reprinted as Frost 42) and the later Companions. It was also set as an anthem for choirs by John Amner (1579–1641), Thomas Tomkins (1572–1656), and William Wigthorpe (fl. 1600); the last is listed in Clifford (1664). An elegant new tune by John Scott (*HTI* 2586a) appeared in the Foundling Hospital Collection in 1760 under the title PSALM 23, and spread to other English and American collections as GOODMAN'S. Isaac Watts borrowed the first line for his paraphrase, and despite the greater early popularity of 23 (1),

---

[30] Byrd, *Collected Works*, 15.5; reproduced online (µ11) by kind permission of Stainer & Bell Ltd.

this version was also printed in psalm and hymn collections through the middle of the 19th century.

Psalm 24
The earth is all the Lord's, with all

Text: The **psalm** was first printed in *1561c*. It is attributed there and in all other early editions to John Hopkins, but is more likely by Thomas Norton. If Hopkins did write this, it is his only versification up through 1561 to use Sternhold's rhyme scheme rather than his own characteristic *abab* pattern. Furthermore, its enjambment and tendency to elide syllables are far more typical of Norton than of Hopkins.[31] Finally, like Ps. 22 (and like Ps. 75, consistently attributed to Norton from *1562a* on) it relies on the Vulgate as well as the Great Bible and the Geneva Bible. The **argument** first appeared as the second half of the very long summary in the 1557 Genevan Psalter, not reprinted in the Geneva Bible. It is based on the summary in Calvin's *Commentary on the Psalms*.

Incipit Domini est terra: The earth is the Lord's
21 brood of travellers: An original expansion on the idea of those seeking God's face.
24 An elaborate rendering of "generation" (in both the Great Bible and Geneva Bible).
25 From the Vulgate, given by Coverdale in his 1540 parallel psalter as "Open your gates, ye princes."
29 glorious: The OED does not record any instances (even this one) of **glorious** as a noun.

Musical settings and later use of the text: Lacking any tune of its own, this psalm was generally referred to PSALM 21; *East 1592* took up this direction, providing a setting by Cobbold, but in later editions East assigned it to Low DUTCH. Ravenscroft's choice of ROCHESTER (275b) proved more popular among later compilers, including Playford. The second half of the text was very extensively reworked in the early 18th century. While it appeared in some other collections into the 19th century, this paraphrase was not a popular one compared to later versions of the psalm.

---

[31] On these features, see *RR*, 293, 296; Ranson, *Hopkins*, 91. Ranson attributes the paraphrase to Sternhold based on its similarity to Pss. 18, 22, and 23, all of which we ascribe to Norton.

Psalm 25
I lift mine heart to thee

Text: The **psalm** was one of Sternhold's original nineteen first printed in *1548* (see p. 826) and was revised for *1556*. This is one of only two paraphrases by Sternhold not in his characteristic meter. Although he did incorporate some readings from the Great and/or Coverdale Bibles, he was unusually reliant here on Coverdale's Englishing of the Vulgate. For *1556*, Whittingham emended several of the verses that did not agree with the Great Bible and added a new quatrain to account for one (v. 9) that Sternhold omitted. In *1556* only, the verses are marked with Hebrew letters rather than numbers. The **argument** was first printed in *1556* and reprinted in both the 1557 Genevan Psalter and the Geneva Bible. It is slightly expanded from the argument in the French metrical psalter, and the note on the alphabetic structure is new. Somewhat unusually, Calvin's commentary seems not to have influenced Whittingham's treatment of this psalm or its apparatus.

Incipit Ad te, Domine, levavi [animam meum]: Unto thee, Lord, have I lift up my soul
i prophet: David.
21 *Marginal note to* **faults**: The Hebrew word signifieth contempt of God. *1556, 1561d*
45 *Marginal note to v. 12*: True felicity standeth in the fear of God. *1556, 1561d, 1562a*
73 *Marginal note to v. 19*: John 15.d [15:25] *1556*

Later use of the text: The paraphrase, lightly modernized and with a rewritten penultimate quatrain, enjoyed much more popularity in psalm and hymn collections through the 18th century than did its proper tune. It was printed outside the *WBP* through the middle of the 19th century.

Tune: DSM, F major (*HTI* 114, Frost 44). First printed in *1558*. This is a tune with an unusually large complement of semibreves, producing a marked irregularity of rhythmic flow that weakens the underlying duple beat. It remained the proper tune for the psalm, and the leading short-meter tune in the book, being generally referred to for Pss. 45, 67, 70 and later Ps. 134 in some editions. The tune was omitted from some editions starting in 1578, though in that very year it was directed to be sung to a special hymn ("Give laud unto the Lord," by "I. C.") in the printed Accession Service, *STC* 16480 (see *MEPC*, 1. 47). It was occasionally appropriated for other DSM texts, following the *WBP* cross-references: for Ps. 45 by East (in 1592 only), and for Ps. 67 in some Middleburg editions, but it lost out soon after 1700. Revived in Victorian times as OLD 25TH in a smoothed-out version, it was then coupled with Emma Toke's hymn "Thou art gone up on high," and is still in common use.

Other musical settings: John Sheppard composed two four-voice settings of Sternhold's unrevised text in Edward VI's time, but in each case only the uppermost voice part survives (see p. 518). The *1556* tune (*HTI* 81, Frost 43) was never reprinted. The first stanza was set as a four-voice anthem by John Mundy in his *Songs and Psalmes* (1594). Daman in 1591 provided settings of the psalm both with its proper tune and with the common tune LONDON (*HTI* 269c): the latter setting is reprinted as Frost 45. Thomas Robinson also used LONDON in an arrangement for solo voice and cithern in *New Citharen Lessons* (1609). That tune was eventually picked up in some late editions of the *WBP*, starting in 1630, while others followed Ravenscroft's choice of CANTERBURY (361). A new tune for the psalm (*HTI* 1088) was provided in James Green's *Book of Psalm-Tunes* (5th edition, London and Gainsborough, 1724) and this text-tune match was followed in 17 other musical publications, the last in 1779.

Psalm 26
Lord, be my judge, and thou shalt see

Text: The **psalm** was first printed in *1561c*. Here, as in most of his Elizabethan paraphrases, Hopkins consulted the Great and Geneva Bibles and intermixes readings from both. The **argument** was first printed in the 1557 Genevan Psalter and subsequently the Geneva Bible. It is an expansion of the summary in Calvin's *Commentary on the Psalms*.

Incipit Iudica me, Domine: Be thou my judge, O Lord
ii integrity toward Saul: A reference to at least one of the two instances when David refused to harm Saul despite getting close enough to do so; see 1 Sam. 24 and 26.
v banished by Saul: See 1 Sam. 19–27.
7 This simile is not in the psalm text.

Musical settings and later use of the text: No *WBP* editions provided music until a Middleburg edition of 1605, which followed *East 1592* in setting it to PSALM 14. East later substituted OXFORD, but Playford's choice of WINDSOR in 1677 became the favorite for this psalm, which maintained some popularity throughout the 18th century. The textual revision in the 1690s replaced a number of lines.

Psalm 27
The Lord is both my health and light

Text: The **psalm** was first printed in *1561c*. Hopkins drew on both the Geneva and Great Bible translations in this paraphrase. The **argument** first appeared in the 1557 Genevan Psalter, and the first part was adopted in the Geneva Bible. It is similar to, but much expanded from, Calvin's summary in his *Commentary on the Psalms*.

Incipit Dominus illuminatio [mea]: The Lord is my light
13–16 The expressions of confidence in ll. 14 and 16 are not in the psalm text.

Musical settings and later use of the text: In the *WBP*, lacking any tune of its own, this psalm was referred to PSALM 18; *East 1592* followed this direction, but in later editions East assigned it to CAMBRIDGE. When Playford revised the music of the *WBP* for the great 1661 edition (Wing B2475A) he set it to YORK, following Ravenscroft's choice. In the 18th century two durable tunes were composed for this text: William Wheall's BEDFORD (*HTI* 930a) in about 1720 and William Tans'ur's EWELL (1403) in 1735. The text continued to appear mainly in psalm collections into the early 19th century. Modernization of the text in the 1690s was light apart from the final quatrains.

Psalm 28
Thou art, O Lord, my strength and stay

Text: The **psalm** was one of Sternhold's original nineteen first printed in *1548* (see p. 828) and was revised for *1556*. The misattribution to Hopkins, originating in *1561d*, remained for a substantial number of subsequent editions of the *WBP*. Sternhold took readings from the Great Bible in this psalm but also chose a relatively large number of cognates to the Latin of the Vulgate. For *1556*, Whittingham eliminated some of these echoes but did not uniformly bring the paraphrase closer to the literal meaning of the text. He seems to have been influenced by Beza's French metrical version in addition to Calvin's commentary. The **argument** was first printed in *1556* and reprinted with minor changes in the 1557 Genevan Psalter and the Geneva Bible. It is translated from the argument in the French metrical psalter.

Incipit Ad te, Domine, clamabo: Unto thee, Lord, will I cry
1 Whittingham's revised first quatrain omits the opening phrase of the literal psalm text (in the Geneva Bible, "Unto thee, O Lord, do I cry"). The French metrical version similarly begins with an address to God as protector ("O Dieu qui es ma forteresse": *Pseaumes octantetrois*, p. 37); in compressing six lines of Beza's verse into an English quatrain, the crying was squeezed out.

8 holy ark: Only Calvin's commentary among Whittingham's sources specifically mentions the ark of the covenant.
29 *Marginal note to* **our**: Meaning himself and his companions. *1556*

Musical settings and later use of the text: John Sheppard composed two four-voice settings of Sternhold's unrevised text in Edward VI's time, but in each case only the uppermost voice part survives (see p. 518). The *1556* tune (*HTI* 82, Frost 28) was not adopted in the *WBP*. The usual cross-reference was to PSALM 21. The psalm was later set to several common tunes, first in *East 1592* to OXFORD. This was followed in Middleburg editions, beginning with *1601b*. Cumulative revisions from the late 17th to early 18th century substantially updated parts of the text, but it seems to have disappeared from collections outside the *WBP* itself by the late 18th century.

Psalm 29
Give to the Lord, ye potentates

Text: The **psalm** was one of Sternhold's original nineteen first printed in *1548* (see p. 829) and was revised for *1556*. Sternhold may have consulted the Coverdale Bible in paraphrasing this psalm, but, very unusually, there are no obvious readings from the Great Bible in his original version. Rather, he relies heavily on the Vulgate and Coverdale's 1540 parallel translation as well as some inventive phrasing. Whittingham for *1556* eliminated the signs of a half-verse at the start of the psalm present in the Septuagint but not in the Hebrew, and brought a few other lines into closer agreement with the literal text, but did not otherwise revise heavily. The **argument** was first printed in *1556*; the 1557 Genevan Psalter reprinted it unchanged and the Geneva Bible adopted it with small verbal emendations. It is in the main a translation from the argument in the French metrical psalter, although the impiety of rulers is new in the English version.

Incipit Afferte Domino[, filii Deo]: Bring unto the Lord, ye children of God
17 *Marginal note to* **voice**: He meaneth the thunderings and tempests. *1556, 1561d, 1562a*
19–20 Sternhold uses these lines to interpolate an explanation of why the cedars of Lebanon are significant; see p. 830 for his moralization in the next verse.
23–24 The literal psalm text gives place names rather than a topographic description, as in the Geneva Bible's "Lebanon *also* and Sirion" (i.e., Mount Hermon).
25 *Marginal note*: the lightening *1556*

Musical settings and later use of the text: John Sheppard composed a four-voice setting of Sternhold's text in Edward VI's time, but only the uppermost voice part survives (see p. 518). The *1556* tune (*HTI* 83, Frost 49) was dropped from the English psalm book after 1560u. The usual cross-reference was to the adjacent

PSALM 30. The psalm was set to several common tunes, first in *East 1592* to Low DUTCH. The text, with second line altered in the 1690s to "give ye with one accord" (*WBP* 1751), was reprinted in psalm and hymn collections through the middle of the 19th century.

Psalm 30
All laud and praise with heart and voice

Text: The **psalm** was first printed in *1549b* as one of John Hopkins's original seven Edwardian paraphrases (see p. 831) and revised in *1556*. Hopkins worked primarily from translations by Coverdale—the Great Bible and either the Coverdale Bible or one of its successors like the Matthew Bible—and appears to have consulted George Joye's English paraphrases. There are also scattered recollections of the Vulgate. For *1556*, Whittingham revised the paraphrase lightly and with little significant change in meaning. The **argument** was first printed in *1556* and reprinted in the 1557 Genevan Psalter; it is slightly abridged in the Geneva Bible. The bulk of the argument translates the one in the French metrical psalter, but the first sentence contextualizing the psalm in relation to David's illness endorses an interpretation that Calvin raises only to dismiss at the beginning of his commentary on it.

Incipit Exaltabo te, Domine: I will magnify thee, O Lord
i When David . . . Lord: This incident is not recounted in the biblical David story.
31 *Marginal note to v. 7b*: From prosperity to adversity the fall is sudden. *1556* [The gloss reflects Whittingham's French sources, probably Louis Budé's translation: "(mais soudain que) tu caches ta face, je fu troublé" (Pidoux, *Psautier huguenot*, p. 42)]

Later use of the text: The text was widely printed in collections of psalms and hymns through the 18th century and up to the middle of the 19th.

Tune: DCM, Dorian/D minor (*HTI* 84b, Frost 51). The original form of the tune in *1556* (84a, Frost 50) had twelve phrases, representing six fourteeners, but phrases 5–8 were dropped in *1558*. (For a discussion of one consequence of this change see Temperley, "'All skilful praises sing,'" 545.) The shorter form became a fixture in the *WBP*. It was also generally referred to for Pss. 32–34 and 65. The increased number of semibreves in phrases 7 and 8, suggesting triple time, is a somewhat disruptive feature. It was one of five tunes selected for Fetherstone's *Lamentations of Jeremie* (1587). It was preserved with its text in all the Companions, in Playford (1677), and on into the early 18th century.

Other musical settings: John Sheppard composed a four-voice setting of Hopkins's text in Edward VI's time, but only the uppermost voice part survives (see p. 518). The first four stanzas formed the text of a verse anthem for six voices by Thomas Weelkes (1576–1623), possibly to mark the Queen's death in 1603; it is listed in Clifford (1663, 1664).[32] Middleburg editions, beginning with Peter Short's (*1601b*), used the common tune Low Dutch. Other short tunes were matched with this text in the 18th century. The most durable was the anonymous one now known as Burford (*HTI* 846a), first printed with Ps. 30 in the 4th edition of James Green's *Collection of Psalm Tunes* and with Ps. 42 in John Chetham's *Book of Psalmody*. Both have an imprint date of 1718 and were published in the North Midlands region. With this tune the psalm appeared in more than 50 tunebooks between 1718 and 1820. An anthem by John Holmes (d. 1629), based on stanzas 1–4 and 8, had its text printed in Clifford (1664).

Psalm 31
O Lord, I put my trust in thee

Text: The **psalm** was first printed in *1561c*. Hopkins chose phrasing from both the Geneva and Great Bibles, with a slight preference for the former. The **argument** was first printed in the 1557 Genevan Psalter and reprinted, in the slightly emended form adopted by the *WBP*, in the Geneva Bible. It derives from Calvin's summary and comments on v. 1 in the *Commentary on the Psalms*.

Incipit In te, Domine, speravi: In thee, Lord, have I put my trust
17 The versification lacks v. 11b, "who seeing me in the street, fled from me" (Geneva).
69 Hopkins did not paraphrase v. 18. *1601b* supplies it in an additional quatrain here from the Scottish psalm book. The insertion originated in the 1599 *WBP* edition printed by Richard Schilders (see p. 578), but was very quickly adopted into most editions of the *WBP*.

Musical settings and later use of the text: This psalm never had a tune of its own in the *WBP*. The usual cross-reference was to Psalm 30. It was set to several common tunes, first by East to Cambridge, but did not become widely popular.

---

[32] See MB 23: 69–74.

Psalm 32
The man is blest whose wickedness

Text: The **psalm** was one of Sternhold's original nineteen first printed in *1548* (see p. 832) and was revised for *1556*. For the original versification, Sternhold drew on and combined Coverdale's three translations. Whittingham's revisions in *1556*, which substantially change four quatrains and some individual lines, usually bring the paraphrase into closer literal agreement with the Great Bible as well as with Whittingham's 1557 Genevan Psalter. The **argument** was first printed in *1556* and was reprinted in the 1557 Genevan Psalter and the Geneva Bible. It translates the argument preceding Marot's versification in the French metrical psalter. There was no significant abridgement to the argument in 1577.

Incipit Beati quorum remissi [*sc.* remissae] sunt [iniquitates]: Blessed are they whose iniquities are forgiven
12 *Marginal note to* **moan**: Heb. roaring. *1556* [Whittingham provided the same alternate translation as a gloss in the 1557 Genevan Psalter.]
16 *Marginal note to end of v. 4:* Selah. *1556*
18 Marginal note to v. 5a: Isa. 65.d [65:23] *1556* [Cross-reference copied from the Olivétan Bible.]
20 *Marginal note to end of v. 5:* Selah. *1556*
23 *Marginal note to* **waters**: The just man shall not shrink for any adversity. *1556, 1561d* [Paraphrasing the note in the Olivétan Bible.]
25 *Marginal note to v. 8:* Selah. *1556, 1561d*

Musical settings and later uses of the text: John Sheppard composed two four-voice settings of Sternhold's unrevised text in Edward VI's time, but in each case only the uppermost voice part survives (see p. 518). The *1556* tune (*HTI* 85, Frost 52) was never reprinted. The usual cross-reference was to PSALM 30. The psalm was set to several common tunes, first in *East 1592* to OXFORD. Even with its nearly-completely rewritten first quatrain (beginning "The man is blest, whose wickedness / The Lord forgiven hath": *WBP* 1751) the text is not found in musical collections after 1757.

Psalm 33
Ye righteous in the Lord rejoice

Text: The **psalm** was first printed in *1549b* (see p. 833) and appeared in *1556* with a small number of primarily cosmetic emendations. Hopkins leaned most heavily on the Great Bible in versifying this psalm, but a few verses show the influence of the Coverdale Bible or possibly Joye's paraphrases. The **argument** was first printed in *1556*, and reprinted in the 1557 Genevan Psalter and the Geneva Bible.

It shares ideas with Calvin's comments in the *Commentary on the Psalms*, but does not closely follow any of Whittingham's favorite sources.

Incipit Exultate iusti in Domino: Rejoice in the Lord, O ye righteous
17 *Marginal note to v. 6:* Gen. 1.a [1:6] *1556, 1561d* [Cross-reference from the Olivétan Bible.]
33 *Marginal note to v. 10:* No counsel can prevail against God, but shall have evil success. *1556;* ill successe *1561d, 1562a* [Echoed by a gloss on the same verse in the 1557 Genevan Psalter.]
53 *Marginal note to v. 16:* God only delivereth and preserveth his people. *1556, 1561d, 1562a*
57–8 The heaps . . . starve: Hopkins elaborates on his sources to actually kill off the horses, which were not harmed in the original psalm text.

Musical settings and later use of the text: John Sheppard composed a four-voice setting of Hopkins's text in Edward VI's time, but only the uppermost voice part survives (see p. 518). The *1556* tune (*HTI* 86, Frost 53) was reassigned to Ps. 96 in *1558*, for no obvious reason, and replaced by the tune of Psalm 42 (*HTI* 89, Frost 61). This was adopted in the Scottish psalm books, but not in the *WBP*, where from *1561c* onwards it lost its tune. The usual cross-reference was to Psalm 30. *Daman 1579* set the psalm to an otherwise unknown 8-line tune (*HTI* 250a, Frost 54), the first half of which became the common tune Low Dutch, assigned to this psalm in *East 1592*. Ravenscroft's choice of the Scottish tune Dukes (276c) was followed in some subsequent editions of the *WBP* and in several 18th-century collections. This psalm surpassed most others in popularity, although it was revised extensively after the first quatrain in the early 18th century. It appeared in 254 musical publications up to the year 1820, set to 37 different tunes.

Psalm 34
I will give laud and honour both

Text: The **psalm** was one of Sternhold's original nineteen first printed in *1548* (see p. 836) and was revised for *1556*. In this paraphrase, Sternhold consulted Coverdale's three English translations but in several places preferred the reading of the Vulgate. *1556* emends a large number of lines, but most of the changes do not create dramatic differences in meaning. Because the psalm is an alphabetic acrostic in Hebrew, the verses in *1556* are signaled by Hebrew letters rather than numbers. The **argument** was first printed in *1556* and was reprinted in the 1557 Genevan Psalter and the Geneva Bible. It begins by translating the argument from the French metrical psalter, but then departs from it to incorporate ideas from Calvin's summary in the *Commentary on the Psalms* as well as some apparently new material.

Incipit Benedicam Domino [*sc.* Dominum]: I will bless the Lord
25 *Marginal note to v. 7:* Gen. 19, 31, 32 / 4 Kings [2 Chron.] 6 / Heb. 1. *1556, 1561d, 1562a* [The same cross-references appear in the 1557 Genevan Psalter.]
45 *Marginal note to v. 12:* 1 Pet. 3.b [3:10] *1556*; 1 Pet. [5:10] 5.b *1561d, 1562a* [*1556* is correct, and echoed in the 1557 Genevan Psalter]
53 *Marginal note to v. 15:* Heb. 4.c [4:13]/ Ecclus 15.d [15:20] *1556, 1561d, 1562a* [Ecclus 15.d also appears as a cross-reference in the 1557 Genevan Psalter]
58 **train:** Paraphrasing the prose originals, "train" means a group of people, but it also puns on the common sixteenth-century meanings of "snare" or "treachery."

Musical settings and later use of the text: John Sheppard composed a four-voice setting of Sternhold's text in Edward VI's time, but only the uppermost voice part survives (see p. 518). The *1556* tune (*HTI* 87, Frost 55), in the Mixolydian mode, was not used again. The usual cross-reference was to PSALM 30. The first English setting was Cosyn's (*Cosyn 1585*) to the tune VENI CREATOR (see p. 915). *East 1592* chose CAMBRIDGE. Ravenscroft's choice of the Scottish tune ABBY (325) was adopted in some late editions of the *WBP* and in several 18th-century collections. Like Ps. 33, this psalm had a longer life than many, and appeared in 228 musical publications up to 1820, with 33 different tunes. The text was lightly modernized in the late 17th century, and then more aggressively updated for style early in the 18th. John Holmes (d. 1629) wrote an anthem based on stanzas 1–4 and 8; its text is listed in Clifford, 2nd edn. (1664).

Psalm 35
Lord, plead my cause against my foes

Text: The **psalm** was first printed in *1562a*. In versifying, Hopkins incorporated readings from both the Geneva and Great Bibles. The **argument** was first printed in the 1557 Genevan Psalter and reprinted in the Geneva Bible. It paraphrases and abridges the summary in Calvin's *Commentary on the Psalms.*

Incipit Iudica, Domine, [nocentes me]: Judge them, O Lord, that hurt me
86 **fleer:** Most early editions spell the word as 'fliere' to signal the rhyme with **desire.**

Tune: DCM, Dorian/D minor (*HTI* 170b, Frost 57). First printed in *1562a*. Its first five phrases are essentially the same as those of HUMBLE SUIT, also dating from 1562. Unlike HUMBLE SUIT it has unusual dotted-minim-crotchet pairs in phrases 4 and 8. For a while Pss. 36–40, 42–43, and 55 were referred to this tune. However, it was dropped from most editions of the *WBP* from 1569 onwards, and replaced by a cross-reference to LAMENTATION OF A SINNER. After a brief revival in five editions of Abraham Barber's *Book of Psalme Tunes in Four Parts* (York, 1687–1715) it disappeared from view.

Other musical settings and later use of the text: With its proper tune fading, *East 1592* set the psalm to PSALM 40, but in 1594 East substituted the common tune OXFORD. Middleburg editions, starting with *1601b*, used CAMBRIDGE instead. Playford chose HEREFORD (276g), but this did not save the psalm from dropping out of use in the 18th century.

Psalm 36
The wicked, with his works unjust

Text: The **psalm** was first printed in *1562a*. In this psalm, Hopkins chose the meaning of the Geneva Bible over the Great Bible in every disagreement. The **argument** was first printed in the 1557 Genevan Psalter and reprinted in the Geneva Bible as well as in *1560b* and its descendants (accompanying Kethe's versification). It is an adaptation of the summary in Calvin's *Commentary on the Psalms*.

Incipit Dixit iniustus [ut delinquat in semetipso]: The unrighteous hath determined within himself to do amiss

Musical settings and later use of the text: This psalm never had its own tune in the *WBP*. The usual cross-reference was to PSALM 35, and later to the similar HUMBLE SUIT. It was set to several common tunes, first in *East 1592* to LOW DUTCH, but did not become widely popular. From the start of the 18th century, its first lines read "The wicked, by his works unjust, / doth thus persuade my heart" (*WBP* 1751), though revision of the text was extremely light overall.

Psalm 37
Grudge not to see the wicked men

Text: The **psalm** was first printed in *1558*. Although it is not a line-by-line translation of the French metrical version, Whittingham's versification incorporates some of Marot's phrasing and English cognates to the French. Other sources were the Great Bible and the 1557 Genevan Psalter. The **argument** was first printed in *1558*, translating the one found in the French metrical psalter. Somewhat unusually, it is not textually related to the arguments in any of the Geneva prose psalms.

Incipit Noli emulari [in malignantibus]: Fret not thyself at the wicked

Musical settings and later use of the text: The *1558* tune (*HTI* 115, Frost 59) was adopted in the Scottish but not the English psalm book. The usual cross-reference was to PSALM 35, and later to the similar HUMBLE SUIT. *East 1592* set it to CAMBRIDGE; Playford chose ROCHESTER (275b). Textual modernization in the 1690s affected phrases and some whole lines, though fewer as a proportion of the

psalm than the most aggressive revisions in the later *WBP*. The psalm was print-
ed with various tunes, but dropped out of most musical publications after 1750.

Psalm 38
Put me not to rebuke, O Lord

Text: The **psalm** was first printed in *1562a*. Although attributed to John Hopkins
in that and most subsequent editions, the attribution in *1562b* to Thomas Norton
is almost certainly correct. Not only is *1562b* a more reliable text in general, the
rhyme scheme is Norton's rather than Hopkins's. In addition, the *1562a* version
lacks verse numbers, which accompany all of the new psalms that are clearly by
Hopkins, but not those by Norton. The paraphrast relied heavily on the Great
Bible, preferring the wording of the Geneva Bible in a small number of cases. The
argument was first printed in the 1557 Genevan Psalter and reprinted in the Ge-
neva Bible. It is constructed from Calvin's summary and parts of the commentary
on individual verses in his *Commentary on the Psalms*.

Incipit Domine, ne in furore [tuo arguas me]: Lord, rebuke me not in thy heavy
indignation

Musical settings and later use of the text: The psalm had no tune of its own in
the *WBP*. The usual cross-reference was to PSALM 35, and later to the similar
HUMBLE SUIT. *Cosyn 1585* followed the latter in a six-voice setting, and Playford
also adopted this choice in 1677, giving that tune a lasting association with Ps.
38 that was followed by William Crotch when he revived it in 1803. The late-
17th-century revision of the text replaced a number of whole lines in addition to
isolated archaic phrases, and included an unusually high number of changes to
verb tenses (reflecting difference between the Great Bible and KJV translations).

Psalm 39
I said, "I will look to my ways"

Text: The **psalm** was first printed in *1562a*. Where Hopkins closely followed any
prose translation of this psalm, he chose the phrasing of the Great Bible. The
argument was first printed in the 1557 Genevan Psalter and reprinted in the Ge-
neva Bible. It was taken entirely from Calvin's summary in his *Commentary on
the Psalms*.

Incipit Dixi custodiam [vias meas]: I said, "I will keep my ways"

Musical settings and later use of the text: This psalm lacked its own tune in the
WBP. The usual cross-reference was to PSALM 35, and later to the similar HUM-
BLE SUIT. It was set to several common tunes, first in *East 1592* to LOW DUTCH;

Ravenscroft chose MARTYRS (330a). Several others were assigned to it in tune-books up to about 1750, but it never became widely popular.

Psalm 40
I waited long and sought the Lord

Text: The **psalm** was first printed in *1562a*. Hopkins consulted and blended readings from the Geneva and Great Bibles in composing his versification. The **argument** was first printed in the 1557 Genevan Psalter and reprinted in the Geneva Bible. It closely paraphrases Calvin's summary in his *Commentary on the Psalms*.

Incipit Expectans expectavi [Dominum]: I waited patiently for the Lord
57 The paraphrase omits v. 11: "Withdraw not thou thy tender mercy from me, O Lord: let thy mercy and thy truth alway preserve me" (Geneva). A quatrain corresponding to this verse is supplied in *1601b*, taken from the Scottish psalm book via Richard Schilders's 1599 edition of the *WBP* (see p. 578). This additional quatrain became a normal part of the text in the first years of the 17th century.

Musical settings and later use of the text: This psalm had no tune to itself in the *WBP*. The usual cross-reference was to PSALM 35, and later to the similar HUMBLE SUIT. The first setting was Cosyn's in 1585, to the tune VENI CREATOR. East set it to HUMBLE SUIT in *East 1592*, before consigning it to CAMBRIDGE in 1594. It retained more than average popularity in the 18th century: the competing tunes for it then were WESTMINSTER (*HTI* 387d), first assigned by Playford in 1677, and a new tune STROUDWATER (794), provided in Timbrell's *Divine Musick Scholars Guide* (1714). The text was modernized and a few lines replaced in the early 18th century. Collections of hymns and psalms continued to reprint the text through the first decades of the 19th century.

Psalm 41
The man is blest that careful is

Text: The **psalm** was one of Sternhold's original nineteen first printed in *1548* (see p. 838) and was revised for *1556*. While Sternhold relied more than usual on either the Vulgate or Coverdale's parallel translation in the first half of the psalm, the second half tends to favor phrasing from either the Coverdale or Great Bible. Whittingham's revision for *1556* is extensive, replacing three entire quatrains (vv. 6–8) and substantially altering three more (vv. 9, 12, and 13). He did remove some readings from the Vulgate in favor of those from the Great Bible, but also sometimes followed the French versification by Beza rather than a more literal English prose translation. The **argument** was first printed in *1556* and was reprinted in the 1557 Genevan Psalter and the Geneva Bible. It translates the argument from the French metrical psalter.

Incipit Beatus qui intelligit [super egenum et pauperum]: Blessed is he that considers the needy and poor
34 *Marginal note to v. 9:* John 13.b [13:18] / Acts 1.c [1:16] *1556*; *om* John 13.b. *1561d, 1562a* [Cross-reference from the Olivétan Bible.]
36 *Marginal note to* **laid wait:** Heb. He lift up his heel against me or used deceit, and therefore Jacob had his name, by taking by the heel and deceiving: Gen. 25.d [25:26], 27.e [27:36] *1556*; Gen. 15.d.17.c. *1561d, 1562a* [Partly derived from Calvin or the Olivétan Bible, but possibly showing influence from Martin Bucer's commentary.[33]]

Later use of the text: This paraphrase was substantially revised at the end of the 17th century, including the opening lines, which became "The man is blest, that doth provide / for such as needy be" (*WBP* 1751). It stopped appearing in most psalm collections other than the *WBP* before the 19th century, however.

Tune: DCM, D minor/F major (*HTI* 88, Frost 60). First printed in *1556*. It begins in D minor but ends in F major; this unusual feature was never modified. Extra syllables at the end of phrases 2 and 4 are accommodated with two minims in editions from 1562 onwards; they only apply, of course, to the first stanza, and so have not been adopted here. The tune was in all early editions of the *WBP*, but was dropped from some later ones, beginning in 1586, when it was referred to HUMBLE SUIT. The proper tune was adopted in the Companions and survived well into the 18th century.

Other musical settings: John Sheppard composed a four-voice setting of Sternhold's text in Edward VI's time, but only the uppermost voice part survives (see p. 518). Middleburg editions and a few other later editions of the *WBP* substituted common tunes, beginning with LOW DUTCH in *1601b*. Playford in 1677 coupled the psalm to TE DEUM and this was followed in a few early-18th-century tunebooks. William Tans'ur composed a new tune, DAINTREE (*HTI* 1396a), in 1735 for the revised text.

Psalm 42
Like as the hart doth breathe and bray

Text: The **psalm** was first printed in *1549b* and revised for *1556*. Hopkins here mingled readings from the Vulgate and the Great Bible, with occasional suggestive echoes of Joye's paraphrase and a good deal of interpretive freedom. Whittingham revised this psalm more extensively for *1556* than any other by Hopkins, replacing two quatrains entirely (v. 4), adding a new one (to v. 5, compressed in

---

[33] See p. 629 above. This is a verse on which the two theologians disagree, and the *1556* gloss incorporates both interpretations.

the *1549b* version), and further revising vv. 6 and 8. These revisions do not necessarily bring the versification closer to literal English prose translations, and in places (e.g., vv. 5–6) seem to reflect French sources, including both the glosses in the French Bible and Beza's metrical version. The **argument** was first printed in *1556* and was reprinted in the 1557 Genevan Psalter and the Geneva Bible. It paraphrases that in the French metrical psalter.

Incipit Quemadmodum desiderat [cervus ad fontes aquarum]: Whenas the wild hart hath a desire to the water springs
9 *Marginal note to v. 3:* It is death to a Christian heart to hear his God blasphemed. *1556* [Derived from Calvin's commentary.]
13 *Marginal note to v. 4:* What grief it is to a godly man to be out of the congregation, where by prayer and confession of faith he might call upon God. *1556*
33 *Marginal note to v. 7:* God trieth his children by divers and often afflictions. *1556, 1561d, 1562a*
44 *Marginal note to v. 9b:* The papists and infidels esteem not God and therefore mock all such as profess his name. *1556, 1561d*

Musical settings and later use of the text: John Sheppard composed a four-voice setting of Hopkins's text in Edward VI's time, but only the uppermost voice part survives (see p. 518). The somewhat insipid *1556* tune for Psalm 33 (*HTI* 89, Frost 61) was set to this text for four voices by Hake in *Day 1563*. But it was not adopted in the *WBP*. The usual cross-reference was to PSALM 35, and later to the similar HUMBLE SUIT. The psalm was set to several common tunes, first in *East 1592* to CAMBRIDGE. The psalm continued to appear in Anglican tunebooks until around 1780. Surprisingly, it had a brief run among dissenters, even carrying its original tune in Nathaniel Gawthorn's *Harmonia Perfecta* (1730). In addition to a handful of other modernized lines, the first line was updated at the end of the 17th century to "Like as the hart doth pant and bray," and the psalm as a whole fell out of use in the late 18th century.

Psalm 43
Judge and revenge my cause, O Lord

Text: The **psalm** was first printed in *1549b* (see p. 841) and revised for *1556*. Sternhold mixed some wording from at least Coverdale's translation of the Vulgate and the Great Bible, but leaned more heavily on the Great Bible throughout. In revising, Whittingham added a final quatrain more fully expressing the second half of v. 5 as well as emending a handful of other lines. The **argument** was first printed in *1556* and was reprinted in the 1557 Genevan Psalter and the Geneva Bible. It translates that in the French metrical psalter. There was no abridgement of the argument in 1577.

Incipit Iudica me, Deus: Be thou my judge, O God

Musical settings and later use of the text: John Sheppard composed a four-voice setting of Sternhold's text in Edward VI's time, but only the uppermost voice part survives (see p. 518). The Geneva tune (*HTI* 90a, Frost 62), as printed in *1556* and later Scottish psalm books, is ostensibly in the Locrian mode transposed, with final on E and a key signature of B flat. This was not one of the church modes and is generally regarded as purely theoretical, since its "tonic triad" would be a diminished-5th chord. Not surprisingly, the tune was never used in the *WBP*, and Hake's four-part setting in *Day 1563* changed the final from E to F and treated it as in F major. The usual cross-reference was to PSALM 35, and later to the similar HUMBLE SUIT. *East 1592* set the psalm to the common tune LOW DUTCH, but after Ravenscroft selected ST. DAVID's (379a), followed by Playford, this became the tune of choice until about 1740. However, the psalm rarely appeared in tunebooks after 1770. Early in the 17th century, in addition to a scattering of other revised lines, the first two lines were changed to "Judge and defend my cause, O Lord, / 'gainst them that evil be" (*WBP* 1751).

Psalm 44
Our ears have heard are fathers tell

Text: The **psalm** was first printed in *1549b* (see p. 842) and revised for *1556*. Sternhold's primary source for his versification was the Great Bible, although at least one cognate from the Vulgate (l. 20, "confound") also appears. The **argument** was first printed in *1556*. It was translated from the French metrical psalter and reprinted in the 1557 Genevan Psalter, but not adopted for the Geneva Bible.

Incipit Deus auribus nostris [audivimus]: We have heard with our ears, O God
22 *Marginal note to end of v. 8:* Selah. *1556, 1561d, 1562a*
39 *Marginal note to vv. 14–15:* The state of God's children in this world. *1556, 1561d*
58 *Marginal note to* **dens:** He meaneth among the infidels. *1556, 1561d* [From the Olivétan Bible.]

Later use of the text: The text appeared in various collections of psalms, but there is little evidence that the paraphrase itself was very popular apart from its tune(s); despite relatively aggressive updating of the language in the early 1700s, it was seldom printed outside the *WBP* after the middle of the 18th century.

Tune: DCM, F major (*HTI* 91a, Frost 63). First printed in *1556*. This strong and memorable tune (μ10), with its varied repeat of phrases 1 and 2, gained a permanent home in both the English and Scottish psalm books, and was also generally referred to for Pss. 63 and 73. It was treated to no less than five 4-voice settings in

Day 1563, perhaps an indication of its early popularity: the most straightforward, by Parsons, is recorded here (µ14).[34] The tune was later also associated with Tate & Brady's version, "O Lord, our fathers oft have told." It was revived in the 19th century and appears as OLD 44TH in *Hymns Ancient & Modern* (1861) with Cecil Frances Alexander's hymn "The roseate hue of early dawn."

Other musical settings: John Sheppard composed a four-voice setting of Stern-hold's text in Edward VI's time, but only the uppermost voice part survives (see p. 518). The psalm's strong association with its proper tune meant that it was not printed with a common tune until 1677, when Playford matched it to PETERBOR-OUGH (*HTI* 539b). This combination was found in some tunebooks up to 1779.

Psalm 45
My heart doth take in hand

Text: The **psalm** was first printed in *1562a*. Hopkins drew on both the Geneva and Great Bibles, although this versification departs frequently from the phrasing and occasionally the literal meaning of either one. An expanded version of the **argument** was first printed in the 1557 Genevan Psalter, and edited to the same text as *1562a* for the Geneva Bible. It was paraphrased from Calvin's summary in his *Commentary on the Psalms*.

Incipit Eructavit [cor meum verbum bonum]: My heart hath composed a good matter
31 pointed: The reading from *1562b* ("oynted," i.e., anointed) probably correctly records the original MS. The Geneva and Great Bibles have identical wording for v. 7b: "because God, even thy God hath anointed thee with the oil of gladness above thy fellows."
33 mirth: Also a misreading by the original compositors, corrected in editions of 1569 to accord with the prose: "All thy garments smell of myrrh and aloes" (Geneva).

Musical settings and later use of the text: This psalm had no proper tune. The usual cross-reference was to the most popular short-meter tune in the *WBP*, PSALM 25. It was first set to the common tune LONDON in *Daman 1579*: the setting is transcribed in Frost, no. 65. Playford's choice of ST. PETER'S (276h), a revision of WINCHESTER, was popular in the early 18th century, and the psalm appeared with various tunes until after 1800. The text itself was little changed, except that lines 65–8 (v. 16) — a set of lines that seems to have caused persistent

---

[34] A more elaborate one by Brimley, with the tune slurring in the bass, was treated as a "second tune" by Frost (Frost 64).

confusion in the Elizabethan editions—were rewritten entirely in the early 18th century.

Psalm 46
The Lord is our defence and aid

Text: The **psalm** was first printed in *1562a*. The paraphrase shows some influence from the Geneva Bible but more frequently echoes the Great Bible. The **argument** was first printed in the 1557 Geneva Psalter and subsequently in the Geneva Bible (with an additional half sentence at the end omitted from the *WBP*). It is paraphrased from Calvin's summary in his *Commentary on the Psalms*. The argument was not significantly abridged in 1577.

Incipit Deus noster refugium: Our God is our refuge
21 folk: Most editions correctly give "flock." The reading from *1565*, "folcke," results either from an accidentally transposed letter or from misconstruing the word as a noun rather than a verb; that semi-plausible misreading allowed the error to persist in some later editions, including *1567*. (The Great Bible source phrase is "The heathen make much ado.")

Later use of the text: This paraphrase was attached to a special order of public and domestic prayers in response to the earthquake of 1580 (see Other musical settings, below). The text saw little of the modernization that most of the psalms underwent in the late 17th and early 18th centuries, but it also appears to have been seldom reproduced outside the *WBP* after the late 18th century.

Tune: DCM, F major (*HTI* 171, Frost 66). First printed in *1562a*. It sounds more like a bass than a tune, and it was so treated in several four-part settings: by Parsons in *Day 1563*, by Daman in *Daman 1591*, and by Allison in *Allison 1599*, though not by Blancks in *East 1592*, who placed it in the tenor like any other tune. In the Scottish psalm book of 1635 it serves as bass to a much more tuneful tenor. Nevertheless the original kept its place in most editions of the *WBP* and was generally referred to for Pss. 47, 48, 53, and 54. It was ignored by Ravenscroft and Playford but survived in many 18th-century tunebooks. The treble part of the four-voice setting in *Allison 1599* (*HTI* 278, Frost 115) had a life of its own as the tune for Ps. 101 in some Scottish psalm books.

Other musical settings: A specially written tune in *WBP* style (*HTI* 256) was published with the psalm and an added doxology in 1580, as part of *The Order of Prayer, and Other Exercises, upon Wednesdayes and Frydayes, to Avert and Turne Gods Wrath from us, Threatned by the Late Terrible Earthquake: To be Used in all Parish Churches and Householdes throughout the Realme, by Order Given from the Queens Majesties Most Honourable Privie Counsel* (London: Christopher Barker,

1580, D3v–4v). Middleburg editions and a few other late editions of the *WBP* assigned common tunes, beginning with Low Dutch in *1601b*. Playford in 1677 chose to set the psalm to a modified version of Nunc dimittis (see p. 638). With various other tunes it was still in use at the end of the 18th century.

Psalm 47
Ye people all, in one accord

Text: The **psalm** was first printed in *1562a*. Where he followed a source closely, Hopkins worked almost exclusively from the Great Bible for this paraphrase. The **argument** was first printed in the 1559 Geneva Book of Psalms and subsequently in the Geneva Bible as well as in *1560b* and its descendants (accompanying Kethe's versification). It is an abridgement of that in the 1557 Genevan Psalter, derived ultimately from Calvin's summary in his *Commentary on the Psalms*.

Incipit Omnes gentes, [plaudite manibus]: All ye heathen, clap with your hands

Musical settings and later use of the text: This psalm had no proper tune in the *WBP*. The usual cross-reference was to Psalm 46; the reference in *1567* to Ps. 45 is erroneous, since that psalm is in short meter and has no tune. The first and sixth stanzas were set as a three-voice anthem by John Mundy in his *Songs and Psalmes* (1594). It was set to Oxford in *East 1592*; the Middleburg editions either did the same, or followed the *WBP* reference to Psalm 46. Playford's choice of London New (*HTI* 497b) was adopted in some early-18th-century tunebooks. A slightly updated version of the text survived into the mid-19th century in other hymnbooks, with the first lines "Ye people all, with one accord, / clap hands, shout and rejoice" (*WBP* 1751).

Psalm 48
Great is the Lord and with great praise

Text: The **psalm** was first printed in *1562a*. As with Ps. 38, that edition and most later ones attribute the versification to Hopkins, when in fact it is almost certainly by Norton. (Unlike Ps. 38, the error is not corrected in *1562b*.) Departing from Hopkins's practice but agreeing with Norton's, the psalm lacks verse numbers in the 1562 editions and the quatrains rhyme *abcb*. Although not conclusive, the fact that it derives mostly from the Geneva Bible translation with only traces of the Great Bible's phrasing is also more characteristic of Norton than of Hopkins, as is the abrupt enjambment of line 23. The **argument** was first printed in the 1559 Geneva Book of Psalms and subsequently in the Geneva Bible, abridged from the version in the 1557 Genevan Psalter which drew on Calvin's summary in his *Commentary on the Psalms*.

Incipit Magnus Dominus: Great is the Lord
23 stayed: probably a compositor's error for "stroyed," corresponding to the Geneva Bible's "so were they destroyed." This is the last word of v. 7.

Musical settings and later use of the text: This psalm had no proper tune in the *WBP*. The usual cross-reference was to PSALM 46. It was set to LOW DUTCH in *East 1592*. Playford's choice of EXETER (*HTI* 397b) was followed in several early 18th-century tunebooks. With various tunes it survived into the 19th century.

Psalm 49
All people, hearken and give ear

Text: The **psalm** was one of Sternhold's original nineteen first printed in *1548* (see p. 844) and was revised for *1556* (*1567* and some later editions misattribute it to Hopkins). Sternhold incorporated readings from all three of the Coverdale translations he consulted. The revision in *1556* was extensive, rewriting nine quatrains in their entirety and emending four more in addition to supplying a quatrain for a missing half-verse (14b). The majority of the revisions bring the text closer to what Whittingham understood as the literal meaning, agreeing with Great Bible or with his own 1557 prose translation. The **argument** was first printed in *1556* and was reprinted in the 1557 Genevan Psalter and the Geneva Bible. It does not closely follow any of Whittingham's ordinary sources, though it agrees with Calvin's reading of the psalm and may echo parts of Bucer's argument in his psalm commentary.

Incipit Audite hæc, omnes [gentes]: Hear these things, all ye nations
vi 1 Thes. 1: Although v. 10 of this chapter refers to waiting for the return of the resurrected Christ, the reference is probably to 2 Thes. 1:4–10, which elaborates on the tribulation faced by the just, their eschatological triumph, and the punishment facing unbelievers.
6 rightwise: Both the Edwardian editions and *1556* print this as two words ("right wyse"), meaning in in this case "very wise" (and corresponding to the Great Bible's "My mouth shall speak of wisdom"). About half of the Elizabethan editions consulted, however, including *1567*, print the words run together into one, forming an archaic but still recognizable spelling of "righteous." This would not, even in the mid-sixteenth century, have rhymed with "exercise," but it is more likely that compositors mistook the phrase for a single word than that they consistently forgot to put a space between those two words in particular.
9 *Marginal note to v. 4:* He will treat of weighty matters and great importance. *1556, 1561d*
21 *Marginal note to v. 7:* The term of man's life is only in God's hands. *1556, 1561d*
33 *Marginal note to v. 11:* They dream an immortality in this life, although daily they see the contrary by experience. *1561d;* The dream . . . the see *1556*

43 *Marginal note to end of v. 13:* Selah *1556*
56 *Marginal note to end of v. 15:* Selah *1556*
61 *Marginal note to v. 17:* Job 27 [27:19] / 1 Tim. 6 *1556* [Cross-reference to Job from the Olivétan Bible.]

Musical settings and later use of the psalms: A unique 4-voice piece in the Wanley partbooks (c. 1547) uses the first stanza of this psalm followed by most of Sternhold's Psalm 4 (omitting only stanza 2); it is set strophically, the same music to be sung nine times. The tenor partbook is missing; one possible reconstruction makes the tenor into a "tune,"[35] another makes it a subordinate part in a motet-like piece with no predominant voice.[36] John Sheppard also composed a four-voice setting in Edward VI's time, but only the uppermost voice part survives (see p. 518). The *1556* tune (*HTI* 92, Frost 68) was never adopted in the *WBP*, but appeared in a four-part setting by Hake in *Day 1563*. The usual cross-reference was to Psalm 45, which, however, is in short meter and has no tune. East's choice of Cambridge was followed by Playford. With various tunes the psalm continued in use through most of the 18th century, with the second line in the lightly modernized text slightly altered to "to that which I shall tell."

<h2 style="text-align:center">Psalm 50 (1)
The mighty God, the eternal, hath thus spoke</h2>

Text: The **psalm** was first printed in *1558*. It was omitted from *1562a* in favor of Ps. 50 (2); *1563* and *1564* include it in a separate section after the metrical psalter proper. It returned to the metrical psalter in *1565* in the same position it holds in *1567* and most later editions, although it follows 50 (2) in the edition of 1566 (*STC* 2437). The versification is for the most part a line-by-line translation of Marot's French metrical version, sometimes in the diction of the Great Bible or the 1557 Genevan Psalter. The **argument** was first printed in *1558*, and is textually unrelated to the arguments in the 1557 Genevan Psalter and Geneva Bible. It translates and adapts the argument in the French metrical psalter. It was not significantly abridged in 1577.

Incipit Deus deorum [Dominum locutus est]: The God of gods, even the Lord, hath spoken

Later use of the text: The paraphrase, in nearly unchanged form, was printed in other psalm collections through the early 19th-century.

---

[35] See *MEPC* 2, no 4, and Leaver, *'Goostly Psalmes'*, 504.
[36] See Wrightson, ed., *The Wanley Manuscripts*, 2: 91–96.

Tune: 10.10.10.10.11.11, Dorian transposed/G minor (*HTI* 116a, Frost 69). This grand tune was first printed with Marot's Ps. 50 ("Le Dieu, le fort, l'Eternel parlera") in *La Forme des prieres et chantz ecclesiastiques* (Strassburg: Jehan Knobloch, 1545) (Pidoux 50a). In this earlier form the 8th note of phrase 2 was f' rather than e'. Otherwise the tune was essentially unchanged in the French Genevan psalter of 1551 (Pidoux 50b), and in its adaptation to Whittingham's translation in *1558*. The lack of a semibreve and rest at the end of phrase 4, in contrast to the otherwise identical phrase 3, reflects an enjambment in the opening stanza of the French text: "Devers Sion Dieu clair et evident / Apparoistra, orné de beauté toute," but serves no purpose with the English text and would be removed in the 1586 revision (see p. 938). The extra syllable in line 4 gave some trouble. The word "Sion" was evidently pronounced as a trochee (cf. Psalm 50(2)), and was so treated here by means of an extra note in *Day 1563, 1565,* and *1567,* allowing "toward" two notes; we rejected this solution because it does not fit the later stanzas. The feminine endings of phrases 5 and 6 were misunderstood by the adapter.

The tune is found in all musical editions of the *WBP*, and continued to be sung with its text well into the 19th century, often with the irrelevant name Llandaff, chosen for it by William Tans'ur in 1743. It was equally popular with dissenters: Ainsworth (1612) and Watts (1719) each wrote his own translation of Ps. 50 to fit the tune, and it became standard for Watts's version in the 19th century. On the high-church side it was revived by William Crotch in 1803. It eventually entered *Hymns Ancient & Modern* (1922) as Old 50th, with another text.

Other musical settings: The first challenge was a tune produced by John Bishop in 1710; seven others were printed in the next century, but none dislodged the French tune.

Psalm 50 (2)
The God of gods, the Lord

Text: The psalm was first printed in *1562a*. Hopkins combined readings from the Geneva and Great Bibles in a relatively loose paraphrase.

49 This 8-syllable line—a slip into common meter in an otherwise poulter's meter text—was corrected to 6 syllables in editions of 1569.

Tune: DSM, F major (*HTI* 172, Frost 70). First printed in *1562a*. It was in all the early editions of *WBP*, but was dropped from most after 1573 and left without a tune suggestion. The only harmonized versions were in *Day 1563, Daman 1579,* and *Daman 1591.*

Other musical settings and later use of the text: Both East and Playford set the psalm to the most common SM tune, London (*HTI* 269c). It was for this text that John Chetham (1718) first printed what would become one of his most wide-ly published tunes, AYLESBURY (*HTI* 848a). With this and other tunes it main-tained some popularity through the 18th century and into the early 19th. Mod-ernization of the text was mainly restricted to the first Part.

Psalm 51 (1)
O Lord, consider my distress

Text: The **psalm** was first printed in *1556*. This is the only psalm to be included as a duplicate in *1562a* with an Elizabethan London version. Whittingham's pri-mary source was the Great Bible, but he also chooses in places to follow the sense of Marot's French versification or to employ cognates of Marot's wording. The **argument** was first printed in *1556* and was reprinted in the 1557 Genevan Psal-ter as well as the Geneva Bible. It adapted from Calvin's summary in his *Com-mentary on the Psalms*.

Incipit 1. Miserere mei, Deus: Have mercy on me, O God [The numeral "1" was traditionally added to this incipit to distinguish this psalm from Pss. 56 and 57, which begin with the same three words.]
13 *Marginal note to v. 4:* Rom. 3 [3:4] *1556* [Cross-reference from the Olivétan Bible.]
23 *Marginal note to v. 7:* Num. 19 / Iea. [Lev.] 14 / Isa. 1 *1556*
54 Misprint "from thus" in *1556* is corrected in the *1558* errata.

Later use of the text: This was one of the more popular paraphrases from the *WBP* carried over into other collections of psalms and hymns. Both the open-ing stanzas and another selection beginning at the modernized line 41 ("Cast me not, Lord, from out thy sight") were printed independently through the middle of the 19th century.

Tune: DLM, Dorian/D minor (*HTI* 93a, Frost 71). First printed in *1556* and present in every musical edition of the *WBP*. In the earliest editions up to 1562 this unusually designed tune began in the strict Dorian mode, with no B-flats; took them on in its 4th and 5th phrases (as if modulating to F major); then gave them up for phrases 6–8. By 1564 it had B-flats throughout. The choice of mode may have been related to the penitential character of its well-known text, often called (*The*) *Miserere*. The unusual frequency of pairs of minims on the same note, occurring eleven times, gives a plaintive character to the tune. As a firmly es-tablished proper tune it appeared in all the Companions. William Lawes used text and tune as one of his *12 Psalms* (c. 1640). Another, anonymous 17th-century setting of text and tune for voice and instrumental bass survives (British Li-brary Add. MS. 29481, fol. 4). This was one of the eight long tunes chosen by

Playford for his *Introduction to the Skill of Musick* in 1658, and it accompanied its text through many later publications. It was revived by William Crotch in 1803.

Julian (*Dictionary of Hymnology*, 2nd edn., 839) states that this is "the earliest known version of a Psalm in L.M." This is strictly true for English, but the tune is coeval with COMMANDMENTS (2), which was adapted to LM from a French tune in 9.8.9.8.

Other musical settings: Several Elizabethan anthems were based on the first few verses of this paraphrase; two of them are listed in Clifford (1664); one, by Thomas Wylkinson, has been recently published.[37] Thomas Call composed a tune for the psalm (*HTI* 2802a) for the Magdalen Chapel collection in 1762, beginning on the 7th degree of the major scale; it spread to many other books, but without its text and deprived of its unconventional opening. The second part of the psalm, beginning "Cast me not, Lord, out from thy face," was set in four parts by William Lawes for his *12 Psalms* and was accorded its own tune, LEMSTER (*HTI* 1421), by William Tans'ur in *A Compleat Melody* (1735).

Psalm 51 (2)
Have mercy on me, God, after

Text: The **psalm** was first printed in *1562a*. Norton consulted and intermixed readings from the Geneva and Great Bibles in his paraphrase.

Musical settings and later use of the text: This version never acquired its own tune in the *WBP*, but *Day 1563* included it with an otherwise unknown tune, headed "Another upon Miserere," by Thomas Caustun (*HTI* 188): the setting is printed as Frost 72. The usual cross-reference to "the Lamentation" must have meant LAMENTATION OF A SINNER, since The Lamentation and its tune are in long meter. The psalm was set to OXFORD in *East 1592* and to CAMBRIDGE by Playford in 1677, but—despite a comprehensive textual revision in the 1690s—barely survived into the 18th century outside of the *WBP*.

Psalm 52
Why dost thou, tyrant, boast abroad

Text: The **psalm** was first printed in *1549b* (see p. 846) and revised for *1556*. Hopkins's main source for his versification was the Great Bible. For *1556*, Whittingham emended a handful of lines, usually to make them slightly more literal as paraphrases of the prose. The **argument** was first printed in *1556* and was reprinted in the 1557 Genevan Psalter as well as the Geneva Bible. It is related to

---

[37] Wylkinson, "O Lord, consider my distress," ed. Peter le Huray [c. 2005].

the argument in the Olivétan Bible and to Calvin's summary in his *Commentary on the Psalms*, although the French sources do not make reference to Antichrist.

Incipit Quid gloriaris [in malitia]: Why rejoiceth thou in malice
ii Abimelech: Or Achimelech; the two names have a complex history of substitution for each other. He was the high priest of Nob who (in 1 Sam. 21) armed and fed David as he fled from Saul, David having carefully given the impression that he was on the king's business. Doeg witnessed the interaction and reported back to Saul in 1 Sam. 22, portraying Abimelech as a rebellious conspirator who had prophesied on David's behalf (the "false surmises" that led Saul to order all the priests at Nob executed).
9–10 On . . . upright?: In the original (and all Hopkins's sources), the wickedness of the addressee is a statement rather than a rhetorical question.
12 *Marginal note to end of v. 3:* Selah *1556*
20 *Marginal note to end of v. 5:* Selah *1556*
24 *Marginal note to* **cry:** Heb. shall laugh or mock. *1556*

Later use of the text: This paraphrase was relatively seldom included in psalm collections outside the *WBP* and seems to have passed out of usage by the mid-18th century.

Tune: DCM, C major (*HTI* 161a, Frost 74). This bland tune was first printed in *1561c*. It appeared in most musical editions of the *WBP*: the first to omit it was *STC* 2540.5 (1578). From 1614, very unusually, it was introduced in the Scottish psalm books as the tune for a different text, Pont's Ps. 57 ("Be merciful to me, O God"). Some *WBP* editions used it for Ps. 85. But as Playford never printed it, it quickly fell out of common use.

Other musical settings: John Sheppard composed a four-voice setting of Hopkins's text in Edward VI's time, but only the uppermost voice part survives (see p. 518). Playford (*Whole Book of Psalms in Three Parts*, 1677) coupled this psalm with the tonally ambiguous tune LITCHFIELD (*HTI* 381b). A few other tunes were used with it in the early 18th century.

Psalm 53
The foolish man, in that which he

Text: The **psalm** was first printed in *1562a*. Norton's main source seems to have been the Geneva Bible, though wording is very occasionally closer to the Great Bible. The **argument** was first printed in the 1557 Geneva Psalter and subsequently in the Geneva Bible. It was paraphrased from the Olivétan Bible, and not significantly abridged in 1577.

Incipit Dixit insipiens [in corde suo]: The unwise man hath said in his heart
4 denied: Spelled "denayed" in early editions in order to make a full rhyme with
said.

Musical settings and later use of the text: This psalm never had its own tune in
the *WBP*. The usual reference was to Psalm 46. It was later set to several com-
mon tunes, first in *East 1592* to Oxford, but did not become widely popular and
seems to have been largely extinct by the late 18th century. The first half of the
psalm was substantially revised in the 1690s, and the first two lines subsequently
appear as "The foolish man within his heart / blasphemously hath said" (*WBP*
1751).

Psalm 54
God, save me for thy holy name

Text: The **psalm** was first printed in *1562a*. Hopkins worked primarily from the
Great Bible in his paraphrase, though he takes a single reading from the Gene-
va version in the last verse ("*my* heart's desire"). The **argument** was first printed
(with substantial variants) in the 1557 Genevan Psalter, and subsequently in the
form adopted by the *WBP* in the Geneva Bible as well as in *1560b* and its descen-
dants (accompanying Kethe's versification). While influenced by Calvin's *Com-
mentary on the Psalms*, it does not paraphrase the summary there.

Incipit Deus, in nomine [tuo salvum me fac]: Save me, O God, in thine own
name
i Ziphims: False form of the already plural "Ziphim," inhabitants of the desert
of Ziph. For the incidents in which they reveal David's hiding place to Saul, see
1 Sam. 23:19 and 26:1.
6 thee: Should be understood as the indirect object of **pray** (i.e., when I do pray
to thee). Editors or typesetters as early as *1564*, however, understandably read it
as the blasphemous indirect object of **give an ear,** and so emended to **me.**

Musical settings and later use of the text: This psalm never had its own tune in
the *WBP*. The usual reference was to Psalm 46. It was later set to several com-
mon tunes, first in *East 1592* to Low Dutch, but did not become widely popular
and rarely appeared outside the *WBP* after the 18th century.

Psalm 55
O God, give ear and do apply

Text: The **psalm** was first printed in *1562a*. In this versification, Hopkins pri-
marily follows the Great Bible when he hews closely to any of his usual sources,
though there is some influence from the Geneva Bible (as in the "double tongue"

of line 38, from the Genevan "divide their tongues," as well as line 45 below). The **argument** was first printed in the 1559 Geneva Book of Psalms and subsequently in the Geneva Bible. It was taken from Calvin's summary in his *Commentary on the Psalms*.

Incipit Exaudi, Deus, [orationem meam]: Hear my prayer, O God
13–16: This quatrain expands the original by interpolating new complaints.
45 her privy parts: An unexpected metaphorical extrapolation from the Geneva Bible's "Wickedness is in the mids [midst] thereof."

Musical settings and later use of the text: This psalm never had its own tune in the *WBP*. *Cosyn 1585* set it to a version of Te Deum (*HTI* 166b), altered so as to end in G minor. It was set to several common tunes: East and Ravenscroft chose Cambridge; Playford chose Manchester (*HTI* 374a), with which it was printed in some early-18th-century collections. William Byrd (1543–1623) set the first two stanzas as a consort song for voices and viols, which he published in 1588 (*Collected Works*, 12:1). The text itself, with the first lines emended in the early 18th century to "O God, give ear, and speedily / hear me when I do pray" (*WBP* 1751), was printed through the early 19th century but not in a large number of publications.

Psalm 56
Have mercy, Lord, on me I pray

Text: The **psalm** was first printed in *1562a*. Hopkins seems to have worked almost entirely from the Great Bible in his paraphrase. The **argument** was first printed in the 1557 Genevan Psalter and subsequently in the Geneva Bible. It agrees with Calvin's *Commentary on the Psalms*, but takes pieces from the whole exposition rather than paraphrasing the summary.

Incipit Miserere [mei, Deus]: Have mercy on me, O God

Musical settings and later use of the text: This psalm never had its own tune in the *WBP*. The reference to "the Lamentation" must have meant Lamentation of a Sinner (cf. Ps. 51 (2)). It was set to several common tunes, first in *East 1592* to Oxford, but did not become widely popular and appeared mainly in the *WBP* itself.

Psalm 57
Take pity for thy promise sake

Text: The **psalm** was first printed in *1562a*. In his paraphrase, Hopkins drew from both the Great Bible and the Geneva Bible for phrasing and interpretation. The **argument** was first printed in the 1557 Genevan Psalter and subsequently in the Geneva Bible. It does not come in any straightforward way from any of Whittingham's usual sources.

Incipit Miserere [mei, Deus]: Have mercy on me, O God
i–ii desert of Ziph . . . Saul: The argument contextualizes the psalm within the events of 1 Sam. 26:1–12, when David, having been hunted by Saul, nevertheless refuses to allow his lieutenant Abishai to kill the sleeping king after they penetrate the Israelite camp.
16 mercy, truth, and might: In apposition to **his aid** (13). Cf. the Great Bible: "He shall send from heaven, and save me from the reproof of him that would eat me up. Selah. God shall send forth his mercy and truth."

Musical settings and later use of the text: This psalm never had its own tune in the *WBP*. The usual reference was to Psalm 44. It was set to several common tunes, first in *East 1592* to Low Dutch, but did not become widely popular.

Psalm 58
Ye rulers that are put in trust

Text: The **psalm** was first printed in *1562a*. In versifying this psalm, Hopkins drew from not only the Geneva and Great Bibles but also the Vulgate in making sense of the difficult v. 9. The **argument** was first printed in the 1559 Geneva Book of Psalms and subsequently in the Geneva Bible as well as in *1560b* and its descendants (accompanying Kethe's versification). It is an abridgement of that in the 1557 Genevan Psalter, which differs significantly from all of Whittingham's usual sources.

Incipit Si vere utque [iustitiam loquimini]: If ye speak of righteousness unfeignedly indeed
16, 17 her, he: The inconsistency in gender is the result of partial emendation by a compositor or proofreader to a familiar formulation from the Great Bible, in which the adder "stoppeth her ears"; Hopkins's versification originally followed the Geneva version in which it is "his ear." The next quatrain, however, escaped revision and remained male (except, among editions collated, in *1599*).

Musical settings and later use of the text: This psalm never had its own tune in the *WBP*. Its *1567* cross-reference is to Psalm 68; it was referred to various psalms in other editions with none predominating. It was set to several common tunes, first in *East 1592* to CAMBRIDGE, but largely gave up its place in other psalm collections to newer paraphrases by the middle of the 18th century.

Psalm 59
Send aid and save me from my foes

Text: The **psalm** was first printed in *1562a*. Hopkins intermingled diction and sense from the Geneva and Great Bibles in his versification. The **argument** was first printed in the 1557 Genevan Psalter, and subsequently in the emended form adopted by the *WBP* in the Geneva Bible. It greatly expands on the summaries (similar to each other) in Calvin's *Commentary on the Psalms* and the Olivétan Bible, but disagrees with Calvin about the purpose of keeping the enemies of God's people alive for a time.

Incipit Eripe me [de inimicis meis]: Deliver me from mine enemies
22, 24 grin, run: Early editions rhyme these words through the variant spellings "grenne" and "renne."

Later use of the text: The text was modernized, though not aggresively revised, in the early 18th century. It was not widely popular, and seems to have fallen out of use before the 19th century.

Tune: DCM, D minor (*HTI* 173, Frost 77). First printed in *1562a*. It begins unusually with four portentous semibreves (μ15), which were modified in the 1586 revisions (p. 942, and μ16). No less than five phrases end on the final, D. It appeared in almost all editions of the *WBP* and was generally referred to for Pss. 61 and 62. Ravenscroft (1621) set it to MAGNIFICAT, which from then on competed with the proper tune in the *WBP*.

Other musical settings: *Cosyn 1585* chose the tune LAMENTATION OF A SINNER (see p. 921). Some editions of the *WBP* from 1636 onwards substituted YORK (*HTI* 331a). Several other tunes appeared with the text in scattered 18th-century publications.

Psalm 60
O Lord, thou didst us clean forsake

Text: The **psalm** was first printed in *1562a*. Hopkins relied chiefly on the Great Bible in versifying the text, although he adopted the sense of the Geneva version in v. 10. The **argument** was first printed in the 1559 Geneva Book of Psalms and subsequently in the Geneva Bible. It is paraphrased from Calvin's *Commentary* *on the Psalms*. The changes during the revision and abridgment of arguments in 1577 were minor.

Incipit Deus repulset [*sc.* repulisti] nos: Thou has cast us off, O God
14 token shall ensue: *1601b*'s "banner thou didst shew" replaces the Great Bible's "token" with the Geneva translation's "banner." It comes from the Scottish psalm book via Richard Schilders's 1599 edition of the *WBP* (see p. 578).

Musical settings and later use of the text: This psalm never had its own tune in the *WBP*. The usual reference was to PSALM 59. It was set to several common tunes, first in *East 1592* to OXFORD, but did not become widely popular and seldom appeared outside the *WBP* after the middle of the 18th century Its slightly emended second line read, by then, "and scatter us abroad" (*WBP* 1751); other changes were restricted to individual words or phrases.

Psalm 61
Regard, O Lord, for I complain

Text: The **psalm** was first printed in *1562a*. The texts in all the English translations that Hopkins normally consulted are very close, and there is no evidence of any other sources. The **argument** was first printed in the 1557 Genevan Psalter and reprinted in the Geneva Bible. It derives from Calvin's summary and comments on v. 1 in the *Commentary on the Psalms*.

Incipit Exaudi, Deus [, deprecationem meam]: Hear mine humble petition, O God

Later use of the text: The very lightly revised text was reprinted for congregational use more frequently and longer than its tune, surviving in psalm and hymn collections outside the *WBP* at least into the second quarter of the 19th century.

Tune: DCM, F major (*HTI* 174a, Frost 78). First printed in *1562a*. This somewhat characterless tune is found in many editions of the *WBP*, but was omitted from some, starting with *STC* 2449.5 (1579). The psalm was then most often referred to PSALM 59. It was in the Companions, but was not used by Playford and had a short life in 18th-century tunebooks.

Other musical settings: Playford in his *Whole Book of Psalms in Three Parts* (1677) set this text to PSALM 119 and was followed in this by some later compilers. At least 18 other tunes were allied to the psalm, showing that it retained some popularity during the 18th century.

Psalm 62
My soul to God shall give good heed

Text: The **psalm** was first printed in *1561c*. Where Hopkins appears to follow a specific prose translation closely, it is nearly always the Great Bible (which is nearly the same as the 1557 Genevan Psalter). The **argument** first appeared in the 1557 Genevan Psalter; the Geneva Bible has a related but distinct headnote.

Incipit Nonne Deo subjecta [erit anima mea]: Shall not my soul be subject unto God?

Musical settings and later use of the text: This psalm never had its own tune in the *WBP*. The usual reference was to PSALM 59. It was set to several common tunes, first in *East 1592* to LOW DUTCH, but did not become widely popular. The revision of the 1690s was light except for the entire replacement of ll. 25–8 (v. 7). There is little evidence of it outside the *WBP* after the 18th century.

Psalm 63
O God, my God, I watch betime

Text: The **psalm** was first printed in *1549b* (see p. 847) and appeared in *1556* with a handful of lines emended, two quatrains replaced, and two further quatrains added to include imagery that Sternhold had omitted in his compression. Some of the imagery in vv. 5 and 10, in fact, Whittingham expanded from the scriptural original after the example of Beza's French metrical version. The **argument** was first printed in *1556* and was reprinted in the 1557 Genevan Psalter and the Geneva Bible. It is modeled on the headnote in the Olivétan Bible.

Incipit Deus, Deus meus [, ad te de luce vigilo]: O God, my God, unto thee do I watch betimes in the morning
v 1. Sam. 3: David's flight to the wilderness of Ziph occurs in 1. Sam. 23, correctly given in the Genevan editions as well as a solitary London printing (1564, *STC* 2433); the marginal note in the Olivétan Bible references 1 Sam 23:14.
31 *marginal note to v. 9:* 1 Sam. 31 *1556*
38 *marginal note to* **profess:** Hebr. that swear by him, that is, which worship him alone *1556* [This combines the literal meaning as translated in the Great Bible with Budé's gloss.]

Musical settings and later use of the text: John Sheppard composed a four-voice setting of Sternhold's text in Edward VI's time, but only the uppermost voice part survives (see p. 518). The *1556* tune (*HTI* 95a, Frost 80) was transferred to Ps. 101 in Scottish psalm books, but was not used in the *WBP*; it did appear in a setting by Hake in *Day 1563*. The usual reference was to PSALM 44. Later the psalm was set to several common tunes, first in *East 1592* to CAMBRIDGE, but did not become widely popular, despite revisions in the early 18th century to eliminate nearly all the expressions that had become archaic. The first line was at that time emended to "O God, my God, I early seek" (*WBP* 1751).

Psalm 64
O Lord, unto my voice give ear

Text: The **psalm** was first printed in *1561c*. The primary source for Hopkins's versification here is the Great Bible. The **argument** first appeared in the 1557 Genevan Psalter and was included with minor changes in the Geneva Bible; the *WBP* follows the 1557 version. It paraphrases and slightly expands on the argument from the Olivétan Bible. There was no abridgement of this argument in 1577.

Incipit Exaudi, Deus, vocem [*sc.* orationem] meam: Hear thou my voice [*sc.* prayer], O God

Musical settings and later use of the text: This psalm never had its own tune in the *WBP*. Its usual cross-reference was to PSALM 18. It was set to several common tunes, first in *East 1592* to OXFORD, but was not widely reproduced outside of the *WBP*. By the end of the 17th century, the second line had become "when I complain and pray."

Psalm 65
Thy praise alone, O Lord, doth reign

Text: The **psalm** was first printed in *1561c*. While the versification most often follows the wording of the Great Bible and very similar 1557 Genevan Psalter, several lines seem to be influenced by the Geneva Bible's translation, most notably in v. 13, where Hopkins's "places plain" resembles the Geneva's "pastures" far more than the other versions' "folds." The **argument** was first printed in the 1557 Genevan Psalter and again with some emendation in the Geneva Bible. The *WBP* follows the 1557 version. It is mainly drawn from the summary in Calvin's *Commentary on the Psalms*. There was no significant abridgement of this argument in 1577.

Incipit Te decet hymnus [deus in Sion]: It beseemeth us to praise thee, O God, in Sion
41 wet: The sense is definitely "moisture," as in the Great Bible's "Thou waterest her furrows." Most early editions, however, spelled the word "wete," which was also a current spelling of the modern "wheat." The variant list records all spellings other than "wet" in the editions collated; a few other 16th-century editions have spellings that unambiguously signify grain (e.g., "wheat" in 1596, *STC*

2490.6), and it is entirely possible that readers and singers frequently interpreted the verse that way in using other editions.

55 valleys: Probably pronounced as one syllable, like "vales."

Musical settings and later use of the psalm: This psalm never had its own tune in the *WBP*. The usual reference was to PSALM 30. It was set to several common tunes, first in *Cosyn 1585* to OXFORD. The text was modernized in the late 17th century, but the psalm did not become widely popular and was essentially out of use before 1800.

Psalm 66
Ye men on earth, in God rejoice

Text: The **psalm** was first printed in *1561c*. Where Hopkins's English sources differed, he opted for the Great Bible or Geneva readings roughly an equal number of times. In v. 20, in fact, he combined the Geneva's "not put back" with "not cast out" from the Great Bible (and 1557 Psalter) to get "not put / nor cast me out." The significant variants in lines 58, 59, and 67 of *1601b* reflect the Scottish text of this psalm, conveyed to the *WBP* through the Schilders 1599 edition (see p. 578). The **argument** was first printed in the 1557 Genevan Psalter and reprinted in the and Geneva Bible without the last phrase of the first sentence. It expands on the headnote in the Olivétan Bible.

Incipit Iubilate Deo, omnis terra: Be joyful in God, all the earth

Musical settings and later use of the text: This psalm never had its own tune in *WBP*, though some Middleburg editions borrowed the Scottish tune (see p. 988). The usual reference was to PSALM 68. It was set to several common tunes, first in *East 1592* to CAMBRIDGE. In the 18th century it was set to at least 28 tunes and persisted in hymn collections with and without printed music into the 19th century.

Psalm 67
Have mercy on us, Lord

Text: The **psalm** was first printed in *1561c*, permanently displacing both versions (by Whittingham and Wisdom, respectively) that appeared in *1560a*. Hopkins clearly worked from the English Protestant translations he usually favored, but they are too close in their own wording to show any preference on his part. The **argument** first appeared in the 1557 Genevan Psalter, and was reprinted in slightly different form from the one here in the Geneva Bible. It is unusually independent from Whittingham's usual sources. (A completely different argument accompanied Whittingham's metrical paraphrase beginning in *1558*, and a third prefaced Wisdom's versification in *1560a*.) The argument was not abridged in 1577.

Incipit Deus misereatur nostri: God have mercy upon us

Musical settings and later use of the text: *1560a* offered new tunes for both Whittingham's and Wisdom's versions of this psalm, but the Hopkins version never had its own tune. Early editions referred it to PSALM 30, which however is in the wrong meter; some later ones suggested PSALM 25. The psalm later gained an association with the SM tune LONDON (*HTI* 269a, 269c), chosen by Cosyn, East, and Ravenscroft, and followed by Playford. It was also set as a consort song for voices and viols by William Byrd (*Collected Works*, 15: 8). William Lawes used text and tune as one of his *12 Psalms* (c.1640). An elementary new tune, GUILFORD (*HTI* 1411a), was provided for it by William Tans'ur in *A Compleat Melody* (1735) and it maintained some popularity, with the text very little changed, through the 18th century.

Psalm 68
Let God arise, and then his foes

Text: The **psalm** was first printed in *1549b* (see p. 848) and extensively revised for *1556*. When hewing closely to prose translations, Sternhold most often chose to follow the Great Bible, though occasional phrasing from the Vulgate appears as well as some attempts at clarification by interpreting rather than paraphrasing metaphors. In reworking the paraphrase, Whittingham significantly changed or replaced 87 lines out of 140 and added two quatrains to the psalm's total length, with the result that the *WBP* version is more his than Sternhold's. Whittingham drew on several Genevan sources, including Calvin's as-yet-unpublished *Commentary on the Psalms* (as for the name "Jah" in v. 4) and Budé's French translation (the "calves and bulls of might" in v. 30 from "forts taureeaux avec les veaux": Pidoux, *Psautier huguenot*, p. 110). The **argument** was first printed in *1556* and was reprinted in the 1557 Genevan Psalter and the Geneva Bible. Unlike the psalm paraphrase, it is unrelated to Whittingham's usual French or Latin sources.

Incipit Exurgat Deus: Let God stand up
15 *marginal note to* **Jah**: Jah is one of the proper names of God and signifieth "evermore" *1556, 1561d*
28 *marginal note to end of v. 7*: Selah *1556*
33 *marginal note to v. 9*: The abundance and plentifulness of the land of Canaan *1556, 1561d* [This summarizes a note in the Olivétan Bible.]
41 *marginal note to* **women**: As Miriam, Deborah, Judith *1556, 1561d* [Calvin mentions only Miriam.]
49 *marginal note to* **pots**: Or trivets *1556, 1561d, 1562a*

57 *marginal note to v. 15*: The Church of God doth excel all worldly things, not in outward pomp but by the grace of God which there remaineth because of his promise *1556, 1561d, 1562a*

65 *marginal note to* **army**: Or chariots *1556*

66 *marginal note to* **warriors**: He understandeth angels *1556* ["Angels" is the literal translation given in all of Whittingham's Reformed Latin and vernacular prose sources; the Vulgate does not specify what or who is being counted.]

73 *marginal note to v. 18b*: God took not taxes to enrich himself but to bestow them on his Church, and therefore in the 4th to the Ephesians [4:8] St. Paul saith he "gave gifts," following the Greek translation. *1556, 1561d, 1562a* [This follows Calvin's commentary on the verse.]

80 *marginal note to end of v. 19*: Selah. *1556, 1561d, 1562a*

89 *marginal note to* **Basan**: He meaneth the victory which David had of Og, king of Basan. *1556, 1561d, 1562a*

109 *marginal note to* **little Benjamin**: Because he was the youngest of the Patriarchs [sic] Jacob's sons, he calleth him little Benjamin. *1556, 1561d, 1562a*

117 **And . . . word**: I.e., We will give you gifts in your temples, O Lord, because of the promise that you made to Jerusalem.

125 *marginal note to v. 30*: He attributeth the victory to God. *1556* [In the Olivétan Bible, the corresponding note glosses v. 28.]

136 *marginal note to end of v. 32*: Selah. *1556*

Later use of the text: This psalm underwent particularly heavy revision in the early 18th century, with four quatrains entirely replaced in addition to smaller changes throughout. Its appearance in hymnals outside the *WBP*, however, seems to have been due more to the success of the tune than any attachment to this particular paraphrase. Hymnbooks without music in the 19th century frequently feature versions of Ps. 68, but almost never Sternhold's.

Tune: DCM, F major (*HTI* 117a, Frost 85). First printed in *1558*. The first two phrases may have been inspired by the French tune for Ps. 134, which was to become PSALM 100. Perhaps for that reason it was one of the most successful of the proper tunes, appearing in every musical edition of the *WBP*; a few, starting with *1585a*, printed it for Ps. 115 as well. It was one of the eight long tunes chosen by Playford for his *Introduction to the Skill of Musick* in 1658, and continued to be widely printed after 1700, carrying its text through most of the influential tunebooks.

Other musical settings: John Sheppard composed a four-voice setting of Sternhold's text in Edward VI's time, but only the uppermost voice part survives (see p. 518). The *1556* tune (*HTI* 66a, Frost 84) became the Scottish tune for Ps. 34, but was never adopted in the *WBP*; it did appear in *Day 1563* in a setting by

Hake. The popularity of the proper tune in the 18th century reduced the incentive for new matches, but a handful were printed.

Psalm 69
Save me, O God, and that with speed

Text: The **psalm** was first printed in *1561c*. Although occasional word choices from the Geneva Bible appear (e.g., "restore" in v. 4), Hopkins largely favored the Great Bible in this paraphrase. The **argument** first appeared in the 1557 Genevan Psalter, and was reprinted with minor emendation in the Geneva Bible; the *WBP* follows the 1557 text. It is loosely modeled on the argument and glosses of the Olivétan Bible.

Incipit Salvum me fac, Domine: Save me, O God

Later use of the text: Like Ps. 68, this one was extensively revised in the early 18th century without achieving its continued success. Few collections outside the *WBP* contained it after the 1750s. During its brief 18th-century life, the second line appeared as "because the waters do" (*WBP* 1751).

Tune: DCM, Dorian transposed/G minor (*HTI* 162a, Frost 86). First printed in *1561c*. This Dorian tune, with a heavy emphasis on the lower 7th degree, remained a fixture in all musical editions of the *WBP* and in all the Companions; it was also referred to as the tune for Ps. 71 in most editions. Playford, from 1671, transferred it to Ps. 71, Timbrell (1723) to Ps. 72; its last known printing was with Ps. 64 in Richard Langdon's *Divine Harmony* (1774).

Other musical settings: The first stanza of this psalm was chosen for a three-voice, madrigalesque anthem by John Mundy in his *Songs and Psalmes* (1594). The first printed setting to a tune other than the proper tune was Playford's (*Whole Book of Psalms in Three Parts*, 1677), to GLASSENBURIE, but it was not copied by other compilers; a few other tunes were matched to the psalm in 18th-century collections.

Psalm 70
O God, to me take heed

Text: The **psalm** was first printed in *1561c*. As usual, Hopkins worked from the Geneva and Great Bibles, though each is clearly chosen over the other only once: the Geneva Bible provided the "rebuke" in l. 8, while the Great Bible inspired the enemies to shout "there" in l. 12. The **argument** first appeared in the 1557 Genevan Psalter and was reprinted in the Geneva Bible. It paraphrases the headnote in the Olivétan Bible.

Incipit Deus, in adiutorium [meum intende]: Have respect to help me, O God

Musical settings and later use of the text: This short-meter psalm never had its own tune in the *WBP*. The usual reference was to PSALM 72, which, however, is in common meter; in some later editions this was corrected to PSALM 25. It was later set to several common tunes, first in *East 1592* to LONDON, but did not become widely popular. In the early 17th century, the second line stabilized as "I help of thee require" (*WBP* 1751).

Psalm 71
My Lord my God, in all distress

Text: The psalm was first printed if *1561c*, replacing an earlier version by Whittingham that first appeared in *1558*. When closely resembling any previous translation, this psalm follows the Geneva Bible more frequently than is usual for Hopkins, although there are also occasional glimpses of the Great Bible. The **argument** first appeared in the 1557 Genevan Psalter; a revised version was reprinted in the Geneva Bible. It is derived from the summary and commentary to v. 1 in Calvin's *Commentary on the Psalms*.

Incipit In te, Domine, speravi: In thee, O Lord, have I put my trust

Musical settings and later use of the text: The *1558* tune (*HTI* 118, Frost 88) was adopted in the Scottish but not the English psalm book. The usual reference was to PSALM 69. It was set to several common tunes, first in *East 1592* to OXFORD, and this was copied in Middleburg editions starting with *1601b*. Ravenscroft set it to PSALM 72, followed in some *WBP* editions. Playford chose PSALM 69, and this became the standard match in many tunebooks of the first half of the 18th century. Nathaniel Giles (c. 1558–1634) wrote a verse anthem in six parts based on stanzas 1–6.[38] It seems to have fallen out of use before the beginning of the 19th century.

Psalm 72
Lord, give thy judgements to the king

Text: The **psalm** first appeared in *1561c*. As in his paraphrase of the previous psalm, Hopkins strongly favored the Geneva Bible most of the way through, including some substantive disagreements (e.g., at v. 6 Geneva has "rain upon the mown grass," as against the Great Bible and 1557 Genevan Psalter which offer "rain into a fleece of wool"). A handful of choices from the Great Bible do,

---

[38] Giles, *Anthems*, 87–101. It begins "O Lord, my God, in all distress."

however, pop up, such as the "little hills" of l. 11 or the king of "Araby" in v. 10. The **argument** first appeared in the 1557 Genevan Psalter and was reprinted in a version slightly expanded from this one in the Geneva Bible. It is modeled on that in the Olivétan Bible.

Incipit Deus, iudicium tuum [regi da]: Give the king thy judgment, O God

Later use of the text: In 1609, this psalm was cannibalized (with the opening quatrain intact) for a broadsheet hymn in honor of James I to be sung by the orphan schoolchildren of Christ's Hospital (see *HTI* 282).[39] The full text of the paraphrase was at best moderately popular in collections of psalms other than the *WBP*, though it continued in some into the 19th century. In the *WBP*, it underwent successive revisions starting in the late 17th and early 18th centuries, resulting in a text with a substantial number of lines completely different from the Elizabethan originals.

Tune: DCM, Aeolian (*HTI* 163a, Frost 89). First printed in *1561c* and *1561d*. This boldly modal tune, characterized by rising and descending 4ths, and with unusual leaps of a 7th and a 6th between later phrases, was printed in nearly all musical editions of the *WBP* before 1622, and was generally referred to as the tune for Ps. 74 as well. Ravenscroft (1621) transferred it to Ps. 71. It was selected, with the text of Ps. 72, by Hawkins as an illustration in his *History of Music* (1776), 3: 516.

Other musical settings: Ravenscroft composed a striking new four-line tune (*HTI* 364a, Frost 233) for this psalm, which he named CHRIST HOSPITAL. This was adopted in 116 editions of the *WBP* between 1622 and 1649, and in a number of early 18th-century collections, despite Playford's restoration of the older tune.

Psalm 73
However it be, yet God is good

Text: The **psalm** was one of Sternhold's original nineteen first printed in *1548* (see p. 852) and was extensively revised for *1556*. It most often follows the Great Bible, though Sternhold occasionally preferred phrasing from the Vulgate or Coverdale's parallel English translation. Whittingham's version for *1556* is three quatrains longer than Sternhold's, in addition to replacing or substantially rewriting more than 40 of the original 92 lines. While the *1556* text in a few places (notably v. 25) brings the paraphrase into more literal agreement with the Great Bible, Whittingham much more frequently followed Beza's metrical French version in his revision. The **argument** was first printed in *1556* and was reprinted in

---

[39] *A Psalme of Prayer and Praise for . . . the King* (London: Edward Allde, 1609).

the 1557 Genevan Psalter and the Geneva Bible. It paraphrases and expands the headnote in the Olivétan Bible.

Incipit Quam bonus [Israel] Deus: Oh, how good is God unto Israel
37 *marginal note to v. 10*: How hard it is for God's children themselves to avoid the temptations of the world. *1556, 1561d*
51 innocents: Both the Geneva and Great Bibles give "in innocency," but Sternhold here followed the Vulgate's "inter innocentes." No editions of the *WBP* consulted change the word into an abstract noun.
57 *marginal note to v. 15*: God's children ought not to be contemned because the worldlings are preferred in dignity and worldly honours. *1556, 1561d*
84 *marginal note to* **in this point**: Heb. before thee. *1556* [This is the literal rendering in the English prose translations.]
89 *marginal note to v. 25*: Neither superstition nor yet fear or subtlety of man could draw him from the true worshipping of God. *1556, 1561d* [The note is derived from Calvin's commentary on this verse.]
97 *marginal note on* **thee forsake**: Heb. go awhoring from thee. *1556* [Translated thus in the Geneva Bible; the Great Bible gives "commit fornication against thee."]

Musical settings and later use of the text: John Sheppard composed a four-voice setting of Sternhold's text in Edward VI's time, but only the uppermost voice part survives (see p. 518). The *1556* tune (*HTI* 97, Frost 90) was not used in the English psalm books after *1560a*. The usual reference was to PSALM 44. The psalm was set to several common tunes, first in *East 1592* to LOW DUTCH, but did not become widely popular. The revision of the late 17th-century changed the opening quatrain the most, giving the psalm a first line of "Truly the Lord is very good" (*WBP* 1751) for the fifty or so years that it was printed outside the *WBP*.

Psalm 74
Why art thou, Lord, so long from us

Text: The **psalm** was first printed in *1561c*. Hopkins clearly consulted both the Geneva and Great Bibles, but followed the Great Bible in diction and/or meaning for long stretches of the psalm. The **argument** first appeared in the 1557 Genevan Psalter and was reprinted in the Geneva Bible. It is paraphrased from the headnote in the Olivétan Bible.

Incipit Ut quid, Deus, [repulisti nos in finem]: Why hast thou utterly cast us away, O God

Musical settings and later use of the text: This psalm never had its own tune in the *WBP*. The usual reference was to PSALM 72. It was later set to several common tunes, first in *East 1592* to CAMBRIDGE, but was infrequently included in other psalm collections, almost never after the 1750s. Revisions to the text in the late 17th century were light, except for wholly replacing the eight lines of vv. 10–11.

Psalm 75
Unto thee, God, we will give thanks

Text: The **psalm** was first printed in *1561c*. Norton worked from the Geneva and Great Bibles, though he favored the latter. The **argument** first appeared in the 1557 Genevan Psalter and was reprinted in the Geneva Bible. It expands on that in Olivétan Bible.

Incipit Confitebimur tibi, Deus: We will give thanks unto thee, O God
41–4 The **Gloria Patri** or doxology ("Glory be to the Father") follows the reading or singing of prose psalms in the *BCP*. This is the only psalm in the *WBP* to have a metrical doxology explicitly appended (Robert Wisdom's Ps. 125 (2) includes an unlabeled Gloria Patri as the last stanza).

Musical settings and later use of the text: This psalm never had its own tune in the *WBP*. The usual reference was to PSALM 44. It was later set to a few common tunes, first in *East 1592* to OXFORD, but did not become widely popular and disappeared in collections other than *WBP* before the end of the 18th century. The first line, from the 1690s on, appears as "To thee, O God, will we give thanks" (*WBP* 1751); in the early 18th century, the doxology was dropped.

Psalm 76
To all that now in Jewry dwell

Text: The **psalm** was first printed in *1562a*. Hopkins worked from the usual sources for his Elizabethan psalms: although the paraphrase is slightly weighted toward readings from the Geneva Bible, the Great Bible is also extremely well represented. A longer version of the **argument** was first printed in the 1557 Genevan Psalter and revised for Geneva Bible; the *WBP* adopted the latter version. It is derived from the summary in Calvin's *Commentary on the Psalms*.

Incipit [Notus] In Iudea [Deus]: God is known in Israel

Musical settings and later use of the text: This psalm never had its own tune in the *WBP*. The usual reference was to PSALM 69. It was set to several common tunes, first in *East 1592* to LOW DUTCH, but none resulted in wide popularity. In the late 17th century, the first half of the psalm in particular was revised to bring the text up to date, with the result that subsequently "Jewry" in the first line appears as "Judah."

Psalm 77
I with my voice to God do cry

Text: The **psalm** was first printed in *1562a*. In this psalm one can see Hopkins weighing the Great Bible against the Geneva verse by verse, and in some places where they disagreed choosing neither. In v. 1, for example, the Geneva translation takes the past tense, the Great Bible takes the future—and Hopkins opts for present. The **argument** first appeared in the 1557 Genevan Psalter and was reprinted in the slightly amended form adopted by the *WBP* in the Geneva Bible. It is derived from the summary in Calvin's *Commentary on the Psalms*.

Incipit Voce mea ad Dominum [clamavi]: With my voice have I cried unto the Lord

Later use of the text: The paraphrase was reprinted in some other collections of psalms into the 19th century. Its first lines changed in the light modernization of the 1690s to "I with my voice to God did cry / who lent a gracious ear" (*WBP* 1751).

Tune: DCM, F major (*HTI* 175a, Frost 93). First printed in *1562a*. This tune and PSALM 81 are a unique pair, in that they have the same succession of pitches but differ in rhythmic scheme. This version is in a strongly marked duple time, reinforced by the five dotted-minim-crotchet pairs. It accompanied its psalm in all early editions of *WBP*, with additional references from Pss. 79, 80, 82–84, 87, 93, 96, and still others in later editions. It was given settings in the Companions, but in Wolfe's revisions of *WBP* in *1586a* and most later editions it yielded to its sister tune PSALM 81. An abridged derivative is the second tune for Ps. 120 (see p. 395). This is also a likely model for WINCHESTER (see p. 1007) and other tunes, as discussed under PSALM 81 below.

Other musical settings: Playford from 1671 set this text to the old tune LAMENTATION OF A SINNER (*HTI* 155, Frost 10), copied in a few other publications. James Green's *Collection of Psalm Tunes* (3rd and 4th editions, Nottingham, 1715, 1718) supplied a curious new tune in the style of the Elizabethan proper tunes (*HTI* 818), but it is not found anywhere else.

Psalm 78
Attend, my people, to my law

Text: The **psalm** was one of Sternhold's original nineteen first printed in *1548* (see p. 854) and relatively lightly revised for *1556*. Sternhold paraphrased concisely but stayed fairly close to his his sources, choosing diction and phrasing from both the Vulgate and the Great Bible. In *1556*, Whittingham adopted several readings from Budé's French translation and notes. The most obvious of these are in v. 61 ("son honneur vint en la main de l'ennemi," in contrast to the Great Bible's "their beauty into the enemy's hand") and v. 65 ("valliant [homme]" vs. Coverdale's "giant"): Pidoux, *Psautier huguenot,* pp. 141, 142. The **argument** first appeared in *1556* and was reprinted verbatim in the 1557 Genevan Psalter and with minor emendations in the Geneva Bible. It is adapted from the summary in Calvin's *Commentary on the Psalms.*

Incipit Attendite, populi [*sc.* popule], [meus legem]: Listen to my law, O my people
15 *marginal note to v. 5b*: Deut. 6.a. [6:7] *1556, 1561d* [The reference also appears in the Olivétan Bible.]
17 *marginal note to v. 6*: God hath left his word for to be understande[d] of all men excepting neither degree nor age. *1556, 1561d* [*1561d* partly cropped]
29 *marginal note to v. 9*: 1 Chron. 7. *1556* [Calvin's commentary specifically rejects the association of this verse with 1 Chron. 7:20–22 as too narrow a reading of the passage.]
44 Thaneos: Thus the Vulgate, a Latinization of the Greek "Tanis." The Hebrew name for this Egyptian city is usually Anglicized as "Zoan," as in both the Great Bible and the Geneva.
45 *marginal note to v. 13*: Exod. 13, 14 / Ps. 105.d [105:39] *1556, 1561d* [The Olivétan Bible correctly references Exod. 14:21 on the divided waters of v. 13 and then Exod. 13:21 for v. 14; the reference to Ps. 105:39 should also apply to v. 14 instead of here.]
53 *marginal note to v. 15*: Exod. 17.b [17:6] / Num. 20.d [20:11] / Ps. 105.d [105:41] *1556, 1561d* [All these references are also given in the Olivétan Bible.]
69 *marginal note to v. 19a*: Num. 11.a [11:4] *1556, 1561d* [The reference is from the Olivétan Bible.]
71 *marginal note to v. 19b*: The distrust of man. *1556* [This boils down a longer note in the Olivétan Bible.]
75 *marginal note to v. 20b*: Num. 11.b [11:13] / 1 Cor. 10.a [10:3–4] *1556, 1561d* [The Olivétan Bible references the passage from 1 Cor. at v. 18.]
87 *marginal note to v. 24*: Exod. 16.c [16:14] / Num. 11.b [11:7] *1556, 1561d* [This note is positioned in the margin as if referring to v. 23. The references are given in the Olivétan Bible at v. 21.]
88 *marginal note to* **food**: Heb. wheat from heaven. *1556, 1561d* [Calvin lingers over the etymology in his commentary on this verse.]
89 *marginal note to* **angels'**: Heb. mighty or strong. / John 6.d [6:31] *1556, 1561d* [These are positioned in the margin as if referring to v. 26. The Olivétan Bible gives "pain des puissants" in the text itself and explains that this refers to the food of angels in the marginal gloss. The reference to John should accompany the translation of manna as "wheat from heaven."]

103 *marginal note to v. 31*: Numb. 11.g [11:33] *1556, 1561d* [In the Olivétan Bible, this more correctly glosses v. 30.]

113 *marginal note to v. 34*: Affliction causeth men to seek unto God. *1556, 1561d*

125 *marginal note to start of v. 38*: In Hebrew the Psalm is here divided. *1556, 1561d*

153 *marginal note to v. 44*: Exod. 7.d [7:20] *1556* [The reference is from the Olivétan Bible.]

157 *marginal note to v. 45*: Exod. 8.a [8:6] *1556* [Also a reference from the Olivétan Bible.]

161 *marginal note to v. 46*: Exod. 20.c. *1556* [An error for Exod 10:16, as given in the Olivétan Bible.]

172 *marginal note to* **thunder bolts:** Heb. darts of fire, or such thunder as is called of Pliny *brontia*. *1556* [Budé provides the literal Hebrew translation but not the reference to Pliny.]

181 *marginal note to v. 51*: Exod. 12. *1556* [The Olivétan Bible here references Exod. 12:20.]

185 *marginal note to v. 52*: Exod. 13.c [13:18] *1556* [The reference is from the Olivétan Bible.]

197 *marginal note to v. 55*: Josh. 11.b [11:7] *1556* [Again taken from the Olivétan Bible.]

209 *marginal note to* **hill altars:** Altars erected in the mountains. *1556, 1561d* [This echoes the note in the Olivétan Bible.]

217 *marginal note to v. 60*: 1 Sam. 4.a [4:11] *1556* [Again repeating a reference from the Olivétan Bible.]

253 *marginal gloss to v. 70*: 1 Sam. 16.b [16:11] *1556* [Taken from the Olivétan Bible.]

Later use of the text: Although reprinted (at least in part) in tunebooks into the early 19th century, the text was not widely popular.

Tune: DCM, Dorian/D minor (*HTI* 164a, Frost 95). First printed in *1561c*. It shares its opening phrase with PSALM 135. The degree of similarity between the tune's two halves, which share 18 out of 28 pitches, is unusual. The tune is in virtually every musical edition of the *WBP*, often with references from Pss. 90, 94, and 114. It is in all the Companions, and in many later musical collections up to about 1775.

Other musical settings: John Sheppard composed a four-voice setting of Sternhold's text in Edward VI's time, but only the uppermost voice part survives (see p. 518). The *1556* tune (*HTI* 98a, Frost 94), in the unusual key of B flat major, was dropped from English editions after *1560a*, but reappeared in *Day 1563* in a setting by Hake. Later, several short tunes were used, beginning with CHESHIRE in a 1636 edition of the *WBP* (*STC* 2694); Playford chose YORK (*HTI* 331a).

Psalm 79
O Lord, the Gentiles do invade

Text: The psalm was first printed in *1549b* (see p. 861) and appeared with only
two lines revised in *1556*. Much of Hopkins's paraphrase reflects the influence of
the Coverdale or Great Bible, although Joye's paraphrase probably contributed
phrases in vv. 7 and 8. Whittingham's *1556* revisions to lines. 23 and 28 make
them more literal representations of the passages as translated in both the Great
Bible and his own 1557 Genevan Psalter. The **argument** first appeared in *1556*,
was reprinted in the 1557 Genevan Psalter, and was slightly revised for the Ge-
neva Bible. It derives from the summary in Calvin's *Commentary on the Psalms*.

Incipit Deus, venerunt gentes [in haereditatem tuam]: O Lord, the heathen are
come into thine inheritance
21 *marginal note to v. 6*: Jer. 10.d [10:25] *1556* [The reference comes from the Ol-
ivétan Bible.]
26 *marginal note to* **destroyed:** Heb. he hath devoured, meaning the enemy. *1556*
["Devoured" is the translation given in the text of all Whittingham's vernacular
sources.]
29 *marginal note to v. 8*: Isa. 64.c [64:9] / An earnest prayer for remission of sins.
1556 [The cross-reference comes from the Olivétan Bible.]
53 *marginal note to v. 12*: The troubled heart uttereth diverse affections in pray-
ing. *1556, 1561d* [This slightly odd comment on a request for vengeance probably
derives from Calvin's discussion in his *Commentary* of the holy zeal that animates
the faithful when they see God traduced.]

Musical settings and later use of the text: Neither the *1556* tune, which was in
triple CM (*HTI* 99, Frost 96), nor the DCM tune of *1558* (*HTI* 119, Frost 97)
was adopted in the *WBP*; the latter became the standard Scottish tune. The usual
reference was to PSALM 77. The psalm was later set to several common tunes, first
in *East 1592* to CAMBRIDGE, but did not become widely popular. It appears in
relatively few collections of psalms other than the *WBP*. In the late 18th century,
the first line was revised to "O God, the Gentiles do invade" (*WBP* 1751).

Psalm 80
Thou herd that Israel dost keep

Text: The psalm was first printed in *1562a*. Hopkins's paraphrase shows close
affinities with both the Geneva and Great Bible versions, but reproduces dic-
tion directly most often from verses where they agree; a small number of distinc-
tive phrases from the Great Bible appear (e.g., the boars that "root" and beasts
that "devour" in v. 13). The **argument** first appeared in the 1559 Geneva Book of

Psalms and then the whole Geneva Bible. It paraphrases the opening sentences of the summary in Calvin's *Commentary on the Psalms*.

Incipit Qui regis Israel, [intende]: O listen, thou that governest Israel
45 The paraphrase omits v. 11, "She stretched out her branches unto the sea, and her boughs unto the river" (Great Bible).

Musical settings and later use of the text: This psalm never had its own tune in the *WBP*. The cross-reference in *1567* is to Psalm 67, a tune in the wrong meter. This was later corrected to Psalm 77. The psalm was set to several common tunes, first in *East 1592* to Oxford, but did not become widely popular. By the start of the 18th century, the first line in the *WBP* had become "Thou Shepherd, that dost Israel keep" (*WBP* 1751).

Psalm 81
Be light and glad, in God rejoice

Text: The **psalm** was first printed in *1562a*. Hopkins drews more or less equally from the Geneva and Great Bibles, with substantive interpretation taken from each (e.g., v. 5b follows the distinct meaning of the Great Bible, while v. 7b follows the Geneva Bible's sense). The **argument** first appeared in the 1559 Geneva Book of Psalms and then the whole Geneva Bible. It condenses the summary in Calvin's *Commentary on the Psalms*. The abridgement of this argument occurred after 1577; a number of later editions that normally include the shorter arguments, including *1577* and *1582*, use the longer original.

Incipit Exultate Deo, [audiutori nostro]: Rejoice before God, our savior

Later use of the text: Beginning in 1580, the Elizabethan service for Accession Day (November 17) included a thanksgiving hymn modeled on this versification and borrowing its first lines (and tune).[40] Although extraordinarily popular, this psalm was borne forward into the 19th century largely on the strength of its proper tune, which survived it by many decades. Perhaps because it was so well known, the early 18th-century revisions were extremely light. A one-word change appears in the second line, "who is our strength and stay" (*WBP* 1751).

Tune: DCM, F major (*HTI* 175a, Frost 99). First printed in *1562a*. This, the triple-time version of Psalm 77, is one of only three *WBP* proper psalm tunes clearly in that rhythm. It possesses a feeling of gaiety happily matched to its opening words and quite distinct from the somber mood of most of the tunes.

---

[40] *Fourme of Prayer to be Used the 17. of Nouember*, sig. C4v–6r.

It was probably the most popular of them all in Elizabethan times, Psalm 100 being the only possible rival. It was present in virtually every musical edition of the *WBP*, with references from Pss. 85–87 and 101. Starting with Wolfe's revision of 1586 it was printed with Ps. 77 as well (see p. 947), replacing the common-time version. In the same year it was selected for *A Godlie Dittie to be Song for the Preservation of the Queenes Most Excellent Majesties Raigne* (London: Abel Jeffes, 1586): "We laud and praise his name always, Who doth our queen defend."[41] *Allison 1599* contains an effective arrangement for four voices and lute (µ28); Ravenscroft (1621) used Allison's voice parts, and for Pss. 105 and 135 as well. Playford adopted the tune in both his *Introduction* (from 1658) and his *Whole Book of Psalms in Three Parts* (from 1677), using it also for Ps. 98 in the latter source.

Tune and text remained together in 112 other publications between 1694 and 1820, a record surpassed only by Psalm 100. The tune was also adapted to Tate & Brady's version of Ps. 92 ("How good and pleasant must it be / To thank the Lord most high"). It found its way into dissenting tunebooks, such as Nathaniel Gawthorn's *Harmonia Perfecta* (1730) and the supplements to Isaac Watts's *Psalms* from 1753 (*HTI* ✳TS WatB). An ornamented version (175c) became popular in the Midlands region after Michael Broome published it in *A Choice Collection of Sixteen Excellent Psalm Tunes* (Birmingham, [c. 1751]), and in this form it was later adopted for a version of Ps. 19 ("Ye worshippers of Jacob's God") at the Asylum for Female Orphans in London.[42]

Another indication of the depth of this tune's assimilation by the singing public is the series of shorter tunes evidently drawn from it: Psalm 120, second tune (see p. 395), in six 6's; and no less than 21 four-line tunes (*HTI* 276a-u). The best known of these are Winchester (276a: see p. 1007) and the short-meter St. Peter's (276h), adopted by Playford for Ps. 45.[43]

The tune persisted in use in the 19th century. As Old 81st it was paired incongruously in *Hymns Ancient and Modern* and elsewhere with Reginald Heber's hymn "The Son of God goes forth to war." A *Fantasia and Fugue on Old 81st* for organ by William Thomas Best was published in 1881. *The English Hymnal* (1906) used it with two hymn texts.

Other musical settings: East used the proper tune in *East 1592*, but in 1594 reset the psalm to Low Dutch. Several other tunes were used with this psalm.

---

[41] Facsimile in Krummel, *English Music Printing*, 163.

[42] See *Psalms and Hymns, for the Chapel of the Asylum for Female Orphans.*

[43] For a detailed discussion of this tune's progeny see Temperley, "Kindred and Affinity," *Musical Times* 113 (1972), 905–9.

Psalm 82
Amid the press with men of might

Text: The **psalm** was first printed in *1549b* (see p. 862) and slightly revised for *1556*. Hopkins appears to have worked mainly from the Coverdale Bible, though he takes a number of interpretive liberties with the text. For *1556*, Whittingham replaced the quatrain paraphrasing v. 5b. The new version interprets the scriptural image of the earth's foundations shaking in light of Budé's gloss to his French translation. The **argument** was first printed in *1556* and appeared verbatim in the 1557 Genevan Psalter and nearly identically in the Geneva Bible. It is based on the argument in the Olivétan Bible.

Incipit Deus stetit in synagoga [deorum]: God hath stood in the congregation of the gods
16 tyrants' force and might: The original (and all Hopkins's sources) identify the threat as the ungodly or sinners. **Tyrant** could mean "ruffian."
25 *marginal note to v. 6:* John 10.c [10:34] *1556* [This echoes the reference in the Olivétan Bible.]

Musical settings and later use of the text: The *1556* tune (*HTI* 100, Frost 101) was never adopted in England. The usual reference was to PSALM 77. The psalm was later set to several common tunes, first in *East 1592* to LOW DUTCH, but it never attained much popularity. The revision of the early 18th century not only eliminated archaisms by substantially rephrasing a number of passages but shortened the psalm by a quatrain. The new first lines ran "Among the princes, men of might, / the Lord himself doth stand" (*WBP* 1751).

Psalm 83
Do not, O God, refrain thy tongue

Text: The **psalm** was first printed in *1562a*. Hopkins's usual sources for his Elizabethan paraphrases, the Geneva and Great Bibles, are very close in this psalm, although a few fragments of differing diction from each find their way into the metrical version. The **argument** first appeared in the 1557 Genevan Psalter and was emended to the form found in the *WBP* for the Geneva Bible. It derives from the summary and discussion in Calvin's *Commentary on the Psalms*.

Incipit Deus, quis similis [erit tibi]: O God, who shall be like unto you

Musical settings and later use of the text: This psalm never had its own tune in the *WBP*. The usual reference was to PSALM 77. It was later set to several common tunes, first by East to CAMBRIDGE, but did not become widely popular and, outside the *WBP*, largely dropped out of sight after the middle of the 18th century.

The text in the *WBP* was modernized in the 1690s, and then further revised in the early 17th century, including a complete replacement of the final quatrain.

Psalm 84
How pleasant is thy dwelling place

Text: The psalm was first printed in *1562a*. As is frequently the case in his Elizabethan paraphrases, Hopkins appears to draw equally from (and expand equally on) the Geneva and Great Bibles in versifying this psalm. The **argument** first appeared in a slightly longer form the 1557 Genevan Psalter and then as here in the Geneva Bible. It follows and expands on the headnote in the Olivétan Bible.

Incipit Quam dilecta tabernacula [tua]: How beloved are thy tabernacles
49 light and defence: These are descriptions of God, not (grammatically) what he is giving; cf. the Great Bible, "For the Lord God is a light and defence."

Musical settings and later use of the text: This psalm never had its own tune in the *WBP*. The reference in *1567* is to PSALM 67, a tune in the wrong meter. This was later corrected to PSALM 77. The psalm was set to several common tunes, first to WINCHESTER in *East 1592*—the only text East assigned to that tune (μ25). He substituted OXFORD in 1594, but Allison, Ravenscroft, and Playford reverted to WINCHESTER. That classic tune (see p. 1007), now chiefly associated with "While shepherds watched their flocks by night," coupled with the appealing nature of the verse, raised the 84th psalm to an uncommon level of popularity. It is a notably modern tune for its date, with a balanced binary form and a midway modulation to the dominant key. Later, Francis Timbrell matched the psalm to BEDFORD (930a), which proved to be another winner. In all the psalm was printed in some 170 musical publications between 1700 and 1820. The text itself changed very little, the late-17th-century revisions being limited to those necessary to eliminate the archaic "eke" and "lust." It also appeared in hymnbooks without the tune into the second half of the 19th century. A related paraphrase from the Scottish metrical psalter of 1650 retained the first quatrain almost unchanged, and that version ("How lovely is thy dwelling place") remains in wide use.

Psalm 85
Thou hast been merciful indeed

Text: The **psalm** was first printed in *1562a*. Unusually, Hopkins could have written the whole paraphrase based only on the Geneva Bible translation; although that frequently overlaps with the Great Bible, his other accustomed source, there are no obvious borrowings of the Great Bible that are not also in the Geneva. The **argument** first appeared in the 1559 Geneva Book of Psalms and then the whole Geneva Bible. It paraphrases the summary in Calvin's *Commentary on the Psalms*.

Incipit Benedixisti, Domine [, terram tuam]: Thou has blessed thy land, O Lord

Musical settings and later use of the text: This psalm never had its own tune in the *WBP*. The usual reference was to Psalm 81. It was later set to several common tunes, first in *East 1592* to Oxford, but did not become widely popular. Despite obvious archaisms and some older verb forms that are difficult to contract into the requisite number of syllables, the text changed very little up to the 19th century.

Psalm 86
Lord, bow thine ear to my request

Text: The **psalm** was first printed in *1562a*. As with most of Hopkins's Elizabethan versifications, this one uses both the Geneva and Great Bibles; in contrast to the previous psalm, however, this one is weighted heavily toward the Great Bible. After numerous distinctive echoes of the Great Bible, there is no sign of any Geneva influence until v. 12 (which at l. 45 employs the Geneva Bible's verb "praise" rather than the Great Bible's "thank"). The **argument** first appeared in the 1557 Genevan Psalter and was shortened to the form found in the *WBP* for the Geneva Bible. While not disagreeing with Calvin's analysis of the psalm, this argument appears to be an independent composition.

Incipit Inclina, Domine, aurem [tuam]: Bow down thine ear, O Lord

Musical settings and later use of the text: This psalm was first set by Thomas Caustun to an otherwise unknown tune in *Day 1563* (*HTI* 189, Frost 105), but it never had its own tune in the *WBP*. The usual reference was to Psalm 81. It was later set to several common tunes, first in *East 1592* to Oxford, but did not become widely popular. The text was thoroughly brought up to date at the end of the 17th century, and by the early 18th the second line had permanently changed to "and hear me speedily" (*WBP* 1751).

Psalm 87
That city shall full well endure

Text: The **psalm** was first printed in *1562a*. The paraphrase is very expansive, so although there are no signs of sources other than the Great Bible and Geneva Bible, neither is followed particularly closely. The **argument** first appeared in the 1559 Geneva Book of Psalms and then the whole Geneva Bible. It succinctly abstracts the very long summary in Calvin's *Commentary on the Psalms*.

Incipit Fundamenta eius [in montibus]: The foundations of her are in holy mountains

30–1 therein . . . and: Hopkins is closer to the Great Bible's "The singers also and trumpeters shall he rehearse. All my fresh springs are in thee." The Scottish psalm book was revised to reflect the Geneva Bible's "As well the singers and the players on instruments shall praise thee: all my springs are in thee," and this reading entered *1601b* via Schilders's 1599 edition (see p. 578).

Musical settings and later use of the text: This psalm never had its own tune in the *WBP*. The usual reference was to PSALM 81. It was later set to several common tunes, first in *East 1592* to LOW DUTCH, but was not widely reprinted outside the *WBP*.

Psalm 88
Lord God, of health the hope and stay

Text: The **psalm** was first printed in *1562a*. The dominant source for this paraphrase is the Great Bible, with a handful of words echoing instead the Geneva Bible (e.g., "cry" at l. 8 or "afflict" at l. 61). The **argument** first appeared in the 1557 Genevan Psalter and was emended to the form found in the *WBP* for the Geneva Bible. It derives from the summary in Calvin's *Commentary on the Psalms*.

Incipit Domine, Deus salutatis [meae]: O Lord, God of my salvation

Later use of the text: There were relatively few printings of the psalm in 18th-century tunebooks, and it soon disappeared outside of the *WBP*.

Tune: DCM, C major, *HTI* 176a, Frost 108. First printed in *1562a*, and chosen for Ps. 141 in the Scottish psalm books. The early editions showed some instability in the key signature and in the endings of the 6th and 8th phrases, but these had settled down by 1565. The tune was replaced in some editions by a reference to PSALM 77, and did not last much beyond the Elizabethan period of the *WBP*, except in one quarto series that ended with *STC* 2572 (1621).

Other musical settings: East chose GLASSENBURIE (274a, Frost 109: see p. 1000, and µ22, stanzas 3, 4); some later editions of the *WBP* used Ravenscroft's choice of ABBY (325).

Psalm 89
To sing the mercies of the Lord

Text: The **psalm** was first printed in *1562a*. Hopkins relied more or less equally on the Geneva and Great Bibles in this paraphrase, in places essentially alternating between them. For instance, v. 1 derives from the Genevan translation, while v. 2 owes several choices to the Great Bible. At v. 6, Hopkins relied on the Great

Bible for the first clause and the Geneva for the second. The **argument** first appeared in the 1557 Genevan Psalter and was emended to the form found in the *WBP* for the Geneva Bible. It derives from the summary and discussion in Calvin's *Commentary on the Psalms*.

Incipit Misericordias Domini [in aeternum cantabo]: My singing shall be always of the loving kindnesses of the Lord
37–40 And . . . abroad: Hopkins followed the Great Bible closely in v. 10a ("Thou hast subdued Egypt and destroyed it"). *1601b*, using the Scottish psalm book text inherited from the Schilders 1599 *WBP* edition (see p. 578), instead reflects the Geneva Bible's "Thou hast beaten down Rahab as a man slain."
114–6 as . . . hold: Line 114 is metrical padding that adds meaning not found in the prose; the *1601b* reading (another borrowing from the Scottish text via Schilders) corrects it.

Musical settings and later uses of the text: This psalm never had its own tune in the *WBP*. The reference in *1567* is to Psalm 67, a tune in the wrong meter. This was later corrected to Psalm 77. The psalm was set to several common tunes, first in *East 1592* to Cambridge. The *WBP* text was lightly modernized in the 1690s, and then more extensively revised early in the 18th century. Although not widely popular, it appeared in some tunebooks into the first decades of the 19th century.

Psalm 90
Thou, Lord, hast been our sure defence

Text: The **psalm** was first printed in *1562a*. As is not unusual for the Elizabethan Hopkins, he here relied more or less equally on the Geneva and Great Bibles. He also took divergence between them as opportunity for further invention. Thus at v. 9 years pass "as a tale that is told" in the Great Bible, "as a thought" in the Geneva, and "as words or blasts [wind]" in Hopkins. The **argument** first appeared in the 1559 Geneva Book of Psalms and then the whole Geneva Bible. It is loosely based on Calvin's summary in his *Commentary on the Psalms*.

Incipit Domine, refugium [factus es nobis]: Thou, O Lord, art become a refuge unto us

Musical settings and later use of the text: This psalm's usual cross-reference was to Psalm 78. It had its own tune in just one edition of the *WBP*: *STC* 2443 (1573), apparently for the purpose of filling up space in the first half of the book so that it could be attached without a break to the second half (quires F–H) that had already been set. The tune chosen was Psalm 6 (*HTI* 65). It never again appeared with this psalm, which was later set to several common tunes, first in *East 1592* to Low Dutch. The psalm did not become widely popular.

Psalm 91
He that within the secret place

Text: The **psalm** was first printed in *1562a*. The paraphrase primarily follows the text of the Great Bible when it has a recognizable source, although the interpretation at v. 9b and some diction in v. 15 come from the Geneva Bible. The **argument** was first printed in the 1557 Genevan Psalter and a final phrase added in the Geneva Bible (the version used in the *WBP*). It essentially agrees with Calvin's discussion in his *Commentary on the Psalms* and may also draw on the argument in Joye's paraphrase of the Psalms, but appears to be an independent composition.

Incipit Qui habitat [in adiutorio altissimi]: Who dwelleth within the help of the most high

Musical settings and later use of the text: This psalm never had its own tune in the *WBP*. The usual reference was to PSALM 69 (misprinted in *1567*). It was later set to several common tunes, first in *East 1592* to CAMBRIDGE, but did not become widely popular, despite modernizing revision in both the late 17th and early 18th centuries.

Psalm 92
It is a thing both good and meet

Text: The **psalm** was first printed in *1562a*. Hopkins worked from both the Geneva and Great Bibles in paraphrasing this psalm, which overlap to a substantial degree. A handful of details like the Great Bible's "lute" in v. 3 and the Geneva Bible's "rock" in v. 15, however, point to selective use of each at different points. The **argument** first appeared in the 1557 Genevan Psalter and was reprinted in the slightly amended form adopted by the *WBP* in the Geneva Bible. It is very loosely drawn from Calvin's discussion in his *Commentary on the Psalms*.

Incipit Bonum est confiteri[, Domino]: It is a good thing to give thanks unto the Lord

Musical settings and later use of the text: A tune of unknown provenance (*HTI* 190, Frost 112) was set to this psalm by Thomas Caustun in *Day 1563*, but never appeared in the *WBP*. It was revived with its text by Abraham Barber, parish clerk of Wakefield, in 1687 and enjoyed some circulation in 18th-century Yorkshire after it was adopted in John Chetham's *Book of Psalmody* (1718). The *1567* reference to PSALM 86 is erroneous; the usual reference was to PSALM 78. In *East 1592* the psalm was set to KENTISH (275a, Frost 111: see p. 1001, and μ22, last stanza). The text was systematically modernized in the early 1700s. It appeared with many other tunes in the course of the 18th century as well as in collections of hymns without printed tunes to the middle of the 19th.

Psalm 93
The Lord as king aloft doth reign

Text: The **psalm** was first printed in *1562a*. Although Hopkins did not stay verbally very close to any of his prose sources in this paraphrase, only v. 1a shows the influence of the Geneva Bible; the rest of the psalms' borrowings are from the Great Bible. The **argument** first appeared in the 1557 Genevan Psalter and was reprinted in the Geneva Bible. It reworks the argument from Joye's paraphrase of the Psalms. The argument was not revised in 1577.

Incipit Dominus regnavit: The Lord is king

Musical settings and later use of the text: This psalm never had its own tune in the *WBP*. The usual reference was to PSALM 77. It was later set to a few common tunes, first in *East 1592* to LOW DUTCH, and survived in occasional use into the 19th century. The text was extensively revised at the end of the 17th century, with the first lines reading "The Lord doth reign and clothed is / with majesty most bright" (*WBP* 1751).

Psalm 94
O Lord, thou doth revenge all wrong

Text: The **psalm** was first printed in *1562a* (a different version by William Kethe appears in *1560b* and *1561b*). Hopkins's paraphrase contains specific verbal echoes of both the Geneva and Great Bibles, and includes phrases found in one but not the other. For example, in v. 1 of the Great Bible, as in Hopkins's version, vengeance "belongeth" to God, whereas in the Geneva God is apostrophized as "the avenger." Similarly, the Geneva Bible adds "shall he not know?" to the psalm's description of God as teacher, which Hopkins rephrases in l. 39. The **argument** first appeared in the 1559 Geneva Book of Psalms and Geneva Bible, adapted from a longer version in the 1557 Genevan Psalter. It paraphrases the headnote in the Olivétan Bible.

Incipit Deus ultionum [Dominus]: God is the Lord of vengeance

Musical settings and later use of the text: This psalm never had its own tune in the *WBP*. The usual reference was to PSALM 78 or 88. It was set to several common tunes, first in *East 1592* to CAMBRIDGE, but did not become widely popular. By 1700, the second line had permanently changed to "vengeance belongs to thee" (*WBP* 1751).

Psalm 95
O come, let us lift up our voice

Text: The psalm was first printed in *1562a*; the version appearing in the *WBP* as the hymn Venite (see pp. 20, 634) was printed among the metrical psalms in *1560a*, accompanied by a different argument. Hopkins's version adopts readings from the Geneva Bible in v. 1, but subsequently appears to be paraphrased nearly exclusively from the Great Bible. He also borrowed phrases and some rhyme words from the version appearing among the hymns as Venite. The **argument** first appeared in the 1559 Geneva Book of Psalms and Geneva Bible, adapting a longer version in the 1557 Genevan Psalter. That original argument was a paraphrase of the summary in Calvin's *Commentary on the Psalms*.

Incipit Venite, exultemus [Domino]: Come, let us rejoice in the Lord

Later use of the text: One of the more lastingly popular paraphrases from the *WBP*, this psalm—or most of it—continued to be printed in a wide range of hymn collections with and without music into the second half of the 19th century. This is a clear case of a psalm long outliving its original tune. Its familiarity must have shielded it from modernization during the changes to the book in the late 17th and early 18th centuries, as even obvious archaisms in the text remained throughout the life of the *WBP*.

Tune: DCM, Aeolian (*HTI* 177, Frost 113). First printed in *1562a*. This modal and rather rootless tune proved to be one of the most vulnerable in the *WBP*, dropped as early as 1569. (*1569a* referred it to PSALM 77, *1569b* to BENEDICTUS, and each was followed in some later editions.) Nevertheless, there were cross-references to the tune in early editions from Pss. 97–9, 105–6, 108–9, 114, and 116–17. Its last English appearance was in 1606 (*STC* 2519), though it continued in the Scottish psalm books until 1640. There are harmonized settings in *Day 1563* and *Daman 1571*.

Other musical settings: The first stanza was set as a three-voice anthem by John Mundy in his *Songs and Psalmes* (1594). The psalm was matched to several common tunes, first in *East 1592* to OXFORD, which was followed in Middleburg editions starting with *1601b*. Ravenscroft's choice of ST. DAVID's (379c) proved to be a winner, especially after it was adopted in Playford's *Brief Introduction* in 1658. It was printed with this tune in the Foundling Hospital collection as late as 1796, and by Francis Roome of Derby in 1801 with BRUNSWICK (1994a, adapted by John Alcock from the song "Sin not, O king" in Handel's *Saul*). Subsequent musical publications paired it with this and yet other tunes. It continued to appear in musical publications well into the 19th century.

Psalm 96
Sing ye with praise unto the Lord

Text: The **psalm** was first printed in *1562a*. In paraphrasing, Hopkins consulted the Geneva Bible but usually preferred the Great Bible. The clearest traces of the Geneva translation is in v. 4a, where Hopkins agrees with the Geneva Bible's "The Lord is . . . much to be praised" rather than the Great Bible's "The Lord . . . cannot worthily be praised." The **argument** first appeared in the 1559 Geneva Book of Psalms and Geneva Bible, paraphrasing the first sentences of Calvin's summary in his *Commentary on the Psalms*. The argument was not abridged in 1577.

Incipit Cantate Domino [canticum novum]: Sing unto the Lord a new song

Musical settings and later use of the text: This psalm never had its own tune in the *WBP*. The usual reference was to Psalm 77. It was later set to several common tunes, first in *East 1592* to Low Dutch, and remained moderately popular with many different tunes through the 18th century. The text in the *WBP* was lightly modernized in the 1690s. The second part of the psalm, "Fall down and worship ye the Lord," was taken up by several 18th-century compilers, first by Richard Willis in his book *The Excellent Use of Psalmody* (Nottingham, 1734), who set it to London New (*HTI* 497b). Tunebooks and collections of hymn texts included this paraphrase well into the 19th century.

Psalm 97
The Lord doth reign, whereat the earth

Text: The **psalm** was first printed in *1562a*. As usual in the last set of psalms that he paraphrased, Hopkins worked from both the Geneva and Great Bibles, here sometimes in the same verse. In v. 11, for example, we find the first half echoing the Genevan diction ("there is springing light") while the second half reflects the Great Bible ("the upright in heart"). The **argument** first appeared in the 1557 Genevan Psalter and was reprinted in the Geneva Bible. It adapts the headnote from the Olivétan Bible. The 1577 revision of the argument changed only the opening words.

Incipit Dominus regnavit: The Lord is king

Musical settings and later use of the text: This psalm never had its own tune in the *WBP*. The usual reference was to Psalm 77. It was later set to several common tunes, first in *East 1592* to Cambridge, but was printed only sporadically outside the *WBP* in the 18th century. Light modernization shortly before 1700 produced

relatively stable first lines reading "The Lord doth reign, for which the earth /
may sing with pleasant voice" (*WBP* 1751).

Psalm 98
O sing ye now unto the Lord

Text: The **psalm** was first printed in *1562a*. While the translations in the Geneva
and Great Bibles are very close, Hopkins in this psalm chose some phrasing from
each in places in which they differ. The **argument** first appeared in the 1557 Ge-
nevan Psalter and was reprinted in the Geneva Bible. It adapts the headnote from
the Olivétan Bible. The argument was not abridged in 1577.

Incipit Cantate Domino [canticum novum]: Sing unto the Lord a new song

Musical settings and later use of the text: This psalm never had its own tune in
the *WBP*. The usual reference was to PSALM 95 (85 in *1567* is probably a misprint).
It was later set to several common tunes, first in *East 1592* to OXFORD. Playford
set it as an additional text to the popular PSALM 81. Perhaps for that reason it was
quite frequently printed in 18th-century books. John Chetham's *Book of Psalmody*
(1718), the leading tunebook in the north of England, provided a successful new
tune SKIPTON (*HTI* 850), to which an alternate one was added in the 8th edition
(1752) and a third in the revised edition of 1811. It continued to turn up in psalm
collections with and without printed tunes further into the 19th century.

Psalm 99
The Lord doth reign, although at it

Text: The **psalm** was first printed in *1562a*. While Hopkins generally follows
the Geneva and Great Bibles in this paraphrase, with some echoes of each, v. 1a
derives from the Vulgate's "irascantur populi." The **argument** first appeared in
the 1557 Genevan Psalter and was reprinted (with a single variant also found in
the *WBP*) in the Geneva Bible. It adapts the headnote from the Olivétan Bible,
which contradicts Calvin's assertion in his *Commentary* that this Psalm primarily
concerns Judea and the Israelites as the chosen people.

Incipit Dominus regnavit: The Lord is king.
3 cherubin: The standard medieval and early modern English form of "cherub"
in either the single or plural, ultimately deriving from the Hebrew plural.
20 for . . . too: In the Geneva Bible, v. 5 reads "Exalt the Lord our God and fall
down before his footstool: *for* he is holy" (the Great Bible uses the same pronoun,
"he"). The reading in *1601b*, taken from the Scottish psalm book via the 1599
Schilders edition of the *WBP* (see p. 578), corrects Hopkins's mistaken reading of
"he" as referring to the footstool.

32 their deeds . . . maintain: I.e., [but] you did not look kindly on their deeds.

Musical settings and later uses of the text: This psalm never had its own tune in the *WBP*. The usual reference was to PSALM 77. It was later set to several common tunes, first in *East 1592* to LOW DUTCH, but did not become widely popular. The text was lightly modernized in the late 17th century.

Psalm 100 (1)
All people that on earth do dwell

Text: The **psalm** by William Kethe was first printed in *1560b* and *1561c*. The most closely related prose version is that in the Geneva Bible. As *1561c* and *1561d* adopt no other texts first appearing in *1560b*, and as the arguments come from different sources, Day almost certainly got a copy of this psalm through some other route. In *1562a*, it was replaced by Psalm 100 (2). Kethe's version was included between the main group of metrical psalms and the second set of hymns in *1564*, the quarto of 1565 (*STC* 2435), and (probably) *1563* (the leaves which would contain it are missing, but a section of alternate psalms beginning with Psalm 50 appears there as in *1564* and the 1565 quarto). It was the only version printed in *The First Parte of the Psalmes* (1564), where it was attributed to Hopkins, and then appeared in its normal numerical order among the psalms in *1565*, the quarto edition of 1566 (*STC* 2437), and after, preceding 100 (2) whenever they appear together. The **argument** was first printed in the 1557 Geneva Psalter and reprinted with minor emendations in the Geneva Bible. (While the *WBP*, beginning with *1561c*, follows the 1557 version, *1560b* uses that from the Geneva Bible.) It paraphrases the headnote in the Olivétan Bible. This argument was not altered in 1577.

Incipit 2. Iubilate Deo, omnis terra: Be joyful in God, the whole earth [The numeral "2" is a traditional way to distinguish this psalm from Ps. 65, which begins with the same four initial words.]

Later uses of the text: The 1570s form of the Elizabethan prayer service for Accession Day (November 17) specifies singing "the C. Psalme after the Sermon," which in practice would have been this version (*Fourme of Prayer to be Used the 17. of November*, sig. B1v). This paraphrase, with almost no changes, is the only psalm from the *WBP* still in extremely widespread use; see notes on Tune and Other musical settings.

Tune: LM, F major (*HTI* 143a, Frost 114). First printed in *1560b*. It is identical to the anonymous tune for Beza's Ps. 134 ("Or sus, serviteurs du Seigneur": μ9), first printed in *Pseaumes octantetrois de David* (Geneva, 1551) (Pidoux 134a). It was also used for The Lord's Prayer (1) in *1560b*. Passed over by Day for the first edition of the *WBP* (*1562a*) and the *Residue* (*1562b*), it appeared in all subsequent musical editions and Companions. Its rhythm was regularized in *1577* and, permanently, in *1586a* (see p. 952).

This psalm and its tune have never lost their position at the center of English-speaking Protestantism. Between 1561 and 1820 they appeared together in 805 printed books. In addition to this robust combination, the tune had its own history, appearing in 1,119 additional printings during the same period, either textless or allied to other texts of every persuasion. A remarkably similar melody (*HTI* 143f), identical in its first half, appeared in John Hall's *Coourte of Vertu* (London, 1565), sig. 161v–162r, with a verse beginning "The dawning day begins to glare, And Lucifer doth shine on high." PSALMS 3 and 68 also share its opening phrase. From *1561c* the tune was assigned by cross-reference to Becon's paraphrases, "Praise the Lord" and "Behold, now give heed" (see p. 771), and *East 1592* set them to Dowland's four-part arrangement of the tune.

Ainsworth used the tune for his own versification of Ps. 100, "Shout to Jehovah, all the earth," later revised for the "Bay Psalm Book" (1640). William Lawes used text and tune for one of his *12 Psalms* (c. 1640). Playford in 1677 matched the tune to Bishop Cosin's translation of *Iam lucis ante terminum*, "Now that the day-star doth arise," and also to Ps. 136 (1), which he altered to fit the meter.[44] In 1700 it was matched to Tate & Brady's Ps. 100 ("With one consent let all the earth"); in 1725 to Isaac Watts's ("Ye nations of the earth, rejoice"), which was to be particularly popular among Independents and Baptists; and in 1754 to John Wesley's revision of the latter ("Before Jehovah's awful throne"). Its association with Bishop Ken's doxology ("Praise God, from whom all blessings flow"), now almost universal in American hymnals, seems to have originated in the second edition of *The Federal Harmony* (Boston: John Norman, 1790).

The tune, today generally called OLD 100 or OLD 100TH, was also sometimes entitled SAVOY, a name first found in *Select Psalms and Hymns for the Use of the Parish-Church . . . of St. James's Westminster* (1697) and therefore probably of local significance. It has been attributed to Le Jeune, Goudimel, Dowland, and Playford, all of whom at least arranged the tune, and, more recklessly, to Luther (this last gaffe can be traced to Ralph Harrison, the Manchester Unitarian minister and editor of *Sacred Harmony*, 2nd edition, 1788). In fact it had entered the Lutheran repertory in about 1600 with the hymn "Nun Lob', mein Seel', den Herren," and so was used by Bach in several contexts—Cantatas 28 and 130, and the motet "Sei Lob und Preis mit Ehren."

OLD 100TH is the only psalm tune that is the basis of a surviving English organ voluntary from the 17th century, which exists in two forms, one attributed to John Blow, the other to his pupil Henry Purcell.[45] A version "broken" for the violin was published in John Playford's *Introduction to the Skill of Musick*, beginning with the 14th edition (1700), while elaborate organ preludes and interludes for

---

[44] See Temperley, "John Playford and the Metrical Psalms," 352–5, 372.

[45] See Blow, *Thirty Voluntaries and Verses*; Purcell, *Organ Works*.

the tune were composed in the early 18th century by Blow, Daniel Purcell, John Reading and others. It was chosen by the expatriate German composer A. F. C. Kollmann (1756–1829) to demonstrate harmonic principles,[46] by the Victorian musicologist John Spencer Curwen (1847–1916) to illustrate past, present, and future modes of performing hymn tunes,[47] and by the Tin Pan Alley composer Henry Lamb to represent the "old-time religion" of an organist falsely accused of drunkenness.[48] Arrangements for choir and orchestra were regularly played at the Concert of Ancient Music, London, from 1810. It is the only tune from the Elizabethan canon that was included in Samuel Sebastian Wesley's *Selection of Psalm Tunes Adapted Expressly to the English Organ with Pedals* (London, 1834). It was by far the most frequently printed tune in all American publications up to 1810.[49] It easily surpassed all other tunes in a count of surviving British barrel-organ tune lists (indicating great popularity from about 1790 to 1860).[50]

There was no decline in popularity in the 20th century. Hubert Parry (1848–1918) published a "Fantasia on the Old Hundredth" for organ in 1915, and Gustav Holst (1874–1934) produced an arrangement of text and tune for chorus and orchestra (c. 1920). It occurs in approximately half the 450 modern hymnals surveyed in D. DeWitt Wasson's *Hymntune Index and Related Hymn Materials* (Lanham, Md., 1998), often with its original text. Its continuing fame is further attested by the satirical use of its name for a private club of doubtful repute in Evelyn Waugh's *Brideshead Revisited* (1945).[51] On the other hand, the tune inspired a work for chorus and orchestra by Ralph Vaughan Williams (1872–1958), *The Old Hundredth Psalm* (1929), which would be chosen for the service celebrating Queen Elizabeth II's diamond jubilee on 5 June 2012. It was also included in Vaughan Williams's communion anthem "O taste and see" for the queen's coronation (1953).

The 32 pitches have changed little over the centuries. A variant form of the last line — c' a f g a b♭ (a) g f — seems to be of German origin, reaching England in *Psalmodia Germanica*, vol. 2 (1732), edited by John Christian Jacobi, organist of the royal Lutheran chapel. The tune in this form (143c) was later set to a "Michaelmass Hymn" beginning "To God let all the human race / Bring humble worship, mixed with grace," and was used with various texts in over 100 English prints, including Edward Miller's influential *Psalms of David* (1790). The rhythm began to be revised in the 19th century, until in *Hymns Ancient & Modern* (1861) it was reduced to 32 minims.

---

[46] Kollmann, *The Melody of the Hundredth Psalm.*

[47] Curwen, *Studies in Worship Music,* [1st series],130–2.

[48] In the 1891 song "The Volunteer Organist." See Scott, "Music, Morality and Rational Amusement," 97–8.

[49] Crawford, *Core Repertory,* lxxvii.

[50] Boston and Langwill, *Barrel-Organs,* 21–38.

[51] Book I, chapter 5.

Other musical settings: It was not until 1682 that anyone ventured to print this psalm with a different tune: William Barton's *Book of Psalms in Metre*, edited posthumously by his son Edward, had it set to Orlando Gibbons's Song 34 (*HTI* 387b, Frost 362a). A number of other new tunes were provided, but none lasted very long. A full anthem on the complete text was composed by Henry Aldrich (1648–1710).[52] Modern anthems have been composed by Ronald Diggle, Anthony Foster, Paul Robinson, and Sydney Thomson.

Psalm 100 (2)
In God the Lord be glad and light

Text: The **psalm** was first printed in *1562a*, and it was omitted from the 1564 *First Parte of the Psalmes*, which was set primarily from an edition similar to *1561c* (see note to Psalm 100 (1) above). This version is by Hopkins, though it lacks any attribution in the early editions. He based his versification primarily on the Great Bible.

Musical settings and later use of the text: This version never had its own tune in the *WBP*. The usual reference was to Psalm 81, misprinted in *1567*. The psalm appeared in only nineteen musical publications before 1820, beginning with *East 1592*, where it was set to Cambridge. The popularity of 100 (1) made this paraphrase almost entirely superfluous.

Psalm 101
I mercy will and judgement sing

Text: The **psalm** was first printed in *1562a* (a different version by William Kethe appears in *1560b* and *1561b*). Norton's paraphrase of this psalm closely follows the Geneva Bible translation. The **argument** first appeared in the 1557 Genevan Psalter and was reprinted with slight emendations in the Geneva Bible; the *WBP* follows the latter version. It adapts the headnote in the Olivétan Bible. The argument was only slightly abridged in 1577 by omitting one phrase and combining the two sentences.

Incipit Misericordiam et iudicium [cantabo]: I will sing of mercy and judgement

Musical settings and later use of the text: This version never had its own tune in the *WBP*. The usual reference was to Psalm 68. It was set to several common

---

[52] The text is printed in *A Collection of Anthems Perform'd. . . in the Cathedral Church of Durham* (1749), 50. The music is in Samuel Arnold's *Cathedral Music* (London, 1790), i, and is probably adapted from an earlier work.

tunes, first in *East 1592* to Oxford, but did not become widely popular. Revision in the 1690s replaced lines 3–6 but was otherwise sparing.

Psalm 102
O hear my prayer, Lord, and let

Text: The **psalm** was first printed in *1562a*. Although *1562a* and a majority of later editions attribute the paraphrase to Hopkins, *1562b*'s attribution to Norton is correct. Not only does the rhyme of this versification match Norton's rather than Hopkins's usual form, but its heavy reliance on the Geneva Bible without significant echoes of the Great Bible is much more characteristic of Norton. Moreover, like Norton's other new contributions in *1562a* and *1562b*, it lacks verse numbers in those editions. The **argument** first appeared in the 1559 Geneva Book of Psalms and then the Geneva Bible; it derives from Calvin's summary in his *Commentary on the Psalms*. The argument was not substantively changed in 1577.

Incipit Domine, exaudi orationem [meam]: Lord, hear thou my prayer

Musical settings and later use of the text: This psalm never had its own tune in the *WBP*. The *1567* reference to Psalm 67 is erroneous, since that psalm is in short meter. The usual reference was to Psalm 30. It was later set to several common tunes, first in *East 1592* to Low Dutch, but did not become widely popular. Nathaniel Giles (c. 1558–1634) wrote a verse anthem for five voices based on the text of the first three stanzas (Giles, *Anthems*, 70–78). The first line changed at the end of the 17th century to "Hear thou my prayer, O Lord, and let" (*WBP* 1751).

Psalm 103
My soul, give laud unto the Lord

Text: The **psalm** was one of Sternhold's original nineteen first printed in *1548* (see p. 864) and was revised for *1556*. Sternhold made use of at least two of Coverdale's English translations in versifying this psalm, the Great Bible and the Latin-English parallel psalter, with phrasing chosen from each; he also preferred the Vulgate Latin at least once, in v. 7. In addition, this paraphrase has more clear debts to Joye's paraphrase than any others that Sternhold wrote, adopting Joye's diction or working with the connotations of his phrasing in parts of vv. 3, 8, 14, and 18, and these survive in the *1567* texts. For *1556*, Whittingham rewrote about fifteen lines, bringing the passages which Sternhold had paraphrased most freely or that corresponded to the Vulgate (rather than to Coverdale or Joye's translations) closer to the Great Bible's text. The Anglo-Genevan *Form of Prayers* directed that after Communion, "The action thus ended, the people singe the 101 [or rather, 103] psal. My soul give laud &c. or some other of thancks givynge" (p. 79). The **argument** first appeared in *1556*; it remained distinct from the arguments in any of the Anglo-Genevan prose translations. Whittingham took his approach to the text from Joye's argument in his paraphrase of the Psalms.

Incipit 1. Benedic anima mea [Domino]: Praise the Lord, O my soul. [The numeral "1" traditionally distinguishes this psalm from Ps. 104, which has identical opening words in the Vulgate.]

19–20 The psalm itself does not specify how the eagle's youth is renewed, but commentary ultimately deriving from Augustine connected this verse to the belief that the eagle's beak never stopped growing; eventually, when it had curved over too far to allow for eating, the eagle would have to break it off in order to restore itself to health. The lines are Sternhold's; the Geneva Bible marginal gloss reframes the metaphor: "As the eagle, when her beak overgroweth, sucketh blood, and so is renewed in strength, even so God miraculously giveth strength to his Church above all man's expectation."

25 *marginal note to* **commandèments:** The law teacheth us all the works of God, and thereby we see God's favour towards us. *1556, 1561d*

29 *marginal note to v. 8:* Num. 14.c [14:18] *1556*; [*cropped*]4. *1561d.* [The reference comes from the Olivétan Bible]

45 *marginal note to v. 12:* God's mercy cannot be comprehended. *1556, 1561d*

53 *marginal note to v. 14:* Man is but dust. *1556, 1561d*

Later use of the text: The text was revised in two stages over the first quarter of the 18th century, by the end of which process the opening lines had become "My soul, give praise unto the Lord, / my spirit do the same." Selections from this emended version were reasonably popular in selections of psalms and hymns without tunes up to the middle of the 19th century.

Tune: DCM, F major (*HTI* 101, Frost 117). First printed in *1556*. This tune accompanied the psalm in all the early editions of the *WBP*, but later began to be replaced by short tunes. In addition to the settings in the Companions there is one based on this tune by Thomas Weelkes (*Collected Anthems*, MB 23). Playford re-adopted the proper tune in his *Whole Book of Psalmes . . . Compos'd in Three Parts* (1677) and it continued to appear frequently with this psalm until the 1730s.

Other musical settings: John Sheppard composed a four-voice setting of Sternhold's text in Edward VI's time, but only the uppermost voice part survives (see p. 518). Henry Denham's choice of CAMBRIDGE in *1588b* was not generally adopted, but a number of other tunes were tried after Playford's *Introduction* selected ST. MARY's (539a) in 1674, and the psalm outlived its proper tune by several decades.

Psalm 104
My soul, praise the Lord, speak good of his name

Text: The **psalm** was first printed in *1560b*, and it was added to the main London corpus in *1562a*. Kethe's versification generally coincides with the sense of the Geneva translation, but contains a good deal of metrical padding to fit the long lines in his borrowed French form. The whole **argument** first appeared in the 1559 Geneva Book of Psalms and then the Geneva Bible, expanding a very similar one from the 1557 Genevan Psalter. The earlier version had been modeled on the headnote in the Olivétan Bible.

Incipit Benedic, anima mea [, Domino]: Praise the Lord, O my soul

Later use of the text: This psalm survived unusually late into the 19th century with almost no modernization. Although published in hymnals without printed music as well as tunebooks, the popularity of tunes associated with it probably played a significant role in its longevity (see below).

Tune: 10.10.11.11.D, Dorian (*HTI* 144a, Frost 118). First printed in *1560b*. It was taken without change from Marot's Ps. 104 ("Sus, sus, mon âme, il te faut dire bien") (Pidoux 104d) as set in the 1551 French Genevan psalter. It had already appeared in earlier editions, the first being *La manyere de faire prieres aux eglises Francoyses* ("Rome" [or rather, Strassburg], 1542) (Pidoux 104a). The first half of the tune was derived from the melody of the medieval hymn *Te lucis ante terminum*. Marot's decasyllables, alternating pairs of masculine and feminine endings, replaced the four-foot iambic meter of the Latin. To accommodate them, repeated or passing notes were added where needed. The second half of the tune was new.

When Kethe decided to write a translation of the psalm to fit this tune, he chose an anapestic meter, rare in English verse of the period (the only other example in the metrical psalm repertory is Pullain's Ps. 149). Most of the half-lines, though not all, have clear stresses on their second and fifth syllables. It was a surprising choice, certainly not suggested by the tune, which imposes numerous false accents on Kethe's verse. Yet it had a large progeny in later hymnological history, as will be seen below. The proper tune played no part in this development. It remained in some editions of the *WBP*, but barely survived into later publications. In 1603 Henry Dod published a DCM reduction of the text, "better fitting the common tunes."

Other musical settings: Thomas Ravenscroft harmonized and published, and probably composed, a strong and stirring new tune for this psalm in 1621 (*HTI* 377a, Frost 119: see Ex. 9), in a triple time that fully recognized the anapestic meter, with line breaks (already implied in the text) that recast the meter as 5.5.5.5.6.5.6.5. Ravenscroft recognized Kethe's lapse from the regular meter in phrase 4 ("Honour and majesty in thee shine most clear") by abandoning the triple-time pattern for that phrase: an unfortunate decision, since it did not fit later stanzas of the text and gave much trouble to future editors.

This immediately competed with the older tune in the *WBP*, appearing in 126 editions after 1621 as against 49 for the old tune, and it was adopted by Playford in 1677. It even became known as OLD 104TH, and has survived to this day in many hymnals, with the rhythm of its last phrase usually revised to match phrase 3. There is a fine organ prelude on it by Hubert Parry.

But OLD 104TH was challenged by the even more successful HANOVER (*HTI* 657a), long misattributed to Handel but almost certainly the work of William Croft (see Table 1). It was first printed in *A Supplement to the New Version of Psalms*, 6th edition (1708), with Ps. 67 (New Version), but with the heading "A New Tune to the 149th psalm of the New Version, and the 104th of the Old." Kethe's psalm soon inveigled HANOVER from its *New Version* texts; tune and text shared enormous popularity until relatively recent times. This tune in its turn, understandably but confusingly, was sometimes also called OLD 104TH: it is so named on eight surviving 19th-century barrel organs, suggesting that it was still being sung to Kethe's words.[53]

The success of these two tunes was probably the main reason for both the psalm's unusual durability and the wide imitation of its verse meter. The tunes appear together in *Hymns Ancient and Modern Revised* (1950) as alternative choices for Robert Grant's hymn "O worship the King / All glorious above," with phrase 4 of Ravenscroft's tune presented in the same rhythm as phrase 2. The *HTI* records 157 different tunes in the meter 5.5.5.5.6.5.6.5 printed in or before 1820, and another 53 in the original meter, 10.10.11.11.

Tune (*HTI* no.)	144a	377a	657a	Others	Total
First printed	1561	1621	1708		
Date range	Number of printings				
1561–1620	321	–	–	–	321
1621–1688*	50	126	–	–	176
1689–1707	3	12	–	–	15
1708–1820	2	45	158	34	239
Totals	376	183	158	34	751

Table 1. Printings of Psalm 104, Old Version, with Tunes. Statistics drawn from the *Hymn Tune Index*.   *1688 is the date of the last edition of the *WBP* with tunes.

---

[53] Boston and Langwill, *Barrel-Organs*: 27.

Ex. 9. Ravenscroft's tune for Psalm 104.

My soul praise the Lord, speak
good of his name; O Lord our great God, how
dost thou ap - pear So pass - ing in
glo - ry that great is thy fame! Ho - nour
and ma - jes - ty in thee shine most clear.

Source of music: Thomas Ravenscroft, *The Whole Booke of Psalmes . . . Composed into 4. Partes by Sundry Authors* (London, 1621).

Psalm 105
Give praises unto God the Lord

Text: The **psalm** was first printed in *1562a*. In paraphrasing, Norton followed the Geneva Bible quite closely with the exception of vv. 16–20a. That section instead reverts to the Great Bible's phrasing, which is closer to the Vulgate than the Genevan translation is and more obviously Christological. The **argument** first appeared in the 1559 Geneva Book of Psalms and then the Geneva Bible (with the word "grace" in place of the *WBP*'s "goodness"). It paraphrases the summary from Calvin's *Commentary on the Psalms*.

Incipit Confitemini Domino: Give thanks unto the Lord
67–8 Whose . . . also: Nearly verbatim from the Great Bible (except for "came into" rather than "pierced"); cf. the Geneva Bible translation, "They held his feet in the stocks, and he was laid in irons."

Musical settings and later use of the text: This psalm never had its own tune in the *WBP*. The usual reference was to Psalm 103 or the Benedictus. It was later set to several common tunes, first in *East 1592* to Cambridge, but none made it widely popular. The text itself was thoroughly revised in the 1690s to minimize archaisms and smooth the meter.

Psalm 106
Praise ye the Lord, for he is good

Text: The **psalm** was first printed in *1562a*. Norton based his versification on the Geneva Bible translation. The **argument** first appeared in the 1557 Genevan Psalter and was revised for the Geneva Bible; the *WBP* uses the latter version. It owes a debt to Bucer's argument in his *Psalmorum libri quinque*, but more directly summarizes consecutive groups of lines.

Incipit Confitemini Domino: Give thanks unto the Lord

Musical settings and later use of the text: This psalm never had its own tune in *WBP*. The usual reference was to Psalm 103 or the Benedictus. It was set to several common tunes, first in *East 1592* to Oxford. Although it did not become widely popular, it appeared in some tunebooks into the early 19th century. The second line changed in the late 17th-century revision to "his mercy lasts alway" (*WBP* 1751).

Psalm 107
Give thanks unto the Lord our God

Text: The **psalm** was first printed in *1560b*, and it was added to the main London corpus in *1562a*. It is based mainly on the 1557 Genevan Psalter. The translation of this psalm is largely identical there to that in the Great Bible, but Kethe's versification reproduces a handful of the small differences between them, like a "for" at the start of v. 14 or beginning v. 24 with "Those men," which has a demonstrative adjective only in 1557. Additionally, there are a very small number of phrases or individual word choices that correspond to the Geneva Bible translation but not to earlier English prose versions. While it is possible that Kethe was working from both the Geneva Bible and the earlier Genevan Psalter, it is more likely that Kethe's paraphrase preceded the MS of the 1559 prose Book of Psalms and that either Kethe himself or his metrical version influenced the composition of the final Geneva translation. The **argument** first appeared in the 1557 Genevan Psalter, though the emended version in the *WBP* came from the Geneva Bible. It is modeled on the headnote in the Olivétan Bible.

Incipit Confitemini Domino: Give thanks unto the Lord

Musical settings and later use of the text: This psalm never had its own tune in the *WBP*. The usual reference was to Psalm 95 or 119. (The *1567* reference is to a psalm that has no tune.) It was later set to several common tunes, first in *East 1592* to Low Dutch, but did not become widely popular and was largely out of use by the 19th century. A fairly light early-18th-century revision changed the second line to "for very kind is he" (*WBP* 1751).

Psalm 108
O God, my heart prepared is

Text: The **psalm** was first printed in *1562a*. Here Norton closely paraphrased the Geneva Bible translation throughout. The **argument** first appeared in the 1557 Genevan Psalter and was reprinted in the Geneva Bible. Calvin's *Commentary on the Psalms* notes that the psalm has already been treated because it is composed of two earlier ones; the remainder of the argument is loosely based on the headnote in the Olivétan Bible.

Incipit Paratum cor meum[, Deus]: My heart is ready, O God
39–40 This sentence, paraphrasing the Geneva Bible's "who will bring me into Edom?," is certainly corrupt. The correction first appearing in *1564*, substituting "how" for "who," may be what Norton meant, but "when" is a more likely candidate, both because the meaning is a better fit and because "whē" could have been easily misconstrued as "who" by the 1562 compositors.

Musical settings and later use of the text: This psalm never had its own tune in the *WBP*. The usual reference was to Psalm 81. (The *1567* reference is to a psalm that has no tune.) It was later set to several common tunes, first in *East 1592* to Cambridge. Although never extremely popular, the paraphrase did survive some decades into the 19th century in collections of psalms and hymn texts. A verse anthem by Richard Hutchinson (1590–1646), based on stanzas 1–4 and 12–13, survives in manuscripts at Durham Cathedral and elsewhere, and its text was listed in Clifford (1664). By the late 17th century, the second line had been amended to "my heart is likewise so" (*WBP* 1751).

Psalm 109
In speechless silence do not hold

Text: The **psalm** was first printed in *1562a* (although vv. 3–22 appeared in the middle of Psalm 115 in *1562a* and not at all in *1562b*). Practically speaking, Norton worked exclusively from the Geneva Bible here. The **argument** first appeared in the 1557 Genevan Psalter and was slightly shortened for the Geneva Bible, which gave its version to the *WBP*. It is based on the headnote in the Olivétan Bible.

Incipit Deus, laudem tuam [ne tacueris]: Keep not thou thy praise in silence, O God. [The Vulgate runs "Deus laudem *meam* ne tacueris," which Coverdale translates as "Keep not thou my praise in silence, O God." The incipit in the *WBP* seems to have been distorted by Norton's adoption of the Geneva Bible reading of this verse: "Hold not thy tongue, O God of my praise."]

Musical settings and later use of the text: This psalm never had its own tune in the *WBP*. The usual reference was to PSALM 81. (The *1567* reference is to a psalm that has no tune.) It was later set to several common tunes, first in *East 1592* to OXFORD, but the lightly modernized 18th-century version was not widely popular.

Psalm 110
The Lord did say unto my Lord

Text: The **psalm** was first printed in *1562a*. Quite unusually for Norton in his 1562 psalms, this paraphrase follows the Great Bible version without any evidence of influence from the Geneva translation. The **argument** first appeared in the 1559 Geneva Book of Psalms and then the Geneva Bible, extensively revising the one in the 1557 Genevan Psalter. It chiefly reflects Calvin's summary in his *Commentary on the Psalms*. Revisions to the argument in 1577 were minor.

Incipit Dixit Dominus Domino [meo]: The Lord said unto my Lord

Musical settings and later use of the text: This psalm never had its own tune in the *WBP*. The usual reference was to PSALM 68 or 95. It was later set to several common tunes, first in *East 1592* to LOW DUTCH, but appeared in relatively few 18th century tunebooks. The text continued to be occasionally reprinted outside the *WBP* into the early 19th century; the *WBP* text received almost no revision in the interim.

Psalm 111
With heart I do accord

Text: The **psalm** was first printed in *1560b* and entered Day's collections in *1562a*. Despite apparently unanimous misattribution in editions after *1562b*, it is Kethe's work. The paraphrase itself is based on the Geneva Bible text. The **argument** first appeared in the 1559 Geneva Book of Psalms and then the Geneva Bible. It paraphrases the headnote in the Olivétan Bible. The argument was not abridged in 1577.

Incipit Confitebor tibi Domine: Unto the Lord will I give thanks

26 judgement, right, and truth: Or possibly "judgement right [i.e., right judgement] and truth." The comma after **judgement** is present in *1560b*, which, unlike any London editions, consistently punctuates the texts as if they were prose (rather than observing metrical pauses), and thus offers a more helpful guide to meaning. Lines 25–7 paraphrase the Geneva Bible's "The works of his hands are truth and judgement: all his statutes are true."

30 Which . . . end: I.e., which makes equity complete.

Later use of the text: Although the French metrical pattern created difficulties for singers, the text itself was not abandoned in favor of new paraphrases. Versions of Kethe's text were in use well into the middle of the 19th century, some adapted to accommodate less challenging tunes (see below). The text found in the *WBP* itself permanently shortened the seven-syllable lines to six in the early 1700s, very belatedly matching the tune cross-reference supplied in some Elizabethan editions (see below).

Tune: 6.6.6. 6.6.6. 6.6.7. 6.6.7, Mixolydian, *HTI* 145a, Frost 123. First printed in *1560b*. From the tune for Marot's Psalm 19, "Les cieulx en chascun lieu," as in the French Genevan psalter of 1551 (Pidoux 19c). The earliest version of the tune, in *La Forme des prieres et chantz ecclesiastiques* (Geneva, 1542), had a completely different form for phrases 4–6 (see Pidoux 19b). Kethe's iambic meter is a serious misfit: in the first stanza every line except one begins with an unstressed function word, which has to be sung to a semibreve on a strong beat. The English adapters at first made an unfortunate amendment of phrase 7 (to g' g' g' f' d' e'), probably a simple misreading; it was corrected from *1565* onwards (μ8). The tune was dropped from some later editions, beginning in 1576 (*STC* 2446), which supplied a cross-reference to the second tune of Ps. 120 in the meter 6.6.6.6.6.6. It was retained in the Companions. Unusual length seems to have discouraged its use. Playford in 1677 devised a shortened version (145e) of six phrases, altering the text to fit. Both this and the original tune are found in 18th-century tunebooks. Playford also offered a new, alternate translation in common meter (as had Dod in 1603), allowing the psalm to be sung to one of the popular short tunes.

Thomas Williams's psalmody collection for dissenters, *Psalmodia Evangelica* (1789), found another way of shortening the tune (145f) by using only the first three and last three lines, while retaining the text more or less intact. This version, under the name VERULAM, was copied in John Rippon's *Selection of Psalm and Hymn Tunes* (London, 1792), the leading Baptist collection of the time, still with the original text. On the Anglican side the original version was revived by William Crotch in 1803.

Other musical settings: Few other tunes in this daunting metre were attempted. The earliest was John Bishop's EXETER (*HTI* 701), in his *Selection of Psalm and Hymn Tunes* (1710)

Psalm 112
The man is blest that God doth fear

Text: The psalm was first printed in *1560b*, and it was added to the main London corpus in *1562a*. The Great Bible, 1557 Genevan Psalter, and Geneva Bible versions agree closely in this psalm, though a handful of words (e.g., "compassion" at l. 6 or "fear" at l. 8) suggest that Kethe was working from the Geneva Bible translation. For this extremely compact versification, however, Kethe largely chose to reword his English prose source, rather than preserve its diction and then pad around it to produce the requisite form. The **argument** first appeared in the 1557 Genevan Psalter and was reprinted in the Geneva Bible. It paraphrases the headnote in the Olivétan Bible; there was no revision in 1577.

Incipit Beatus vir [qui timet Dominum]: Blessed is the man that feareth the Lord

Musical settings and later use of the text: From the first this psalm was designed to be sung to the Lutheran *Vater unser* tune, LORD'S PRAYER (2) (*HTI* 130a: see pp. 462, 773). They were printed together in *1560b*, *1561c*, and *1562a*, but from *1563* onwards the tune was replaced with the direction "Sing this as the Lord's Prayer," presumably to avoid printing it twice. It reappeared in musical notation with this psalm in a harmonized version by George Kirby published in *East 1592* and adopted by Ravenscroft, and in monophonic form in the 1661 folio edition of the *WBP* (Wing B2475A, *STC* ✳P E84 a) revised and edited by Playford, who also printed it with the tune in his *Whole Booke of Psalms Compos'd in Three Parts* (1677). In the later 18th century it was still in use with the psalm at the Magdalen Chapel, London, and only two lines—the final couplet—were noticeably changed by that time. In modern English usage it is often known as OLD 112TH rather than VATER UNSER, even in the *English Hymnal* (1906), which adopted J. S. Bach's harmonization.

    William Byrd (1543–1623: *Collected Works*, 15:11) set the first stanza of the psalm as a consort song for voices and viols. *Daman 1579* provided a new tune (*HTI* 252, Frost 124), but this was not reprinted. The psalm remained popular through the 18th century and beyond; several new tunes were assigned to it, and it also appeared in collections of hymns and psalms without music well into the 19th century.

Psalm 113
Ye children which do fear the Lord

Text: The psalm was first printed in *1560b*, and Day adopted it for the *WBP* in *1562a*. Although the Great Bible and 1557 Genevan Psalter are very close to the Geneva Bible translation, Kethe's echo of the latter's distinctive verb "abaseth" in

l. 13 suggests that he was using the Geneva Bible or its sources. (In addition, the 1557 prose lacks the final sentence of the psalm, which Kethe paraphrases in l. 24.) The **argument** first appeared in the 1557 Genevan Psalter and was revised for the Geneva Bible; the *WBP* uses the later version. It derives from the summary and discussion in Calvin's *Commentary on the Psalms*.

Incipit Laudate, pueri [, Dominum]: Praise the Lord, O ye children

Later use of the text: The paraphrase remained in use through the early 19th century. Only a few lines of this text were emended by this point, but editions of the *WBP* and other collections of psalms and hymns printed without tunes began in the middle of the 18th century to print it in half-length stanzas. These correspond to changes in the tune used (see below).

Tune: 8.8.8. 8.8.8.D, F major (*HTI* 146a, Frost 125). First printed in *1560b*. The famous tune is the work of one of the originators of Reformed singing styles, the German cantor Matthäus Greiter (c. 1494–1550). He wrote it for "Es sind doch selig alle, die / Im rechten Glauben wandeln hie," a paraphrase of Ps. 119:1–16 (Zahn 8303), with which it was printed in 1525, in a publication no longer extant; the earliest surviving source is *Psalmen, Gebett und Kirchenübung* (Strassburg: Wolff Köpphel, 1526).[54] Bach used the melody in the chorus that ends Part I of the *Matthew Passion* ("O Mensch, bewein dein Sünde groß").

It was borrowed, with minor changes, by Calvin for his Psalm 36 ("En moy le secret pensement") in *Aulcuns Pseaulmes et cantiques mys en chant* (Strassburg, 1539). With the substitution of Marot's version ("Du malign les faicts vicieux"), and further slight changes in the melody, it reached the Genevan psalter of 1551 (Pidoux 36d), which was no doubt Kethe's source. The German and French versions had seven, not eight, syllables in phrases 3, 6, 9 and 12. In each case the sixth syllable was a semibreve: substituting two minims allowed for Kethe's wholly iambic meter.

The tune has a structural formality not found in the English psalm tunes, resulting from the partial repetition of phrase 1 in phrase 2, the identity of 7 and 8, sequential repetition of 9 in 10 and 11, reuse of a three-note cadence formula at several pitch levels, and (on a higher time level) the exact repetition of phrases 1–3. The striking leap to the upper tonic at the halfway point was imitated in many a later tune, both French and English (e.g. PSALMS 104, 111).

At 96 notes this is the longest tune in the *WBP*. Its prominence throughout the Reformed world supplied an international dimension: it was a war song during the religious conflicts in France, and was dubbed "the Huguenot Marseillaise" by Douen.[55] All the Companions adopted it, despite its unusual length:

---

[54] See Stalmann et al., *Das deutsche Kirchenlied*, III, 1/2: 121, 125–6, tune Eh14

[55] Douen, *Clément Marot et le psaultier huguenot*, 1: 658.

Cosyn 1585 made a spacious consort song out of it, with accompaniment for viols (μ18). The Presbyterian William Barton in the 1640s printed no less than five versions, shortened in different ways (*HTI* 146c-g), to fit various psalm paraphrases of his own. It was one of eight long tunes chosen by Playford for the selection in his *Introduction to the Skill of Musick* in 1658. He left it untouched, but many later compilers found it unwieldy (especially at the extraordinarily slow pace that had become customary) and devised their own ways of reducing it (146h–q). The original form was revived by William Crotch in 1803. It was printed as OLD 113TH in *Hymns Ancient & Modern* (1861) with Henry Baker's hymn "From highest heaven the eternal Son." By that time congregations were singing fast again, the original rhythm had disappeared, and the tune was presented in notes of equal duration.

Other musical settings: The exalted standing of the proper tune discouraged alternatives, and it was not until 1708 that Elias Hall of Oldham set the psalm to a different tune, one that John Blow had composed for John Patrick's translation of Ps. 113 in 1701 (*HTI* 612). Several later attempts were made, but none came near to rivaling the old tune in public esteem.

Psalm 114
When Israel by God's address

Text: The **psalm** was first printed in *1556*. In his versification, Whittingham seems to have worked primarily from the Great Bible and the French paraphrase by Marot. The **argument** also first appeared in *1556*, was reprinted in the 1557 Genevan Psalter, and was slightly emended for the Geneva Bible. It probably owes the emphasis on memory to the summary in Calvin's *Commentary on the Psalms*, but otherwise largely resembles both the headnote in the Olivétan Bible and Joye's argument. None of the sources, however, mention ingratitude for God's gifts.

Incipit In exitu Israel [de Aegypto]: At the departing of Israel out of Egypt
9 *marginal note to v. 3a*: Exod. 14.f [14:21] / Ps. 78:106 *1556*
11 *marginal note to v. 3b*: Josh. 3.c. [3:13] *1556* [The reference is from the Olivétan Bible.]
13 *marginal note to v. 4a*: Exod. 19.c [19:18] *1556*
15 *marginal note to v. 4b*: If insensible creatures see God and tremble, how great is our wickedness, if we open not our eyes and reverence him. *1556*
29 *marginal note to v. 8*: Ps. 78. *1556* [See Ps. 78:15–16.]

Musical settings and later use of the text: The *1556* tune (*HTI* 102, Frost 126) was not included in the English psalm book after 1560, though there is a four-voice setting of it by Hake in *Day 1563*. The usual reference is to PSALM 68 or 77. It was later set to several common tunes, first in *East 1592* to Oxford, but did not become widely popular. As modernized in the late 17th century, the first line runs "When Isräcl by God's command" (*WBP* 1751).

Psalm 115
Not unto us, Lord, not to us

Text: The **psalm** was first printed in *1562a*, where it replaced a version by William Whittingham that appeared from *1556* through all the editions of 1561. This is the only case in which a psalm paraphrase new to *1562a* was not also printed in *1562b*, an omission that was probably an oversight. It is also missing from the 1564 *First Parte of the Psalmes*, which copies Whittingham's version from *1561c* (or another lost edition sharing variants with it). Norton's version primarily versifies the Geneva Bible translation, though the first two quatrains choose the Great Bible's diction where the two versions differ. The **argument** first appeared in *1556*, and was reprinted in the 1557 Genevan Psalter as well as the Geneva Bible. It is expanded from Calvin's summary in his *Commentary on the Psalms*.

Incipit Non nobis, Domine: Not unto us, O Lord

Musical settings and later use of the text: The *1556* tune (*HTI* 103, Frost 126: see App. 5, p. 985) was printed with Whittingham's version in the English psalm book *1561c, 1561d*, and their 1564 reprint, *The First Parte*, but thereafter only in the Scottish psalm book. Norton's version had no tune until *1585*, when John Wolfe supplied it with Psalm 68 (*HTI* 117a, Frost 85); this was copied in only nineteen of the hundreds of later editions, the last in 1638. Thirty-three other editions followed East, who had set it to Low Dutch, or Ravenscroft, who had chosen York (331a); eight used an unintelligible "nonsense" tune (324), and the remainder left it with only a cross-reference, usually to Psalm 119. The few 18th-century tunebooks that included this psalm generally followed Playford's choice of Westminster (387b). The text was revised, with the heaviest alterations in the second half, in the 1690s, and then lightly modernized again in the early years of the 18th century.

Psalm 116
I love the Lord because my voice

Text: The **psalm** was first printed in *1562a*. Norton relied nearly exclusively on the Geneva Bible translation for his paraphrase. A single exception—"hell" rather than the Geneva's "the grave" in v. 3—shows either a recollection of the Great Bible translation or a traditional interpretive preference that the Great Bible shared. The **argument** first appeared in the 1557 Genevan Psalter, where it occupies the first half of a longer headnote; the shortened version comes from the Geneva Bible. The main source appears to be Bucer's *Psalmorum libri quinque*, which alone of the texts that Whittingham most often followed identifies the location of David's danger. There was no revision of the argument in 1577.

Incipit Dilexi quoniam [exaudiet Dominus]: I am in love with the Lord, for he will hear
i Mammon: Corrected to "Maon" in the editions of 1569 and thereafter. See 1 Sam. 23:24–26.

Musical settings and later use of the text: Like Norton's Psalm 115, this text had no music in the *WBP* until *1585*, when it, too, was set to the tune of PSALM 68 (*HTI* 117a, Frost 85); but this match was repeated only once, in a 1592 edition. In *1586c* the first 58 notes of PSALM 111 (*HTI* 145c) were fitted (more or less) to this text, with different line breaks, making a nonsense tune that ends on the 5th degree—a labor-saving trick by an irresponsible typesetter, corrected in subsequent editions in the same series to the proper tune for PSALM 69 (*HTI* 162a). The psalm was often referred to PSALM 95. *Daman 1591* and *East 1592* chose WINDSOR, and this was followed in the Middleburg editions and some others from *1602* onwards, and by Playford in his *Introduction* from 1658. In his 1671 and 1677 psalm books, however, Playford provided an eight-line, *WBP*-like tune of unknown origin (*HTI* 538, Frost 130). The text was modernized in the early 18th century, with the first lines permanently amended to "I love the Lord, because the voice / of my pray'r heard hath he" (*WBP* 1751). Later metrical paraphrases of the psalm were, however, longer-lived outside of the *WBP*.

Psalm 117
O all ye nations of the world

Text: The **psalm** was first printed in *1562a*. Norton's versification is essentially an expansion of the Geneva Bible translation into eight lines. The **argument** first appeared in the 1559 Geneva Book of Psalms and the Geneva Bible. The Geneva Bible editors, like both Calvin and Bucer, accept Paul's contextualization of this psalm in Rom. 15:11 as confirming Christ's promise to the Gentiles. The argument was not abridged in 1577.

Incipit Laudate Dominum, [omnes gentes]: Praise the Lord, all ye nations

Musical settings and later use of the text: This psalm never had its own tune in the *WBP*. In many editions, including *1567*, it was referred to a psalm that also had no tune. It was later set to several common tunes, first in *East 1592* to CAMBRIDGE, and appeared in compilations of psalm and hymn texts through the middle of the 19th century.

Psalm 118
O give [ye] thanks unto the Lord

Text: The **psalm** was first printed in *1562a*. In paraphrasing, Marckant remained very close to the Great Bible translation, echoing diction and syntax verbatim wherever doing so could be made compatible with the verse form. The **argument** first appeared in 1557 Genevan Psalter and then, in the slightly emended version found in the *WBP*, in the Geneva Bible. Variations on this summary are found in Calvin's *Commentary on the Psalms* and Bucer's *Psalmorum libri quinque* as well as Joye's English paraphrase of Bucer. Abridgement of the argument in 1577 was limited to one phrase.

Incipit Confitemini Domino: Give thanks unto the Lord
37–9 In the original, v. 12 offers two unrelated metaphors, men as bees and their lives as a fire quickly exhausted because of inadequate fuel: the Great Bible gives "They came about me like bees, and are extinct even as the fire among the thorns." Marckant's rephrasing at least suggests, however, that the fiery "thorns" extinguished by the Lord are the bees' stings.
51 wealth: The 1562 reading, "health," corresponds to the Great Bible source.

Musical settings and later use of the text: This psalm never had its own tune in the *WBP*. In many editions, including *1567*, it was referred to a psalm that also had no tune. It was later set to a few common tunes, first in *East 1592* to Ox-FORD, but was surpassed in popularity by other metrical versions of the psalm and not widely reprinted outside the *WBP* after the middle of the 18th century. The substantial early-18th-century revision left the first lines as "O give ye thanks to God the Lord, / for very kind is he" (*WBP* 1751).

Psalm 119
Blessed are they that perfect are

Text: The **psalm** was first printed in *1558*. Whittingham drew much of the diction for his paraphrase from his own prose version, the 1557 Genevan Psalter, including some material that there appears as marginal glosses. At the same time, the versification regularly departs from its English prose source to emulate Beza's French metrical paraphrase, as in v. 25, a nearly complete translation of the passage as Beza gave it. Less frequently the psalm reflects Budé's translation and notes without Beza's mediation (e.g., the unexpected word "idiots" in l. 509). The **argument** also first appeared in *1558*, and closely paraphrases the argument in the French metrical psalter.

Incipit Beati immaculati [in via]: Blessed are the undefiled in the way

287 Their hearts . . . wealth: Cf. Whittingham's marginal gloss from the 1557 Genevan Psalter: "Their heart is indurate and hardened, puffed up with prosperity."

Later use of the text: Portions of this paraphrase continued to be popular past the middle of the 19th century. Two different methods of abridging it emerged in tunebooks and selections of psalm texts. A number of its alphabetically-separated parts began to circulate as independent hymns, some with considerable use in the 18th century (see Musical settings below). In other collections, selected verses from the whole psalm appear as new "parts" that can be used separately in worship, sometimes mixed with verses from other CM paraphrases.[56]

The length also made the idea of singing this psalm a source of remark and witticism. It is likely but not certain that the diarist Thomas Hearne refers to Whittingham's paraphrase in his 1725 anecdote of a priest using the time spent singing Ps. 119 to travel several miles home to retrieve a forgotten sermon text (for a fuller account, see p. 593). By the middle of the 18th century, a story was circulating that during the English Civil Wars "one of the Chaplains to the famous Montrose," having been condemned to death in Scotland, "being upon the Ladder, and order'd to set out a Psalm, expecting a Reprive [sic], he named the 119th Psalm." The reporter dryly notes that the reprieve was long enough in coming that "any other Psalm would have hang'd him."[57] As the Scottish psalm book shares the version in the *WBP*, the account, apocryphal or not, refers to this text.

Tune: DCM, Dorian (*HTI* 120a, Frost 132). First printed in *1558*. The first four phrases and the last are based on the Lutheran creed, "Wir glauben all" (Zahn 7971), which is in ten 8's. Martin Luther, with Johann Walter's likely assistance, had prepared this tune for Walter's *Geystliches gesangk Buchleyn* (1524). It was adapted in turn from a Latin Credo trope, found as early as 1417 in Wroclaw, Biblioteka Uniwerstyecka, MS. I. Q. 466, p. 27.[58] Coverdale, in *Goostly Psalmes* [c. 1535–6], had adapted that version to an English translation of the creed, "We believe all upon one God" (*HTI* 7, Frost 258), but in an irregular meter which necessitated some musical changes.

Other musical settings: Because of the continued popularity of the proper tune, only a handful of others were printed with the first eight-verse "part" of the

---

[56] See, for instance, the 26-verse version in Dalton, *A Selection of Psalms and Hymns*, 75–80.

[57] Butler, *Hudibras*, Vol. 2, annotated by Zachary Grey (1744), 112.

[58] For a modern edition see *Denkmäler deutscher Tonkunst* 34, p. X, no. 21; for Luther's adaptation see Frost, *Psalm Tunes*, 301–2, or Herl, *Worship Wars*, 12. Herl discusses the use of the hymn in Lutheran practice (11–13, 58–9). See also Stalmann, *Das deutsche Kirchenlied*, III, 1/2: 146, 177–8, tune Ec18.

psalm, and none of them were widely used. However, eight of the other 21 parts were printed with their own tunes in various 18th-century tunebooks. Most popular was the second ("By what means may a young man best / his life learn to amend?"), which was linked with ten different tunes, some old, some new, in 22 publications. It was launched as a separate hymn by Richard Willis of Nottingham: his 1734 collection *The Excellent Use of Psalmody* included five of these self-contained portions, using pre-existing tunes. For "By what means" he chose CANTERBURY (*HTI* 250h), Playford's revision of Low DUTCH.

Psalm 120
In trouble and in thrall

Text: The **psalm** was one of Sternhold's original nineteen first printed in *1548* (see p. 866) and was relatively lightly revised for *1556*. In his original paraphrase, Sternhold drew not only on the Great Bible but on both the Vulgate (or Coverdale's English translation) and Joye's paraphrase. He also allowed himself considerable latitude for interpolation, as in ll. 16–18, which appear in none of his sources. When Whittingham revised the versification, he actually brought it closer to Joye's version (e.g., "vantage" in l. 7). The **argument** first appeared in *1556* and was reprinted in the 1557 Genevan Psalter and later, with emendations, the Geneva Bible. It is an expanded version of the argument in the French metrical psalter.

Incipit Ad Dominum cum tribularer [clamavi]: When I was in trouble, I cried unto the Lord
13 *marginal note to v. 5*: He meaneth the shepherds' tents of Arabia, which were black with weather. Cant. 1. *1556* [See Song Sol. 1:5.]

Later use of the text: This paraphrase appears in tunebooks primarily before the middle of the 18th century. Later versions of the psalm generally supplanted Sternhold's in later collections.

First tune: 6.6.6.6.6.6, Dorian transposed (*HTI* 121, Frost 134). It was first printed in *1558*, reduced from Marot's Ps. 107 "Donnez au Seigneur gloire" (7.6.7.6.6.7.6.7) in the French Genevan psalter of 1551 (Pidoux 107c, Frost 120) by ruthlessly omitting the 3rd and 6th phrases and modifying others. It was adopted in the early editions up to and including *1567*. But it had a short English life: in 1569 it was displaced by the second tune (see below) and thereafter appeared in only three Elizabethan editions, one of which is *1583b*. There is a four-voice setting by Parsons in *Day 1563*, and it was revived in a few tunebooks between 1698 and 1715.

Second tune: 6.6.6.6.6.6, F major (*HTI* 175b, Frost 135). This is an abridgement of PSALM 77, no doubt due to the process of reduction quite often found when songs are orally transmitted (see *MEPC* 1: 70–71). It appeared in three of the four 1569 editions of the *WBP*[59] and in most subsequent editions. Comparison of the two tunes is instructive. The first is modal and archaic, whereas the second is distinctly modern for its date. It is firmly in F major, with even a modulation to the dominant key in phrases 3–4 (if the two B♭'s are raised to B natural). It had the advantage of a close resemblance to the immensely popular PSALM 81, the triple-time version of PSALM 77. The text-tune combination was in all the Companions from *Cosyn 1585* onwards, and was adopted by Playford. Nevertheless, Dod in 1603 printed a version in DCM "better fitting the common tunes." Eventually the tune was used for Tate & Brady's Ps. 120 ("In trouble and distress / To God I did address"). In modern revival it has become quite popular again as OLD 120TH, but the playful syncopations of phrases 3, 4, and 5 have long since gone.

Other musical settings: John Sheppard composed a four-voice setting of Sternhold's text in Edward VI's time, but only the uppermost voice part survives (see p. 518). The original *1556* tune (*HTI* 104, Frost 133) was not reprinted. Several other tunes were tried in the 18th century, but none caught on.

Psalm 121
I lift mine eyes to Sion hill

Text: The **psalm** was first printed in *1558*. Whittingham took the verse form of this paraphrase from Beza's version, and the English for the most part follows the sense of the French line by line. The diction, however, owes a significant debt to the Great Bible (which Whittingham reproduced almost unchanged in the 1557 Genevan Psalter). As the expansion on the literal text at the beginning of v. 8 shows, the poet also consulted Calvin's *Commentary*. The **argument** was also first printed in *1558*, and translates the argument in the French metrical psalter; it is textually distinct from the arguments in either of the Geneva prose versions of the psalms. It was not revised in 1577.

Incipit Levavi oculos meos [in montes]: I have lift up mine eyes unto the mountains
1 Sion hill: The identification of the hills or mountains in v. 1 with Mount Sion is not present in any of Whittingham's usual sources, nor is it to be found in the early Church Fathers or prominently among contemporary English Reformation sources. The gloss in the Matthew Bible succinctly explains "hylles for heauen"; the Geneva Bible shares this interpretation. (Calvin, on the contrary, reads the

---

[59] Including the reprint of *The First Part of the Booke of Psalmes*, *STC* 2439.7.

first verse as asking *whether* help shall come from the mountains, a question which the second verse answers in the negative.) Later commentators as diverse as John Wesley and Benedict XVI, however, agree that the psalm primarily refers to the literal topography of Jerusalem and thus the divine presence in the Temple.[60]

Later use of the text: The paraphrase was frequently reprinted in the 18th century, but collections of psalm and hymn texts in the 19th century largely preferred Tate & Brady's version.

Tune: 8.6.6.8.7.7, Mixolydian (*HTI* 122a, Frost 136). First printed in *1558*. From the tune to Beza's Ps. 121, "Vers les monts j'ay levé mes yeux," in the French Genevan psalter of 1551 (Pidoux 121a), for which the English text was designed. The French tune was unchanged in early editions (see the list of variants), but in *1564* some adjustments were made, apparently to make the phrases more equal in duration. It appeared in every musical edition of the *WBP* and in all the Companions. The two 7-syllable lines presented an awkward ambiguity between iambic and trochaic rhythm that meant nothing to French singers but may have confused English ones. Dod (1603) offered a DCM paraphrase to replace this one. Playford (1677) changed the meter of both text and tune to 8.6.6.8.8.8 (*HTI* 122b), probably to encourage their revival. Mostly in this form the text-tune combination remained in use through the 18th century, reaching the Magdalen Chapel tunebook in 1762.

Other musical settings: The first to attempt a new tune in this unusual meter was John Bishop (1710). Several others were tried, but none displaced the proper tune.

Psalm 122
I did in heart rejoice

Text: The **psalm** is first printed in *1560b*, and entered the London canon in *1562a*. Of the available prose versions, Kethe's versification is closest to the Geneva Bible. It is, however, significantly expanded in several verses, relying for the interpretation that it offers on Calvin's *Commentary on the Psalms*. The **argument** was first printed in the 1559 Geneva Book of Psalms. It is loosely drawn from Calvin's discussion in his *Commentary on the Psalms*.

Incipit Letatus sum [in his quae dicta]: I rejoice in the words that were said
7 wide: While it is possible that the word means "astray" in a moral sense, it is more likely that Kethe intended to echo Calvin on the significance of standing

---

[60] Matthew Bible, sig. Ff5r; Kelly and Brown, eds.,"John Wesley's Notes on the Bible"; Benedict XVI, "Commentary on Psalm 120."

in one place after the long, meandering sojourn in the desert: "the faithfull doo with thanksgiuing declare that theyr feete shal henceforth stande stedfast in the gates of Ierusalem, wheras heeretofore they wer wont too trot vp and downe" (Calvin, *Commentaries*, fol. 195v).

Later use of the text: A very wide range of tunebooks through the 18th century included this paraphrase. Hymnals after the early 19th century, however, were much more likely to use Isaac Watts's CM version ("How did my heart rejoice").

Tune: 6.6.8.6.6.8.D, F major (*HTI* 147a, Frost 137). First printed in *1560b*. It was taken from the tune for Marot's Ps. 3, "O Seigneur, que de gens / A nuire diligens" (6.6.7.6.6.7.D) as it appeared in the French Genevan psalter of 1551 (Pidoux 32c). In each 7-syllable phrase the 6th note was changed from a semibreve to two minims, equipping the tune for a wholly iambic verse, as in PSALM 113. Its joyous character and regularity of rhythm may have made it more acceptable to English singers than some of the French tunes, although Dod in 1603 felt it necessary to print a version of the psalm in DCM. The tune was matched with new texts in the 18th century, most notably to Isaac Watts's Ps. 122 ("How pleas'd and blest was I"), with which it appeared from 1780 as UXBRIDGE in Stephen Addington's popular *Collection of Psalm Tunes* for dissenters. It was also revived by William Crotch in 1803. The tune is in the *English Hymnal* (1906) as O SEIGNEUR, with a translated German hymn.

Other musical settings: Not until 1710 was this text printed with another tune: CHICHESTER, by John Bishop. James Green (1715) adapted the French Nunc dimittis (*HTI* 112b), and 17 other tunes were used in the next 100 years, attesting to the continuing popularity of the psalm.

Psalm 123
O Lord that heaven dost possess

Text: The **psalm** was first printed in *1548* (see p. 867). Sternhold probably worked from several sources, including both the Great Bible and Coverdale's parallel English translation of the Vulgate as well as the Vulgate itself. The most important disagreement of meaning between these sources is in the final verse, where Sternhold preferred the Great Bible's interpretation. This psalm is the only one of Sternhold's that did not materially change in *1556*. The **argument** first appeared in *1556*, essentially translating the one in the French metrical psalter. The version found here was reprinted in the 1557 Genevan Psalter and expanded in the Geneva Bible. It remained the same in *1577* and subsequent Elizabethan editions.

Incipit Ad te levavi oculos [meos]: Unto thee have I lift up mine eyes

Musical settings and later use of the text: John Sheppard composed a four-voice setting of Sternhold's text in Edward VI's time, but only the uppermost voice part survives (see p. 518). The *1556* tune (*HTI* 105, Frost 138), in the Mixolydian mode, was not used in English editions of the *WBP*. The *1567* tune reference is to PSALM 23, but neither version of that psalm carried a tune. The usual reference was to PSALM 119. It was later set to several common tunes, first in *East 1592* to LOW DUTCH, and later by Playford to WINDSOR, but was not widely popular. From the end of the 17th century on, the first lines were "O thou that in the heav'ns dost dwell, / I lift my eyes to thee" (*WBP* 1751).

Psalm 124
Now Israel may say, and that truly

Text: The **psalm** was first printed in *1558*. It is, in the main, a line-by-line translation from Beza's metrical version, with influence from the Great Bible on phrasing and diction. The **argument** also first appeared in *1558*, translating the one in the French metrical psalter. While it agrees in substance with the arguments in the Genevan prose psalters, it is textually distinct.

Incipit Nisi quia Dominus [erat in nobis]: Except the Lord had been among us
13 loved by God: Corrupted from Whittingham's unexpected "loved be God." The phrase derives from a false visual cognate in Beza's French version, "loué soit Dieu" (praised be God).

Later use of the text: This version was reprinted into the second half of the 19th century in hymnbooks other than the *WBP*, with only a few words revised (l. 13 did eventually shift to "Praised be God": *WBP* 1751), and it was revived for purposes of both historical illustration and non-denominational Protestant use, in the four-voice setting from *Daman 1579*, by Albert Christ-Janer and Charles W. Hughes in their 1980 *American Hymns Old and New*. In addition, the 1650 revision of the Scottish psalm book retained not only the distinctive meter and the first line but more than half of the phrasing from Whittingham's rendition. That adaptation survived in Presbyterian use into the early 20th century, and was was sung at the House of Commons' thanksgiving service for the Japanese surrender in 1945.[61]

Tune: 10.10.10.10.10, C major (*HTI* 123a, Frost 139). First printed in *1558*. This famous tune, distinguished by its five-phrase structure, came from Beza's Ps. 124 in the French Genevan psalter of 1551 (Pidoux 124c), "Or peut bien dire Israel maintenant." Whittingham's paraphrase was designed to fit the tune: the only

---

[61] *Hansard* 5th Series (Commons), Vol. 413, col. 51

change lay in regularizing the rhythms of phrase 2. Later, in *1564*, the syncopation in phrase 3 was ironed out. Dod in 1603 printed a version of the text adapted to DCM. But tune and text remained firmly wedded through all *WBP* editions and Companions, and in many other musical sources until the mid-18th century. The tune was one of those chosen by Sir John Hawkins to illustrate ancient psalmody in his *General History of Music* (1776), 3. 517. A few other texts were set to it, and it has proved popular since its revival in the later 19th century as OLD 124TH or GENEVA, but with no predominant text.

Other musical sources: The whole text was set as a five-voice verse anthem by Nathaniel Giles (c.1558–1634). Later, a handful of new tunes were tried, beginning with Bishop's IPSWICH (*HTI* 705) in 1710, but none became well established as a rival to the proper tune.

Psalm 125 (1)
Such as in God the Lord do trust

Text: The **psalm** was first printed in *1560b*, and was first published by Day in *1562a*. It was displaced by Ps. 125 (2) in the 1564 *Firste Parte of the Psalmes*, but otherwise remained the preferred version in the *WBP*, either appearing first or, occasionally, alone. There is no clear evidence that Kethe worked from any source other than the translation in the Geneva Bible, although some expansions (as at the end of v. 3) draw either on the glosses from the Geneva Book of Psalms or from their source in Calvin's *Commentary on the Psalms*. The **argument** first appeared in the 1557 Genevan Psalter and was reprinted in the Geneva Bible. It translates the argument from the Olivétan Bible, and was not revised in 1577.

Incipit Qui confidunt [in Domino]: They that put their trust in the Lord

Later use of the text: This version of the psalm was reprinted with regularity outside the *WBP* into the 19th century. The relatively light early-18th-century revision changed the second line to "as Sion mount shall firmly stand" (*WBP* 1751).

Tune: 8.8.8.8.6.6, F major (*HTI* 148a, Frost 144). First printed in *1561c* and entering the *WBP* from the earliest editions, it was adapted from the tune for Beza's Ps. 21, "Seigneur le Roy s'enjouira," first printed in the French Genevan psalter of 1551 (Pidoux 21). Kethe fitted the original 8.7.7.8.6.6 meter to iambic verse by the usual means of splitting semibreves into two minims in the penultimate notes of phrases 2 and 3. Four other pairs of semibreves were replaced by minims in editions from *1564* onwards. The tune was dropped from some *WBP* editions, starting in 1579, and it gradually lost popularity. Dod in 1603 printed a version of the text adapted to DCM. The tune gained a new lease of life in America in 1778 when Andrew Law printed a version in six 8's by extending the last two lines (*HTI* 148e), and set it to Isaac Watts's Psalm 146 ("I'll praise my maker with my breath"). On the high-church side it was revived by William Crotch in 1803.

Other musical settings: The only other tune linked with this psalm with any frequency was John Bishop's CHIEVELY (1710).

Psalm 125 (2)
Those that do put their confidence

Text: The first known printing of the **psalm** is in *1560a*, with a completely different argument from that for Ps. 125 (1). Wisdom translated, often line by line, the anonymous German metrical paraphrase of Ps. 125 first appearing in the *Strassburg Church Order* in 1525 and reprinted in numerous subsequent Lutheran collections. It was printed in the London lineage of partial metrical psalters (*1561c* and *1561d*), but was replaced by 125 (1) in *1562a*. In *1563*, Day brought it back into the *WBP* in a section after the main body of metrical psalms, along with Pss. 23 (1) and 100 (1). That group was placed after the last of the hymns in *1564*, but followed Ps. 150 again in the 1565 quarto (*STC* 2435). In the 1564 *First Parte of the Psalmes*, which largely reprinted *1561c* or a closely-related lost edition, this version displaced 125 (1). Beginning in *1565* and then in the quarto of 1566 (*STC* 2437) and after, this versification usually appeared, as here, immediately after 125 (1). It is, however, absent from some 32° editions, including *1577*, *1593*, and *1601b*. This psalm alone in the numerically-ordered psalm section of the *WBP* lacks verse numbers throughout its Elizabethan printing history.

31–40 Glory . . . Amen: An extended versification of the doxology recited at the end of psalms in both the *BCP* and in Lutheran liturgies. This stanza is present in the German original.

Musical settings and later use of the text: The tune in *1560a* (*HTI* 133, Frost 141), based on a German melody perhaps adopted by the exiles in Strassburg, was not used again. In the *WBP* the tune was referred to "the 10 Commandments," presumably the second version (COMMANDMENTS (2)) that follows after the psalms. *Daman 1579* produced an otherwise unknown melody (*HTI* 253, Frost 142), but *Cosyn 1585* and *East 1592* adopted COMMANDMENTS (2) (*HTI* 111); Ravenscroft named the tune FRENCH. *Allison 1599*, however, selected a new tune, partly of his own composition (see p. 1020). East's combination eventually reached the *WBP* in some later editions, starting with *STC* 2583.5 (1623). With the waning of the custom of singing the Commandments the tune became chiefly associated with this psalm, and it was named OLD 125TH in some late-19th-century revivals. The text was revised in two stages, first in the 1690s and then in the early years of the 17th century. This version of the psalm text also survived outside the *WBP* into the 19th century.

Psalm 126
When that the Lord against his Sion had forth brought

Text: The psalm was first printed in *1560b*, and adopted by Day for his collection in *1562a*. Kethe appears to have used the Geneva Bible as the primary source for his paraphrase, but, as with Ps. 125, he interpolated explanation and elaboration from either the Geneva Bible marginal notes or from Calvin's *Commentary on the Psalms*. The argument first appeared in the 1559 Geneva Book of Psalms and Geneva Bible, based on Calvin's discussion (primarily of the first verse) in his *Commentary*. The argument was not abridged in 1577.

Incipit In convertendo [Dominus captivitatem Sion]: When the Lord turned again the captivity of Sion
17 But much more we: Cf. the Geneva Bible's gloss: "If the infidels confess God's wonderful work, the faithful can never show themselves sufficiently thankful."
23–4 As . . . send: Literally, in the Geneva version, "as the rivers in the south," but glossed thus: "It is no more impossible to God to deliver his people than to cause the rivers to run in the wilderness and barren places."

Later use of the text: While reprinted in tunebooks somewhat regularly during the 18th century (with three single-word alterations), this version was not included in many later collections of hymns.

Tune: 12.12.12.12.10.10, Dorian (HTI 149a, Frost 145a). First printed in *1560b*. It was adapted from the tune for Beza's Ps. 90 ("Tu as esté, Seigneur, nostre retraicte") in the 1551 French Genevan psalter (see Pidoux 90). Each of the first four phrases, originally eleven syllables, was expanded by an extra note to accommodate English iambic verse. Unlike other French tunes with awkwardly long lines, this one kept its place in the *WBP* in all but the Middleburg editions. Dod in 1603 printed a version of the text adapted to DCM. But the original tune was later supplied with a new version of Ps. 126 by Tate & Brady ("When Zion's God her captive sons from bondage freed").

Other musical settings: Several new tunes were written for this text in the 18th century, but none lasted long.

Psalm 127
Except the Lord the house do make

Text: The psalm was first printed in *1558*. Whittingham followed Beza's metrical French version nearly line for line, although there are word choices drawn directly from the Great Bible (or his own nearly identical 1557 Genevan Psalter). The argument was also translated from the French metrical psalter, and was composed separately from either that in the 1557 Genevan Psalter or the different argument in the Geneva Bible. There was no revision to the argument in 1577.

Incipit Nisi Dominus [aedificaverunt domum]: Except the Lord be the builder of the house

Musical settings and later use of the text: The *1558* tune (*HTI* 124a, Frost 146), based on the French tune for the same psalm (Pidoux 127a), was dropped from the English psalm books after *1560a*, though it appeared in *Day 1563* in a setting by Hake. *Cosyn 1585* followed the reference in most *WBP* editions by using LORD's PRAYER (2), in a six-voce setting (μ20). Evidence that this pairing was in common use is its surprising appearance next year in George Whetstone's book of advice for men at arms.[62] The same match was adopted in *East 1592* and hence entered some Middleburg editions of the *WBP*. The psalm had dropped out of regular use by the mid-18th century. Beginning in the late 17th century, the first two lines read "Except the Lord the house doth make, / and thereunto doth set his hand" (*WBP* 1751).

Psalm 128
Blessed art thou that fearest God

Text: The **psalm** was one of Sternhold's original nineteen first printed in *1548* (see p. 868) and very lightly revised for *1556*. Sternhold's versification derives primarily from the Great Bible, although the phrase "olive buds" at l. 7 may indicate the influence of the Vulgate's "novelle olivarum" (as opposed to the Great Bible's "olive branches"). This is the only isolated word that Whittingham changed in *1556*. In addition, he replaced Sternhold's final two lines with a pair that translate the final lines of Marot's metrical French version. The **argument** bears no resemblance to any of Whittingham's common sources. Rather, it reflects the practice, inherited from the Sarum missal and retained in the *BCP*, of reciting this psalm at the conclusion of the marriage ceremony. The *Form of Prayers* of 1556, unlike the French Genevan order of prayers, specifies that the congregation sing this metrical version ("or some other appertaynyng to the same purpose") at the end of weddings.

Incipit Beati omnes qui timent [Dominum]: Blessed are all they that fear the Lord

Later use of the text: The association of this versification with weddings persisted for about three centuries. Set as an anthem, it was sung at the marriage service of

---

[62] Whetstone, *The Honourable Reputation of a Souldier* (1586), 100.

Princess Elizabeth in 1613.[63] At some social and ceremonial distance from that occasion, the paraphrase is fondly mentioned in an 1825 evangelical tract as part of a country wedding.[64]

Musical settings: Perhaps Sternhold chose to paraphrase this psalm because it was customary for weddings; at any rate, his version was soon set to music. There is an anonymous through-composed setting of the whole of Sternhold's unrevised text for four male voices, headed "Wedding," in the Wanley partbooks.[65] Another Edwardian example is by Philip van Wilder (d. 1554): a 5-part anthem, which survives in several Elizabethan manuscript sources and was still in use in 1664 (see p. 524; and μ4).[66] Either of these could have been sung by choirs at marriage ceremonies. John Sheppard also composed a four-voice setting, but only the uppermost voice part survives (see p. 518). In the 1556 *Form of Prayers*, where it was specifically prescribed for weddings, it had a tune (*HTI* 106a, Frost 147) adapted from Marot's Ps. 128 in the French Genevan psalter (Pidoux 128a): the original 7.6.7.6.D meter was converted to DCM by simply splitting the sixth note of each seven-note phrase into two. This tune was adopted in the Scottish psalm book, and also appeared in *Day 1563* in a setting by Hake.

Having no tune in the *WBP*, however, it was usually referred to PSALM 137. It was set to CAMBRIDGE in *East 1592*. The first half was used for a three-voice anthem by John Mundy in his *Songs and Psalmes* (1594), and the second half for another ("Thus art thou blest that fearest God"), both doubtless for use at weddings. Playford chose a four-line tune, which he named LONDON (536a), and several other CM tunes were attached to it in the 18th century.

Psalm 129
Oft they, now Israel may say

Text: The **psalm** was first printed in *1562b*, replacing thenceforth the version by Whittingham that appeared in all editions from *1558* through *1562a*. It represents the only instance where a *1562b* replacement for a paraphrase in *1562a* permanently displaced the earlier version; either the compositors for *1562a* overlooked it or, more likely, it was a late delivery from Norton which arrived after *1562a* had been cast off or even printed. The 1564 *First Parte of the Psalmes*, which in the main reprinted *1561c* or a closely-related lost edition, reverted to Whittingham's version and omitted this one. Norton's versification is taken entirely and very literally from the Geneva Bible. The **argument** first appeared in 1558,

---

[63] Nichols, *Progresses of King James the First*, 2:547.

[64] *Evangelical Rambler*, 102 (1825), 5.

[65] Oxford, Bodleian Library, MS Mus. Sch. 323–5. For a modern edition, with reconstructed tenor part, see MB 1: 146ff.

[66] Wilder, *Collected Works*, 1: 1–9. See Clifford, *Divine Services*, 2nd edn., 1664.

and translates that in the French metrical psalter. Because the argument in the 1557 Genevan Psalter, reprinted in the Geneva Bible, is a modification of this one, rather than drawn from one of Whittingham's prose sources, it is likely that Whittingham composed his paraphrase of this psalm (which borrows the tune and much of its phrasing from Beza's metrical version) with its argument late in 1556 or early in 1557.

Incipit Sepe expugnaverunt me: Many a time have they fought against me
7 cut the cords: The phrase is from the 1559/1560 Geneva translation. The marginal gloss clarifies thus: "Because God is righteous, he cannot but plague his adversaries and deliver his, as oxen out of the plow." The relationship between cords and plows, in turn, comes from Calvin's *Commentary on the Psalms* (fol. 508v), which explains that "hee alludeth to a plough, which we knowe to bee fastened with lynes to the neckes of the oxen."

Musical settings and later use of the text: The *1558* tune (*HTI* 125, Frost 148) was adopted in the Scottish but not the English psalm book. There were only cross-references in *WBP* editions, mostly to PSALM 137, until *East 1592* matched the psalm to CAMBRIDGE; this was followed in Middleburg editions, starting with *1601b*. It was set to a few other tunes up to the mid-18th century, with the original wording nearly entirely intact.

Psalm 130
Lord, to thee I make my moan

Text: The **psalm** was first printed in *1556*. Although Whittingham adopted the French tune (and thus stanzaic form) and borrowed occasional metaphors and adjectives from Marot, only a few lines directly translate the French. The Great Bible, too, exercises less influence over Whittingham's diction than usual; this psalm is, in general, more freely composed than most of his paraphrases. In addition to these sources, Whittingham clearly consulted Calvin's as-yet-unpublished psalm commentaries. The **argument**, by contrast, quite literally translates that in the French metrical psalter. It was not reproduced in either of the prose psalters prepared in Geneva.

Incipit De profundis clamavi: Out of the deep have I cried
9 *marginal note to v. 3*: No man is just in God's sight. *1556*
15–16 That . . . face: The causal relationship between God's mercy and fear of God comes from Calvin's *Commentary on the Psalms*, where the theologian explains that only those convinced of God's grace can bear to contemplate God's justice and serve him; all others experience such overwhelming fear that they shun him.

Later use of the text: In the early 18th century, the paraphrase was rewritten into CM (the first line became "Lord, unto thee I make my moan": *WBP* 1751). Nevertheless, Tate & Brady's New Version of this psalm enjoyed much more popularity.

Tune: 7.6.7.6.D, Dorian transposed/G minor (*HTI* 107a, Frost 149a). First printed in *1556*. It was the tune for Marot's Ps. 130, "Du fonds de ma pensée," from *La Forme des prieres et chants ecclesiastiques* ([Geneva, 1542]), which was apparently based in turn on a Dutch folksong, "O radt van aventuren."[67] The revised version in the French Genevan psalter of 1551 (Pidoux 130c) was taken without change for Whittingham's translation, creating an uncertainty in the stress pattern of the seven-syllable lines; it is the only tune in the canon with a *prosodic* stress on its first note. Psalm and tune gained a permanent place in the *WBP* and the Companions, surviving well into the 18th century. Dod (1603) modified the text to DCM; Ainsworth (1612) did the same to the tune by the well-tried method of repeating the sixth note of each 7-note phrase. Revived as OLD 130TH, the original tune was paired in the *English Hymnal* (1906) with J. M. Neale's translation of a hymn by Thomas à Kempis, "Our Father's home eternal."

Other musical settings: John Mundy set the first two stanzas as a four-voice anthem in his *Songs and Psalmes* (1594) (μ26); William Byrd (1543–1623: *Collected Works*, 15: 14) left a consort song on the same text. Thomas Weelkes (1576–1623), some time soon after 1600, set the same verses as a full anthem for five voices (μ29), which is listed in Clifford (1663) and is often performed today.[68] John Bishop's READING (*HTI* 702b), dating from 1710, was the only other tune printed with the original text. Two tunes were specially compoed for the revised DCM text, by John Chetham in 1717 (*HTI* 854a, named simply PSALM 130) and by William Tans'ur in 1735 (1417a, KENCHESTER). These and other tunes kept the revised psalm alive until after 1800.

Psalm 131
O Lord, I am not puffed in mind

Text: The **psalm** was first printed in *1562a*. Marckant worked primarily from the Great Bible, though ll. 7–8 borrow from the Geneva Bible instead ("I have behaved myself . . . and kept silence" as opposed to the Great Bible's "I refrain my soul and keep it low"). The **argument** first appeared in the 1557 Genevan Psalter and was reprinted in the Geneva Bible. It paraphrases the beginning of Calvin's discussion of v. 1 in his *Commentary on the Psalms*.

---

[67] See Douen, *Clément Marot*, 1: 630–1; Blankenburg, "Church Music," 522.
[68] Weelkes, *Collected Anthems*: 31–3.

Incipit Domine, non est [exaltatum cor meum]: Lord, my heart is not exalted

Musical settings and later use of the text: This psalm never had a tune of its own in the *WBP*. The usual reference was to "Lamentation," presumably meaning LAMENTATION OF A SINNER (LAMENTATION is in long meter).[69] It was set to several common tunes, first in *East 1592* to LOW DUTCH and later by Playford to WINDSOR. These and other short tunes were matched with it in various later collections up to the 1750s.

Psalm 132
Remember David's troubles, Lord

Text: The **psalm** was first printed in *1562a*. Marckant most closely followed the Great Bible in paraphrasing, though he did choose scattered readings from the Geneva Bible as well. Some verses combine the two: l. 49, for instance, includes both "deck" from the Great Bible and "clothe" from the Geneva. He also expanded fairly freely in order to fill out his quatrains (e.g., l. 24, which is not present in the original). The **argument** first appeared in the 1559 Geneva Book of Psalms and then the Geneva Bible; it derives from Calvin's summary and the opening of his discussion in his *Commentary on the Psalms*. It was not abridged in 1577.

Incipit Memento, Domine [, David]: Lord, remember David

Later use of the text: This version continued to be reprinted in collections other than the *WBP* to at least the middle of the 19th century. Its second line was altered early in the 18th century to "how unto thee he swore" (*WBP* 1751).

Tune: DCM, F major (*HTI* 178a, Frost 150). First printed in *1562a*. This is one of the more robust and well-constructed of the English tunes. It lasted through all the musical editions of the *WBP* and the Companions and survived until the mid-18th century, gaining the anomalous name PARIS in one source. *East 1592* used it also for Ps. 138, and this was copied in some Middleburg editions beginning with *1602*. *Barley 1598* also set it to Ps. 138, but (perhaps accidentally) omitted the second half of the tune. On the revival of the complete tune as OLD 132ND in *Hymns Ancient & Modern* (1861) its note-lengths were equalized, and it was coupled with Henriette Auber's paraphrase of Ps. 78, "O praise our great and gracious Lord." But Barley's stunted version replaced the complete tune in later editions of *Hymns Ancient & Modern*, starting in 1875, as ST. FLAVIAN, with F.

---

[69] *HTI* 155 rather than 184a (Duguid, *Metrical Psalmody*, 241–4).

W. Faber's hymn "Most ancient of all mysteries." This version was approved by
Erik Routley among others.

Other musical settings: A consort song for voices and viols by William Byrd
(1543–1623) based on stanzas 8 and 9 of this psalm ("Arise, O Lord") was pub-
lished in his *Psalmes, Songs and Sonnets* (1611: *Collected Works*, 11:1). For no obvious
reason Playford in 1677 substituted VENI CREATOR for the proper tune, and this
was followed in some 18th-century tunebooks.

Psalm 133
Oh, how happy a thing it is

Text: The **psalm** was first printed in *1556*. The main English source is the Great
Bible, contributing a handful of word choices. Although Whittingham did not
use the tune or stanzaic form of Beza's metrical version, he did refer to it while
paraphrasing; the most obvious echo is in line 5, where "It calleth to mind" is
closer to "Cela me fait de . . . souvenir" than to the Great Bible's "Is it like."
Whittingham also followed Beza's lead in expanding the psalm considerably,
albeit in largely different ways. The **argument**, too, first appeared in *1556*, was
reprinted in the 1557 Genevan Psalter, and appears in a shortened version in the
Geneva Bible. It is not taken in any direct way from Whittingham's usual sourc-
es, although it essentially agrees with both the argument in the Olivétan Bible
and with Calvin's discussion in his *Commentary on the Psalms*.

Incipit Ecce quam bonum: Behold how good
19–20 Early editions offered instructions about how to adapt the tune to the fi-
nal quatrain. In *1556*, an asterisk printed before these lines corresponded to an
asterisk before phrase 7 of the tune, and the marginal note specifies that "These
two last verses are sung as this mark." The instruction is wrong, however: the
asterisk should have been placed before l. 17 and phrase 5 to include the whole
quatrain. *1558* retained the asterisks, but discarded the marginal note along with
all the other marginal glosses from *1556*. The matter was somewhat clarified in
1560a, *1560b*, and *1561b*, which drop the asterisk but carry a note at the end of the
psalm stating that "This last verse is sung with the last two clauses." Odd qua-
trains occur in many of the psalms. In Ps. 15 Whittingham had created the same
situation by adding a quatrain to Sternhold's text, but saw no need to point it out.

Musical settings and later use of the text: The *1556* tune (*HTI* 108, Frost 151) was
not used in the English psalm books after *1560a*, though it was set by Hake in
Day 1563. The usual reference was to PSALM 137. The psalm became the text of a
verse anthem for six voices by Nathaniel Giles (c. 1558–1634). It was printed with
several common tunes, first in *East 1592* to CAMBRIDGE. Ravenscroft substituted
WINCHESTER; Playford in some sources used a revised version of that tune (276e,

Frost 152a), which he named HEREFORD. A verse-anthem setting by Adrian Batten (1591–1637) was often sung in the later 17th century, especially at charity meetings.[70] In the early 17th century, a wholesale revision modernized the text and shortened it by a quatrain. With its first line of "O what a happy thing it is," the emended versification (*WBP* 1751) continued to be printed in tunebooks and psalm collections into the 19th century. Chetham's tune (855a), written for the psalm, gained currency in dissenting and American tunebooks, where it was sometimes named RINETON.

Psalm 134
Behold and have regard

Text: The **psalm** was first printed in *1560b*, and it was added to the main London corpus in *1562a*. Kethe probably worked from the Geneva Bible version in composing his versification, although he padded rather than compressed in fitting the sense to the metrical form. The **argument** first appeared in the 1557 Genevan Psalter and was reprinted in the Geneva Bible; the argument for the metrical psalm differs from these in substituting "that watch" for "watching." It translates (and slightly truncates) the headnote from the Olivétan Bible; no further abridgement was undertaken in 1577.

Incipit Ecce, nunc [benedicite Domino]: Behold, now praise the Lord

Later use of the text: This version retained its popularity through the 18th century and continued to be printed in psalm collections outside the *WBP* past the middle of the 19th with only minor alterations to the text.

Tune: SM, F major? (*HTI* 150a, Frost 153a). First printed in *1560b*. It is based on the first two phrases of the tune to Beza's Ps. 101, "Vouloir m'est pris de mettre en escriture" (Pidoux 101c), as printed in the French Genevan psalter of 1551. This was in the meter 11.11.10.4 and in a clear F major. In the English adaptation the first phrase was turned into 6.6. by repeating one note, the second cut off to 8 notes for the third line of SM verse, and the remainder was replaced by simply descending the scale to an incongruous cadence on C. The result is an awkward and modally ambiguous tune in short meter. The last phrase gave great trouble to music editors. It was changed to end on E in *1565* and on D in the first solfa edition, *1569b*. In one edition (*1573*), the proper F final was restored (*HTI* 150c), and this became the norm with the 1586 revision (see p. 967). A growing number of *WBP* editions, starting with *STC* 2446 (1576), omitted the tune altogether; *Cosyn 1585* and *Allison 1599* followed suit. It was revived in 1836 by William Crotch as

---

[70] Its text is included in Clifford, *Divine Services*, 2nd edn. (1664), with the heading "This is to be sung at the charitable Meeting of each County."

St. Michael, with the final on F, and in that form it is found in some modern hymnals.

Other musical settings: *Cosyn 1585* substituted the short tune London, and this was imitated in Henry Denham's edition of the *WBP* (*1588b*) and its successors in the same series. It was also adopted by Ravenscroft and, in revised form, by Playford (1677), and from there reached many 18th-century tunebooks. The psalm, as a simple SM verse, retained popularity longer than many. One of its most successful pairings was by James Green (1724) to an improved version (848b) of a tune introduced a few years earlier by John Chetham, known at first as Psalm 134 and later as Aylesbury.

Psalm 135
O praise the Lord, praise him, praise him

Text: The **psalm** was first printed in *1562a*. For this paraphrase, Marckant relied primarily on the Geneva Bible version, with a small number of verses adopting the diction of the Great Bible instead. The **argument** first appeared in the 1557 Genevan Psalter, where it contained an additional final sentence; the Geneva Bible shortened it to the form adopted by the *WBP*. It paraphrases the summary from Calvin's *Commentary on the Psalms*.

Incipit Laudate nomen [Domini]: Praise ye the name of the Lord
30 that took rest: In Exod. 12:29 (referenced in the margin at this verse in the Geneva Bible), the Lord smote the Egyptian firstborn at midnight.

Later use of the text: This versification was regularly printed in 18th-century tunebooks and appeared outside the *WBP* into the 19th century. The first line was altered in the early-18th-century revision to "O praise the Lord, praise ye his name" (*WBP* 1751).

Tune: DCM, D minor (*HTI* 179a, Frost 155). First printed in *1562a*. This tune, like Psalm 81, has a strong suggestion of triple time (with a regular syncopation in every phrase but the last), though this is not supported by a time signature in any source, and it is interrupted by a rest after phrase 4. Perhaps for that reason, the revisers of *1586a* did not recognize it as a fundamentally triple-time tune, and recast it into something close to the standard pattern (see p. 968). It was used in all Elizabethan editions of the *WBP*, and in the Companions (*Daman 1591b* altered the last line to end on C), but is rarely found after 1640.

Other musical settings: Ravenscroft substituted the popular triple-time Psalm 81, and this was followed in the majority of *WBP* editions after 1621. Playford chose the short tune LONDON NEW (497b). A number of 18th-century tunes were associated with the revised text.

Psalm 136 (1)
Praise ye the Lord for he is good

Text: The **psalm** was first printed in *1562a*. Norton based his versification on the Geneva Bible translation with the exception of the final two lines, which restate v. 26 in the phrasing of the Great Bible. This paraphrase is omitted from *1601b* in favor John Craig's Ps. 136 (2) (see pp. 578–9). The **argument** first appeared in the 1559 Geneva Book of Psalms and Geneva Bible, revising a similar one from the 1557 Genevan Psalter. The later version combines the first part of the headnote in the Olivétan Bible with the end of Calvin's summary in his *Commentary on the Psalms*. It was shortened in 1577 by eliminating the final clause.

Incipit Confitemini [Domino]: Give thanks unto the Lord

Later use of the text: This version of the psalm continued to be printed in tune-books into the early 19th century.

Tune: 8.10.8.10.D, Dorian (*HTI* 180a, Frost 156). First printed in *1562a*. This tune responds to the unique structure of the psalm, yet the "refrain" is not quite a refrain: phrases 4 and 8 are not identical to 2 and 6, though carrying the same words. Despite this potential difficulty for congregations the tune survived through the musical history of the *WBP* and was in all the Companions. Caustun's setting in *Day 1563* is unusual in allotting the odd-numbered phrases to two or three voices and only the "refrains" to all four. The tune was later adopted for Tate & Brady's very similar version of Ps. 136 ("O praise the Lord, for he is good") and, with the old version, in the Magdalen Chapel tunebooks from 1762. It was revived by William Crotch in 1803.

Other musical settings: Several other tunes were matched with this psalm in the 18th century, but none caught on to any great extent.

Psalm 136 (2)
O laud the Lord benign

Text: The **psalm** was first printed in *Scot1564*, the Scottish psalm book, and adopted into the *WBP* in 1577. It was a permanent addition to the English metrical psalms, though a few quarto and folio printing series continued to reproduce texts from which it was missing up to the end of the 16th century. (The series containing *1567* did include this version after the 1570s.) The initials in the *WBP* were wrong from the start: the author is John Craig, referred to in the Scottish editions as "I.C."

Musical settings and later use of the text: From its first inclusion in the *WBP* in 1577, this version was given a cross-reference to the only other tune with the same meter, PSALM 148, which had been matched with it in the Scottish psalm books from the beginning (1564). *East 1592* used Kirby's harmonization of that tune for both psalms; from there it was taken into the Middleburg editions and Playford's *Whole Book of Psalms* (1677). In the early 18th century, the first line was emended to "O praise the Lord benign" (*WBP* 1751). Several new tunes were adopted before the psalm fell out of common use; it was considerably less popular than Norton's version.

Psalm 137
Whenas we sat in Babylon

Text: The **psalm** was first printed in *1556*. Whittingham used Sternhold's meter, but he drew considerably on Marot's French metrical paraphrase for diction and for figurative color. This influence is strongest in the second half of the psalm, as in l. 32 where "On, sack!" echoes Marot's "A sac, à sac." The other primary source was the Great Bible; in a handful of verses, however, this versification anticipates the Geneva Bible's translation (where it differs from the Great Bible) or marginal notes. The **argument** was first printed in *1556*, then reprinted in the 1557 Genevan Psalter and subsequently in the Geneva Bible. It is largely derived from the introductory remarks that Calvin makes in beginning the discussion of the first verse of the psalm. Whittingham's version differs, though, in affirming that true religion was in fact currently decaying; Calvin merely treats the psalm as a prudent precaution on the part of the prophet in circumstances in which the Israelites were "in hazard too grow heathenishe among the Bablylonians." (Calvin, *Commentaries*, fol. 236v).

Incipit Super flumina Babilonis: Upon the rivers of Babylon
9 *marginal note to v. 3*: God suffereth sometimes the wicked to vex and torment his children with new and sundry affliction. *1556*
21 *marginal note to v. 6*: The zeal that God's children have towards their Father's glory. *1556*
29 *marginal note to v. 7b*: Jer. 4.9. [i.e., 49:7]; Ezek. 25.c. [25:13] *1556* [Both are mentioned in Calvin's discussion of v. 7 in his *Commentary on the Psalms*.]
33 *marginal note to v. 8a*: Isa. 13.d. [13:16] *1556* [Given in the marginal note in the Olivétan Bible and also Calvin's *Commentary*.]

Later use of the text: There were two stages of revision to this text, and the second in the early 18th century changed the first line to "When we did sit in Babylon" (*WBP* 1751). The psalm dropped out of common use after 1750.

Tune: DCM, C major (*HTI* 109a, Frost 157). First printed in *1556*. This is one of the finest, as well as the most popular, of the English psalm tunes; it is said that Robert Bridges thought it so good that he assumed it was French. Among its attractive features are the apparent move to triple time in phrases 5 and 7 and the melodic sequence between those two phrases. The tune was in all musical editions of the *WBP*, and was also generally referred to for Pss. 128, 129, 133, 138, 139, and 146, and still others in some editions. It was also designated as the tune for "Our living God, to thee we cry," *A Godly Ditty or Prayer to be Song unto God for the Preservation of his Church, our Queene and Realme, against all Traytours, Rebels, and Papisticall Enemies* (London: John Awdely, [1569?]). It enjoyed four distinct settings in *Day 1563* as well as those in the other Companions: for Kirby's setting in *East 1592* see μ21. The text-tune combination maintained popularity to the mid-18th century. The tune was revived as OLD 137TH in *Hymns Ancient & Modern* (1861) with F. W. Faber's hymn "Jesus is God, the solid earth," and in *The English Hymnal* (1906) with John Mason's "How shall I sing that majesty."

Other musical settings: A verse anthem on this text by Richard Farrant (d. 1581) exists in manuscript, and may be the one listed anonymously in Clifford (1663, 1664). There was no successful rival to the proper tune, though several others were printed with the text in the 18th century.

Psalm 138
Thee will I praise with my whole heart

Text: The **psalm** was first printed in *1562a*. Norton closely paraphrased the Geneva Bible translation throughout. The **argument** first appeared in the 1557 Genevan Psalter and was reprinted in the Geneva Bible. Whittingham's summary appears to be based on Bucer's in his *Psalmorum libri quinque*.

Incipit Confitebor tibi[, Domine]: I will give thanks unto thee, O Lord

Musical settings and later use of the text: This psalm had no tune of its own in the *WBP*. The usual reference was to PSALM 137; that in *1567* is to Ps. 47, which carried no tune. *East 1592* set it to PSALM 132. *Barley 1598* used only the first half of that tune (*HTI* 178b). East reverted to OXFORD in 1594. The Schilders edition of 1599 (*STC* 2499.9) chose PSALM 3 (see p. 57). Short's Middleburg edition (*1601b*) compromised, using OXFORD plus the second half of PSALM 3 (see p. 1010). Ravenscroft 1621 preferred YORK (331a). This assortment is reflected in later editions of the *WBP*, and was gradually augmented to a total of 23 different tunes printed with the psalm before 1820.

Psalm 139
O Lord, thou hast me tried and known

Text: The psalm was first printed in *1562a*. Norton paraphrased the Geneva Bible translation very closely. The **argument** first appeared in the 1559 Geneva Book of Psalms and the Geneva Bible. It paraphrases and abridges the summary in Calvin's *Commentary on the Psalms*. *1577* and most subsequent editions abridged the argument by omitting a phrase.

Incipit Domine, probasti [me]: Thou hast tried me, O Lord
11 me . . . before: As is usually the case, the *1601b* alternate reading of this line derives from the Scottish psalm book via the 1599 Schilders edition of the *WBP* (see p. 578). Unusually, however, it is less like the Geneva Bible's wording ("Thou holdest me strait behind and before") than the standard English text had been.
29 Yea . . . also: *1601b*'s text, again Scottish via Schilders, emends the line to emphasize the Geneva Bible's "Yet thither."

Musical settings and later use of the text: This psalm had no tune of its own in the *WBP*, but three motet settings based on otherwise unknown tunes were printed, two by Thomas Caustun in *Day 1563* (*HTI* 191, 192, Frost 159, 160) and one in *Daman 1579* (*HTI* 254, Frost 161). In the *WBP* the usual reference was to PSALM 137. East set it to the common tune LOW DUTCH, which was then adopted in some Middleburg editions; Ravenscroft, followed by Playford, chose ROCHESTER (175a, b). The psalm remained current with various tunes until about 1780. The text was liberally emended at the end of the 17th century, though without successfully removing all of what were by then its conspicuous archaisms; the second line became "my sitting down dost know" (*WBP* 1751).

Psalm 140
Lord, save me from the evil man

Text: The psalm was first printed in *1562a*. Norton here again followed the Geneva translation extremely closely. The **argument** first appeared in the 1559 Geneva Book of Psalms and then the Geneva Bible. The first sentence echoes Calvin's summary in his *Commentary on the Psalms*. The second sentence, although in agreement with Calvin's discussion of the psalm's final verse, is not part of the argument in any of the Geneva Bible compilers' usual sources. The 1577 revision is less an abridgement than a syntactical clarification.

Incipit Eripe me[, Domine]: Deliver me, O Lord

2–5 and . . . war: The second verse begins in the middle of l. 2, at "which." Despite the change from singular in v. 1 to plural in v. 2 (a feature of the original), the evil imagination and war-making belong to the "cruel wight."

Musical settings and later use of the text: This psalm had no tune of its own in the *WBP*. The usual reference was to "Lamentation," presumably meaning Lamentation of a Sinner (Lamentation is in long meter). It was set to several common tunes, first in *East 1592* to Cambridge; Ravenscroft chose Wells (274c), Playford Gloucester (368a), and a few others were printed with the text up to the 1750s. The text was revised in the late 17th century, lightly over all but nearly entirely rewriting lines 2–5; the new second line was "and from his pride and spite."

Psalm 141
O Lord, upon thee do I call

Text: The **psalm** was first printed in *1562a*. Norton appears to have worked exclusively from the Geneva Bible translation, although the paraphrase includes more metrical filler than is ordinary for Norton's new 1562 compositions. The **argument** first appeared in the 1559 Geneva Book of Psalms and then the Geneva Bible. While derived from the summary in Calvin's *Commentary on the Psalms*, it is more definite than Calvin was about the circumstances of David's troubles: he says at the opening of his discussion that "although I dare not poynt vppon any time, yet mislike I not the coniecture of them that will haue this psalme to be made vppon the persecutions which he suffered vnder Saule" (Calvin, *Commentaries*, fol. 236v).

Incipit Domine, clamavi [ad te]: Unto thee, O Lord, have I cried

Later use of the text: The psalm was printed in tunebooks to nearly the end of the 18th century, but was less popular than later versifications. The late-17th-century revision changed the second line to "then haste thee unto me" (*WBP* 1751).

Tune: DCM, F major (*HTI* 181, Frost 163). First printed in *1562a*. This tune had the distinguishing feature of dotted rhythms near the end of each long phrase, but they began to be evened out in some editions, starting as early as *1564*, perhaps because they sounded too secular for those with strict Calvinist views. The tune itself was omitted from some editions, beginning with with *STC* 2450.5 (1578), though it was usually referred to as the tune for Pss. 142–144 and featured in all the Companions. It lost its rhythmic individuality in the 1586 revision. It was not used by Playford and thus barely survived the Restoration.

Other musical settings: Henry Denham's edition (*1588b*) and those in the same series substituted Oxford (µ22) for the proper tune. Playford chose Westminster (275b) for his *Introduction*, but in his *Whole Book of Psalms in Three Parts* (1677) he reverted to Lamentation of a Sinner, which was adopted in some later tunebooks.

Psalm 142
Before the Lord God with my voice

Text: The **psalm** was first printed in *1562a*. There is no evidence that Norton consulted versions other than the Geneva translation, but he did expand short verses to fill up whole quatrains. The **argument** first appeared in the 1559 Geneva Book of Psalms and the Geneva Bible, although the version in the *WBP* altered the first words from "The Prophet" to "David." It is a paraphase of the summary in Calvin's *Commentary on the Psalms*.

Incipit Voce mea ad Dominum [clamavi]: With my voice have I cried unto the Lord

Musical settings and later use of the text: This psalm had no tune of its own in the *WBP*. The usual reference was to Psalm 141. *Daman 1591* used a tune not found elsewhere (*HTI* 272, Frost 165) in a motet setting. The psalm was set to several common tunes, first in *East 1592* to Oxford, but it was not in frequent use after 1700. At the end of the 17th century, the first line was emended to "Unto the Lord God with my voice" (*WBP* 1751).

Psalm 143
Lord, hear my prayer, hark the plaint

Text: The **psalm** was first printed in *1562a*. In versifying, Norton remained very close to the language of the Geneva Bible translation. The **argument** first appeared in the 1559 Geneva Book of Psalms and the Geneva Bible, with the first phrase retained from the otherwise different argument in the 1557 Genevan Psalter (which itself translated the headnote from the Olivétan Bible). The rest of the argument paraphrases Calvin's summary from his *Commentary on the Psalms*. It was not abridged in 1577.

Incipit Domine, exaudi [orationem meam]: Hear my prayer, O Lord

Musical settings and later use of the text: This psalm had no tune of its own in the *WBP*, but two tunes in four-voice settings by Thomas Caustun (*HTI* 193, 194, Frost 166, 167) appeared in *Day 1563*. In the *WBP* the usual reference was to Psalm 141. East set it to Low Dutch, which was followed in the Middleburg editions; Ravenscroft and Playford chose other common tunes. The psalm fell out of common use by the mid-18th century. The extensive late-17th-century revision changed the opening lines to "Lord, hear my pray'r and my complaint / which I do make to thee" (*WBP* 1751).

Psalm 144
Blest be the Lord, my strength, that doth

Text: The **psalm** was first printed in *1562a*. Norton's versification here is so compact and faithful to the phrasing of the Geneva Bible translation that the meaning is occasionally opaque without reference to his source. The **argument** first appeared in the 1557 Genevan Psalter, and was revised for the 1559 Geneva Book of Psalms and the Geneva Bible. In turn, the editor who inserted it into the *WBP* made some minor verbal emendations to the 1559 version. Originally paraphrased from the headnote in the Olivétan Bible, by 1559 it intermixed some elements of the opening of the discussion in Calvin's *Commentary on the Psalms*.

Incipit Benedictus Dominus [Deus meus]: Blessed be the Lord my God
45 corners: The Geneva Bible explains this locution in the margin: "That the very corners of our houses may be full of store for the great abundance of thy blessings." From the 1569 editions on, the *WBP* substituted the Great Bible's more comprehensible "garners" (i.e., granaries).

Musical settings and later use of the text: This psalm had no tune of its own in the *WBP*. The usual reference was to PSALM 141. East set it to LOW DUTCH, which was followed in the Middleburg editions; Ravenscroft and Playford chose other common tunes. Despite a modernizing and smoothing revision in the late 17th century, the psalm did not achieve wide popularity with any of these.

Psalm 145
Thee will I laud, my God and king

Text: The **psalm** was first printed in *1562a*. The majority of the paraphrase is very close to the Geneva Bible translation, although Norton also consulted the Great Bible. At v. 7b, Norton used the Geneva diction but replaced the third person plural with the Great Bible's first person subject. The **argument** first appeared in the 1559 Geneva Book of Psalms and Geneva Bible. It derives from Calvin's summary and the opening of his discussion in his *Commentary on the Psalms*.

Incipit Exaltabo te, Deus [meus rex]: I will magnify thee, O my God my King
29 Verse 11 begins at "and."
31 Verse 12 begins at "to cause."

Later use of the text: The text persisted in hymn and psalm collections into the early 19th century, though as time went on it was less popular that Tate & Brady's "Thee I'll extol, my God and King." The second line was altered in the psalm's very light late-17th-century revision to "and bless thy Name alway" (*WBP* 1751).

Tune: DCM, F major (*HTI* 182, Frost 169). This lively tune was first printed in *1562a*. Though it began to lose its dotted rhythms in some "reformist" editions such as *1569a* and *1577* and was dropped altogether from some editions, starting with *STC* 2446 (1576), it was used in the Companions, except *Cosyn 1585*, which chose Psalm 72 instead. It was often suggested as the tune for Ps. 149. A variant with a different opening phrase (*HTI* 208, Frost 177) was the standard Scottish tune for Ps. 150 from 1564 onwards.

Other musical settings: Playford set the psalm to Martyrs (*HTI* 330a) in 1671, but in his *Whole Book of Psalms in Three Parts* (1677) he used Psalm 119. The psalm remained popular through most of the 18th century, with many different tunes.

Psalm 146
My soul, praise thou the Lord; always

Text: The **psalm** was first printed in *1549b* (see pp. 868) and slightly revised for *1556*. Hopkins relied predominantly on the Great Bible, but there are traces of both the Vulgate and Joye's prose paraphrase. At line 11, in fact, each of these sources contributes to the phrase "counsels of their heart" ("counsels" from Joye, the rest from the Vulgate's "cogitationem corum"). For the Geneva editions, Whittingham altered only five words in three lines, all of which look more like aesthetic tinkering than disagreement over meaning. The **argument** also first appeared in *1556*; the 1557 Genevan Psalter and Geneva Bible share a revised version of it, while the *WBP* retains the original. It paraphrases and expands on the argument from the Olivétan Bible.

Incipit Lauda, anima mea [, Dominum]: Praise the Lord, O my soul
17 *marginal note to v. 6*: Acts 14 [14:15]; Apoc. 14 [Rev. 14:7] *1556* [An error in printing placed these next to v. 7. The same references are given in the 1557 Genevan Psalter.]
26 *marginal note to* **lame**: They that are grieved and troubled with any kind of sickness or affliction. *1556* [Echoes the marginal note in the Olivétan Bible.]

Musical settings and later use of the text: The *1556* tune (*HTI* 110a, Frost 171) was not adopted in the English editions, but two settings of it, by Hake and Brimley respectively, are found in *Day 1563*. The usual reference was to Psalm 137. *East 1592* set it to a new and rather striking short tune, Cheshire (see p. 999), which was adopted by Ravenscroft and became a popular tune in its own right. In the

18th century the psalm was most often associated with William Tans'ur's tune ZEALAND (*HTI* 1400a). With only a few words revised, it remained in occasional use into the 19th century.

Psalm 147
Praise ye the Lord, for it is good

Text: The **psalm** was first printed in *1562a*. Norton's versification closely paraphrases the Geneva Bible translation. The **argument** first appeared in the 1557 Genevan Psalter, and was revised for the Geneva Bible; the *WBP* adopted the latter version. It was modeled on the headnote in the Olivétan Bible but adds to that the contention that this is a post-exilic composition. Calvin discusses this context at length in his *Commentary on the Psalms*, but as Whittingham does not seem to have had access to the final section of Calvin's work when he was finishing his own 1557 Psalter, the original form of the argument is probably indebted to Bucer's *Psalmorum libri quinque*. By contrast, the 1559 revision does take Calvin's summary into account, particularly in changing the phrase "his people Israel" to "his Church." It was not abridged in 1577.

Incipit Laudate Dominum [, quoniam bonus est psalmos]: Praise ye the Lord, for it is good to sing psalms
39–40 flour of wheat: I.e., the best part, not the bran.

Later use of the text: The text remained virtually unchanged, and it was occasionally reprinted outside the *WBP* into the 19th century. It was, nevertheless, surpassed in popularity by later metrical versions.

Tune: DCM, D minor (*HTI* 183a, Frost 173). First printed in *1562a*. It was adopted in most later editions, and also referred to as the tune for Ps. 150, but began to be omitted in some, starting with *STC* 2446 (1576). Its unusual ending on the sharpened third degree, as well as its secular-sounding dotted notes, suggest that it originated in a harmonized setting. Possible candidates are the two versions in *Day 1563*, by Southerton and Caustun respectively. The implied D-major ending was rejected in *Daman 1579* and *East 1592*; both treated F as the tonic. Wolfe's revision in 1586 (see p. 973) changed the last line to end on D, and this was adopted in *Allison 1599*. The last known printing of the tune in its original form was in a 1647 edition of the *WBP* (Wing B2422A). Like PSALMS 141 and 145 it began to lose its dotted-note rhythms in some editions, starting with *1569c*.

Other musical settings: The first stanza was set as a three-voice anthem by John Mundy in his *Songs and Psalmes* (1594). Ravenscroft chose MANCHESTER (*HTI* 374a), and this was adopted in some later editions of the *WBP*, but Playford substituted St. David's (379c). A number of other short tunes were adopted during the 18th century.

Psalm 148
Give laud unto the Lord

Text: The psalm was first printed in *1558*, one of the two that John Pullain contributed to that volume (the other, Ps. 149, was replaced in 1562 with Norton's version). Excluding the conventional 8-syllable lines of Ps. 51 and Ps. 136, with its refrain in every verse that poses a novel formal problem to the versifier, this is the only psalm in the *WBP* that uses neither a pre-existing Continental tune nor one of Sternhold's verse forms. Pullain, that is, invented his own stanza, apparently in imitation of the variety found in the French metrical psalter. The paraphrase is based on the 1557 Genevan Psalter, which reproduces the Great Bible exactly except for omitting the phrases found only in the Septuagint. The argument first appeared in 1557 Genevan Psalter and was slightly emended for the 1559 Geneva Book of Psalms and the Geneva Bible, although the *WBP* retains the original version. It is related to both the headnote in the Olivétan Bible and to Bucer's summary in his *Psalmorum libri quinque*, adding to them a paraphrase of part of the last verse as rendered in the Olivétan Bible, where praise belongs "aux enfants d'Israel, qui est le peuple prochain de lui." The abridgement of 1577 consisted primarily of omitting the argument's final clause.

Incipit Laudate Dominum: O praise ye the Lord

Later use of the text: This text in very nearly its original form was popular through the 18th century and continued to appear in printed collections of psalm texts outside the *WBP* through the middle of the 19th.

Tune: 6.6.6.6.4.4.4.4, Mixolydian transposed (*HTI* 126a, Frost 174). First printed in *1558*. This bold and distinctive tune, composed for its psalm, remained a permanent feature in the *WBP* and the Companions. A five-voice setting by John Mundy, found in cathedral sources, is a rare case of a psalm *tune* (as well as text) being used as the basis of an anthem, suggesting that the tune was a popular one.[71] When Craig's alternate version of Ps. 136 was introduced to the *WBP* in 1577, it was in the same meter and was naturally referred to this tune. East and Ravenscroft printed it with both psalms, and this was also done in some Middleburg editions, starting in 1603. It was one of the eight long tunes chosen by Playford for his *Introduction to the Skill of Musick* in 1658. Its exceptional popularity lasted through the 18th and into the 19th century. It was the fifth most frequently

---

[71] Durham Cathedral Library, MSS. C 2–18; York Minster Library, MS. M. 29. See Le Huray, *Music and the Reformation*, 380.

printed tune associated with any English-language texts up to 1820, appearing in 1,067 printings (*Hymn Tune Index*, 1:61). A partial explanation is its innovative verse meter, with the four short lines at the end, which is not found in either French or German tunes of the day, nor in English secular songs.

The meter caught on with a vengeance. The *HTI* records over 500 other English tunes in either 6.6.6.6.4.4.4.4 or 6.6.6.6.8.8 printed before 1821. It inspired many new texts, beginning with Tate & Brady's Ps. 148 ("Ye boundless realms of joy"), which was at first sung to the same tune. William Croft in 1707 printed a tune with Ps. 136 (2) (*HTI* 645), which has become popular only in recent times under the misleading name CROFT's 148TH. But the Tate & Brady version generated one of the most famous of all English hymn tunes, DARWALL'S 148TH (*HTI* 3503), by John Darwall (1767). That tune, in turn, is today most often coupled with William Baxter's hymn "Ye holy angels bright," but the name remains to attest its ultimate indebtedness to Pullain's catchy verse meter. Another fine exemplar of the meter is John Ireland's LOVE UNKNOWN (1925), set to a 17th-century hymn by Samuel Crossman, "My song is love unknown."

Other musical settings: An anonymous anthem setting of stanzas 1–2 and 11–12 is listed in Clifford (1664), p. 294. The tune seems to have carried the psalm through the 18th century, but a number of other tunes were successfully matched with it, most notably James Green's PSALM 148 (*HTI* 1197a), later known as NORWICH.

Psalm 149
Sing ye unto the Lord our God

Text: The **psalm** was first printed in *1562a*, replacing a version by John Pullain that appeared in all editions from *1558* through 1561. Norton's version is very close to the Geneva Bible translation. The **argument** first appeared in the 1557 Genevan Psalter and was reprinted in the Geneva Bible. It translates the headnote in the Olivétan Bible. This argument was not shortened in 1577.

Incipit Cantate Dominum [*sc.* Cantate Domino canticum novum]: O sing ye unto the Lord a new song

Musical settings and later use of the text: The tune in *1558* (Frost 175), related to Luther's "Ein' feste Burg," was not adopted in England. The usual reference was to PSALM 145. The first musical setting is in *Daman 1579*, to a tune not found elsewhere[72] (*HTI* 255, Frost 176). The first stanza was set as a four-voice anthem by John Mundy in his *Songs and Psalmes* (1594). The psalm was matched to several

---

[72] Frost (*Psalm Tunes*, pp. 207, 227) states that the tune was also used by Daman for a communion hymn, "With glory and with honour now," but this is merely the second

common tunes, first in *East 1592* to Low Dutch (μ23), which was adopted in the Middleburg editions, while Ravenscroft and Playford preferred Martyrs (330a). The psalm retained some currency in the 18th century, partly owing to its association with William Wheal's Bedford (930a). The *WBP* text changed very little during this time. It survived into psalm and hymn collections of the 19th century, though sometimes in abridged form.

Psalm 150
Yield unto God the mighty Lord

Text: The **psalm** was first printed in *1562a*. The paraphrase does not show evidence of any sources other than the Geneva Bible translation, to which it is very close. The **argument** first appeared in the 1557 Genevan Psalter and, with emendations, the Geneva Bible; the *WBP* uses the latter version. Originally a paraphrase of the headnote in the Olivétan Bible, the argument as it appears here has been modified to reflect Calvin's insistence in his *Commentary on the Psalms* that the many musical instruments named in the psalm are a figural way of emphasizing that all means should be used to praise God. No abridgement was made in 1577.

Incipit   Laudate Dominum [in sanctis eius]: O praise ye the Lord in his holiness

Musical settings and later use of the text: This psalm had no tune of its own in the *WBP*. The usual reference was to Psalm 147. *Cosyn 1585* set it to Psalm 77. It was later matched with several common tunes, first in *East 1592* to Cambridge. In the 18th century the psalm was frequently printed in tunebooks, the favorite tunes being London New (497b: Playford's choice) and Tans'ur's Colchester (1393a), composed for the revised text in 1735. The early-18th-century revision made most of its changes in the first eight lines, resulting in a new second line "praise in his holiness" (*WBP* 1751). It was printed outside the *WBP* into the 19th century, but eventually overtaken in popularity by later paraphrases of this psalm.

---

half of the first stanza of Ps. 149. It was never a separate text and has no connection with communion.

HYMNS AFTER THE PSALMS

"Praise the Lord"

Text: This versification of Ps. 117 was first printed in *1561c*. It is missing from *1562a*, where Day eliminated most duplicate psalm paraphrases. Extant copies of *1563* lack the gatherings where "Praise the Lord" and its companion "Behold, now give heed" would have been found, but it was probably restored there as Venite was in the front of the volume. It was certainly present in *1564* and later Elizabethan and Jacobean editions, except in small-format versions that reduced the number of hymns. The author, Thomas Becon, had a long-standing professional relationship with Day, who would publish Becon's *Worckes* in 1564. This hymn and "Behold, now give heed" are exceptionally literal responses to the Elizabethan Injunctions of 1559, which allowed "an hymn or such like song to the praise of Almighty God" to be sung "in the beginning or in the end of common prayers, either at morning or evening," and follow the lead of the *BCP* in concluding the Psalms with a doxology. Both hymns show the influence of the Vulgate. They were omitted from Elizabethan and Jacobean editions that reduced the number of hymns.

Musical settings and later use of the text: East, following the *WBP* cross-reference, set this and the following text to PSALM 100, though they are not consistently iambic. They are, indeed, the only paraphrases that seem to adopt the French model of meterless syllable count. The first line of the doxology, for instance, comes out as a purely trochaic tetrameter. By 1603 some editions began to emend the first line to "Praise the Lord, O Gentiles all" (*STC* 2509) and shortly after to "Praise ye the Lord, ye Gentiles all" (e.g., the 1615 *STC* 2550). Both produced a defective syllable count but much more satisfactorily iambic first line, and the latter version became the standard form of the text. For "Praise the Lord" Ravenscroft in 1621 made the strictly iambic choice of TALLIS's CANON (*HTI* 246a, Frost 316), originally composed for Matthew Parker's Psalm 67 ("God grant with grace he us embrace"). Thomas Tallis (c. 1505–1585) had devised this eight-line tune in canon at the unison, repeating each phrase in the form AABBCCDD. Ravenscroft now omitted the repeats, producing an LM tune (*HTI* 246b, Frost 316a) which still worked perfectly in canon, the second voice entering on the fifth note. The hymn text had disappeared from the *WBP* by the middle of the 18th century, but Ravenscoft's tune was revived and soon used with other texts that fitted it better. An altered version (246c) in John Wesley's *Collection of Tunes Sung at the Foundery* (1742) led, after further evolution, to a tune variously named EVENING HYMN, SUFFOLK, or BRENTWOOD (246f), first printed in the Magdalen Chapel tunebook in 1760 with Bishop Ken's Evening Hymn ("Glory to thee, my God, this night") and associated with it in hundreds of tunebooks and organ barrels over the next century. This version no longer worked in canon. When the canon proper was discovered in early Victorian times, Ravenscroft's version was revived with Ken's words, and the EVENING HYMN version was summarily dismissed.[73] But it still hung on in popular use, now fully transformed into trochaic meter and reduced to its first half. In this form it was collected in Northumberland by Ralph Vaughan Williams, then freely arranged by Martin Shaw as WATTS's CRADLE SONG ("Hush! my dear, lie still and slumber") in *The Oxford Book of Carols* (1928), no. 130, without a suspicion of its origin. It was then extended to eight lines again by the editors of *The New Oxford Book of Carols* (1992), no. 121.

"Behold, now give heed"

Text: A paraphrase of Ps. 134, first printed in *1561c*. For printing history and context, see the Text notes to "Praise the Lord," above.

Musical settings and later use of the text: East, following the *WBP* cross-reference, set this to PSALM 100, though it is not consistently iambic. Ravenscroft followed suit. No other settings are known. Like "Praise the Lord," this text appears to have been abandoned by the mid-1700s, even in the *WBP*.

The Ten Commandments (2)

Text: First printed in *1556*. The paraphrase itself is a quatrain-by-quatrain adaptation of Marot's version in nearly the same form (Whittingham shortened the first and third lines by one syllable). It was included in *1560a* after the psalms and with a new "Addition," renamed "A Prayer" in *1562a*. The Prayer is an elaboration of the congregational response following each of the first nine commandments in the *BCP*: "Lord, have mercy upon us, and incline our hearts to keep this law." Though The Prayer was never printed independently of The Ten Commandments (2) through the middle of the 17th century, it was sometimes detached in use (see Other musical settings, below). From 1575 (*STC* 16579.5) until 1650, this paraphrase with The Prayer also appeared in nearly all editions of the Scottish service and psalm book after the metrical psalms.

Later use of the text: Although apparently more popular than The Ten Commandments (1) during the Elizabethan period, this version began to be omitted from editions of the *WBP* before 1640, and was rarely included after 1700. The Prayer was a different story. In the 18th century, with the new first line "Thy spirit grant to us, O Lord," it frequently followed immediately after The Ten

---

[73] "The outrageous corruption which this fine Melody has undergone, renders the immediate adoption of the *Original*, indispensably necessary" (Hackett, *The National Psalmist*, 1842). See Temperley, "Adventures," 375–6.

Commandments (1) (see *WBP* 1751, sig. G2v). Although it could still be considered a response, it was obviously not a continuation of Norton's CM versification. By the mid-1700s, its title had changed to "The Petition" and its typesetting no longer held any clue that it was not an independent hymn.

Tune: LM, C major (*HTI* 111a, Frost 178). First printed in *1556*. It was based on the tune for Marot's Ten Commandments, "Leve le cueur, ouvre l'aureille" (Pidoux 201c), probably composed by Guillaume Franc (c. 1505–70) and first published in the lost 1543 edition of Calvin's *La forme des prières et chants ecclésiastiques*; it survives in the 1545 Strassburg edition. It was essentially unchanged in the French Genevan psalter of 1551 (Pidoux 201d). Converted from 9.8.9.8 to LM by omitting notes in the first and third phrases, it won a permanent place in the *WBP* and the Companions, and was also used by East and Ravenscroft for Ps. 125 (2). As a memorable tune in long meter, it was easily transferred to other texts, including Kethe's Ps. 100 (first by Thomas Wanless in 1702), Tate & Brady's version of the Commandments ("All they whose hopes on God depend"), and Ps. 51 in both old and new versions. The tune also recurred in Dissenting and American tunebooks, was christened OLD ENGLAND by Thomas Walker in a Baptist tune supplement dated 1811,[74] and showed no signs of losing ground in 1820 (the closing date of the *HTI*). Smoothed out to even minims, it reappeared in *Hymns Ancient and Modern*, matched in the 1875 edition to Bishop Ken's morning hymn ("Awake, my soul, and with the sun"). *Hymns Ancient & Modern Revised* (1950) restored the original 9.8.9.8 version with a different text, "O rock of ages, one foundation," by H. A. Martin.

Other musical settings: None are known for the Commandments themselves. The Prayer that follows was, as a continuation, evidently intended to be sung to the same tune. It was also, however, used as a response to the prose Commandments in the ante-communion service (see p. 590 for evidence of this practice). This became explicit in Playford's *Whole Booke of Psalms in Three Parts* (1677), where The Prayer is printed without the Commandments and the tune is headed "Prayer after the X. Commandments. Proper Tune." An anthem setting of The Prayer by William Child (1606–97) is lost, but its text survives in British Library Harley MS. 4142, fol. 28v.

The Lord's Prayer (2)

Text: First printed with the metrical psalms in *1556w*, although it was also attached in 1556 to Laurence Saunders's *A Trewe Mirrour or Glase Wherin We Maye Beholde the Wofull State of Englande*, sig. 3v–4r. It is a translation by Richard Cox

---

[74] *Walker's Companion to Dr. Rippon's Tune Book* (1811) (*HTI* WalkTWC 1).

of Luther's "Vater unser im Himmelreich," and was probably used by the English exiles at both Strassburg and Frankfurt before its printed publication. It entered the London metrical psalters in *1560a*, and was reprinted in all Day's subsequent collections. The copy text probably came from a source different from that for the other hymns first printed in *1556w* (see *RR*, 121, n. 42). That the printer of *1560a* had it in multiple versions, along with its publication in *The Trewe Mirrour*, suggests that this was an unusually popular hymn in Protestant communities during the Marian period. That popularity must have continued to a degree in the Elizabethan period, given that editions of the *WBP* which reduced the number of hymns chose to include this one in preference to The Lord's Prayer (1). From 1575 (*STC* 16579.5) until 1650, it also appeared in nearly all editions of the Scottish service and psalm book after the metrical psalms.

Later use of the text: As with the two versions of The Ten Commandments, Norton's more literal paraphrase of The Lord's Prayer (1) was more frequently printed after the Restoration. Cox's version appears to have dropped out of the *WBP* altogether by the middle of the 18th century.

Tune: 8.8.8.8.8.8, Dorian/D minor (*HTI* 130a, Frost 180). First printed in *1560a*. It was directly based on the German "Vater unser im Himmelreich" (Zahn 2561; µ19), whose first extant printing is in Luther's *Geistliche Lieder, auffs new gebessert und gemehrt, zu Witte[n]berg* (Leipzig: Balten Schumann, 1539). Traditionally attributed to Luther himself,[75] it is now suspected to have originated in Strassburg. It may well have been adopted by the English exiles there in 1554 for use with Cox's translation. It was present in all musical editions of the *WBP*, and in *1562a* was also printed with Ps. 112, which (along with 127) was referred to it in most later editions. There are three harmonizations by different composers in *Day 1563*. *Cosyn 1585* wrote a six-voice setting with Ps. 127 (µ20) and *East 1592* also used it for that text. In the 18th century, when the practice of singing a metrical Lord's Prayer had died out, the tune remained in frequent use with Ps. 112 and a few other texts. So when it was incorporated in Victorian hymn books it tended to be named OLD 112TH: for instance in *Hymns Ancient & Modern* (1861). It is often associated with Lawrence Tuttiett's hymn "O quickly come, dread judge of all."

Other musical settings: None are known.

---

[75] This has been questioned. See Stalmann et al., *Das deutsche Kirchenlied*, III, 1: 129, 141–44, tune Eb35; Jenny, *Luthers geistliche Lieder*, 4, 114–15. See also Leaver, *'Goostly psalmes,'* 194.

The Creed

Text: First printed in *1556w*. Although never attributed, this paraphrase of the Apostles' Creed may be by William Samuel (see Text note to Venite, p. 634). It was reprinted in *1560a*, although all after l. 43 is lacking in the imperfect unique exemplar. As a result, it is not clear whether the two highly sectarian quatrains omitted in *1561c* and all subsequent editions were first removed in *1560a* or in the 1561 editions. Nor is it immediately obvious why Day did not place this hymn in the section before the psalms, with all the other DCM versifications of *BCP* texts from *1556w*. (The Apostle's Creed is recited at both Morning and Evening Prayer except on those feasts days when the Athanasian Creed, "Quicunque vult," is substituted.) The most likely explanation is that, even without the explicitly anti-Catholic interpolations, Day decided that the hymn expanded too much on the Creed and would not promote the image of conformity to the *BCP* that he desired. That Norton did not provide a rigorously literal alternative may indicate that Day made that decision too late to commission one. It was, however, included in all Elizabethan and Jacobean editions of the *WBP*. From 1575 (*STC* 16579.5) until 1650, it also appeared in nearly all editions of the Scottish service and psalm book after the metrical psalms.

Later use of the text: The text was substantially revised in the 1690s, without altering the first lines. Though it was included in editions of the *WBP* into the 19th century, it was not popular enough to be included in other collections.

Tune: DCM, F major (*HTI* 129, Frost 181). First printed in *1560b*. Very unusually, the note values of this tune tend to increase, rather than diminish, after its opening phrase. It occupied a permanent place in the *WBP* and the Companions, except in *Barley 1598* where the Creed was set to Low Dutch. Efforts to make its rhythms more consistent were made in some editions, notably *1577* and *1586a* (see p. 977). It was not used by Playford, but it was adapted to Tate & Brady's version of the Creed ("I stedfastly believe in God") in 1700.

Other musical settings: Only one is known, the Welsh tune St. Mary's (*HTI* 542a), in James Leman's *A New Method of Learning Psalm-Tunes, with an Instrument of Musick Call'd the Psalterer* (London, 1729).

"Come, Holy Spirit"

Text: First printed in *1561c*. This hymn was never attributed, and the (inconsistent) internal rhyme scheme is unlike any other text in the *WBP*. It combines an invocation to the Holy Ghost appropriate for a prayer before the sermon with a version of a prayer for the whole estate of the church, present in the *BCP* as a post-sermon prayer and in the *WBP* as "A prayer for the whole state of Christ's Church." For its controversial use in place of *BCP* prayers, see p. 590.

Musical settings and later use of the text: Although in the *WBP* this hymn was generally referred to PSALM 119, the first tune actually printed with it was CAM-BRIDGE, in *East 1592*; Ravenscroft chose YORK (331a). It is not found with music in any later publication. The text printed in the *WBP* was revised in the early 18th century (including an altered first line, "Come, Holy Spirit, God of might"). With yet more substantial revision and abridgment, the hymn found its way into a large number of hymn collections up to the middle of the 19th century. Several associated it with Ember Week: for instance, *A Selection of Psalms and Hymns for Public Worship* (1832), 60.

"Da pacem, Domine"

Text: First printed in *1561c*, this hymn is a translation of Wolfgang Capito's hymn "Gieb Fried zu unser Zeit, o Herr." The first line, but not the rest of the text, was based on the Latin antiphon "Da pacem Domine in diebus nostris." In this English version by Edmund Grindal, it was probably used by the Marian exiles at Strassburg and Frankfurt. It was omitted from most small-format Eliza-bethan editions that reduced the number of hymns.

Later use of the text: The hymn seems not to have been popular, and dropped out of the *WBP* in the early 18th century.

Tune: 8.7.8.7.D, modified Phrygian (*HTI* 154a, Frost 183). First printed in *1561c*. It was taken from "Gieb Fried zu unser Zeit, o Herr" (Zahn 7556), first printed in *Psalmen, Gebett und Kirchenübung* (Strassburg: Wolff Köphl, 1533).[76] The fine tune has been attributed to Mathias Greitter (c. 1494–1550) on stylistic grounds (see Jenny, *Geschichte der deutsch-schweizerischen evangelischen Gesangbuches*, 83–4), and may well have been adopted by the English exiles at Strassburg in 1554. As the Phrygian mode was obsolescent in English use, the last note was changed from E to G, with the result that the tune begins on the 6th scale degree (in relation to the final), inviting confusion in the second and subsequent stanzas. Another unfamiliar feature for English congregations was the presence of melis-mas, represented here by slurs; those in phrases 2 and 4 were dropped from the start, but those in phrases 1 and 3 remained. The ending even shows an expansive cadence of the kind one might find in a courtly song of the time, which clearly gave editors some trouble (see the list of variants). Parsons's setting in *Day 1563* retained these features, but the 1586 revision and the later Companions elimi-nated them (see p. 978). Not surprisingly, given its increasing distance from the developing tonal system, the tune tended to drop out of use after the last musical

---

[76] This source is no longer extant. See Stalmann et al., *Das deutsche Kirchenlied*, III, 1/ 2: 125, tune Eb21.

edition of the *WBP* (1688), but not before Luke Milbourne (1698) had written for it a new translation of Ps. 24 ("The earth is God's, the fulness too").

Other musical settings: *Barley 1598* matched this text (or its first half) to the common tune OXFORD. He treated the extra syllable in lines 2 and 4 by simply printing two syllables under the 5th note.

The Complaint of a Sinner

Text: First printed in *1561c* but (uniquely among the new additions) not included in *1561d*. We have found no source for this penitential hymn. From *1562a* through *1567*, it was printed after the psalms; in *1569b* and *1569c* it moved to the first section of hymns, following The Ten Commandments (1) and immediately preceding the psalms. It subsequently remained there in all editions which placed hymns before the psalms. Elizabethan and Jacobean editions that consolidated all hymns after the psalms and reduced their number omitted this one. From 1575 (*STC* 16579.5) until 1650, it also appeared in some editions of the Scottish service and psalm book after the metrical psalms.

Later use of the text: In the early years of the 18th century, the text received considerable revision (primarily to the second half). Additionally, some *WBP* editions beginning in the middle of the century began to print a second version in "Another Metre" (DSM) with the same first lines (see *WBP* 1751, sig. G3r-v). Both versions were uncommon by 1800.

Tune: 6.6.6.6.6.6.6.6.(6), Dorian/D minor (*HTI* 153a, Frost 185). First printed in *1561c*. This tune is atypical in several ways: the voice range (alto or "mean"), the textual repetition required at the end, the glaring false relation between the C sharp of phrase 8 (not found in the earliest editions) and the C natural of phrase 9, and the ending on a sharpened 3rd. These features all point to an origin in a setting composed in parts, or with instrumental accompaniment, by a professional musician for private domestic use (for a reconstruction of this see μ12). The last note hardly makes sense for a monophonic melody of this period: it calls for harmonization, with a D in the bass to provide the final of the mode. The melody does not sound like a psalm or hymn tune. It could well be a parody of a secular song, yet no antecedent has been discovered. Attempts to mitigate its uncongregational irregularities can be seen in the variant readings, and in altered versions of the tune (*HTI* 153b–e). It attracted two harmonized settings in *Day 1563*: the first, by Thomas Caustun, may have been the source of the tune. It lasted through all the musical editions of the *WBP* and beyond.

Other musical settings: None are known.

The Lamentation

Text: First printed in John Day's *Certaine Notes* (1560), a set of four partbooks. That work was not published until 1565, under the new title *Mornyng and Evenyng Prayer and Communion* (see Aplin, "The Origin of John Day's 'Certaine Notes'.") There the hymn is titled "A Prayer" ("A Godly Prayer" in the contratenor part). The text seems to be patterned after (a much-abridged) Ps. 51, though it stops short of paraphrase. It entered the metrical psalter without attribution in *1562a*, headed by a new short prose argument rather than a title ("The Lamentation" appears as the running head). Unlike the other two hymns new in *1562a* (The Humble Suit of a Sinner and Benedicite), it was not also printed in *1562b*, probably to avoid beginning another half sheet of paper. The ending hymns are missing from extant copies of *1563*, but The Lamentation is present in editions from *1564* on, with that title. From 1575 (*STC* 16579.5) until 1650, it also appeared in nearly all editions of the Scottish service and psalm book after the metrical psalms.

Later use of the text: The text was lightly revised shortly after 1700. By the middle of the 18th century, it appeared under the title The Lamentation of a Sinner, or simply followed Marckant's hymn headed as a variation in "Another Metre" (*WBP* 1751, sig. G3v). A few other collections of psalms and hymns up through the early 19th century included The Lamentation, and it remained a fixture in the *WBP* until it ceased publication.

Tune: DLM, Dorian/D minor (*HTI* 184a, Frost 186). The tune was first printed in a four-voice setting designed for *Certaine Notes* (1560), which was eventually published as *Mornyng and Evenyng Prayer and Communion* (1565), with an attribution to "M[aster] Talys." The tune is in the uppermost voice, where it is headed "This Meane part is for children" (see μ13). The three verses of the hymn are printed there, each with music, in succession, with slight musical differences among the verses and an added Amen at the end. The first verse of the same setting was printed in *Day 1563*, with the same title and attribution. But text and tune had already appeared anonymously in *1562a*, referred to as "The Lamentation," and they are found with that title in all musical editions of the *WBP*, where they retain the relatively high vocal range of the original.

Thomas Tallis (c. 1505–1585), who was undoubtedly responsible for the four-voice arrangement, almost certainly composed the melody as well. He was the leading English composer of his generation. In contrast to most of the English tunes, this one has a purposeful form and direction, and by design reflects the anguished cry for mercy in the text. It rises gradually to an almost despairing climax on the 7th scale degree. Other harmonizations are found in the Companions. Kirby's (from *East 1592*) found its way into William Bathe's *Brief Introduction to the Skill of Song* [1596]. William Lawes used text and tune as one of his *12*

Psalms (c. 1640). Playford printed them together under the title Penitential Hymn, and the tune carried that name in many 18th-century tunebooks, generally retaining its proper text. Meanwhile the tenor part of Tallis's setting developed into an independent tune (*HTI* 210b), which reached the Foundling Hospital Collection in 1796, with its original text but with no sign of Tallis's melody.

John Amner (1579–1641), organist of Ely cathedral, wrote a set of eight variations on the tune for keyboard, the earliest known set based on a tune from the *WBP*. It survives in manuscript at New York Public Library; there is a modern edition by Anthony Greening.

Other musical settings. There is an independent, through-composed setting of the whole text as a five-voice full anthem by Orlando Gibbons (1583–1625). It is listed in Clifford (1664) and is still in use today (Gibbons, *Anthems II*, 73–87).

"The Lord be thanked"

Text: First printed in *1556w*, where it is attributed to W.S., identified as William Samuel (see Temperley, "The Anglican Communion Hymn"). The text allusively recalls a number of psalms (e.g., Ps. 8:3–4, 14:3), but no other source is known. The Geneva *Form of Prayers* prescribed Ps. 103 to be sung after communion, but it is likely that at least the exile church that began at Wesel sang this hymn in that context, a congregational adaptation of the Latin choral *post-communio* verses. It was probably included in *1560a*, but the surviving copy lacks the leaves where it would be found. It reappears in *1561c* and in Day's subsequent editions. In England, this hymn was used after or during the administration of communion (see p. 590). It was omitted from a 24° series with the first surviving exemplar from 1603 (*STC* 2510.5), though the selection of hymns in that series suggests hasty cutting among the hymns at the end of the volume in order to fit into the final gathering.

Later use of the text: The hymn was printed with the *WBP* well into the 19th century. It was also adopted by a small number of other collections of hymns, though primarily before 1800.

Musical settings: Though the ancient tradition of the communion hymn persisted in England for centuries after the Reformation, this, the earliest vernacular specimen, never had its own tune in the *WBP*, being generally referred to Psalm 137. *Daman 1579* presented a harmonized tune (Frost 191) which was not seen again. *East 1592* set it to Oxford in a harmonization by John Dowland; Ravenscroft substituted Martyrs (*HTI* 330a). The only known later printing with music was in *The Psalm-Singer's Compleat Companion* by Elias Hall of Oldham, Lancashire (London, 1708). Hall chose *HTI* 546a (Frost 199), the CM tune Playford had attached to "All glory be to God on high," an anonymous paraphrase of the *Gloria in excelsis* that he included for "After Holy Communion" in his *Whole Book of Psalms in Three Parts* (1677). It is found with this tune in several American Episcopal sources from 1752 into the early 19th century.

"Preserve us, Lord"

Text: This text first survives in *1561c,* though it was probably also included in *1560a,* where Wisdom's psalm paraphrases were first printed—the final leaves of the unique exemplar are lacking. It translates Luther's dismissal hymn "Erhalt uns, Herr, bei deinem Wort / und steur des Papsts und Türken Mord." It seems to have been a popular hymn, though it drew the indignation of Elizabethan and Jacobean Catholic polemicists (see p. 591). It was omitted from a 24° series starting in 1603 (see Text note on "The Lord be thankèd").

Later use of the text: Of all the texts in the *WBP*, this one was eventually the most notorious. Combined with the fact that it never acquired a title or heading other than Wisdom's name or initials, that meant that by the mid-1630s, his name was as much a short-hand for the perceived flaws of the *WBP* as the names of Sternhold and Hopkins. A poem attributed to Richard Norbet, Bishop of Norwich, for example, was entitled "To the Ghost of Rob. Wisdome," and addressed him as "Arch-botcher of a *Psalme* or *Prayer*" (Corbet, *Certain Elegant Poems*, 49). The hymn was printed in the *WBP* increasingly rarely over the 18th century, disappearing well before 1800. At least one attempt, however, was made to revive it subsequently. In the 6th edition (1838) of *Psalms and Hymns, Selected and Revised,* John Bickersteth included seven "hymns extracted from a Prayer Book, 1636"—that is, an edition of the *WBP* bound with the *BPC*. Among them is a revised version of the text beginning "Preserve us, Lord, with thy blest word, / From ev'ry foe defend us, Lord." This more ecumenical version did not catch on, and Luther's hymn would not become popular in English again until Catherine Winkworth's Victorian translation, "Lord, keep us steadfast in thy word." That version, with no mention of Turk or Pope, is still in common use.

Tune: LM, Aeolian/A minor (*HTI* 157a, Frost 184). First survives in *1561c.* The tune was directly based on "Erhalt uns, Herr, bei deinem Wort" (Zahn 350a), first published in *Geistliche Lieder zu Wittemberg* (Wittenberg: Joseph Klug, 1543).[77] This in turn came from the medieval tune for St. Ambrose's hymn *Veni redemptor gentium.*[78] The tune was probably adopted in 1554 by the English exiles in Strassburg, in ignorance of its origins. It was in all musical editions of the *WBP* until

---

[77] The earliest extant edition is dated 1544. See Stalmann et al., *Das deutsche Kirchenlied,* III, 1/2: 161, 207–8, tune Ee21. For the Lutheran use of this hymn, with its controversial second line, see Herl, *Worship Wars,* 62, 66, 260.

[78] For one version of this see Frost, *Historical Companion,* 190.

the hymn itself was omitted. Several later compilers, beginning with Henry King (1654), used the tune with other LM texts. Playford in 1671 set it to a new paraphrase of Ps. 6, "Rebuke me not in wrath, O Lord." It was revived in some editions of *Hymns Ancient & Modern* (1889, 1904).

Other musical settings: Two tunebooks from the 1690s set the hymn to PSALM 100, and a new tune (*HTI* 824) was contributed by James Green in his *Collection of Psalm Tunes* (1715). The hymn's last known printing in a musical publication was in Matthew Wilkins's *Introduction to Psalmody* (c. 1744), as "A Hymn of Thanksgiving," with Green's tune.

FORM OF PRAYER

A form of prayer to be used in private houses every morning and evening

This section of private prayers originated in *1556*, with a selection of only four prayers (for morning, evening, and before and after eating respectively); it would be expanded in subsequent editions of the *Form of Prayers*. The earliest prayers largely imitated the prayers that concluded Calvin's 1542 catechism, and the *Form of Prayers* thus printed them next after the translation of the *Catéchisme*.[79] These prayers also appear in another, even more basic, pedagogical text, the *A.B.C. françois*. The first surviving edition of the Genevan *A.B.C.* (1551) contains the same prayers as the 1542 *Catéchisme*, albeit not in the order shared by the *Catéchisme* and *1556*. The next surviving *A.B.C. françois*, from (probably) 1562, is greatly expanded and includes not only an assortment of prayers for children but "The exercise of the father of the family, and of all Christians."[80] The Anglophone editors of *1556* seem to have taken their cue for a household prayer book from a version of the *A.B.C.* also containing this "exercise," and they adopted some of the text and much of the darker tone found in those French domestic prayers.

The "Form of prayer to be used in private houses" as found in *1567* (except for "A prayer to be said before a man begin his work") first appeared in *1561a*,

---

[79] Jean Calvin, *Catéchisme de l'église de Genève* (Geneva: Jules-Guillaume Fick, 1853), 106-13. This is a reprint of the 1553 edition.

[80] *L'ABC françois* (Geneva: Jean Crespin, 1551); *ABC et chrestienne instruction bien utile* (Geneva: Antoine Davodeau and Lucas de Mortière, [1562]). It is not clear whether all the prayers from the *Catéchisme* appear in the 1562 edition, because the unique exemplar is missing a crucial handful of pages. On the bibliography of these books and for an edition of the 1551 *A.B.C.*, see Peter Rodolphe, "L'abécédaire ou catéchisme élémentaire de Calvin," *Revue d'histoire et de philosophie religieuses* 45.1 (1965): 11–45.

and was first appended to the metrical psalms without the formal Anglo-Genevan liturgy in *1561d*. In these editions, some prayers specific to the Marian context—"A prayer made at the first assembly of the congregation" (*1556*) and "A complaint of the tyranny used against the saints of God" (*1558*)—were omitted, and two prayers from the congregational service added to the household collection. The contents then remained basically unchanged until 1577. At that point, many editions began to print only selections from the original set (most commonly, omitting the six prandial prayers). One surviving edition prior to that, *1569c*, added nine additional prayers, of which three reappeared in *1577*. The only long-lived additions to this section of the *WBP*, however, were "A Prayer Made for the Church" by John Foxe and the pseudo-Augustinian "Prayer Against the Devil," both of which are printed in App. 3. Before the Restoration, at least one private prayer was usual in editions of the *WBP*; after, editions that omitted the domestic "Form of prayers" entirely became relatively common. None of the prayers for before or after eating seem to have survived in the *WBP* after the 1640s.

For all prayers except the Morning and Evening Prayers and "A prayer to be said before a man begin his work," the first phrase is given to help alleviate the confusion caused by similar titles and the variation in headings among editions of the *WBP*. In the *Form of Prayers*, all of these texts supplied copious scriptural cross references in the margins. Unlike glosses for the psalms from *1556*, none of them were ever printed with London editions of the texts, so they have not generally been recorded here.

Morning Prayer

This text was first printed in *1556*. The author skillfully adapted parts of at least three French Genevan prayers in order to create a basically original composition responding to the situation of the Anglo-Genevan exiles. It was reprinted among the prose prayers in *1556w* as well as in subsequent editions of the *Form of Prayers*. In *1560b*, a section referring to the "afflictions of our country" resulting from "contempt of thy word" was replaced with a general confession of sins more suitable to the new Elizabethan context; the section was omitted entirely in *1561a*, from which the text in the *WBP* derives (see pp. 544, above).

14–19 And seeing . . . heavenly Father: Paraphrases from the morning prayer in Calvin's catechism (*Catéchisme*, 106–7).
28 And because thou hast . . . : In *1556*, *1558*, and *1560b*, a mark—(.)—is placed here to indicate the passage that may be inserted into the Evening Prayer as well (see note on that text, below). This section partly condenses and paraphrases a prayer to be said "after the evening prayer, as the morning" from the 1562 *A.B.C.* (49–57). This French prayer also notes the command to pray for others, expresses a hope for conversion and consolation, and asks protection from

"ravening wolves" for those under the Roman Antichrist. (See also note, above, on the whole private "Form of prayer.")

47–50 For thy people Israel . . . to mercy: Translates a passage from the prayer in the French Genevan service book for occasions when God punishes the sins of the people through adversity (*La forme des prières*, sig. K6v; see note to Evening Prayer, below). In the English prayer, this is the conclusion of the section referring to the punishment that England and Scotland were enduring, and it was omitted from *1560b*.

Later use of the text: The prayer appears in Bentley's 1582 *Monument of Matrones*, headed as "Another forme of Confession and praier to be vsed of the Maister and Mistresse with their families in priuate houses euerie morning" (Bentley, 389–92).[81] In the *WBP*, the Morning and Evening prayers always appeared together, and the vast majority of *WBP* editions before the Restoration included them. From the late 18th century until the *WBP* ceased publication, this pair, along with the "Prayer before a man begin his work," frequently formed the only contents of the "Form of prayers to be used in private houses."

A prayer to be said before meals ("All things depend upon thy providence, O Lord")

This prayer was first printed in *1556*. It is a translation of the "Oraison pour dire avant le repas" at the end of Calvin's 1542 catechism (*Catéchisme*, 106–7). As both the *Catéchisme* and the annotation in *1556* indicate, the first sentence paraphrases Ps. 104:27–8. The prayer was reprinted in *1556w* as well as subsequent editions of the *Form of Prayers*. This prayer was always accompanied by "A thanksgiving after meals." As the prandial prayers began to drop out of some editions of the *WBP* in the late 1570s, these two were initially favored, but by the mid-1580s found very rarely in editions that omitted any of the *1567* prayers, with the exception of longer or more deluxe 32° series.

Later use of the text: It was included in Henry Bull's popular *Christian Prayers*, which survives in nine editions from 1568 to 1612.[82]

---

[81] Thomas Bentley, *The Monument of Matrones: Containing Seven Severall Lampes of Virginitie* (London: Henry Denham, 1582), 389–92.
[82] Henry Bull, *Christian Prayers and Holy Meditations* (London: Thomas East for Henry Middleton, 1568), 114–15.

A thanksgiving after meals
("Let all nations magnify the Lord")

This prayer was first printed in *1556*. Like the preceding prayer, it is a translation from Calvin's 1542 catechism, in this case the "Actions de graces apres le repas" (*Catéchisme*, 107–8). The first two sentences translate Ps. 117 (as noted in both the *Catéchisme* and in *1556*). Its printing history is essentially identical to that of "A prayer to be said before meals" (see note, above).

Later use of the text: With the preceding prayer, it was included in Henry Bull's *Christian Prayers* (115–16).

Another thanksgiving before meals (1)
("Eternal and everliving God, Father of our Lord Jesus Christ")

In this form, the prayer was first printed in *1558*. Its general meaning strongly resembles "A prayer before supper" printed in *1556w* (P3v), although it is not clear whether both were translated from the same source or whether the *1558* version represents a thorough revision of *1556w*. When the prandial prayers began to drop out of *WBP* editions in the late 1570s, this one was the single most likely to be excluded (although it was one of only two, with "Glory, praise, and honour be unto thee, most merciful and omnipotent Father," to be included in a one-column quarto series running from at least 1588 until at least 1614).

Another [thanksgiving before meals] (2)
("The eyes of all things do look up and trust in thee, O Lord")

First printed in *1558*. Like the first Prayer to be said before meals ("All things depend upon thy providence, O Lord"), it paraphrases from Ps. 104; the use of these psalm verses as a grace before eating preceded the Reformation, and versions are to be found among most of the mid-Tudor primers in English. In this case, the paraphrase is almost identical to the opening of "A prayer before supper" from *1556w* (P3v). After 1577, this and the following two prandial prayers were very frequently omitted from the *WBP* altogether, but tended to be printed without the preceding three in Elizabethan and Jacobean octavo editions in particular, with occasional survival into the 1640s.

Another thanksgiving after meat (1)
("Glory, praise, and honour be unto thee, most merciful and omnipotent Father")

First printed in *1558*. This is another case in which the primary sentiments echo those in a prayer from *1556w*, "A thankes geuinge after supper" (P4r), though in substantially different words. After 1577, this prayer was usually included in the *WBP* only when the full *1567* range of prayers were printed, although it could be found in Elizabethan and Jacobean octavos formats with the two prayers surrounding it or, in at least one series of one-column quartos, paired with Another thanksgiving before meals (1) ("Eternal and everliving God, Father of our Lord Jesus Christ").

Later use of the text: Henry Bull adopted the prayer in his *Christian Prayers* (119–20). It survived occasionally into the 1640s in the *WBP*.

Another [thanksgiving after meat] (2)
("The God of glory and peace, who hath created, redeemed, and presently fed us")

The prayer was first printed in *1558*. The first half significantly resembles the "Grace before diner or supper" in Huycke's translation of the Genevan liturgy (fol. 206r), suggesting that both are adapted from a common unidentified Genevan source. The references to current persecution are not shared with the version in Huycke. Its printing history in the *WBP* is essentially the same as Another [thanksgiving before meals] (2) ("The eyes of all things do look up and trust in thee, O Lord").

Later use of the text: This thanksgiving was also reproduced in the full range of editions of Henry Bull's *Christian Prayers* (121). With the preceding two prayers, it is occasionally found in the *WBP* until the mid-1640s.

Evening Prayer

This text was first printed in *1556*. Like the Morning Prayer, it is indebted to at least two distinct French Calvinist prayers. The last paragraph closely paraphrases most of the prayer before sleep from the end of Calvin's catechism (*Catéchisme*, 112–3). The first paragraph, however, comes from a much more unexpected source: the prayer stipulated in the French Genevan service book for times when extraordinary repentance is required in the face of "plagues, wars, and other such adversities" sent by God for the punishment of sins.[83] The French penitential prayer is longer, and the editors of the Anglo-Genevan *Form of Prayers* chose to translate the opening quite literally and then to paraphrase or adapt pieces from the rest.

The prayer was reprinted in *1556w* as well as in subsequent editions of the *Form of Prayers*.

33 holy prophet.: At this point in *1556, 1558,* and *1560b*, a mark—(.)—is inserted, with the marginal direction that "This mark directeth us to that part of the Morning Prayer that is for the increase of the gospel, which also may be said here as time [s]erveth."

Later use of the text: See note to Morning Prayer, above. In addition to its appearances with the Morning Prayer, this Evening Prayer was included in the many editions of Henry Bull's *Christian Prayers* (107–11) as well as in Bentley's *Monument of Matrons* (982–4)

A godly prayer to be said at all times
("Honour and praise be given to thee, O Lord God almighty")

This prayer was first printed in *1556w*, and adopted among the Anglo-Genevan household prayers in *1558*. Among Elizabethan editions after 1577, this prayer was rarely omitted, and the first extant edition to have done so is a 1593 octavo (*STC* 2484.3).

Later use of the text: By the middle of the 17th century, a pared-down selection of five prayers—those for Morning and Evening, this one, "A prayer to be said before a man begin his work," and A confession for all estates and times ("O eternal God and most merciful Father, we confess and acknowledge")—had become one of the most common configurations of the *WBP* domestic Form of prayer in editions that included any. In this set and occasionally with some others, this prayer was printed well into the 18th century.

---

[83] *La Forme des prières* [Geneva, 1542], sig. K4r–7r. For context, see *RR*, 186.

A confession for all estates and times
("O eternal God and most merciful Father, we confess and acknowledge")

An adaptation of the general confession in Calvin's French liturgy, this prayer was first printed in *1556* as one of two possible confessions to be used at the start of common prayers. It did not enter the domestic Form of prayer to be used in private houses until *1561a* (where it was also printed in the service book itself). It was, however, included among the private prayers in *1556w* (O2r–v), together with Coverdale's paraphrase of Daniel 9, the other public general confession included in the Anglo-Genevan *Form of Prayers*. With the exception of an octavo series beginning by 1593 (*STC* 2484.3), this prayer was included in all extant Elizabethan editions of the *WBP*.

Later use of the text: Henry Bull included it in his *Christian Prayers* as "An other confession of our sinnes" (G3r–v). Its 17th- and 18th-century printing history in the *WBP* is nearly identical to that of A godly prayer to be said at all times (see Note, above).

A prayer to be said before a man begin his work

The first known source for this prayer is *1561b*, where it is the only prose prayer included along with the 87 Anglo-Genevan psalm paraphrases from *1560b*. As *1561b* included one other addition to the Genevan materials, The Lord's Prayer (2), the prayer may have originated, like Cox's hymn, in a different exile community during the Marian diaspora. Day first incorporated it into the domestic Form of prayers in *1562a*. It began to be omitted from various editions in different formats in the mid-to-late-1580s, but it was still one of the more frequently printed prayers in the Elizabethan period.

Later use of the text: Through the 1640s, its pattern of publication looked very much like the late Elizabethan one. After the Restoration, this was one of the three most common prayers found in editions that included any, and by the 18th century often one of only three or five included. It continued to be printed until the demise of the *WBP* in the 19th century.

A prayer for the whole estate of Christ's Church
("Almighty God and most merciful Father, we humbly submit ourselves")

First printed in *1556* as the prayer following the sermon in the Anglo-Genevan liturgy. It resembles the prayer following the sermon in Calvin's service book in praying for those in authority and in asking help for those in distress as well as deliverance for churches and persons under Catholic tyranny. The opening reference to the parable of the sower (Matt. 13:3–23) is original, however, and the English prayer is both shorter and, at least as originally written, more focused on the specific plight of England than its French analogue. *1556w* extracted it from the *Form of Prayers* to print with the private prayers in that volume (O3r–6r).

When it was inserted among the private prayers in *1561a*, the passages referring to England's tragic Catholicism were removed (the changes can be seen in the list of variant readings). Nevertheless, the public, congregational section of *1561a* retained the original, obviously Marian version. The collation for *1561a* in the list of variant readings reflects the edited text among the household Form of prayer. Only this version appeared in English printings of the *WBP*. The prayer began to be omitted from some editions of the *WBP* in the mid-1580s, across several different printing formats. Subsequently, it was less common than the other *1567* prayers not for meal times.

Later use of the text: Henry Bull inserted it in his *Christian Prayers* as "A prayer to be sayde after the preaching and hearing of gods word for the Whole state of Christes Churche" (224–9). Appearances in the *WBP* from the late Elizabethan period on were usually limited to editions with a substantial collection of prayers. It occasionally resurfaced in post-Restoration editions (e.g., 1673, Wing B2510B and 1675, Wing B2517) but disappeared entirely from the *WBP* before the end of the 17th century. A Victorian revival, in the spirit of the Oxford Movement, can be found in Leopold John Bernays's 1845 *Manual of Family Prayers and Meditations*.[84]

---

[84] L[eopold] J[ohn] Bernays, *A Manual of Family Prayers and Meditations* (London: Peacock and Mansfield, Bowdery and Kirby, 1845), 104–7.

Appendix 1

(B. Q.)

A List of Predecessors, Editions, and Companions to 1603

The following table lists all known editions of the *WBP*, along with the partial metrical psalters and liturgies that contributed to it and the musical Companions that followed its initial publication. Because the purpose is to capture editions up to the death of Elizabeth, we have included volumes nominally dated 1603; all surviving editions from that year were printed for assigns of Richard Day, although the Company of Stationers was granted the patent by James I on October 29, 1603.

 STC numbers are those given in the online *ESTC*, which in a few cases updates or adds to the revised printed *STC*. *STC* numbers with an asterisk represent editions definitely or likely printed abroad. Because they represent rather different market decisions than those made by the Days or the Stationers' Company, foreign editions after 1562 have not been included in the production statistics given in the Historical Essay, but are included here to provide the most complete list of volumes containing the texts. The printing series are those established in the revised *STC*, including quarto series numbers devised earlier by John R. Hetherington (all numbers given in the form of hundreds rather than format/ series of that format). They are included primarily to provide information about the printing format, but may also be cross-referenced with Appendix 8 to determine the textual contents of any individual volume. (Where a printing series is unknown or unassigned, the format only is given.) Incomplete and inaccessible editions are included; brackets around the date indicate uncertainty about the date. *STC* dates have been revised when a colophon has a later date. Years given in italics (with or without a subsequent letter) represent the codes that we gave to those volumes in recording our collations, and greater detail about those volumes may be found in pp. xxxix–xlvii. Musical Companions to the psalm book (e.g., *Day 1563*) are described in detail in Appendix 6.

 The *HTI* source codes are based on tune content, the lowercase letters (if any) identifying individual editions that have the same tunes. The number in the "*WBP* texts set" column reflects the number of psalms or hymns that are provided with printed tunes, whether or not the same tunes are also printed with other texts in the same book. For instance, our copy-text (*1567*) is shown as having 66 tunes, whereas the *HTI* assigns it only 65: this is because the tunes for Psalms 77 and 81 differ only in rhythm, and so are only counted once for *HTI* purposes. Bracketed question marks represent best guesses based on other information about the printed book.

STC#	Year	Series	Columns/Type	*HTI* source	*WBP* texts set
2419.5	[*1548*]	8/30	1 BL	—	—
2419	[*1549a*]	8/30	1 BL	—	—
2420	*1549b*	8/31	1 BL	—	—
2422	1551	8/31	1 BL	—	—
2423	[1551]	8/31	1 BL	—	—
2424	1551	8/31	1 BL	—	—
2424.1	1552	8/31	1 BL	—	—
2424.2	*1553*	8/31	1 BL	—	—
2424.4	[1553]	8/31	1 BL	—	—
2424.6	[1553]	8/31	1 BL	—	—
2424.8	[1553]	8/31	1 BL	—	—
2425	1553	8/32	1 BL	—	—
2426	1553	8/32	1 BL	—	—
2426.5	1554	8/33	1 BL	—	—
16561*	*1556*	8°	1 rom.	*P AG1	52
2426.8*	[*1556w*]	16/41	1 BL	—	—
16561a*	*1558*	16°	1 rom.	*P AG2	41
2427	*1560a*	8/35	1 BL	*P E1	48
16561a.5*	*1560b*	8°	1 rom.	*P AG4	61
16562*	*1561a*	8°	1 rom.	—	—
2428	*1561b*	16/42	1 BL	*P AG6 b	62
—*	*1561c*	8°	1 rom.	*P AG5	41
2429	*1561d*	101	1 BL	*P E2	40
16563*	1561	16°	1 rom.	*P AG6 a	62
2430	*1562a*	102.1	1 BL	*P E4	65
2429.5	*1562b*	8/39	1 BL	*P E3	23
2430.5	*1563*	103.1	1 BL	*P E5	58 [62?]
2431	*Day 1563*	obl. 8°	4 ptbks.	#WPFP	79
2432	*1564*	8/40	1 BL	*P E6	67

STC#	Year	Series	Columns/ Type	HTI source	WBP texts set
2433	1564	8/37	1 BL	✱P E7	43
2434	*1565*	2/40	1 BL	✱P E8 a	66
2435	1565	105.1	1 BL	✱P E8 b	66
2437	1566	106.1	1 BL	✱P E8 c	66
2437.5	1566	16/44	1 BL	—	43[?]
2438	*1567*	2/40	1 BL	✱P E8 d	66
2106*	1569	291.68	2 rom.	✱P E13	61
2439.3	*1569a*	107	1 BL	✱P E9 a	65
2439.5	*1569b*	221.1	1 BL	✱P E10 a	63
2439.7	1569	8/37	1 BL	✱P E11	42
2440	*1569c*	32/40	1 BL	✱P E12	64
2440a	1569	4°	2 rom.	✱P E13	61
2441	1570	8/42	1 BL	✱P E14 a	67
2441.5	[1570]	16/46	1 BL	✱P E15	64
2441.7	[1571]	107.3	1 BL	✱P E9 b	65
2442	*1572*	221.4	2 BL	✱P E10 b	63
2442.5	1572	8/42	1 BL	✱P E14 b	67[?]
2442.7	[1573]	2/40	1 BL	✱P E16 a	66
2443	1573	230.1	2 BL	✱P E17	64
2443.5	[1573]	107.5	1 BL	✱P E9 c	65
2444	1574	231.4	2. BL	✱P E10 c	63
2445	1575	2/40	1 BL	✱P E16 b	66
2445a.5	1575	107.7	1 BL	✱P E9 d	65
2446	1576	2/50	2 rom.	✱P E18 a	53
2447	1576	221.8	2 BL	✱P E10 d	63
2448	1577	107.9	1 BL	✱P E9 e	65
2448.5	1577	231.7	2 BL	✱P E10 e	63
2449	1578	8/43	1 BL	✱P E21 a	60
2449.3	*1577x*	16/47	1 BL	✱P E19 a	55
2449.5	*1577*	32/50	1 rom.	✱P E20a	57
2449.7	1578	2/50	2 rom.	✱P E18 b	53
2450	1578	232.1	2 BL	✱P E10 f	63
2450.5	1578	201.1	2 rom.	✱P E22a	50
2451	1578	16/53	1 rom.	✱P E22b	50

STC #	Year	Series	Columns/Type	*HTI* source	*WBP* texts set
2451.5	1578	16/47	1 BL	✳P E23 a	62
2452	1579	108.2	1 BL	✳P E24 a	65
2452.5	1579	232.2	2 BL	✳P E10 g	63[?]
2452.7	1579	222.3	2 BL	✳P E10 h	63[?]
6219	*Daman 1579*	obl. 4°	4 ptbks.	DamaWPD	68
— [1]	1579	8/60[?]	2 rom.	—	47[?]
2453	1580	2/40	1 BL	✳P E8 e	66
2454	1580	108.3	1 BL	✳P E24 b	65
2456	1580	232.3	2 BL	✳P E10 h	63
2456.2	1580	232.4	2 BL	✳P E10 j	63
2456.4	1580	8/43	1 BL	✳P E21 b	60
2456.6	[1580]	16/48	1 BL	✳P E23 b	62
2457	1581	108.4	1 BL	✳P E24 c	65[?]
2458	1581	232.5	2 BL	✳P E10 k	63
2458.3	1581	232.6	2 BL	✳P E10 l	63
2459	1581	8/45	1 BL	✳P E21 c	60
— [2]	1581	8°	1 BL	—	?
2459.3	*1581b*	8°	2 rom.	✳P E25 a	47
2459.5	1581	16/48	1 BL	✳P E23 c	62
2459.7	*1581a*	16/53	1 rom.	✳P E22 c	50
2460.5	1582	8/45	1 BL	✳P E21 d	60
2461	*1582*	12/50	1 rom.	✳P E23 d	62
[2461] [3]	1582	12/50	1 rom.	✳P E23[?]	62[?]
2461.3	1582	16/57	1 rom.	✳P E22 d	50
2461.5	1582	32°	1 rom.	—	47
2460	*1583*	222.6	2 BL	✳P E10 m	63
2462	1583	2/50	2 rom.	✳P E18 c	53
2463	1583	2/40	1 BL	✳P E16 c	66
2464	1583	233.1	2 BL	✳P E10 n	63
2465	1583	232.7	2 BL	✳P E10 o	63

---

[1] Held at Magdalene College, Cambridge, and assigned *ESTC* number s505819.

[2] Imperfect (lacking all after Bb8); held at the National Library of Scotland.

[3] The *ESTC* conflates two distinct impressions under this number.

STC#	Year	Series	Columns/ Type	HTI source	WBP texts set
2466	1583	234.1	2 BL	✱P E18 d	53
2466.5	1583/84	108.6	1 BL	✱P E24 d	65
2466.7	*1583x*	8/45	1 BL	✱P E21 e	60
2466.9	1583	16/47	1 BL	✱P E23 f	62[?]
2467	1584	108.7	1 BL	✱P E24 e	65
2467.3	1584	232.8	2 BL	✱P E10 p	63
2468	1584	8/60	2 rom.	✱P E25 b	47
2468.5	1584	222.8	2 BL	✱P E10 q	63[?]
2469	1585	2/46	2 BL	✱P E26 a	56
2470	1585	109.1	1 BL	✱P E27	62
2470a	1585	240.1	2 BL	✱P E10 rom.	63
2470a.3	1585	8/61	2 rom.	✱P E25 c	47
2470a.6	1585	16/49	1 BL	✱P E28	50
5828	*Cosyn 1585*	obl. 8°	6 ptbks.	CosyJMSFP	43
2471	*1586a*	2/40	1 BL	✱P E16 d	66
2472	*1586b*	241.1	2 BL	✱P E29 a	61
2472.5	*1586c*	221.2	2 BL	✱P E30 a	56
2473	*1586d*	8/61	2 rom.	✱P E25 d	47
2473a	*1586e*	16/55	1 rom.	✱P E25 e	47
2474	1587	261.1	2 rom.	✱P E29 b	61
2475	*1588a*	241.3	2 BL	✱P E29 c	61
2475.2	*1588b*	110.1	1 BL	✱P E31 a	59
2475.3	1588	8/61	2 rom.	✱P E32	38
2475.5 [4]	1589	109.5	1 BL[?]	?	?
2475.7	1589	211.5	2 BL	✱P E30[?]	56[?]
2476	1589	8/61	2 rom.	✱P E33 a	47
— [5]	1589	8/47	1 BL	✱P E35[?]	60[?]
2476.5	1590	241.5	2 BL	✱P E29 d	61
2477	1590	8/61	2 rom.	✱P E33 b	47[?]

---

[4] This edition is only known to survive as a single-leaf title page fragment. Based on its resemblance to other title pages in the 109 series, Hetherington designated it 109.5, but there is no way to confirm either number of columns or contents.

[5] Examined by Aaron Pratt in 2012, and not yet recorded in the *ESTC*. Held at the Beinecke Library, Yale University.

STC #	Year	Series	Columns/Type	HTI source	WBP texts set
2477.5	1590	32/52	1 rom.	—	—
2477.7	1591	261.3	2 rom.	*P E29 e	61
2478	1591	8/61	2 rom.	*P E33 c	47
2478.5	1591	16/57	1 rom.	*P E34	24
2479	1591	241.6	2 BL	*P E29 f	61[?]
2479.5	1591	110.4	1 BL	*P E31 b	59
6220	*Daman 1591 (1)*	4º	4 ptbks.	DamaWBM1	68
6221	*Daman 1591 (2)*	4º	4 ptbks.	DamaWBM2	67
2480	1592	2/48	2 BL	*P E26 b	56
2481	1592	241.7	2 BL	*P E29 g	61
2481.5	1592	8/47	1 BL	*P E35 a	60
2482	*East 1592*	8º	score	EastWBP a	179
2483	1593	241[.8]	2 BL	*P E29[?]	61[?]
2483.5	1593	211.9	2 BL	*P E30 b	56
2484	1593	8/47	1 BL	*P E29[?]	61[?]
2484.3	1593	8/62	2 rom.	*P E25 f	47
2484.5	1593	16/48	1 BL	*P E23 [?]	62[?]
2485	*1593*	32/45	1 BL	*P E20 b	57
2486	1594	241.9	2 BL	*P E29 h	61
2487	1594	261.5	2 rom.	*P E29 i	61
2487.3	1594	110.7	1 BL	*P E31 c	59
2487.6	1594	32/52	1 rom.	—	—
2488	*East 1594*	8º	score	EastWBP b	179
2489	*1595*	2/41	1 BL	*P E36 a	64
2490	1595	241.10	2 BL	*P E29 j	61
2490.2	1595	211.1	2 Bl	*P E30.5 a	56
2490.3	1595	211.11	2 BL	*P E30 c	56
2490.4	1595	8/62	2 rom.	*P E25 g	47
2490.5	1595	32/52	1 rom.	—	—
2490.6	1596	211.12	2 BL	*P E30.5 b	56
2490.7	1596	8/47	1 BL	*P E35 b	60[?]
2490.8	1596	8/62	2 rom.	*P E25 h	47
2491	1597	2/58	2 rom.	*P E31 d	59
2492	1597[5]	241.12	2 BL	*P E29 k	61[?]

STC #	Year	Series	Columns/Type	HTI source	WBP texts set
2492a	1597	16/57	1 rom.	✳P E37	50
2492a.5	1597	32/56	1 rom.	—	—
2493	1598	110.11	1 BL	✳P E31 e	59
2494	1598	241.13	2 BL	✳P E29 l	61
2494a	1598	8/62	2 rom.	✳P E25 i	47[?]
2494a.5	1598	16/48	1 BL	✳P E23 g	62[?]
2495	Barley 1598	16°	score	#WBPWT	179
2497	Allison 1599	2°	table format	AlliRPD	69
2497.3	1599	2/41	1 BL	✳P E36 b	64
2497.5	1599	241.14	2 BL	✳P E29 m	61
2497.7	1599	8/47	1 BL	✳P E35 c	60[?]
2498	1599	32/52	1 rom.	—	—
2498.5	1599	32/45	1 BL	✳P E20 c	57
2499.9*	1599	16/60	1 rom.	✳P E38	80
2500	1600	241.15	2 BL	✳P E29 n	61
2500.3	1600	241.16	2 BL	✳P E29 o	61
2500.5	1600	8/62	2 rom.	✳P E25 j	47
2500.7	1600	8/47	1 BL	✳P E35 d	60
2501	1600	32/52	1 rom.	—	—
2502	1601a	262.1	2 rom.	✳P E29 p	61
2503	1601	8/62	2 rom.	✳P E25 k	47
2503.5	1601	8/47	1 BL	✳P E35 e	60[?]
2504	1601	32/52	1 rom.	—	—
2505	1601b	16/60	1 rom.	✳P E39	80
2506	1602	241.18	2 BL	✳P E29 q	61[?]
2506.5	1602	110.15	1 BL	✳P E31 f	59
2507	1602	8/62	2 rom.	✳P E25 l	47
2507.5*	1602	8/55	1 rom.	✳P E40	92
2508	1603	2/42	1 BL	✳P E36 c	64[?]
2509	1603	241.19	2 BL	✳P E29 r	61
2510	1603	8/47	1 BL	✳P E35 f	59
2510.5	1603	24/40	1 rom.	✳P E41 a	46[?]
2511	1603	16/60	1 rom.	✳P E42 a	80
2511.5	1603	16/60	1 rom.	✳P E42	78

Appendix 2
(B. Q.)
The 1549 Sternhold and Hopkins Psalm Texts

The Text and Editorial Policies

This appendix provides a critical edition of the forty-four Edwardian psalm texts as they circulated before the revisions undertaken by William Whittingham for *1556*. It is not comprehensive in that it collates only the earliest and one of the latest Edwardian editions. We have not attempted to discover precisely which edition Whittingham took with him to Frankfurt and Geneva, but instead given the beginning and ending states of the text, which are, in any event, quite close.

The copy text is *1549b*, *Al Such Psalmes of Dauid as Thomas Sternholde, Late Grome of y[e] Kinges Maiesties Robes, Didde in his Life Time Draw into English Metre*. The colophon is dated 24 December, 1549; as Thomas Sternhold died on 23 August of the same year, and John Hopkins's seven psalms were solicited after Sternhold's death, it must be the first edition of the enlarged collection. It is certainly the earliest of Whitchurch's dated editions of *Al Such Psalmes*. Although nine editions from Edward Whitchurch's press survive, only five have intact, dated colophons: *1549b*, *STC* 2422 (22 June 1551), *STC* 2424 (1551), *STC* 2424.1 (1552), and *STC* 2424.2 (18 March 1553). Whitchurch's press ceased production in the summer of 1553,[1] so 2424.2 is very likely to have been either the latest or next-to-latest edition that he printed, and we have collated it as *1553* to show the (very small) number of changes in the Edwardian text after *1549b*.

In addition to *1549b* and *1553*, we have collated and provided variant readings from the two extant editions of Sternhold's first collection of nineteen paraphrases, *Certayne Psalmes Chose[n] out of the Psalter of Dauid, and Drawe[n] into Englishe Metre by Thomas Sternhold Grome of the Kinges Maiesties Roobes* (*1548* and *1549a*). Neither of these editions is dated. On the basis of a handful of unique readings and errors in lineation resulting from breaking long fourteener lines into quatrains, it is evident that *STC* 2419.5 (*1548*) was printed from Sternhold's

---

[1] Peter W.M. Blayney, *The Stationer's Company and the Printers of London, 1501–1557* (New York: Cambridge University Press, 2013), 756.

manuscript, while the other edition (*1549a*) is the reprint. Because the purpose of the edition is to provide a comparison text for the Elizabethan *WBP*, rather than to ascertain Sternhold's original intention, we have not restored authorial variants from *1548* in the main text. (For further discussion of dating and the form of these volumes, see pp. 510–13.)

We have also departed from the printed format of *1549b* where doing so makes comparison to *1567* and to prose versions of the Book of Psalms more convenient. The Edwardian editions of *Al such Psalmes* printed Sternhold's thirty-seven psalms together, followed by the seven by Hopkins. We have placed all of the paraphrases in numerical order, with initials in brackets to identify the author of each. The Edwardian editions also lacked verse numbers to the psalms, as no English (or Latin) Bible yet included them, but we have supplied them in brackets. The dedication by Sternhold to Edward VI, published in *Certayne Psalmes* and all editions of *Al such Psalmes* through 1553, has been omitted, as has the epistle by Hopkins "To the Reader" that prefaced his psalms in the Edwardian editions.

Editorial principles and the conventions for listing variant readings are essentially the same as those for the *1567* texts, described on pp. xxix–xxxvii. The exceptions are as follows:

- When a psalm is misnumbered in *1549b*, the correct number is given in the main text and the *1549b* reading in the variants, even when the error is common to the early editions.

- When *1549b* disagrees with all three other collated editions and also with *STC* 2422 (1551), the reading of the other four editions is given in the main text.

Commentary on Sternhold's and Hopkins's sources and on specific passages of the paraphrases that remained intact in the Elizabethan versions is found in the Notes on the Individual Texts and Tunes (beginning on p. 623), though a few are repeated here where the reader might otherwise be puzzled. Latin incipits are also translated there. In the interest of minimizing further dispersal of information, any additional notes specific to the *1549b* psalm texts follow each individual psalm.

Psalm Texts and Notes

Beatus vir. Psalm 1. [T.S.]

How happy be the righteous men,
this Psalm declareth plain
And how the ways of wicked men
be damnable and vain.

[1]	The man is blest that hath not gone		
	by wicked rede° astray,		°counsel
	Ne sat in chair of pestilence,		
	nor walked in sinners' way;		
[2]	But in the law of God the Lord	5	
	doth set his whole delight		
	And in that law doth exercise°		°employ
	himself both day and night.		
[3]	And as the tree that planted is		
	fast by the riverside,	10	
	Even so shall he bring forth his fruit		
	in his due time and tide°;		°season
	His leaf shall never fall away,		
	but flourish still and stand:		
	Each thing shall prosper wondrous well	15	
	that he doth take in hand.		
[4]	So shall not the ungodly do:		
	they shall be nothing so,		
	But as the dust which from the earth		
	the winds drive to and fro.	20	
[5]	Therefore shall not the wicked men		
	in judgement stand upright		
	Ne° yet in council of the just,		°Nor
	but shall be void of might.		
[6]	For why° the way of godly men	25	°Because
	unto the Lord is known,		
	And eke° the way of wicked men		°also
	shall quite be overthrown.		

Text sources: *1548, 1549a, 1549b, 1553*
Psalm: 17 not] *om 1549a*

Quare fremuerunt. Psalm 2. [T.S.]

How heathen kings did Christ withstand,
yet he was king of all,
And of the counsel that he gave
to kings terrestrial.

[1]   Why did the Gentiles fret and fume,
What rage was in their brain?
Why did the Jewish people muse
On matters that were vain?

[2]   The kings and rulers of the earth   5
stood up and did convent°   °conspire
Against the Lord and Christ his Son
which he among us sent.

[3]   "Shall we be bound to them?" say they,
"Let all their bonds be broke,   10
And of their doctrine and their law
let us reject the yoke."

[4]   But he that in the heaven dwelleth
their doings will deride
And make them all as mocking° stocks   15   °laughing
throughout the world so wide.

[5]   For in his wrath the Lord will speak
to them upon a day
And in his fury trouble them,
and then the Lord will say: 20

[6]   "Of him was I appointed king
upon his holy hill
To preach the people his precepts
and to declare his will.

[7]   For in this wise the Lord himself   25
did say to me, I wot°:   °know
'Thou art my dear and only son,
today I thee begot.

[8]   All people I shall give to thee
as heirs at thy request;   30
The ends and coasts° of all the earth   °limits
by thee shall be possessed.

[9]   Thou shalt them rule and govern all
and break them like a God,

As thou wouldst break an earthen pot   35
even with an iron rod.'"
[10]   Now ye, O kings and rulers all,
be wise therefore and learned,
By whom the matters of the world
be judgèd and discerned.   40
[11]   See that ye serve the Lord above
in trembling and in fear;
See that with reverence ye rejoice
to him in like manner.
[12]   See that ye kiss and eke° embrace   45   °also
his blessed Son, I say:
Lest in his wrath ye perish all
and wander from his way.
        For when his wrath full suddenly
shall kindle in his breast,   50
Then all that put their trust in him
shall certainly be blest.

Text sources: *1548, 1549a, 1549b, 1553*
Psalm: 14 deride] deuide *1548*

Notes
21 I was appointed: Following the Vulgate's reading here, rather than the Great Bible (or subsequent Protestant bibles).

Domine, quid multiplicati. Psalm 3. [T.S.]

        The passion here is figurèd
and how Christ rose again;
So is the Church and faithful men,
their trouble and their pain.

[1]   O Lord, how many do increase
and trouble me full sore:
[2]   How many say unto my soul,
"God will him save no more."
[3]   But thou, O Lord, art my defence   5
when I am hard bested°:   °beset
My worship° and mine honour both,   °source of honour
and thou holdest up my head.

[4]   And with my voice upon the Lord
        I do both call and cry,   10
        And he out of his holy hill
        doth hear me by and by.
[5]   I laid me down, and quietly
        I slept and rose again,
        For why° I know assuredly   15   °Because
        the Lord will me sustain.
[6]   Ten thousand men have compassed° me,   °encircled
        yet am I not afraid,
        For thou art still° my Lord my God,   °always
        my saviour and mine aid.   20
[7]   Thou smitest all thine enemies
        even on the hard cheek bone,
        And thou hast broken all the teeth
        of each ungodly one.
[8]   Salvation only doth belong   25
        to thee, O Lord above;
        Bestow therefore upon thy folk
        thy blessing and thy love.

Text sources: *1548, 1549a, 1549b, 1553*
Psalm: 8 my] myne *1553*   **11** his] the *1553*   **18** I not] not I *1549b*

Notes
21 Sternhold omits the first half of v. 7 ("Up Lord, and help me, O my God" in the Great
Bible).

Cum invocarem. Psalm 4. [T.S.]

        God heard the prayèr of the Church,
        men's vanities are shent°;   °ruined, disgraced
        With sacrifice of righteousness
        the Lord is best content.

[1]   O God that art my righteousness,
        Lord, hear me when I call:
        Thou hast set me at liberty
        when I was bond and thrall°.   °oppressed
[2]   O mortal men, how long will ye   5
        the glory of God despise?

Why wander ye in vanity
and follow after lies,
[3]   Knowing that good and godly men
the Lord doth take and choose?   10
And when to him I make my plaint,
he doth me not refuse.
[4]   Sin not, but stand in awe therefore,
examine well thine heart,
And in thy chamber quietly   15
thou shalt thyself convert°.   °turn to godliness
[5]   Offer to God the sacrifice
of righteousness, I say,
And look that in the living Lord
thou put thy trust alway.   20
[6]   The greater sort crave worldly goods
and riches do embrace;
But, Lord, grant us thy countenance,
thy favour and thy grace,
[7]   Wherewith thou shalt make all our hearts   25
more joyful and more glad
Than they that of thy corn and wine
full great increase have had.
[8]   In peace therefore lie down will I,
taking my rest and sleep: 30
For thou art he that only dost
all men in safety keep.

Text sources: *1548, 1549a, 1549b, 1553*
Psalm: **12** me not] not me *1549b*

Notes
4 Sternhold omits the second half of v. 1 (in the Great Bible "have mercy upon me and harken unto my prayer").

Verba mea auribus. Psalm 5. [T.S.]

    The Church doth pray and prophesy
    that God doth not regard
    Liars and bloody schismatics,
    but good men have reward.

[1]   Ponder my words, O Lord above,
    my study, Lord, consider;
[2]   And hear my voice, my King, my God,
    to thee I make my prayer.
[3]   Lord, thou shalt hear me call betime°,   5   °early
    for I will have respect
    My prayèr early in the morn
    to thee for to direct.
[4]   And only thee I will behold,
    thou art the God alone   10
    That is not pleased with wickedness,
    and ill in thee is none.
[5]   And in thy sight there shall not stand
    these furious fools, O Lord:
    Vain workers of iniquity   15
    of thee shall be abhorred.
[6]   The liars and the flatterers,
    thou shalt destroy them then,
    And God will hate the bloodthirsty
    and the deceitful man.   20
[7]   But I will come into thy house
    trusting upon thy grace,
    And reverently will worship thee
    toward thine holy place.
[8]   Lord, lead me in thy righteousness   25
    for to confound my foes,
    And eke° the way that I shall walk   °also
    before my face disclose.
[9]   For in their mouths there is no truth,
    their heart is foul and vain,   30
    Their throat an open sepulchre,
    their tongues do gloze° and feign.   °flatter deceitfully
[10]   Condemn them and their counsels all,
    let their device° decay;   °plot, scheme
    Subvert° them in their heaps of sin,   35   °vanquish
    for they did thee betray.

[11] But those that put their trust in thee,
let them be glad always,
And render thanks for thy defence
and give thy name the praise.   40
[12] For thou with favour followest
the just and righteous still°,   °always
And with thy grace, as with a shield,
defendest him from ill.

Text sources: *1548, 1549a, 1549b, 1553*
Argument: **iii** and] add *1548*
Psalm: **12** ill] euill *1548, 1549a* **24** toward] towardes *1548*

Domine, ne in furore. Psalm 6. [T.S.]

The troubled soul with sin oppressed
on God for grace doth call;
Though he sometime turn back his face,
from faith it doth not fall.

[1] Lord, in thy wrath reprove me not,
though I deserve thine ire;
Ne° yet correct me in thy rage,   °Nor
O Lord, I thee desire.
[2] For I am weak; therefore, O Lord,   5
of mercy me forbear°,   °have patience with
And heal me, Lord, for why thou knowest
my bones do quake for fear.
[3] My soul is troubled very sore
and vexèd vehemently.   10
But Lord, how long wilt thou delay
to cure my misery?
[4] Lord, turn thee to thy wonted grace,
my silly° soul up take: °defenceless
O save me, not for my deserts,   15
but for thy mercy's sake.
[5] For why° no man among the dead   °Because
remembereth thee one whit;
Or who shall worship thee, O Lord,
in the infernal pit?   20
[6] So grievous is my plaint and moan
that I wax wondrous faint

And wash my bed whereas° I couch   °where
with tears of my complaint.
[7]   My beauty fadeth clean away   25
with anguish of mine heart
For fear of those that be my foes
and would my soul subvert°.   °destroy
[8]   But now away from me all ye
that work iniquity,   30
For why the Lord hath heard the voice
of my complaint and cry.
[9]   He heard not only the request
and prayèr of my heart,
But it receivèd at my hand   35
and took it in good part.
[10]   And now my foes that vexèd me
the Lord will soon defame
And suddenly confound them all,
to their rebuke and shame.   40

Text sources: *1549b, 1553*
Argument: iii turn] turue *1549b*
Psalm: 34 my] mine *1553*

Domine Deus meus, in te. Psalm 7. [T.S.]

The Church against her foes to God
her sufferance° doth declare;   °long-suffering
The wicked which would work deceit
are trapped in their own snare.

[1]   O Lord my God, I put my trust
and confidence in thee:
Save me from them that me pursue,
and eke° deliver me;   °also
[2]   Lest like a lion they devour   5
my soul in pieces small
Whiles there is none to succour me
and rid° me out of thrall°.   °release / °oppression
[3]   O Lord my God, if I have done
the thing that is not right;   10
Or else if I be found in sin,
or guilty in thy sight;

[4]   Or have rewarded ill for ill
to those that harmèd me;
Or rashly robbed mine enemy   15
with great extremity:
[5]   Then let my foes pursue my soul,
and eke° my life down thrust   °also
Unto the earth, and also lay
mine honour in the dust.   20
[6]   If not, start up, Lord, in thy wrath,
and put my foes to pain:
Perform thy vengeance promisèd
to such as me disdain.
[7]   And that thy flock may come to thee   25
and know thee by this thing,
Exalt thy self in majesty
as their chief Lord and king.
[8]   That art revenger of all folk,
O Lord, revenge thou me,   30
According to my righteousness
and mine integrity.
[9]   Lord, cease the hate of wicked men,
and be the just man's guide,
By whom the secrets of all hearts   35
are searchèd and descried.
[10]   I take my help to come of God
in all my grief and smart°,   °pain
That doth preserve all those that be
of pure and perfect heart.   40
[11]   For God a right revenger is
and patient with his power:
He threateneth still°, yet we provoke   °continually
his vengeance every hour.
[12]   And if we will not turn to him,   45
the Lord will then begin
His sword to whet, his bow to bend,
and strike us for our sin.
[13]   He will prepare his killing tools
and sharp his arrows prest°   50   °ready
To strike and pierce with violence
the persecutors' breast.
[14]   For why° the wicked travailèd°   °Because / °laboured
in mischief men to cast,

Conceivèd sorrow and brought forth   55
ungodly fraud at last,
[15]   And digged a cave and cast it up
in hope to hurt his brother;
But he shall fall into the pit
that he digged up for other.   60
[16]   Thus wrong returneth to the hurt
of him in whom it bred,
And all the mischief that he wrought
shall fall upon his head.
[17]   I will give thanks to God, therefore,   65
that judgeth righteously,
And with my song shall praise the name
of him that is most high.

Text sources: *1549b, 1553*

Domine, Dominus noster. Psalm 8. [T.S.]

God's glory is so great in earth
that babes do it declare;
So doth the state of man, to whom
all creatures subject are.

[1]   In earth, O Lord, how wonderful
is thy great majesty
That lifteth up thy laud and praise
above the heavens high!
[2]   For why° the mouths of sucking babes   5   °Because
thine honour do disclose;
Thou makest infants overcome
thy mighty mortal foes.
[3]   And when I see the heavens high,
the works of thine own hand,   10
The sun, the moon, and all the stars
in order as they stand,
[4]   What thing is man, Lord, think I then,
that thou dost him remember?
Or what is man's posterity,   15
that thou dost it consider?
[5]   For thou hast made him little less
than angels in degree,

And thou hast crownèd him at last
with glory and dignity.   20
[6]   Thou hast preferred° him to be lord   °promoted
of all thy works of wonder,
And at his feet hast set all things,
that he should keep them under:
[7]   All sheep and neat°, and all beasts else   25   °ox or cow
that in the fields do feed,
[8]   Fowls of the air, fish in the sea
and all that therein breed.
[9]   Therefore must I say once again,
O Lord that art our Lord,   30
How famous is thy majesty
esteemèd through the world!

Text sources: *1549b, 1553*

Notes
7–8 The idea that the babes not only praise God but themselves overcome his enemies is
not in the original psalm.

Confitebor tibi. Psalm 9. [T.S.]

The faithful give great thanks to God,
for that he doth destroy
Their enemies all, and help the poor,
that none doth them annoy.

[1]   O Lord, with all my heart and mind
I will give thanks to thee
And speak of all thy wondrous works
unsearchable of me.
[2]   I will be glad and much rejoice   5
in thee, O God most high,
And make my songs extol thy name
above the starry sky:
[3]   For that my foes are driven back
and turnèd unto flight;   10
They fall down flat and are destroyed
by thy great force and might.
[4]   Thou hast revengèd all my wrong,
my grief and all my grudge;

Thou dost with justice hear my cause   15
most like a righteous judge.
[5]   Thou dost rebuke the heathen folk
and wicked so confound
That afterward the memory
of them cannot be found.   20
[6]   The force and weapon of thy foes
thou takest clean away;
When cities were destroyed by thee,
their name did eke° decay.   °also
[7]   But evermore in dignity   25
the Lord doth rule and reign,
And in the seat of equity
true judgement doth maintain.
[8]   With justice he doth keep and guide
the world and every wight°   30   °person
With conscience and with equity
he yieldeth folk their right.
[9]   He is protector of the poor
what° time they be oppressed: °whatever
He is in all adversity   35
their refuge and their rest.
[10]   All they that know thy holy name
therefore do trust in thee,
For thou forsakest not their suit
in their necessity.   40
[11]   Sing psalms, therefore, unto the Lord
that dwelleth in Sion hill;
Publish among the people plain°   °clearly
his counsels and his will.
[12]   For he is mindful of the blood   45
of those that be oppressed
And printeth still the poor man's plaint
within his blessed breast.
[13]   And though my foes do trouble me,
thy mercy doth remain: 50
Yea, from the gates of death, O Lord,
thou raisest me again,
[14]   In Sion that I should set forth
thy praise with heart and voice;
And that in thy salvation, Lord,   55
my soul should much rejoice,

[15]   When heathen folk fall in the pit
that they themselves prepared,
And in the net that they do set
their own feet find they snared.   60

[16]   Thus when ye see the wicked man
lie trapped in his own work,
God showeth his judgement which were good
for wordly men to mark.

[17]   The wicked and the sinful men   65
go down to hell for ever,
And all the people of the world
that will not God remember.

[18]   But sure the Lord will not forget
the poor man's grief and pain: 70
The patient people never look
for help of God in vain.

[19]   Then, Lord, arise, lest men prevail
that be of worldly might,
And let the heathen folk receive   75
their judgement in thy sight.

[20]   Lord, strike such terror, fear, and dread
into the hearts of them
That they may know assuredly
they be but mortal men.   80

Text sources: *1549b, 1553*

Ut quid, Domine. Psalm 10. [T.S.]

      This Psalm doth show the grievous plaint
of an afflicted mind
And setteth forth the wicked works
of persecutors blind.

[1]   What is the cause that thou, O Lord,
art now so far from thine
And keepest close° thy countenance   °hidden
from us this troublous time?

[2]   The poor doth perish by the proud   5
and wicked men's desire:
Let them be taken in the craft
that they themselves conspire.

[3] For of the lust° of his own heart   °pleasures, will
    the ungodly man doth boast   10
    And praiseth much the covetous,
    whom God abhorreth most.
[4] The ungodly is so proud that he
    of God accounteth naught:
    He will not call on God to know   15
    his counsel and his thought,
[5] But walketh wrong, for Lord, thy ways
    be far out of his sight;
    Wherefore he runneth to revenge
    his enemies with despite.   20
[6] And "Tush," he saith unto himself,
    as one devoid of grace;
    "I will let slip no time," quoth he,
    "when malice may take place."
[7] His mouth is full of cursedness,   25
    of fraud, deceit, and guile:
    Under his tongue doth sorrow sit
    and travail° all the while.   °work
[8] He lieth hid in secret streets
    to slay the innocent;   30
    Against the poor that pass him by
    his cruël eyes are bent.
[9] And like a lion privily°   °stealthily
    lieth lurking in his den,
    If he may snare them in his net   35
    to spoil° poor simple men.   °rob
[10] And for the nonce° full craftily   °express purpose
    he croucheth down, that they
    By colour of his humbleness
    may soon become his prey.   40
[11] "Tush, God forgetteth this," saith he,
    "therefore may I be bold;
    His countenance is cast aside,
    he doth it not behold."
[12] Arise, O Lord, O God in whom   45
    the poor man's hope doth rest;
    Lift up thine hand, forget not, Lord,
    the poor that be oppressed.
[13] What blasphemy is this to thee?
    Lord, dost not thou abhor it,   50

To hear the wicked in their hearts
say, "Tush, thou carest not for it"?
[14]   But thou seest all this wickedness
and well dost understand
That friendless and poor fatherless   55
are left into thy hand.
[15]   Of wicked and malicious men
then break the power for ever,
That they with their iniquity
may perish altogether.   60
[16]   For thou dost reign for evermore
as Lord and God alone,
But all the heathen of the earth
shall perish every one.
[17]   Lord, harken to the poor men's plaint,   65
their prayèr and request;
Give ear to that that thou hast wrought
within the poor man's breast.
[18]   Revenge the poor and fatherless
and help them to their right,   70
That they may be no more oppressed
with men of worldly might.

Text sources: *1549b, 1553*
Argument: iii forth] out *1553*
Psalm: 7 the] their *1553*   **23** quoth] quod *1553*

Notes
21–4 All of Sternhold's sources depict the oppressor as unmoved by the idea of divine punishment (Great Bible: "Tush, I shall never be cast down, there shall no harm happen unto me"), but the idea of actively turning his time to malice is original.

In Domino confido. Psalm 11. [T.S.]

Though faithful men that trust in God
be here in earth oppressed,
Yet he from heaven seeth their grief
and doth prepare them rest.

[1]   I trust in God, how dare ye then
say thus my soul until°:   °unto
"Flee hence as fast as any fowl,
and hide thee in thine hill"?

[2]   Behold, the wicked bend their bows   5
             and make their arrows prest°   °ready
             To shoot in secret and to hurt
             the sound and harmless breast,
[3]   That they may bring all godliness
             to ruin and decay;   10
             For as for just and righteous men,
             what can they do or say?
[4]   But he that in his temple is,
             most holy and most high,
             And in the heaven hath his seat   15
             of royal majesty,
                  The poor and simple man's estate
             considereth in his mind,
             And searcheth out full narrowly
             the manners° of mankind,   20   °conduct, morals
[5]   And with a cheerful countenance
             the righteous man doth use°.   °treat
             But in his heart he doth abhor
             all such as mischief° muse,   °evil
[6]   And on the sinners casteth snares   25
             as thick as any rain
             Of tempests, storms, and brimstone fires
             appointed for their pain.
[7]   Ye see then how a righteous God
             doth righteousness embrace,   30
             And unto truth and equity
             showeth forth his pleasant face.

Text sources: *1549b, 1553*

Salvum me fac, Domine. Psalm 12. [T.S.]

             The want° of good men is bewailed,   °lack
             ill tongues are threatened sore;
             God's word is true, who saith he will
             the poor to right restore.

[1]   Help, Lord, for good and godly men
             do perish and decay,
             And faith and truth from worldly men
             is parted clean away.

[2]	Whoso doth with his neighbour talk,	5
his talk is all but° vain:	°only
For every hart bethinketh how
to flatter, lie, and feign.
[3]	But flattering and deceitful lips
and tongues that be so stout	10
To speak proud things against the Lord,
the Lord will sure cut out.
[4]	Yet say they still, "We will prevail,
our tongues shall us extol;
Our tongues are ours, we ought to speak,	15
what lord shall us control?"
[5]	But for the great complaint and cry
of poor and men oppressed,
"Arise will I now," saith the Lord,
"and help them all to rest."	20
[6]	God's word is like to silver pure
that from the earth is tried°	°extracted, purified
And hath no less than seven times
in fire been purified.
[7]	Now since thy promise is to help,	25
Lord, keep thy promise then,
And save us from the cursedness
of this ill kind of men.
[8]	For now the wicked world is full
of mischiefs° manifold,	30	°evils
When vanity with mortal men
so highly is extolled.

Text sources: *1549b, 1553*

Usquequo, Domine. Psalm 13. [T.S.]

Though God sometime seem to forget
the affliction of the just,
At him alone they seek relief
and in his mercy trust.

[1]	How long wilt thou forget me, Lord,
shall I never be remembered?
How long wilt thou thy visage hide
as though thou were offended?

[2]   In heart and mind how long shall I   5
with care tormented be?
How long eke° shall my deadly foe   °as well
thus triumph over me?
[3]   Behold me now, my Lord my God,
relieve me with thy breath.   10
Lighten mine eyes in such a wise
that I sleep not in death;
[4]   Lest thus mine enemy say to me,
"Behold, I do prevail";
Lest they also that hate my soul   15
rejoice to see me quail°.   °waste away
[5]   But from the mercy of the Lord,
my hope shall never start°,   °pass away
In whose relief and saving health
right joyful is mine heart.   20
Who dealt with me so lovingly
that I have cause to sing
In praise of his most holy name,
that is most mighty king.

Text sources: *1549b, 1553*
Psalm: **20** mine] my *1553*

Notes
10 relieve me with thy breath: Not in any of Sternhold's sources.

Dixit insipiens. Psalm 14. [T.S.]

The wicked say there is no God;
man's works are all infect°:   °morally polluted
Perish shall they that trust therein.
Grace saveth the elect.

[1]   "There is no God," as foolish men
affirm in their mad mood°;   °pride
Their study is corrupt and vain,
not one of them doth good.
[2]   The Lord beheld from heaven high   5
the manners° of mankind,   °conduct, morals
And saw not one that sought about
his living God to find.

[3]   They went all wide° and were corrupt,   °astray
    and truly there was none   10
    That in the world did any good:
    I say there was not one.

[4]   Did they know God or worship him,
    that were so swiftly led
    My people to devour and spoil°   15   °rob, plunder
    and eat them up like bread?

[5]   But they shall feel a fearful time,
    when God shall say to them,
    Standing among the company
    of good and righteous men,   20

[6]   "Ye mocked the counsel of the poor
    on God when they did call,
    But they did put their trust in God,
    and he did help them all."

[7]   But who shall give thy people health,   25
    and when wilt thou fulfill
    The promise made to Israel
    from out of Sion hill?
    And turn their thrall° to liberty   °bondage
    in bond that long are lad°,   30   °led
    That Jacob may therein rejoice
    and Israel may be glad.

Text sources: *1549b, 1553*

Notes

13 Sternhold here skips three verses' worth of material present in the Vulgate, the parallel English-Latin translation, and (in the small font reserved for material from the Septuagint) the Great Bible.

Domine, quis habitabit. Psalm 15. *[T.S.]*

    To those that lead a godly life,
    the Lord doth promise rest;
    The fruits of their unfeignèd faith
    are lively here expressed.

[1]   O Lord, within thy tabernacle
    who shall inhabit still°?   °always
    Or whom wilt thou receive to rest
    in thy most holy hill?

[2]   The man whose life is uncorrupt,   5
whose works are just and straight,
Whose heart doth speak the very truth,
whose tongue doth no deceit;
[3]   Nor to his neighbour doth none ill
in body, goods, or name,   10
Ne° seeketh not to bring his friend   °Nor
to take rebuke and shame;
[4]   That in his heart regardeth not
malicious wicked men,
But those that love and fear the Lord,   15
he maketh much of them;
            His oath and all his promises
that keepeth faithfully,
Although he make his covenant so
that he doth lose thereby;   20
[5]   That putteth not to usury
his money and his coin,
Ne for to hurt the innocent
doth bribe or else purloin.
[6]   Whoso doth all thing as ye see   25
that here is to be done
Shall never perish in this world
nor in the world to come.

Text sources: *1549b, 1553*

Conserva me, Domine. Psalm 16. [T.S.]

            We need no bloody sacrifice:
Christ once for all was slain
And rose again from death and hell,
they could him not retain.

[1]   Lord, keep me, for I trust in thee
and do confess indeed
[2]   Thou art my God; and of my good,
O Lord, thou hast no need.
[3]   I give my goodness to the saints   5
that in the world do dwell,
And namely° to the faithful flock   °especially
in virtue that excel.

[4]   As for their bloody sacrifice
           and offerings of that kind,   10
           I will have none, nor yet their name
           for to be had in mind.
[5]   For why° the Lord the portion is   °Because
           of mine inheritance,
           And he it is that will restore   15
           to me my lot° and chance.   °destiny, portion
[6]   The place wherein my lot did fall
           in beauty did excel:
           Mine heritage assigned to me
           doth please me wonders° well.   20   °wondrous
[7]   I thank the Lord that counseled me
           to understand the right,
           By whose advice I seek remorse
           of conscience in the night.
[8]   I set the Lord before mine eyes   25
           and trust him over all:
           And he doth stand on my right hand,
           lest I might haply° fall.   °by chance
[9]   Wherefore my heart is very glad,
           my glory much increased,   30
           That at the last I shall be sure
           my flesh in hope shall rest.
[10]   Thou wilt not leave my soul in hell,
           for, Lord, thou lovest me;
           Nor yet wilt give thine holy one   35
           corruption for to see;
[11]   But rather to the path of life
           wilt gladly me restore,
           For at thy right hand is my joy,
           and shall be evermore.   40

Text sources: *1549b, 1553*
Psalm: 20 wonders] wonderous *1553*

Notes
i **bloody sacrifice:** I.e., the Catholic mass.
9 Sternhold omits the first half of v. 4 (in the Great Bible, "But they that turn after another god shall have great trouble").

Exaudi, Domine. Psalm 17. [T.S.]

God's Church man's doctrine doth despise,
his word alone to trust;
The worldly wish none other wealth,
but here to live at lust°.   °i.e., as they wish

[1]   O Lord, hear out my right request,
attend when I complain,
And hear the prayer that I put forth
with lips that do not feign.

[2]   And let the judgement of my cause   5
proceed alway from thee,
For thou dost ponder and perceive
what thing is equity.

[3]   Search out and try° me in the night,   °test, assess
and thou shalt nothing find   10
That I have spoken with my tongue
that was not in my mind:

[4]   But from the works of wicked men
and paths perverse and ill,
For love of thy most holy word   15
I have refrainèd still°.   °at all occasions

[5]   Then in thy paths that be most pure,
Lord, thou mayst me preserve,
That from the way wherein I walk
my steps may never swerve.   20

[6]   For I do call to thee, O Lord,
for succour and for aid:
Then hear my prayer, and weigh right well
the words that I have said.

[7]   Be good to those that trust in thee   25
and in thy faith do stand,
But pity not those that resist
the power of thy right hand.

[8]   And keep me, Lord, as thou wouldst keep
the apple of thine eye,   30
And under covert of thy wings
defend me secretly

[9]   From wicked men that trouble me
and daily me annoy°,   °harm
And from my foes that go about   35
my soul for to destroy:

[10]   Which wallow in their worldly wealth,
so full and eke° so fat   °also
That in their pride they do not spare
to speak they care not what.   40

[11]   They lie in wait where I should pass,
with craft me to confound°;   °overcome
And musing mischief° in their minds,   °injury
They cast their eyes to ground,

[12]   Much like a lion greedily   45
that would his prey embrace,
Or lurking like a lion's whelp
within some secret place.

[13]   Up, Lord, and overturn these folk,
disperse them like a God: 50
Redeem my soul from wicked men,
which are thy sword and rod.

[14]   I mean from worldly men, to whom
all worldly goods are rife,
That have no hope nor part of joy   55
but in this present life,
     But of thy store for to be filled
with pleasure to their mind
And to have children unto whom
they may leave all behind.   60

[15]   But I shall come before thy face
both innocent and clear,
And all my joy shall be when thou
in glory shalt appear.

Text sources: *1549b, 1553*
Psalm: 3 the] my *1553*   58 pleasure] pleasures *1553*

Notes
27–8 None of Sternhold's sources here suggest punishment of those who resist the Lord.

Coeli enarrant. Psalm 19. [T.S.]

     All creatures set God's glory forth:
his word and law doth fill
The world throughout, as honey sweet
converting souls from ill.

[1]   The heavens and the firmament
do wondersly° declare   °wondrously
The glory of God omnipotent,
his works and what they are.

[2]   Each day declareth by his course   5
another day to come,
And by the night we know likewise
a nightly course to run.

[3]   There is no language, tongue, or speech
where their sound is not heard;   10

[4]   In all the earth and coasts° thereof   °regions
their knowledge is conferred°.   °collected
        In them the Lord made royally
a settle° for the sun,   °seat

[5]   Where like a giant joyfully   15
he might his journey run.

[6]   And all the sky from end to end
he compassed° round about: °encircled
No man can hide him from his heat
but he will find him out.   20

[7]   So perfect is the law of God,
his testimony sure:
Converting souls and maketh wise
the simple and obscure.

[8]   Just is the judgement of the Lord   25
and gladdeth heart and mind;
Pure his precept and giveth light
to eyes that be full blind.

[9]   The fear of God is very clean
and doth endure for ever.   30
The judgements of the Lord are true
and righteous altogether,

[10]   And more to be embraced of thee
than finèd° gold, I say;   °refined
The honey and the honey comb   35
are not so sweet as they.

[11]   By them be all thy servants taught
to have thee in regard,
And in performance of the same
there shall be great reward.   40

[12]   But, Lord, what earthly man doth know
how oft he doth offend?

Then cleanse my soul from secret sin,
my life that I may mend,
[13]   And keep me that presumptuous sins   45
prevail not over me,
And then shall I be innocent
and great offences flee.
[14]   Accept my mouth and eke° my heart,   °also
my words and thoughts each one: 50
For my redeemer and my strength,
O Lord, thou art alone.

Text sources: *1549b, 1553*
Psalm: 2 wondersly] wonderously *1553*

Exaudiat te Deus. Psalm 20. [T.S.]

As God preservèd Christ his Son
in trouble and in thrall°,   °oppression
So when we call upon the Lord,
he will preserve us all.

[1]   In trouble and adversity
the Lord will hear thee still°:   °at all times
The majesty of Jacob's God
will thee defend from ill
[2]   And send thee from his holy place   5
his help at every need,
And so in Sion stablish thee
and make thee strong indeed;
[3]   Remembering well the sacrifice
that thou to him hast done,   10
And doth receive right thankfully
thine offerings every one.
[4] According to thy heart's desire
the Lord will give to thee,
And all thy counsel and device°   15   °will
full well perform will he.
[5]   In thy salvation we rejoice
and magnify the Lord,
That thy petitions and request
preservèd with his word.   20

[6]   The Lord will his annointed save,
         I know well, by his grace,
         And send him health from his right hand
         out of his holy place.
[7]   In charets° some put confidence,   25   °(war) chariots
         and some in horses trust:
         But we remember God our Lord
         that keepeth promise just.
[8]   They fall down flat, but we do rise
         and stand up steadfastly.   30
[9]   Now save and help us, Lord and King,
         on thee when we do cry.

Text sources: *1548, 1549a, 1549b, 1553*
Psalm: 32 do] shall *1548, 1549a*

Domine, in virtute tua. Psalm 21. [T.S.]

         Christ's kingdom here he doth describe,
         with his eternal power;
         All that rise up him to resist
         his right hand shall devour.

[1]   O Lord, how joyful is the king
         in thy strength and thy power:
         How vehemently he doth rejoice
         in thee, his savïour!
[2]   For thou hast given unto him   5
         his godly heart's desire:
         To him hast thou nothing denied
         of that he did require.
[3]   Thou didst prevent° him with thy gifts   °anticipate, prepare for
         and blessings manifold,   10
         And thou hast set upon his head
         a crown of perfect gold.
[4]   And when he askèd life of thee,
         thereof thou madest him sure
         To have long life, yea, such a life   15
         as ever should endure.
[5]   Great is his glory by thy help,
         thy benefit and aid:

Great worship and great honour both
thou hast upon him laid.   20
[6]   Thou wilt give him felicity
that never shall decay,
And with thy cheerful countenance
wilt comfort him alway.
[7]   For why° the king doth strongly trust   25   °For
in God for to prevail;
Therefore his goodness and his grace
will not° that he shall quail°.   °i.e., do not will / °wither
[8]   But let thine enemies feel thy force
and those that thee withstand: 30
Find out thy foes, and let them feel
the power of thy right hand.
[9]   And like an oven burn them, Lord,
in fiery flame and fume;
Thine anger will destroy them all,   35
and fire will them consume.
[10]   And thou wilt root out of the earth
their fruit that should increase,
And from the number of thy folk
their seed shall end and cease.   40
[11]   For why much mischief did they muse
against thine holy name,
Yet did they fail and had no power
for to perform the same.
[12]   Therefore shalt thou right valiantly   45
put them to flight and chase,
And charge° thy bowstrings readily   °aim
against thine enemies' face.
[13]   Be thou exalted, Lord, therefore,
in thy strength every hour: 50
So shall we sing right solemnly,
praising thy might and power.

Text sources: *1549b, 1553*
Psalm: 42 thine] thy *1553*

Notes
20 hast: Sternhold's version creates a coherent Christological interpretation by departing
from all his sources (which here employ a future tense).

Ad te, Domine, levavi. Psalm 25. [T.S.]

For aid against her enemies
the faithful Church doth pray,
For patience in adversity,
and for the perfect way.

[1]   I lift mine heart to thee,
my God and guide most just;
[2]   Now suffer me to take no shame,
for in thee do I trust.
       Let not my foes rejoice   5
nor make a scorn of me,
[3]   And let them not be overthrown
that put their trust in thee.
       Confounded° are all such   °shamed; overcome
whose doings are but vain;   10
[4]   O Lord, therefore, thy paths and ways
declare unto me plain.
[5]   Direct me in thy strength
and teach me, I thee pray;
Thou art my God and saviour   15
that helpest me every day.
[6]   Thy mercies manifold
I pray thee, Lord, remember,
And eke thy pity plentiful
that doth endure for ever.   20
[7]   Remember not the faults
and frailty of my youth;
Remember not how ignorant
I have been of thy truth.
       Nor after my deserts   25
let me thy mercy find,
But of thine own benignity,
Lord, have me in thy mind.
[8]   His mercy is full sweet,
his truth the perfect way;   30
Therefore the Lord will give a law
to them that go astray.
[10]   For all the ways of God
are truth and mercy both
To them that seek his testament,   35
the witness of his troth°.   °faithfulness; covenant

[11]   Now for thy holy name,
O Lord, I thee entreat
To grant me pardon for my sin,
for it is wondrous great.   40
[12]   Whoso doth fear the Lord,
the Lord doth him direct
To lead his life in such a way
as he doth best accept.
[13]   His soul shall evermore   45
in goodness dwell and stand;
His seed and his posterity
inherit shall the land.
[14]   To those that fear the Lord,
he is a firmament°,   50   °support, foundation
And unto them he doth declare
his will and testament.
[15]   My ears and eke° my heart   °also
to him I will advance
That plucked my feet out of the snare   55
of willful ignorance.
[16]   With mercy me behold,
to thee I make my moan:
For I am poor and solitary,
comfortless alone.   60
[17]   The troubles of mine heart
are multiplied indeed:
Bring me out of this misery,
necessity, and need.
[18]   Behold my poverty,   65
mine anguish and my pain;
Remit my sin and mine offence,
and make me clean again.
[19]   O Lord, behold my foes,
how they do still° increase,   70   °continuously
Pursuing me with deadly hate
that fain° would live in peace.   °gladly
[20]   Preserve and keep my soul,
and eke° deliver me;   °also
And let me not be overthrown,   75
because I trust in thee.
[21]   The just and innocent,
by me do stick and stand,

Because I look for to receive
my succour at thy hand.   80
[22]   Deliver, Lord, thy folk
that be of thy belief:
Deliver, Lord, thine Israel
from all his pain and grief.

Text sources: *1548, 1549a, 1549b, 1553*
Psalm: 6 nor] and *1548, 1549a*   **40** is] *om 1553*

Notes
33 Sternhold omits v. 9. In Coverdale's translation of the Vulgate, which Sternhold relied on heavily for this paraphrase, the missing text reads "Them that are gentle herted, wyll he ordre ryghte in judgement, he will teach the meke his wayes" (fol. 19r).
59 solitary: This is the one instance in which *1549b* and later editions permitted a syllable division of 9 and 5 between the two short lines of a fourteener, rather than dividing the word with a hyphen across the printed lines.
72 that . . . peace: Sternhold's addition to the psalm text.

Ad te, Domine, clamabo. Psalm 28. [T.S.]

This Psalm setteth out the Pharisees
with flattering hearts unclean
And showeth how God is all our strength,
by Christ, our only mean°.   °means

[1]   O Lord, I call to thee for help,
and if thou me forsake
I shall be likened unto them
that fall into the lake.
[2]   The voice of thy suppliant hear   5
that unto thee doth cry,
When I lift up my heart and hands
unto thy heavens high.
[3]   Repute not me among the sort
of wicked and pervert   10
That speak right fair unto their friends
and think full ill in heart.
[4]   According to their handiwork,
as they deserve indeed,
And after their inventions   15
let them receive their meed°.   °deserts

[5]   They not regard the works of God,
his law ne° yet his lore;   °nor
Therefore will he their works and them
destroy for evermore.   20

[6]   To render thanks unto the Lord
how great a cause have I,
My voice, my prayer, and my complaint
that heard so willingly.

[7]   He is my shield and fortitude,   25
my buckler in distress;
My hope, my help, my heart's relief
my song shall him confess.

[8]   He is our strength and our defence
our enemies to resist,   30
The health and the salvatïon
of his elect by Christ.

[9]   Thy people and thine heritage,
thy blessed word preserve;
Extol° thy flock with faithful food,   35   °lift up, fortify
that they may never swerve.

Text sources: *1548, 1549a, 1549b, 1553*
Heading: 28] xxvii *1549a*
Psalm: 12 ill] euill *1548, 1549a*

Afferte Domino. Psalm 29. [T.S.]

      As David did the temple deck
with earthly sacrifice,
So Christ's Church with spiritual gifts
ye must adorn likewise.

[1]   Give to the Lord, ye potentates
and princes of the world,
Ye rams that guide the Christian flock,
give laud unto the Lord.

[2]   Give glory to his holy name   5
and honour him alone;
Worship him in his majesty
within his holy throne.

[3]   His voice doth rule the waters all
even as himself doth please;   10

He doth prepare the thunderclaps
and governeth all the seas.

[4]   Of virtue° is the voice of God   °strength, efficacy
and wondrous excellent:
Of full great purpose and effect   15
and much magnificent.

[5]   His voice doth break in Libanus°   °Lebanon
the cedar trees full long,
Which for their highness are compared
to mighty men and strong,   20

[6]   Whom God will strike with fearfulness
and make them all as mild
As calves that come to sacrifice
or unicorns full wild.

[7]   His voice divideth flames of fire   25
and shaketh the wilderness;

[8]   He maketh the desert quake for fear
that callèd is Cades°.   °Kadesh

[9]   His voice doth make the wild harts tame
and maketh the covert plain°;   30   °exposed
And in his temple every man
his glory doth proclaim.

[10]   He stayed the rage of Noah's flood,
and stoppèd the Red Sea,
And keepeth his seat as Lord and king   35
in his eternity.

[11]   The Lord doth give his people power
in virtue to increase;
The Lord doth bless his people eke°   °also
with everlasting peace.   40

Text sources: *1548, 1549a, 1549b, 1553*
Heading: 29] xix *1549a*
Psalm: 15 full] *om 1548, 1549a*

Notes
19–20 The comparison to **mighty men** is not in the original text.
21–4 This peculiar paraphrase, in which the cedars (or mighty men?) are as mild as sacrificial calves and also like **unicorns full wild** is the result of an unsuccessful combination of two sources. In Coverdale's translation of the Vulgate, these two things are separate, as the Lord "shal hew the[m] [the cedars] in peces as a calfe of Libanus, and the beloved shall be as a yonge unycorne"; in the Great Bible, the landscape is all one scene of shaking, where the cedars "skip like a calf: Libanus also, and Syrion like a young unicorn."

Exaltabo te, Domine. Psalm 30. [J.H.]

	The Church, that ghostly° Israel,	°spiritual
	Her Lord and God doth praise,	
	Which from the dread of death and hell	
	Doth her defend always.	

[1]   All laud and praise with heart and voice,
        O Lord, I give to thee,
    Which wilt not see my foes rejoice,
        Nor triumph over me.

[2]   O Lord my God, to thee I cried   5
        In all my pain and grief:
    Thou gavest an ear and didst provide
        To ease me with relief.

[3]   Of thy good will thou hast called back
        My soul from hell to save;   10
    Thou dost relieve when strength doth lack
        To keep me from the grave.

[4]   Sing praise, ye saints that prove° and see   °experience
        The goodness of the Lord;
    In memory of his majesty,   15
        Rejoice with one accord.

[5]   For why° his anger but a space   °Because
        Doth last and slake° again,   °die down
    But yet the favour of his grace
        For ever doth remain.   20
    Though gripes° of grief and pangs full sore   °spasms
        Do chance us overnight,
    The Lord to joy shall us restore
        Before the day be light.

[6]   When I enjoyed the world at will,   25
        Thus would I boast and say:
    "Tush, I am sure to feel none ill,
        This wealth shall not decay."

[7]   For thou, O Lord, of thy good grace
        Hadst sent me strength and aid;   30
    But when thou turnedst away thy face,
        My mind was sore dismayed.

[8]   Wherefore again yet did I cry
        To thee, O Lord of might:

My God with plaints I did apply°   35   °continuously address
    And prayed both day and night.
[9]   "What gain is in my blood," said I
    "If death destroy my days?
Doth dust declare thy majesty,
    Or yet thy truth doth praise?   40
[10] "Wherefore, my God, some pity take,
    O Lord, I thee desire;
Do not this simple soul forsake,
    Of help I thee require°."   °i.e., I ask help from thee
[11] Then didst thou turn my grief and woe   45
    Unto a cheerful voice;
The mourning weed° thou tookest me fro°   °garment / °from
    And madest me to rejoice.
[12] Wherefore my soul uncessantly
    Shall sing unto thy praise: 50
My Lord my God, to thee will I
    Give laud and thanks always.

Text sources: *1549b, 1553*

Beati quorum. Psalm 32. [T.S.]

God promiseth salvatïon
to the repentant heart
Of his mere mercy and his grace,
not for the man's desert.

[1]   The man is blest whose wickedness
the Lord hath clean remitted,
And he whose sin and wretchedness
is hid also and covered.
[2]   And blest is he to whom the Lord   5
imputeth not his sin,
Which in his heart hath hid no guile,
nor fraud is found therein.
[3]   For whiles that I kept close my sin
in silence and constraint,   10
My bones did wear and waste away
with daily moan and plaint.
[4]   For night and day thy hand on me
so grievous was and smart°   °painful

	That all my blood and humours° moist	15	°bodily fluids
	to dryness did convert.		
[5]	But when I had confessed my faults		
	and shrove° me in thy sight,		°performed confession
	My self accusing of my sin,		
	thou didst forgive me quite.	20	
[6]	Let every good man pray therefore		
	and thank the Lord in time,		
	And then the floods of evil thoughts		
	shall have no power of him.		
[7]	When trouble and adversity	25	
	do compass me about,		
	Thou art my refuge and my joy,		
	and thou dost rid° me out.		°release, rescue
[8]	"I shall instruct thee," saith the Lord,		
	"how thou shalt walk and serve;	30	
	And bend mine eyes upon thy ways,		
	and so shall thee preserve."		
[9]	Be not, therefore, so ignorant		
	as is the ass and mule,		
	Whose mouth without a rein or bit	35	
	ye cannot guide or rule.		
[10]	For many be the miseries		
	that wicked men sustain;		
	Yet unto them that trust in God,		
	his goodness doth remain.	40	
[11]	Be merry therefore in the Lord;		
	ye just, lift up your voice,		
	And ye of pure and perfect heart,		
	be glad and eke° rejoice.		°also

Text sources: *1548, 1549a, 1549b, 1553*
Psalm: 11 wear and waste] wast and weare *1553*   **37** For] Full *1548*

Exultate iusti.   Psalm 33.   [J.H.]

To praise the Lord with joy they ought
    Which are accept through faith;
God by his word each thing hath wrought,
    All man's defence decayeth.

[1]   Ye righteous in the Lord, rejoice:
        It is a seemly sight
    That upright men with thankful voice
        Should praise the God of might.

[2]   Praise ye the Lord with harp and song,   5
        In psalms and pleasant things,
    With lute and instrument among
        That soundeth of ten strings.

[3]   Sing to the Lord a song most new,
        With courage° give him praise: 10   °liveliness, energy

[4]   For why° his word is ever true,   °Because
        His works and all his ways.

[5]   To judgement, equity, and right
        He hath a great good will,
    And with his gifts he doth delight   15
        The earth throughout to fill.

[6]   For by the word of God alone
        The heavens all were wrought:
    Their hosts and powers every one
        His breath to pass hath brought.   20

[7]   The waters great gathered hath he
        On heaps within the shore,
    And hid them in the depth, to be
        As in an house of store.

[8]   All men on earth, both least and most,   25
        Fear ye the Lord his law:
    Ye that inhabit in each coast°,   °region
        Dread him and stand in awe.

[9]   What he commanded, wrought it was
        At once with present speed: 30
    What he doth will is brought to pass
        With full effect indeed.

[10] The counsels of the nations rude
        The Lord doth drive to naught;
    He doth defeat the multitude   35
        Of their device° and thought.   °will

[11] But his decrees continue still°,   °at all times
        They never slack° or swage°:   °delay / °abate
    The motions of his mind and will
        Take place in every age.   40

[12] Oh, blest are they to whom the Lord,
        A God and guide, is known,

	Whom he doth choose of mere accord°		°i.e., by his will alone
	To take them as his own.		
[13]	The Lord from heaven cast his sight	45	
	On men mortal by birth,		
[14]	Considering from his seat of might		
	The dwellers on the earth:		
[15]	The Lord, I say, whose hand hath wrought		
	Man's heart and doth it frame,	50	
	For he alone doth know the thought		
	And working of the same.		
[16]	A king that trusteth in his host		
	Shall naught prevail at length;		
	The man that of his might doth boast	55	
	Shall fall, for all his strength.		
[17]	The heaps of horsemen eke° shall fail,		°also
	Their sturdy steeds shall starve°:		°die
	The strength of horse shall not prevail		
	The rider to preserve.	60	
[18]	But lo, the eyes of God intend°		°are directed
	And watch to aid the just,		
	With such as fear him to offend		
	And on his goodness trust:		
[19]	That he of death and all distress	65	
	May set their souls from dread,		
	And if that dearth the land oppress,		
	In hunger them to feed.		
[20]	Wherefore our soul doth still depend		
	On God, our strength and stay:	70	
	He is the shield us to defend		
	And drive all darts away.		
[21]	Our soul in God hath joy and game°,		°pleasure
	Rejoicing in his might:		
	For why° in his most holy name	75	°Because
	We hope and much delight.		
[22]	Therefore let thy goodness, O Lord,		
	Still present with us be,		
	As we always, with one accord,		
	Do only trust in thee.	80	

Text sources: *1549b, 1553*
Psalm: 38 slack] slake *1553*

Notes
36 Hopkins omits a phrase from the Septuagint present in the Vulgate and (in the usual smaller type) in the Great Bible, "and casteth out the counsels of princes."
57–8 The heaps . . . starve: An addition to the original psalm text.

Benedicam Dominum. Psalm 34. [T.S.]

The prophet David praiseth God,
warning us to forebear
From evil, and exhorteth us
to live in godly fear.

[1]   I will give laud and honour both
unto the Lord always,
And eke° my mouth for evermore   °also
shall speak unto his praise.
[2]   I do delight to laud the Lord   5
in soul and eke in voice,
That simple men that suffer pain
may hear and so rejoice.
[3]   Therefore see that ye magnify
with me the living Lord,   10
And let us now exalt his name
together with one accord.
[4]   For I myself besought the Lord;
he answered me again°   °in return
And me delivered incontinent°   15   °immediately
from all my fear and pain.
[5]   Whoso they be that him behold
and show him their unrest;
He dasheth not their countenance,
but granteth their request.   20
[6]   Whoso in their afflictïons
unto the Lord doth call,
He heareth their suit without delay
and riddeth° them out of thrall.   °rescues
[7]   The angel of the Lord doth pitch   25
his tents in every place
To save all such as fear the Lord
that nothing them deface°.   °destroy, harm
[8]   See and consider well, therefore,
that God is good and just,   30

And they be blest that put in him
their only faith and trust.

[9]   Fear ye the Lord, his holy ones,
above all earthly thing,
For they that fear the living Lord   35
are sure to lack nothing.

[10]   The mighty and the rich shall want,
yea, thirst and hunger much;
But as for them that fear the Lord,
no lack shall be to such.   40

[11]   Come near, therefore, my children dear,
And to my word give ear:
I shall you teach the perfect way
how you the Lord should fear.

[12]   Whoso would lead a blessed life   45
must earnestly devise

[13] His tongue and lips from all deceit
to keep in any wise,

[14]   And turn his face from doing ill,
and do the godly deed;   50
Inquire for peace and quietness,
and follow her with speed.

[15]   For why° the eyes of God above   °For
upon the just are bent;
His ears likewise are given much   55
to hear the innocent.

[16]   The Lord doth frown and bend his brows
upon the wicked train°,   °retinue, group
And cutteth away the memory
that should of them remain.   60

[17]   But when the just do call and cry,
the Lord doth hear them so
That out of pain and misery
forthwith he letteth them go.

[18]   The Lord is kind and merciful   65
to such as be contrite;
He saveth also the sorrowful,
the meek and poor in sprite°.   °spirit

[19]   Full many be the miseries
that righteous men do suffer,   70
But out of all adversities
the Lord doth them deliver.

[20]   The Lord doth so preserve and keep
          the bones of his alway
          That not so much as one of them   75
          doth perish or decay.
[21]   The wicked die full wretchedly,
          they seek none other boot°;   °alternative
          And those that hate the righteous men
          are plucked up by the root.   80
[22]   But they that serve the living Lord,
          the Lord doth save them sound;
          And who that put their trust in him,
          nothing shall them confound°.   °defeat

Text sources: *1548, 1549a, 1549b, 1553*
Heading: 34] xxxiii *1548, 1549a*
Psalm: 22 doth] do *1548, 1549a*

Beatus qui intelligit. Psalm 41. [T.S.]

          The Lord will help that man again°   °in return
          that helpeth poor and weak;
          The passion here is figurèd
          and resurrection eke°.   °also

[1]   The man is blest that careful is
          the needy to consider:
          For in the season perilous,
          the Lord will him deliver.
[2]   The Lord will make him safe and sound   5
          and happy in the land,
          And he will not deliver him
          into his enemies' hand.
[3]   And in his bed when he lieth sick
          the Lord will him restore,   10
          And thou, O Lord, wilt turn to health
          his sickness and his sore.
[4]   And in my sickness thus say I:
          "Have mercy, Lord, on me,
          And heal my soul, which is full woe   15
          that I offended thee."
[5]   Mine enemies gave me ill report
          and thus of me they say:

       "When shall he die, that all his name
       may vanish quite away?"   20
[6]   And whereas they go in and out
       for to behold and see,
       They muse much mischief° in their hearts,   °evil
       whatso° their sayings be.   °whatever
[7]   Mine enemies run against me still°   25   °continuously
       together on a throng
       To take a council and conspire
       how they may do me wrong,
[8]   Agreeing on a wicked word,
       and do determine plain: 30
       "Be he destroyed with death," say they,
       "he shall not rise again."
[9]   The man eke that I trusted most
       with me did use deceit:
       Which eat° with me the bread of life,   35   °ate
       the same for me laid wait.
[10]   Have mercy, Lord, on me therefore,
       and let me be preserved,
       That I may render unto them
       the things they have deserved.   40
[11]   By this I know assuredly
       to be beloved of thee,
       When that mine enemies have no cause
       to triumph over me.
[12]   Because that I am innocent,   45
       Lord, strength me, I thee pray,
       And in thy presence point° my place   °appoint
       where I shall dwell for ay°.   °ever
[13]   The Lord, the God of Israel,
       be praisèd now therefore,   50
       Which hath been everlastingly
       and shall be evermore.

Text sources: *1548, 1549a, 1549b, 1553*
Psalm: 17 ill] euil *1548*

Quemadmodum desiderat. Psalm 42. [J.H.]

The faithful soul afflicted here
    Doth sigh, complain, and cry
Unto the Lord for to draw near,
    Whom wicked men defy.

[1]   Like as the hart doth breathe° and bray   °pant
    The wellsprings to obtain,
So doth my soul desire alway
    With thee, Lord, to remain.

[2]   My soul doth thirst and would draw near   5
    The living God of might;
Oh, when shall I come and appear
    In presence of his sight?

[3]   The tears all times are my repast
    Which from mine eyes do slide   10
When wicked men cry out so fast,
    "Where now is God, thy guide?"

[4]   For comfort this I call to mind
    And stretch my strength abroad,
That with the holy I shall find   15
    Health in the house of God:
Enjoying with a joyful voice
    There full quiet and rest,
As with a sort that do rejoice
    And celebrate a feast.   20

[5]   My soul, why art thou sad and sour?
    Why troublest me so sore?
Trust in the Lord and praise his power
    That doth thy health restore.

[6]   When that my soul in me, O Lord,   25
    Doth faint, I think upon
The land of Jordan and record°   °remember
    the little hill Hermon.

[7]   One grief another in doth call,
    As clouds burst out their voice;   30
The floods of evils that do fall
    Run over me with noise.

[8]   But yet the Lord of his goodness
    Doth help at all assays°:   °trials, afflictions
Wherefore each night I will not cease   35

   The living God to praise.
[9] I am persuaded thus to say
    To him with pure pretence°:   °(rightful) claim
   "O Lord, thou art my guide and stay,
    My rock and my defense."   40
   Why do I then in pensiveness,
    Hanging the head, thus walk,
   While that mine enemies me oppress
    And vex me with their talk?
[10] For why° they pierce mine inward parts 45   °For
    With pangs to be abhorred
   When they cry out with stubborn hearts,
    "Where is thy God thy Lord?"
[11] So soon why dost thou faint and quail°,   °fade, wither
    My soul, with pains oppressed?   50
   With thoughts why dost thyself assail
    So sore within my breast?
   Trust in the Lord thy God always,
    And thou the time shalt see
   To give him thanks with laud and praise 55
    For health restored to thee.

Text sources: *1549b, 1553*

Iudica me. Psalm 43. [T.S.]

   The woeful mind whom wicked men
   would with their ill infect°   °pollute
   Doth call to God for light and truth,
   his steps for to direct.

[1]   Judge and defend my cause, O Lord,
   from those that evil be:
   From wicked and deceitful men,
   O Lord, deliver me.
[2]   For of my strength thou art the God; 5
   why puttest me thee fro°?   °away from
   And why walk I so heavily,
   oppressèd with my foe?
[3]   Send out thy light and eke° thy truth,   °also
   and lead me with thy grace,   10

Bring me unto thy holy hill
and to thy dwelling place.
[4]   That I may to the altar go
of God, my joy and cheer,
And on my harp give thanks to thee,   15
O God, my God most dear.
[5]   Why art thou then so sad, my soul,
thus troubled and afraid?
Still° trust in God, for yet will I   °Always
give thanks to him for aid.   20

Text sources: *1549b, 1553*
Psalm: **11** unto] into *1553*

Deus auribus. Psalm 44. [T.S.]

God's people show how wondersly°   °wondrously
he holp° their fathers old   °helped
And much lament that now from them
his hand he doth withhold.

[1]   Our ears have heard our fathers tell
and reverently record
The wondrous works that thou hast done
in older time, O Lord:
[2]   How thou didst weed the Gentiles out   5
and stroyed° them with strong hand,   °destroyed
Planting our fathers in their place,
and gavest to them their land.
[3]   It was not, Lord, our fathers' sword
that purchased them that place: 10
It was thy hand, thine arm, thy light,
thy countenance and grace.
[4]   Thou art the king, our God, that holp
Jacob in sundry wise°;   °ways
[5]   Led with thy power, we threw down such   15
as did against us rise.
[6]   We trusted not in bow ne° sword,   °nor
they could not save us sound:
[7]   Thou keptst us from our enemies' rage,
thou didst our foes confound°.   20   °defeat; put to shame

[8]   And still we boast of thee our God
and praise thine holy name,

[9]   Yet now thou goest not with our host
but leavest us to shame.

[10]   Whereby we flee before our foes,   25
and so be overtrod,

[11]   Yea, killed of heathen folk like sheep
and scattered all abroad.

[12]   Thy people thou hast sold like slaves
in open marketstead°   30   °market place
For no reward, as though they were
of none account indeed.

[13]   And to our neighbours thou hast made
of us a laughing stock,
And those that round about us dwell   35
at us do grin and mock.

[15]   The Gentiles talk, the people scorn,
we be ashamed to see

[16]   How full of slander and reproach
our wicked enemies be.   40

[17]   For all this, we forgot not thee
nor yet thy covenant brake:

[18]   We turn not back our hearts from thee
nor yet thy paths forsake.

[19]   Yet thou hast trod us down to dust,   45
where dens of dragons be,
And covered us with deadly dark
and great adversity.

[20]   And if we had forgot thy name
and help of idols sought,   50

[21]   Then hadst thou cause us to correct;
but, Lord, thou knowest our thought,

[22]   And how that for thy sake, O Lord,
we be tormented thus:
As sheep were to the shambles sent,   55
right so they deal with us.

[23]   Up, Lord: why sleepest thou? Awake,
and leave us not for all:

[24]   Why hidest thou thy countenance
and dost forget our thrall°?   60   °misery

[25]   For down to dust our soul is brought,
our womb to earth doth take;

[26] Arise, help, and deliver us,
    Lord, for thy mercies' sake.

Text sources: *1549b, 1553*
Psalm: *22* thine] thy *1553*

Audite haec, gentes. Psalm 49. [T.S.]

      Though rich men do oppress the poor,
discourage° not therefore,   °lose courage
For, vainly trusting in their goods,
they perish evermore.

[1]   All people, hearken and give ear
    to that that I shall tell,
[2]   Both high and low, both rich and poor,
    that in the world do dwell:
[3]   For why° my mouth shall make discourse   5   °Because
    of many things right wise;
    In understanding shall my heart
    his study exercise.
[4]   I will incline mine ear to know
    the parables so dark,   10
    And open all my doubtful speech
    in metre on my harp.
[5]   The wicked days and evil time
    why should I fear and doubt,
    When the oppressors mischievous°   15   °evil
    do compass me about?
[6]   For some there be that riches have
    in whom° their trust is most,   °which
    And of their treasures infinite
    themselves do brag and boast.   20
[7]   No man can yet by any mean
    his brother's death redeem;
    Or make agreement accepta-
    ble unto God for him;
[8]   Or pay the ransom for his soul,   25
    that he may live for ever
[9]   And taste of no corruption:
    this lieth in no man's power.

[10] We see that wise men die as soon
  as foolish men and fond°,   30   °weak-minded
  And both do leave to other men
  their goods and eke° their lond°.   °also / °land

[11] Although they build them houses fair
  and do determine° sure   °settle beforehand
  To make their name right great in earth, 35
  for ever to endure;

[12] We see again it is not given
  with riches to have rest,
  But in that point a rich man is
  comparèd to a beast.   40

[13] This is the foolish way they walk,
  with pomp to get them fame,
  And all their friends° that follow them   °family and allies
  do much commend the same;

[14] Whom death will soon devour like sheep, 45
  when they are brought to hell:
  Then shall the just in light rejoice,
  when they in darkness dwell.

[15] Yet for all this I trust that God
  will save my soul from pain   50
  And from all such infernal power,
  and comfort me again.

[16] If any man wax wonders° rich,   °wondrously
  fear not, I say, therefore,
  Although the glory of his house   55
  increaseth more and more.

[17] For when he dieth, of all these things
  nothing shall he receive:
  His glory will not follow him,
  his pomp will take her leave.   60

[18] Yet in this life he taketh° himself   °reckons
  the happiest under sun,
  And doth commend all other men
  that doth as he hath done.

[19] But when he shall go to his kind°, 65   °kin; sort
  where his forefathers be,
  He shall his fellows find full dark
  that light shall never see.

[20] A foolish man whom riches hath
  to honour thus preferred°,   70   °advanced

> That doth not know and understand,
>   is to a beast compared.

Text sources: *1548, 1549a, 1549b, 1553*
Psalm: 10 parables] parable *1553*   **32** lond] lande *1548*   **53** wonders] wundrous *1548, 1553*   **62** sun] the sun *1548*   **64** doth] do *1548*

Notes
23–4 acceptable: Unusually, the word is not broken across these two lines in *1549a* despite being divided in *1548*.
45–6 When . . . hell: Not divided metrically in 1548, but rather as prose squeezed into 2 lines' space: "When death will soone deuoure, / lyke sheepe whan they are brought to (hel."
49 Sternhold omits the second half of v. 14, which in the Great Bible reads "their beauty shall consume in the sepulchre out of their dwelling."

Quid gloriaris. Psalm 52. [J.H.]

> The wicked that the Lord despise
>   And trust in worldly strength
> With such as use deceit and lies
>   Shall be destroyed at length.

[1]   Why dost thou, tyrant, boast abroad,
        Thy wicked works to praise?
    Dost thou not know there is a God
        Whose strength doth last always?

[2]   Why doth thy mind yet still° devise   5   °always
        Such wicked wiles to warp°?   °lay (as an egg)
    Thy tongue untrue in forging lies
        Is like a razor sharp.

[3]   On mischief° why dost set thy mind   °evildoing
        And wilt not walk upright?   10
    Thou hast more lust° false tales to find   °delight
        Than bring the truth to light.

[4]   Thou dost delight in fraud and guile,
        In craft, deceit, and wrong;
    Thy lips have learned the flattering style,   15
        O false deceitful tongue.

[5]   Therefore shall God thy strength confound
        And pluck thee from thy place,
    Thy seed and roots from of° the ground   °i.e., out of
        At once he shall deface.   20

[6]   The just when they behold thy fall
            With fear will praise the Lord,
        And in reproach of thee withal
            Cry out in one accord:
[7]   "Behold the man which would not take   25
            The Lord for his defence,
        But of his goods his god did make
            And trust his own pretence°."   °claim of merit
[8]   But I an olive fresh and green
            Shall spring and spread abroad,   30
        For why° my trust all times hath been   °Because
            Upon the living God.
[9]   For this therefore will I give praise
            To him with heart and voice:
        I will set forth his name always,   35
            Wherein his saints rejoice.

Text sources: *1549b, 1553*

Deus, Deus meus. Psalm 63. [T.S.]

        Whereas° Christ's kingdom is oppressed,   °Where
    the just desire of God
    Above all wealth that his pure word
    may freely come abroad.

[1]   O God, my God, I watch to come
    to thee in all the haste:
    For why° my soul and body both   °Because
    do thirst of thee to taste.
            As drought of earth would water have,   5
    so I desire each hour
[2]   For to behold thy holy house,
    thy glory and thy power.
[3]   Thy goodness passeth worldly life
    and these uncertain days;   10
    My lips therefore shall give to thee
    due honour, laud, and praise.
[4]   And whiles I live I will not fail
    to worship thee alway,
    And in thy name I shall lift up   15
    my hands when I do pray.

[5]   My soul is greatly satisfied
and fareth wonders° well   °wondrously
When that my mouth with joyful lips
thy laud and praise doth tell.   20
[6]   Both in my bed I think of thee
and in the evening-tide,
[7]   For under covert of thy wings,
thou art my joyful guide.
[8]   My soul doth surely stick to thee,   25
thy right hand is my power;
[9]   And those that seek my soul to stroy°   °destroy
[10]   the sword shall them devour.
[11]   The king and all men shall rejoice
that do profess God's word,   30
For liars' mouths shall now be stopped
that have the truth disturbed.

Text sources: *1549b, 1553*

Exurgat Deus. Psalm 68. [T.S.]

Christ's glorious kingdom is declared
And how he should ascend;
The Church throughout the world doth joy,
the Jews' law taketh his end.

[1]   Let God arise, and then his foes
will turn themselves to flight:
His enemies then will run abroad
and scatter out of sight.
[2]   And as the fire doth melt the wax   5
and wind blow smoke away,
So in the presence of the Lord,
the wicked shall decay.
[3]   But when the Lord shall come to us,
let righteous men rejoice;   10
Let them be glad and merry all
and cheerful in their voice;
[4]   And sing out laud unto the Lord,
his name to magnify
That sitteth as a saviour   15
above the starry sky.

[5]   That same is he that is above
within the holy place,
That father is of fatherless
and judge of widows' case.   20
[6]   That same is he that in one mind°   °i.e., in agreement
the household doth preserve,
that bringeth bondmen out of thrall°   °slavery
when wicked men do starve°.   °die
[7]   When thou wentest out in wilderness,   25
thy majesty did make
[8]   The earth to quake, the heavens drop°,   °rain
the mount Sinai to shake.
[9]   Thine heritage with drops of grace
full liberally is washed,   30
And when thy people mourn and plain°,   °wail, complain
by thee they be refreshed.
[10]   There shall thy congregation dwell,
where thou dost point° the place;   °appoint
Yea, for the poor thou dost prepare   35
of thine especial grace.
[11]   Thou dost commend thy word, O Lord,
and give thine Holy Sprite°   °Spirit
To all that preach thy gospel pure,
thy glory and thy might.   40
[12]   Kings with their hosts° shall flee away,   °armies
Thy ward° shall give the foil°,   °defence / °defeat
The household of the living Lord
shall then divide the spoil.
[13]   Then shall the Church be innocent   45
and white as silver fine
And in good life more oriently°   °lustrously
than beaten gold shall shine.
[14]   When he that ruleth earthly kings
the earth shall order so,   50
Then shall the hill of Salmon be
as white as milk or snow.
[15]   Since Basan is the hill of God
and fruitful every whit,
[16]   Then ye, the members of that hill,   55
why hop ye out of it?
      Since God is pleasèd wonders° well   °wondrously
to dwell within this hill

And therein doth determine plain
for to continue still°:   60   °always
[17]   Whose charets° and his angels eke°   °(war) chariots / °also
be thousands on a throng,
As in his mount of Sinaï
the Lord is them among.
[18]   The Lord ascended up on high   65
and led them bound with him
That long before in bondage lay
of death and deadly sin,
      And as a man receivèd gifts
and gave them unto men: 70
Yea, to his foes he gave his Spirit
that God might dwell in them.
[19]   Now praisèd be the Lord therefore,
and daily let us praise
Our God that with his benefits   75
doth prosper us always.
[20]   He is the God from whom alone
salvation cometh plain;
He is the God by whom we scape
from everlasting pain.   80
[21]   This God will wound his enemies' head
and break the hairy scalp
Of those that in their wickedness
continually do walk.
[22]   "From Basan will I bring," said he,   85
"my people and my sheep,
And all mine own, as I have done
from danger of the deep,
[23]   And make them dip their feet in blood
of those that hate my name;   90
And dogs shall have their tongues imbrued°   °stained
with licking of the same."
[24]   All men may see how thou, O God,
thine enemies dost deface°,   °defeat
And how thou goest as God and king   95
into thy holy place.
[25]   The singers go before with joy,
the minstrels follow after,
And in the mids° the damsels play   °midst
with timbrel and with tabor.   100

[26]   Now in thy congregatïons,
    O Israel, praise the Lord,
    And from the bottom of thy heart,
    give thanks with one accord.
[27]   Thy chief is little Benjamin,   105
    thy council princes been
    of Judah and of Zabulon
    and eke° of Nephthalim.   °also
[28]   As God hath given power to thee,
    so, Lord, make firm and sure   110
    The thing that thou hast wrought in us,
    for ever to endure.
[29]   Then for thy temple's sake shall kings
    give gifts to thee always,
    Greater than at Jerusalem,   115
    of everlasting praise,
[30]   When thou shalt waste the wavering folk
    that rage against all right:
    The stout°, the nice°, the money men,   °proud / °lascivious
    and those that love to fight.   120
[31]   Then out of Egypt shall they come
    that long have been full blind;
    The Gentiles then shall reconcile
    to God their sinful mind.
[32]   Then shall the kingdoms of the earth   125
    sing praises to the Lord
[33] That over all doth sit and send
    to us his mighty word.
[34]   Therefore the strength of Israel
    ascribe to God on high,   130
    Whose might and power doth far extend
    above the cloudy sky.
[35]   God's holiness is wonderful
    and drad° for evermore,   °dreaded
    And he will give his people power: 135
    praisèd be God therefore.

Text sources: *1549b, 1553*
Psalm: 42 ward] worde *1553*   **57** wonders] wondrous *1553*

Notes
iv Jews' law: In the context of the 1540s, the reference is to a doctrine of merit through good works rather than faith and free grace.

Quam bonus Israel. Psalm 73. [T.S.]

He wondereth how the foes of God
do prosper and increase
And how the good and godly men
do seldom live in peace.

[1]   How good is God to such as be
of pure and perfect heart!
[2]   Yet slip my feet away from him,
my steps decline apart.
        And why, because I fondly° fall   5   °foolishly
[3]   in envy and disdain
That wicked men all things enjoy
without disease or pain;
[4]   And bear no yoke upon their neck,
nor burden on their back;   10
And as for store of worldly goods,
they have no want or lack;
[5]   And free from all adversity
when other men be shent°;   °ruined
And with the rest they take no part   15
of plague or punishment.
[6]   Whereby they be full gloriously
in pride so high extolled,
And in their wrong and violence
be wrapped so manifold,   20
[7]   That by abundance of their goods
they please their appetite
And do all things accordingly
unto their heart's delight.
[8]   All things are vile in their respect,   25
saving themselves alone;
They brag their mischief° openly   °evildoing
to make their power be known.
[9]   The heavens and the living Lord
they care not to blaspheme;   30
And look what° thing they talk or say,   °i.e., whatever
the world doth well esteem.
[10]   The flock therefore of flatterers
do furnish up their train°,   °entourage
For there they be full sure to suck   35
some profit and some gain.

[11]   "Tush, tush," say they unto themselves,
          "is there a God above
          That knoweth and suffereth all this ill
          and will not us reprove?"   40

[12]   Lo, ye may may see how wicked men
          in riches still° increase,   °continually
          Rewarded well with worldly goods
          and live in rest and peace.

[13]   Then why do I from wickedness   45
          my fantasy° refrain,   °imagination
          And wash my hands with innocents,
          and cleanse my heart in vain?

[14]   And suffer scourges every day,
          as subject to all blame,   50
          And every morning from my youth
          sustain rebuke and shame?

[15]   And I had almost said as they,
          misliking mine estate,
          But that I should thy children judge   55
          as folk unfortunate.

[16]   Then I bethought me how I might
          this matter understand,
          But yet the labour was too great
          for me to take in hand   60

[17]   Until the time I went into
          thy holy place, and then
          I understood right perfectly
          the end of all these men.

[18]   And namely°, how thou settest them   65   °particularly
          upon a slippery place,
          And at thy pleasure and thy will
          thou dost them all deface.

[19]   Then, Lord, how soon do they consume
          and fearfully decay,   70

[20] Much like a dream when one awaketh
          their image passeth away.

[21]   Thus grievèd was my heart full sore,
          my mind was much oppressed:

[22] So fond° was I and ignorant,   75   °foolish
          and in thy sight a beast.

[23]   Yet nevertheless, by my right hand
          thou holdst me always fast,

[24]   And with thy counsel dost me guide
       to glory at the last.   80
[25]   What place is there preparèd, then,
       for me in heaven above?
       There is nothing in earth like thee
       that I desire or love.
[26]   My flesh and eke° my heart do fail,   85   °also
       but God doth fail me never:
       For of my heart God is the strength,
       my portion eke for ever.
[27]   And lo, all such as thee forsake
       shall perish every one,   90
       And those that trust in anything
       saving in thee alone.

Text sources: *1548, 1549a, 1549b, 1553*
Psalm: 27 They] The *1549a*   66 upon] vnto *1549a*

Attendite. Psalm 78. [T.S.]

          The covenant and the wondrous works
       of God in Israel;
       And how he provèd° them with plagues,   °tested
       and yet how oft they fell.

[1]   Attend, my people, to my law,
       and to my words incline:
[2]   My mouth shall speak strange parables
       and sentences divine
[3]   Which we ourselves have heard and seen   5
       even of our fathers old,
       And which for our instructïon
       our fathers have us told:
[4]   Because we should not keep it close
       from them that should come after,   10
       But show the power and glory of God
       and all his works of wonder.
[5]   With Jacob he the covenant made
       how Israel should live,
       And made their fathers the same law   15
       unto their children give:

[6]　　　That they and their posterity
　　　that were not sprung up tho°　　　　　　　　　　　　　°then
　　　Should have the knowledge of the law
　　　and teach their seed also;　　　　　　　　20
[7]　　　That they might have the better hope
　　　in God that is above,
　　　And not forget to keep his laws
　　　and his precepts in love;
[8]　　　Not being, as their fathers were,　　　　25
　　　a kind° of such a sprite°　　　　　　　°people, race / °spirit
　　　That would not frame their wicked hearts
　　　to know their God aright.
[9]　　　How went the people of Ephraim
　　　their neighbors for to spoil:　　　　　30
　　　Shooting their darts the day of war,
　　　and yet they took the foil°?　　　　　　°i.e., were defeated
[10]　　　For why° they did not keep with God　　　°Because
　　　the covenant that was made
　　　Nor yet would walk or lead their lives　　　35
　　　according to his trade°,　　　　　　　　°way, path
[11]　　　But put into oblivion
　　　his counsel and his will
　　　And all his works most magnific
　　　which he declarèd still°.　　　　　　　40　　　　°at all times
[12]　　　What wonders to our forefathers
　　　did he himself disclose,
　　　In Egypt land within the field
　　　that called is Thaneos!
[13]　　　He did divide and cut the sea　　　　45
　　　that they might pass at once
　　　And made the water stand as still
　　　as doth an heap of stones.
[14]　　　He led them secret in a cloud
　　　by day when it was bright,　　　　　　50
　　　And all the night when dark it was,
　　　with fire he gave them light.
[15]　　　He brake the rocks in wilderness
　　　and gave the people drink
　　　As plentiful as when the deeps　　　　55
　　　do flow up to the brink.
[16]　　　He drew out rivers out of rocks
　　　that were both dry and hard,

	Of such abundance that no floods°		°rivers, waterways
	to them might be compared.	60	
[17]	Yet for all this, against the Lord		
	their sin did still° increase,		°continually
	And stirrèd him that is most high		
	to wrath in wilderness,		
[18]	Attempting° him within their hearts	65	°Tempting
	like people of mistrust,		
	Requiring° such a kind of meat		°demanding
	as servèd to° their lust°:		°i.e., gratified / °appetite; will
[19]	Saying with murmuratïon		
	in their unfaithfulness,	70	
	"Cannot this God prepare for us		
	a feast in wilderness?		
[20]	Behold, he strake° the stony rock,		°struck
	and floods forthwith did flow;		
	Doubt not that he can give his folk	75	
	both bread and flesh also."		
[21]	When God heard this, he waxèd wroth°		°angry
	with Jacob and his seed;		
	So did his indignatïon		
	on Israel proceed,	80	
[22]	Because they did not faithfully		
	believe and hope that he		
	Could always help and succour them		
	in their necessity.		
[23]	Wherefore he did command the clouds:	85	
	forthwith they brake in sunder		
[24]	And rained down manna for them to eat,		
	a food of mickle° wonder.		°great
[25]	When earthly men with angels' food		
	were fed at their request,	90	
[26]	He bade the east wind blow away		
	and brought in the southwest,		
[27]	And rained down flesh as thick as dust		
	and fowl as thick as sand,		
[28]	Which he did cast amid the place	95	
	where all their tents did stand.		
[29]	Then did they eat exceedingly,		
	and all men had their fills;		
	Nothing did want° to their desire,		°lack
	he gave them all their wills.	100	

[30] But as the meat was in their mouths,
his wrath upon them fell
[31] And slew the flower of all the youth
and choice of Israel.
[32] Yet fell they to their wonted sin,   105
and still they did him grieve:
For all the wonders that he wrought,
they had no fast belief.
[33] Their days, therefore, he shortenèd
and made their honour vain;   110
Their years did waste and pass away
with terror and with pain.
[34] But ever when he plaguèd them,
they sought him by and by,
[35] Remembering then he was their strength, 115
their help and God most high.
[36] Though in their mouths they did but gloze°   °speak insincerely
and flatter with the Lord,
And with their tongues and in their hearts
dissembled every word.   120
[37] For why° their hearts were nothing bent   °Because
to him nor to his trade°,   °path
Nor yet to keep or to perform
the covenant that was made.
[38] Yet was he still° so merciful   125   °always
when they deserved to die,
That he forgave them their misdeeds
and would not them destroy.
    Yea, many a time he turned his wrath
and did himself advise   130
And would not suffer all his whole
displeasure to arise,
[39] Considering that they were but flesh,
and even as a wind
That passeth away and cannot well   135
return by his own kind°.   °natural action
[40] How oftentimes in wilderness
did they their Lord provoke!
How did they move and stir their Lord
to plague them with his stroke!   140
[41] Yea, when they were converted well,
of purpose they would move.°   °anger

The holy one of Israel,
his power for to prove°;   °test

[42]   Not thinking of his hand and power,   145
nor of the day when he
Delivered them out of the bond-
age of the enemy;

[43]   Nor how he wrought his miracles,
as they themselves beheld,   150
In Egypt, and the wonders that
he did in Zoan field;

[44]   Nor how he turnèd by his power
their waters into blood,
That no man might receive his drink   155
at river ne° at flood°;   °nor / °river, stream

[45]   Nor how he sent them flies and lice
which did upon them crawl,
And filled the country full of frogs
to trouble them withal;   160

[46]   Nor how he did commit their fruits
unto the caterpillar,
And all the labour of their hands
he gave to the grasshopper.

[47]   With hailstones he destroyed their vines,   165
so that they were all lost;
And also their mulberry trees
he did consume with frost.

[48]   And yet with hailstones once again
the Lord their cattle smote,   170
And all their flocks and herds likewise
with thunderbolts full hot.

[49]   He cast upon them in his ire
and in his fury strong
Displeasure, wrath, and angels ill   175
to trouble them among.

[50]   Then to his wrath he made a way
and sparèd not the least,
But gave unto the pestilence
the man and eke° the beast.   180   °also

[51]   He strake also the firstborn all
that up in Egypt came,
And all that they had laboured for   °best
within the tents of Ham.

[52] But as for all his own dear folk,   185
he did preserve and keep
And carried them through wilderness,
even like a flock of sheep.

[53] Without all fear both safe and sound
he brought them out of thrall°,   190   °slavery
Whereas their foes with rage of sea
were overwhelmèd all;

[54] And brought them out into the bor-
ders of his holy land,
Even to the mount which he had pur- 195
chasèd with his right hand;

[55] And there cast out the heathen folk
and did their land divide,
And in their tents he set the tribes
of Israel to abide.   200

[56] Yet for all this, their God most high
they stirred and tempted still,
And would not keep his testament
nor yet obey his will.

[57] But as their fathers turnèd back, 205
even so they went astray,
Much like a bow that would not bend,
but brake and start away,

[58] And grieved him with their hill altars,
their lights and with their fire, 210
And with their idols vehemently
provokèd him to ire.

[59] Therewith his wrath began again
to kindle in his breast,
The naughtiness° of Israel 215   °sinfulness
he did so much detest.

[60] Then he forsook the tabernacle
of Silo, where he was
Right conversant with earthly men,
even as his dwelling place. 220

[61] Then suffered he their might and power
in bondage for to stand,
And gave the beauty of his folk
into their enemy's hand,

[62] And did commit them to the sword, 225
wroth with his heritage:

[63] The young men were devoured with fire,
       maids had no marrïage.
[64]   And with the sword the priests also
       did perish every one,   230
       And not a widow left alive
       their fault for to bemoan.
[65]   And then the Lord began to wake,
       like one that slept a time,
       Or like a soldier that had been   235
       refreshèd well with wine.
[66]   With haemorroids in the hinder parts
       he strake his enemies all,
       And put them then unto a shame
       that was perpetual.   240
[67]   Then he the tent and tabernacle
       of Joseph did refuse;
       As for the tribe of Ephraim,
       he would in no wise choose;
[68]   But chose the tribe of Judah,   245
       whereas° he thought to dwell: °Where
       Even the mount of Sion,
       which he did love so well,
[69]   Whereas he did his temple build
       both sumptuously and sure,   250
       Like to the ground which he hath made
       for ever to endure.
[70]   Then chose he David him to serve,
       his people for to keep,
       Which he took up and brought away   255
       even from the folds of sheep.
[71]   As he did follow the ewes with young,
       the Lord did him advance
       To feed his people of Israel
       and his inheritance.   260
[72]   Then David with a faithful heart
       his flock and charge did feed,
       And prudently with all his power
       did govern them indeed.

Text sources: *1548, 1549a, 1549b, 1553*
Psalm: 2 words] woorde *1549a*   **19** the law] that lawe *1548*   **48** an] a *1548,*
1549a   **119** hearts] lippes *1553*   **125** was he] he was *1548, 1549a*   **147** the] *om 1548*
171 herds] herbes *1548, 1549a*   **193** into] vnto *1548*   **196** his] *om 1549a*   **233** then]
that *1549a*

Notes
147–8 bondage: Divided "bond-age" in *1549a*, *1549b*, and *1553*. Not divided across lines
in *1548* due to the omission of another syllable ("the"), although l. 148 was thus left with
only 5 syllables.

Deus, venerunt. Psalm 79. [J.H.]

Here are set forth the sore assaults
    That wicked men invent
Against God's Church, which showeth her faults
    And doth to him lament.

[1]   O Lord, the Gentiles do invade,
        Thine heritage to spoil;
    Jerusalem an heap is made,
        Thy temple they defoil°.   °profane; trample

[2]   The bodies of thy saints most dear   5
        Abroad to birds they cast;
    The flesh of such as do thee fear
        The beasts devour and waste.

[3]   Their blood throughout Jerusalem
        As water spilt they have,   10
    So that there is not one of them
        To lay their dead in grave.

[4]   Thus are we made a laughing stock
        Almost the world throughout:
    The enemies at us jest and mock   15
        Which dwell our coasts° about.   °borders

[5]   Wilt thou, O Lord, thus in thine ire
        Against us ever fume,
    And show thy wrath as hot as fire,
        Thy folk for to consume?   20

[6]   Upon those people pour the same
        Which did thee never know;
    All such as call not on thy name
        Consume and overthrow.

[7]   For they have got the upper hand   25
        And Jacob's seed destroyed;
    His habitation and his land
        By them is sore annoyed°.   °harmed

[8]   Bear not in mind our former faults,
        With speed some pity show;   30

And aid us, Lord, in all assaults,
    For we are weak and low.
[9]   O God that givest all health and grace,
    On us declare the same;
    Weigh not our works, our sins deface°   35   °blot out
    For honour of thy name.
[10]   Why shall the wicked still° alway   °invariably
    to us, as people dumb,
    In thy reproach rejoice and say
    "Where is their God become?"   40
    Require, O Lord, as thou seest good,
    Before our eyes in sight
    Of all these folk thy servants' blood
    Which they spilt in despite.
[11]   Receive into thy sight in haste   45
    The clamours, grief, and wrong
    Of such as are in prison cast,
    Sustaining irons strong.
    Thy force and strength to celebrate,
    Lord, set them out of band°   50   °imprisonment
    Which unto death are destinate°   °appointed
    And in their enemy's hand.
[12]   The nations which have been so bold
    As to blaspheme thy name,
    Into their laps with seven fold   55
    Repay again the same.
[13]   So we thy folk, thy pasture sheep,
    Will praise thee evermore,
    And teach all ages for to keep
    For thee like praise in store.   60

Text sources: *1549b, 1553*

Deus stetit. Psalm 82. [J.H.]

God doth rebuke the worldly wise
    And tell them all their due;
    To such as will his words despise
    He showeth what shall ensue.

[1]   Amid the press° with men of might,   °throng
    The Lord himself did stand

To plead the cause of truth and right
 With judges of the land.
[2] "How long," said he, "will you proceed   5
 False judgement to award,
And have respect, for love or meed°,   °bribery
 The wicked to regard?
[3] Whereas of due ye should defend
 The fatherless and weak,   10
And when the poor man doth contend,
 In judgement justly speak.
[4] If ye be wise, defend the cause
 Of poor men in their right,
And rid° the needy from the claws   15   °rescue
 Of tyrant's force and might.
[5] But nothing will they know or learn,
 In vain to them I talk;
They will not see or aught discern
 But still° in darkness walk.   20   °always
Wherefore be sure the time will come,
 Since ye such ways do take,
That all the earth from the bottom
 My might shall move and shake.
[6] I had decreed it in my sight   25
 As gods to take you all,
And children to the most of might
 For love I did you call.
[7] But notwithstanding, ye shall die
 As men and so decay;   30
Like tyrants I shall you destroy
 And pluck you quite away."
[8] Up, Lord, and let thy strength be known,
 And judge the world with might:
For why° all nations are thine own   35   °For
 To take them as thy right.

Text sources: *1549b, 1553*
Psalm: 5 you] ye *1553*

Notes
16 tyrants' force and might: The original identifies the threat as the ungodly or sinners.
Tyrant could mean "ruffian."

Benedic anima mea. Psalm 103. [T.S.]

> To God for all his benefits
> we render thanks each one,
> Who knoweth the frailty of us all
> and helpeth us alone.

[1]   My soul, give laud unto the Lord,
my spirit shall do the same;
And, all the secrets of my heart,
praise ye his holy name.

[2]   Give thanks to God for all his gifts,   5
show not thyself unkind°,   °ungrateful
And suffer not his benefits
to slip out of thy mind:

[3]   That gave thee pardon for thy fault
and thee restored again   10
For all thy weak and frail disease
and healed thee of thy pain;

[4]   That did redeem thy life from death,
from which thou couldst not flee
(His mercy and compassion both   15
he did extend to thee);

[5]   That filled with goodness thy desire
and did prolong thy youth,
Like as the eagle casteth° her bill°,   °sheds / °beak
whereby her age reneweth.   20

[6]   The Lord with justice doth revenge
all such as be oppressed:
The patience of the perfect man
is turnèd to the best.

[7]   His ways and his commandèments   25
to Moses he did show;
His counsels eke° with his consents   °also
the Israelites do know.

[8]   The Lord is kind and merciful
when sinners doth him grieve,   30
The slowest to conceive a wrath
and readiest to forgive.

[9]   He chideth not us continually,
though we be full of strife,
Nor keepeth our faults in memory   35
for all our sinful life.

[10]   Nor yet according to our sins
the Lord doth us regard,
Nor after our iniquities
he doth not us reward.   40

[11]   But as the space is wondrous great
twixt earth and heaven above,
So is his goodness much more large
to them that do him love.

[12]   He doth remove our sins from us   45
and our offences all
As far as is the sun rising
full distant from his fall.

[13]   And look what° pity parents dear   °i.e., whatever
unto their children bear,   50
Like pity beareth the Lord to such
as worship him in fear.

[14]   The Lord that made us knoweth our shape,
our mould° and fashion just: °character; earth, soil
How weak and frail our nature is   55
and how we be but dust;

[15]   And how the time of mortal men
is like the withering hay
Or like the flower right fair in field
that fadeth full soon away,   60

[16]   Whose gloss° and beauty stormy winds   °surface loveliness
do utterly disgrace
And make that after their assaults
such blossoms have no place.

[17]   But yet the goodness of the Lord   65
with his shall ever stand;
Their children's children do receive
his righteousness at hand,

[18]   That they may keep their promises
with all their whole desire   70
And not forget to do the thing
that he did them require.

[19]   The heavens high are made the seat
and footstool of the Lord,
And by his power imperial   75
he governeth all the world.

[20]   Ye angels and ye virtuous men,
laud ye the Lord, I say,

That ye may both fulfill his hests
and to his words obey.   80
[21]   His host and eke° his minsters,   °also
cease not, but laud him still°,   °always
And ye also that execute
his pleasure and his will.
[22]   Let all his works in every place   85
give laud unto the Lord;
My heart, my mind, and eke my soul
shall thereunto accord.

Text sources: *1548, 1549a, 1549b, 1553*
Psalm: 9 fault] synne *1553* **14** not] *om 1548* **30** doth] do *1548* **33** not us] vs not
1548 **48** from] from all *1549a* **52** in] with *1548, 1549a* **67** do] dyd *1549a*

Ad dominum cum tri. Psalm 120. [T.S.]

The good men cry and much lament
that they so long do dwell
In company of carnal men,
the sons of Ishmael.

[1]   In trouble and in thrall°,   °oppression
Unto the Lord I call,
And he doth me comfort.
[2]   Deliver me, I say,
From liar's lips alway   5
And tongue of false report.
[3]   How hurtful is the thing
Or else how doth it sting,
The tongue of such a liar?
[4]   It hurteth no less, I ween°,   10   °think
Than arrows sharp and keen
Of hot consuming fire.
[5]   Alas, too long I dwell
With the son of Ishmael,
That Kedar is to name,   15
By whom the folk elect
And all of Isaac's sect°   °race; Church
Are put to open shame.

[6]　　　With them that peace did hate,
　　　I came a peace to make　　　　　　20
　　　And set° a quiet life;　　　　　　　　　　　°settle, establish
[7]　　　But when my word was told,
　　　Causeless I was controlled°　　　　　　　　°rebuked
　　　By them that would have strife.

Text sources: *1548, 1549a, 1549b, 1553*

Ad te levavi. Psalm 123. [T.S.]

　　　The poor in spirit wait for the Lord
till they some grace attain;
The proud and wealthy Pharisees
the simple folk disdain.

[1]　　　O Lord that heaven dost possess,
　　　I lift mine eyes to thee,
[2]　　Even as the servant lifteth his
　　　his master's hands to see.
　　　　　As handmaids watch their mistress' hands,　5
　　　some grace° for to achieve,　　　　　　　　　°act of favour
　　　So we behold the Lord our God
　　　till he do us forgive.
[3]　　　Lord, grant us thy compassïon
　　　and mercy in thy sight,　　　　　　　　10
　　　For we be filled and overcome
　　　with hatred and despite.
[4]　　　Our minds be stuffed with great rebuke:
　　　the rich and worldly wise
　　　Do make of us their mocking° stock,　　　15　　　°laughing
　　　the proud do us despise.

Text sources: *1548, 1549a, 1549b, 1553*
Heading: 123] cxxii *1548, 1549a, 1549b*

Beati omnes.   Psalm 128.   [T.S.]

God blesseth with his benefits
the man and eke° the wife   °also
That in his ways do rightly walk
and fear him all their life.

[1]   Blessed art thou that fearest God
and walkest in his way,
[2]   For of thy labour thou shalt eat:
happy art thou, I say.
[3]   Like fruitful vines on the house sides,   5
so doth thy wife spring out;
Thy children stand like olive buds
thy table round about.
[4]   Thus art thou blest that fearest God,
and he shall let thee see   10
[5]   The promisèd Jerusalem
and his° felicity.   °i.e., Jerusalem's
[6]   Thou shalt thy children's children see,
to thy great joy's increase,
Full quietly in Israel,   15
to pass their time in peace.

Text sources: *1548, 1549a, 1549b, 1553*
Psalm: 11   promisèd] promise of *1548*

Notes
11 promisèd: The *1548* reading "promise of" is almost certainly correct, though never
reprinted. It derives from the Vulgate's "bona Hierusalem" (where "Hierusalem" is an in-
declinable noun), translated in Coverdale's parallel Latin-English psalter as "prosperitie
of Hirusale[m]."

Lauda anima mea.   Psalm 146.   [J.H.]

A praise of God: in him alone
All folk should hope and trust,
And not in worldly men, of whom
The chief shall turn to dust.

[1]   My soul, praise thou the Lord; always
My God I will confess:

[2]   While breath and life prolong my days,
        My mouth no time shall cease.
[3]   Trust not in worldly princes then,   5
        Though they abound in wealth,
    Nor in the sons of mortal men,
        In whom there is no health°.   °salvation
[4]   For why° their breath doth soon depart,   °For
        To earth anon° they fall,   10   °shortly
    And then the counsels of their heart
        Decay and perish all.
[5]   O happy is that man, I say,
        Whom Jacob's God doth aid,
    And he whose hope doth not decay   15
        But on the Lord is stayed°:   °sustained, held up
[6]   Which made the earth and waters deep,
        The heavens high withal;
    Which doth his word and promise keep
        In truth, and ever shall.   20
[7]   With right always doth he proceed
        For such as suffer wrong;
    The poor and hungry he doth feed
        And loose the fetters strong.
[8]   The Lord doth ease the blind with sight,   25
        The lame to limbs restore;
    The Lord, I say, doth love the right
        And just man evermore.
[9]   He doth defend the fatherless,
        The strangers sad in heart,   30
    And quit° the widow from distress   °release
        And all ill ways subvert°.   °overturn
[10]   Thy Lord and God eternally,
        O Sion, still° shall reign   °always
    In time of all posterity,   35
        For ever to remain.

Text sources: *1549b, 1553*

Appendix 3

(B.Q.)

Texts Absent from *1567*, but Commonly Included in Sixteenth-Century Editions of *The Whole Book of Psalms*

Selection and Editorial Policies

This appendix provides critical editions of the six prose texts that appeared with regularity in the *WBP* for some or all of the Elizabethan period but are not included in the main critical edition because they are absent from the *1567* copy text. Only one, "A Short Introduction into the Science of Music," is included in any editions of the *WBP* before 1567; the rest were added to some editions later on. They are printed here in the order in which one would encounter them in an individual edition of the *WBP*, starting with the three texts that only appeared before the psalms and ending with the three that only appeared after them. Excluded from this appendix are texts which appear in only one or two extant editions of the *WBP*. Specifically, the two earliest surviving 32° editions, *1569c* and *1577*, each contain additional private prayers at the conclusion of the volume; *1577* and *1593*, a later deluxe 32°, add some ancient comments on the psalms by way of additional preface (see p. 882, below). While the high loss rates of such editions may mean that some of these materials were more frequently reprinted than the surviving sample suggests (see pp. 567–8), they do not seem to have crossed into other formats.

The copy text for each item is the first surviving appearance in the *WBP* (or, in the case of "A Short Introduction into the Science of Music," in one of John Day's printed metrical psalm books). Each text is preceded by an explanatory headnote and followed by any necessary notes on particular passages. Editorial principles and the conventions for listing variant readings are the same as those for the *1567* texts, described on pp. xxiv–xxxi, except where specified in the headnote to a particular text. The copy text and rationale for texts selected for collation are also given in the individual headnotes.

A Short Introduction into the Science of Music

This text was first printed in *1561c*. It was reprinted in *1561d*, the woodcut gamut having been chipped in the interim, and then in the three one-column quarto editions from 1562 to 1565 (*1562a, 1563,* and *STC* 2435), as well as the 1564 *First Parte of the Psalmes*. Subsequently, it survives only in BL octavo editions. The last extant example of a printing series containing the text is *STC* 2466.7 (*1583x*).

The terminology used in this anonymous music primer is likely to cause some confusion for modern readers; for instance, the word "key" does not carry its modern meaning, but more nearly means "note" or a related concept. We have tried to clarify some of the terms by means of explanatory footnotes. The last portion of the essay, "Divers forms of notes," is a clear enough explanation of note forms and their meaning with regard to duration, but the earlier portion, dealing with the more difficult matter of pitch, is an inadequate exposition of the traditional treatment. The woodblock illustration of the gamut, with its picturesque organ pipes carrying the seven hexachords, is derived, probably at some distance, from the title page of Franchinus Gaffurius's *Theorica Musicae* (Milan, 1492). But some aspects of the diagram are not fully explained in the text, while others contradict the narrative and examples. Nowhere does the writer point out the basic fact that in all seven hexachords the interval from *mi* to *fa* is a half step (semitone), whereas the others are whole steps. The novice learner is left to find this out from someone who possesses a virginals. Nor does the treatise explain mutation (moving from one hexachord to another), a theoretical necessity in any melody extending over more than six notes, hence in nearly all the tunes in the *WBP*.

Because it is unclear where or by whom *1561c* was printed, our copy text is *1561d*. Of the other editions completely collated with *1567*, only *1562a* also contains "A Short Introduction into the Science of Music." We have also collated the text with *1583x* in order to show the small changes (and remaining errors) over the course of its relatively infrequent publication. Numbering of examples and figures is editorial.

To the Reader
A short introduction into the science of music,
made for such as are desirous to have the knowledge thereof
for the singing of these Psalms.

For that the rude* and ignorant in song may with more delight, desire, and
goodwill be moved and drawn to the godly exercise of singing of psalms,
as well in common place of prayer, where all together with one voice render
thanks and praises to God, as privately by themselves or at home in their
5   houses, I have set here in the beginning of this book of psalms an easy and
most plain way and rule of the order of the notes and keys of singing, which
commonly is called the scale of music or the *gamma ut*†. Whereby (any dili-
gence given thereunto) every man may in a few days, yea, in a few hours, eas-
ily without all pain, and that also without aid or help of any other teacher,
10   attain to a sufficient knowledge to sing any psalm contained in this book, or
any such other plain and easy songs as these are.

    In this table or *gamma ut* [Fig. 7] is contained all what is necessary to
the knowledge of singing. Wherefore it must be diligently weighed and must
also be perfectly committed to memory so that ye can readily and distinctly
15   say it without book, both forward and backward: that is, upward and down-
ward. And this is the greatest pain that ye need to take in this travail‡.

    Ye must also note that the letters ascending on the left hand of the table
are called keys§ or *claves*, of which the first is a Greek letter signifying *g* and
is called *gamma* (of whom the whole table or scale is called the *gamma ut*).
20   All the other are Latin letters, seven in number: *a, b, c, d, e, f, g,* then repeat-
ing the same again beginning at *a*, and the third time repeating the same
till ye come to *ee, la*, which is the last. But all these keys are not signed or set
in these psalms, but only two or three, most commonly *C* or *F* or *B*. *C* hath
this form or sign 𝕭; *F* is signed after this manner 𝄢; *B* hath thus ♭ or thus ♮ .
25   The keys of this scale or table are divided and set forth by three divers¶
orders of letters. From *gamma ut* to *G, sol, re, ut* are signed with capital let-
ters and are called grave, bass, or capital keys; from *G, sol, re, ut* to *g, sol, re,
ut,* they are written with small letters and are called mean or small keys; and
from *g, sol, re, ut* to *ee, la*, they are written with double letters and are called
30   double keys and treble keys.

    When it chanceth two keys to be of one letter, as *G, sol, re, ut* and *g, sol,
re, ut; A, la, mi, re* and *a, la, mi, re; F, fa, ut* and *f, fa, ut; E, la, mi* and *e, la, mi,*

---

* unsophisticated
† gamut
‡ work
§ notes
¶ separate

Behold this table:

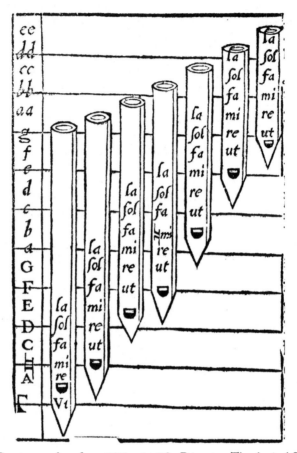

Fig. 7: Gamut woodcut from *1562a*, sig. ✠2v. Princeton Theological Seminary, Princeton, NJ.

ye may (to put difference and distinction between them) call the one "capi-
35   tal *G*" or "*G, sol, re, ut* the lower" and the other "small *g*" or "*g, sol, re, ut* the higher," and so of others.

      They are called keys because they open, as it were, the door and make a way into song: for by the sight and place of the key, ye shall know easily the whole song, the nature of every note, in what key or place it standeth, and
40   how ye shall name it. Ye see also in the table that some of the keys be set in lines or rules and other are set in spaces between the lines: as *gamma ut* is set in rule; *a, re* in space; *b, mi* in rule; *c, fa, ut* in space; *d, sol, re* in rule, and so ascending to the end. So also in the songs of your book, ye see rules and

spaces, so that every rule and space in your book answereth to some one rule
45   or space of your table or scale and taketh the name of the same, which ye
may easily find out either by ascending or descending from the key set* and
marked in your song.

     Moreover, it is to be noted that there are six voices or notes signified and
expressed by these six syllables *ut, re, mi, fa, sol, la,* by which, through repeti-
50   tion of them, may be sung all songs of what compass soever they be; which
six notes ye must learn to tune aptly of someone that can already sing or by
some instrument of music, as the virginals or some other such like. Which
thing well learned, ye shall need none other teaching of any.

     And for a plainer learning thereof, I have set before your eyes those six
55   notes ascending and descending [Exx. 10 and 11], and again with a little va-
riety from their natural order, to the end ye may attain to the just tunes of
them howsoever they be placed. For these two examples well had and tuned
aright, all other songs and psalms with little use and a small labour will soon
be attained unto.

Ex. 10.

Ex. 11.

60   First, ye must diligently search out in what key every note of your song
standeth, which ye may easily do in beholding your signed key (commonly
called the clef) which is set in the beginning of every song, and that line or
space wherein the signed key is set beareth the name of the same key, and
all notes standing in the line or space are said to stand in that key; and so
65   ascending or descending from that key, ye shall straightway see wherein or
in what key every note of your song standeth. As in this present example: if
ye will know wherein your first note standeth, consider your key, signed and
marked with this letter *C* in the second rule† (and because it standeth in rule,
ye find by your table that it is *C, sol, fa, ut*: for the other two *c, c,* which are
70   *C, fa, ut* and *cc, sol, fa* stand in space), wherefore that second line throughout
is called *c, sol, fa, ut*, and all the notes placed in that line are counted to stand
in *c, sol, fa, ut*. Then descend from that key to the next space, which (as your
table telleth you) is *b, fa, ♮, mi;* from thence to the next rule, which is *a, la,*

---

*   i.e., clef
†   i.e., the third line in modernized examples.

mi, re; and from thence to the next space, wherein your first note standeth,
75   which is *G, sol, re, ut.* So find ye by descending in order, beginning at your
signed key, after this sort: *c, sol, fa, ut; b, fa, ♯, mi; a, la, mi, re; G, sol, re, ut.* Ye
find that your first note standeth in *G, sol, re, ut,* wherefore ye may sing it by
any of these three notes: *sol, re,* or *ut.* But because this note *ut* in this place is
most aptest to ascend withal, ye shall call it *ut.* By the same trial, ye shall find
80   that your second note standeth in *a, la, mi, re;* ye shall express it in singing
by this voice *re* rather than by *la* or *mi,* because *re* is in order next above *ut.*
So shall ye find the third note to stand in *b, fa, ♯, mi,* which ye shall express
by *mi.* The fourth standeth in the signed key or clef, wherefore it standeth
in *c, sol, fa, ut,* which ye must express by *fa.* The fifth in *d, la, sol, re,* and is to
85   be expressed by *sol.* The sixth and highest note ye shall, by ascending from
your key, find to stand in *e, la, mi,* and is to be expressed by voice by *la.* So
have you the whole compass of your song, and as in order of notes and sound
of voice ye ascended, so contrariwise ye must descend till ye come to the last
note of your song.

90   Here note that when *b, fa, ♯, mi* is formed and signed in this manner
with this letter *b,* which is called *b flat,* it must be expressed with this voice
or note *fa,* but if it be formed and signed with this form ♯, which is called *b
sharp,* or if it have no sign at all, then must ye express it in singing with this
voice or note *mi.*

95   Likewise may ye practice placing your first note *ut* in any other key
wherein ye find *ut,* which are seven: *gamma, ut; C, fa, ut; F, fa, ut* grave; *G,
sol, re, ut* grave; *c, sol, fa, ut; f, fa, ut* sharp*; *g, sol, re, ut* sharp, ascending up
to *la,* and descending as in your former example. These seven several ascen-
sions and descensions upon divers grounds or clefs are commonly called of
100   writers seven deductions, which ye may plainly and distinctively behold in
your table or scale.

One example more have I set [Ex. 12] , wherein ye sing fa in *b, fa, ♯, mi.*
Whose deduction beginneth in *ut* placed in *F, fa, ut* grave or capital as ye see.

Ex. 12.

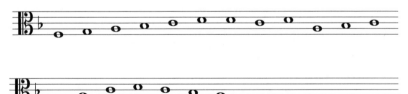

* the higher

Ye have also in your songs divers forms and figures of notes. Of which
105   all, it behoveth* you to know both the names and value.

Divers forms of notes

Ex. 13.

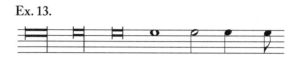

The first of these is called a large; the second, a long; the third, a breve; the
fourth, a semibreve; the fifth, a minim; the sixth, a crotchet; the seventh and
last, a quaver. The first is worth in value two of the second, that is, two longs;
110   and one long is worth two breves; and one breve is two semibreves; and one
semibreve, two minims, and hath twice the time in pronouncing in singing
that the minim hath. One minim is worth two crotchets, and one crotchet is
two quavers, as appeareth in this table following [Fig. 8].

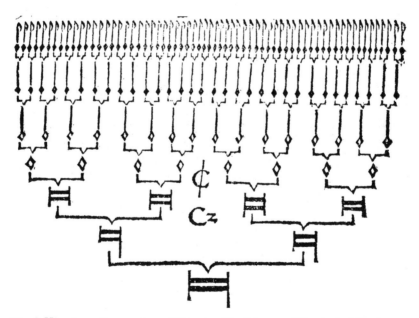

Fig. 8: Woodcut of note values, *1562a*, sig. ✠6r. Princeton Theological Seminary,
Princeton, NJ.

* is necessary to

If there chance any prick* to be set by any of these notes, the prick is
115 worth in value the note next following it. As a prick set by a semibreve, as
thus o. , is worth this note ⌡, which is a minim; and a prick by a minim, as
here ⌡. , is worth a ♩. There are also oftentimes in singing pauses or rests set
in songs, sometime for ease of the singer and comely stay of the songs, some-
time, where divers† parts are, for sweetness of the harmony and apt repeti-
120 tions and reports‡, which are signified by little strikes or lines or half lines
between the rules, as thus [see Ex. 14]. The first, which is drawn from the
first line to the third, is called a long rest and signifieth that ye must pause
while that a long is sung, which is worth four plain song notes or four semi-
breves. The second, which is from one line to another, is called a breve rest
125 and requireth the pausing of a breve or of two semibreves. The third, which
is from a line to the half space underneath, is called a semibreve rest and re-
quireth the pause or space while a semibreve is in singing. The fourth, which
is ascending from the line to the half space above, is called a minim rest and
is but the drawing of a breath while a minim may be sung. The fifth and last,
130 which is like unto the minim rest but crooked at the top, requireth the pause
of a crotchet.

Ex. 14.

To set out a full and absolute knowledge of the nature of the scale,
the differences between notes and half-notes, and half-notes between them-
selves; of intervals, proportions, and which notes concord and agree together
135 and which disagree; what modes there are and how many; what is perfec-
tion, what imperfection; how notes ought to be bound together, and what
their value is so bound, tailed upward or downward, pertaineth to a just§ in-
troduction to the art of music. These things before taught seem at this time,
for the poor, unlearned, and rude, sufficient and enough to the attaining of
140 such knowledge in singing as shall be requisite to the singing of psalms con-
tained in this book, for which cause only they are set out.

Text sources: *1561d, 1562a, 1583x.*
Text: **3** place] places *1583x* **7–8** any diligence] and diligence *1583x* **12** table
or] table of *1583x* **18** claves] cleuis *1561d, 1562a*; cleues *1583x* **22** signed]

* dot
† different, the various
‡ responses
§ full, proper

signified *1583x*   23 C or F or B] c, or e, or b *1562a*   24 *F* is] *E* is *1562a*   thus]
thus sharpe *1562a*   27 to *g, sol*] to *G, sol 1562a*   29 from *g, sol*] from *G, sol 1583x*
33 F, fa] E, fa *1562a, 1583x*   36 so of] so *1583x*   38 into song] into the song
1583x   44–5 rule or] rule of *1561d*   54 none other] no other *1583x*   58 aright,
all] all right, a *1561d*   a small] small *1583x*   60 ye] you *1583x*   76 *b, fa*] *be, fa*
1583x   76–7 Ye find] *om 1583x*   80 express it] expresse *1562a*   82 *b, fa*] *be fa*
1583x   84 by fa] by *la 1583x*   85 be expressed] by expressed *1561d*   96 *F, fa*]
E, fa 1562a   97 *f, fa*] *F, fa 1562a*   103 deduction] deductions *1562a*   *F*] *E 1562a*
104–5 which all] all which *1583x*   106 called] *om 1583x*   111 semibreve, two]
Semibreve is woorth two *1583x*   pronouncing] pronouncing and *1583x*   112 One
minim] and one Minime *1583x*   crotchet is] crotchet is worth *1583x*   115 a
prick] prick *1561d*   116 note] none *1562a*   117 set] om *1583x*   127 in singing] a
singing *1583x*   130 like unto] like to *1583x*

Notes

12 In collated editions, the gamut woodblock immediately precedes this paragraph.
20 b: The text here does not match the woodblock, which gives a natural sign rather than a B. This is because in the lowest hexachord the B can only be *mi* (B natural). In addition, all collated editions use lower case letters here and at l. 18, though they refer to the upper case letters in the illustration.
22 signed or set: I.e., used for a clef or accidental.
24 In fact only C clefs are used in the psalm book, replaced in this edition by modern G clefs. Only B flat is used in key signatures, but accidentals (sharp, flat, or natural) are to be found on B, C, E, and F in some tunes as edited.
25 keys: here the word "key" is expanded to mean the note in the lefthand column modified by the solfa syllables in the hexachords opposite.
27 from *G, sol, re, ut*: Or rather, less confusingly, from *a, la, mi, re*.
29 from *g, sol, re, ut*: Or rather, less confusingly, from *aa, la, mi, re*.
32 All editions collated give, incorrectly, *A, la, mi, re* and *a, la, mi, re*; these should instead be *a, la, mi, re* and *aa, la, mi, re*, respectively.
42 As at l. 20 above, the printed texts use lower case letters where the woodblock shows capitals.
49–50 through repetition of them: If a tune exceeds a compass of six notes from *ut* to *la* (which the examples given do not), it is necessary to shift to a new hexachord. This process, known as *mutation*, is not explained.
[Ex. 10 and 11] In *1583x*, these musical phrases have been placed on three staves and jumbled such that the ascending and descending scales fall on the stave between two sets of ascending and descending interval pairs. As a result, the figure does not match the text describing it.
62–3 line or space: In fact clefs are invariably placed on a line.
68 standeth in rule: I.e., falls on a line.
69 *C, sol, fa, ut*: Correctly should be *c, sol, fa, ut*; all collated editions are erroneous here. For **the other two c, c,** the writer means "the other two C's" [i.e., the pitch class].

73 ♯: The sharp sign here—and all other note sequences that use it—once again fails to match the woodblock gamut, which gives a natural instead (with the same meaning, however).

79 The writer fails to convey how a beginner would know that *ut* is the "most aptest" choice for naming the note G here.

82–3 The reason for the choice of *mi* rather than *fa* for the note *b*, where the woodblock offers a choice, is given below (lines 90–4).

90–4 The woodcut correctly shows a natural for *b, mi* in the 4th hexachord (starting on G, *sol, re, ut*) but fails to mark *b, fa* with a flat in the 3rd hexachord (starting on F, *fa, ut*). Neither mark is given for *bb, fa, mi* in the two uppermost hexachords.

96–7 grave, sharp: I.e., in the lower or upper octave.

135 "The difference between notes [i.e., whole tones] and half-notes [semitones]" is exactly what the reader needed to know but this essay failed to explain.

Introduction to Solfa Notation ("To the Reader")

This text was first printed in *1569b*, accompanying a new music type. (For discussion of this innovation, see pp. 583–4). This type and the brief introduction appeared in the majority of two-column BL quartos through the end of the Elizabethan period and well into the 17th century. They were also common, if not as ubiquitous, in BL 16° editions during the same time frame. At some point after 1603, however, the type and its explanation became separated, such that the reader is instructed in how to use notation that is not in fact printed in that volume (e.g., *STC* 2685 from 1639).

The *1569b* printing, inexplicably, did not include the solmization syllables themselves below the notes of the sample lines of music in the Introduction. We have thus used the second surviving edition with the new type as the copy text, *STC* 2442 (*1572*), and included those sample lines here. It is collated with *1569b* and with *1588a*, which demonstrates textual changes that persist to the end of the Elizabethan period.

To the Reader

Thou shalt understand, gentle reader, that I have for the help of those that are desirous to learn to sing caused a new print of note to be made, with letters to be joined by every note; whereby thou mayest know how to call every note by his right name, so that with a very little diligence (as thou art taught
5   in the introduction printed heretofore in the psalms) thou mayest the more easily by the viewing of these letters come to the knowledge of perfect *solfaing*, whereby thou mayest sing the psalms the more speedily and easilier. The letters be these: *V* for *Vt* [*Ut*], *R* for *Re*, *M* for *Mi*, *F* for *Fa*, *S* for *Sol*, *L* for *La*. Thus where thou seest any letter joined by the note, you may easily call
10 him by his right name, as by these two examples you may the better perceive.

Vt Re My Fa Sol La La Sol Fa My Re Vt.

Vt Re My Fa Sol La Fa Sol La La Sol Fa La Sol Fa My Re Vt

Fig. 9: Illustration of solfa music font, *1572*, sig. A1v. University of Illinois at Urbana-Champaign.

Thus I commit thee unto him that liveth for ever, who grant that we may sing with our hearts and minds unto the glory of his holy name. *Amen.*

Text sources: *1569b, 1572, 1588a*
Text: **3** by every] to euery *1588a*   **6–7** sol-faing] Solfying *1569b*; Solfyng *1572*
7 speedily and easilier] easlier *1569b*; speedilie and easilie *1588a*   **9** thou seest]
you see *1588a*   **11** I commit] committing *1569b*   **12** and minds] *om 1588a*

Notes
8 In *1569b* the names of the solfa notes are not provided. In all known editions from *STC* 2442 (*1572*) to *STC* 2448.5 (1577), the C clef on the upper staff is erroneously printed on the top line instead of the second line — as in Fig. 9.

Of the use and virtue of the Psalms.

This text replaced "A Treatise Made by Athanasius the Great" in *1577* and all subsequent *WBP* editions that included Athanasian commentary. It was first printed not in the *WBP*, but in Matthew Parker's *Whole Psalter Translated into English Metre* (1567). Parker modeled his text on the *WBP* "Treatise," however: it is a nearly identical set of selections from Athanasius of Alexandria's *Letter to Marcellinus*, and in some places seems to borrow phrasing in translation. It also frequently agrees with the original *WBP* "Treatise" in the psalms specified where they differ from those given by Athanasius. For a description of the *WBP* selection, see p. 624. (Parker also added to his book, as a separate prefatory item, a slightly abridged translation of the first third of the Athanasian *Letter*, omitted from the *WBP* "Treatise"; this accompanied Parker's "Of the Use and Virtue of the Psalms" into *1577* and the printing series represented by *1593*).

If Parker worked from the original *WBP* "Treatise," however, he also did a nearly wholesale retranslation and re-editing of the text. In addition to numbering the sets of instructions (which we will refer to as "items"), Parker reordered them so that (usually) the psalms in successive items follow their numerical order — or at least the first psalm mentioned in each item does. He also included an Athanasian item omitted in the *1567* "Treatise" and added two at the end based on other sections of *A Letter*. Finally, he inserted a handful of wholly novel items, at least one (item 29, lines 69–70) based on the *WBP* "The use of the rest."

Parker's text gives English incipits of each psalm rather than simply numbers. When a *WBP* editor — probably Richard Day — substituted Parker's translation for the one that was first printed in *1562a*, he removed these and sometimes changed the syntax slightly to accommodate their removal. (For discussion of replacing the original "Treatise" with this one, see pp.

574–5.) As a result, collation against Parker's *Whole Psalter* is complex. Rather than recording differences from the *Whole Psalter* in the list of variant readings, then, any alterations beyond changing the syntax to shift the position of the psalm numbers are given in the notes that follow the text.

The notes also record significant differences from the Athanasian text in meaning, order, and psalm selection, based on Migne's edition in the *Patrologia graeca* and its English translation by Robert C. Gregg. As in the notes to the *1567* "Treatise made by Athansius the Great," Jan van Campen's 1534 Latin edition of the first two-thirds of *A Letter to Marcellinus* is also referenced as a comparison when it may indicate differences from Athanasius already present in Parker's intermediate source. Athanasius used the Septuagint psalm numbering, and Campen did not convert them in his edition; psalm numbering in the notes is given as in the *WBP* and KJV, unless otherwise indicated.

This list of suggested uses appears in some editions through the 1640s. In the later part of the 17th century, it seems to be printed only in folio editions with music, ending by 1800.

The copy text for this edition is *1577*. Of the texts selected for collation with *1567*, only *1582* also includes "Of the Use and Virtue of the Psalms." We have thus also collated it with *1593* as an example of its textual state in the late Elizabethan period.

Of the use and virtue of the Psalms by Athanasius.

All holy scripture is certainly the teacher of all virtue and of the true faith, but the Book of the Psalms doth express after a certain manner the very state and condition of the soul. For as he which intendeth to present himself to a king first will compound* with himself to set in good order both his gesture
5   and speech, lest else he might be reputed rude† and ignorant, even so doth this godly book inform all such as be desirous to lead their life in virtue and to know the life of our saviour which he led in his bodily conversation, putting them in mind in the reading thereof of all their affections and passions whereto their soul is inclined.
10   Moreover, the Psalms form and teach every man with divers instructions, whereby he may not only espy the affections and state of his soul and, to win a good pattern and discipline, how he may please God, but also with what form of words he may amend himself and how to give God due thanks: lest if he should speak otherwise than were convenient‡, he should

---

* devise
† unsophisticated; insulting
‡ befitting

15   fall into impiety by his unreverent estimation to God, for we must all make
      an account to the judge as well of our evil deeds as of our idle words.

1   If therefore thou wouldst at any time describe a blessed man, who he
      is and what thing maketh him to be so, thou hast the 1st, 32nd, 41st,
      112th, 128th Psalms.

20   2   If thou wouldst rebuke the Jews for their spite they have to Christ,
      thou hast the 2nd Psalm.

3   If thine own familiars* pursue thee and if many rise against thee, say
      the 3rd, 143rd Psalms.

4   If thus in trouble thou hast called on God and hast tarried upon his
25   help, and wouldst give him thanks for that he hath heard thee with his
      help, sing the 4th, 116th, 40th Psalms.

5   If that thou seest that evil men lay snares for thee, and therefore de-
      sirest God's ears to hear thy prayer, sing the 5th Psalm.

6   If thou feelest God's dreadful threats and seest thyself afraid of them,
30   thou mayest say the 6th, 38th, 88th Psalms.

7   If any take counsel against thee, as Achitophel did against David, if
      thou be admonished thereof sing the 7th Psalm.

8   If thou in beholding the grace of our saviour so spread on every side,
      specially for the restoring of mankind to salvation, and wouldst speak
35   thereof in meditation to God, sing the 8th Psalm.

9   If so again thou wilt sing in giving thanks to God for the prosperous
      gathering of thy fruits, use the 8th Psalm.

10   If thou wouldst have thine adversary kept back and thy soul saved,
      trust not in thyself but in the Son of God, singing the 9th Psalm.

40   11   If thou perceivest God to be wroth† with his people, as though he re-
      garded‡ them nothing, thou hast to pacify him to complain thereof the
      10th, 60th, 74th Psalms.

12   If any man would put thee in fear, have thou thy hope in God and sing
      the 11th Psalm.

45   13   If thou beholdest the pride of many men and seest malice to abound so
      that there is no godliness among men, repair thou to God and say the
      12th Psalm.

14   If thine adversary lie long in wait against thee, despair not as though
      God had forgotten thee, but call upon the Lord and sing the 13th, 61st,
50   22nd Psalms.

15   If thou hearest any to blaspheme God in his providence, be not par-
      taker with them in wickedness, but make haste to God and say the
      14th, 53rd Psalms.

* close companions
† wrathful
‡ valued

16   If thou desirest to know who is a citizen of heaven, sing the 15th
55   Psalm.

17   If thou hast need of prayer for such as be against thee and have closed*
thy soul on every side, sing the 16th, 17th, 86th, 141st Psalms.

18   If thou hast escaped from thine enemies and art delivered from them
who pursued thee, sing thou the 18th, 89th Psalms.

60   19   If thou dost wonder at the order of things created by God, considering
the grace of the divine providence sing the 19th, 24th Psalms.

20   If thou seest any man in adversity, comfort him and pray for him with
the 20th Psalm.

21   If thou perceivest thyself to be defended and fed by God and to live
65   prosperously, rejoice therein and sing the 23rd Psalm.

22   If thine enemies conspire against thee, lift up thy soul to God and say
the 23rd Psalm, and thou shalt espy them to labour but in vain against
thee.

23   If thine enemies cluster against thee and go about with their bloody
70   hands to destroy thee, go not thou about by man's help to revenge
it, for all men's judgements are not trusty, but require God to be the
judge, for he alone is judge, and say the 26th, 35th, 43rd Psalms.

24   If they press more fiercely on thee, though they be in numbers like an
armed host, fear them not which thus reject thee, as though thou were
75   not annointed and elect by God, but sing the 27th Psalm.

25   If they be yet so impudent that lay wait against thee so that it is not
lawful for thee to have any vocation by them, regard them not, but sing
to God the 28th Psalm.

26   If thou wilt exhort and provoke kings and princes to submit their pow-
80   ers to God and to regard his honour, sing the 29th, 82nd Psalms.

27   If thou renew and build thine house, both of thy soul, whereto thou
receivest God to host, and of thy temporal habitation, sing the 30th,
48th, 127th Psalms.

28   If thou seest thyself had in hate for the truth's sake of† thy friends and
85   kinsfolk, leave not off thy purpose nor fear them which be against
thee, but think on them which follow and sing the 31st Psalm.

29   If thou beholdest such as be baptized and so delivered from the cor-
ruption of their birth, praise thou the bountiful grace of God and sing
the 32nd Psalm.

90   30   If thou delightest to sing among many, call together righteous men of
godly life and sing the 33rd Psalm.

---

* enclosed, shut in
† by

31   If by chance thou fallest amongst thine enemies and yet hast fortunately escaped them, if therefore thou wilt give thanks, call together meek men and sing the 34th Psalm.

95 32   If thou seest wicked men contend among themselves to do mischief, think not that their nature doth impel them by necessity to work sin against their will, as certain heretics suppose, but consider the Psalm 36, and thou shalt perceive that they be to themselves their own occasion* of sinning.

100 33   If thou seest how wicked men do much wickedness and that yet simple folk praise such, when thou wilt admonish any man not to follow them, to be like unto them, because they shall be shortly rooted out and destroyed, speak to thyself and to other the 37th Psalm.

34   If thou hast decreed to take heed of thyself† and seest thine enemy ap-
105 proach nigh thee, as to such the adversary is more provoked to come with assault, and therefore wilt prepare thyself, sing the 39th Psalm.

35   If thou seest many poor men to beg and wilt show pity to them, thou mayst both thyself receive them to mercy and also exhort other to do the same saying the 41st Psalm.

110 36   If thou hast a desire to Godward and hearest thine enemies to upbraid thee, be not troubled, but consider what fruit of immortality riseth to thee for this desire: comfort thy soul with hope to God, and so therein relieving and assuaging the heaviness of thy life, say the 42nd Psalm.

37   If thou wilt remember of God's benefits which he did to their fathers,
115 both in their outgoing from Egypt as in the desert, and how good God was to them but they unthankful to him, thou hast the 44th, 78th, 89th, 102nd, 106th, 107th, 114th Psalms.

38   If thou hast made thy refuge to God and hast escaped such trouble as was prepared against thee, if thou wilt give thanks and show out his
120 kindness to thee, sing the 46th Psalm.

39   If thou wilt know how to give thanks to God when thou dost resort to him with understanding sound, sing the 47th, 48th Psalms.

40   If thou wilt exhort men to put their trust in the living God, who ministreth all things abundantly to good men's use, and blameth the mad-
125 ness of the world, which serveth their god Mammon‡ so inordinately, sing the 49th Psalm.

41   If thou wouldst call upon the blind world for their wrong confidence of their brute sacrifices and show them what sacrifice God most hath required of them, sing the 50th Psalm.

* cause
† i.e., be cautious of your own safety
‡ i.e., wealth

130   42   If thou hast sinned and art converted and moved to do penance, desirous to have mercy, thou hast words of confession in the 51st Psalm.

43   If thou hast suffered false accusation before the king and seest the Devil to triumph thereof, go aside and say the 52nd Psalm.

44   If they which persecute thee with accusations would betray thee, as
135   the Pharisees did Jesus and as the aliens* did David, discomfort† not thyself therewith, but sing in good hope to God the 54th, 69th, 57th Psalms.

45   If thine adversaries which trouble thee do upbraid thee and that they which seem to be thy friends speak most against thee, whereupon if in thy meditation thou art somewhat grieved thereat, thou mayest call on
140   God saying the 55th Psalm.

46   If persecution come fierce on thee and unbewares chance to enter into the cave where thou hidest thyself, fear not: for in this strait thou shalt have expedient words both to comfort thee and put thee in old remembrance with the 57th, 142nd Psalms.

145   47   If thou wilt confound hypocrites which make glorious shows outwardly, speak their conversion with the 58th Psalm.

48   If thy pursuers command thy house to be watched, when thou art escaped give thanks to God and grave it in the tables of thy heart for perpetual remembrance, and say the 59th Psalm.

150   49   If thine enemies cruelly assault thee and would catch thy life, offer the subjection to God against them and be of good comfort, for the more they rage, the more shall God subdue them, and say the 62nd Psalm.

50   If thou flyest persecution and gettest thee into wilderness, fear thou not as though thou were there alone, but having God nigh unto thee,
155   rise to him early in the morning, singing the 63rd Psalm.

51   If thine enemies would put thee in fear and never cease to lay trains‡ for thee and pick all manner of quarrels against thee, though they be very many give no place to them, for the darts of babes shall be their destruction if thou sayest the 61st, 68th, 70th, 71st Psalms.

160   52   If thou wilt laud God with a psalm or hymn, sing the 65th, 66th Psalms.

53   If thou askest mercy of God, sing the 67th Psalm.

54   If thou wouldst sing to the Lord, thou hast what to say in the 96th, 98th Psalms.

165   55   If thou hast need to confess God with thanks, sing the 71st, 75th, 92nd, 105th, 118th, 136th, 108th, 111th, 138th Psalms.

---

*   strangers

†   discourage

‡   snares

56   If thou seest wicked men prosper in peace, be not offended nor moved thereat but say the 73rd Psalm.

57   If thine enemies have beset the ways whither thou fleest and art there-
170   by in great anguish, yet in this trouble despair not, but pray: and if thy prayer be heard, give God thanks and say the 77th Psalm.

58   If they persevere still and defile the house of God, kill his elects and cast their bodies to the fowls of the air, fear not their cruelty, but show pity to them which be in such agony and say the 79th Psalm.

175   59   If thou wilt inform any man with the mystery of the resurrection, sing the 80th Psalm.

60   If thou wilt sing to the Lord, call together God's servants on the feast-ful* day and sing the 81st, 95th, 134th Psalms.

61   If the adversaries flock together on every side and threat to destroy the
180   house of God and make their conspiracies against his religion, let not their numbers and power trouble thee, for thou hast an anchor of the words of the Psalm 83.

62   If thou castest an eye to God's house and to his eternal tabernacles and hast a desire thereto as the apostle had, say thou also 84th Psalm.

185   63   If God's wrath be ceased and the captivity ended, thou hast cause how to give thanks to God with David, recounting his goodness to thee and others with the Psalms 85, 116, and 76.

64   If thou wilt rebuke paynims† and heretics for that they have not the knowledge of God in them, thou mayest have an understanding to
200   sing to God the 86th, 115th Psalms.

65   If thou wilt see and know the dissent that the catholic Church have from schisms and wouldst convert them, or to discern the Church concerning the outward appearance and forms thereof, thou mayest say the 87th Psalm.

205   66   If thou wouldst know how Moses prayed to God and in his medita-tion, recounting the brittle state of man's life, desired God to direct so his short life, that he might follow wisdom, read the 90th Psalm.

67   If thou wouldst comfort thyself and others in true religion and teach them that hope in God will never suffer a soul to be confounded,
210   but make it bold and without fear for God's protection, sing the 91st Psalm.

68   If thou wilt sing on the Sabbath day, thou hast the 92nd Psalm.

69   If thou wilt sing on the Sunday in meditation of God's word, desiring to be instructed therein whereby thou mayest rest in God's holy will
215   and cease from all the works and doctrines of vain man, revolve that notable Psalm 119.

---

* festival
† pagans

70   If thou wilt sing in the second day of the Sabbath, thou hast 95th Psalm.

71   If thou wouldst sing to the Lord, thou hast what to say in the 96th, 98th Psalms.

72   If thou wilt sing the fourth day of the Sabbath, sing the Psalm 94, for then when the Lord was betrayed, he began to take vengeance on death and to triumph of it. Therefore, when thou readest the gospel wherein thou hearest the Jews to take counsel against the Lord and that he standeth boldly against the Devil, then sing the foresaid Psalm.

73   If thou wilt sing on Good Friday, thou hast a commendation of the Psalm 93, for then was the house of God's Church builded and groundly* founded, though the enemies went about to hinder it: for which cause, sing to God the songs of triumphant victory, with the said Psalm and with 129th and 98th Psalm.

74   If there be any captivity wherein thy house is laid waste and yet builded again, sing the 96th Psalm.

75   If the land be vexed with enemies and after come to any rest by the power of God, if thou wilt sing therefore, sing the 97th Psalm.

76   If thou considerest the providence of God in his governance so over all and wilt instruct any with true faith and obedience, when thou hast first persuaded them to confess themselves, sing the 100th, 147th Psalms.

77   If thou dost acknowledge in God his judicial power and that in judgement he mixeth mercy, if thou wilt draw nigh unto him, thou hast the words of this Psalm 101 to this end.

78   If, for the imbecility† of thy nature, thou art weary with the continual miseries and griefs of this life and wouldst comfort thyself, sing the 102nd Psalm.

79   If thou wilt give thanks to God as it is most convenient‡ and due for all his gifts, when thou wilt so do, thou hast how to enjoin thy soul thereunto with these: 103rd and 104th Psalms.

80   If thou wilt praise God and also know how, and for what cause and with what words thou mayest best do it, consider the 113th, 117th, 133rd, 146th, 147th, 148th, 149th, 150th Psalms.

81   If thou hast faith to such things as God speaketh and believest that which in prayer thou utterest, say the Psalm 116 in the end.

82   If thou feelest thyself to rise upward in degrees of well-working, as though thou saidst with St Paul, "I forget those things which be be-

---

* firmly
† weakness
‡ befitting

hind me and set mine eyes on things which be before me," thou hast the 120th Psalm.

83   If thou beest holden in thralldom* under straying and wandering thoughts and feelest thyself drawn by them, whereof thou art sorry, then stay thyself from thenceforth and tarry where thou hast found thyself in fault: sit thee down and mourn thou also as the Hebrew people did, and say with them the 137th Psalm.

84   If thou perceivest that temptations be sent to prove† thee, thou oughtest after such temptations give God the thanks and say the 139th Psalm.

85   If yet thou be in bondage by thine enemies and wouldst fain be delivered, say the 140th Psalm.

86   If thou wouldst pray and make supplication, say the 141st, 142nd, 143rd Psalm.

87   If any tyrannous enemy rise up against the people, fear thou not, no more than David did Goliath, but believe like David and sing the 144th Psalm.

88   If thou art elect out of low degree, specially before other to some vocation to serve thy brethren, advance not thyself too high against them in thine own power, but give God his glory who did choose thee, and sing thou the 145th Psalm.

89   If thou wilt sing of obedience, praising God with *Alleluia*, thou hast these: 105th, 106th, 107th, 111th, 112th, 113th, 114th, 115th, 117th, 135th, 136th, 146th, 147th, 148th, 149th, 150th Psalms.

90   If thou wilt sing specially of our saviour Christ, thou hast of him in every Psalm, but most chiefly in the 25th, 45th, 110th Psalms.

91   Such Psalms as show his lawful generation of his Father and his corporal presence be these: 11th, 69th Psalm.

92   Such as do prophesy before of his most holy cross and passion, telling how many deceitful assaults he sustained for us and how much he suffered, be these: 2nd, 119th Psalms.

93   Such as express the malicious enmities of the Jews and the betraying of Judas are the 55th, 109th, 21st, 50th, 72nd, 69th Psalms.

94   Such as describe his agony in his passion, death, and sepulture be 22nd, 88th Psalms.

95   For his dominion and presence in the flesh, read 16th Psalm.

96   Such as show his glorious resurrection of body be 24th, 47th Psalms.

97   Such as set out his ascension into heaven, read the 93rd, 96th, 98th, 99th Psalms.

---

* bondage
† test

295   98   And that he sitteth on the right hand of his Father, the 110th Psalm
            maketh manifest.
      99   Such as show that he hath authority of his Father to judge, expressing
            his judicial power both in condemning the Devil and all wicked na-
            tions, are the 72nd, 50th, 82nd Psalms.

300   **FINIS.**

Text sources: *1577, 1582, 1593*
Heading: Of . . . Athanasius] A Treatise made by Athanasius the great, concerning
the vse and vertue of the Psalmes *1582*
Text: 4 first will] will first *1582*   **7** bodily] *om 1582*   **8** all their] all other *1593*
10 form] enforme *1582*   **15** to God] of God *1582*   **16** evil . . . words] idle wordes,
as of our euill deedes *1582*   **17** 1] *om 1582*   **26** 116th, 40th] 40. 116. *1582, 1593*
27 that] *om 1593*   **30** 6th] 9. *1593*   **33** so] *om 1582*   **34** and wouldst] wouldest
1582   **46** thou] then *1582*   **49** 61st] 16. *1582*   **53** 53rd] 55. *1582, 1593*   **72** the
judge] iudge *1582*   **78** 28th] 48. *1582*   **81** renew] renne *1593*   **97** consider the]
consider this *1582*   **105** to such] agaynst one whom *1582*   **114** of] *om 1582, 1593*
their fathers] the fathers *1582*   **116** was to] was vnto *1582*   **117** 107th, 114th] 114.
117. *1582*   **122** understanding sound] sound vnderstanding *1582*   **124** blameth]
blame *1582*   **128** God] Gost *1577*   **131** words] the wordes *1582*   **143** old re-
membrance] remembraunce of his olde mercy *1582*   **148** thy heart] thine hart
1582   **149** perpetual] a perpetual *1582*   **150** the] thy *1582*   **153** flyest] fleest
1582; seest *1593*   **157** of] *om 1593*   **162** askest] aske *1582*   **166** 105th . . . 138th]
108. 111. 118. 136. 138. 195. *1582*; 105. 108. 111. 118. 136. 138. *1593*   **167** nor moved]
om 1582   **172** his elects] the elect *1582*; his elect *1593*   **176** 80th] 81. *1582,*
1593   **177–8** feastful] feastiuall *1582, 1593*   **179** the adversaries] thine aduer-
saries *1582*   threat] threaten *1582*   **180** his religion] the religion *1582*; religion
1593   **181** numbers] number *1582*   **182** Psalm 83] 83. Psalme *1582*   **187** Psalms
. . . 76] 76. 85. 116. psa. *1582*; Psalmes 76. 85. and 116. *1593*   **201** have] hath *1582,*
1593   **202** schisms] schisme *1582*   **215** man] men *1582, 1593*   **217** 95th] the 95.
1582, 1593   **225** foresaid] aforesaid *1593*   **231** 129th . . . Psalm] the 98. and 129.
Psalmes *1582*; the 129. and 89. Psalmes *1593*   **241–2** thou . . . end] sing the 101.
Psalme. *1593*   **242** this end] the end *1582*   **247–8** when . . . these] sing the *1593*
247 enjoin] reioyce *1582*   **248** these] the *1582*   Psalms] Psal. *1577*   **250** 113th]
13. *1593*   **253** the Psalm 116] the 116. Psal. *1593*   in the end] to the end *1582*; *om*
1593   **254** well-working] well doing *1593*   **255–6** which be behind] that be be-
hind *1593*   **256** which be before] before *1593*   **257** Psalm] *om 1577*   **258** beest]
be *1582*   and wandering] *om 1593*   **260** thenceforth] henceforth *1593*   **261** thou
also] *om 1593*   as the] as he *1577*   **264** give . . . thanks] to geue God the thankes
1582; giue to God thankes *1593*   **269** Psalm] Psalmes *1582, 1593*   **276** thou the]
the *1593*   **277** 89] 88 *1577*   of] *om 1593*   **278** these] the *1582, 1593*   **281** most]
om 1593   **283** these] the *1582*; these, the *1593*   Psalm] Psalmes *1582, 1593*
284 most] *om 1593*   **286** these] the *1582*   **288** of Judas] by Iudas *1593*   55th

... 69th] 21. 50. 55. 69. 72. 109. *1582*   **290** 22nd] the 22. *1582*   **291** 16th] the
116. *1582, 1593*   **292** his] the *1582*   body] his body *1582*   be] be the *1582, 1593*
293 read] are *1582, 1593*   **298–9** both ... nations] *om 1593*   **300** FINIS] *om*
1582

Notes

19 Omits Ps. 119.

23 Adds Ps. 143.

26 Replaces Ps. 75 with Ps. 40.

30 Adds Ps. 88.

31 Achitophel ... David: David's counselor Achitophel joined Absolom's rebellion
against David (2 Sam. 15:12).

37 Omits Ps. 84. (Campen and *1567* replace it with Ps. 81.)

40–2 In *A Letter* (and the *1567* text), Parker's item 11 immediately follows item 56
(ll. 167–8). Parker seems to have moved it here because he adds Pss. 10 and 60.

48–50 Adds Pss. 61 and 22.

57 141st: Should be 142nd (incorrect translation from 140th in Septuagint). Omits
Ps. 88 and adds Ps. 16.

59 Adds Ps. 89.

67 23rd: Should be 25th.

76–7 so that ... by them: An interpolation into the Athanasian text, but also pres-
ent in Campen.

79–80 If thou ... Psalms: Not present in *A Letter*. Cf. "The use of the rest" (p. 15).
This replaces an Athanasian instruction: "And if in giving thanks, you wish to learn
what it is necessary to offer to the Lord, while you think spiritually, chant the twen-
ty-eighth [KJV 29th]" (Gregg, 116).

81–2 Adds Ps. 48. Campen and *1567* replace Ps. 30 with 49.

95–9 In the 4th century, this was a warning against particular Gnostic doctrines.
In the context of 16th-century debates about the implications of predestination so-
teriology, it would probably have struck readers as a comment on the culpability of
the reprobate. **Psalm 36** should be Psalm 37 (36 in Septuagint), although Campen
and *1567* give Ps. 36.

114 Omits an Athanasian item (also omitted in Campen and *1567*): "And if, when
the enemies set upon you, you persevere in the face of the trials, and you want to
learn the advantage of endurance, sing Psalm 39 [40]." Parker assigned Ps. 40 above
at l. 26.

117 102nd: Replaces the Athanasian 105. Campen and *1567* do the same, although
1567 has further differences in the psalms specified.

121–9 Items 39–41 are not in *A Letter*.

134–5 as ... Jesus: Not in Migne, though present in Campen and *1567*.

135 aliens: the Ziphites, who reported David's hiding place to Saul (1 Sam. 23:
19–20).

136 69th, 57th: Added in place of Ps. 56.

138–49 In *A Letter* (and in the *1567* text), the order of Parker's items is 46, 48, 45, 47.

144 142nd: Replaces Ps. 116. Campen and *1567* make the same replacement.

159 61st, 68th: Replacing Pss. 64 and 65. In Campen and *1567*, 68 also replaces 65.

160 Adds Ps. 66. Parker then omits the Athanasian item for that psalm: "And if you wish to instruct some people about the resurrection, sing the words in Ps. 65 [66]" (Gregg, 119).

163 In *A Letter* and *1567*, item 54 immediately precedes item 88. Parker reiterated it verbatim as item 71. He also follows *1567* in replacing Ps. 93 with 96.

165–6 71st: Replaces Ps. 10 (as in Campen and *1567*). Omits Ps. 106. In *A Letter* and in *1567*, this item follows rather than preceding item 56.

175–6 In *A Letter* and in *1567*, item 59 immediately follows 52. Parker follows *1567* in replacing Ps. 66 with Ps. 80.

177–8 Adds Ps. 134.

185–7 Follows *1567* in replacing Ps. 126 with Ps. 116, and adds Ps. 76.

198–200 In *A Letter* and *1567*, item 64 immediately follows item 55 and precedes item 57. Follows *1567* in omitting mention of truth residing in the Catholic Church and in replacing Ps. 76 with Ps. 86 (see p. 11 and p. 626). Parker adds Ps. 115.

205–7 In *A Letter* and *1567*, item 66 immediately follows item 17. Parker's summary of the psalm considerably expands on the Athanasian text.

213–16 The incipient Sabbatarianism here is Parker's, expanding on the brief direction to "return thanks in the Lord's Day" (Gregg, 120). He also replaces the Athanasian Ps. 24 with Ps. 119 (*1567* gives 13).

217–8 95th: Follows *1567* in replacing Ps. 48.

219–20 See note to l. 163 above.

227–31 In *A Letter* and *1567*, item 73 immediately follows item 75.

236–9 Adds Ps. 147.

250–1 113th, 117th, 133rd: Replaces the Athanasian selections of Pss. 105, 107, and 135; in *1567*, the replacements are 113, 117, and 133 (in Campen, 118, 119, and 135).

253 in the end: Athanasius specifies Septuagint Ps. 115, which corresponds to the second half of Ps. 116 in Protestant Bibles.

256–7 thou hast . . . 120th: The version in the *Whole Psalter* better reflects the original: "thou has in eueryc exaltation of thy progresse what thou mayest saie in the xv. songes of the stayers. 120" (Parker, sig. D3r). The reference is to the Gradual Psalms or Song of Ascents (Pss. 120–134).

268 141st, 142nd, 143rd: *A Letter* gives Pss. 6 and 143 (5 and 142 in the Septuagint); *1567* gives Pss. 5, 141, 142, 143, and 144; Campen offers Pss. 141, 142, 143, and 146.

271 David did Goliath: See 1 Sam. 17:1–51.

276 145th: Replaces Ps. 151, which does not appear in Protestant Bibles.

277–9 This version only partially corrects the list given in *1562a* and *1567*, which appears to have gotten confused in converting numbers from the Septuagint. The Athanasian list lacks the equivalents of Pss. 111 and 117, but contains Pss. 116, 118, and 119. Campen adds Ps. 117.

280–3 In *A Letter*, Athanasius notes that Christ can be found in nearly every psalm, but that his generation and incarnation are shown in Pss. 45 and 110. The text in *1567* divides that statement the same way that Parker does in this version. Where *1567* replaced Ps. 45 with 25 and added Ps. 11 to the next sentence, Parker keeps Ps. 45, restores Ps. 25, and adds Ps. 69 to item 91.

284–6 Follows *1567* in replacing Pss. 22 and 69 with Pss. 2 and 119.

287–8 Combines one of the two psalms specified by Athanasius (3 and 109) with those that replaced them in *1567* (21, 50, and 72), and adds Pss. 55 and 69.

289–90 In this item, Parker paraphrased Athanasius's discussion of Christ in the Book of Psalms from ¶7 of *A Letter*. The *WBP* radically abridges the text from *The Whole Psalter* (Parker, sig. D4r).

291 This item follows *1567* in replacing Pss. 21, 50, and 72 with 16. Parker also truncates the item to reduce overlap with item 99, taken from another part of *A Letter*.

292 Follows *1567* in replacing Ps. 15 with two discussed earlier (¶8) with reference to the resurrection.

295 6 This item draws on a discussion in an earlier section about Christ in the Psalms (¶8).

297–9 Summarizes Athanasius' comments from the middle of ¶8, and adds Pss. 50 and 82. Parker's *Whole Psalter* (sig. D4r) then concludes with two additional sentences of summary about the utility of the psalms inspired by, but not directly translating, Athanasius.

A Prayer Made for the Church

This prayer by John Foxe was first printed at the end of his *Sermon of Christ Crucified* (*Foxe1570*), which he had delivered at St. Paul's Cross on Good Friday of 1570 and which Day quickly and copiously put into print, with three impressions dated 1570. It continued to be popular, surviving in four further English editions up to 1609 in addition to a 1571 Latin translation. The sermon was delivered a month after Pius V issued his bull of excommunication against Elizabeth, and it is, like the prayer, an argument for Catholics to become reconciled to the true (Protestant) religion. Foxe's emphasis in the prayer and to a lesser extent in the sermon on the threat from "the Turk" was probably stoked by his recent preparation of a history of the Ottoman Empire for inclusion in the 1570 edition of *The Acts and Monuments*.[1]

The "Prayer Made for the Church" first appears in the *WBP* in *1577*, one of the innovations in that volume probably attributable to Richard Day. Richard also included it in his 1578 revised edition of *A Booke of Christian Prayers* (25–31; see p. 576, above). After one 1578 quarto (*STC* 2450.5), it appeared only in small format editions, including a brief octavo printing series in the early 1580s but chiefly 16° and 32° editions. It continued to be occasionally printed with the *WBP* until at least the late 1630s, but does not seem to have been reprinted after the Restoration.

The copy text is *1577*. The prayer does not appear in other editions selected for collation with *1567*. We have collated it with *Foxe1570* to establish changes as it entered the *WBP*, and with *1593* to demonstrate its textual state near the end of the 16th century.

A prayer made for the Church and all the states thereof.
J.F.

Lord Jesus Christ, Son of the living God, who was crucified for our sins and didst rise again for our justification, and, ascending up to heaven, reignest now at the right hand of thy Father, with full power and authority ruling and disposing all things according to thine own gracious and glorious purpose: we sinful creatures, and yet servants and members of thy Church, do prostrate ourselves and our prayers before thy imperial majesty, having no other patron nor advocate to speed our suits or to resort unto but thee alone, beseeching thy goodness to be good to thy poor Church militant here in this wretched earth; sometimes a rich Church, a large Church, an universal

5

---

[1] On this preparation, see Evenden and Freeman, *Religion and the Book in Early Modern England* (Cambridge: Cambridge University Press, 2011), 135, 141.

10   Church, spread far and wide through the whole compass of the earth, now
driven into a narrow corner of the world, and hath much need of thy gra-
cious help. First the Turk with his sword, what lands, nations and countries,
what empires, kingdoms and provinces with cities innumerable hath he won,
not from us but from thee! Where thy name was wont to be invocated, thy
15   word preached, thy sacraments administered, there now reigneth barbarous
Mahomet*, with his filthy Alcoran†. The flourishing churches in Asia, the
learned churches of Grecia, the manifold churches in Africa which were
wont to serve thee now are gone from thee. The seven churches of Asia with
their candlesticks (whom thou didst so well forewarn) are now removed.
20   All the churches where thy diligent apostle St. Paul, thy apostle Peter and
John and other apostles so laboriously travailed, preaching and writing to
plant thy gospel, are now gone from thy gospel. In all the kingdom of Syr-
ia, Palestina, Arabia, Persia, in all Armenia, and the empire of Capadocia,
through the whole compass of Asia, with Egypt and with Africa also (unless
25   amongst the far Ethiopians some old steps of Christianity peradventure yet
do remain), either else in all Asia and Africa, thy Church hath not one foot
of free land, but all is turned either to infidelity or to captivity, whatsoever
pertaineth to thee. And if Asia and Africa only were decayed, the decay were
great, but yet defection were not so universal. Now in Europa a great part
30   also is shrunk from the Church. All Thracia with the empire of Constanti-
nople, all Grecia, Epirus, Illiricum, and now of late all the kingdom almost
of Hungaria with much of Austria with lamentable slaughter of Christian
blood is wasted and all become Turks.

    Only a little angle of the west parts yet remaineth in some profession
35   of thy name. But here, alack, cometh another mischief as great or greater
than the other. For the Turk with his sword is not so cruel, but the Bishop
of Rome on the other side is more fierce and bitter against us, stirring up
his bishops to burn us, his confederates to conspire our destruction, set-
ting kings against their subjects and subjects disloyally to rebel against their
40   princes, and all for thy name. Such dissention and hostility Satan hath set
amongst us, that Turks be not more enemies to Christians than Christians
to Christians, papists to Protestants; yea, Protestants with Protestants do not
agree, but fall out for trifles. So that the poor little flock of thy Church, dis-
tressed on every side, hath neither rest without, nor peace within, nor place
45   almost in the world where to abide, but may cry now from the earth, even
as thine own reverence cried once from thy cross, "My God, my God, why
hast thou forsaken me?"

    Amongst us Englishmen here in England, after so great storms of per-
secution and cruel murder of so many martyrs, it hath pleased thy grace

* Muhammed
† Koran

50   to give us these halcyon days, which yet we enjoy and beseech thy merci-
ful goodness still* they may continue. But here also, alack, what should we
say? So many enemies we have that envy us this rest and tranquility and do
what they can to disturb it. They which be friends and lovers of the Bishop
of Rome, although they eat the fat of the land, and have the best preferments
55   and offices, and live most at ease, and ail nothing, yet are they not therewith
content. They grudge, they mutter and murmur, they conspire and take on
against us. It fretteth them that we live by them or with them, and cannot
abide that we should draw the bare breathing of the air, when they have all
the most liberty of the land. And albeit thy singular goodness hath given
60   them a Queen so calm, so patient, so merciful, more like a natural mother
than a princess to govern over them, such as neither they nor their ancestors
ever read of in the stories of this land before, yet all this will not calm them:
their unquiet spirit is not yet content, they repine and rebel and needs would
have, with the frogs of Aesop, a *ciconia*†, an Italian stranger, the Bishop of
65   Rome, to play rex over them, and care not if all the world were set on fire
so they with their Italian lord might reign alone. So fond are we English-
men of strange and foreign things; so unnatural to ourselves; so greedy of
newfangle novelties, never contented with any state long to continue, be it
never so good; and furthermore, so cruel one to another that we think our
70   life not quiet unless it be seasoned with the blood of other. For that is their
hope, that is all their gaping and looking, that is their golden day, their day
of Jubilee which they thirst for so much: not to have the Lord to come in the
clouds, but to have our blood and to spill our lives.

        That, that is it which they would have, and long since would have had
75   their wills upon us had not thy gracious pity and mercy raised up to us this
our merciful queen, thy servant Elizabeth, somewhat to stay their fury. For
whom as we most condignly‡ give thee most hearty thanks, so likewise we
beseech thy heavenly majesty that as thou hast given her unto us, and hast
from so manifold dangers preserved her before she was queen, so now in
80   her royal estate she may continually be preserved, not only from their hands
but from all malignant devices wrought, attempted, or conceived of enemies
both ghostly§ and bodily against her. In this her government be her gov-
ernor, we beseech thee: so shall her majesty well govern us, if first she be
governed by thee. Multiply her reign with many days and her years with
85   much felicity, with abundance of peace and life ghostly. That as she hath now
doubled the years of her sister and brother, so (if it be thy pleasure) she may
overgrow in reigning the reign of her father.

   *   always
   †   stork
   ‡   deservedly
   §   spiritual

And because no government can long stand without good counsel, nei-
ther can any counsel be good except it be prospered by thee, bless therefore,
90   we beseech thee, both her majesty and her honourable Council, that both
they rightly may understand what is to be done and she accordingly may ac-
complish that they do counsel, to thy glory and furtherance of thy gospel and
public wealth of this realm.

Furthermore, we beseech thee, Lord Jesu (who with the majesty of thy
95   generation* dost drown all nobility, being the only son of God, heir and
Lord of all things), bless the nobility of this realm and of other Christian
realms, so as they Christianly agreeing among themselves may submit their
nobility to serve thee; or else let them feel, O Lord, what a frivolous thing is
that nobility which is without thee.

100   Likewise to all magistrates, such as be advanced to authority or placed
in office by what name or title soever, give, we beseech thee, a careful con-
science uprightly to discharge their duty, that as they be public persons to
serve the commonwealth, so they abuse not their office to their private gain
nor private revenge of their own affections; but that, justice being admin-
105   istered without bribery and equity balanced without cruelty or partiality,
things that be amiss may be reformed, vice abandoned, truth supported,
innocency relieved, God's glory maintained and the commonwealth truly
served.

But especially to thy spiritual ministers, bishops and pastors of thy
110   Church, grant, we beseech thee (O Lord, Prince of all pastors) that they,
following the steps of thee, of thy apostles and holy martyrs, may seek those
things which be not their own, but only which be thine: not caring how
many benefices nor what great bishoprics they have, but how well they can
guide those they have. Give them such zeal of thy Church as may devour
115   them, and grant them such salt wherewith the whole people may be sea-
soned and which may never be unsavoury, but quicken daily by thy Holy
Spirit whereby thy flock by them may be preserved.

In general give to all the people and the whole state of this realm such
brotherly unity in knowledge of thy truth and such obedience to their su-
120   periors as they neither provoke the scourge of God against them nor their
prince's sword to be drawn against her will out of the scabbard of long suffer-
ance, where it hath been long hid. Especially give thy gospel long continu-
ance amongst us. And if our sins have deserved the contrary, grant, we be-
seech thee, with an earnest repentance of that which is past to join a hearty
125   purpose of amendment to come.

And forasmuch as the Bishop of Rome is wont on every Good Friday to
accurse us as damned heretics, we here curse not him but pray for him, that

* lineage

he with all his partakers either may be turned to a better truth, or else, we pray thee, gracious Lord, that we never agree with him in doctrine, and that
130 he may so curse us still and never bless us more as he blessed us in Queen Mary's time. God of his mercy keep away that blessing from us.

Finally, instead of the Pope's blessing, give us thy blessing, Lord, we beseech thee, and conserve the peace of thy Church and course of thy blessed gospel. Help them that be needy and afflicted. Comfort them that labour
135 and be heavy-laden. And above all things, continue and increase our faith. And forasmuch as thy poor little flock can scarce have any place or rest in this world, come, Lord, we beseech thee, with thy *factum est* and make an end, that this world may have no more time nor place here, and that thy Church may have rest for ever. Our Father, which art etc.

Text sources: *Foxe1570, 1577, 1593*
Heading: A . . . thereof. J.F.] The Prayer in this Sermon. *Foxe1570*
Text: 2 rise] so rise *1593* reignest] reigning *1593* 9 an universal] and vniuersall *1593* 18 serve] receiue *1593* 19 removed] reuoked *1593* 25 amongst] among *1593* 26 all Asia] Asia *1593* 27 to captivity] captiuitie *1593* 29 defection] destruction *1593* 31 kingdom] kingdoms *1593* 33 all become] become the *1593* 42 with Protestants] to Protestants *1593* 53 They which] The which *1593* 59 thy] by thy *1593* 61 princess] Prince *1593* 65 on fire] a fire *Foxe1570* 70 other] others *1593* 72 thirst] trust *1593* 77 most] must *1593* 80 their hands] the handes *Foxe1570* 85 peace] grace *1593* 86 may] may also *Foxe1570* 89 except] accept *1577* 92 thy gospel] the Gospell *1593* 94 Jesu] Iesus *1593* 104 private revenge] the fulfilling *1593* 111–2 seek . . . not] not seek those things which be *1593* 112 only] only those *1593* 113 benefices nor] benefites not *1593* 115–6 salt . . . and] seasoned zeale *1593* 116 never] euer *1593* 117 quicken] quickened *Foxe1570* 121 scabbard] scraped *1593* 124 a hearty] an hearty *1593* 126 every] this Godfridy, and euery *Foxe1570* 133 thy Church] the Church *1593* 139 have rest] hast rest *Foxe1570* Our Father] For these and all other necessities requisite to be begged & prayed for asking in Christes name, and as he hath taught vs let vs saye the Lordes prayer. Our Father *Foxe1570*

Notes
18–9 seven churches . . . forewarn: Rev. 1:20–3:22 concerns messages to seven specific congregations in Asia minor, containing varying degrees of praise, admonition, and warning of punishment to come.
31 Epirus, Illyricum: Northwestern Greece and an historical Roman territory covering most of the western Balkans (Illyria), respectively.
64 frogs . . . ciconia: In Aesop's fable, the frogs ask Zeus for a king, and he first offers a log. After they ridicule it and request a different king, he sends a predator (water snake or heron) which promptly and predictably begins to eat the frogs. By the 16th century, the predatory king was usually a stork.
72–3 Lord to come in the clouds: Christ's return as described in Rev. 1:7.
137 factum est: From Rev. 8:1, "factum est silentio in caelo" (there was silence in heaven); this follows the opening of the seventh seal.

A Prayer Against the Devil

This text first appears in an ornate little book printed by John Day in 1574, *Certaine Select Prayers Gathered Out of S. Augustines Meditations*.[1] The volume is part of a set of 13th-century pseudo-Augustinian devotional works, from which Day published other pieces beginning in 1567.[2] Day reprinted the 1574 collection in 1575, and again, claiming to be "corrected, and compared with an old auncient written Copye," in 1577 (*Augustine* in our Editions Collated, p. xlvii; "A Prayer Against the Devil" changes by a few words in this edition). Whether it was John or Richard Day who decided to insert "A Prayer Against the Devil" into the *WBP* beginning with *1577x,* he was probably motivated at least in part by the fact that *Certaine Select Prayers* was such a brisk seller. The prayer was also included in Bentley's 1582 *Monument of Matrones,* which mined other materials from the *WBP,* among the Lenten prayers (Bentley, 776–8).

By the early 1580s, this text was an expected part of most *WBP* editions that included more than three or four prayers (for reasons that are not clear, it seems to have been excluded from Elizabethan 32°s), and it was regularly reprinted through the middle of the 17th-century and then rarely, until disappearing before 1700.

The copy text is *1577x.* Of the editions chosen for collation with *1567,* only *1582* contains this text; we have added to the collation *Augustine* as the source text and *1588a* as a later example from a different, common format (two-column quarto).

A prayer against the Devil and his manifold temptations made by St. Augustine.

There wanted* a tempter, and thou wert the cause that he was wanting; there wanted time and place, and thou wert the cause that they wanted. The tempter was present, and there wanted neither place nor time, but thou heldest me back that I should not consent. The tempter came full of darkness as
5　he is, and thou didst hearten me that I might despise him. The tempter came

---

* lacked, was not

---

[1] *Certaine Select Prayers Gathered Out of S. Augustines Meditations* (London: John Day, 1574), F1r–3v. *STC* 924.

[2] On the history and context of these publications, see Julia D. Staykova, "Pseudo-Augustine and Religious Controversy in Early Modern England," in *Augustine Beyond the Book: Intermediality, Transmediality and Reception* (Leiden: Brill, 2011), 147–66.

armed and strongly, but to the intent he should not overcome me, thou didst
restrain him and strengthen me. The tempter came transformed into an an-
gel of light, and to the intent he should not deceive me, thou didst rebuke
him, and to the intent I should know him, thou didst enlighten me. For he
10 is that great red dragon, the old serpent, called the Devil and Satan, which
hath seven heads and ten horns, whom thou hast created to take his pleasure
in this huge and broad sea wherein there creep living wights innumerable
and beasts great and small: that is to say, divers sorts of fiends which practice
nothing else day nor night but to go about seeking whom they may devour,
15 except thou rescue him, O Lord Jesus. For it is that old dragon which was
bred in the paradise of pleasure, which draweth down the third part of the
stars of heaven with his tail and casts them to the ground, which with his
venom poisoneth the waters of the earth that as many men as drink of them
may die, which trampleth upon gold as if it were mire, and is of opinion that
20 Jordan shall run into his mouth, and which is made of such a mould* as he
feareth no man.

And who shall save us from his chaps†, O Lord Jesus? Who shall pluck
us out of his mouth, saving thou, O Lord, who hast broken the heads of the
great dragon? Help us, Lord. Spread out thy wings over us, O Lord, that we
25 may flee under them from the face of this dragon that pursueth us, and fence
thou us from his horns with thy shield. For this is his continual endeavour,
this is his only desire, to devour the souls which thou hast created.

And therefore we cry unto thee, my God, deliver us from our daily ad-
versary, who whether we sleep or wake, whether we eat or drink, or whether
30 we be doing of anything else, presseth upon us by all kind of means, assault-
ing us day and night with trains‡ and policies§ and shooting his venomous
arrows at us, sometime openly and sometime privily¶ to slay our souls.

And yet such is our great madness, O Lord, in that whereas we see the
dragon continually in a readiness to devour us with open mouth, we never-
35 theless do sleep and riot in our own slothfulness, as though we were out of
his danger, who desireth nothing else but to destroy us. Our mischievous en-
emy, to the intent to kill us, watcheth continually and never sleepeth, and yet
will not we wake from sleep to save ourselves. Behold, he hath pitched infi-
nite snares before our feet and filled all our ways with sundry traps to catch
40 our souls. And who can escape, O Lord Jesu, so many and so great dangers?
He hath laid snares for us in our riches, in our poverty, in our meat, in our
drink, in our pleasures, in our sleep, and in our waking. He hath set snares

---

* character
† jaws
‡ entrapments
§ stratagems
¶ secretly

for us in our words, and in our works, and in all our life. But thou, O Lord, deliver us from the net of the fowlers and from hard* words, that we may give
45   praise to thee, saying: Blessed be the Lord, who hath not given us up to be a prey for their teeth; our soul is delivered as a sparrow out of the fowler's net, the net is broken and we escaped.

Text sources: *Augustine, 1577x, 1582, 1588a*
Header: A prayer . . . and] Of the deuill and of *Augustine*   made . . . Augustine] *om Augustine*
Text: 1 wert] wast *1582, 1588a*   **2** wert] wast *1582, 1588a*   **5** hearten] harden *1582, 1588a*   **10** that great] the great *1582, 1588a*   **11** pleasure] pleasures *1582*   **13** fiends] frendes *1577x*   practice] practiceth *1588a*   **14** day nor] day or *1582, 1588a*   to go] goeth *1588a*   they may] he may *1582, 1588a*   **15** rescue] resist *1588a*   **15–6** which . . . pleasure] *om 1582, 1588a*   **17** casts] casteth *1582, 1588a* with his] his *1582*   **20** mould] moulde that *1582, 1588a*   **23** heads] head *1582, 1588a*   **23–4** the great] this great *1582, 1588a*   **27** only] odely *1577x*   **28** my God] O God *1582, 1588a*   **30–1** upon us . . . assaulting] vpon *1582*   **32** sometime openly and] *om 1582*   **35** riot] reioyce *1582, 1588a*   **38** wake] awake *1582, 1588a*   **40** so great] great *1582, 1588a*   **43** in our works] our workes *1582, 1588a*   **46** fowler's net] nette of a fouler *Augustine*   **47** escaped] bee escaped *Augustine*

Notes
7–8 angel of light: As in 2 Cor. 11:14.
10–2 great red dragon . . . sea: Combines the ten-headed dragon of Rev. 12 with the ten-headed beast from the sea in Rev. 13.
16–9 draweth . . . die: Drawing from Rev. 12:4, 12:15, and 8:11.
46 out of the fowler's net: Ps. 124:7.

* cruel

The Confession of Christian Faith

First printed in *1556* as the first item after the Preface in the Anglo-Genevan *Form of Prayers* (and thenceforth in subsequent editions). Unlike the majority of the *Form of Prayers*, the Confession has no textual precedent in the French Genevan service book, or, indeed, in Calvin's church. The model is, instead, the confession written by Valerand Poullain for the exile Francophone congregation he superintended at Glastonbury from 1551–53, and to which the English congregation at Frankfurt subscribed when they arrived there and shared a church building with Poullain's transplanted congregation in 1554.[1] The English confession is much shorter than the French one, and much more obviously an expansion and adaptation of the Apostles' Creed, the articles of which are printed, in the *Form of Prayers*, at the inside margins next to the corresponding sections of the confession. Most of that adaptation consists of interpreting the Creed in light of Calvinist theology. But the final section on the marks of the true Visible Church is strongly indebted to Poullain's confession, especially the non-Calvinist insistence that discipline is a third necessary condition (along with the word of God and the two sacraments of baptism and communion). The marginal annotation printed with it in the Genevan *Form of Prayers* does not, however, make reference to any theologians, but instead builds a dense lattice of scriptural proof texts. (Because the *WBP* copies of the confession never make use of any of the Genevan annotation, we have not included it here.)

"The Confession of Christian Faith" was first printed with a London edition of the *WBP* in *1569c*, where it precedes the private prayers. Although it retained that position in 32° Elizabethan editions that included it, it was more usually placed at the very end of the volume. It can be found in some printing series of every Elizabethan format other than octavos, and was one of the most common prose items included after the psalms. It became much less common after the Restoration, appearing only in copies with unusually long sets of household prayers, and seems to have disappeared from the book by the early 18th century.

The copy text is *1569c*. For the list of variant readings, we have collated it against *1556* (as the original), *1577*, and *1582*, which were chosen for collation for the critical edition of *1567*, and *1588a*, which represents a different and later line of textual transmission representative of the very common two-column quarto format.

---

[1] See *RR*, 117. Poullain's confession was first printed in *L'ordere des prieres et ministere ecclesiastique* (London: [T. Gaultier?], 1552), D5v-E4v.

The confession of Christian faith.

I believe and confess my Lord God eternal, infinite, unmeasurable, incomprehensible, and invisible, one in substance and three in person, Father, Son, and Holy Ghost, who by his almighty power and wisdom hath not only of nothing created heaven, earth, and things therein contained, and man af-
5 ter his own image that he might in him be glorified, but also by his fatherly providence governeth, maintaineth, and preserveth the same, according to the purpose of his will.

I believe also and confess Jesus Christ the only saviour and messiah, who, being equal with God, made himself of no reputation but took on him
10 the shape of a servant and became man in all things, like unto us (except sin) to assure us of mercy and forgiveness. For when, through our father Adam's transgression, we were become children of perdition, there was no means to bring us from that yoke of sin and damnation but only Jesus Christ our Lord: who giving us that by grace which was his by nature, made us (through faith)
15 the children of God; who, when the fullness of time was come, was conceived by the power of the Holy Ghost, born of the Virgin Mary (according to the flesh), and preached in earth the gospel of salvation, till at length by tyranny of the priests he was guiltless condemned under Pontius Pilate, then president of Jewry, and most slanderously hanged on the cross between two
20 thieves as a notorious trespasser, where, taking upon him the punishment of our sins, he delivered us from the curse of the law.

And forasmuch as he, being only God, could not feel death, neither, being only man, could overcome death, he joined both together and suffered his humanity to be punished with most cruel death, feeling in himself the
25 anger and severe judgement of God even as if he had been in extreme torments of hell, and therefore cried with a loud voice, "My God, my God, why hast thou forsaken me?"

Thus of his free mercy without compulsion he offered up himself as the only sacrifice to purge the sins of all the world, so that all other sacri-
30 fices for sin are blasphemous and derogate from the sufficiency hereof. The which death, albeit it did sufficiently reconcile us to God, yet the scriptures commonly do attribute our regeneration to his resurrection. For as by rising again from the grave the third day he conquered death, even so the victory of our faith standeth in his resurrection, and therefore without the one we
35 cannot feel the benefit of the other. For as by his death sin was taken away, so our righteousness was restored by his resurrection. And because he would accomplish all things and take possession for us in his kingdom, he ascended into heaven to enlarge that same kingdom by the abundant power of his Spirit, by whom we are most assured of his continual intercession towards
40 God the Father for us.

And although he be in heaven as touching his corporal presence, where
the Father hath now set him at his right hand, committing unto him the ad-
ministration of all things as well in heaven above as in earth beneath, yet is
he present with us his members, even to the end of the world, in preserving
45 and governing us with his effectual power, and grace; who, when all things
are fulfilled which God hath spoken by the mouth of all his prophets since
the world began, will come in the same visible form in the which he ascend-
ed, with an unspeakable majesty, power, and company to separate the lambs
from the goats, the elect from the reprobate. So that none, whether he be
50 alive then or dead before, shall escape his judgement.

Moreover, I believe and confess the Holy Ghost, God equal with the
Father and the Son, who regenerateth and sanctifieth us, ruleth and guideth
us into all truth, persuading most assuredly in our consciences that we be
the children of God, brethren to Jesus Christ and fellow heirs with him of
55 life everlasting. Yet notwithstanding, it is not sufficient to believe that God
is omnipotent and merciful, that Christ hath made satisfaction or that the
Holy Ghost hath his power and effect, except we do apply the same benefits
to ourselves which are God's elect.

I believe therefore and confess one holy Church, which as members of
60 Jesus Christ, the only head thereof, consent in faith, hope, and charity, us-
ing the gifts of God, whether they be temporal or spiritual, to the profit and
furtherance of the same. Which Church is not seen to man's eye, but only
known to God: who of the lost sons of Adam hath ordained some, as vessels
of wrath, to damnation and hath chosen others, as vessels of his mercy, to be
65 saved, the which in due time he calleth to integrity of life and godly conver-
sation* to make them a glorious Church in himself.

But that Church which is visible and seen to the eye hath three tokens
and marks whereby it may be known. First, the word of God contained
in the Old and New Testament, which, as it is above the authority of the
70 same Church and only sufficient to instruct us in all things concerning sal-
vation, so is it left for all degrees of men to read and understand. For without
this word neither Church, council, or decree can establish any point touch-
ing salvation. The second is the holy sacraments, to wit, of baptism and the
Lord's Supper, which sacraments Christ hath left unto us as holy signs and
75 seals of God's promises. For as by baptism once received is signified that we
(as well infants as others of age and discretion), being strangers from God
by original sin, are received into his family and congregation with full assur-
ance that, although this root of sin lie hid in us, yet to the elect it shall not
be imputed: so the Supper declareth that God, as a most provident father,
80 doth not only feed our bodies, but also spiritually nourisheth our souls with

---

* behaviour

the graces and benefits of Jesus Christ, which the scripture calleth eating of his flesh and drinking of his blood. Neither must we in the administration of these sacraments follow man's fantasy, but as Christ himself hath ordained, so must they be ministered, and by such as by ordinary vocation
85   are thereunto called. Therefore, whosoever reserveth and worshipeth these sacraments or, contrariwise, contemneth* them in time and place, procureth to himself damnation.

The third mark of this Church is ecclesiastical discipline, which standeth in admonition and correction of faults; the final end whereof is excom-
90   munication, by the consent of the Church determined, if the offender be obstinate. And besides this ecclesiastical discipline, I acknowledge to belong to this Church a politic magistrate, who ministereth to every man justice, defending the good and punishing the evil. To whom we must render honour and obedience in all things which are not contrary to the word of
95   God. And as Moses, Ezechias, Josias, and other godly rulers purged the Church of God from superstition and idolatry, so the defence of Christ's Church appertaineth to the Christian magistrates against all idolaters and heretics, as papists, Anabaptists, with such like limbs of Antichrist, to root out all doctrine of devils and men, as the mass, purgatory, *limbus patrum*,
100   prayer to saints and for the dead, free will, distinction of meats, apparel, and days, vows of single life, presence at idol service, man's merits, with such like, which draw us from the society of Christ's Church, wherein standeth only remission of sins, purchased by Christ's blood to all them that believe, whether they be Jews or Gentiles, and lead us to vain confidence in creatures
105   and trust in our own imaginations. The punishment whereof, although God oftentimes deferreth in this life, yet after the general resurrection, when our souls and bodies shall rise again to immortality, they shall be damned to unquenchable fire; and then we, which have forsaken all man's wisdom to cleave unto Christ, shall hear that joyful voice, "Come, ye blessed of my Fa-
110   ther, inherit the kingdom prepared for you from the beginning of the world," and so shall go triumphing with him, in body and soul to remain everlastingly in glory, where we shall see God face to face and shall no more need to instruct one another, for we shall all know him, from the highest to the lowest: to whom with the Son and the Holy Ghost be all praise, honour, and
115   glory now and ever. So be it.

FINIS.

---

* treats contemptuously

Text sources: *1556, 1569c, 1577, 1582, 1588a*
Heading: Christian faith] our faithe, Which are assembled in the Englishe
co[n]gregation at Geneua *1556*; the Christian fayth *1582, 1588a*
Text: 4 earth] & earth *1582, 1588a* things] al thinges *1582, 1588a* **10** except sin] synne except *1556* **13** that yoke] the yoke *1582, 1588a* our Lord] the
Lord *1582* **15** the fullness] that fulnesse *1582, 1588a* **17** length] the length
1577 **19** between] betwixt *1556* **20** where] when *1577* **25** as if] as *1582,
1588a* extreme] the extreme *1556* **27** free] *om 1582, 1588a* **31–2** The which]
Which *1582, 1588a* **35** benefit] benefites *1582, 1588a* his death] death *1556*
38 that same] the same *1582, 1588a* **42** at his] on his *1556* **43** earth] the earthe
1556, 1582 **46** all his] his holy *1582* **53** into all] vnto all *1582, 1588a* **57** his
power] this power *1556* **58** ourselves] vs *1582, 1588a* **65** which] whiche also
1556 **66** make them] make *1577* in himself] to him selfe *1556* **68** and marks]
or markes *1556* known] discerned *1556* **81** the graces] graces *1582* **86** contemneth] contemned *1569c* **87** to himself] himselfe *1582, 1588a* **91** discipline]
censure *1556* **92** politic] politicall *1556* **93** punishing] punisheth *1569c* **94** in]
in in *1577* **95** godly] good *1582, 1588a* **97** the Christian] Christian *1582, 1588a*
100 prayer] praiers *1582, 1588a* **101** presence] present *1577* **108** unquenchable]
inquencheable *1556* **109** that joyful] the ioyfull *1582, 1588a* **110** inherit] inherite ye *1556* **111** so shall] so will *1582* **113** to instruct one] one to instructe *1556*
for we] we *1582, 1588a* **116** FINIS] *om 1556*

Notes

23–7 This represents Calvin's interpretation of the *decensus*, a much-debated article
of the Creed in the 16th century. For discussion, see Catherine Ella Laufer, *Hell's
Destruction: An Exploration of Christ's Descent to the Dead* (2013; rpt. Abingdon and
New York: Routledge, 2016), 80–100.

62–3 The distinction between the Visible and Invisible Church was a Protestant accommodation of the Creed's insistence on a (continuously extant) catholic Church
while repudiating the medieval institutional church. For discussion, see Randall
Otto, "The Remnant Church," *Journal for Christian Theological Research* 7 (2002):
15–29.

63–6 With phrasing from Romans 9:22–3, this is a statement of Calvinist "double
predestination," in which God's eternal will has already determined the full number
of people who will receive the grace necessary for repentance and regeneration; see
Institutes Book 3, chp. 21. The Thirty-Nine Articles of the English Church are much
less clear on this point. See, for one discussion of the ambiguities of the Articles
regarding predestination, Beth Quitslund, "Protestant Theology and Devotion," in
Andrew Escobedo, ed., *Spenser in Context* (Cambridge and New York: Cambridge
University Press, 2016), 293–5.

82–5 Restricting the administration of sacraments to those do so by "ordinary vocation" is a prohibition both on the Catholic practice of reserving the consecrated host
for administration by non-priests later (e.g., to the sick) and also on practices accommodated by the *BCP*, such as baptism by midwives.

88–91 The Anglo-Genevan *Form of Prayers* included such an order for ecclesiastical discipline. The failure of the English Church to adopt one either in Edward or

Elizabeth's reign was a continual complaint from the more radical puritan community. (See pp. 570–71 above, as well as *RR*, 235–40.)

99–101 This is a fairly standard list of Catholic practices and beliefs attacked by Protestants in the course of 16th-century sectarian skirmishing. The Elizabethan Settlement would remove nearly all of them from the English Church, at least until the Arminian wing moved the question of free will back into contention in the 1620s. The exception is "distinction of meats, apparel, and days," which each retained some currency in either the *BPC* or in royal injunctions. The vestiarian controversy of the 1560s over ministerial garments, in fact, was the catalyst for early Calvinist puritan separatism. For a traditional view of the controversy, see Patrick Collinson, *The Elizabethan Puritan Movement* (Berkeley and Los Angeles: University of California Press, 1967), 61–83; for more recent insights, see Karl Gunther, *Reformation Unbound: Protestant Visions of Reform in England, 1525–1590* (Cambridge: Cambridge University Press, 2014), 189–217.

Appendix 4

(N.T.)

The Musical Revision of 1586

Background

In 1586 John Wolfe, under Richard Day's patent, published five editions of the *WBP* in which the tunes were systematically revised and corrected. They are as follows:

Edition	*STC* no.	Series	Columns/ Type	*HTI* Source	*WBP* texts set	Notes
1586a	2471	2/40	1 BL	✳P E16 a	66	–
1586b	2472	241.1	2 BL	✳P E29 a	61	With solfa letters
1586c	2472.5	241.2	2 BL	✳P E30 a	55?	Only copy incomplete
1586d	2473	8/61 (1.)	2 rom.	✳P E25 d	47	–
1586e	2473a	16/55	1 rom.	✳P E25 e	47	–

These are the only known editions printed in 1586, and they represent a full range of sizes, formats, and printing styles, from reading-desk folio to pocket 16°, and from the full canon of 66 tunes to the smallest number in any Elizabethan edition. They share some 238 changes of musical details not found in any earlier edition. The great majority of these were adopted in all but a few subsequent editions, and in the later Elizabethan Companions produced by East, Barley, and Allison. For these reasons we have thought it appropriate and practical to provide a separate edition of the tunes based on the revised versions, and to collate it with the later sources, rather than record the changes in the already substantial lists of variant readings attached to the *1567* tunes.

This revision has until now escaped attention. Musicologists have tended to lose interest in editions later than *1562a*, and to assume that the tunes thereafter were simply copied from that edition or its successors. That is the assumption of Frere, Frost, Illing, and Leaver. Historians of printing have found nothing unusual about the editions of 1586; nor have literary scholars, since the comprehensive revision did not extend to the texts. It first came to light in the 1980s when it became necessary to examine all musical editions of the *WBP* for the purposes of the *Hymn Tune Index*.

The extent and systematic character of the 1586 overhaul leaves no room for doubt that it was a planned and deliberate undertaking. But no mention or discussion of it has been found in contemporary documents, so we cannot be sure who supervised the process, or precisely why it was undertaken. Presumably Wolfe himself, as the effective heir to Day's privilege, at least approved the revision, and may have initiated it. The typesetters must have copied the revised tunes from a musical editor's script, whether it was a handwritten score, an annotated printed edition, or a list of revisions. Who was that musical editor?

The nature and likely motive of the changes allow for a reasonable conjecture. On the practical side, recent editions of the *WBP* had been disfigured by a growing number of misprints in the tunes. They largely failed to record melodic changes, including modernizing accidentals, that had taken place over more than twenty years of oral transmission. Above all, they reflected a lack of consistent underlying beats (as described on pp. 557–9) which would certainly have made difficulties for congregations attempting to maintain unity. The practice in London churches was no doubt the predominant influence and concern.[1] Any professional musician who was familiar with the tunes sung in a London parish church on Sundays, year in, year out, would have had reason to be provoked by the many anomalies and inadequacies in the printed tunes.

Some of the changes, however, reflect an ideological motive: a desire to restore the gravity emphasized by Calvin, by clearly distinguishing the psalm singing from secular music. The editor is likely to have been a musician with practical experience of directing psalm singing, who supported puritan ideas about congregational worship.

John Cosyn (d. 1609) was just such a man. He was a distinguished and highly reputed composer, in the contemporary opinion of Thomas Whythorne.[2] He lived in the parish of St. Martin Vintry, London, at least from 1569 to 1575, and may have been its parish clerk, the official appointed to lead the singing in

---

[1] All editions were supervised by the Days, assignees in close tandem with the Company of Stationers in the City of London, or the Company itself until Cambridge University challenged the Company's monopoly in 1628. The City itself harbored more than 100 parish churches. Evidence of varying versions of *WBP* tunes arising outside of London is not found in print until 1687: the first were printed at York in a tunebook compiled by Abraham Barber, parish clerk of Wakefield (see, for instance, *HTI* 90b, 153d–e, 161c, 162b).

[2] James M. Osborn, ed., *The Autobiography of Thomas Whythorne* (Oxford: Clarendon Press, 1961), 302, cited in Susi Jeans, "Cosyn, John," *The New Grove Dictionary of Music and Musicians* (London, 2001).

church.[3] He had just brought out his own Companion to the psalm book, *Musike in Six, and Five Partes*, and dedicated it to Francis Walsingham, praising him as a "patron of godliness and mainteiner of true religion."[4] His known puritan leanings made him more likely to take a serious interest in popular psalm singing than most of his peers. His Companion, like the five *WBP* editions of 1586, was published by John Wolfe.

In the thirty-eight tunes common to *1586a* and *Cosyn 1585* the great majority of revisions in pitch and rhythm correspond exactly, as is confirmed by the relative paucity of variants ascribed to *Cosyn 1585* in the list of readings below. The main differences are in text (Cosyn in his Companion substituted psalms for all six hymns whose tunes he used, showing a Calvinistic disapproval of unscriptural songs), key (he transposed fifteen tunes to suit the range of whichever voice part was to sing it in his arrangement), and added sharps (his harmonies often required them).[5]

It seems more than likely, then, that Cosyn himself was the musical editor who prepared the revised versions of 1586, under Wolfe's authority. If it was not he, it was someone who knew his work and used it as principal model.

Character of the Revisions

(1) *Rhythm.* Most notably, a systematic and determined effort was made to eliminate the rhythmic problems found in many of the tunes (see pp. 558–9). In *1556* Whittingham, apparently overimpressed by Calvin's edict against tunes that sounded too much like "table" music, had tended to avoid any sense of a strong regular beat, often by lengthening notes bearing important words such as "Lord" in the printed first stanza (for example Psalm 30, p. 119). This impediment to learning the tunes was partially corrected in *1558*, and haphazard improvements were made in some later editions (see pp. 539–41). Now came a systematic effort to return to the original model: the French psalter.

---

[3] See Brett Usher, "The Silent Community: Early Puritans and the Patronage of the Arts," *The Church and the Arts* (Diana Wood, ed.), Studies in Church History, 28 (Oxford: Blackwell, 1992), 295–7; cited in Mark C. Reagan, "John Cosyn's *Musike in Six and Five Partes* Newly Notated and Completed," master's thesis, Washington State University, 2010. We are indebted to Mr. Reagan for kindly placing his work at our disposal. For parish clerks' musical duties see *MEPC*, 1. 88–9.

[4] For further details of Cosyn's puritan views see below, p. 1015.

[5] For example, each of these variants, but no other, is present in *Cosyn 1585* as a source for Veni Creator. One group of consecutive tunes (Psalms 18, 21, 25, 30), especially Psalm 25, does show substantial rhythmic differences between *1586a* and *Cosyn 1585*, perhaps due to the carelessness of the printer who was assigned that group in *1586a*. But there are very few such differences elsewhere.

Many of these changes had been anticipated in *1577*, but not adopted in most subsequent editions. The degree of uniformity in the 1586 editions implies a positive editorial policy. The first tune in the book, Veni Creator, was turned into a perfect model of the standard common-meter psalm tune (called Pattern C on p. 558), with French-style semibreves at the beginning and end of every phrase, minims elsewhere, and rests after all phrases. This set the trend for the rest of the book. In Psalm 135 all traces of triple time were removed. Total war was waged on dotted notes: thirty-five dotted semibreves were replaced by minims, and only one retained; all thirty-one examples of the dotted-minim-and-crotchet pattern were replaced by two even minims. This was clearly a puritan initiative, obeying Calvin's strictures on anything suggesting domestic music-making (see p. 530).

The drive towards a uniform Pattern C was not absolute, however. Pairs of semibreves were treated more leniently: fifty-three removed, twenty-one retained.[6] (In Lord's Prayer (2), the trend was reversed, each line *gaining* a pair of semibreves.) Syncopations and "fourteener" patterns were retained; a few were even added. The other categories were also changed rather lightly. Some widely popular tunes of French or German origin, most notably Psalms 100, 104, and 111, were brought closer to the prevailing rhythmic pattern. An effort was made to clarify tunes whose rhythms had baffled earlier editors (Magnificat, Creed, Da pacem). Two tunes seem to have escaped the sweeping rhythmic reform (Lord's Prayer (1) and Psalm 88). Overall, however, the plan seems to have been to retain only two note lengths, as in the French psalter: semibreve and minim (with the exception of the final long).

(2) *Mode.* Efforts to modernize—or anglicize—the modal system are clearly present. Twenty-four sharps were added as accidentals, generally at cadences; it is more than likely that they were already in use, especially in London churches, where leading citizens would have been familiar with current trends in English secular art music. The endings of three tunes were drastically altered. Psalm 95, in its *1567* form a purely Aeolian melody that was losing popularity, had its final note changed from A to D and two C-sharps added elsewhere, converting it to D minor. Psalm 134, whose ending had given trouble to earlier editors, was transformed from a Mixolydian anomaly into a firm F major by a change in the final cadence. The last phrase of Psalm 147 was altered to avoid ending on a sharpened third degree. These larger changes, unlike the added sharps, would not have occurred spontaneously in the course of oral transmission, and again suggest deliberate action by an editor such as Cosyn.

In *1586b*, however, these changes could not easily be made without a thorough revision of the solfa notation, which, however desirable, was not attempted. Cadences with flat 7th degrees were allowed to remain in Psalms 18, 21, 68, 69,

---

[6] These figures are drawn from all 66 tunes, and thus are not directly related to those on p. 558, which refer only to the 46 tunes using 8- and 6-syllable iambic lines.

81, 119, 120, 121, 122, 124, 145, COMPLAINT, CREED, DA PACEM, LAMENTATION, and PRESERVE US, while they were usually sharpened in the other editions that retained those tunes. Only in PSALMS 126, 130, and 148 was a solfa letter changed to M (Mi) to sharpen a cadential leading note.

(3) *Melodic revisions.* The pitch of 45 other notes was altered. In some but not all cases there is an obvious reason. Some reduce or eliminate an unusual melodic leap;[7] many make a phrase more conventional.[8] It is difficult to be sure whether these are editorial innovations or spontaneous changes that had already happened.[9] Five of them had appeared in at least one earlier edition, *1583*. Nearly all are in tunes of English or Anglo-Genevan origin; the French and German tunes were mostly left alone. Probably this is because most of the French and German tunes were little used, owing to their unpopular meters. Also, of course, the French tunes had been approved by Calvin, and were not to be freely tampered with.

(4) *Tune selection.* In two cases, a different tune replaces the one in *1567*. The new PSALM 120 had already appeared in most editions, starting in 1569 (it has been collated below with *1569b*). Psalm 77 was now, for the first time, provided with the more popular triple-time version of its tune, identical to PSALM 81.[10]

(5) *Notation.* Time signatures were now consistently provided, ¢ in most cases. The proper signature was used for the three surviving triple-time tunes (PSALM 77, PSALM 81, and LAMENTATION). Note-values were modernized (i.e., halved) in all seven tunes where the semibreve had been the unit in *1567*.

Most later editions and Companions adopted these revisions. The main exceptions were those printed by Henry Denham, starting with *1588b*, which has therefore been collated with the tunes of *1567* in the main body of this edition. Thomas East carried out his own revision for *East 1592*, which drew on both the *1567* and *1586a* versions as well as those in *Day 1563*. Some of his changes, like those in *Cosyn 1586*, were due to harmonic considerations. *Barley 1598* and *Allison 1599* generally followed *East 1592*. Allison transposed many more tunes than East, so that he could comfortably assign them to the treble voice.

---

[7] For instance, two revisions in PSALM 77, phrase 6, and one in Psalm 135, phrase 4.

[8] For instance PSALM 88, phrase 6; PSALM 103, phrase 8.

[9] The 7th note of PSALM 1 may well have shifted in common use, because the opening phrase was otherwise identical to LAMENTATION OF A SINNER. A similar reason may have led to some other changes that replace unusual melodic formulations with more conventional ones. This type of change is common in secular folk songs.

[10] Surprisingly, three extra tunes appeared in *1586c* only, for Psalms 10 (the first half of PSALM 3), 115 (the whole tune of PSALM 3), and 116 (a "nonsense" tune based on PSALM 111). These presumably owe their existence to the whim of an individual printer. See pp. 1009–10 for further discussion of them.

Editing policy

The edition below is of the tunes, not the texts. It treats *1586a* as the copy-text for the tunes, since it is there that the revisions were most consistently applied. The other 1586 editions have been collated for variants.[11] In most later Elizabethan editions the standard of music printing declined steeply, and they have so many misprints that we did not think them worth considering. Two of the least faulty ones have been collated: *1595* and *1601a*. The Companions of Cosyn, East, and Allison have also been compared and collated. Some tunes in *Cosyn 1585* had two or more distinct settings, which are distinguished in the list of sources: for instance *Cosyn 1585 (1: a6 sextus; 2: a5 altus)* means that *"Cosyn (1)"* in the list of variants refers to the six-part portion of the book, in which this tune is carried by the sextus part, and *"Cosyn (2)"* refers to the five-part portion, in which this tune is carried by the altus part.

Editorial principles and the conventions for listing variant readings are the same as those for the *1567* tunes, described on pp. xxxiv–xxxvii. Transpositions of tunes in the Companions are mentioned if they involve a key change, but not if the transposition interval is an octave. Rests between phrases are not recorded for the Companions, as they are often due to contrapuntal treatment of the melody.

The underlaid texts are those of the copy text, *1586a*. They differ in wording from the critical edition in Volume 1 in only four places.[12] In spelling and pronunciation the critical edition has been followed without change. The other sources of the tune have not been collated for details of the text, but if any of them has a wholly different text this fact has been noted under "text."

---

[11] The only surviving copy of *1586c*, at Winchester Cathedral, lacks its last gathering, and ends in the middle of the CREED tune. A later edition in the same format (*STC* 2483.5, *HTI* ✳P E30 b [c.1593]) shows the likely tune content of the missing pages, but it has not been collated here.

[12] Ps. 59, line 8: *still thirst* for *thirsteth*; Ps. 68, line 2: *in flight* for *to flight*; Ps. 113, line 7: *people* for *peoples*; Ps. 141, line 5: *prayer* for *prayers*.

Veni, Creator

Come Ho - ly Ghost, e - ter - nal God

pro - ceed - ing from a - bove,

Both from the Fa - ther and the Son,

the God of peace and love.

Vi - sit our minds, and in - to us

thy heaven - ly grace in - spire,

That in all truth and god - li - ness

we may have true de - sire.

Sources: *1586a, 1586b, 1586c, 1586d, 1586e, 1595, 1601a, Cosyn 1585 (1: a6 sextus; 2: a5 altus), East 1592, Allison 1599*

text Ps. 34 *Cosyn (1)*, Ps. 40 *Cosyn (2)* **key** A minor *Cosyn (1, 2)* **1** 3 ♯ *Cosyn (1), Allison* / 9 *no rest 1601a* **2** 2–3 *s s 1601a* / 4 f' *1586c* / 7 *no rest 1601a* **3** 9 *no rest 1601a* **4** 2 c' *1601a* / 4–5 *s s 1601a* **5** 3 ♯ *Allison* / *no rest 1601a* **6** 5 e *1601a, East, Allison* **8** 1–2 *s m Allison*

Te Deum

We praise thee, God, we know-ledge thee

the on - ly Lord to be,

And as e - ter - nal Fa - ther all

the earth doth wor - ship thee.

To thee all an - gels cry, the heavens

and all the powers there - in:

To thee che - rub and se - ra - phin

to cry they do not lin.

Sources: *1586a, 1586b, 1586c, 1586d, 1586e, 1595, 1601a, Cosyn 1585 (a6 altus), East 1592, Allison 1599*

text Ps. 55 *Cosyn* **t-s** none *1586b, 1601a* **1** 8 *s East, Allison* **2** 1 *s East, Allison* **3** 4–5 *s s East, Allison* / 8 *s East, Allison* **4** 1 *s East, Allison* **7** 2 *s East, Allison* / 8 *s East, Allison* **8** 1 *s East, Allison* (*Cosyn, East* and *Allison* harmonize the final d with a G-major chord.)

BENEDICITE

O all ye works of God the Lord,

bless ye the Lord,

praise him and mag - ni fy him for e - ver.

Sources: *1586a, 1586b, 1586c, 1586d, 1586e, 1595, 1601a, East 1592, Allison 1599*
k-s open *1586d, 1586e* **1** 7 ♯ *Allison* **2** 3 ♯ *East, Allison* **3** 1 *no rest 1601a* / 1–2 *as East, Allison* / 5–7 *m. c m East, Allison* / 9 *s East, Allison*

BENEDICTUS

The on - ly Lord of Is - ra - el

be prais - ed e - ver - more;

For, through his vi - si - ta - ti - on

and mer - cy kept in store,

His peo - ple now he hath re - deemed

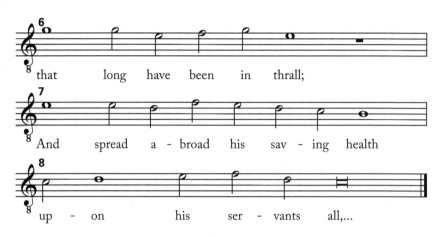

that   long   have   been   in   thrall;

And   spread a - broad   his   sav - ing   health

up - on   his   ser - vants   all,...

Sources: *1586a, 1586b, 1586c, 1586d, 1586e, 1595, 1601a, East 1592, Allison 1599*
text Venite (Ps. 95) *East, Allison*   **key** F major *East*; B♭ major *Allison*   **1** 4 s *East, Allison / 6 s East, Allison*   **8** 4–5 s s *East, Allison*

MAGNIFICAT

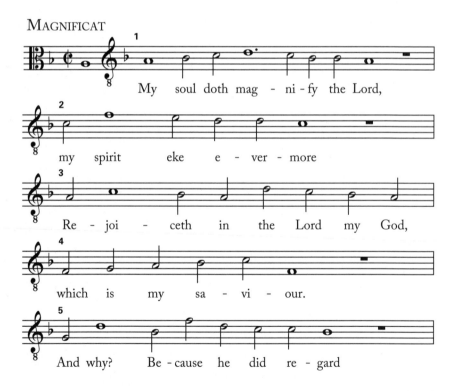

My   soul doth mag - ni - fy the Lord,

my   spirit   eke   e - ver - more

Re - joi - ceth   in   the   Lord   my   God,

which   is   my   sa - vi - our.

And why?   Be - cause   he   did   re - gard

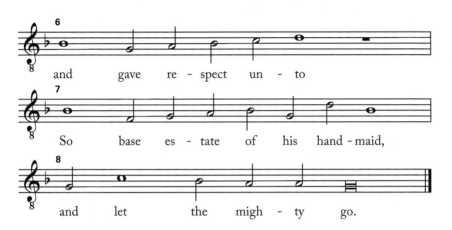

and gave re - spect un - to

So base es - tate of his hand - maid,

and let the migh - ty go.

Sources: *1586a, 1586b, 1586c, 1586d, 1586e, 1595, 1601a, East 1592, Allison 1599*
1 *4 s 1586a, East* **3** *1–2 s m East, Allison / 8 s East, Allison* **4** *1 s East, Allison / 2 g 1586b, 1601a, East, Allison*

NUNC DIMITTIS

O Lord, be - cause my heart's de - sire

hath wish - ed long to see

My on - ly Lord and sa - vi - our,

thy Son, be - fore I die,

The joy and health of all man - kind

de - sir - ed long be - fore,

Which now is come in - to the world,

of mer - cy bring - ing store,...

Sources: *1586a, 1586b, 1586c, 1586d, 1586e, 1595, 1601a, East 1592, Allison 1599*
1 *1–2 m s East, Allison / 6 s East, Allison*   **2** *5 ♯ East, Allison*   **3** *6 s East, Allison*
4 *7 no rest 1586b*   **5** *1–8 m s m s m s m s East, Allison / 4–5 s s 1586b, 1586e*   **8** *2 ♯ East,*
Allison

QUICUNQUE VULT

What man so - e - ver he be that

sal - va - tion will at - tain,

The ca - tho - lic be - lief he must

be - fore all things re - tain,

Which faith un - less he ho - ly keep

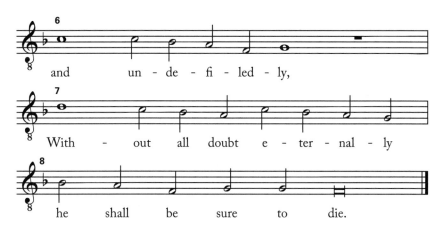

and un - de - fi - led - ly,

With - out all doubt e - ter - nal - ly

he shall be sure to die.

Sources: *1586a, 1586b, 1586c, 1586d, 1586e, 1595, 1601a, East 1592, Allison 1599*
1 1 c' *1586c* / 7 ♯ *Allison* **6** 7 no rest *1601a* **7** 8 s *East, Allison* **8** 1 s *East, Allison*

LAMENTATION OF A SINNER

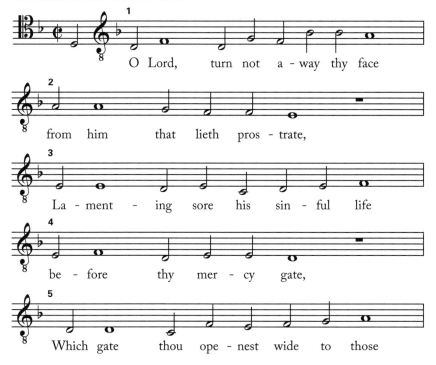

O Lord, turn not a - way thy face

from him that lieth pros - trate,

La - ment - ing sore his sin - ful life

be - fore thy mer - cy gate,

Which gate thou ope - nest wide to those

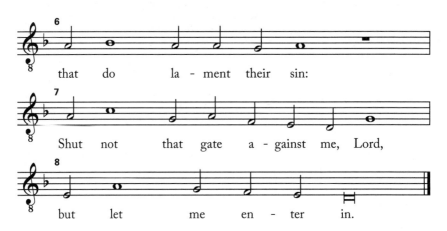

that do la - ment their sin:

Shut not that gate a - gainst me, Lord,

but let me en - ter in.

Sources: *1586a, 1586b, 1586c, 1586d, 1586e, 1595, 1601a, Cosyn 1585 (a6 sextus), East 1592, Allison 1599*

text Ps. 59 *Cosyn*   **key** G minor *Allison*   **t-s** none *1586a–e*   **1** 1–2 s s *East, Allison*
3 1–2 *m m 1601a*; *s m Allison*   **4** 1 d *East, Allison*   **5** 1–2 *s m East, Allison*; *m s. 1586b*
7 8 *m Allison*   **8** 1 s *East* / 2 g *1595* / 5 s *East, Allison* / 6 f *1586e*

Humble Suit

O Lord, of whom I do de -pend,

be - hold my care - ful heart,

And when thy will and plea - sure is,

re - lease me of my smart.

Thou seest my sor - rows what they are,

my grief is known to thee;

And there is none that can re - move,

or take the same from me,...

Sources: *1586a, 1586b, 1586c, 1586d, 1586e, 1595, 1601a, Cosyn 1585 (a6 quintus), East 1592, Allison 1599*

text Ps. 38 *Cosyn* **key** A minor *Cosyn*; G minor *Allison* **t-s** none *1586a* **1** 2 *s. East, Allison* **3** 1–2 *m s East, Allison* / 8 *s East, Allison* **4** 2 *s East, Allison* **6** 4–5 *m. c Allison* **7** 8 *s East, Allison* **8** 1 *s East, Allison*

LORD'S PRAYER (1)

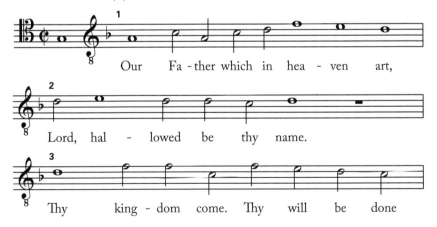

Our Fa - ther which in hea - ven art,

Lord, hal - lowed be thy name.

Thy king - dom come. Thy will be done

Sources: *1586a, 1586b, 1586c, 1586d, 1586e, 1595, 1601a, East 1592, Allison 1599*
t-s none *1601*

2 1-2 *s m East, Allison* / 5 ♯ *East, Allison* / 7 *no rest 1586b* **3** 8 ♯ *East* **4** 3 *s 1586e, 1595, East, Allison* / 4 ♯ *East* **5** 4 +*s-rest 1586b–d, 1601a* / 7 e' *1586a, 1595;* c♯ *East, Allison* **6** 2 *m. East, Allison* / 3 f *1586b–c;* bc *East, Allison* **7** 8 *m East, Allison* **8** 2 *m East, Allison* **9** 2 *m East, Allison* /4–6 -ta- *m.* -tion *c East, Allison* **10** 1 *s 1601a* / 2–3 bs c'*m 1586a* / 2 *s 1586b–d, 1601a* **11** 1 *m 1586b,* d *1595* / 3 f *1601a* / 4 f *1586b, s 1601a* **12** 1 c' *East, Allison* / 5 ♯ *East, Allison*

COMMANDMENTS (1)

Hark, Is - ra - el, and what I say

give heed to un - der - stand.

I am the Lord thy God that brought

thee out of E - gypt land,

Ev'n from the house where - in thou didst

in thrall - - dom live a slave:

None o - ther gods at all be - fore

my pre - sence shalt thou have.

Sources: *1586a, 1586b, 1586c, 1586d, 1586e, 1595, 1601a, East 1592, Allison 1599*
5 8 +*s-rest 1586db–d*　**6** 6 +*s-rest 1586b, 1601a*　**7** 3 b *East, Allison* / 7 ♯ *East, Allison*
8 4–5 a g♯ *Allison*

PSALM 1

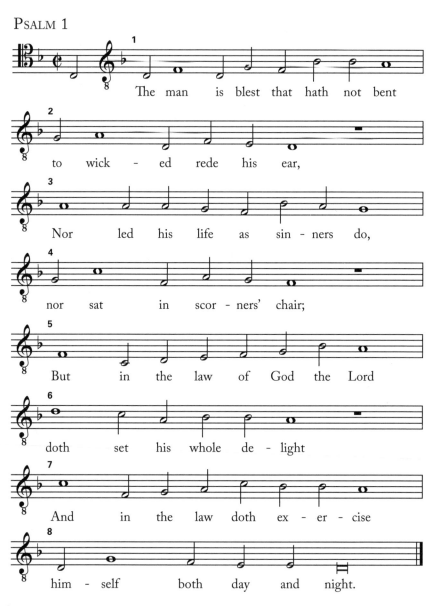

The man is blest that hath not bent

to wick - ed rede his ear,

Nor led his life as sin - ners do,

nor sat in scor - ners' chair;

But in the law of God the Lord

doth set his whole de - light

And in the law doth ex - er - cise

him - self both day and night.

Sources: *1586a, 1586b, 1586c, 1586d, 1586e, 1595, 1601a, Cosyn 1585 (a6 quintus), East 1592, Allison 1599*
key G minor *Allison*

PSALM 3

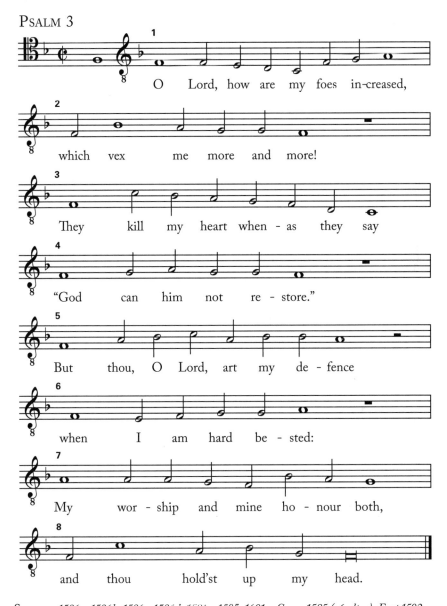

O Lord, how are my foes in-creased,

which vex me more and more!

They kill my heart when - as they say

"God can him not re - store."

But thou, O Lord, art my de - fence

when I am hard be - sted:

My wor - ship and mine ho - nour both,

and thou hold'st up my head.

Sources: *1586a, 1586b, 1586c, 1586d, 1586e, 1595, 1601a, Cosyn 1585 (a6 altus), East 1592, Allison 1599*

additional text Ps. 115 *1586c*   **key** C major *Allison*   **5** 8 m *1601a* / 9 no rest *1586e, 1595, 1601a*   **7** 8 +rest *1586b, 1601a*   **8** 3–4 f g *East, Allison*; f b *Cosyn*

PSALM 6

Lord, in thy wrath re-prove me not,
though I de-serve thine ire;
Ne yet cor-rect me in thy rage,
O Lord, I thee de-sire.
For I am weak; there-fore, O Lord,
of mer-cy me for-bear,
And heal me, Lord, for why thou knows't
my bones do quake for fear.

Sources: *1586a, 1595, East 1592, Allison 1599*
key A minor *Allison*   **4** *2–5 gs fm gs es East, Allison*   **5** *4 s East, Allison / 7 s East, Allison*   **7** *4–6 s s m East, Allison*   **8** *1 s East / 2 s Allison, ♯ East, Allison / 4–5 s s East, Allison*

PSALM 14

"There is no God," as fool - ish men
af - firm in their mad mood;
Their drifts are all cor - rupt and vain,
not one of them doth good.
The Lord be - held from hea - ven high
the whole race of man - kind,
And saw not one that sought in - deed
the liv - ing God to find.

Sources: *1586a, 1586b, 1586c, 1595, 1601a, East 1592, Allison 1599*
1 *4–5 s s East, Allison* **3** *4–5 s s East, Allison* **5** *4–5 s s East, Allison* **7** *4–5 s s East, Allison / 7 a 1586c, 1601a, East, Allison*

PSALM 18

O God, my strength and for - ti - tude,

of force I must love thee;

Thou art my cas - tle and de - fense

in my ne - ces - si - ty:

My God, my rock in whom I trust,

the wor - ker of my wealth;

My re - fuge, buck - ler and my shield,

the horn of all my health.

Sources: *1586a, 1586b, 1586c, 1586d, 1586e, 1595, 1601a, Cosyn 1585 (a6 quintus), East 1592, Allison 1599*

key D minor *Allison*   **1** 3 no ♯ *1586b, 1586d–e, 1601a, Cosyn, East, Allison* / 8 s *East, Allison*   **2** 1 s *East, Allison* / 6 +rest *1586b, 1601a, Cosyn*   **3** 8 s, ♯ *East, Allison*   **4** 1 s *East, Allison* / 5 no ♯ *1586b, 1586d–e, 1601a*   **5** 7 no ♯ *1586d–e, East, Allison* / 8 m *Cosyn*   **6** 1 m *Cosyn* / 6 ♯ *Cosyn, East, Allison*   **7** 8 m *Cosyn*   **8** 1 m *Cosyn* / 5 ♯ *East, Allison*

PSALM 21

O Lord, how joy - ful is the king

in thy strength and thy power:

How vehe - ment - ly doth he re - joice

in thee, his sa - vi - our!

For thou hast gi - ven un - to him

his god - ly heart's de - sire:

To him no - thing hast thou de - nied

of that he did re - quire.

Sources: *1586a, 1586b, 1586c, 1595, 1601a, Cosyn 1585 (a6 altus), East 1592, Allison 1599*
key A minor *Cosyn* **3** 5 g *1595, East, Allison* / 8 m *1586a, 1586c, 1601a* **4** 2 m *1586a,*
1586c, 1601a / 5 no ♯ *1586b, 1595, 1601a* **5** 1–2 s m *Cosyn* / 5 g *East, Allison* **7** 1–2 s m
1586a–b, 1601a, Cosyn

PSALM 25

I lift my heart to thee,

my God and guide most just;

Now suf - fer me to take no shame,

for in thee do I trust.

Let not my foes re - joice

nor make a scorn of me,

And let them not be o - ver - thrown

that put their trust in thee.

Sources: *1586a, 1586b, 1586c, 1586d, 1595, 1601a, Cosyn 1585 (1: a6 altus, 2: a5 altus), East 1592, Allison 1599*

key C major *Cosyn (1, 2)* **1** 7 no rest *1586c, 1595, 1601a, Cosyn (1)* **2** 1–2 s m *Cosyn (2)* / 4–5 s s *Cosyn (2)* **3** 4–6 m m m *Cosyn (1), East, Allison* **4** 1–2 m s *Cosyn (1), Allison* / 4–5 s s *Cosyn (2)* **5** 4–5 s s *Cosyn (2)* / 6 +rest *1586b, 1601a, Cosyn (2)* **6** 4–5 s s *Cosyn (2)* **7** 4–6 s m s *1586b–c, 1595, 1601a, Cosyn (2)* / 8 +rest *Cosyn (2)* **8** 4–5 m m *Cosyn (1), East, Allison*

Psalm 30

All laud and praise with heart and voice,

O Lord, I give to thee,

Which didst not make my foes re - joice,

but hast ex - alt - ed me.

O Lord my God, to thee I cried

in all my pain and grief:

Thou gav'st an ear and didst pro - vide

to ease me with re - lief.

Sources: *1586a, 1586b, 1586c, 1586d, 1586e, 1595, 1601a, Cosyn 1585 (a6 quintus), East 1592, Allison 1599*

key G minor *Allison* **1** 3 ♯ *East, Allison* **3** 8 ♯ *Allison* **5** 1 *s Cosyn, East, Allison / 2 m Cosyn; s. East, Allison* **7** 4 *s East, Allison / 6 s East, Allison / 7 ♯ East* **8** 4 *s Allison / 5 s East, Allison*

PSALM 35

1 Lord, plead my cause a-gainst my foes,

2 con - found their force and might:

3 Fight on my part a - gainst all those

4 that seek with me to fight.

5 Lay hand up - on thy spear and shield,

6 thy - self in ar - mour dress:

7 Stand up for me and fight the field

8 to help me from dis - tress.

Sources: *1586a, 1595*
2 *7 no rest 1595*

PSALM 41

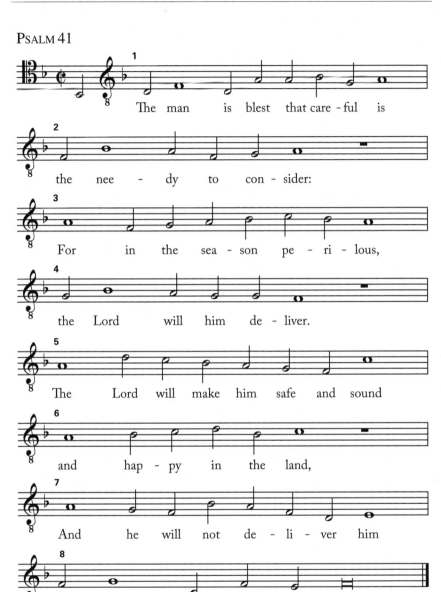

The man is blest that care - ful is

the nee - dy to con - sider:

For in the sea - son pe - ri - lous,

the Lord will him de - liver.

The Lord will make him safe and sound

and hap - py in the land,

And he will not de - li - ver him

in - to his en' - mies' hand.

Sources: *1586a, 1586b, 1586c, 1595, 1601a, East 1592, Allison 1599*
1 1–2 *s m East, Allison*   **2** 6 *m m East*   **4** 5 e *East, Allison* / 6 *m m East*   **5** 4–5 *m m*
6 5 ♯ *Allison*

PSALM 44

Our ears have heard our fa - thers tell

and rev' - rent - ly re - cord

The won - drous works that thou hast done

in ol - der time, O Lord:

How thou didst cast the Gen - tiles out

and stroy'dst them with strong hand,

Plant - ing our fa - thers in their place,

and gav'st to them their land.

Sources: *1586a, 1586b, 1586c, 1586d, 1586e, 1595, 1601a, Cosyn 1585 (a6 quintus), East 1592, Allison 1599*
key F major *Cosyn*

PSALM 46

The Lord is our de-fence and aid,
the strength where - by we stand:
When we with woe are much dis - mayed,
he is our help at hand.
Though th'earth re - move, we will not fear,
though hills so high and steep
Be thrust and hurl - ed here and there
with - in the sea so deep.

Sources: *1586a, 1586b, 1586c, 1586d, 1595, 1601a, East 1592, Allison 1599 (bassus)*
1 1–2 *s s. East, Allison* **2** 7 no rest *1586b, 1601a* **5** 1–2 *s s. East, Allison / 7 f 1601a*
6 4 e *East /* 7 no rest *1586b, 1601a* **7** 6–7 c d *East*

Psalm 50 (1)

The migh-ty God, th'e-ter-nal, hath thus spoke,

And all the world he will call and pro-voke:

Ev'n from the east and so forth to the west.

From toward Si-on, which place him lik-eth best,

God willl ap-pear in beau-ty most ex-cell-ent;

Our God will come, be-fore that long time be spent.

Sources: *1586a, 1586b, 1586c, 1586d, 1586e, 1595, 1601a, Cosyn 1585 (1: a6 tenor, 2: a5 altus), East 1592, Allison 1599*
key D minor *Cosyn (1, 2)* **t-s** none *1586e, 1601a* **5** 5 ♯ *East*

Psalm 50 (2)

The God of gods, the Lord,

hath called the earth by name

From where the sun doth rise un - to

the set - ting of the same.

From Si - on, his fair place,

his glo - ry bright and clear,

The per - fect beau - ty of his grace,

from thence it did ap - pear.

Sources: *1586a, 1595*
5 4 e *1595*

PSALM 51 (1)

O Lord, con - si - der my dis - tress,

and now with speed some pi - ty take:

My sins de - face, my faults re - dress,

good Lord, for thy great mer - cies' sake.

Wash me, O Lord, and make me clean

from this un - just and sin - ful act,

And pu - ri - fy yet once a - gain

my hei - nous crime and bloo - dy fact.

Sources: *1586a, 1586b, 1586c, 1586d, 1586e, 1595, 1601a, Cosyn 1585 (a6 quintus), East 1592, Allison 1599*
key G minor *Allison* **t-s** none *1601a*   **1** 4–5 *s. s 1595; s. m East, Allison*   **2** 1 f *1586c*
3 5 a *East, Allison*

PSALM 52

Why dost thou, ty - rant, boast a - broad,

thy wick - ed works to praise?

Dost thou not know there is a God

whose mer - cies last al - ways?

Why doth thy mind yet still de - vise

such wick - ed wiles to warp?

Thy tongue un - true in forg - ing lies

is like a ra - zor sharp.

Sources: *1586a, 1586b, 1586c, 1595, 1601a, East 1592, Allison 1599*
1 *6 c' 1586a / 8 s East*; *ds Allison* **2** *1 s East, Allison*; *m 1577 / 7 no rest 1586a* **3** *8 s East, Allison* **4** *1 s East, Allison* **7** *8 s East, Allison* **8** *1 s 1586b, East, Allison*

Psalm 59

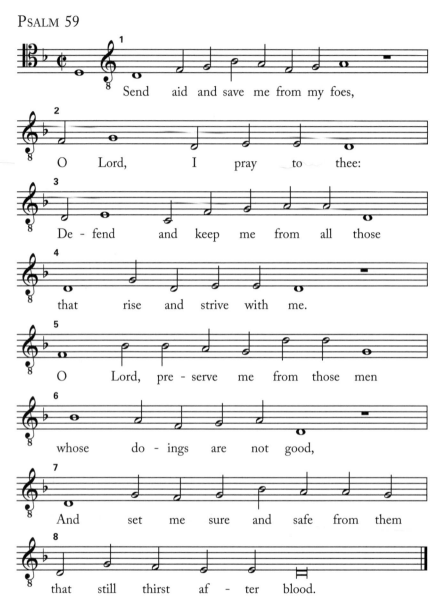

Send aid and save me from my foes,

O Lord, I pray to thee:

De - fend and keep me from all those

that rise and strive with me.

O Lord, pre - serve me from those men

whose do - ings are not good,

And set me sure and safe from them

that still thirst af - ter blood.

Sources: *1586a, 1586b, 1586c, 1586d, 1586e, 1595, 1601a, East 1592, Allison 1599*
key *G minor Allison* **1** *4 m. 1586b, s. East, Allison / 9 no rest 1586b, 1595* **2** *1–2 s m
East, Allison* **3** *1 s East, Allison / 2 fs. East, Allison* **5** *2 s. East, Allison* **6** *7 no rest
1601a* **7** *8 s East, Allison* **8** *1 s 1586b, East, Allison / 2 m. 1586b, East, Allison / 3 c East,
Allison*

PSALM 61

Re - gard, O Lord, for I com-plain
and make my suit to thee:
Let not my words re - turn in vain,
but give an ear to me.
From off the coasts and ut - most parts
of all the earth a - broad,
In grief and an - guish of my heart
I cry to thee, O God.

Sources: *1586a, 1586c, 1595, East 1592, Allison 1599*
key C major *Allison* **1** 2 *s. East, Allison* **3** 8 *s East, Allison* **4** 1 *s East, Allison* **7** 8
s East, Allison **8** 1 *s East, Allison*

PSALM 68

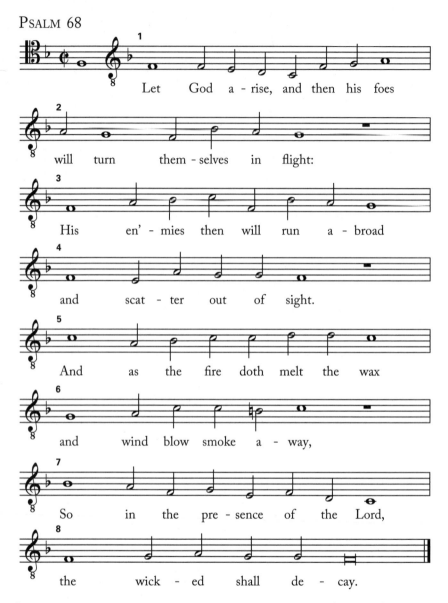

Let God a - rise, and then his foes
will turn them - selves in flight:
His en' - mies then will run a - broad
and scat - ter out of sight.
And as the fire doth melt the wax
and wind blow smoke a - way,
So in the pre - sence of the Lord,
the wick - ed shall de - cay.

Sources: *1586a, 1586b, 1586c, 1586d, 1586e, 1595, 1601a, Cosyn 1585 (a6 quintus), East 1592, Allison 1599*

t-s none *1586b, 1601a* **1** 6–7 *s s East, Allison* **2** 1–2 *s m Cosyn* **4** 3 f *East, Allison* **5** 3 ♯ *East* **6** 5 *no* ♯ *1586b, 1586d–e, 1601a, East* **8** 1 *m*-rest, *m Cosyn*; *es East, Allison* / 2 f *1595, East, Allison*

PSALM 69

Save me, O God, and that with speed,

the wa - ters flow full fast:

So nigh my soul do they pro - ceed

that I am sore a - ghast.

I stick full deep in filth and clay

where - as I feel no ground:

I fall in - to such floods, I say,

that I am like be drowned.

Sources: *1586a, 1586b, 1586c, 1586d, 1586e, 1595, 1601a, Cosyn 1585 (a6 altus), East 1592, Allison 1599*

key D minor *Allison* **t-s** none *1601a* **1** 4 *s. East, Allison* **2** 6 *no ♯ 1586b, 1586d–e, 1601a / 7 no rest 1586b, 1601a* **3** 7 ♯ *Cosyn, Allison / 8 s East, Allison* **4** 1 *s East, Allison / 5 no ♯ 1586b–e, 1601a* **6** 6 *no ♯ 1586b, 1586d–e, 1601a* **7** 8 ♯ *Cosyn, Allison* **8** 5 *no ♯ 1586b, 1586d–e, 1601a*

PSALM 72

Lord, give thy judge-ments to the king,

there - in in - struct him well;

And with his son (that prince - ly thing),

Lord, let thy jus - tice dwell:

That he may go - vern up - right - ly

and rule thy folk a - right,

And so de - fend through e - qui - ty

the poor that have no might.

Sources: *1586a, 1586b, 1586c, 1586d, 1586e, 1595, 1601a, East 1592, Allison 1599*
1 *4 s. East, Allison* **3** *2 s East, Allison / 8 m East, Allison* **6** *1 d' Allison/ 6 g♯ East, Allison / 7 no rest 1601a* **7** *7 f East, Allison*

PSALM 77

I with my voice to God do cry

with heart and hear - ty cheer:

My voice to God I lift on high,

and he my suit doth hear.

In time of grief I sought to God,

by night no rest I took

But stretched my hands to him a - broad;

my soul com - fort for - sook.

Sources: *1586a, 1586b, 1586c, 1586d, 1586e, 1595, 1601a, East 1592*
t-s ¢ *1586b, 1586d, East*; ¢3 *1586c, 1586e*   **1** *two m-rests before* 1 *1586c* / 2 *m East*   **2** 7–8 *s-rest 1601a*   **3** 6 *m 1586d*   **4** 4–5 *m s East* / 5 *no* ♮ *1586b, 1586d–e, 1601a, East* / 7–8 *s-rest 1601a*   **6** 7–8 *s-rest 1601a*   **7** 2 *s. 1586b*   **8** 4–5 *m s East*

Psalm 78

At-tend, my peo-ple, to my law,

and to my words in-cline:

My mouth shall speak strange pa - ra - bles

and sen - ten - ces di - vine

Which we our - selves have heard and learned

ev'n of our fa - thers old,

And which for our in - struc - ti - on

our fa - thers have us told:...

Sources: *1586a, 1586b, 1586c, 1586d, 1586e, 1595, 1601a, Cosyn 1585 (a6 sextus), East 1592, Allison 1599*

key *G minor Allison* **1** *1–2 s s. East, Allison / 8 s East, Allison; s, m-rest Cosyn* **2** *1 s East, Allison / 7 no rest 1595* **3** *6 s East, Allison; m, m-rest Cosyn* **4** *1 s East, Allison / 5 e East, Allison / 7 no rest 1595* **5** *8 s East, Allison* **6** *1 s East, Allison / 7 no rest 1595* **7** *1 m-rest, m Cosyn / 8 s East, Allison; s, m-rest Cosyn* **8** *1 s East, Allison*

PSALM 81

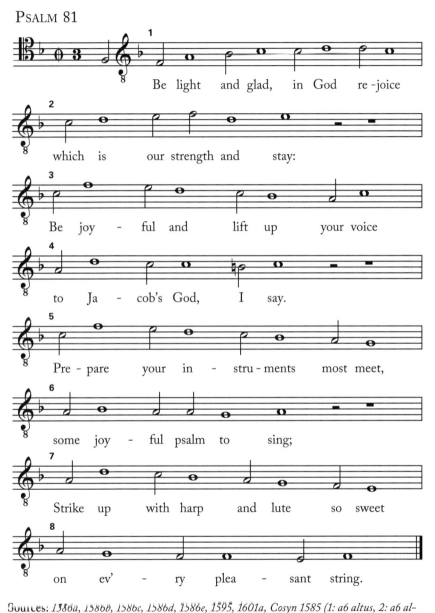

Be light and glad, in God re-joice

which is our strength and stay:

Be joy - ful and lift up your voice

to Ja - cob's God, I say.

Pre - pare your in - stru - ments most meet,

some joy - ful psalm to sing;

Strike up with harp and lute so sweet

on ev' - ry plea - sant string.

Sources: *1586a, 1586b, 1586c, 1586d, 1586e, 1595, 1601a, Cosyn 1585 (1: a6 altus, 2: a6 altus, 3: a5 altus), East 1592, Allison 1599*

text *Ps. 150 Cosyn (2, 3)*   t-s ¢ *East*; ¢3 *1586c, 1586e, none 1601a*   **1** *2 m East, Allison*
2 *7–8 no rests 1601a*   **3** *6 m 1586a–b, 158 d–e*   **4** *4–5 m s East, Allison / 5 no ♯ 1586b–e, 1595, 1601a, East*   **5** *2 m 1586a*   **6** *7–8 no rests 1595; s-rest only 1601a*   **7** *2 m 1586a*
8 *4–5 m s East, Allison*

PSALM 88

Lord God, of health the hope and stay

thou art a - lone to me:

I call and cry through - out the day

and all the night to thee.

O let my pray - ers soon as - cend

un - to thy sight on high;

In - cline thine ear, O Lord, in - tend

and hear - ken to my cry.

Sources: *1586a, 1586b, 1595, 1601a, Cosyn 1585 (a5 altus)*
key G major *Cosyn* **6** 3 b *1595* **7** 2 a*m 1586b*, d' *1595*

PSALM 95

Sources: *1586a, 1595*
No significant variants

PSALM 100

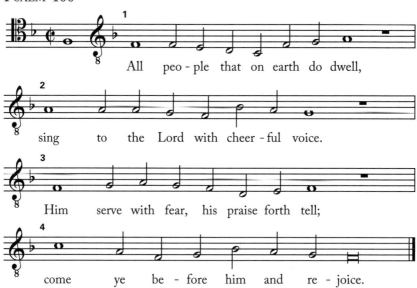

All   peo - ple   that   on   earth   do   dwell,

sing   to   the   Lord   with   cheer - ful   voice.

Him   serve   with   fear,   his   praise   forth   tell;

come   ye   be - fore   him   and   re - joice.

Sources: *1586a, 1586b, 1586c, 1586d, 1586e, 1595, 1601a, Cosyn 1585 (a6 altus), East 1592*
key C major *Cosyn*   **3** 1 *m 1601a*   **4** 6–7 *s s Cosyn, East*

Psalm 103

My soul, give laud un - to the Lord,

my spirit shall do the same;

And, all the sec - rets of my heart,

praise ye his ho - ly name.

Give thanks to God for all his gifts,

show not thy - self un - kind,

And suf - fer not his be - ne - fits

to slip out of thy mind:...

Sources: *1586a, 1586b, 1586c, 1586d, 1586e, 1595, 1601a, Cosyn 1585 (a6 quintus), East 1592, Allison 1599*

key C major *Allison*   **4** *2 s 1601a* / *6 +rest 1601a*   **6** *3 d' 1586a, 1595*

PSALM 104

My soul praise the Lord, speak good of his name;

O Lord our great God, how dost thou ap - pear

So pas -sing in glo - ry that great is thy fame.

Ho - nour and ma -jes - ty in thee shine most clear.

With light as a robe thou hast thee be -clad,

Where -by all the earth thy great -ness may see;

The hea -vens in such sort thou al - so hast spread

That it to a cur -tain com -pa - red may be.

Sources: *1586a, 1586b, 1586c, 1586d, 1586e, 1595, 1601a, Cosyn 1585 (1: a6 quintus, 2: a5 altus), East 1592, Allison 1599*

key G minor *Cosyn (1)*, D minor *Cosyn (2)* **4** 4–5 *s s East, Allison* **7** 4–5 *s s East, Allison* **8** 4–5 *s s East, Allison*

PSALM 111

With heart I do ac - cord

to praise and laud the Lord

In pre - sence of the just,

for great his works are found;

To search them such are bound

as do him love and trust.

His works are glo - ri - ous;

al - - - so his righ - teous - ness,

It doth en - dure for e - ver.

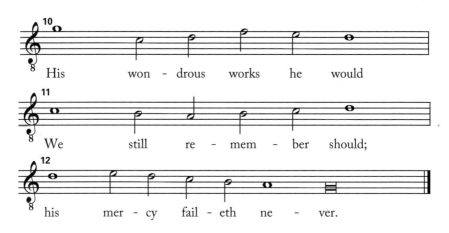

His   won - drous   works   he   would

We   still   re - mem - ber   should;

his   mer - cy   fail - eth   ne - ver.

Sources: *1586a, 1586b, 1586d, 1601a, Cosyn 1585 (a6 quintus), East 1592, Allison 1599*
1 6 *+rest 1586b*   **7** 1 g *(not g') East, Allison*   **9** 8 *no rest Allison*   **11** 5 ♯ *Cosyn, Allison*

PSALM 113

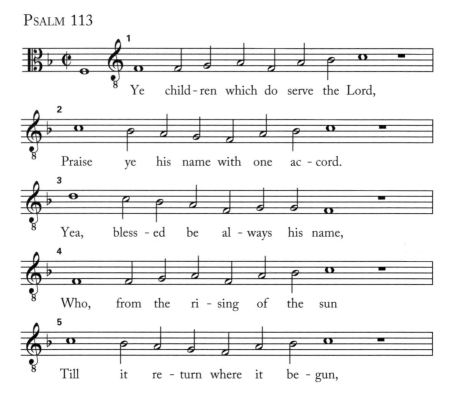

Ye   child - ren   which do   serve the Lord,

Praise   ye   his   name with   one   ac - cord.

Yea,   bless - ed   be   al - ways   his   name,

Who,   from   the   ri - sing   of   the   sun

Till   it   re - turn   where   it   be - gun,

6 Is to be prais - ed with great fame.

7 The Lord all peo - ple doth sur mount;

8 As for his glo - ry, we may count

9 A - bove the hea - vens high to be.

10 With God the Lord who may com -pare?

11 Whose dwel -lings in the hea - vens are,

12 Of such great pow'r and force is he.

Sources: *1586a, 1586b, 1586c, 1586d, 1586e, 1595, 1601a, Cosyn 1585 (1: a6 tenor, 2: a5 altus), East 1592, Allison 1599*
key C major *Cosyn (1, 2)*

PSALM 119

Blessed are they that perfect are
and pure in mind and heart,
Whose lives and conversation
from God's laws never start.
Blessed are they that give themselves
his statutes to observe,
Seeking the Lord with all their heart,
and never from him swerve.

Sources: *1586a, 1586b, 1586c, 1586d, 1586e, 1595, 1601a, Cosyn 1585 (a6 altus), East 1592, Allison 1599*

key G minor *Allison* t-s none *1601a* **1** 1–2 *m s East, Allison* / 3 ♯ *Allison* **2** 5 ♯ *Cosyn, East, Allison* **3** 4 d' *1586a* / 9 *no rest 1601a* **4** 5 ♯ *Cosyn, East, Allison* / 9 *no rest 1601a* **5** 3 ♭ *Cosyn* / 4 ♯ *Allison* / 7 *no* ♯ *1586b, 1586d–e, 1601a* **6** 2 ♭ *1586a* / 9 *no rest 1586b* **8** 5 ♯ *Cosyn, East, Allison* **11** 9 *no rest 1601a*

PSALM 120 (2)

1. In trou - ble and in thrall,
2. Un - to the Lord I call,
3. And he doth me com - fort.
4. De - li - ver me, I say,
5. From li - ar's lips al - way
6. And tongue of false re - port.

Sources: *1569b, 1586a, 1586b, 1586c, 1588b, 1595, 1601a, Cosyn 1585 (a6 tenor), East 1592, Allison 1599*

t-s none *1601a*   **2** *7 no rest 1586c, 1595, 1601a*   **3** *6 no ♯ 1586a–b, 1601a / 6 +rest 1588b*
4 *5 no ♯ 1586b, 1601a / 7 no rest 1601a*

PSALM 121

I lift mine eyes to Si - on hill,

From whence I do at - tend

That suc - cour God me send.

The migh - ty God me suc - cour will,

Which hea - ven and earth fram - ed

And all things there - in nam - ed.

Sources: *1586a, 1586b, 1595, 1601a, Cosyn 1585 (a6 quintus), East 1592, Allison 1599*
1 3 b *Allison,* 9 no rest *1601a*   **3** 1 c' *1586a* / 7 no rest *1601a*   **4** 7 no ♯ *1586b, 1601a*
5 7 s *Cosyn, East, Allison*   **6** 1 s *Cosyn, East, Allison*

PSALM 122

1 I did in heart re - joice

2 To hear the peo - ple's voice

3 In of - fer - ing so wil - ling - ly,

4 For "Let us up," say they,

5 "And in the Lord's house pray";

6 Thus spake the folk full lo - ving - ly.

7 Our feet that wan - dered wide

8 Shall in thy gates a - bide,

9 O thou Je - ru - sa - lem full fair,

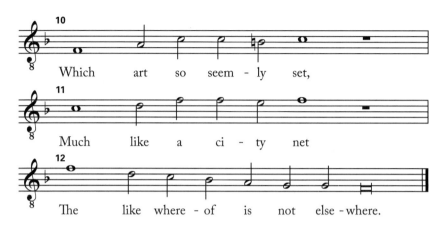

Which art so seem - ly set,

Much like a ci - ty net

The like where - of is not else - where.

Sources: *1586a, 1586b, 1586c, 1586d, 1586e, 1595, 1601a, Cosyn 1585 (1: a6 tenor, 2: a5 altus), East 1592, Allison 1599*

key C major *Cosyn (2)* **t-s** none *1601a* **1** *7 no rest 1586a, 1586c, 1595, 1601a* **2** *5 no ♯1586b–d, 1601a* **3** *9 no rest 1601a* **7** *7 no rest 1601a* **8** *2 f' 1586a* **10** *5 no ♯ 1586b–e, 1601a / 7 no rest 1601a* **11** *7 no rest 1601a*

PSALM 124

Now Is - ra - el may say, and that tru -ly,

If that the Lord had not our cause main -tained, -

If that the Lord had not our right sus -tained

When all the world a - gainst us fur -ious - ly

Made their up -roars, and said we should all die,...

Sources: *1586a, 1586b, 1586c, 1586d, 1586e, 1595, 1601a, Cosyn 1585 (1: a6 altus, 2: a5 altus), East 1592, Allison 1599*
key F major *Cosyn (1)*, G major *Allison* **2** 11 *no rest 1601a* **3** 11 *no rest 1601a* **4** 9 *no* ♯ *1586d–e, 1601a /* 11 *no rest 1601a* **5** 4–5 *s s 1586a, 1601a, East, Allison /* 8–9 *m m East*

PSALM 125 (1)

1 Such as in God the Lord do trust,

2 as Mount Si - on shall firm - ly stand

3 And be re - mov - ed at no hand;

4 the Lord will count them right and just,

5 So that they shall be sure

6 for e - ver to en - dure.

Sources: *1586a, 1586b, 1595, 1601a, Cosyn 1585 (a6 tenor), East 1592, Allison 1599*
No significant variants

Psalm 126

When that the Lord a-gain his Si-on had forth brought

From bon-dage great and al-so ser-vi-tude ex-treme,

His work was such as did sur-mount man's heart and thought,

So that we were much like to them that use to dream.

Our mou-thes were with laugh-ter fil-led then,

And eke our tongues did show us joy-ful men.

Sources: *1586a, 1586b, 1586c, 1586d, 1586e, 1595, 1601a, Cosyn 1585 (1: a6 altus, 2: a5 altus), East 1592, Allison 1599*

key G minor *Allison* **1** 11 ♯ *Cosyn (1, 2), Allison* / 13 *no rest 1601a* **2** 1 *m 1586b* / 11 no ♯ *1586b–e, 1601a* **3** 13 *no rest 1586b* **4** 3 ♯ *Cosyn (1), Allison* **5** 8–9 *m m East, Allison* **6** 2 b *1586a–e, 1595* / 4–5 *m m East, Allison* / 8–9 *m m East, Allison*

Psalm 130

1 Lord, to thee I make my moan

2 when dan - gers me op - press:

3 I call, I sigh, plain, and groan,

4 trust - ing to find re - lease.

5 Hear now, O Lord, my re - quest,

6 for it is full due time,

7 And let thine ears ay be prest

8 un - to this pray - er mine.

Sources: *1586a, 1586b, 1586c, 1586d, 1586e, 1595, 1601a, Cosyn 1585 (1: a6 altus, 2: a5 altus), East 1592, Allison 1599*
key D minor *Cosyn (1, 2)* **1** *8 no rest 1586c–e, 1595, 1601a, Cosyn (1)* **2** *4–5 s s Allison*
3 *2 ♯ Cosyn (1) / 8 no rest 1601a, Cosyn (1)* **4** *4–5 m m East* **5** *2–3 s s Allison / 8 no rest 1586c–e, 1595,1601a, Cosyn (1)* **7** *8 no rest 1586c–e, 1601a, Cosyn (1)*

PSALM 132

Re - mem - ber Da - vid's trou - bles, Lord,

how to the Lord he swore

And vowed a vow to Ja - cob's God

to keep for e - ver - more:

"I will not come with - in my house,

nor climb up to my bed,

Nor let my tem - ples take their rest

or the eyes in my head,..."

Sources: *1586a, 1586b, 1586d, 1586e, 1595, 1601a, Cosyn 1585 (a6 altus), East 1592, Allison 1599*
key C major *Allison*   **1** *2 s. East, Allison*   **5** *1 as Allison / 2 m Allison*   **6** *7 no rest 1586b, 1601a*

PSALM 134

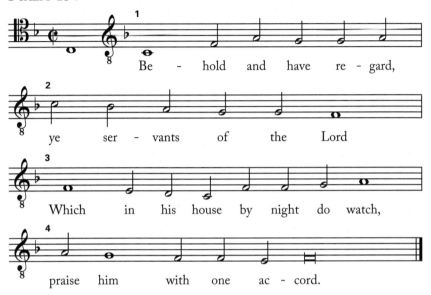

Sources: *1586a, 1586b, 1595, 1601a, East 1592*
1 *6 s East* **2** *1 s East / 6 +rest 1586b, 1601a* **4** *4–6 d e d East*

Psalm 135

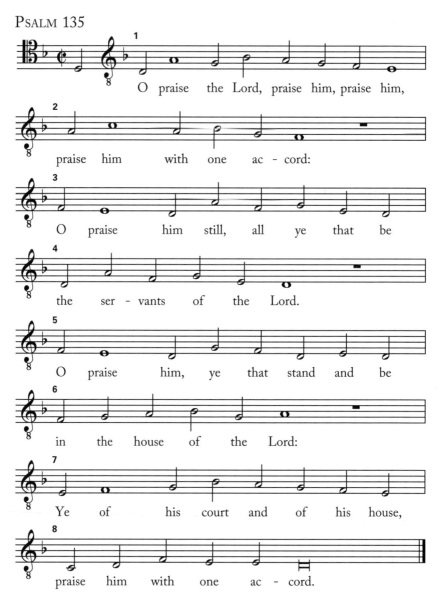

O praise the Lord, praise him, praise him,

praise him with one ac - cord:

O praise him still, all ye that be

the ser - vants of the Lord.

O praise him, ye that stand and be

in the house of the Lord:

Ye of his court and of his house,

praise him with one ac - cord.

Sources: *1586a, 1586b, 1586c, 1586d, 1586e, 1595, 1601a, East 1592, Allison 1599*
key G minor *Allison* **1** 7 a *1586a* **3** 4 s *East, Allison* / 7–8 s s *East, Allison* **4** 1 b
East, Allison / 2 s *East, Allison* **5** 4 s s *East, Allison* / 7–8 s s *East, Allison* **6** 2 s *East,*
Allison / 7 no rest *1586d, 1601a* **7** 4 e *1586b–e, 1601a* / 8 s *East, Allison* **8** 1 s *East, Al-*
lison

PSALM 136 (1)

Praise ye the Lord for he is good,

for his mer - cy en - dur - eth for e - ver:

Give praise un - to the God of gods,

for his mer - cy en - dur - eth for e - ver.

Give praise un - to the Lord of lords,

for his mer - cy en - dur - eth for e - ver:

Which on - ly doth great won - ders work,

for his mer - cy en - dur - eth for e - ver....

Sources: *1586a, 1586b, 1586c, 1595, 1601a, Cosyn 1585 (a6 tenor), East 1592, Allison 1599*
1 *2 ♯ Cosyn / 3 a 1586b / 5 s Cosyn / 7 s Cosyn / 9 no rest 1595, Cosyn*   **2** *4 ♯ East / 9 no rest 1595*   **3** *2–3 m m Allison / 9 no rest Cosyn*   **4** *7 ♯ East / 9 no rest 1595*   **5** *2–3 m m East, Allison / 6 c' 1586c / 9 no rest 1595, Cosyn*   **6** *4 ♯ East / 9 no rest 1595*   **7** *2–3 m m East, Allison / 9 no rest 1586a–c, 1595, 1601a, Cosyn*   **8** *7 ♯ East, Allison*

Psalm 137

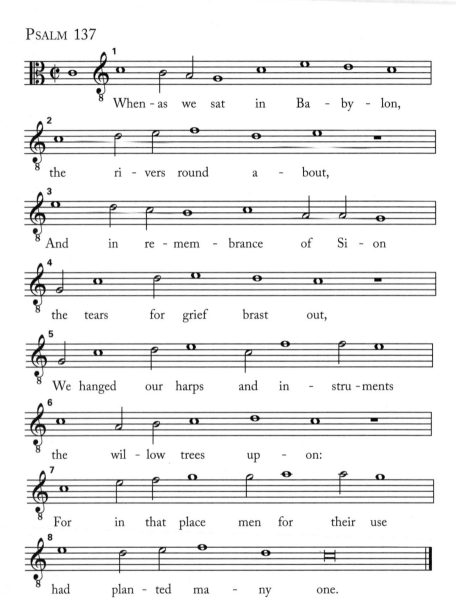

When-as we sat in Ba - by - lon,

the ri - vers round a - bout,

And in re - mem - brance of Si - on

the tears for grief brast out,

We hanged our harps and in - stru -ments

the wil - low trees up - on:

For in that place men for their use

had plan - ted ma - ny one.

Sources: *1586a, 1586b, 1586c, 1586d, 1586e, 1595, 1601a, Cosyn 1585 (1: a6 tenor, 2: a5 altus), East 1592, Allison 1599*

key B♭ major *Allison* **2** 7 *no rest 1601a* **5** 8 +*rest 1586b*

Psalm 141

1 O Lord, up - on thee do I call,

2 Lord haste thee un - to me;

3 And hear - ken, Lord, un - to my voice

4 when I do cry to thee.

5 As in - cense let my pray - er be

6 di - rec - ted in thine eyes,

7 And the up - lift - ing of my hands

8 as eve - ning sa - cri - fice.

Sources: *1586a, 1586b, 1595, 1601a, East 1592, Allison 1599*
key C major *Allison* **1** 6–7 *m. c East, Allison* / 8 *s East, Allison* **2** 1 *s East, Allison*
3 6–8 *m. c s East, Allison* **4** 1 *s East, Allison* **5** 7 *g East, Allison* / 8 ♯ *East,* s *East, Al-
lison* **6** 1 *s East, Allison* / 5 no ♯*1586b, 1595, 1601a* **7** 6–8 *m. c s East, Allison* **8** 1 *s
East, Allison*

Psalm 145

Thee will I laud, my God and King,

and bless thy name for ay:

For e - ver will I praise thy name

and bless thee day by day.

Great is the Lord, most wor - thy praise,

his great - ness none can reach:

From race to race they shall thy works

praise and thy pow - er preach.

Sources: *1586a, 1586b, 1586d, 1586e, 1595, 1601a, Cosyn 1585 (a6 quintus), East 1592, Allison 1599*

key C major *Cosyn,* G major *Allison* **1** 8 s *East, Allison* **2** 1 s *East, Allison / 2 c' Cosyn, East, Allison* **3** 8 s *East, Allison* **4** 1 s *East, Allison* **5** 8 m *1586e, 1595, Cosyn* **6** 1–3 s m. c *East, Allison / 5 g no* ♯ *1586b, 1586d, 1595, 1601a* **7** 8 s *East, Allison* **8** 1 s *East, Allison*

Psalm 147

Praise ye the Lord, for it is good
un - to our God to sing:
For it is plea - sant and to praise
it is a come - ly thing.
The Lord his own Je - ru - sa - lem
he build - eth up a - lone,
And the dis - persed of Is - ra - el
doth ga - ther in - to one.

Sources: *1586a, 1586b, 1586d, 1586e, 1601a, East 1592, Allison 1599*
key G minor *Allison* **1** 6–7 *m.c East* / 8 *s East, Allison* **2** 1–3 *s m. c East, Allison* **3** 8 *s East, Allison* **4** 1 *s East, Allison* **5** 8 *s East, Allison* **6** 1 *es East, Allison*; *em 1601a* / 7 *no rest 1601a* **7** 8 *s East, Allison* / 9 *m-rest 1564* **8** 1 *s East, Allison* / 1–6 c' b a g g f *(ends on F-major chord) East*

Psalm 148

Give laud un-to the Lord
From heaven, that is so high:
Praise him in deed and word
A-bove the star-ry sky.
And al-so ye, His an-gels all,
Ar-mies roy-al, Praise him with glee.

Sources: *1586a, 1586b, 1586c, 1586d, 1586e, 1595, 1601a, Cosyn 1585 (1: a6 altus, 2: a5 altus), East 1591 (1, 2), Allison 1599*
text Ps. 136 (2) *East (1)* **key** F major *Cosyn (1, 2)* **4** 2 *no* ♭ *1595 /* 4–5 *m m 1586a, Cosyn* **5** 4 *m Cosyn (1, 2) /* 5 *no rest 1601a, Allison, Cosyn (1, 2);* *m-rest 1586e* **6** 1 *s Allison / 3 no* ♭*1595*

COMMANDMENTS (2)

At - tend my peo - ple, and give ear,

Of fer - ly things I will thee tell;

See that my words in mind thou bear,

And to my pre - cepts lis - ten well.

Sources: *1586a, 1586b, 1586c, 1586d, 1586e, 1595, 1601a, Cosyn 1585 (a6 tenor), East 1592, Allison 1599*

text Ps.125 (2), stanzas 1, 2 *Cosyn* **1** *9 no rest 1586a, 1601a, East, Allison* **3** *9 no rest 1595, 1601a* **4** *8 s, s-rest Cosyn* (stanza 1)

Lord's Prayer (2)

Our Fa -ther which in hea - ven art

And mak'st us all one bro - ther - hood

To call up - on thee with one heart,

Our heav'n -ly Fa - ther and our God,

Grant we pray not with lips a - lone

But with the heart's deep sigh and groan.

Sources: *1586a, 1586b, 1586c, 1586d, 1586e, 1595, 1601a, Cosyn 1585 (1: a6 quintus, 2: a5 altus), East 1592, Allison 1599*
text *Ps. 127 Cosyn (1, 2)* **1–6** *4–7 m m m m East, Allison* **1** *9 no rest 1601a* **3** *7 no ♯ 1586d–e, 1595, 1601a* **4** *2–3 m. c Allison / 7 ♯ Cosyn (1), East, Allison*

CREED

Sources: *1586a, 1586b, 1586c* [incomplete], *1586d, 1586e, 1595, 1601a, East 1592, Allison 1599*

key C major *East* **1** *9 no rest 1601a* **3** *9 no rest 1601a* **6** *3 no ♯ 1601a, Allison* / 4–5 ma- d*m* -ny d*m* a d*m 1586e* **7** 1 c' *East, Allison*

DA PACEM

Give peace in these our days, O Lord,

Great dan - gers are now at hand:

Thine e - ne - mies with one ac - cord

Christ's name in eve - ry land

Seek to de - face, Root out and race

Thy true right wor - ship in - deed:

Be thou the stay, Lord, we thee pray:

Thou helpst a - lone in all need.

Sources: *1586a, 1586b, 1586d, 1586e, 1595, 1601a, East 1592, Allison 1599*
key G minor *Allison* **1** *6–7 m m East, Allison / 9 no rest 1595, 1601a* **2** *8 no rest 1601a*
3 *6–7 m m East, Allison / 9 no rest 1586e, 1601a* **4** *4 e- am -ve- em East, Allison / 8 no rest 1601a* **5** *4–5 m m East, Allison / 7 no ♯ 1586b, 1586d, 1601a / 9 no rest 1601a* **7** *7 ♯ East, Allison / 9 no rest 1601a*

COMPLAINT

Sources: *1586a, 1586b, 1586c, 1586d, 1586e, 1595, 1601a, East 1592, Allison 1599*
key G minor *East, Allison*   **1** *1–3 s m. c East, Allison*   **2** *1 m-rest, m 1586e, East, Allison
/ 5 ♯ East, Allison / 7 no rest 1601a*   **3** *1–3 m-rest m. c East, Allison*   **4** *1 m-rest, m East,
Allison / 5 no ♯ 1586c–e, 1601a / 7 no rest 1601a*   **5** *1 m-rest m East, Allison / 6 m 1586c /
7 no rest 1601a*   **6** *1 m-rest, m East, Allison*   **7** *1 m-rest, m East, Allison / 5 -nu- fm -al-
gm 1586c / 7 no rest 1601a*   **8** *1 m-rest m East, Allison / 2 s 1586b / 2–3 m m 1601a / 6 no
♯ 1586b–e, 1601a / 7 no rest 1586c*   **9** *1 m-rest, m East, Allison / 2 no ♯, m 1586b, 1601a / 3
no ♯ 1586b, 1586c, 1601a / 6 no ♯ 1586b–e, 1601a; d 1586d*

LAMENTATION

1. O Lord, in thee is all my trust:
2. Give ear un - to my woe - ful cry.
3. Re - fuse me not that am un - just,
4. But bow - ing down thy heaven - ly eye,
5. Be - hold how I do still la - ment
6. My sins where - in I do of - fend.

O Lord, for them I shall be shent,

Sith thee to please I do in - tend?

Sources: *1586a, 1586b, 1586d, 1586e, 1595, 1601a, East 1592, Allison 1599*
key G minor *East, Allison* t-s ¢ +inverted 3 *586e*; c *1586b, 1601a* **no sharps** *1586b,*
1586d, 1595, 1601a **1** 5 c♯ *East, Allison* / 8 +rest *1601a* **2** 8 +rest *1601a* **3** 8 +rest
1601a **4** 8 +rest *1601a* **6** 7 7 ♯ *East, Allison*

PRESERVE US

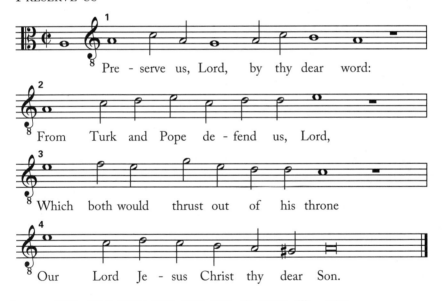

Pre - serve us, Lord, by thy dear word:

From Turk and Pope de - fend us, Lord,

Which both would thrust out of his throne

Our Lord Je - sus Christ thy dear Son.

Sources: *1586a, 1586b, 1586d, 1586e, 1595, 1601a, East 1592, Allison 1599*

key G minor *Allison* **1** 4 m *East, Allison* / 8 m *1586b, 1601a* / 9 no rest *1601a* **2** 9 *no*
rest 1601a **3** 9 *no rest 1601a* **4** 7 *no* ♮ *1586b, 1586d, 1601a*

APPENDIX 5
(N.T.)
OTHER TUNES FOUND IN
THE WHOLE BOOK OF PSALMS

This appendix encompasses all tunes that appeared in any edition of the psalm book published in England up to 1603, but are not among the sixty-six tunes of *1567*. (The exception is the 1569 tune for Psalm 120, which is included in the main sequence.)

Tunes of *1560a*

The first surviving Elizabethan edition, *1560a*, has no publisher's name on it. It may well have been issued by William Seres in an effort to assert his publishing privilege in rivalry with John Day. Two features of the music make this likely. One is that the musical editor, whoever he was, attempted a complete overhaul of all the tunes, making hundreds of changes, especially in the area of rhythm, as discussed on pp. 540–1. These were ignored in all Day's later editions, and have not been collated for this edition.

The other reason is that *1560a* contains nineteen tunes that were not taken up by Day in any edition from 1561 onwards. They are among those listed in Table 2. Most of them survived in the Scottish psalm book. They can be found in Frost in edited form, and are also presented in facsimile in Illing's *English Metrical Psalter 1562* (Adelaide, 1583), vol. 3. However, three tunes from *1560a* (PSALMS 1, 22, and 115), also listed in the table, were reprinted in some later editions of the *WBP*, but not in *1567*: these will be discussed in the next section.

Of the seven tunes that were new in *1560a*, four (BENEDICTUS, MAGNIFICAT, CREED, and LORD'S PRAYER (2)) were permanently adopted in the *WBP* along with their texts, and hence are found in their places in the edition. The other three (for the two versions of Psalm 67 and for Psalm 125) were never reprinted in the English psalm book, and so are included in this table.

Table 2. Tunes in *1560a* not in *1567*

Text	Author	Tune: HTI	Frost	First printing	Notes
Ps. 1	Sternhold	60	14	*1556*	Reprinted in *1564*: see below
Ps. 7	Sternhold	66a	23	*1556*	µ7
Ps. 9	Sternhold	68	26	*1556*	-
Ps. 10	Sternhold	61	16	*1556*	Originally for Ps. 2
Ps. 15	Sternhold	74	33	*1556*	-
Ps. 21	Sternhold	79	39	*1556*	-
Ps. 22	Norton?	75	34	*1556*	Originally for Ps. 16; and some later editions (see below); reprinted in *1564*; set by J. Hake in *Day 1563*
Ps. 23	Whittingham	80	41	*1556*	-
Ps. 29	Sternhold	83	49	*1556*	-
Ps. 37	Whittingham	115	59	*1558*	-
Ps. 67	Whittingham	26b	83	*1560a*	Adapted from a German hymn (Zahn 7247)
Ps. 67	Wisdom	132	82	*1560a*	-
Ps. 71	Whittingham	118	88	*1556*	-
Ps. 73	Sternhold	97	90	*1556*	-
Ps. 78	Sternhold	98a	94	*1556*	Set by J. Hake in *Day 1563*
Ps. 114	Whittingham	102	126	*1556*	Influenced by French Ps. 118 (Pidoux 66a, 118c); set by J. Hake in *Day 1563*
Ps. 115	Whittingham	103	127	*1556*	Reprinted in *1564*: see below
Ps. 125	Wisdom	133	141	*1560a*	From German Ps. 125 (Zahn 751)
Ps. 127	Whittingham	124a	146	*1558*	From French Ps. 127 (Pidoux 117a)
Ps. 129	Whittingham	125	148	*1558*	From French Ps. 129 (Pidoux 129a)
Ps. 133	Whittingham	108	151	*1556*	Set by J. Hake in *Day 1563*
Ps. 149	Pullain	127	175	*1558*	-

Other proper tunes not found in *1567*

The *1556* tunes for Psalms 1, 22, and 115 survived in English editions until 1564. But Psalm 1 was then superseded by another tune; Psalm 115 was eliminated; and Psalm 22 led a shadowy existence, recurring from time to time in certain editions and Companions.

In *1585* a new, short tune for Psalm 10 suddenly appeared, full of evident misprints; when properly printed in *1586c* it turned out to be the first half of Psalm 3. *1586c* repeated the tune of Psalm 3 for Psalm 115 and attempted to transfer that of Psalm 111 to Psalm 116, which did not fit its meter, resulting in a "nonsense" tune. These unexplained changes were copied in three later editions in the same format (see *HTI* ✳P 30).

In 1599 Thomas Schilders of Middelburg published an unauthorized edition of the *WBP*.[1] His innovation of printing the prose psalms in the margin proved to be popular in puritan circles, and was imitated by Peter Short in *1601b*. But his allocation of tunes was radically different from that of the *WBP*. Short, while following Schilders's format page by page, replaced many of his tunes. In particular, 20 tunes from the Scottish psalm book were unknown to English congregations. (Many of them were the very same tunes in *1560a* that Day had dropped, listed in Table 2 above.) Short replaced most of these. But Psalm 66 survived in several post-Elizabethan editions—almost, it seems, by accident.

Psalm 1 (Old Tune)

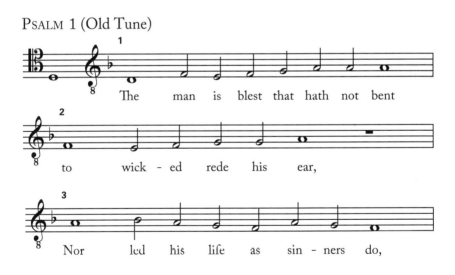

The man is blest that hath not bent

to wick - ed rede his ear,

Nor led his life as sin - ners do,

---

[1] Thomas Schilders, *The Psalms of David in Metre, with the Prose. For the Use of the English Church in Middelburgh*, Middelburg [United Provinces]: Richard Schilders, 1599. See Temperley, "Middleburg Psalms," and pp. 578–9 above

nor   sat   in   scor - ners'   chair;

But   in   the   law   of   God   the   Lord

doth   set   his   whole   de - light

And   in   that   law   doth   ex - er - cise

him - self   both   day   and   night.

Sources: *1556, 1558, 1560b, 1561b, 1561c, 1564*
k-s 1 flat *1556–61*   t-s ¢ *1556–61*
1 1 *m 1561b, 1561c* / 2 *s 1556–61* / 6 *s 1560b, 1564, s m 1561b, 1561c* / 8 *m 1561b, 1561c*
3 2 no ♭ *1564*   **4** 1 *m 1556* / 3 a *1561c* **5** 4 *s 1556–58* **6** 1 *m 1556* / 2–5 no ♭ *1564* /
7 no rest *1564* **8** 4 *s 1558–60, 1561c* / 5 *s 1556–60*

PSALM 10

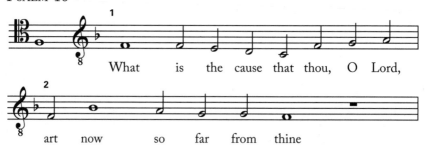

What   is   the   cause   that   thou,   O   Lord,

art   now   so   far   from   thine

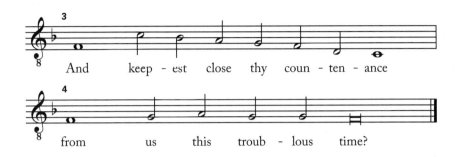

And keep - est close thy coun - ten - ance

from us this troub - lous time?

Sources: *1585, 1586c, 1592a*
clef on 3rd line *1585, 1592a*
1 6–8 a a f *1585, 1592a* **2** 1–3 b*s* a*m* g*m 1585, 1592a* **3** 3–8 b*m* a*s* g*m* g*m* d*m 1585, 1592a* **4** 1–2 c*s* f*s 1585*, m m *1592a* / 6 c's d*breve 1585, 1592a*

PSALM 22

O God, my God, where -fore dost thou

for - sake me ut - ter - ly,

And help - est not when I do make

my great com - plaint and cry?

To thee, my God, ev'n all day long

I do both cry and call;

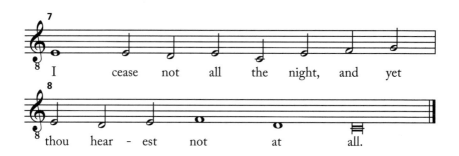

Sources: *1556, 1558, 1560b, 1564, 1570a, 1578a, 1601b, Day 1563, East 1592, Allison 1599*
text Ps. 16 *1556–60*, Ps. 20 *1601b*   **key** F major *1601b, East, Allison*   **t-s** ¢ *1556–60, 1601b, East* **1** *2–3 s s 1556–60 / 5 s 1601b, East, Allison*   **2** *2 s 1556–60, 1601b, East, Allison / 4–5 m m 1556–60, East / 7 no rest 1556–58, Day*   **3** *8 s 1556–60, 1601b, East, Allison* **4** *1 s 1601b, East, Allison / 2 s 1556–60 / 4–5 m m 1556–60*   **5** *6 m 1556–58 / 8 s. 1578a* **6** *1 s 1556–60, 1601b, East, Allison / 2 s 1560b / 4–5 s m 1556–60, m m 1601b, East, Allison* **7** *8 s 1556–60, 1601b, East, Allison* **8** *1 s 1601b, East, Allison / 2 s 1556–60 / 4 m 1556–58 / 5 m 1556 / 6 e 1556*

PSALM 66 (Scottish Tune)

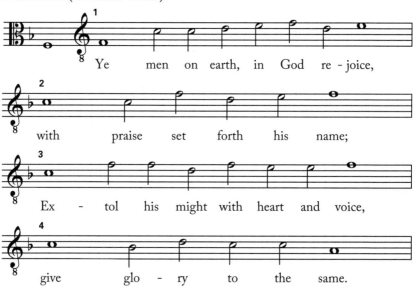

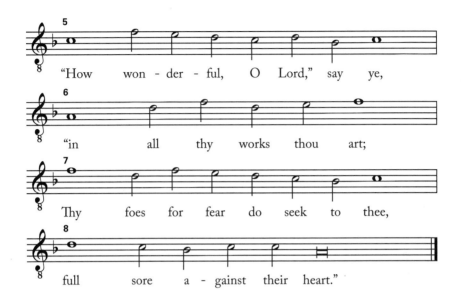

"How won - der - ful, O Lord," say ye,

"in all thy works thou art;

Thy foes for fear do seek to thee,

full sore a - gainst their heart."

Sources: *Scot1564, 1601b*
3 8 d' *Scot1564*   **6** 2 e' *Scot1564*

PSALM 115 (Whittingham's version)

Not un - to us, O Lord,

I say, to us give none,

But give all praise of grace and truth

un - to thy name a - lone.

Why   shall   the   Gen - tiles   say
to   us   as   in   de - spite,
"Where   is   the   God   they   call   up - on?
where   is   their   heart's   de - light?"

Sources: *1556, 1558, 1560a, 1561a, 1561c, 1561d*
t-s ¢ *1556–61* **3** 5 f' *1561c* **7** 2, 6 ♭ *1561a, 1561c, 1561d*

Common tunes

The ten tunes that follow represent an important trend that grew steadily in the latter half of Elizabeth's reign. Popular singing in the churches moved away from the proper tunes represented in the *WBP*, towards simpler, more memorable four-line common tunes, designed to be sung with any texts that fitted their meter. Because the texts were interchangeable, these tunes eventually acquired names, by which they are still known in many cases.

The common tunes never fully replaced the old ones in the printed psalm books. Indeed they could not replace those in irregular meters (mostly French in origin). Yet in 1594 Thomas East declared that "the Psalmes are song to these 4 tunes in most churches of this Realm" (*East 1594*, p.1), referring to three CM tunes (later named Oxford, Low Dutch, Cambridge) and one in SM (later named London). These were the only two meters sufficiently frequent among the *WBP* texts for common tunes to be useful. In 1592 East had set 92 texts to those four tunes, a number increased to 106 in his 1594 edition. These most popular tunes shared one characteristic: a small vocal range. East set a few psalms to other short tunes (see table). Slightly different selections of the short tunes were also printed in the Companions *Daman 1579, 1591, Cosyn 1585, Barley 1598,* and *Allison 1599*, all of them collections of psalm settings for domestic use (see

Appendix 6 below). Daman's editor in 1591 claimed that he had included "all the tunes of David's psalms, as they are ordinarily sung in the Church," suggesting that the common tunes he included were already in use there, even if they were not yet in the psalm books. Allison, adopting a more patrician stance, included at the end of his book "tenne short Tunnes . . . for the use of such as are of mean skill, and whose leysure least serveth to practice." Indirect evidence of the decline of the proper tunes in public worship lies in the increasingly negligent printing of them in the *WBP*, which by the 1590s had become so inaccurate that it can no longer have been serviceable for singers who wished to learn or perform tunes from the book.

In most cases the origins of the common tunes are unknown. With two exceptions,[2] they have not been positively identified with courtly songs, ballads, or any other secular source. Several seem to have come into existence by a process of reduction, or as subordinate voice parts to existing tunes.

To judge by East's collections, the common tunes were used only with those psalms and hymns for which the *WBP* did not provide proper tunes. The inference is that when the leading singers in a congregation—especially those who could read music—had the tune in front of them, however badly printed, the musical notation was a sufficient aid to their memories. If no tune was printed, but only a cross-reference to another long tune, it was easier to sing a shorter, simpler one by heart.

However, the *WBP* gradually accommodated a small number of the new common tunes here and there. Editions that did so, beginning with Henry Denham's of 1588, generally printed each tune only once, or at most a few times. The Middleburg editions, starting with *1601b*, used them more freely. A few new tunes appeared in *STC 2522* (1607), 2536.5 (1611), 2564.2 (1619). Yet most editions excluded them altogether, until the publication of Ravenscroft's Companion in 1621 provided a new stimulus.

Why were the publishers so reluctant to follow a popular trend? Apart from mere indolence or conservatism, it did make practical sense. If most of the psalms formerly lacking tunes were now being sung to the new tunes, the only way to cater fully for this would be to print a tune with every psalm (as East had). But this would greatly increase the size and expense of the book. If, on the other hand, people were singing the new tunes from memory anyway, there was no need to print them at all. The same reasoning lay behind the introduction and gradual increase of editions without any tunes, from 1590 onwards. Since almost everybody knew the tunes, only the words were strictly necessary.

---

[2] WINDSOR is markedly similar to a traditional tune for the song "How should I your true love know?", used in Shakespeare's *Hamlet*. This tune can be seen at http://www/8notes.com/scores/6679.asp (consulted October 4, 2011). OXFORD may have originated in the song "Pastime with good company," attributed to Henry VIII but also found as a French chanson printed in 1529. See *MEPC* 1: 69–70

The Elizabethan common tunes were augmented in 1621 by many more of the same kind, printed by Ravenscroft. Common tunes proved to be more durable than most of the proper tunes (the chief exception among the latter being OLD 100TH, which is itself a four-liner). By the late 17th century a group of about a dozen had become almost universal, and several of these, including three of the ten Elizabethan common tunes and OLD 100TH, have remained in continuous use until the present. It is difficult to think of any other Elizabethan music of which this can truly be said, though of course much has been revived in recent times.

We may now consider each of the ten Elizabethan common tunes that eventually reached the *WBP*, in chronological order of their first printing. The information is summarized in Table 3.

OXFORD, alone of the ten, originated in the Scottish psalm book. (See below, p. 1005. It can be heard at µ20, first stanza.) Uniquely, it begins on F and ends on G. It sounds vaguely Gregorian, but it is not close enough to any of the traditional psalm tones to suggest derivation from them. Thomas Campion wrote about OXFORD as follows:

> There is a tune ordinarily used, or rather abused, in our Churches, which is begun in one key and ended in another, quite contrary to nature; which errour first crept in through the ignorance of some parish Clarks, who understood better how to use the keyes of their Church-doores, then the keyes of Musicke, at which I not much mervaile, but that the same should passe in the booke of Psalmes set forth in foure parts, and authorised by so many Musitions [i.e., *East 1592*], makes me much amazed . . . What a strange unaireable change must the key then make from F. with the first third sharp [i.e., F major] to G. with B. flat [i.e., G minor].[3]

Campion quotes the tune as it had occurred in all printings to date, with F sharps in the second half only. He offers the solution of making all the F's sharp, so that the whole tune is in G minor. This advice was taken by Ravenscroft in 1621.

The Scottish psalm book, *Daman 1579, Cosyn 1585, East 1592,* and Denham's edition of the *WBP* (*1588b*) all chose different texts for the tune, and East treated it as one of the four most popular tunes "in this Realme." It was Ravenscroft who named it OXFORD. The Scottish name for it, from 1615, was OLD COMMON. Playford extended its compass a little (*HTI* 201e). He and later compilers most often set it to Psalm 4. After 1750 it rapidly dropped out of use in England, no doubt sounding archaic. Perhaps for the same reason William Cross's attempt to revive it in 1818 was unsuccessful. It is unknown to modern hymnals.

---

[3] Thomas Campion, *A New Way of Making Fowre Parts in Counter-point* (London: T. S. for John Browne, 1610), sig. D6v–7v.

Table 3. Common Tunes in Print by 1603

| Tune | | | | Origin and first printing | Texts set to tune in *East 1594* | In *WBP* Editions* | | English printings by 1820§ |
Name	Meter	Frost	*HTI*			first	no. by 1603	
Oxford	CM	121	201a	Ps. 108 in Scottish psalm book (1564)†	32	*1588*	15	486
Cambridge	CM	42b	249a,b	Ps. 23 (2) in *Daman 1579*	34	*1588*	18	761
Low Dutch	CM	19	250b	1st half of Ps. 33 in *Daman 1579*	36	*1588*	30	870
Southwell	SM	65	251	Ps. 45 in *Daman 1579*	0	*1588*	6	78
London	SM	45	269c	Ps. 65 in *Cosyn 1585*	4	*1605*	0	495
Windsor	CM	129	271a	Reduction of chap. 3 in Tye's *Actes of the Apostles* (1553) (Frost 297); Ps. 116 in *Daman 1591*	1	*1604*	0	837
Cheshire	CM	172	273a	Ps. 146 in *East 1592*	2	*1605*	0	98
Winchester	CM	103	276a	Reduction of chap. 2 in Tye's *Actes of the Apostles* (1553) (Frost 296), or of Ps. 77 in *WBP*, Ps. 84 in *East 1592*	0	*1605*	0	675
Glassenburie	CM	109	274a	counterpoint to Oxford Ps. 88 in *East 1592*	1	*1608*	0	158
Kentish	CM	111	275a	counterpoint to Glassenburie Ps. 92 in *East 1592*	1	*1622*	0	198

† *The Forme of Prayers and Ministration of the Sacraments . . . with the Whole Psalmes of David in Englishe Meter* (Edinburgh: Robert Lekprevik, 1564).

* Not counting editions published abroad.

§ In all forms: statistics compiled from the *Hymn Tune Index*

CAMBRIDGE appeared in three forms (see below, p. 996–8). Version A (μ22), the earliest, was printed in *Daman 1579* with Psalm 23 and was set to various texts in the later Companions, and in the Middleburg editions from *1601b*. Version B (and its double, version C) has a substantially different second half; it was the first to enter the *WBP*, with Psalm 103 in *1588b*, but version A soon prevailed. It was named CAMBRIDGE by Ravenscroft. It entered the Scottish psalm book in 1625 as LONDON. In England and America it lasted longest as a standard tune for Psalm 2 in Ravenscroft's or Playford's setting, but it began to fade from English collections after 1775. It is not in common use today.

Low DUTCH has a similar history, but more tangled. It originated as the first half of a tune introduced in *Daman 1579* (*HTI* 250a), but was first printed as a separate tune in *Cosyn 1585*, for Psalm 6. Cosyn's setting incorporated the four-line version (250b) twice, with the melody first in the tenor and then in the quintus voice. Henry Denham took it from there in *1588b*, printing it as an 8-line tune (Version B) but with the second half no longer quite identical to the first. This form was adopted by Windet in several later *WBP* editions. In its short form (Version A, μ21) it became the third of the all-pervading CM tunes in *East 1592*. It is unusual in being clearly in triple time in most early sources. It was one of two tunes (the other being Tallis's LAMENTATION) cited as an example by William Bathe in 1596.[4] The Scots named it ENGLISH in 1615. Ravenscroft called it DUTCH, then LOW DUTCH (meaning from the Netherlands as opposed to Germany, though there is no concrete evidence that it came from there). By the time Playford published it in 1658 (250h), the second half (lines 3–4) had changed to a form that may well have originated as a partial descant, and he called this version CANTERBURY. For a while both CM forms survived, sometimes in the same publication; they were popular with dissenters in the 18th century. CANTERBURY had won out by 1800, and remained in favor well into the 19th century, especially in North America, but it is no longer in common use.

SOUTHWELL naturally had far fewer printings than the other early common tunes, because its meter (SM) matched only a handful of texts in the *WBP*; moreover, it was passed over by both East and Playford. Named by Ravenscroft, it was only occasionally revived in the 18th century.

LONDON, with many minor changes, has maintained its popularity until the present time. East chose it as the common tune for SM texts. Ravenscroft's name for it, however, was overridden by Playford, who confusingly called it both CAMBRIDGE SHORT and SOUTHWELL; the latter name soon prevailed and still survives. In later editions of the *WBP*, and subsequently, the tune was often set to

---

[4] William Bathe, *A Brief Introduction to the Skill of Song* (London: Thomas Este, [1596]), sig. B4r.

Psalm 25. As Southwell it was by far the most popular SM tune in the 18th century.

Windsor, named Suffolk in the incipit index of *East 1594*, Windsor or Eaton by Ravenscroft, and Dundie in Scottish sources, was at first chiefly associated with Psalm 116 but acquired many other texts later. A variant, or partial bass, to the tune (271c) arose in an Irish source in 1698 under the name Dublin, also named Coleshill in England. Windsor was the most popular four-line common-meter tune in English-language publications up to 1820, the third most popular of all tunes, with 1,451 printings (see *HTI*, printed edition, 1. 61), and the seventh most frequently printed in American publications up to 1810.[5] The tune survived intact into *Hymns Ancient & Modern* (1861) and is still to be found in many modern hymnals.

Cheshire was given some currency by East, who named it on its first publication, and by Ravenscroft, but was passed over by Playford and was only moderately popular in the 18th century. It was successfully revived in *Hymns Ancient & Modern* (1861) with Edward Caswall's translation of a Latin hymn, "My God, I love thee; not because / I hope for heaven thereby."

Winchester (µ23) sounds like a revival of the lively domestic settings of Edwardian times, with its purposeful rhythm and dotted notes. Indeed, Frost believed that it originated in the second half of the tune for chapter 8 in Christopher Tye's *Actes of the Apostles* (*HTI* 53, Frost 302: see Frost 1962, p. 165), but it could equally be a reduction of the tune for Psalm 77,[6] and has a strong resemblance to part of Edwards's partsong "In going to my naked bed" (see p. 518). Possibly because of its secular, un-Calvinist character, East timidly assigned it to only one psalm and dropped it from later editions. But Ravenscroft named it Winchester and allocated it to seven psalms, and it has remained popular since his time. He also introduced a variant version named Dukes (*HTI* 276c). It took many other forms, some in different meters. A short-meter version (276d) introduced by Playford was favored in 18th-century dissenting circles; it was usually named Farnham and sung to Watts's paraphrase of Psalm 19, "Behold the lofty sky." The decisive triumph of Winchester (Old) came in 1861 when *Hymns Ancient & Modern* attached it to Tate & Brady's Christmas hymn, "While shepherds watched their flocks by night," which had been sung to many other tunes. This combination is now a permanent feature of the English Christmas season.

Glassenburie (µ20, stanza 3), later spelled Glastenbury or renamed after nearby Wells, originated as a descant or subordinate part to Oxford. Charles

---

[5] Crawford, *Core Repertory of Early American Psalmody*, lxxvii.

[6] Leaver, '*Goostly Psalmes*,' 305; Temperley, "Adventures of a Hymn Tune—I."

Butler in 1636 cited this as a happy example of melodious part writing: "Such as are all the four Parts of that *Oxford* Tune: the mean and Tenor whereof, in the Psalms set out by *Tho. East*, are (for their melodies) made two several Tunes, (under the names of Glassenburie and Kentish Tunes) with other Parts set unto them."[7] East named it on its first publication, but set it to only one psalm. It was used for several others before falling out of common use after about 1740.

KENTISH (μ20, stanza 5) works as a subordinate part to GLASSENBURIE, though not (despite Butler) to OXFORD. This also was set by East to only one psalm. Ravenscroft rechristened it ROCHESTER, a name that stuck. Playford drastically revised the second half of the tune (*HTI* 275b). In this form it retained some currency until about 1740.

CAMBRIDGE (Version A)   Psalm 9

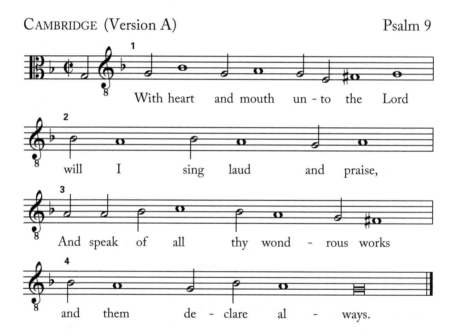

Sources: *1601b, Daman 1579, Cosyn 1585 (a6 altus*, stanza 1; *cantus*, stanza 2 [partbook missing]), *East 1592, East 1594, Allison 1599*
text Ps. 23 *Daman, Cosyn*, Ps. 12 *Allison* additional texts Ps. 23, 35, *1601b*; 29 psalms, Come, Holy Spirit *East 1592–94*; 4 further psalms, *East 1594*
t-s Ø *Cosyn* 1 6–7 *s m Daman* 2 6 *s. Cosyn* / *m*-rest at end *East 1592–94*, 3 *m*-rests *Cosyn* 4 6 *s Cosyn*

---

[7] Charles Butler, *The Principles of Musik, in Singing and Setting* (London: John Haviland, 1636), 44: spelling standardized.

CAMBRIDGE (Version B)   Psalm 103

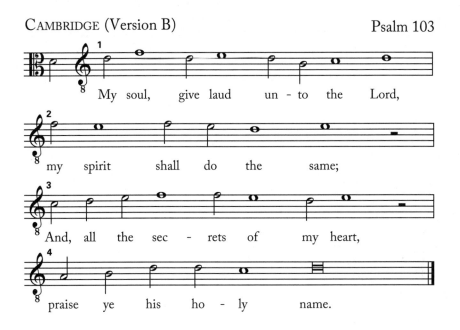

My soul, give laud un - to the Lord,
my spirit shall do the same;
And, all the sec - rets of my heart,
praise ye his ho - ly name.

Sources: *1588b, 1597a*
tune name first used in *Ravenscroft 1621* **2** 5 b *1597a*

CAMBRIDGE (Version C)   Psalm 103

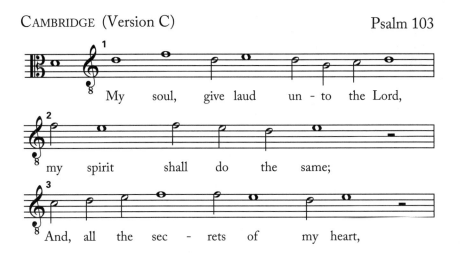

My soul, give laud un - to the Lord,
my spirit shall do the same;
And, all the sec - rets of my heart,

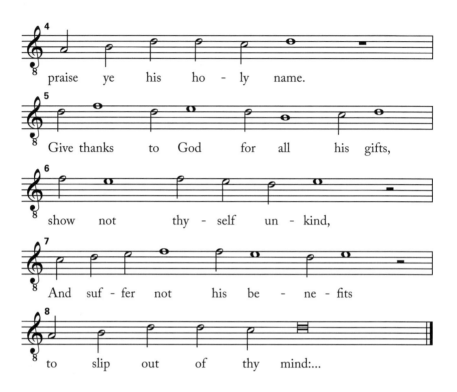

praise ye his ho - ly name.

Give thanks to God for all his gifts,

show not thy - self un - kind,

And suf - fer not his be - ne - fits

to slip out of thy mind:...

An 8-line version derived from Version B by nearly exact repetition
Sources: *1589, 1591, 1597b*
3 8 *m 1597b* / 9 no rest *1597b*   **6** 6 a*m 1597b*   **7** 8 c' *1597b*

CHESHIRE

Psalm 146

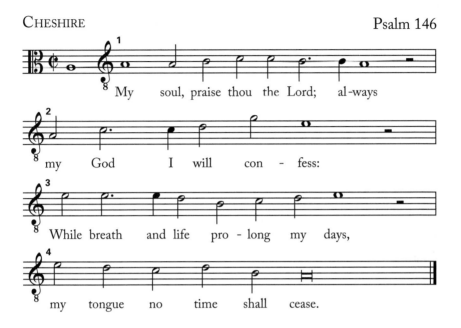

Sources: *East 1592, East 1594*
tune name first used in *East 1592*
additional text A Prayer for the Queen *East 1592–94*

GLASSENBURIE   Psalm 88

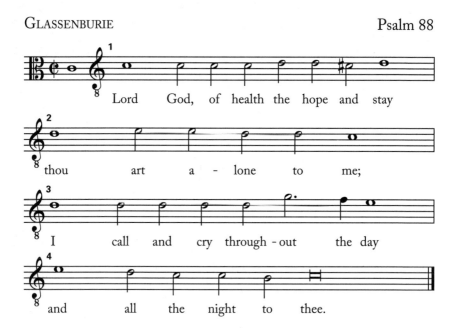

Lord God, of health the hope and stay thou art alone to me; I call and cry throughout the day and all the night to thee.

Sources: *East 1592, East 1594, Allison 1599*
tune name first used in *East 1592*

KENTISH

Psalm 92

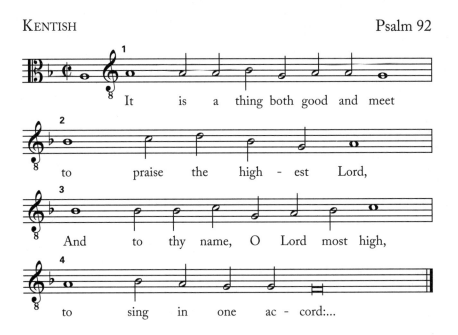

It is a thing both good and meet

to praise the high - est Lord,

And to thy name, O Lord most high,

to sing in one ac - cord:...

Sources: *East 1592, East 1594, Allison 1599*
tune name first used in *East 1592*
3 7 ♯ *Allison*

LONDON   Psalm 67

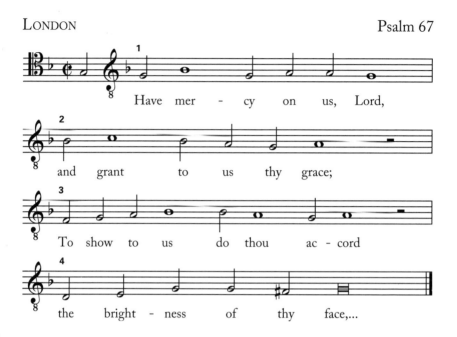

Have mer - cy on us, Lord,

and grant to us thy grace;

To show to us do thou ac - cord

the bright - ness of thy face,...

Sources: *Cosyn 1585 (a6 quintus,* stanza 1; *sextus,* stanza 2), *Daman 1591, East 1592, East 1594, Allison 1599*
tune name first used in *Ravenscroft 1621*; later named SOUTHWELL
additional texts Ps. 50, 70, *East 1592–94*; Ps. 45, *East 1594*
2 1 a *Daman 1591,* g *East 1592–94*

Low Dutch (Version A)

Psalm 15

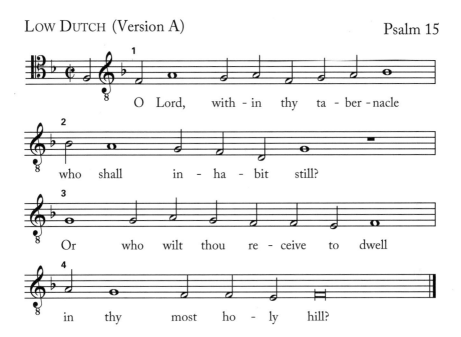

O Lord, with-in thy ta-ber-nacle
who shall in-ha-bit still?
Or who wilt thou re-ceive to dwell
in thy most ho-ly hill?

Sources: *1601b, Cosyn 1585 (a6 tenor, stanza 1; quintus, stanza 2), East 1592, East 1594, Allison 1599*

tune name first used in *Ravenscroft 1621*

text Ps. 6 *Cosyn,* Ps. 4 *Allison*

additional texts 9 psalms, *1601b*; 32 psalms, *East 1592–94*; 3 further psalms, *East 1594*

key C major *Cosyn, Allison* **2** 7 no rest *East 1592–94, Allison* **4** 1–2 s m *East 1592–94, Allison* / 4 d *Allison*

LOW DUTCH (Version B)   Psalm 6

An 8-line version produced by nearly exact repetition
Sources: *1588b, 1597a*
No significant variants (but compare **5** 5 with **1** 5)

OXFORD　　　　　　　　　　　　　　　　　　　　　　　　　　　Psalm 141

O Lord, up-on thee I do call,
Lord, haste thee un-to me:
And hear-ken, Lord, un-to my voice
when I do cry to thee.

Sources: *1588, 1597, 1601b, Daman 1579, Cosyn 1585 (a6 altus, stanza 1; [cantus, stanza 2, partbook missing]), East 1592, East 1594, Allison 1599*

tune name first used in *Ravenscroft 1621*

text Ps. 7 *1601b*, Ps. 26 *Daman*, Ps. 65 *Cosyn*, Ps. 17 *East 1592–94, Allison*

additional texts Ps. 28, 71, 95, 138, *1601b*; 24 psalms and A Thanksgiving after the Lord's Supper, *East 1592–94*; 6 further psalms, *East 1594*

key F major *1601b, East 1592–94*　　**t-s** Ø3 *Cosyn*, ¢ *East 1592–94*　　**1** 8 s. *Allison* / 9 no rest *Allison*　　**2** 6 s. *Cosyn, Allison* / 7 no rest *East 1592–94, Allison*　　**3** 6 ♯ *Cosyn, East 1592–94, Allison* / 8 ♯ *Allison*　　**4** 4 s *Cosyn* / 5 s *East 1592–94*; ♯ *Cosyn, East 1592–94, Allison* / 6 s *Cosyn*

SOUTHWELL   Psalm 134

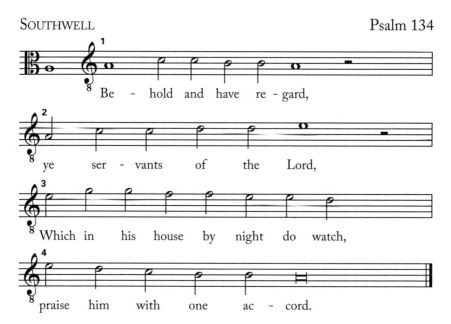

Be - hold and have re - gard,

ye ser - vants of the Lord,

Which in his house by night do watch,

praise him with one ac - cord.

Sources: *1588, 1597, Daman 1579, Cosyn 1585* (*a6 quintus*, stanza 1; *sextus*, stanza 2)
tune name first used in *Ravenscroft 1621*
text Ps. 45 *Daman*
key g *Daman*   **1** 1 *m*-rest *m Cosyn*   **3** 2–3 *m. c Daman* / 6–7 *m. c Daman* / rest at end *Daman*

WINCHESTER   Psalm 84

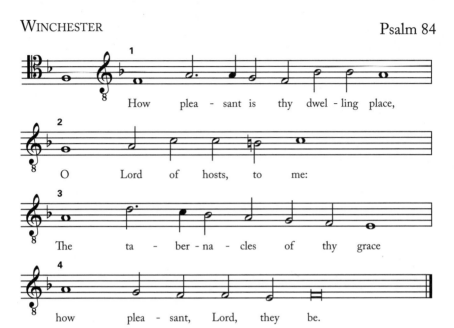

How   plea - sant is   thy   dwel - ling place,

O   Lord   of   hosts,   to   me:

The   ta - ber - na - cles   of   thy   grace

how   plea - sant,   Lord,   they   be.

Sources: *East 1592, East 1594, Allison 1599*
tune name first used in *Ravenscroft 1621*
key G major *Allison*

WINDSOR   Psalm 116

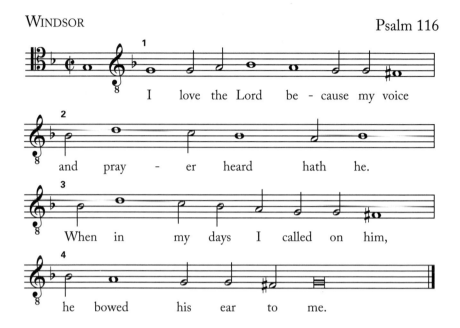

1. I love the Lord be-cause my voice
2. and pray - er heard hath he.
3. When in my days I called on him,
4. he bowed his ear to me.

Sources: *East 1592, East 1594, Allison 1599*
tune name first used in *Ravenscroft 1621*
2 1 preceded by *m*-rest *East 1592–94* / 7 no rest *Allison*

"Nonsense" tunes

These were the result of typesetters' incompetence. Thomas Schilders of Middelburg allocated some familiar proper tunes to additional psalms with which they were not previously associated. Peter Short, when imitating this edition with the prose psalms in the margin, decided to replace these—sometimes with more familiar long tunes, sometimes with common tunes from *East 1592*. His edition (*1601a*) was prepared by two different typesetters, each being assigned half the book, as is clear from the change of music font after quire P. Since they had no experience in setting up pages with prose in the margins, Short must have instructed them to copy Schilders's format page by page. When the intruding tunes were to be replaced with other long tunes, there was no problem with the layout. But what were they to do when they were replaced with common tunes, only half as long as the original ones?

The first typesetter solved the problem correctly by modifying page breaks, gradually using up the extra space. The second preserved the exact format of each page, following Short's instructions to the letter. To replace a long tune with a short one he needed four more phrases of music to fill the vacant space. If he had had any understanding of music he could have simply repeated the tune, as was done in some editions (see examples on pp. 997–8 and 1004). Instead, he followed the short tune with the second half of the long tune occupying the corresponding space in Schilders's edition, without any regard to musical considerations such as key, form, range, or melodic transition. Eight psalms were printed with such constructs, dubbed "nonsense" tunes in the *Hymn Tune Index* (see Table 4). Three of them were even copied in subsequent editions of the *WBP*. It may be doubted, though, whether they were ever sung.[8]

---

[8] For an earlier example of a "nonsense" tune see the note on Ps. 116 (p. 740).

Table 4. "Nonsense" Tunes in *1601a*

Psalm	*HTI*	Make-up of nonsense tune	Tune used from Schilders (1599)	Subsequent printings
95	201b	Oxford + 2nd half of Psalm 95	Psalm 95	none
96	250c	Low Dutch + 2nd half of Psalm 77	Psalm 77	3 editions, 1607–1640
115	250d	Low Dutch + 2nd half of Psalm 44	Psalm 44	12 editions, 1603–1643
129	249c	Cambridge + 2nd half of Psalm 137	Psalm 137	12 editions, 1603–1643
138	201c	Oxford + 2nd half of Psalm 3	Psalm 3	none
143	250e	Low Dutch + 2nd half of Psalm 119	Psalm 119	none
144	250f	Low Dutch + 2nd half of Psalm 145	Psalm 145	none
149	250f	same	Psalm 145	none

Appendix 6
(N. T.)
The Musical Companions to the Psalms

Between 1563 and 1633, several books were published that offered settings of the psalm tunes for four or more voices, with the option of doubling with instruments. For want of a contemporary term we have adopted Robert Illing's term "(Musical) Companions (to the Psalms)" as a generic name for these publications. They were designed for domestic use, for devout recreation, as their titles and prefaces clearly indicate, or possibly to accompany family prayers. There is little evidence that they were used in public worship in Elizabethan times, though John Milson reports that Brasenose College, Oxford, owned a copy of Day's Companion in 1588 and apparently used it in college services. The distinction between monophonic singing of the psalms in church and polyphonic singing at home was widespread in the Calvinist tradition. The settings described here correspond to those of Continental composers such as Bourgeois, Le Jeune, Goudimel, and Sweelinck, for multiple voices with or without instrumental accompaniment.[1]

The Companions cannot be called editions of the *WBP*. Until *East 1592* (a borderline case) they printed only the first stanza of each text with the music. But several of them influenced the selection and exact form of tunes printed in the *WBP*. Moreover they were produced by professional musicians, or at least skilled amateurs, and so represent a higher standard of accuracy and competence than was usually attained in the *WBP* itself. For these reasons they have been collated with the *WBP* for the present edition of the tunes: *Day 1563* in the main edition, the rest in Appendix 4.

The table distinguishes between "plain" and "motet" settings. Plain settings could serve to accompany singers, congregational or domestic, who are singing the tune in the simple form printed in the psalm book. Motet settings use the tunes phrases freely in one or more parts of vocal or instrumental polyphony, and would include consort songs for solo voice and instruments.

---

[1] See "Psalms, metrical, II," in *The New Grove Dictionary of Music and Musicians*; Louis Peter Grijp, "Psalms for the Lute in the Dutch Republic and Elsewhere," in Jan W. J. Burgers, Tim Crawford and Matthew Spring, eds., *The Lute in the Netherlands in the Seventeenth Century* (Cambridge: Cambridge Scholars Publishing, 2016).

Table 5. Summary of Contents of the Musical Companions

Publication	No. of voice parts	No. of texts set	No. of distinct tunes	No. of distinct settings	Composers of settings	Type of setting
Day 1563	4	79	89	143	Parsons + 6 others	134 plain, 9 motet
Daman 1579	4	68	67	67	1 (Daman)	motet
Cosyn 1585:						
part 1	6	43	42	43	1 (Cosyn)	plain
part 2	5	14	14	14	1 (Cosyn)	motet
Daman 1591 (1)	4	68	67	67	1 (Daman)	motet
Daman 1592 (2)	4	67	66	66	1 (Daman)	motet
East 1592	4	180	72	72	10	plain
East 1594	4	180	70	71	10	plain
East 1604	4	179	70	70	10	plain
East 1611	4	179	70	70	10	plain
Barley 1598	4	180	66	74	12	plain
Allison 1599	4	69	69	69	1 (Allison)	plain
Ravenscroft 1621	4	179	98	102	Ravenscroft + 21 others	plain
Ravenscroft 1633	4	179	98	102	Ravenscroft + 21 others	plain

Day 1563

Medius [etc.] *of the Whole Psalmes in Foure Partes, whiche may be Songe to Al Musicall Instrumentes, Set Forth for the Encrease of Vertue: and Aboleshyng of Other Vayne and Triflyng Ballades.* Imprinted at London by John Day. 1563.
　　4 partbooks: Medius, Contra Tenor, Tenor, Bassus.
　　STC 2431; on EEBO; *HTI* #WPFP. Modern edition in facsimile, also edited in score: Robert Illing (Adelaide, 1986).

John Day published this collection with the stated aim of replacing the "vain and trifling ballads" with which some young gentlemen entertained themselves. At the same time it served to introduce the recently developed body of psalm and hymn tunes to the more educated and influential portion of society.

Day claimed his royal privilege on the title page, but there is no evidence that he himself commissioned, supervised, or revised these four-voice tune settings. Some indeed have called the book "Parsons's Psalter," on the grounds that it contains far more settings attributed to "Parsons" than to any other musician (81 out of a total of 143; for an example see μ14). This is thought to be the William Parsons who was on the musical staff at Wells cathedral between 1552 and 1560. Three other substantial contributors, Richard Brimle(y) (11 settings), Thomas Caustun/Causton (26), and John Hake (18), also held positions at choral foundations; little is known of Nicholas Southerton (4). Of the two remaining pieces, one, Thomas Tallis's setting of The Lamentation (μ13), had already been printed in *Certaine Notes* (1560). The other, a setting of The Lord's Prayer (2), is attributed to "Edwards," identified by some scholars as Richard Edwards (1525–66), the prominent court poet and playwright who wrote the words and possibly the music of the still well-known partsong "In going to my naked bed."

All the texts that carry tunes in *1562a* are included in *Day 1563*, but only the first stanza of each is set, unless there is room for two on one page. The placing of Psalm 50 (1) and Psalm 100 (1) after the main numerical sequence points to *1563* as the *WBP* edition used as the main source. However, the selection of tunes is not identical to that of any edition. Indeed 13 of the 89 tunes, taken from earlier editions of the psalms, had already been excluded from *1562a* and are not to be found in any later edition or Companion. Most of these were arranged by Hake; if he died in 1559, as Peter le Huray tells us,[2] that offers a partial explanation. There are also ten new tunes (*HTI* 185–194) which were never adopted in the *WBP*, and may well have originated with Brimley and Caustun, who are credited with their settings.

All the tunes that eventually found their way into *1567* are here, but some are allotted to different texts. (These matters have been recorded in detail in the

---

[2] Peter le Huray, "Hake, John," in *The New Grove Dictionary of Music and Musicians* (London: Macmillan, 2001).

Notes on individual texts and tunes.) The book finally contains four prose an-
thems (Frost 187–90), each called a "Prayer," suggesting choral performance in
church. On the other hand the fact that only the first stanza of each metrical
psalm or hymn was printed made the book unpractical for church use. In con-
trast, the manuscript choir book described on pp. 518–20 had several stanzas of
each psalm in succession, all provided with music.

Some tunes are presented in more than one setting, often by different mu-
sicians: Psalm 44 has as many as five. The great majority have their tune in the
tenor, the normal choice in a culture where men dominated chamber singing:
the bass was needed to provide the harmonic foundation. Nine allot the tune to
the medius or mean (the topmost voice, normally sung by boys), two to the con-
tratenor, and five to the bass. Some settings preserve the irregular rhythms of
tunes taken from *1562a* or *1563*, others standardize them.

The musical level of the settings is mediocre at best, especially when com-
pared with other examples of a harmonized tune by leading composers of the
period, John Sheppard (μ5) and Tallis (μ13).

Daman 1579

> *The Psalmes of David in English Meter, with Notes of Foure Partes Set unto
> them, by Guilielmo Daman, for John Bull, to the Use of the Godly Christians for
> Recreatyng them Selves, in Stede of Fond and Unseemely Ballades.* At London:
> Printed by John Daye. 1579.
> 4 partbooks: Treble, Contratenor [lacking], Tenor, Bassus
> *STC* 6219; not on EEBO; *HTI* DamaWPD. Modern editions of se-
> lected tunes: Frost, nos. 42, 54, 65, 124, 142, 161, 176, 191

William Daman/Damon (c. 1525–91) was an Italian musician who came to Eng-
land in about 1565 as a servant of Thomas Sackville. A recorder player, he became
one of the Queen's musicians in 1579. This collection of his harmonizations, writ-
ten for the private enjoyment of friends, was published by John Bull without the
composer's permission.

The psalms and hymns are all opening stanzas of texts from the *WBP*. In ad-
dition to most of the proper tunes, Daman presented eight new ones (*HTI* 249–
256). Five of these are not found elsewhere, and hence are of little consequence,
but two are the earliest known sources of CAMBRIDGE and LONDON, which were
later to be among the most popular of common tunes (see Table 3, p. 996); the re-
maining one was the germ of a third common tune, LOW DUTCH. This suggests
that in 1579 these tunes were already in use in some churches. Fourteen settings
have the tune in the treble, one in the contratenor, 52 in the tenor, and one in
the bass. Most are of the motet variety: some have codas repeating the last line
of verse. But others present the tune in a simple form that has allowed collation
with the *WBP* version.

Cosyn 1585

> *Musike of Six, and Five Partes. Made upon the Common Tunes Used in Sing-ing of the Psalmes.* By John Cosyn. London: Imprinted by John Wolfe. 1585. (In two sections, the second with its own half-title, *Musike of Five Partes.*)
>   6 partbooks: Cantus [lacking], Altus, Medius, Tenor, Quintus, Bassus.
>   *STC* 5828; *HTI* CosyMSFP. All five surviving partbooks are on EEBO, but in incomplete form.
>   Not mentioned in Frost or reproduced by Illing.

John Cosyn (d. 1609) was a composer of high reputation who was closely associ-ated with several leading puritan families. This collection, however, is his only surviving musical work. In dedicating it to Francis Walsingham, the Queen's principal secretary, Cosyn praised him as a "patrone of godliness, and mainteiner of true religion"—that is, a staunch Protestant with puritan leanings.[3] In the preface Cosyn wrote: "Howsoever the abuse of Musicke may be great, when it is made an instrument to feed vaine delightes, or to nourish and entertaine su-persticious devotion: yet the right use thereof is commanded in singing Psalmes, and making melodie to God in our hearts." This is a classic statement of the pu-ritan approach to music, reflecting Calvin's views. In this case it appears that "supersticious devotion" included, for Cosyn, the singing of liturgical texts and original hymns that were not psalms. Accordingly, his selection from the *WBP* is confined to the psalms; and although he used six of the tunes associated with the hymns and canticles, in each case he replaced the *WBP* text (even if it came from the New Testament) with a psalm. Cosyn demonstrated superior skill in his arrangements, and a fondness for the French tunes that was not shared by the wider public.

The two halves of the collection differ in several respects. The first has 43 ar-rangements for six voices, all of the plain or homophonic variety; they cover more than half of the 66 proper tunes. In 37 of them the text of the first stanza is fully underlaid in all the voice parts, with the tune allotted to one of the four middle voices (an example is PSALM 113, μ19). The remaining six settings are of short tunes (OLD 100TH and five common tunes) which accommodate two four-line stanzas on the page; in these Cosyn switched the tune from one voice to another of similar range for the second stanza.

The second section, preceded by a half-title, adapts 14 of the same tunes for extended settings in five parts. The melodies are all printed in the altus book, though three of them have a higher range and are labeled "Cantus." The tune is fully underlaid with one stanza. But in the other three surviving partbooks, only

---

[3] For a full account of Cosyn's life and political position see Mark C. Reagan, "John Cosyn's *Musike in Six and Five Partes* Newly Notated and Completed" (master's thesis, Washington State University, 2010), Introduction.

the first few words of the text are provided. This suggests that these five-part settings were intended for a solo voice accompanied by viols, at least as an alternative to voices; and they do, indeed, have the character of consort songs, with freely contrapuntal accompaniments (example: μ20).

Cosyn made many minor changes in the tunes themselves, as compared with the *1567* versions. These are closely related to the deliberate revisions made in the five *WBP* editions of 1586, all of them printed by John Wolfe, who had printed Cosyn's Companion the year before. Evidently the musical editor responsible for the 1586 revisions was either Cosyn himself or someone who gave great weight to his readings. For the tune revisions and further discussion see Appendix 4.

Daman 1591 (1)

> *The Former Booke of the Musicke of M. William Damon . . . Conteining All the Tunes of Davids Psalmes, as they are Ordinarily Sung in the Church; Most Excellently by him Composed into 4. Parts. In which Sett the Tenor Singeth the Church Tune. Published for the Recreation of Such as Delight in Musicke: by W. Swayne Gent.* [London:] Printed by T. Este, the assigne of W. Byrd. 1591.
>   4 partbooks: Cantus, Altus, Tenor, Bassus.
>   *STC* 6220; on EEBO; *HTI* DamaWBM1. Modern edition of selected tunes: Frost, nos. 45, 129, 142

Daman 1591 (2)

> *The Seconde Booke of the Musicke of M. William Damon . . . In which Sett the Highest Part Singeth the Church Tune.* [London:] Printed by T. Este, the assigne of W. Byrd. 1591.
>   4 partbooks: Cantus, Altus, Tenor, Bassus.
>   *STC* 6221; on EEBO; *HTI* DamaWBM2.

This complementary pair of publications ("Former" here means "First" [of two], not "Previous") appeared shortly after Daman's death, on the initiative of one of his musical friends, William Swayne, who explains in the preface that the arrangements are improved from the 1579 publication, which "was not purposed or framed for the learned eares of our times." The wording of the title pages clearly shows the distinction between the tunes, as sung publicly in church, and the other voice parts in the arrangements, which are for private recreation. The text and tune content is virtually identical in the two books (the *Seconde Booke* omits Psalm 50 (1)). It is updated, in comparison with *Daman 1579,* by leaving out some of the hymns that were probably no longer in common use (Ten Commandments (1), Lord's Prayer (1), "Da Pacem, Domine,") as well as the ever controversial "Preserve us, Lord," and two tunes that had been dropped from most editions of the *WBP* (Psalms 6 and 95). It also passes over those new tunes in *Daman 1579* that had not caught on. A tune for Psalm 142 (*HTI* 272, Frost 165), now printed for the first time, is not found elsewhere. The setting of Psalm 116, on the other hand, is the first printing of what was to be the common tune called WINDSOR, which would become one of the most popular in English history (see p. 995).

Most of the arrangements from the *Former Booke* were adapted in the *Seconde Booke* so that the tune could be carried in the cantus voice. Often this required transposition and hence a change of key. In ten cases, however, the cantus carries the tune in both books, while Psalm 46 has the tune in the bassus in the *Former Booke*. The settings are mostly of the "motet" variety and hence could not be collated in our edition.

East 1592

> *The Whole Booke of Psalmes: with their Wonted Tunes, as they are Song in Churches, Composed into Foure Partes: All which are so Placed that Foure may Sing Ech One a Several Part in this Booke. Wherein the Churche Tunes are Carefully Corrected, and thereunto Added Other Short Tunes Usually Song in London, and Other Places of this Realme* . . . . Compiled by sondry authors who have so laboured heerein, that the unskillful with small practice may attaine to sing that part, which is fittest for their voice. Imprinted at London by Thomas Est, the assigne of William Byrd. 1592.
>
> *STC* 2482; on EEBO; *HTI* EastTWPB a. Modern edition: Robert Illing, Adelaide 1969–72.

Thomas East (Est, Este) (c. 1540–1608) was "the leading music printer of his day, and may be considered the father of English music printing," in the words of Miriam Miller and Jeremy L. Smith in *The New Grove*. His influential collection differs in important respects from the earlier companions. Instead of partbooks it is a single octavo book using a small music type, with the four vocal parts printed separately, but so placed that they can be read simultaneously in each opening, as the title page boasts. Instead of printing only the first stanzas, East includes the rest of each psalm and hymn, printed after the music. In both respects the format follows that of Tye's *Actes of the Apostles* (1553). The result might have been considered an edition of the *WBP*; yet East acknowledges William Byrd's patent for printing music rather than Richard Day's for printing psalms.[4] He may have hoped that the book would be used in church, but he did not venture to recommend such a heterodox practice in his preface. Since his livelihood depended on the publication of sacred music, he could not afford to alienate either potential high-church customers who did not want metrical psalms in worship at all, or the puritan party that wanted the psalms but disapproved of choirs or polyphony in church. By 1592 parish choirs had virtually disappeared, so any church use

---

[4] See Krummel, *English Music Printing*, 20.

would have been in a cathedral or other choral foundation; no evidence of it has come to light.

East's policy in assigning tunes also differed from his predecessors'. For the first time in England, *every* psalm and hymn was provided with a tune, as had been the plan in many Continental Reformed books from the start. As East says in his preface, "I have not onely set downe in this booke all the Tunes usually printed heretofore, with as much truth as I could possibly gather among divers of our ordinary Psalme bookes, but also have added those, which are commonly song now adayes, and not printed in our common psalme books with the rest." Note that East makes no claim to have originated any tune. In the Epistle Dedicatory he adds: "In this booke the Church Tunes are carefully corrected." Those texts that had a proper tune in the *WBP* were allowed to retain it, but for each of the 108 psalms and five hymns that lacked a tune East now provided one. For some he simply adopted the tune named in the cross-reference in the *WBP*, but for the majority (98 texts) he used one of the ten short tunes "which are commonly song now adayes" — the common tunes described in Appendix 4. Four of these, with their arrangements, were repeated for a number of different texts. The fact that these were *common* tunes[5] was recognized by two innovations: an incipit index, allowing readers to find a tune of their choice regardless of text; and the novelty of giving some tunes names that were independent of their texts.

The 72 distinct tunes resulting were all arranged in homophonic four-voice settings provided by ten musicians: Richard Allison (10 settings), Edward Blanks (7), Michael Cavendish (1), William Cobbold (5), John Dowland (5), John Farmer (15), Giles Farnaby (9), Edmund Hooper (4: for an example see µ24), Edward Johnson (3), and George Kirby (12: for examples see µ21, µ25). With the exception of Hooper, who was master of the choristers at Westminster Abbey, these men were not church musicians, and were known chiefly for their secular music. Although the assignment allowed no room for flights of fancy, the overall artistic standard is fairly high. The distribution of tunes among the arrangers appears to be arbitrary. Some were assigned consecutive blocks of texts. For instance, all the hymns before the psalms were allotted to Farmer. The tune CHESHIRE appears in two different arrangements, one by Farmer for Psalm 146, the other by Dowland for a non-*WBP* text, "A Prayer for the Queenes most excellent Majestie."

East 1594

> *The Whole Booke of Psalmes: with their Wonted Tunes* . . . . London: Printed by Thomas Est, the assigné of William Byrd. 1594.
>   *STC* 2488; on EEBO; *HTI* EastTWPB b.

---

[5] For definitions of "proper" and "common" tunes see the Glossary, pp. 1041, 1038.

In this edition East increased still further the predominance of the four most popular common tunes, in twelve cases substituting them for other tunes—the ones based on *WBP* cross-references. To the incipit index he added this significant comment relating to the tunes that would later be named OXFORD, CAMBRIDGE, LOW DUTCH (all CM) and LONDON (SM): "The psalmes are song to these 4 tunes in most churches of this Realme." (If this was literally true, it would exclude from use all psalms adapted to fit French meters and others not in common or short meter.) He discarded one common tune, WINCHESTER (μ25), that he had used only once in 1592 (see p. 995 for a possible reason).

Barley 1598

> *The Whole Booke of Psalmes. With their Woonted Tunes, as they are Sung in Churches, Composed in Foure Parts.* Printed at London by W. Barley, the assigne of Thomas Morley [c. 1598].
> *STC* 2495; on EEBO; *HTI* #WBPWT. Not included in Frost.

William Barley (1565?–1614) was a music printer of questionable integrity. This was an unauthorized revision of *East 1594*, relying on Thomas Morley's patent (Byrd's had expired in 1596). It has been aptly dubbed a "pocket edition" by Illing, since it is even smaller than its model. There was no room in it for East's format, where all four parts were visible on the same opening, so Barley printed the parts successively, making it impossible to sing the four-voice arrangements by reading from a single copy. He also saved space by omitting the two upper parts at the second and subsequent appearances of a tune. The book is carelessly printed, with many errors. Barley made a handful of changes in the allocation of tunes to texts. He introduced no new tunes, but in nine cases he substituted new arrangements of existing ones, five by John Bennet and four by Thomas Morley. (For details see Illing 1969 or the *HTI.*)

Allison 1599

> *The Psalmes of David in Meter, the Plaine Song Beeing the Common Tunne to be Sung and Plaide upon the Lute, Orpharyon, Citterne or Base Violl, Severally or Altogether, the Singing Part to be either Tenor or Treble to the Instrument, According to the Nature of the Voyce, or for Fowre Voyces:* With tenne short Tunnes in the end, to which for the most part all the Psalmes may be usually sung, for the use of such as are of mean skill, and whose leysure least serveth to practice: By Richard Allison Gent. Practitioner in the Art of musicke: and are to be solde at his house in the dukes place near Alde-gate. London: Printed by William Barley, the assigne of Thomas Morley. 1599.
> *STC* 2497; on EEBO; *HTI* AlliRPD. Modern editions: R. E. Anderson, "Richard Allison's Psalter," PhD diss., University of Iowa, 1974; Robert Illing, Adelaide 1985.

Richard Allison (c. 1565–1610), who was employed as a musician in the house-hold of the Earl of Warwick, chiefly composed music for mixed instrumental consorts, and it was this that distinguished his collection from the other Com-panions, and also definitively ruled it out for use in church. He had already con-tributed settings to *East 1592*, but he now composed fresh arrangements, placing the tune in the top voice (with one exception) and providing well-conceived ac-companiments for both voices and instruments (for examples see µ27, µ28).

He chose 58 of the 66 proper tunes, printing them with the first stanzas of their *WBP* texts (except for Benedictus, which carries the text of the Venite), and adding Psalm 22 with its tune (see p. 987). Most of the seven tunes omitted were losing popularity (Psalms 35, 50 (2), 88, 95) or were problematic (Psalm 134). Psalm 77 had the same tune as Psalm 81, which he therefore did not need to print twice. Curiously, he also omitted Psalm 100. Finally, he set nine psalms not provided with tunes in the *WBP* to four-line common tunes (see pp. 996–1008): eight from *East 1592* and one new one, for Psalm 125 (1), in long meter. The latter (*HTI* 279a) was, perhaps, influenced by Preserve us. It never reached the *WBP*, but it was lifted without attribution by Playford in 1671 for use with a new LM paraphrase of Psalm 121. Playford later reduced it to a CM version (279b), which became popular under the name Salisbury.

East 1604

> *The Whole Booke of Psalmes: with their Wonted Tunes* . . . In London: Printed by Thomas Este, for the Companie of Stationers. 1604.
>   *STC* 2515; on EEBO; *HTI* EastTWPB c.

This edition has the same content as *East 1594*, except for the omission of prefa-tory matter and the prayer for the Queen.

East 1611

> *The Whole Booke of Psalmes: with their Wonted Tunes* . . . Printed at London for the Companie of Stationers. 1611.
>   *STC* 2538.5; on EEBO; *HTI* EastTWPB d.

An essentially unchanged reissue of the 1604 edition.

Ravenscroft 1621

> *The Whole Book of Psalmes: with the Hymns Evangelicall, and Songs Spiri-tuall. Composed into 4. Parts by Sundry Authors, with such Severall Tunes as have beene, and are Usually Sung in England, Scotland, Wales, Germany, Italy, France, and the Nether-lands* . . . Newly corrected and enlarged by Tho: Ra-venscroft. Printed at London for the Company of Stationers. 1621.

STC 2575, 2575.3; on EEBO; *HTI* RavePWBP a. Later editions: William Turner, London 1728, 1746; W. H. Havergal, London 1845; Maurice Frost, London 1953 (the new four-line tunes only, as nos. 227–251); Robert Illing, Adelaide 1985

This book, compiled and published by a musician already well known for his editions of secular music, was a revision of *East 1592*. Thomas Ravenscroft (c. 1588–1635) adopted East's format and followed his general policy by selecting a tune for every *WBP* text and presenting the first stanza in the tenor voice of a four-part homophonic arrangement in score, with the rest of the text printed after it. But the musical content is extensively revised. Ravenscroft, a highly competent and gifted musician, preserved most of East's proper and common tunes, but added 25 new ones, thus greatly reducing the need to reprint the same tunes with so many texts. He used some of East's arrangements, commissioned others from contemporary composers, and provided 48 of his own. He contributed a historically important new tune to Psalm 104 (see p. 731). He developed East's tentative use of tune names in a more systematic fashion, naming or renaming 31 common tunes after English and Welsh cathedrals and choral foundations. Many still retain these names in modern hymnals.

Ravenscroft's collection was extremely influential. It established a high standard of accuracy and musical literacy. It was in a sense both the culmination of Elizabethan psalmody and the main musical vehicle carrying that culture into the future. But its detailed contents lie outside the scope of this book.

Ravenscroft 1633

> *The Whole Book of Psalmes: . . . Composed into 4. Parts by Sundry Authors.* London: Printed by Thomas Harper for the Company of Stationers. 1633.
> *STC* 2648; on EEBO; *HTI* RavePWBP b.

An essentially unchanged reissue of the 1621 edition. This was the last Companion based on the *WBP* until Playford's efforts, beginning in 1658.

APPENDIX 7
(N. T. AND B. Q.)
REFERENCES TO *WBP* ITEMS IN CHURCHWARDENS' ACCOUNTS, 1558–1568

Table 6 is based on information kindly provided by Dr. Jonathan Willis. He reported only those churchwardens' accounts that were available for the entire period of Elizabeth I's reign. The table lists only those items that are evidently copies of the *WBP* (normally referred to as "psalm books") or can be identified as parts of it. Entries of "psalters" are excluded, as they are likely to refer to the prose psalter, which was not part of the *BCP* until 1662 and had to be acquired separately if a choir was to chant the psalms. (Compare evidence gathered from Edwardian accounts, p. 522, footnote 52.) A clear case of this customary usage of the two terms is an entry in the Stationers' Company Court Minutes of September 7, 1600: "Mr. Hooke declareth unto A Court holden this day: that he Received from mr Eldridge A m[er]chant xij books of psalters & psalmes printed at Myddllebourgh by Ric' Skilders." This referred to a new type of edition which combined the metrical psalms with the prose psalms. See Temperley, "Middleburg Psalms," 163.

This information has been checked and augmented by Anne Heminger, who is preparing a Ph.D dissertation for the University of Michigan entitled "Confession Carried Aloft: Music, Sound, and Religious Identity in London, c. 1540–1560." She kindly shared what she has found regarding the twenty-two London churches whose records survive for the period 1558–60.

For source citations see Jonathan Willis, *Church Music and Protestantism in Post-Reformation England* (Farnham: Ashgate, 2010), 245–49.

Table 6. Purchases of Printed Metrical Psalms Recorded in Church Accounts, 1558–1568

Date	Parish (in London unless otherwise noted)	Entry	Cost per item[1]	Likely identification[2]
1558[–59]	St. Benet Gracechurch	2 psalm books	. . .	*1558*
		2 books of the psalms of "Jenevay"	1s.	*1558*
	St. Botolph Aldgate	The psalms in meter	5s.	*1558?*
	St. Margaret Pattens	5 "Genova books"	10d.+	*1558?*
1559[–60]	St. Andrew Hubbard	2 psalm books	1s. 4d.	*1558*
		4 papers of psalms to be song before the service or sermon	¾d.	sheets
	St. Margaret Pattens	6 "Ballettes of the pater noster and ye ten commaundementes"	1s. 3d.	sheets
		"A songe of the holly ghoste" [Veni, Creator?]	1d.	sheet
	St. Mary Woolnoth	2 psalm books in meter for the church	8d.	*1558*
	St. Matthew Friday St.	A psalm book with notes	10d.	*1558*
1559, Aug. 17	St. Martin in the Fields	2 psalm books in meter by note	10d.	*1558*

[1] 12d. (pence) = 1s. (shilling). Where the number of items is unclear, the total cost is given; where the cost for psalms is consolidated with other items, we give no price.

[2] Some may have been from editions that have not survived. Those identified as *1558* could easily be the Genevan 1559 reprint or Day's confiscated 1559 edition; other prices cannot correspond to any known editions.

Date	Parish (in London unless otherwise noted)	Entry	Cost per item[1]	Likely identification[2]
1560[–61]	St. James Garlickhythe	Te deum & other psalms in English meter	4d.	sheets
	St. Margaret Pattens	4 psalm books "of Awstyne"	1d.	sheets
		4 "Ballettes"	1d.	sheets
		A table for the psalms	1d.	sheet
		4 great psalm books for the choir	1s. 6d.	*1560a?*
	St. Mary Woolchurch Haw	2 books of psalms	. . .	?
	St. Matthew Friday St.	book with psalms	. . .	?
	St. Michael Cornhill	8 "genevian books"	1s. (?)	*1558* or *1560a?*
	St. Stephen Walbrook[3]	2 psalm books	10d.(?)	*1558* or *1560a*
	Coventry: Holy Trinity	4 psalm books in meter	4d.	sheets?
	Reading: St. Lawrence	3 psalm books in meter	. . .	?
1560, Sept. 18	St. Mary Woolnoth	6 psalm books	1s. 10d.	*1560a*
1561[–62]	All Hallows Staining	2 psalm books of Geneva town of the greatest [size]	1s. 8d.	*1562a* (4to)
	St. Benet Gracechurch	[Inventory] 4 psalm books with notes to sing	. . .	(see 1558 entry)
	St. Dunstan in the West	psalms	1d.	sheet

---

[3] Thomas Becon, translator of two *WBP* texts, was restored to his position as vicar of St. Stephen Walbrook in 1558 (Garrett, *Marian Exiles*, 84–5).

Date	Parish (in London unless otherwise noted)	Entry	Cost per item[1]	Likely identification[2]
	St. Margaret Moses	3 psalm books for the choir	1s.	*1561d*
	St. Mary Wool-church Haw	A book of psalms	10d.	*1561d* or *1562a*
	Leicester: St. Martin	2 pair of "geneves" for the choir	6½d.	sheets?
		2 pair of "geneves" to the choir	3d.	sheets
		psalm books with notes	. . .	?
1562[–63]	St. Margaret Westminster	4 books of psalms in meter for the choir	1s. 2d.	*1561d*
1563[–64]	St. Andrew Hubbard	2 psalm books	1s. 2d.	*1562a*
	St. Margaret Westminster	2 books for meter psalms of the great-est volume for the choir	1s. 4d.	*1562a or 1563*
1564[–65]	St. Margaret Westminster	2 psalm books for the choir	1s. 8d.	?
	St. Margaret Pattens	Mending and clasp-ing 4 psalm books	10d.	(see 1558 and 1560 entries)
1565[–66]	St. Benet Gracechurch	3 psalm books with notes to sing	. . .	?
	St. Margaret Westminster	2 psalm books for the choir	2s.	*1565*
	St. Matthew Friday St.	Service book with psalm book	4s. 4d.	*BPC + WBP*
1566[–67]	All Hallows Staining	2 books of Genevas psalms	3s. 3d.	*1565*

Date	Parish (in London unless otherwise noted)	Entry	Cost per item[1]	Likely identification[2]
1567[–68]	St. Margaret Westminster	[Inventory] 3 new psalm books of the Geneva		(see 1562 and 1563 entries)
1568[–69]	St. Mary Woolnoth	3 psalm books of the ? and largest volume bound in leather	10s.	*1567*
	Salisbury: St. Edmund	1 psalm book for the priest	2s. 6d.	*1567*
		2 little psalm books	9d.	*1569c?*
	Crediton (Devon)	6 books of metre psalms bought for the parish this year	6s.	?

Appendix 8
(B. Q.)
A List of Textual Contents in Each Printing Series of the *WBP* to 1603

The printing series are those established in the revised *STC*, including quarto series numbers devised earlier by John R. Hetherington. Editions not assigned to a series (chiefly Anglo-Genevan publications, but also some editions located after 1986) are listed instead by *STC* number among the series in the same format and chronologically before the next numbered series. Series dates as shown here reflect extant or known editions catalogued in the *STC*, or up to 1640 in the *ESTC*. When the contents of a series changes, the series is divided and each part distinguished by a letter, e.g. "2/40 (a)." The dates then reflect the years during which a given set of contents are consistent. After 1562, only editions published in England are listed. Incomplete and inaccessible editions are included; brackets around the date indicate uncertainty about the date, while a question mark represents an inaccessible edition that probably belongs to the series. *STC* dates have been revised when a colophon has a later date. Codes in brackets with a question mark are suppositions from imperfect exemplars.

Given the number of different texts that can vary among the parts of the *WBP*, prose descriptions of each series would prove unworkably long. The following table can make clear at a glance which editions have the same contents (or the same contents in one category among the prefatory prose, psalms, hymns, or prayers); the key for each code follows the table itself.

Series	Dates	Prefatory	Psalms	Hymns	Prayers
2/40 (a)	1565, 1573–5	T1U	J1o	H1a	P
2/40 (b)	1567	T1U+	J1o	H1a	P
2/40 (c)	1580–86	T2	J1o	H1a	P
2/41	1595–99	T2	K1o/a	H1a	p6
2/46	1585	—	K1o	H4	p6DC
2/48	1592	—	K1o	H4	p6D[C?]
2/50	1576–83	S	J1o	H4	PC
Heth. 101	1561	I	F1om	h7	P
Heth. 102	1562	IT1U	Gom	h9	P
Heth. 103	1563	IT1U	Iom	[H1a?]	[P?]
Heth. 105	1565	IT1U	Iom	H1a	P
Heth. 106	1566	T1U	J1om	H1a	P
Heth. 107	[1571?]–77	T1U	J1o	H1a	P
Heth. 108	1579–84	T2	J1o	H1a	P
Heth. 109	1585–89?	T2	K1a	H1b	p6DC
Heth. 110	1588–1614	T2	J1a	H1b	p10
Heth. 201	1578	—	K1n	H1b	p1FD
Heth. 211	1586–96	—	K1o	H1b	p6DC
Heth. 221 (a)	1569–76	S	J1o	H1b	P
Heth. 221 (b)	1586	—	K1o	H4	p6DC
Heth. 222	1579–84	S	K1a	H1b	PC
Heth. 230	1573	S	J1o	H1b	PC
Heth. 231	1574–77	S	J1o	H1b	[PC?]
Heth. 232	1578–84	S	J1a	H1b	PC
Heth. 233	1583	S	J1a	H1b	
Heth. 234	1583	—	J1o	H4	[P?]C
Heth. 240–7	1585–1639	S	K1a	H1b	p6DC
Heth. 261	1587–1594	—	K1a	H1b	p6DC
Heth. 262–4	1601–1619	—	K1a	H1b	p6DC
8/30	1548–49	+	Av	—	—
8/31–33	1549–54	+	Bv	—	—
STC 16561	1556	+	C1o	h1	p1

Series	Dates	Prefatory	Psalms	Hymns	Prayers
8/35	1560	—	D2o	h4	[—?]
STC 16561a.5	1560	+	Eo	h5	
STC 16562	1561	—	—	—	P+
	1561	I	F1om	h8	—
8/37	1564–69	I+	F2o	H2	P+
8/39	1562	—	H	h10	—
8/42	1570–72	IT1U	J2o	H1a	P
8/43	1578–80	IT2	K1a	H1b	p7F
8/45	1581–83	IT2	K1a	H1b	p7F
8/47	1589–1603	T2	K1a	H1b	p7
STC 2459.3	1581	—	K1n	H1b	p6
8/55	1602	—	M	—	—
8/60	[1579?]–1584	—	K1n	H1b	p6
8/61	1585–91	—	K1n	H1b	p6
8/62	1584–1604	—	K1n	H1b	p9
12/50	1582	T2	K1a	H1b	p6DC
16/40	1551	+	B	—	—
16/41	[1556?]	—	C2	h2	p2
STC 16561a	1558	+	D1	h3	p3
16/42	1561	—	E	h6	p4
STC 16563	1561	+	E	h6	p5
16/44	1566	[I?]	[F2o?]	[H2?]	[P?]
16/46	[1570?]	T1U	J1o	H1b	PC
16/47 (a)	1577	ST2	K1a	H1b	p6D
16/47 (b)	1578–83	ST2	K1a	H1b	p6DC
16/48	[1580?]–1640	ST2	K1a	H1b	p6DC
16/49	1585	—	K1n	H1b	p8F
16/53	1578–1581	—	K1n	H1b	p6FD
16/55	1586	—	K1n	H1b	p9
16/57	1582–97	—	K1n	H1b	p6FD
16/60	1599–1631	—	Ln	H1c	p12
24/40	1603–40+	—	K1n	h6	p13

Series	Dates	Prefatory	Psalms	Hymns	Prayers
32/40	1569	T1U	J1o	H3	CP+
32/45	1582?[1]–1622	T2+	K2a	H1b	Cp8F
32/50	1577–1582?	T2+	K2a	H1b	CPF+
32/52	1590–1639	—	K1n	H5	p12

---

[1] *STC* 2461.5, a 32° volume in 8s, collated in 1934, is in private hands with current location unknown; the *ESTC* conjectures that it belongs to either 32/45 or 32/50.

Keys to the List of Series Contents

Prefatory Texts

For each series, codes are combined to list all prefatory texts in the order in which they appear.

Code Text
I   "A short introduction to the science of music" [App. 3]
S   "To the Reader" [introducing solfa notation; App. 3]
T1   "A Treatise made by Athanasius the Great"
T2   "Of the use and virtue of the Psalms by Athanasius" [App. 3]
U   "The use of the rest of the Psalms"
+   Any other texts not regularly included in the *WBP*

Metrical Psalter

Psalm numbers in italics are versions which do not appear in the metrical psalter portion of *1567*. Only psalms printed in their numerical order in the metrical psalter portion of the volume or in a separate section explicitly labeled as "other psalms" are shown in this chart; psalms found among the hymns are shown there. The lower-case codes indicating whether and which arguments preface the psalms are appended to the psalm content codes; when a series or part of a series mixes two kinds of arguments, both are given with a slash between (e.g., "C2v/o"). Series with marginal glosses on some psalms end in "m."

Code Contains
A   19 psalms: 1–5, 20, 25, 28, 29, 32, 34, 41, 49, 73, 78, 103, 120, 123, 128 [versions in App. 2]
B   44 psalms: **A** + 6–17, 19, 21, 30, 33, 42–44, 52, 63, 68, 79, 82, 146 [versions in App. 2]
C1   51 psalms: **B** + 23, 51, 114, *115*, 130, 133, 137 [B versions as in *1567*]
C2   51 psalms + 1 psalm as hymn: **C1** [but **B** versions as in App. 2]
D1   62 psalms: **C1** + 37, 50 (1), *67 (a)*, 71, 119, 121, 124, 127, *129*, 148, *149*
D2   65 psalms: **D1** + *67 (b)*, 95 [*1567* Venite], 125 (2)
E   87 psalms: **D1** + *27, 36, 47, 54, 58, 62, 70, 85, 88, 90, 91, 94*, 100 (1), *101*, 104, 107, 111, 112, 113, 122, 125 (1), 126, 134, *138, 142*
F1   80 psalms: **D1** [lacking *67 (a)*] + 18, 21, 23 (2), 24, 26, 27, 31, 62, 64, 65, 66, 67, 69, 70, 72, 74, 75, 100 (1), 125 (2)
F2   78 psalms: **F1** lacking 23 (1), *149*

G   151 psalms: **F1** [lacking 23 (1), 50 (1), 100 (1), *115*, 125 (2), *149*] + **H** [lack-
        ing 129] + 115
H   77 psalms: 35, 36, 38–40, 45–48, 51 (2), 50 (2), 52–61, 76, 77, 80, 81, 83–99,
        100 (2), 101, 102, 104–113, 116–118, 122, 125, 126, 129, 131, 132, 134–136,
        138–145, 147, 149, 150
I   154 psalms: **G** [lacking *129*] + 129 + [separately] 50 (1), 100 (1), 125 (2)
J1   155 psalms: **I** + 23 (1) [psalms integrated in numerical order]
J2   154 psalms: **J1** lacking 125 (2)
K1   156 psalms: **J1** + 136 (2)
K2   155 psalms: **K1** lacking 125 (2)
L   152 psalms: **K1** lacking 50 (2), 100 (2), 125 (2), 136 (1)
M   150 psalms; **L** lacking 23 (2), 51 (2)
v   verse quatrain arguments
o   prose arguments mainly or entirely as in *1567*
a   abridged prose arguments
n   no arguments

Hymns

Hymns include psalm versions not normally printed in their numerical order
in the metrical psalter portion of the *WBP*. Only hymns eventually included in
the *WBP* are identified; those given in italics are not versions that appear in the
WBP.

Code Contains
h1   The Ten Commandments (2) only
h2   12 (?) hymns: Benedictus, Magnificat, [Nunc dimittis?], The Lord's Prayer
        (2), The Creed, The Ten Commandments (2), "The Lord be thanked," 5
        others
h3   2 hymns: Nunc dimittis, The Ten Commandments (2)
h4   6 (?) hymns: Benedictus, Magnificat, Nunc dimittis, The Ten Command-
        ments (2), The Lord's Prayer (2), The Creed [exemplar lacking unknown
        number of final leaves]
h5   4 hymns: The Ten Commandments (2), Nunc dimittis, 2 others
h6   5 hymns: **h5** + The Lord's Prayer (2)
h7   19 hymns (10 before and 9 after the metrical psalter): **h4** + Veni, Creator,
        Venite, Te Deum, "Quicunque vult," The Lamentation of a Sinner, The
        Lord's Prayer (1), The Ten Commandments (1), "Praise the Lord," "Behold,
        now give heed," "Come, Holy Spirit," "Da pacem, Domine," "The Lord be
        thanked," and "Preserve us, Lord"
h8   20 hymns (10 before and 8 after the metrical psalter: **h7** + The Complaint of
        a Sinner

h9   20 hymns (11 before and 9 after the metrical psalter): **h8** [lacking Venite, "Praise the Lord," "Behold, now give heed"] + Benedicite, The Humble Suit of a Sinner, and The Lamentation

h10   2 hymns: The Humble Suit of a Sinner and Benedicite

H1a   23 hymns (12 hymns before and 11 after metrical psalter): **h9** + Venite, "Praise the Lord," and "Behold, now give heed"

H1b   23 hymns (13 hymns before and 10 after metrical psalter): contents as **H1a**

H1c   23 hymns (all after metrical psalter): contents as **H1a**

H2   21 hymns: **H1a** omitting Benedicite and The humble suit of a sinner

H3   21 hymns: **H1a** omitting as "Praise the Lord" and "Behold, now give heed"

H4   22 hymns: **H1b** omitting "Come, Holy Spirit"

H5   14 hymns (all after metrical psalter): The Ten Commandments (2), The Lord's Prayer (2), The Creed, Te Deum, Benedictus, Magnificat, Nunc dimittis, Veni, Creator, "Come, Holy Spirit," The Lamentation of a Sinner, The Humble Suit of a Sinner, The Lamentation, "The Lord be thanked," and "Preserve us, Lord"

H6   19 hymns: **H3** omitting "The Lord be thanked" and "Preserve us, Lord"

Private Prayers

For each series, codes are combined to list all texts or sets of texts in the order in which they appear.

Code   Text(s)

P   "A form of prayer to be used in private houses" [complete as *1567*]

p1   6 prayers from **P**: Morning prayer, A prayer to be said before meals ("All things depend upon thy providence"), A thanksgiving after meals ("Let all nations magnify the Lord"), Evening prayer; "A confession for all estates and times" and "A prayer for the whole estate of Christ's Church" as public prayers

p2   **p1** omitting the two public prayers

p3   **P** omitting "A prayer to be said before a man begin his work"; with, as public prayers, "A confession for all estates and times" and "A prayer for the whole estate of Christ's Church"

p4   "A prayer to be said before a man begin his work" (only)

p5   **P** with, as public prayers, "A confession for all estates and times" and "A prayer for the whole estate of Christ's Church"

p6   **P** omitting all 6 prandial prayers

p7   **P** omitting first 3 prandial prayers: "All things depend upon thy providence," "Let all nations magnify the Lord," and "Eternal and everliving God, Father of our Lord"

p8   **P** omitting last 4 prandial prayers: "Eternal and everliving God, Father of our Lord," "The eyes of all things do look up," "Glory, praise and honour be unto thee," and "The God of glory and peace, who hath created"

p9   2 prayers from **P**: Morning prayer and Evening prayer

p10   6 prayers from **P**: Morning prayer, Another thanksgiving before meals (1) ("Eternal and everliving God, Father of our Lord"), Another thanksgiving after meat (1) ("Glory, praise and honour be unto thee"), Evening prayer, "A godly prayer to be said at all times," and "A confession for all estates and times"

p11   5 prayers from **P**: Morning prayer, Evening prayer, "A godly prayer to be said at all times," "A confession for all estates and times," and "A prayer for the whole estate of Christ's Church"

p12   2 prayers from **P**: "A godly prayer to be said at all times" and "A confession for all estates and times"

p13   "A confession for all estates and times" (only)

C   The confession of Christian faith [App. 3]

F   "A prayer made for the Church and all the states thereof" by John Foxe [App. 3]

D   "A prayer against the Devil and his manifold temptations" [App. 3]

+   Any other private prayers not regularly included in the *WBP*

Glossary of Musical Terms
(N. T.)

This glossary is narrowly based on the way terms are used in this book. It is intended to forestall possible ambiguities or misunderstandings and to assist readers who are not familiar with the language of musical scholarship and practice. It does not cover technical terms used in the didactic introduction to the *WBP*, discussed and reproduced on pp. 871–80. A word printed in italics in a definition here is generally a cross-reference to another entry.

accidental: a sharp, flat, or natural placed before a note to alter its pitch. In modern music and in this edition it applies until the next *barline*, unless contradicted. In some Elizabethan sources it is not clear how long it applies, and sometimes it is not placed immediately in front of its note but appears earlier, unattached to any note. See also *key-signature*.

Aeolian mode: the *scale* on the white notes of a piano with a *final* on A. It is essentially the same as the modern key of A minor, with semitones between steps 2 and 3 and between steps 5 and 6. When the scale has a B flat instead of B natural, the Æolian mode is transposed, so that its final is now on D.

altus: a moderately high voice part, below the *cantus*

anthem: a setting, without strophic repetition, of a sacred text, most often from the prose psalms (though metrical texts were not unknown), designed for singing by a choir without congregational participation

barline: a vertical line through the staff. In this edition, contrary to its use in modern music, it is used solely to separate *phrases* of a tune, without reference to meter, duration, or stress.

bar: see *measure*

breve (US *double whole note*): two semibreves; four minims

cadence: a formula marking the end of a tune, chant, or phrase

canon: (1) a composition in which two or more voices sing the same melody, beginning at different times, requiring contrapuntal skill for a harmonically satisfactory result; (2) a group of compositions widely accepted for normal use in a certain context (e.g., "the Elizabethan canon of psalm tunes")

cantus: a high voice part, often bearing the tune in a harmonized setting

cantus firmus: a pre-existent melody in one voice that is the basis for a multi-voice composition

clef: a symbol at the beginning of a staff defining one line as a particular *note* (generally f, g, c' or g') from which the pitches of the other notes can be determined

common meter: see *meter*

common tune: a tune not linked to a specific text (cf. *proper tune*)

consort song: a song with accompaniment for several viols

contra tenor / countertenor: a high adult-male voice part in the alto compass

copy-text: the principal source of an edition

counterpoint (adj. *contrapuntal*): two or more melodies sung simultaneously to form satisfactory harmony

crotchet (US *quarter note*): a quarter of a semibreve; half a minim

diatonic scale: a scale made up of whole and half steps, using only the white notes of a keyboard, or a *transposition* of them

Dorian mode: the *scale* on the white notes of a piano with a *final* on D. Like the modern D minor it has a semitone between steps 2 and 3, but differs from it in that its usual steps 6 and 7 are B and C rather than B flat and C sharp. When the scale has a B flat instead of B natural, the Dorian mode is transposed, so that its final is now on G.

dotted note: a note followed by a dot, which increases its duration by half

faburden: a technique of improvised harmonization by a choir, in which the tenors sang a known or written melody and the other voices followed conventional rules

final: the last note of a melody, or the note on which it is expected to end, which is the primary factor defining *mode* in medieval and Renaissance music

flat: a sign (♭) placed before a note that lowers its pitch by a semitone

half-cadence: a form marking the end of the first half a tune or chant

homophonic: with all voices sounding simultaneously, sharing the same rhythm and text distribution

incipit: the first few notes of a tune in music notation. (When used in relation to *text*, the incipit is the first words, *line*, or phrase.)

Ionian mode: the *scale* on the white notes of a piano with a *final* on C. Like the modern key of C major, it has semitones between steps 3 and 4 and between steps 7 and 8. When the scale has a B flat instead of B natural, the Ionian mode is transposed, so that its final is now on F.

key: the note in the scale on which a melody, or the bass of a polyphonic piece, is expected to end, the expectation being created primarily by which notes of the chromatic scale (black and white notes) are in use. (Cf. *mode*.) Key, or tonality, was in an early stage of development in the 16th century. The keynote, when named, is often followed by *major* or *minor*, indicating that the third note of the scale in use is four or three semitones above the keynote, respectively: e.g., G major (sometimes abbreviated as G) has B as its third note, while G minor (sometimes abbreviated as g) has B flat.

key-signature (**k-s**): one or more flats or sharps (or the absence of any, called an "open" key signature) placed after the clef at the beginning of a staff and applying to the notes indicated, or their octave transpositions, throughout the staff. In modern music the key signature applies throughout a piece or movement unless contradicted. But in Elizabethan tunes, it may appear only on some of the staves. Cf. *accidental*.

leading note: the note below the *final*

line: a portion of a verse text beginning on a new line of print, corresponding to a phrase of the tune

long: two breves; eight minims. In the sources considered here, however, it is used only for the last note of a tune and indicates a note of indeterminate length.

mean / medius: a treble voice part usually sung by boys, often the highest in an ensemble

measure (Brit. *bar*): one of the equal sections into which a tune is divided, containing a specified number of beats, usually two, three or four. (Measures are not used in this edition, except in some musical examples: see *barline*.)

melisma: two or more notes sung to one syllable

meter: the pattern of syllables and stresses of a single stanza of text, or of a tune, e.g. "common meter" (CM) for an iambic verse with four lines of 8, 6, 8, and 6 syllables or "double common meter" (DCM) for eight lines in the same pattern. Other frequently found iambic meters are LM (long meter, 8.8.8.8), SM (short meter, also called "poulter's meter," 6.6.8.6) and their doubles. (A second possible meaning, the rhythmic pattern of a tune or other music, e.g. 3/2, is here denoted by *time* or *time signature*.)

minim (US *half note*): A relative measure of time. In most vocal music of the later 16th century, this was the standard note-length for a single syllable, and it is so used here (see *semibreve*).

Mixolydian mode: the scale on the white notes of a piano with a *final* on G. Like the modern key of G major it has a semitone between steps 3 and 4, but its usual 7th degree is F rather than F sharp. When the scale has a B flat instead of B natural, the Mixolydian mode is transposed, so that its final is now on C.

mode: a classification based on the note in the *scale* on which a chiefly *diatonic* melody, or the bass of a polyphonic piece, is expected to end. For melodies not already familiar to the singer or hearer, such expectation is created by the pitch range of the melody, the notes on which individual phrases begin and end, and more generally the relative prominence given to the different notes of the diatonic scale (white notes). (Cf. *key*.) The system of modes was declining in the 16th century; the number of modes in practice tended to be reduced to two, major (formerly Ionian) and minor (formerly Æolian). But some melodies are still recognizably in the *Dorian*, *Phrygian*, or *Mixolydian* mode.

motet: a piece for several voices that are rhythmically independent

natural: a sign (♮) placed before a note that cancels a flat or sharp affecting that pitch

note: A note is defined by pitch and duration. The pitch is shown by its position on the staff in relation to the *clef*, and is referred to here by the Helmholtz system: c–b for the white notes in the octave below middle C, c'–b' for the octave beginning on middle C, c"–b" for the octave above that; flats or sharps following a letter define black notes. A capital letter is used for a pitch class (where the octave is not defined) and hence for a *key*. Duration, in relative terms, is shown by the form of a note, and is referred to here by the historical English terms rather than the current American ones: see *long*, *breve*, *semibreve*, *minim*, *crotchet*, *quaver*, each twice as long as the next; see also *dotted note*. Absolute duration is defined by *tempo*.

note-value: the length of a note, such as *minim*

octave: eight notes of the *diatonic scale*, counting inclusively; notes an octave apart have the same letter name.

open: see *key-signature*

phrase: a division of a tune corresponding to a line of text, here numbered in sans serif boldface and separated from adjoining phrases by a *barline*

Phrygian mode: The scale on the white notes of a piano with a *final* on E. It shares the flat 3rd degree (G) with the modern key of E minor, but differs from it in that its 2nd degree is F rather than F sharp and its 7th degree is D rather than

D sharp. Its semitones are between the 1st and 2nd degrees and between the 5th and 6th degrees. When the scale has a B flat instead of B natural, the Phrygian mode is transposed, so that its final is now on A.

poulter's meter: short or double short meter; see *meter*

proper tune: a tune attached to a specific text (cf. *common tune*)

psalm tone: one of eight ancient Gregorian melodies, each in a different *mode*, used for chanting prose psalms

quaver (US *eighth note*): one fourth of a minim

rest: a period of silence in a tune, whose length is theoretically measured by its form. In these tunes, however, it often merely indicates a break of indeterminate length between phrases.

scale: all the notes available for use in a given melody, in ascending or descending order

semibreve (US *whole note*): a relative measure of time, worth two minims; the normal *tactus* (beat) in 16th-century music

semitone: the pitch interval between any two adjacent notes on the keyboard

sharp: a sign (♯) placed before a note that raises its pitch by a semitone

slur: a curved line placed above or below two or more notes, here indicating that the notes within the slur are to be sung to the same syllable

source: one of the printed editions on which an edited tune is directly based. (A second possible meaning — the original or earliest known form of a tune — is avoided here.)

staff (US plural *staves*): the set of five lines on which notes are placed, their pitch being determined by the lines and spaces and by the *clef* at the beginning of the staff

stanza: one of a number of equal portions of a verse text, separated by a space from adjoining stanzas and generally corresponding in length to one statement of a tune

syncopation: the anticipation of a stressed beat on the previous half-beat, as on the word "vex" in the second phrase of Psalm 3

tactus: the underlying beat of a piece of music, as in a walking step. In this edition the tactus is the length of a *semibreve.*

tempo: the actual time between two beats; hence, the time occupied by a given note value, such as a *minim*. Tempo is not precisely defined in Elizabethan musical sources, nor, therefore, in this edition.

text: (1) the words of a song; (2) words elsewhere in a book, not for singing; (3) a written work. (A fourth possible meaning — a source that is the basis of an edition — is not used here, except in the expression *copy-text*.)

time signature (US *meter signature*) (t-s): a representation of the regular division of a tune into portions (*bars* or *measures*), where the first note in each portion carries a musical stress: e.g. 3/2, ¢. In Elizabethan use the signs were often ambiguous, retaining earlier connotations relating to tempo and to the relative durations of different note forms.

transposition: the raising or lowering of the pitch of an entire tune or piece of music

underlay: the placing of sung words immediately below a staff, showing how they are linked to the music. In this edition each syllable is vertically aligned with its note. In some Elizabethan sources the underlay is imprecise or absent.

verse: (1) text ordered by meter and rhyme; (2) a numbered portion of a prose psalm, hymn, or other biblical text. (A third possible meaning — one of a number of equal portions of a verse text — is here denoted by *stanza*.)

verse anthem: an *anthem* including, and generally beginning with, substantial portions for solo voices

BIBLIOGRAPHY

Editions of *The Whole Book of Psalms* collated for the critical edition are not listed here, but on pp. xxxix–xlvii. Encyclopedia articles are cited in footnotes only. Abbreviated citations are shown here in parentheses after full citations.

Manuscripts

Durham Cathedral Library, MSS. C 2–18

London, British Library, Add. MS. 5465 (the "Fayrfax MS.")

———, Add. MS. 15166

———, Add. MS. 29481

———, Add. MS. 30513 (the "Mulliner Book")

———, Add. MS. 31922 ("Henry VIII's MS")

———, Egerton MS. 2711

———, Harley MS. 442

———, Lansdowne MS. 10

———, Royal 17. A. xxi (William Forrest, "Certaigne Psalmes of David in Meeatre")

———, Royal 18. B. xix

———, Royal Appendix 74–76 (the "Lumley partbooks")

London, Lambeth Palace Library, MS. 2523

New Haven, Conn., Yale University, James Marshall and Marie-Louise Osborn Collection, Music MS. 13

Oxford, Bodleian Library, MS. Mus. Sch. 323–5 (the "Wanley partbooks")

——— ,Tanner MS. 131

Oxford, Christ Church, Mus. MSS. 768–70

——— , Mus. MSS. 984–8

Wroclaw, Poland. Biblioteka Uniwerstyecka, MS. I. Q. 466

York Minster Library, MS. M. 29

Primary printed sources (including modern facsimiles)

ABC et chrestienne instruction bien utile. Geneva: Antoine Davodeau and Lucas de Mortière, [1562].

The A.B.C. with the Catechisme that is to say, an Instruction to be Taught and Learned of Every Childe Before He Be Brought to be Confirmed by the Bishop. London: for the Company of Stationers, 1605. (*STC* 20.8)

Addington, Stephen. *A Collection of Psalm Tunes for Publick Worship, Adapted to Dr. Watts's Psalms and Hymns*. 3rd edn. London: for the author, 1780.

A[insworth], H[enry]. *The Book of Psalmes: Englished both in Prose and Metre*. Amsterdam: Giles Thorp, 1612. (*STC* 2407)

All the French Psalm Tunes with English Words. . . . Accorded to the Verses and Tunes Generally Used in the Reformed Churches of France and Germany. London: Thomas Harper, 1632. (*STC* 2734)

Allison, Richard. *The Psalmes of David in Meter, the Plaine Song Beeing the Common Tunne to be Sung and Plaide upon the Lute, Orpharyon, Citterne or Base Violl*. London: William Barley, 1599. (*STC* 2497) (*Allison 1599*)

Angliæ Ruina: or, England's Ruine. [London: n.p.], 1647 [i.e., 1648]. (Wing R2447)

Aulcuns Pseaulmes et cantiques mys en chant. Strassburg, 1539.

Avison, Charles. *An Essay on Musical Expression*. 2nd edn. London: C. Davis, 1753.

Baldwyn, William. *The Canticles or Balades of Salomon, Phraselyke Declared in Englysh Metres*. [London: William Baldwyn,] 1549. (*STC* 2768)

Barber, Abraham. *A Book, of Psalme Tunes in Four Parts*. York: John White, 1687. 3rd edn., 1698. 4th edn., 1700. 6th edn., 1711. 7th edn., 1715.

Barley, William. *The Whole Book of Psalmes. With their Woonted Tunes, as they are Sung in Churches, Composed in Foure Parts*. London: W. Barley, [c. 1598]. (*STC* 2495) (*Barley 1598*)

Barnard, John. *Theologo-Historicus, or, The True Life of the Most Reverend Divine and Excellent Historian, Peter Heylyn*. London: Daniel Brown, 1683. (Wing B854A)

Barton, William. *The Book of Psalms in Metre, Close and Proper to the Hebrew*. London: Matthew Simmons for the Companie of Stationers, 1644. (Wing B2401)

———. *The Book of Psalms in Metre, Lately Translated, with Many Whole Ones, and Choice Collections of the Old Psalms Added to the First Impression*. London: G[eorge] M[iller], 1645. (Wing B2407)

Bathe, William. *A Brief Introduction to the Skill of Song*. London: Thomas Este, [1596]. (*STC* 1589)

Bayly, Lewis. *The Practise of Pietie*. London: John Hodgets, 1613. (*STC* 1602)

Bentley, Thomas. *The Monument of Matrones: Containing Seven Severall Lampes of Virginitie.* London: Henry Denham, 1582. (*STC* 1892)

Bernays, L[eopold] J[ohn]. *A Manual of Family Prayers and Meditations.* London: Peacock and Mansfield, Bowdery and Kirby, 1845.

Beveridge, William. *A Defence of the Book of Psalms, Collected into English Metre, by Thomas Sternhold, John Hopkins, and Others.* London: R. Smith, 1710.

[Bible.] *Biblia: The Bible, that is, the Holy Scripture.* [Cologne?: E. Cervicornus and J. Soter?,] 1535. (*STC* 2063) (The Coverdale Bible)

———. *The Boke of Psalmes.* Geneva: Rowland Hall, 1559. (*STC* 2384) (The Geneva Bible)

———. *The Byble in Englishe.* London: Edward Whitchurch, 1540. (The Great Bible) (*STC* 2070)

———. *The Byble, whych is All the Holy Scripture.* [Antwerp: Matthew Crom for Richard Grafton and Edward Whitchurch,] 1537. (*STC* 2066) (The Matthew Bible)

———. *The Holy Bible and Scriptures Conteyned in the Olde and Newe Testament.* Geneva: Rowland Hall, 1560. (*STC* 2093) (The Geneva Bible.)

———. *La sainte Bible.* Lyon: Jean de Tournes, 1564. (The Olivétan Bible)

———. [Whittingham, William, trans.]. *The Psalmes of Dauid Translated accordyng to the Veritie and Truth of th'Ebrue.* [Geneva: M. Blanchier], 1557. (*STC* 2383.6).

The Boke of Psalmes [from the Geneva Bible]. Geneva: Rowland Hall, 1559. (*STC* 2384)

Bolton, Robert. *Two Sermons Preached at Northampton at Two Severall Assises There.* London: George Miller, 1635. (*STC* 3256)

A Booke of Christian Prayers. London: John Daye, 1578. (*STC* 6429)

Bourgeois, Louis. *Pseaulmes cinquante. . . traduicts en vers francois par Clement Marot, & mis en musique par Loys Bourgeois à quatre parties à voix de contrepoinct égal consonante au verbe.* Lyon: Godefroy et Marcelin Beringer, 1547.

Bownd, Nicholas. *The Doctrine of the Sabbath Plainely Layde Forth.* London: John Porter and Thomas Man, 1595. (*STC* 3436)

Boys, John. *An Exposition of the Dominical Epistles and Gospels Used in our English Liturgie. . .; the Winter Part from the First Aduentuall Sunday to Lent.* London: William Aspley, 1610. (*STC* 3460.2)

A Brieff Discours off the Troubles Begonne at Franckford in Germany anno Domini 1554 abowte the Booke off off [sic] *Common Prayer and Ceremonies* [Heidelberg: M. Schirat], 1575. (*STC* 25443)

Broome, Michael. *A Choice Collection of Sixteen Excellent Psalm-Tunes, which are Used in the Parish-Churches of London &c.* Birmingham: Mich[ael] Broome, [c. 1751].

Brown, Thomas. *Amusements Serious and Comical.* London: for John Nutt, 1700. (Wing B5051)

Bull, Henry. *Christian Prayers and Holy Meditations*. London: Thomas East for
    Henry Middleton, 1568. (*STC* 4028)

Bunyan, John. *Grace Abounding to the Chief of Sinners*. London: George Larkin,
    1666. (Wing B5523)

Burroughs, John. *A Narrative of the Conversion of Thomas Mackernesse*. London:
    John Dunton, 1694. (Wing B6128)

Burton, William. *A Sermon Preached in the Cathedrall Church in Norwich, the xxi.
    Day of December, 1589*. [London: Robert Waldegrave, 1590.] (*STC* 4178)

———. *Ten Sermons vpon the First, Second, Third and Fourth Verses of the Sixt of
    Matthew*. London: Thomas Man, 1602. (*STC* 4178.5)

Butler, Charles. *The Principles of Musik, in Singing and Setting*. London: John
    Haviland, 1636. (*STC* 4196)

Byrd, William. *Psalmes, Sonets, and Songs of Sadnes and Pietie, Made into Musicke
    of Fiue Parts*. [London:] Thomas East, 1588. (*STC* 4253.3)

———. *Psalmes, Songs and Sonnets Some Solemne, Others Joyfull. . . Fit for Voyces
    or Viols of 3. 4. 5. and 6. Parts*. London: Thomas Snodham, the assigne of
    W. Barley, 1611. (*STC* 4255)

Calvin, Jean. *La Forme des prières et chants ecclésiastiques*. [Geneva, 1542.]

———. *The Institution of Christian Religion*. Trans. Thomas Norton. London:
    Reynold Wolfe and Richard Harrison, 1561. (*STC* 4415)

———. *In Librum Psalmorum commentarius*. Geneva: Robert Estienne, 1557.

———. *The Psalmes of Dauid and Others. With M. Iohn Caluins Commentaries*.
    [Trans. Arthur Golding.] London: [Thomas East and Henry Littleton],
    1571. (*STC* 4395)

Campion, Thomas. *A New Way of Making Fowre Parts in Counter-point*. Lon-
    don: T. S. for John Browne, 1610. (*STC* 4542)

Campen, Jan van. *Psalmoru[m] omnium*. Paris: F. Regnault for Thomas Berthe-
    let, 1534. (*STC* 2354)

Certaine Notes Set Forth in Foure and Three Parts. London: John Day, 1560
    (1565). (*STC* 6418) (*Certaine Notes*)

Certaine Select Prayers Gathered out of S. Augustines Meditations. London: John
    Day, 1574. (*STC* 924) (*Augustine*)

Chapman, George. *Eastward Hoe: As it was Playd in the Black-friers*. London:
    William Aspley, 1605. (*STC* 4973)

Chetham, John. *A Book of Psalmody*. London: William Pearson, 1718.

Cinquante Pseaumes en francois par Clement Marot. Geneva, 1543.

C[lifford], J[ames]. *The Divine Services and Anthems Usually Sung in the Cathe-
    drals and Collegiate Choires in the Church of England*. London: Henry Brome,
    1663. (Wing C4703)

——— *The Divine Services and Anthems Usually Sung in His Majesties Chappell,
    and in all Cathedrals and Collegiate Choirs in England and Ireland*. 2nd ed.
    London: Nathaniel Brooke and Henry Brome, 1664. (Wing C4704)

A Collection of Anthems, as the Same are Now Perform'd in the Cathedral Church of Durham. Durham: S. Isaac Lane, 1749.

Corbet, Richard. *Certain Elegant Poems*. London: R. Cotes for Andrew Crooke, 1647. (Wing C6269C)

Cosyn, John. *Musike of Six, and Five Partes. Made upon the Common Tunes Used in Singing of the Psalmes*. 6 partbooks: Cantus [lacking], Altus, Medius, Tenor, Quintus, Bassus. London: John Wolfe, 1585. (*STC* 5828) (*Cosyn 1585*)

Coverdale, Miles, ed. *Goostly Psalmes and Spiritual Songes*. [London:] Johan Gough, [1535–6]. (*STC* 5872)

———. *The Psalter or Booke of Psalmes both in Latyne and Englyshe*. London: Ricardus Grafton, 1540. (*STC* 2368)

Cowley, Abraham. *The Foure Ages of England*. London: n.p., 1648. (Wing C6671)

Crowley, Robert. *The Psalter of David Newely Translated into Englysh Metre in Such Sort that it Maye the More Decently, and wyth More Delyte of the Mynde, be Reade and Songe of All Men*. [London:] Robert Crowley, 1549. (*STC* 2725)

Cuningham, William. *The Cosmographical Glasse*. London: John Day, 1559. (*STC* 6119)

Daman, [William]. *The Psalmes of David in English Meter, with Notes of Four Partes*. 4 partbooks: Treble, Contratenor (lacking), Tenor, Bassus. London: John Daye, 1579. (*STC* 6219) (*Daman 1579*)

———. *The Former Booke of the Musicke of M. William Damon. . . Conteining All the Tunes of Davids Psalmes,. . . Composed into 4. Parts. In which Sett the Tenor Singeth the Church Tune*. 4 partbooks: Cantus, Altus, Tenor, Bassus. [London:] T. Este, 1591. (*STC* 6220) (*Daman 1591 (1)*)

———. *The Seconde Booke of the Musicke of M. William Damon. . . In which Sett the Highest Part Singeth the Church Tune*. 4 partbooks: Cantus, Altus, Tenor, Bassus. [London:] T. Este, 1591. (*STC* 6221) (*Daman 1591 (2)*)

Dammee, Agamemnon Shaglock van. *The Speech of a Cavaleere to his Comrades, in Answer to the Wardens Speech*. London, 1642. (Wing S4858)

[Davantes, Pierre.] *Pseaumes de David, mis en rhythme francoise par Clement Marot, & Théodore de Besze*. [Geneva:] Pierre Dauantes, 1560.

A Directory for the Publique Worship of God. London: Company of Stationers, 1644. (Wing D1547.) Repr. Philip Hall, ed., *Reliquiae liturgicae*, 5 vols. (Bath: Binns and Goodwin, 1847), vol. 3.

D[od], H[enry]. *Certaine Psalmes of David, Heretofore Much out of Use: Because of Their Difficult Tunes. . . . Reduced into English Meter Better Fitting the Common Tunes*. [Edinburgh]: Robert Walde-grave, 1603. (*STC* 2730)

Duffet, Thomas. *New Poems, Songs, Prologues and Epilogues* (London: for Nicholas Woolfe, 1676. (Wing D2449)

Duncon, John. *The Returns of Spiritual Comfort and Grief in a Devout Soul*. London: for R. Royston, 1649. (Wing D2606)

[East, Thomas.] *The Whole Booke of Psalmes; with their Wonted Tunes, as they are Song in Churches, Composed into Foure Partes.* London: Thomas Est, 1592. (*STC* 2482) (*East 1592*)
Later editions: 1594, 1604, 1611.

Egerton, Stephen. *The Boring of the Eare Contayning a Plaine and Profitable Discourse by Way of Dialogue.* London: William Stansby, 1623. (*STC* 7527.5)

Felinus, Aretinus [i.e., Martin Bucer], ed. *Psalmorum libri quinque ad Ebraicam veritatem versi.* Strassburg: George Ulricher, 1529.

[Fetherstone, Christopher.] *The Lamentations of Ieremie in meeter, with apt notes to sing them withall.* London: John Wolfe, 1587. (*STC* 2779)

The First Parte of the Psalmes Collected into Englishe Meter. London: John Day, 1564. (*STC* 2433)

The Forme and Maner of Makyng and Consecratyng of Archebishoppes Bishoppes, Priests and Deacons. [London: Richard Grafton], 1549. (*STC* 16462) (*Ordinal*)

La Forme des prieres et chantz ecclesiastiques. [Geneva, 1542.]

―――. Strassburg: Jehan Knobloch, 1545.

The Forme of Prayers and Ministration of the Sacramentes, &c., Used in the Englishe Congregation at Geneva. . . .. [Title page of second part] *One and Fiftie Psalms of David in Englishe Metre, whereof, 37. were made by Thomas Sterneholde: and the Rest by Others.* Geneva: J. Crespin, 1556. (*STC* 16561). Note: This and later editions of the complete Genevan service book are referred to as [the] *Form of Prayers.* The psalm book alone is cited by date: for a list of editions see pp. xl, xli.

The Forme of Prayers and Ministration of the Sacraments &c Used in the English Church at Geneva, Approved and Received by the Churche of Scotland. . . with the Whole Psalmes of David in Englishe Meter. Edinburgh: Robert Lekprevik, 1564. (*STC* 16577) (*Scot1564*)

A Fourme of Praier with Thankes Giving, to be Used Every Yeare, the 17. of November, being the Day of the Queenes Majesties Entrie to her Raigne. London: Richard Jugge, 1576. (*STC* 16479)

Foxe, John. *The First Volume of the Ecclesiasticall History Contaynyng the Actes and Monuments of Thynges Passed in Euery Kynges Tyme in this Realme.* London: John Daye, 1570. (*STC* 11223)

―――. *A Sermon of Christ Crucified, Preached at Paules Crosse the Friday Before Easter.* London: John Daye, 1570. (*STC* 11242.6) (*Foxe1570*)

Gaffurius, Franchinus. *Theorica musicae.* Milan, 1492.

Galis, Richard. *A Brief Treatise Containing the Most Strange and Horrible Cruelty of Elizabeth Stile.* London: J. Allde, 1579. (*STC* 11537.5)

Gascoigne, George. *The Droomme of Doomes Day.* London: [T. East for] Gabriel Cawood, 1576. (*STC* 11641)

Gawthorn, Nathaniel. *Harmonia Perfecta.* London: William Pearson, 1730.

Gayton, Edmund. *Wil: Bagnal's Ghost. Or the Merry Devill of Gadmunton.* London: W. Wilson for Thomas Johnson, 1655. (Wing G422)

Geistliche Lieder, auffs new gebessert und gemehrt, zu Witte[n]berg. Leipzig: Balten Schumann, 1539. (*Ger1839*)

A Godlie Dittie to be Song for the Preservation of the Queenes Most Excellent Majesties Raigne. London: Abel Jeffes, 1586. (*STC* 23926)

Golding, Arthur. See Calvin, John, *The Psalmes of Dauid and Others.*

Green, James. *A Collection of Psalm Tunes.* 3rd edn. Nottingham, 1715. 4th edn. Nottingham, 1718.

Hall, Elias. *The Psalm-Singer's Compleat Companion.* London: J. Heptinstall for D. Midwinter, 1708.

Hall, John. [*The Courte of Vertue.* London: Thomas Marshe, 1565.] (*STC* 12632)

Hall, Joseph. *Holy Observations. Lib. I. Also Some Fewe of Davids Psalmes Metaphrased, for a Taste of the Rest.* London: Samuel Macham, 1607. (*STC* 12671)

Harington, John. *The Elegant and Witty Epigrams of Sir John Harrington, Knight.* London: G[eorge] P[urslowe] for John Budge, 1618. (*STC* 12776)

Harrab, Thomas. *Tessaradelphus: or the Four Brothers.* [Lancashire? Birchley Hall Press?], 1616. (*STC* 12797)

Harrison, Ralph. *Sacred Harmony.* [2nd edn.] London: Messrs. Thompson, [c. 1788].

Hawkins, Sir John. *A General History of the Science and Practice of Music.* 5 vols. London, 1776.

Heylyn, Peter. *Aerius redivivus: or the History of the Presbyterians. . . from the Year 1536 to. . . 1647.* London: for John Crosley, 1670. (Wing H1681)

———. *Ecclesia restaurata: or, the History of the Reformation of the Church of England.* London: H. Twyford et al., 1660–1. (Wing H1701)

———. *Examen historicum: or, a Discovery and Examination of the Mistakes. . . in Some Modern Histories.* 2 vols. London: for Henry Seile and Richard Royston, 1659. (Wing H1706)

Higford, William. *Institutions, or Advice to a Grandson.* London: Edmund Thorn, 1658. (Wing H1947)

Holinshed, Raphael. *The Chronicles of England, Scotlande, and Irelande.* 2 vols. London: John Harrison, 1577. (*STC* 13568b)

Hooker, Richard. *Of the Lawes of Ecclesiasticall Politie.* 5 books. London: John Windet, [1593]–97.

Jackson, Thomas. *Dauids Pastorall Poeme: or Sheepeheards Song.* London: Edmund Weaver, 1603. (*STC* 14299)

Joye, George, ed. *The Psalter of Dauid in Englishe Purely a[n]d Faithfully Tra[n]slated aftir the Texte of Feline.* Argentine [i.e., Antwerp]: Francis Foxe [i.e., Martin de Keyser], 1530. (*STC* 2370).

Lawes, Henry and William. *Choice Psalmes Put into Musick.* London: Humphrey Moseley, 1648. (Wing L640)

Le Jeune, Claude. *Les cent cinquante Pseaumes de David: mis en musique a quatre parties.* Paris, 1601.

Leman, James. *A New Method of Learning Psalm-Tunes, with an Instrument of Musick Call'd the Psalterer.* London: G. Smith, 1729.

The Lives, Apprehensions, Arraignments, and Executions, of the 19. Late Pyrates. London: [E. Alldes] for John Busby the Elder, [1609]. (*STC* 12805)

L[owe], E[dward]. *A Short Direction for the Performance of Cathedral Service.* London: Richard Davis, 1661. (Wing L3305)

[Luther, Martin, ed.] *Geistliche Lieder, auffs new gebessert und gemehrt, zu Witte[n]berg.* Leipzig: Balten Schuman[n]n, 1539. (*Ger1539*)

Mace, Thomas. *Musick's Monument.* London: T. Ratcliffe, and N. Thompson for Thomas Mace, 1676. (Wing M120)

La Manyere de faire prieres aux eglises Francoyses. "Rome" [or rather Strassburg], 1542.

Marot, Clément. *Cinquante Pseaumes de David mis en françoys selon la vérité hébraïque.* Geneva: Jean Gérard, 1543.

Marston, John. *The Metamorphosis of Pigmalions Image. And Certaine Satyres.* London: Edmond Matts, 1598. (*STC* 17482)

M[athew], T[homas]. *The Whole Booke of Psalms as they are Now Sung in the Churches: With the Singing Notes of Time and Tune Set to Every Syllable.* London: R. Everingham for the Company of Stationers, 1688. (Wing B2565, *HTI✱P* E85)

M[offett], T[homas]. *The Silkewormes, and Their Flies.* London: Nicholas Ling, 1599. (*STC* 17994)

Morley, Thomas. *A Plaine and Easie Introduction to Practicall Musicke.* London: Peter Short, 1597. (*STC* 18133)

Mornyng and Euenyng Prayer and Communion, Set Forthe in Foure Partes, to be Song in Churches, both for Men and Children, wyth Dyuers other Godly Prayers & Anthems, of Sundry Mens Doynges. (Later edition of *Certayne Notes.*) 4 partbooks. London: John Day, 1565. (*STC* 6419.)

The Most Cruell and Bloody Murther Committed by an Inkeepers Wife. London: William Finebrand, John Wright, 1606.

Mundy, John. *Songs and Psalmes Composed into 3. 4. and 5. Parts for the Vse and Delight of All Such as either Love or Learne Musicke.* London: Thomas Est, 1594. (*STC* 18284)

"Nautical Rambles: The Leeward Station During the War." *The Nautical Chronicle and Naval Magazine,* 11 (1842), 319–25, 384–91, 461–68, 543–52, 628–32, 746–53, 828–25.

Of the Endes and Deaths of Two Prisoners, Lately Pressed to Death in Newgate. London: John Awdely, 1569. (*STC* 18492)

Openshaw, Robert. *Short Questions and Answeares, Conteyning the Summe of Christian Religion.* London: Thomas Dawson, 1579. (*STC* 18816)

The Order of Prayer, and Other Exercises, vpon Wednesdayes and Frydayes, to Auert and Turne Gods Wrath from vs, Threatned by the Late Terrible Earthquake: To be vsed in all Parish Churches and Householdes throughout the Realme, by Order giuen from the Queens Majesties Most Honourable Priuie Counsel. London: Christopher Barker, 1580. (*STC* 16513)

L'ordere des prieres et ministere ecclesiastique. London: [T. Gaultier?], 1552. (*STC* 16573)

[Parker, Matthew.] *The Whole Psalter Translated into English Metre.* London: John Daye, 1567. (*STC* 2729)

Parrot, Henry. *Laquei Ridiculosi: or Springes for Woodcocks.* London: Thomas Snodham for John Busby, 1618. (*STC* 19332)

Parsons, Robert. *A Brief Discours Contayning Certayne Reasons why Catholiques Refuse to Goe to Church.* Doway: John Lyon, 1580. (*STC* 19394)

P[ayne], B[enjamin]. *The Parish-Clerk's Guide: or, the Singing Psalms Used in the Parish-Churches Suited to the Feasts and Fasts of the Church of England, and Most Other Special Occasions.* London: Benj[amin] Motte, for the C[o]mpany of Parish-Clerks, 1709.

Pett, Peter, *A Discourse Concerning Liberty of Conscience.* London: Nathaniel Brook, 1661. (Wing P1881A)

Phillips, John. *The Religion of the Hypocritical Presbyterians in Meeter.* London, 1661. (Wing P2097)

———. *A Satyr Against Hypocrites.* London: N. B., 1655. (Wing P2101–3)

Playford, John. *A Brief Introduction to the Skill of Music.* London: W. Godbid, 1658. (Wing P2448)

———. *Psalmes & Hymns in Solemn Musick of Four Parts on the Common Tunes to the Psalms in Metre Used in Parish-Churches.* London: W. Godbid, 1671. (Wing P2527)

———. *The Whole Book of Psalms. . . Compos'd in Three Parts.* London: W. Godbid for the Company of Stationers, 1677. (Wing B2527)

A Psalme of Prayer and Praise for the Prosperous and Good Estate of our Soueraigne Lord the King. London: Edward Allde, 1609. (*HTI* ✳CHP A; *STC* 5208)

Psalmen, Gebett und Kirchenübung. Strassburg: Wolff Köpphel, 1526. (*Ger1526*) Strassburg: Wolff Köphl, 1533, (*Ger1533*)

The Psalmes of Dauid and Others. With M. Iohn Caluins commentaries. Arthur Golding, ed. London: [Thomas East and Henry Littleton, 1571]. (*STC* 4395)

The Psalmes of Dauid Translated accordyng to the Veritie and Truth of th'Ebrue. [Geneva: M. Blanchier], 1557. (*STC* 2383.6)

Psalms and Hymns, for the Use of the Chapel of the Asylum, or House of Refuge, for Female Orphans. William Riley, ed. London: By the editor, [1767].

The Psalms and Hymns, Usually Sung in the Churches and Tabernacles of St. Martins in the Fields and St. James's Westminster. London: R. Everingham for Ric. Chiswell, 1688. (Wing P4148A)

The Psalter or Boke of Psalmes both in Latyne and Englyshe. London: Ricardus Grafton, 1540. (*STC* 2368)

Pseaumes de David, mis en rhythme francoise par Clement Marot, & Théodore de Besze. [Geneva:] Pierre Davantes, 1560.

Pseaumes de David mis en rime francaise par Clement Marot et Theodore de Beze. Paris: Adrian le Roy & Robert Ballard, 1562.

Pseaumes octantetrois de David, mis en rime françoise par Clément Marot et Théodore de Bèze. La forme des prières ecclésiastiques et Catéchisme par Jean Calvin. Geneva: Jean Crespin, 1551. Repr. New Brunswick, N. J.: Friends of the Rutgers University Libraries, 1973. (*Fr1551*)

Rainolds, William. *A Refutation of Sundry Reprehensions, Cauils, and False Sleightes.* Paris, 1583. (*STC* 20632)

Ravenscroft, Tho[mas]. *The Whole Booke of Psalmes. . . Composed into 4. Partes by Sundry Authors.* London: Company of Stationers, 1621. (*STC* 2575, 2575.3) (*Ravenscroft 1621*)

———. London: Thomas Harper for the Company of Stationers, 1633. (*STC* 2648) (*Ravenscroft 1633*)

Reading, John. *Dauid's Soliloquie.* London: Robert Allot, 1627. (*STC* 20788)

Rippon, John. *A Selection of Psalm and Hymn Tunes.* [London, c. 1792.]

Rogers, Richard. *Seven Treatises Containing Such Direction as is Gathered out of the Holie Scriptures. . . : and may be Called the Practise of Christianitie.* London: Felix Kyngston, 1603. (*STC* 21215)

Rous, Francis. *Psalmes of David in English Meter.* London: Philip Nevill, 1643. (Wing B2396)

S[andys], G[eorge]. *A Paraphrase vpon the Psalmes of David.* London, [1636]. (*STC* 21724)

Saunders, Lawrence. *A Trewe Mirrour or Glase Wherin We Maye Beholde the Wofull State of Englande.* [Wesel?]: [H. Singleton?], 1556). (*STC* 21777)

Schilders, Thomas. *The Psalms of David in Metre, with the Prose. For the Use of the English Church in Middelburgh.* Middelburg [United Provinces]: Richard Schilders, 1599. (*STC* 2499.9)

Seager, Francis. *Certayne Psalmes Select out of the Psalter of David and Drawen into Englyshe Meter with Notes to Every Psalme in iiii Partes to Synge.* London: Wyllyam Seres, 1553. (*STC* 2728)

Select Psalms and Hymns for the Use of the Parish-Church and Tabernacle of St. James's Westminster. London: J. Heptinstall for the Company of Stationers, 1697. (Wing B2604A)

A Selection of Psalms and Hymns for Public Worship. London: Rivington's, 1832.

Sergeant, John. *Schism Dis-arm'd of the Defensive Weapons, Lent it by Doctor Hammond, and the Bishop of Derry by S. W.* Paris: M. Blageart, 1655. (Wing S2589)

Sibthorp, Christopher. *A Friendly Advertisement to the Pretended Catholickes of Ireland.* Dublin: Societie of Stationers, 1622. (*STC* 22522)

S[latyer], W[illiam]. *The Psalmes of David in 4 Languages and in 4 Parts Set to ye Tunes of our Church.* London: George Thomason and Octavian Pullen, 1543. (Wing B2798)

Souter Liedekens Ghemaect ter eren Gods op alle die Psalmen van David. Antwerp: Simon Cock, 1540. Facsimile edition with introduction and notes by Jan van Biezen and Marie Veldhuyzen. Facsimiles of Dutch Songbooks, 2. The Netherlands: Frits Knuf, 1984.

The Speech of a Cavaleere to his Comrades, in Answer to the Wardens Speech written by Agamemnon Shaglock van Dammee. London, 1642. (Wing S2589)

Stow, John. *The Annales, or a General Chronicle of England. . . Augmented by Edmund Howes.* London: Thomas Adams, 1615. (*STC* 23338)

———.———. London: Richard Meighan, 1631 [1632]. (*STC* 23340)

Strype, John. *Annals of the Reformation and Establishment of Religion.* 4 vols, 7 pts. Oxford: Clarendon Press, 1822.

———. *The History of the Life and Acts of the most Reverend Father in God Edmund Grindal.* London: John Hartley, 1710.

Stubbes, Philip. *A Perfect Pathway to Felicitie.* London: Humfrey Lownes, 1610. (*STC* 23399)

A Supplement to the New Version of Psalms. See Tate and Brady.

Tans'ur, William. *A Compleat Melody; or, The Harmony of Sion.* London: W. Pearson, for James Hodges, 1735.

Tate, Nahum, and Nicholas Brady. *A New Version of the Psalms of David, Fitted to the Tunes Used in Churches.* London: M. Clark for the Company of Stationers, 1696. (Wing B2598)

———. *A Supplement to the New Version of Psalms.* London: J. Heptinstall, 1700. (Wing B2624)

———.———. 6th edn. In the Savoy [London]: John Nutt, 1708.

A Thankes Geuing to God Vsed in Christes Churche on the Monday, Wednisday and Friday. [London:] Richard Grafton, [1551] (*STC* 16504)

Timbrell, Francis. [*The Divine Musick Scholars Guide.* n.p., 1714.] (*HTI* TimbFDM a)

Todd, Henry John. *Observations upon the Metrical Versions of the Psalms, Made by Sternhold, Hopkins and Others.* London: for F.C. & J. Rivington, 1822.

Tye, Christopher. *The Actes of the Apostles, translated into Englyshe metre,. . . wyth Notes to Eche Chapter, to Synge and Also to Play upon the Lute.* London: Nycolas Hyll, for Wyllyam Seres, 1553. (*STC* 2984)

Walter, Johann. *Geystliche Gesangbüchlin.* Wittenberg, 1524.

Watson, Richard. *The Right Reverend Doctor John Cosin, late Lord Bishop of Durham his Opinion.* London: F. Leach for Nicholas Woolfe, 1684. (Wing W1094)

[Wedderburn, John and Robert.] *Ane Compendious Buik of Godlie Psalmes and Spiritual Sangis.* Edinburgh: Iohne [Ros] for Henrie Charter[is], 1576. (*STC* 2996.7)

[Wesley, John, ed.] *A Collection of Tunes, Set to Music, as they are Commonly Sung at the Foundery.* London: A. Pearson, 1742.

Whetstone, George. *The Honourable Reputation of a Souldier.* Leyden: Jan Paedst Jacobzoon, ende Jan Bouwenzoon, 1586. (*STC* 25340)

[Whittingham, William.] *The Psalmes of Dauid Translated accordyng to the Veritie and Truth of th'Ebrue.* [Geneva: M. Blanchier,] 1557. (*STC* 2383.6)

The Whole Booke of Psalmes Faithfully Translated into English Metre. [Cambridge, Mass.: Stephen Day,] 1640. (*STC* 2738) ("The Bay Psalm Book")

The Whole Book of Psalms, Collected into English Metre, by Thomas Sternhold, John Hopkins, and Others. Cambridge: Joseph Bentham, Printer to the University, 1751. (*ESTC* T180242) (*WBP* 1751)

The Whole Psalmes in Foure Partes, whiche may be Songe to Al Musicall Instrumentes, Set Forth for the Encrease of Vertue: and Aboleshyng of Other Vayne and Triflyng Ballades. 4 partbooks (Medius, Contra Tenor, Tenor, Bassus). London: John Day, 1563. (*STC* 2431) (*Day 1563*; also referred to as "Day's Companion")

Wilkins, Matthew. *An Introduction to Psalmody.* London: J. Johnson, [c. 1744].

Williams, Thomas. *Psalmodia Evangelica.* London: S. A. & P. Thompson, 1789.

Willis, Richard. *The Excellent Use of Psalmody.* Nottingham: George Ayscough and Richard Willis, 1734.

Wither, George. *The Hymnes and Songs of the Church.* London: for G. W., 1623. (*STC* 25908)

———. *A Preparation to the Psalter.* London: Nicholas Okes, 1619. (*STC* 25914)

———. *The Psalmes of David Translated into Lyrick-Verse.* [Amsterdam:] Cornelis Gerritis van Breughel, 1632. (*STC* 2735)

Wyatt, Sir Thomas. *Certayne Psalmes. . . Drawen into Englyshe Meter.* London: Thomas Raynald, and John Harryngton. 1549. (*STC* 2726)

Secondary printed sources
(including modern editions of primary sources)

Addy, John. "The Archdeacon and Ecclesiastical Discipline in Yorkshire, 1598–1714: Clergy and Churchwardens." Borthwick Institute, St. Anthony's Hall Publications, 24. York: St. Anthony's Press, 1963.

Amner, John. *Variations for Keyboard on "O Lord, in Thee is all my trust,"* ed. Anthony J. Greening. London: Schott & Co., 1970.

Aplin, John. "The Fourth Kind of Faburden: The Identity of an English Four-Part Style." *Music & Letters* 61 (1980), 245–65.

———. "The Origin of John Day's 'Certaine Notes,'" *Music & Letters* 62 (1981), 295–98.

Arber, Edward, ed. *A Transcript of the Registers of the Company of Stationers of London: 1554–1640 A. D.* 5 vols. Birmingham: privately printed, 1875–94. Repr. New York: P. Smith, 1950.

———, ed. *A Brief Discourse of the Troubles at Frankfort: 1554–1558* . London: privately printed, 1907.

Arten, Samantha. "The Origin of Fixed-Scale Solmization in *The Whole Booke of Psalmes*." *Early Music*, 46:1 (Feb. 2018), 148–66.

———. "*The Whole Booke of Psalmes*, Protestant Ideology, and Musical Literacy in Elizabethan England," Ph.D. diss., Duke University, 2018.

Athanasius of Alexandria. *Epistola ad Marcellinum*, in *Patrologia graeca*. Jacques-Paul Migne, ed. 162 vols. Paris: J-P Migne, 1857–86. 27: cols. 11–46.

———. *The Life of Anthony* and *The Letter to Marcellinus*, trans. Robert C. Gregg. New York: Ramsey; Toronto: Paulist Press, 1980.

Barnard, John. "The Stationers' Stock 1663/4 to 1705/6: Psalms, Psalters, Primers and ABCs." *The Library*, ser. 6, vol. 21 (1999), 369–75.

———. "The Survival and Loss Rates of Psalms, ABCs, Psalters and Primers from the Stationers' Stock, 1660–1700." *The Library*, ser. 6, vol. 21 (1999), 148–50.

Barrow, Henry. "A Few Observations to the Reader of Mr. Giffard His Last *Replie* [1591/2]". In Leland H. Carlson, ed., *The Writings of John Greenwood and Henry Barrow, 1591–1593*. Elizabethan Nonconformist Texts, vol. 6. London: Leland H. Carlson, 1970; rpt. Routledge, 2003.

Baskervill, Charles Read. *The Elizabethan Jig and Related Song Drama*. Chicago: University of Chicago Press, 1929.

Blayney, Peter W.M. *The Stationers' Company and the Printers of London, 1501–1557*. New York: Cambridge University Press, 2013.

Berens, Rev. E. *Observations on Parochial Psalmody, with a Selection of Psalms from the Old Version*. Oxford: W. Baxter, for C. and J. Rivington, 1825.

Beveridge, William. *A Defence of the Book of Psalms, Collected into English Metre, by Thomas Sternhold, John Hopkins, and Others*. London: R. Smith, 1710.

Bèze, Théodore de. *Psaumes mis en vers français (1551–1562), accompagnés de la version en prose de Loïs Budé*. Pierre Pidoux, ed. Geneva: Librairie Droz, 1984.

Bickersteth, John, ed. *Psalms and Hymns, Selected and Revised for Public, Social, Family, or Secret Devotion*. 6th edn. London: L. and G. Seeley, 1838.

Billings, William. *Complete Works*. 4 vols. Boston: American Musicological Society & The Colonial Society of Massachusetts, 1977–90.

Blagden, Cyprian. *The Stationers' Company: A History, 1403–1959*. Cambridge, Mass.: Harvard University Press, 1960.

Blankenburg, Walter. "Church Music in Reformed Europe." In Friedrich Blume and others, eds., *Protestant Church Music: A History* (New York and London: Victor Gollancz Ltd., 1975), 507–90.

Blezzard, Judith, ed. *The Tudor Church Music of the Lumley Books.* Recent Researches in the Music of the Renaissance, 65. Madison, Wis.: A-R Editions, 1985.

Blow, John. *Thirty Voluntaries and Verses,* ed. Watkins Shaw. London: Schott & Co., [1972].

Boston, Noel, and Lyndesay G. Langwill. *Church and Chamber Barrel-Organs.* Edinburgh: Lyndesay G. Langwill, 1967.

Bray, Gerald, ed. *Tudor Church Reform: The Henrician Canons of 1535 and the* Reformatio Legum Ecclesiasticarum. Church of England Record Society, 8. Bury St. Edmunds: The Boydell Press, 2000.

Bray, Roger, ed. *The Blackwell History of Music in Britain: The Sixteenth Century.* Oxford: Blackwell, 1995.

Bridges, Robert. "A Practical Discourse on Some Theories of Hymn-Singing." *Journal of Theological Studies* 1 (1899–1900), 40–63.

Brigden, Susan. *London and the Reformation.* Oxford: Clarendon Press, 1989.

Bruce, John, ed. *Calendar of State Papers, Domestic Series, of the Reign of Charles I.* 23 vols. London: Longman, Brown, Green, Longman, & Roberts, 1858–67.

Bull, John. "Attend unto my tears, O Lord" and "O Lord, turn not away thy face,"ed. R. Thurston Dart. London: Stainer & Bell, [1963].

Butler, Katherine. "Printed Borders for Sixteenth-Century Music Paper and the Early Career of Music Printer Thomas East," The Library 19:2 (June 2018), pp. 174–202.

Butler, Samuel. *Hudibras,* Vol. 2, annotated by Zachary Grey. Dublin: A. Reilly for Robert Owen and William Brien, 1744.

Byrd, William. *Collected Works,* general editor Philip Brett. 17 vols. London: Stainer & Bell, c. 1970–2004.

Caldwell, John, ed. *The Mulliner Book* (revised edn.). MB 1. London: Royal Musical Association, 2011.

———. *The Oxford History of English Music.* 2 vols. Oxford: Clarendon Press, 1991, 1999.

Calvin, Jean. *Catéchisme de l'église de Genève.* 1553. Geneva: Jules-Guillaume Fick, 1853.

Chambers, Bettye Thomas. *Bibliography of French Bibles: Fifteenth- and Sixteenth-Century French Language Editions of the Scriptures.* Geneva: Librairie Droz, 1983.

Christ-Janer, Albert, and Charles W. Hughes. *American Hymns Old and New.* New York: Columbia University Press, 1980.

Collinson, Patrick. "Ecclesiastical Vitriol: Religious Satire in the 1590s and the Invention of Puritanism." In John Guy, ed., *The Reign of Elizabeth I: Court and Culture in the Last Decade* (Cambridge: Cambridge University Press, 1995), 150–70.

———. *The Elizabethan Puritan Movement*. Berkeley and Los Angeles: University of California Press, 1967.

Cosin, John. *The Correspondence of John Cosin, D.D., Lord Bishop of Durham*, ed. George Ormsby. Publications of the Surtees Society, vols. 52–3. Durham: Andrews & Co., 1869–72.

Cowan, William. *A Bibliography of the Book of Common Order and Psalm Book of the Church of Scotland: 1556–1644*. Edinburgh: Edinburgh Bibliographical Society, 1913.

Crawford, Richard. *The Core Repertory of Early American Psalmody*. Recent Researches in American Music, 11–12. Madison: A-R Editions, 1984.

Crotch, William, ed. *Tallis's Litany. . . A Collection of Old Psalm Tunes. . . for the Use of the University Church, Oxford*. Oxford: for the Editor, 1803.

Cummings, Brian, ed. *The Book of Common Prayer: The Texts of 1549, 1559, and 1662*. Oxford: Oxford University Press, 2011.

Curwen, John Spencer. *Studies in Worship Music*. [1st series.] London: J. Curwen, 1880.

Dalton, William. *A Selection of Psalms and Hymns Designed for Social and Public Worship*. 5th edn. Wolverhampton and London: T. Simpson and Hamilton, Adams and Co., 1853.

Dawson, Jane E.A. "The Early Career of Christopher Goodman and his Place in the Development of English Protestant Thought." Ph.D. diss., Durham University, 1968.

Deloffre, Frédéric. *Le Vers français*. 3rd edn. Paris: Société d'édition d'enseignement supérieur, 1973.

Denkmäler deutscher Tonkunst. 65 vols. Leipzig: Breitkopf und Härtel, 1892–1931.

Di Cristo, Albert. "Vers une modélisation de l'accentuation du français." *French Language Studies* 9 (1999), 143–79; 10 (2000), 27–44.

Donne, John. *The Sermons of John Donne*, ed. Evelyn Simpson and George Potter. 10 vols. Berkeley and Los Angeles: University of California Press, 1953–62.

Doe, Paul, ed. *Elizabethan Consort Music I*. MB 44. London: Royal Musical Association, 1979.

Douen, Orentin. *Clément Marot et le psautier huguenot*. 2 vols. Paris: L'Imprimerie Nationale, 1878–9. Repr. Nieuwkoop: B. de Graaf, 1967.

Duguid, Timothy. *Metrical Psalmody in Print and Practice: English 'Singing Psalms' and Scottish 'Psalm Buiks', c. 1547–1640*. St. Andrews Studies in Reformation History. Farnham: Ashgate, 2014.

The English Hymnal with Tunes. Percy Dearmer, general editor; Ralph Vaughan Williams, musical editor. London: Oxford University Press and A. R. Mowbray, [1906].

Evenden, Elizabeth. *Patents, Pictures and Patronage: John Day and the Tudor Book Trade*. Farnham: Ashgate, 2008.

———— and Thomas L. Freeman. *Religion and the Book in Early Modern England: The Making of Foxe's 'Book of Martyrs.'* Cambridge Studies in Early Modern British History. Cambridge: Cambridge University Press, 2011.

Fellowes, Edmund, ed. *The English Madrigal School.* 36 vols. London: Stainer & Bell, Ltd., 1913–24.

Fiedrowicz, Michael. "Introduction." *Expositions of the Psalms 1–32.* The Works of Saint Augustine: a Translation for the 21st Century, part 3, vol. 15. Brooklyn, N. Y.: New City Press, 2000.

Fincham, Kenneth, ed. *Visitation Articles and Injunctions of the Early Stuart Church.* 2 vols. Woodbridge, Suffolk: Boydell & Brewer, 1994–8.

Flescher, Jacqueline. "French," in *Versification: Major Language Types,* ed. W. K. Wimsatt (New York: Modern Language Association, 1972), 177–90.

Frere, Walter H. *The English Church in the Reigns of Elizabeth and James I.* London, 1904.

————, ed. *Hymn-Melodies for the Whole Year from the Sarum Service-Books and Other Ancient English Sources.* London: Plainsong & Medieval Music Society, 1903.

————, ed. *Hymns Ancient and Modern: Historical Edition.* London: William Clowes, 1909.

————, ed. *Visitation Articles and Injunctions of the Period of the Reformation.* 3 vols. Vol. 2 with the assistance of W. M. Kennedy. Alcuin Club Collections, 14–16. London: Longmans Green & Co., 1910.

Frost, Maurice, ed. *English & Scottish Psalm & Hymn Tunes* c. *1543–1677.* London: S. P. C. K. and Oxford University Press, 1953. (Frost)

————, ed. *Historical Companion to Hymns Ancient & Modern.* London: Hymns Ancient & Modern, 1962.

Garrett, Christina H. *The Marian Exiles.* Cambridge: Cambridge University Press, 1938.

Garside, Charles, Jr. *The Origins of Calvin's Theology of Music: 1536–43.* Philadelphia: American Philosophical Society, 1979.

Gibbons, Orlando. *Anthems II,* ed. David Wulstan. Early English Church Music 21. London: Stainer & Bell, 1978.

Giles, Nathaniel. *Anthems,* ed. J. Bunker Clark. Early English Church Music 23. London: Stainer & Bell, 1979.

Grabo, Norman S. "How Bad is the *Bay Psalm Book*?" *Papers of the Michigan Academy of Science, Arts and Letters,* 56 (1961), 605–15.

Green, Ian. *Print and Protestantism in Early Modern England.* Oxford: Oxford University Press, 2000.

Green, Mary Anne Everett, ed. "Life of Mr William Whittingham, Dean of Durham." *Camden Miscellany* 6. London: Camden Society, 1870.

Greene, Richard L. *The Early English Carols.* 2nd edn. Oxford: Clarendon Press, 1977.

Greg, Walter W., and Eleanore Boswell, eds. *The Records of the Court of the Stationers' Company, 1576–1602*. London: The Bibliographical Society, 1930.

Grijp, Louis Peter. "Psalms for the Lute in the Dutch Republic and Elsewhere." In Jan W. J. Burgers, Tim Crawford and Matthew Spring, eds., *The Lute in the Netherlands in the Seventeenth Century* (Proceedings of the International Lute Symposium, Utrecht, 30 August 2013. Cambridge: Cambridge Scholars Publishing, 2016), 1–38.

Gunther, Karl. *Reformation Unbound: Protestant Visions of Reform in England, 1525–1590*. Cambridge: Cambridge University Press, 2014.

Haar, James. "Monophony and the Unwritten Tradition." In *Performance Practice I: Music Before 1600*, ed. Howard Mayer Brown and Stanley Sadie (New York: W.W. Norton, 1990), 240–7.

Hackett, Charles D. *The National Psalmist*. London: Jefferys & Co., 1842.

Hall, Edward, and Richard Grafton. *Hall's Chronicle: Containing the History of England, during the Reign of Henry the Fourth, and the Succeeding Monarchs, to the End of the Reign of Henry the Eighth. . .. Carefully Collated with the Editions of 1548 and 1550*. Ed. Sir Henry Ellis. London: J. Johnson, 1809. Repr. New York: AMS Press, 1965.

Hamlin, Hannibal. *Psalm Culture and Early Modern English Literature*. Cambridge: Cambridge University Press, 2004.

Haraszti, Zolan. *The Enigma of the Bay Psalm Book*. Chicago: University of Chicago Press, [1956].

The Harvard University Hymn Book. 2nd edn., Cambridge, Mass.: Harvard University Press, 1926; 3rd edn., 1965.

Hearne, Thomas. *Remarks and Collections*. C. E. Doble, D. W. Rannie, and H. E. Salter, eds. 11 vols. Oxford: Clarendon Press, 1885–1921.

Heitz, Paul. *Genfer Buchdrucker und Verlegerzeichen im XV., XVI. und XVII. Jahrhundert*. Strassburg: J. H. Heitz, 1908.

Herl, Joseph. *Worship Wars in Early Lutheranism: Choir, Congregation, and Three Centuries of Conflict*. Oxford: Oxford University Press, 2004.

Horgan, Kate. *The Politics of Songs in Eighteenth-Century Britain*. London: Pickering and Chatto, 2014.

Houle, George. *Meter in Music, 1600–1800*. Bloomington, Ind.: Indiana University Press, 1987.

Hughes, Paul L., and James F. Larkin, eds. *Tudor Royal Proclamations*. 3 vols. New Haven: Yale University Press, 1964–9.

The Hymn Tune Index: A Census of English-Language Hymn Tunes in Printed Sources from 1535 to 1820, ed. Nicholas Temperley with the assistance of Charles G. Manns and Joseph Herl. 4 vols. Oxford: Clarendon Press, 1998. Online at hymntune.library.illinois.edu. (*HTI*)

Hymns Ancient and Modern for Use in the Services of the Church. Ed. William H. Monk. London: Novello & Co., 1861. [See also Frere, Walter H.]

Hymns Ancient and Modern Revised. London: William Clowes and Sons Ltd., 1951.

Illing, Robert, ed. *Allison's Companion 1599 to the English Metrical Psalter.* Adelaide: Robert Illing, 1985.

———. *Day's Companion 1563 to the English Metrical Psalter.* 2 vols. Adelaide: Robert Illing, 1986.

———. *English Metrical Psalter 1562.* 3 vols. Adelaide: Robert Illing, 1983.

———. *Est's Psalter.* 2 vols. Adelaide: Library Board of South Australia, 1969.

Jahn, Robert. "Letters and Booklists of Thomas Chard (or Chare) of London, 1583–4." *The Library,* ser. 4, vol. 3 (1923), 219–37.

Jeanneret, Michel. *Poésie et tradition biblique.* Paris: J. Cortis, 1969.

Jenny, Markus. *Geshichte der deutsch-schweizerischen evangelischen Gesangbuches im 16. Jahrhundert.* Basel: Bärenreiter-Verlag, 1962.

———. *Luthers geistliche Lieder und Kirchengesänge.* Archiv zu Weimarer Ausgabe der Martin Luther: Texte und Untersuchungen, 4. Cologne: Böhlau, 1985.

Julian, John. *A Dictionary of Hymnology.* 2 vols. 2nd edn., London: John Murray, 1907. Repr. New York: Dover Publications, 1957.

Kennedy, William Paul McClure. *Elizabethan Episcopal Administration: An Essay in Sociology and Politics.* 3 vols. Alcuin Club Collections, 25–27. London: A. R. Mowbray & Co., 1924.

Kettle, Ann J., and D. A. Johnson, "House of Secular Canons – Lichfield Cathedral: from the Reformation to the 20th century." In The Victoria History of the County of Stafford (20 vols.), vol. 3, *Ecclesiastical History,* ed. Michael W. Greenslade. London: Oxford University Press, 1970.

Kirkpatrick, Alexander F., ed. *The Cambridge Bible: The Book of Psalms.* Cambridge: Cambridge University Press, 1903.

Kisby, Fiona. "Books in London Parish Churches before 1603: Some Preliminary Observations." In Caroline M. Barton and Jenny Stratford, eds., *The Church and Learning in Late Medieval Society: Essays in Honour of Professor R. B. Dobson.* Proceedings of the 1999 Harlaxton Symposium. Donington, Lincolnshire: Shaun Tyas, 2002.

Kollmann, Augustus Frederick Christopher. *The Melody of the Hundredth Psalm, with Examples and Directions for an Hundred Different Harmonies.* Op. 9. London: for the author, [1809].

Krummel, Donald W. *English Music Printing, 1553–1700.* London: The Bibliographical Society, 1975.

Lander, Jesse. *Inventing Polemic: Religion, Print, and Literary Culture in Early Modern England.* Cambridge: Cambridge University Press, 2006.

Latrobe, John Antes. *The Music of the Church Considered in its Various Branches, Congregational and Choral.* London: Thames Ditton, 1831.

Laufer, Catherine Ella. *Hell's Destruction: An Exploration of Christ's Descent to the Dead.* Farnham: Ashgate, 2013. Rpt. Abingdon and New York: Routledge, 2016.

Lawes, William. *12 Psalms "to Comon Tunes."* Ed. Paul Gameson. York: York Early Music Press, 2002.

Leaver, Robin A. *'Goostly Psalmes and Spirituall Songes': English and Dutch Metrical Psalms from Coverdale to Utenhove, 1535–1566.* Oxford Studies in Church Music, ed. Nicholas Temperley. Oxford: Clarendon Press, 1991.

le Huray, Peter G. *Music and the Reformation in England, 1549–1660.* London: Herbert Jenkins, 1967.

Lewalski, Barbara Kiefer. *Protestant Poetics and the Seventeenth-Century Religious Lyric.* Princeton: Princeton University Press, 1979.

Long, Kenneth. *The Music of the English Church.* London: Hodder & Stoughton, 1972.

Lowe, Roger. *The Diary of Roger Lowe of Ashton-in-Makerfield, Lancashire*, ed. William L. Sachse. New Haven: Yale University Press, 1938.

Luther, Martin. *Luther's Works*, 55 vols, ed. Jaroslav Pelikan. Saint Louis: Concordia Publishing House, [1955–1986].

MacCullough, Diarmid. *Tudor Church Militant: Edward VI and the Protestant Reformation.* Harmondsworth: Penguin Books, 1999.

Machyn, Henry. *The Diary of Henry Machyn, Citizen and Merchant-Taylor of London, from A.D. 1550 to A. D. 1563*, ed. John Gough Nichols. London: Camden Society, 1848.

Marsh, Christopher. *Music and Society in Early Modern England.* Cambridge: Cambridge University Press, 2010.

Martz, Louis. *George Herbert and Henry Vaughan.* Oxford: Oxford University Press, 1985.

May, Steven W., and William A. Ringler, Jr. *Elizabethan Poetry: A Bibliography and First-Line Index of English Verse, 1559–1603.* 3 vols. London and New York: Thoemmes Continuum, 2004.

Mayer, Claude A. *Clément Marot.* Paris: Editions A.-G. Nizet, 1972.

McGraw, Hugh, et al., eds. *The Sacred Harp: 1991 Revision.* [Bremen, Ga.:] Sacred Harp Publishing Company, [c.1991].

McKinnon, James. "The Book of Psalms, Monasticism, and the Western Liturgy." Nancy Van Deusen, ed., *The Place of the Psalms in the Intellectual Culture of the Middle Ages* (Albany, N. Y.: SUNY Press, 1999), 43–58.

———. *Music in Early Christian Literature.* Cambridge: Cambridge University Press, 1987.

McKitterick, David. *A History of Cambridge University Press.* Vol. 1: *Printing and the Book Trade in Cambridge, 1534–1698.* Cambridge: Cambridge University Press, 1992.

McMeeken, John W. *The History of the Scottish Metrical Psalms.* Glasgow: M'Culloch & Co., 1872.

Miller, Josiah. *Singers and Songs of the Church.* [London:] Longmans, Green & Co., 1869.

Milsom, John. "Songs, Carols and *Contrafacta* in the Early History of the Tudor Anthem." *Proceedings of the Royal Musical Association* 107 (1980–1), 34–45.

———. "Tallis, the Parker Psalter, and Some Unknowns." *Early Music* 44/2 (2016), 1–13.

Mitchell, A. F., ed. *A Compendious Book of Godly and Spiritual Songs.* Scottish Text Society, 1/39. Edinburgh: W. Blackwood and Sons, 1897, repr. New York: Johnson, 1966.

More, Mother Thomas. "The Performance of Plainsong in the Later Middle Ages and the Sixteenth Century." *Proceedings of the Royal Musical Association* 92 (1965–6), 121–34.

Morehen, John. "English Church Music." In Roger Bray, ed., The Blackwell History of Music in Britain, vol. 5: *The Sixteenth Century* (Oxford: Blackwell, 1995), 94–146.

Moyise, Steve, and Maarten J. J. Mencken, eds., *The Psalms in the New Testament.* London and New York: T. & T. Clark International, 2004.

Musica Britannica. (Series in progress.) London: Stainer & Bell for the Royal Musical Association, 1951–. (MB)

The New Grove Dictionary of Music and Musicians, ed. Stanley Sadie. 29 vols. London: Macmillan, 2001.

The New Oxford Book of Carols, ed. Hugh Keyte and Andrew Parrott. Oxford: Oxford University Press, 1992. (*The New Grove*)

Nichols, John. *The Progresses, Processions, and Magnificent Festivities, of King James the First.* 4 vols. London: J. B. Nichols, printer to the Society of Antiquaries, 1828.

Oastler, Christopher L. *John Day, Elizabethan Printer.* Oxford: Oxford Bibliographic Society, 1975.

Ollard, Sidney L. *Fasti Wyndesorienses: The Deans and Canons of Windsor.* Windsor: Otley and Son, 1950.

Osborn, James M., ed. *The Autobiography of Thomas Whythorne.* Oxford: Clarendon Press, 1961.

Otto, Randell. "The Remnant Church." *Journal for Christian Theological Research* 7 (2002): 15–29.

Owens, Jessie Ann. "Concepts of Pitch in English Music Theory, c. 1560–1640." In Cristal Collins Judd, ed., *Tonal Structures in Early Music*, Criticism and Analysis of Early Music, 1 (New York and London: Garland, 1998), 191–215.

The Oxford Book of Carols, ed. Percy Dearmer, R. Vaughan Williams, and Martin Shaw. London: Oxford University Press; Humphrey Milford, 1928.

The Oxford Companion to Music, ed. Percy A. Scholes. London: Oxford University Press, 1938.

Page, Christopher. *The Guitar in Tudor England: A Social and Musical History.* Cambridge: Cambridge University Press, 2015.

Patrick, Millar. *Four Centuries of Scottish Psalmody.* London: Oxford University Press, 1949.

Pepys, Samuel. *The Diary of Samuel Pepys*, ed. G. Gregory Smith. London: Macmillan, 1905.

Peter, Rodolphe. "L'abécédaire ou catéchisme élémentaire de Calvin." *Revue d'histoire et de philosophie religieuses* 45/1 (1965), 11–45.

——, trans. Gervase E. Duffield. "Calvin and Louis Budé's Translation of the Psalms." In G[ervase] E. Duffield, ed., *John Calvin*, Courtenay Studies in Reformation Theology, 1 (Appleford, Abingdon, Berkshire: Sutton Courtenay Press, 1966), 191–200.

Pidoux, Pierre. *Le Psautier huguenot du xvie siècle: Mélodies et documents.* 2 vols. Basle: Editions Bärenreiter, 1962. (Pidoux)

Poole, Kristin. *Radical Religion from Shakespeare to Milton: Figures of Nonconformity in Early Modern England.* Cambridge: Cambridge University Press, 2000.

Powell, Jason. "Thomas Wyatt's Poetry in Embassy: Egerton 2711 and the Production of Literary Manuscripts Abroad." *Huntington Library Quarterly* 67/2 (2004), 261–82.

Pratt, Waldo Selden. *The Music of the French Psalter of 1562.* New York: Columbia University Press, 1939.

Pritchard, Allan. "George Wither's Quarrel with the Stationers: an Anonymous Reply to *The Schollers Purgatory*." *Studies in Bibliography* 16 (1963), 28–43.

Proctor, Francis. *A History of the Book of Common Prayer.* London: Macmillan, 1864.

Purcell, Henry. *Organ Works*, ed. Hugh McLean. Borough Green: Novello, 1957.

Purvis, John S., ed. *Tudor Parish Documents of the Diocese of York.* Cambridge: Cambridge University Press, 1948.

Quitslund, Beth. "Protestant Theology and Devotion." In Andrew Escobedo, ed., *Spenser in Context* (Cambridge and New York: Cambridge University Press, 2016), 291–300.

——. *The Reformation in Rhyme: Sternhold, Hopkins and the English Metrical Psalter, 1547–1603.* Aldershot: Ashgate, 2009. (*RR*)

——. "Singing the Psalms for Fun and Profit." In Alec Ryrie and Jessica Martin, eds., *Private and Domestic Devotion in Early Modern Britain* (Aldershot: Ashgate, 2012), 237–58.

Ranson, Susan. *John Hopkins, Metrical Psalmist and Rector of Great Waldingfield.* Norwich: Border Editions, 2004.

Reagan, Mark C. "John Cosyn's *Musike in Six and Five Partes* Newly Notated and Completed." Master's thesis, Washington State University, 2010.

Robinson, Hastings, ed. *Original Letters Relative to the English Reformation.* 2 vols. Cambridge: Cambridge University Press, 1842–5.

———. *The Zurich Letters.* 2 vols. London: Parker Society, 1846.

Routley, Eric. *The Music of Christian Hymns.* Chicago: G. I. A. Publications, 1981.

Ryrie, Alec. "The Psalms and Confrontation in English and Scottish Protestantism," *Archiv für Reformationsgeschichte,* 101 (2010), 114–37.

Scholes, Percy A. *The Oxford Companion to Music.* London: Oxford University Press, 1938.

Scott, Derek B. "Music, Morality and Rational Amusement in the Victorian Middle-Class Soirée." In Bennett Zon, ed., *Music and Performance Culture in Nineteenth-Century Britain* (Farnham: Ashgate, 2012), 83–101.

Selections from Ordinances for the Regulation of the Churches Dependent upon the Seigniory of Geneva (1547), in George L. Burns, ed., *Translations and Reprints from the Original Sources of European History,* 6 vols. (Philadelphia: University of Pennsylvania History Department, 1898–1912), 1, no.3:10–11.

Shakespeare, William. *1 Henry IV* in G. Blakemore Evans, ed., *The Riverside Shakespeare* (Boston: Houghton Mifflin), 847–85.

Shaw, Watkins. "Church Music in England from the Reformation to the Present Day," in Friedrich Blume et al., *Protestant Church Music: A History* (London: Victor Gollancz Ltd., 1975), 691–732.

A Short-Title Catalogue of Books Printed in England, Scotland, & Ireland and of English Books Printed Abroad, 1475–1640. 2nd edn. begun by W.A. Jackson & F.S. Ferguson, completed by Katharine F. Pantzer. 3 vols. London: Bibliographical Society, 1976–1991. (*STC*)

Smith, Alan, ed. "Parish Church Musicians in England in the Reign of Elizabeth I: An Annotated Register." *Royal Musical Association Research Chronicle* 4 (1964), 42–92.

———. "The Practice of Music in English Cathedrals and Churches, and at the Court, during the Reign of Elizabeth I." Ph.D. diss., University of Birmingham, 1967.

Special Prayers, Fasts and Thanksgivings in the British Isles 1533–1688, ed. Natalie Mears, Alasdair Raffe, Stephen Taylor and Philip Williamson (with Lucy Bates). Church of England Record Society, 20. National Prayers: Special Worship since the Reformation. 3 vols. Woodbridge, Suffolk: The Boydell Press, 2013.

Spink, Ian. *Restoration Cathedral Music, 1660–1714.* Oxford Studies in British Church Music, ed. Nicholas Temperley. Oxford: Clarendon Press, 1995.

Stalmann, Joachim, et al. *Das deutsche Kirchenlied: Kritische Gesamtausgabe der Melodien.* Kassel: Bärenreiter, 1993–2010.

Staykova, Julia D. "Pseudo-Augustine and Religious Controversy in Early Modern England," in *Augustine Beyond the Book: Intermediality, Transmediality and Reception* (Leiden: Brill, 2011), 147–66.

Stevens, Denis, ed. *The Mulliner Book.* MB 1. London: Royal Musical Association, 1951.

Stevens, John, ed. *Music at the Court of Henry VIII.* MB 18. London: Royal Musical Association, 1962.

———. *Music and Poetry at the Early Tudor Court.* (Corrected edition.) Cambridge: Cambridge University Press, 1979.

Stokes, James, and Robert L. Alexander, eds. *Records of Early English Drama: Somerset.* 2 vols. Toronto: University of Toronto Press, 1996.

Sutcliffe, Peter. *The Oxford University Press: An Informal History.* Oxford: Clarendon Press, 1978.

Tacaille, Alice. "Faire chanter l'assemblée au temps des premiers exils: la musique et la nécessité (Genève, Londres, Édimbourg, 1535–1564)." *Bulletin de la Société de l'histoire du protestantisme français,* 158 (2012), 405–32.

Targoff, Ramie. *Common Prayer: The Language of Public Devotion in Early Modern England.* Chicago: University of Chicago Press, 2001.

Temperley, Nicholas. "The Adventures of a Hymn Tune—I." *Musical Times* 112 (1971), 375–76. Repr. in *Hymnology in the Service of the Church: Essays in Honor of Harry Eskew,* ed. Paul R. Powell (Fenton, Mo.: MorningStar Music Publishers, 2008), 307–10.

———. "'All Skillful Praises Sing': How Congregations Sang the Psalms in Early Modern England." *Renaissance Studies* 29 (2015), 531–53.

———. "The Anglican Communion Hymn." *The Hymn* 30 (1979), 178–86. Repr. *SECM* 122–30.

———. "John Playford and the Metrical Psalms." *Journal of the American Musicological Society* 25 (1972), 331–78. Repr. *SECM,* 21–68.

———. "Kindred and Affinity in Hymn Tunes." *Musical Times* 113 (1972), 905–9. Repr. in *Hymnology in the Service of the Church: Essays in Honor of Harry Eskew,* ed. Paul R. Powell (Fenton, Mo.: MorningStar Music Publishers, 2008), 311–14.

———. "Middleburg Psalms." *Studies in Bibliography* 30 (1977), 162–70. Repr. *SECM,* 10–19.

———. "The Music of Dissent." In Isabel Rivers and David Wright, eds., *Dissenting Praise* (Oxford: Oxford University Press, 2011), 197–228.

———. *The Music of the English Parish Church.* 2 vols. Cambridge: Cambridge University Press, 1979. Repr. 2005. (*MEPC*)

———. "The Old Way of Singing: Its Origins and Development." *Journal of the American Musicological Society* 34 (1981), 511–44. Repr. *SECM,* 69–102.

———. *Studies in English Church Music, 1550–1900.* Farnham: Ashgate, 2009. (*SECM*)

——— and David Temperley. "Stress-Meter Alignment in French Vocal Music." *Journal of the Acoustical Society of America* 134 (2013), 520–7.

——— and Sally Drage, eds. *Eighteenth-Century Psalmody.* MB 85. London: Royal Musical Association, 2007.

———— with the assistance of Charles G. Manns and Joseph Herl. *The Hymn Tune Index: A Census of English-Language Hymn Tunes in Printed Sources from 1535 to 1820.* 4 vols. Oxford: Clarendon Press, 1998. (*HTI*)

Tudor Church Music, ed. Percy C. Buck et al. 10 vols. London: Oxford University Press, 1923–9.

Tye, Christopher. *English Sacred Music,* ed. John Morehen. Early English Church Music, 19. London: Stainer & Bell, 1977.

Usher, Brett. "The Silent Community: Early Puritans and the Patronage of the Arts," in *The Church and the Arts,* ed. Diana Wood, Studies in Church History, 28 (Oxford: Blackwell, 1992), 287–302.

Walter, Johann. Preface to *Geystliche Gesangbüchlin* (1524), tr. Paul Zeller Strodach, rev. Ulrich S. Leopold. In Martin Luther, Works, 53: *Liturgy and Hymns* (Philadelphia: American Philosophical Society, 1976), 33.

The Wanley Manuscripts, ed. James Wrightson. 3 vols. Recent Researches in the Music of the Renaissance, 99–101. Madison, Wis.: A-R Editions, [c.1995].

Ward, John. *Music for Elizabethan Lutes.* 2 vols. Oxford: Clarendon Press, 1992.

Wasson, D. DeWitt. *Hymntune Index and Related Hymn Materials.* 3 vols. Studies in Liturgical Musicology, 6. Lanham, Md.: Scarecrow Press, 1998.

Waugh, Evelyn. *Brideshead Revisited.* London: Chapman & Hall, 1945.

[Wedderburn, John, James and Robert.] *A Compendious Book of Godly and Spiritual Songs, Commonly Known as 'The Gude and Godlie Ballatis',* Reprinted from the Edition of 1567, ed. A.F. Mitchell. Scottish Text Society, ser. 1, vol. 39. Edinburgh: W. Blackwood and Sons, 1897. Repr. London and New York: Johnson Reprint Corp., 1966.

Weelkes, Thomas. *Collected Anthems,* ed. David Brown, Walter Collins and Peter le Huray. MB 23. London: Royal Musical Association, 1966.

White, Helen Constance. *English Devotional Literature (Prose), 1600–1640.* University of Wisconsin Studies in Language and Literature, 29. New York: Haskell House, 1966.

Wieck, Roger S. *Painted Prayers: The Book of Hours in Medieval and Renaissance Art.* New York: George Braziller in association with the Pierpont Morgan Library, 1997.

Wilder, Philip van. *Collected Works,* ed. Jane A. Bernstein. Masters and Monuments of the Renaissance, ed. Leeman L. Perkins, 4. New York: Broude Bros., 1991.

Willis, Jonathan. *Church Music and Protestantism in Post-Reformation England: Discourses, Sites and Identities.* Farnham: Ashgate, 2009.

Wing, Donald G. *Short-Title Catalogue of Books Printed in England, Scotland, Ireland, Wales, and British America and of English Books Printed in Other Countries.* 3 vols. New York: The Index Society, 1945–51. (Wing)

Woodfield, Ian. *English Musicians in the Age of Exploration.* Stuyvesant, N. Y.: Pendragon Press, 1995.

Wrightson, James, ed. *The Wanley Manuscripts*. 3 vols. Recent Researches in the Music of the Renaissance, 99–101. Madison, Wis.: A-R Editions, [c. 1995].

Wylkinson, Thomas. "O Lord, consider my distress," ed. Peter le Huray. Altamonte Springs, Fl.: Anglo-American Music Publishers, [c. 2005].

Zahn, Johannes. *Die Melodien der deutschen evangelischen Kirchenlieder*. 6 vols. Gütersloh: C. Bertelsmann, 1888–93. (Zahn)

Zim, Rivkah. *English Metrical Psalms: Poetry as Praise and Prayer, 1535–1601*. Cambridge: Cambridge University Press, 1987.

—— and M. B. Parkes, "'Sacvyles Olde Age': A Newly Discovered Poem by Thomas Sackville, Lord Buckhurst, Earl of Dorset &c. (1536–1608)." *Review of English Studies*, 40 (1989), 1–25.

Electronic and online sources

Benedict XVI, Pope. "Commentary on Psalm 120," "Documents: Pope Benedict XVI," *Catholic News Agency*, 4 May 2005. www.catholicnewsagency.com/document/commentary-on-psalm-120-83

The Canterbury Dictionary of Hymnology. Norwich, England: Canterbury Press, 2013. www.hymnnology.co.uk. (*CDH*)

Duguid, Timothy. "Early Modern British Metrical Psalters." *Edinburgh Research Archive*, 2013. www.era.lib.ed.ac.uk/handle/1842/6684

Early English Books Online. Ann Arbor, Michigan: ProQuest LLC, 2003–2014. www.eebo.chadwyck.com. (EEBO)

English Short Title Catalogue. London: The British Library, n.d. www.estc.bl.uk. (*ESTC*)

Hansard 5th Series (Commons), Vol. 413 http://hansard.millbanksystems.com/commons/1945/aug/15/isaiah-lxi-1-4-and-11

The Hymn Tune Index. Urbana, Illinois: The University of Illinois, 2001–. www.hymntune.library.illinois.edu. (*HTI*)

"John Wesley's Notes on the Bible: Notes on The Book of Psalms," ed. Sulu Kelley and Bill Brown, *Wesley Center Online*, 1993–2011

The Oxford Dictionary of National Biography. Oxford: Oxford University Press. www.oxforddnb.com. (*ODNB*)

Oxford Music Online. Oxford: Oxford University Press. (Including *The New Grove Dictionary of Music and Musicians*.) www.oxfordmusiconline.com

Primary Sources on Copyright (1450–1900). Lionel Bently and Martin Kretschmer, eds. www.copyrighthistory.org

INDEX OF PSALM AND HYMN TUNES

Both volumes are indexed. Page numbers in bold type refer to the tune in music notation; page numbers in regular type refer to mentions, discussions, or descriptions; μ numbers refer to the Audio Supplement at https://www.retsonline.org/psalms.audiosupplement.html where the tune may be heard. Cases where a tune is merely identified are not indexed unless of special interest.

Many tunes, especially common tunes, were given different names in various publications. We have chosen the name that ultimately prevailed for each tune and listed only that name in the index "By Name" below. If you look up a tune by name here and it leads to the wrong tune, look it up by name in the *Hymn Tune Index* at www.hymntune.library.illinois.edu, where you can check the notes of the tune. This will provide the definitive *HTI* number, which you can then find in the second index below.

1. By Name

2. By Hymn Tune Index number

Index of Biblical Passages

This index locates references to or quotations of biblical passages in the apparatus and texts of the *WBP*; *1567* psalm texts presented in numerical order in the main body of the critical edition are omitted. Numbered items preceded by "μ" are recordings in the audio supplement, available at https://www.retsonline.org/psalms.audiosupplement.html.

General Index

The main critical edition of the *1567* text is not indexed here. To prevent multiple lists that include the majority of the Notes on individual psalms, it also excludes references to the most common sources of the psalm texts and arguments within those Notes.

Renaissance English Text Society

Officers and Council

International Advisory Council

Lukas Erne, University of Geneva
Sergio Rossi, University of Milan
Helen Wilcox, University of Wales, Bangor

Editorial Committee for The Lyrics of Henry VIII Manuscript.
  Steven May, chair
  Roy Flannagan
  Elizabeth H. Hageman
  Margaret Hannay
  Arthur F. Marotti

The Renaissance English Text Society was established to publish literary texts, chiefly nondramatic, of the period 1475–1660. Dues are $50.00 per annum ($35.00, graduate students; life membership is available at $750.00). Members receive the text published for each year of membership. The Society sponsors panels at such annual meetings as those of the Modern Language Association, the Renaissance Society of America, and the Medieval Congress at Kalamazoo.

General inquiries and proposals for editions should be addressed to the president, Arthur Kinney, Massachusetts Center for Renaissance Studies, PO Box 2300, Amherst, Mass., 01004, USA. Inquiries about membership should be addressed to William Gentrup, Membership Secretary, Arizona Center for Medieval and Renaissance Studies, Arizona State University, Box 874402, Tempe, Ariz., 85287–4402.

Copies of volumes x–xii may be purchased from Associated University Presses, 440 Forsgate Drive, Cranbury, N.J., 08512. Members may order copies of earlier volumes still in print or of later volumes from xiii, at special member prices, from the Treasurer.

FIRST SERIES

VOL. I. *Merie Tales of the Mad Men of Gotam* by A. B., edited by Stanley J. Kahrl, and The History of Tom Thumbe by R. I., edited by Curt F. Buhler, 1965. (o.p.)

VOL. II. *Thomas Watson's Latin Amyntas,* edited by Walter F. Staton, Jr., and Abraham Fraunce's translation The Lamentations of Amyntas, edited by Franklin M. Dickey, 1967.

SECOND SERIES

VOL. III. *The dyaloge called Funus, A Translation of Erasmus's Colloquy (1534),* and *A very pleasaunt & fruitful Diologe called The Epicure, Gerrard's Translation of Erasmus's Colloquy (1545),* edited by Robert R. Allen, 1969.

VOL. IV. *Leicester's Ghost* by Thomas Rogers, edited by Franklin B. Williams, Jr., 1972.

THIRD SERIES

VOLS. V–VI. *A Collection of Emblemes, Ancient and Moderne*, by George Wither, with an introduction by Rosemary Freeman and bibliographical notes by Charles S. Hensley, 1975. (o.p.)

FOURTH SERIES

VOLS. VII–VIII. *Tom a' Lincolne* by R. I., edited by Richard S. M. Hirsch, 1978.

FIFTH SERIES

VOL. IX. *Metrical Visions* by George Cavendish, edited by A. S. G. Edwards, 1980.

SIXTH SERIES

VOL. X. *Two Early Renaissance Bird Poems*, edited by Malcolm Andrew, 1984.

VOL. XI. *Argalus and Parthenia by Francis Quarles*, edited by David Freeman, 1986.

VOL. XII. Cicero's *De Officiis*, trans. Nicholas Grimald, edited by Gerald O'Gorman, 1987.

VOL. XIII. *The Silkewormes and their Flies* by Thomas Moffet (1599), edited with introduction and commentary by Victor Houliston, 1988.

SEVENTH SERIES

VOL. XIV. John Bale, *The Vocacyon of Johan Bale*, edited by Peter Happé and John N. King, 1989.

VOL. XV. *The Nondramatic Works of John Ford*, edited by L. E. Stock, Gilles D. Monsarrat, Judith M. Kennedy, and Dennis Danielson, with the assistance of Marta Straznicky, 1990.

SPECIAL PUBLICATION. *New Ways of Looking at Old Texts: Papers of the Renaissance English Text Society, 1985–1991*, edited by W. Speed Hill, 1993. (Sent gratis to all 1991 members.)

VOL. XVI. *George Herbert, The Temple: A Diplomatic Edition of the Bodleian Manuscript (Tanner 307)*, edited by Mario A. Di Cesare, 1991.

VOL. XVII. Lady Mary Wroth, *The First Part of the Countess of Montgomery's Urania*, edited by Josephine Roberts, 1992.

VOL. XVIII. Richard Beacon, *Solon His Follie*, edited by Clare Carroll and Vincent Carey, 1993.

VOL. XIX. An Collins, *Divine Songs and Meditacions*, edited by Sidney Gottlieb, 1994.

VOL. XX. *The Southwell-Sibthorpe Commonplace Book: Folger MS V.b.198*, edited by Sr. Jean Klene, 1995.

SPECIAL PUBLICATION. *New Ways of Looking at Old Texts II: Papers of the Renaissance English Text Society, 1992–1996*, edited by W. Speed Hill, 1998. (Sent gratis to all 1996 members.)

VOL. XXI. *The Collected Works of Anne Vaughan Lock,* edited by Susan M. Felch,1996.

VOL. XXII. Thomas May, *The Reigne of King Henry the Second Written in Seauen Books,* edited by Götz Schmitz, 1997.

VOL. XXIII. *The Poems of Sir Walter Ralegh: A Historical Edition,* edited by Michael Rudick, 1998.

VOL. XXIV. Lady Mary Wroth, *The Second Part of the Countess of Montgomery's Urania,* edited by Josephine Roberts; completed by Suzanne Gossett and Janel Mueller, 1999.

VOL. XXV. *The Verse Miscellany of Constance Aston Fowler: A Diplomatic Edition,* by Deborah Aldrich-Watson, 2000.

VOL. XXVI. *An Edition of Luke Shepherd's Satires,* by Janice Devereux, 2001.

VOL. XXVII. *Philip Stubbes: The Anatomie of Abuses,* edited by Margaret Jane Kidnie, 2002.

VOL. XXVIII. *Cousins in Love: The Letters of Lydia DuGard, 1665–1672, with a new edition of* The Marriages of Cousin Germans *by Samuel DuGard,* edited by Nancy Taylor, 2003.

VOL. XXIX. *The Commonplace Book of Sir John Strangways (1645–1666),* edited by Thomas G. Olsen, 2004.

SPECIAL PUBLICATION. *New Ways of Looking at Old Texts, III: Papers of the Renaissance English Text Society, 1997–2001,* edited by W. Speed Hill, 2004. (Sent gratis to all 2001 members.)

VOL. XXX. *The Poems of Robert Parry,* edited by G. Blakemore Evans, 2005.

VOL. XXXI. *William Baspoole's 'The Pilgrime',* edited by Kathryn Walls, 2006.

VOL. XXXII. *Richard Tottel's 'Songes and Sonettes': The Elizabethan Version,* edited by Paul A. Marquis, 2007.

VOL. XXXIII. *Cælivs Secvndus Curio: his historie of the warr of Malta: Translated by Thomas Mainwaringe (1579),* edited by Helen Vella Bonavita, 2008.

SPECIAL PUBLICATION. *New Ways of Looking at Old Texts, IV: Papers of the Renaissance English Text Society, 2002–2006,* edited by Michael Denbo, 2008. (Sent gratis to all 2006 members.)

VOL. XXXIV. *Nicholas Oldisworth's Manuscript (Bodleian MS. Don.c.24),* edited by John Gouws, 2009.

VOL. XXXV. *The Holgate Miscellany: An Edition of Pierpont Morgan Library Manuscript MS 1057,* edited by Michael Denbo, 2012.

VOL. XXXVI. *The Whole Book of Psalms Vol. I,* edited by Beth Quitslund and Nicholas Temperley, 2018.

VOL. XXXVII. *The Whole Book of Psalms Vol. II,* edited by Beth Quitslund and Nicholas Temperley, 2018.

VOL. XXXVIII. *Averrunci or The Skowrers,* edited with Introduction and Commentary by Patricia Osmond and Robert W. Ulery, Jr., 2017.

VOL. XXXIX. *The Lyrics of the Henry VIII Manuscript,* edited by Raymond G. Siemens, 2018.